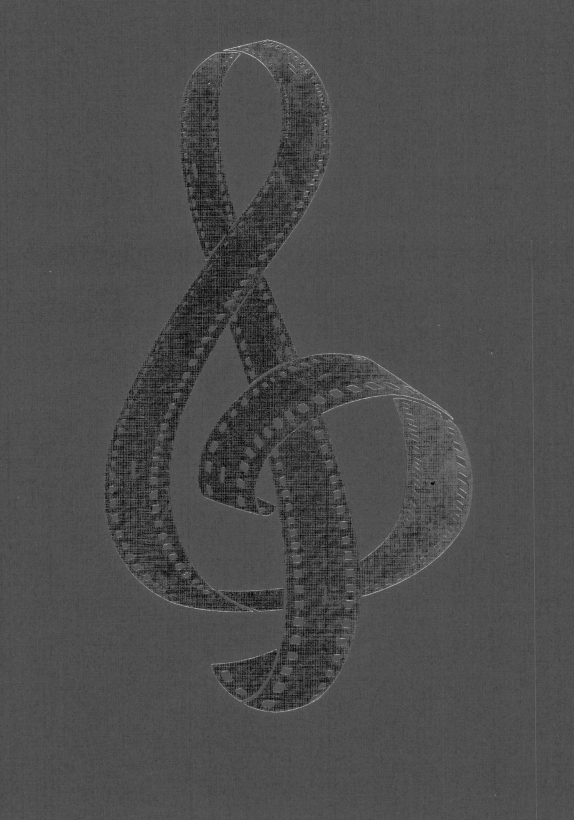

**Detroit Studies in
Music Bibliography**

Editor
J. Bunker Clark
University of Kansas

A

COMPREHENSIVE BIBLIOGRAPHY

of

MUSIC for FILM and TELEVISION

compiled by

Steven D. Wescott

DETROIT STUDIES IN MUSIC BIBLIOGRAPHY   NUMBER FIFTY-FOUR
INFORMATION COORDINATORS   1985   DETROIT

Printed and bound in the United States of America
Published by
Information Coordinators, Inc.
1435-37 Randolph Street
Detroit, Michigan 48226

Cover design by Nicholas Jakubiak
Preliminary pages:
Photocomposition by Kristin Gorzelski
Editing by J. Bunker Clark

Library of Congress Cataloging in Publication Data

Wescott, Steven D., 1950-
    A comprehensive bibliography of music for film and television.

    (Detroit studies in music bibliography ; no. 54)
    Includes index.
    1. Moving-picture music — Bibliography.   2. Television
music — Bibliography.   I. Title.   II. Series: Detroit
studies in music bibliography ; 54.
ML128.M7W47   1985   016.7828´5   85-27184
ISBN 0-89990-027-5

CONTENTS

I. HISTORY

II. COMPOSERS

III. AESTHETICS

IV. SPECIAL TOPICS

V. RESEARCH

VI. INDEX

INTRODUCTION

In his introduction to Clifford McCarty's *Film Composers in America: A Checklist of Their Work* (1953), critic Lawrence Morton observed:

> The tasks of criticism are many. One of the most altruistic but thankless of them is the gathering together of those materials which make possible the more showy and rewarding tasks.
>
> . . . It represents the patient labor of the sort that every serious critic of film music has so far shunned, in the hope that somebody else would do it. Meanwhile its need has grown more and more urgent.*

Almost as long as there has been film, there has been film music. Though widely disregarded, often mis-perceived, and relegated by many to a subsidiary status among the "higher" filmic arts, this very specialized cinematic appendage has never lacked its own enthusiastic critical observers, proponents, doomsayers, and devotees. It is not surprising, however, that much of their reportage, locked within the purview of an industry seemingly and, perhaps, innately prone to a simultaneous pursuit of both the superlative and the superficial, reveals a far greater capacity for "show" than substance. Secured by only the slimmest, most tentative factual and methodological tethers, like a once-impressive though transient Hollywood facade, this abundant but less-than-insightful commentary has generally overshadowed the relatively few truly sound and "rewarding" contributions made to the literature of film music.

Historical distance has now, of course, imbued even the least perceptive of these documents with greater relevance as primary source materials for the study of film music history. At the same time, however, a more substantive vein of film music criticism, less encumbered by the demands of commercial exigency, has gradually emerged, exhibiting a determined appetite for more erudite and enduring exegesis of music's historical and aesthetic role in the development of the so-called "visual" media of the 20th century.

---

* See #6270, p. xi.

Not necessarily for lack of trying, however, this pursuit has been consistently plagued by a dearth of essential scholarship. Basic research tools, for example, including bibliographies, filmographies, discographies, and other resource guides, remain uncataloged, widely dispersed, elusive, and often unavailable. Many exist only as unpublished manuscripts. Others are tucked away in obscure periodicals, or lost in the yellowing mimeography of film society newsletters. Many primary source materials have been irretrievably misplaced or destroyed: recordings, musical manuscripts, cue sheets, scripts, and most important, the films themselves. Those which exist are, for the most part, uncataloged and inaccessible. Even at best, they are difficult and cripplingly expensive to acquire for use.

Lacking some of the most basic materials for continuing research, then, it is little wonder that "serious" musicologists and film scholars remain at a skeptical distance. Glancing hesitantly at the nascent discipline, they await more compelling evidence of its potential as a viable academic pursuit, and a more convincing appraisal of its value as a truly valid form of 20th century art.

Thirty years after Morton's admonition for urgent action, it is apparent that the future of the discipline, if not the ultimate development of the genre itself, still rests upon long-delayed efforts to establish a more secure and substantive foundation for further research. Those who see the need must first engage in the unavoidable, if not wholly "altruistic," scholarly legwork which will provide a ready pool of essential data concerning sources, film credits, archival resources, and the like. A second, far more Herculean effort will be required to physically secure the primary documents themselves, making them available to those who are committed and capable of accomplishing the more "showy *and* rewarding" tasks of film music research.

Recognizing the many projects which have already been undertaken, and those now in progress which seek to effect these goals, this volume was prepared in order to meet one of the most basic needs of film music scholarship. It is an attempt to provide, in a single, useable volume, a compendium of all the basic materials, resources, and references which inform the study of music as it has collaborated in the 100-year development of film and television, both as art and as media for the communication of information and art.

Begun as a catalog of sources relevant to the more specific question of music's role as *dramatic* element in film and television, the listing was soon expanded to include a number of closely interrelated topics: music in documentary films; music in television and radio advertising; music in radio drama; the social and cultural influence of film, television, and radio music; experimental use of film itself as a medium for musical composition; and use of the "visual" media as a vehicle for musical performance and for the dissemination and marketing of both contemporary and popular music.

As the title indicates, this is a *comprehensive listing*. It attempts to embrace the whole field of film and television music by offering a reliable and accurate overview of the literature based upon a thorough and systematic search of the materials available to this compiler. It is by no means *complete*, however, and a number of specific topics and sources excluded from the listing are carefully noted below.

At the same time, no attempt was made to select articles directed toward a particular readership or any predetermined research goal or need. As a result, entries in a single category often present an odd mixture of authorship, audience appeal, and scholarly intent, obviating neither the question nor the opportunity for interpretation of materials and sources juxtaposed historically, geographically, or categorically. Likewise, subject headings are deliberately broad, in an effort to avoid the inadvertent overlay of any inherent organizational bias through the selection and categorization of the materials cited.

Every effort was made to compile a truly international listing, citing contributions by over 3700 authors in 28 countries and 18 languages. Appropriate caution should be exercised, however, in dealing with countries outside the U.S., Canada, and Western Europe, making allowance for the understandably limited accessibility of these sources. Nevertheless, many Russian titles are provided, and sources pertinent to the study of other film centers (India, Japan, South American countries, etc.) may be traced through regional film and film music surveys cited throughout.

While this volume thus represents the most extensive attempt to compile a listing of film music sources, it is by no means, of course, the first. It builds, in fact, upon a broad foundation of significant bibliographic research conducted by Rubsamen (#6247-6248), Lissa (#4733), Sharples (#6252-6254), Marks (#6195), Comuzio (#20), Birett (#6200), and many others (some are listed in Section V: *Bibliographies*). All of the previous film music bibliographies have, in turn, to some extent borrowed from one another. Unfortunately, however, the result has often been a repeated citation of less-than-valuable sources, a sharing of bias in the selection of materials, and the propagation of erroneous information. The otherwise impressive and extemely valuable listing by Zofia Lissa, for example, contains significant errors, even in the citation of her own works. Most are not corrected in subsequent borrowings. Another example may be noted in Grove's 5th edition and *The New Grove Dictionary* which, together with compilations by Manvell (#82), Verdone (#6255), and others, rely heavily upon an incomplete and error-prone listing by John Huntley (#51) for information concerning sources in English. Lissa and Comuzio, consulting Manvell for these same sources, repeat and even compound Huntley's mis-information. A great many errors and omissions found in these compilations have been rectified in this volume, however, through the actual location and verification of the sources themselves.

At the same time, more than 50% of the sources cited here are new, and have never before appeared in a catalog of film music literature. Many were culled from footnotes, journal articles, periodical indexes, reference works, union catalogs, and library files. Others were drawn from obscure and significantly dated material generally inaccessible to the broader audience of film music devotees. A large number of new citations were collected from bibliographic references which are, in fact, easily accessible to film and music scholars (*RILM Abstracts*, *Music Index*, *Film Literature Index*, *Reader's Guides*, etc.). Nevertheless, since many of these works lack even annual accumulations, their use in investigating a topic of this size has become extremely cumbersome and time consuming. These sources were, however, invaluable in serving to update and greatly expand the number of sources cited in several important categories. Citations in this volume are, therefore, essentially current to January 1984.

This volume thus presents a broadly inclusive, yet reliable and accurate compendium of the materials of film music history. It is, first of all, a book of sources: an aid to the location of necessary facts and statistics. At the same time, it is itself a survey of the history and methodology of film music research, and a revealing guide to the many possibilities and opportunities for continuing study of this significant and singular genre of 20th-century music.

Sources / Citations

Several basic guidelines were established to direct the selection of sources and the format of source citations presented in the bibliography. Most were designed to promote the easiest possible use of the volume, while preserving its broad scope and ultimately controlling its size and complexity. They further address the very practical needs of the researcher by providing sufficient information to allow an accurate pre-assessment of the content and value of sources, and their applicability to a particular research problem—thus also facilitating, in every possible way, his/her acquisition of the materials themselves.

1. Every effort was made to provide *complete* and *accurate* citations for each source, including full author names, titles (with subtitles), series titles, volume and issue numbers, publisher locations and names, complete dates, page numbers, and any other pertinent information. Where all of the publication data was unavailable or indecipherable, sources were nevertheless cited with all the information known to this compiler.

2. In order to reflect a more accurate view of the history of film music literature, each source is noted first with publication data which describes its *original publication*. Subsequent reprints, revised editions, and translations are cited chronologically just below the original entry, and carry added letters (for example, #4573a, #4573b, etc.) only if the content or publication data has been substantially altered from the original publication.

3. Citations appear *only once*, listed under the subject heading which most accurately reflects the principal topic and focus of the source. Sources which also include information pertinent to a second or third topic are *cross-referenced*. These are listed numerically (with the author's name and, in some cases, the composer's name) following all other citations under that heading. A brief annotation will generally direct the user to these additional categories.

4. *Annotations* are also provided, when necessary, to clarify complex entries, and to enumerate specific contents. They also serve to cross-reference related materials: source anthologies, subsequent references to the work, original sources, dissertation abstracts, etc.

5. A number of sources are cited which *relate only marginally* to the subject of film music. These may refer indirectly to a film music topic, or may serve as a philosophical or methodological foundation for film music research noted elsewhere in the catalog. These sources were cited only when two or more "non-dependent" bibliographic sources suggested their inclusion. In these cases, the annotation will describe the work as having "implications for the study of film music."

6. *Book reviews* of works with special historical interest or scholarly merit appear with complete citations throughout the catalog. These references accompany the original book citation, and do not appear as separate entries.

7. *Film reviews*, except those which concern films of musical performance or films on musical subjects, are not cited in this volume. To locate additional film reviews, many of which contain glancing references to a film's musical score or music credits, the user should refer to specific film titles listed in an important reference compiled by Stephen Bowles (#6224), and similar listings cited at #6219, #6443, and #6249.

8. For the most part, *reviews of soundtrack recordings* have not been included in the catalog, except where they provide especially insightful commentary, or serve as the *only* source of information on a particular composer or topic. Users should consult *Music Index* (#6242) as a first source for locating additional record reviews.

9. *Record jacket and record liner notes* are an especially rich source of information, and contain many valuable contributions to the literature of film music. Because of the extreme difficulty in consistently locating these materials, however, only a few are listed here. The user must necessarily initiate the process of discovery, therefore, by referring to the discographies noted in individual topic and composer citations, and in Section V: *Discographies*.

10. Similarly, a wealth of information remains hidden in *program notes* which have accompanied concert performances of film music, and in *reviews* of these concerts. Again, awaiting a greatly determined effort to unearth these sources, it was impossible to cite more than a few in this listing.

11. *Citation numbers* have been *underlined* throughout the volume to indicate sources judged by this compiler to reflect a relatively greater historic interest or special scholarly merit. These purely editorial suggestions are intended only to assist the "new" student of film music, by identifying the more authoritative and informative documents of film music history. These indications may be safely ignored, therefore, by those more familiar with the literature.

Subject Headings

Subject headings were designed, once again, to facilitate the use of the volume by imposing a seemingly necessary organization upon the large and otherwise unwieldy volume of material presented. Revealing the essential content of each source, these subject headings segregate articles of similar topical focus, while attempting to preserve the relationship of sources to other materials grouped in similar and often closely related categories.

Section I, HISTORY, provides information about specific historical events and developments in the field. It presents a wide variety of historical reportage, discussion of compositional and performance technique, and even includes some practical materials and manuals for film music performance.

The subject heading *Surveys* cites books, articles, and chapters in volumes of film and music history which summarize historical and technical developments over a period of two or more decades. Surveys of historical developments in certain special topics (or sub-categories) of film music are also cited. (Surveys of the work of individual composers, film music research, and special subjects listed in Sections III and IV are cataloged under those headings, however, and are not cross-referenced here.)

Subsequent subject headings group sources which deal with the history film music in the *Silent and Early Sound Era*, and the so-called "Golden Age" of Hollywood film, roughly *1935-1949*. Although the grouping of later film music materials *by decade* reflects a certain unavoidable arbitrariness, such a delineation was judged to be as viable and justifiable as any. It quite adequately reflects, in fact, many of the major historical shifts which mark the ever-changing focus of both the film and film music genres.

Within these broad chronological divisions, sub-headings highlight sources which focus upon the impact of developments in *sound recording techniques and technology*, and the history of music composed specifically for *television*. Users who seek additional information on sound technology, however, are directed to a useful listing by Claudia Gorbman (#6234), *RILM Abstracts* (#6245), and additional references cited at #6225, #6233, #6236, and #6246.

It is important to note that most sources which deal with the history of *legal*, *commercial*, and other *business* aspects of the profession have *not* been included in this volume. Although this important and interesting facet of film music history is plentifully documented in publications like *Variety, Billboard, Rolling Stone, Village Voice*, and others, these materials are, in fact, more easily accessible through reference to chronological listing of sources in *Music Index* (#6242), and only important articles which pre-date that index are included here. (See, however, listings for the topic *film music copyright, performance right, etc.* in the index to this volume.)

Section II, COMPOSERS, lists sources which focus upon the work of individual composers, including books and articles written by the composers themselves. In considering the work of composers renowned well beyond their contributions to film (Copland, Honegger, Prokofiev, Shostakovich, etc.), citations are limited, however, to those which specifically address the topic of film music.

If a number of truly important composers seem to have been slighted in this listing, it should be noted that this specific selection of 114 composers merely reflects a certain quantity and quality of critical commentary which has been devoted to their work, and does not necessarily imply an assessment of their contribution to the field. Nevertheless, literally hundreds of film music composers remain, in fact, without mention in the literature. The user is directed, however, to the section *Additional Composer Profiles* (pp. 250-53) and to the *Index*, where many more composers are listed (their names designated by an asterisk).

Again, cross-references are included for each composer listed, but specific information found in film music surveys is not cross-referenced, except where such a work devotes a significant section to the work of a particular composer. Also, composer bibliographies, filmographies, and discographies are indicated by annotations which accompany citations for the composer listing, but are not cross-referenced in Section V, RESEARCH.

Section III, AESTHETICS, includes sources embracing a wide range of divergent and somewhat nebulous issues regarding musical and filmic artistry, creativity, communication, and influence. If the section on film music *history* may have dealt with the concrete question of "what happened?," this section may be characterized as pertaining more specifically to the theoretical issues of "why?" and "how?," or perhaps, "so what?," and "who cares?"

First, sources are cited which attempt to explain questions of propriety, creativity, and function in the underscoring of "live" accompaniment for *silent films*. Additional sources proffer directives in "specially designing" scores for silents, eventually confronting the many new challenges encountered during the complex transition to film sound.

Studies are then noted which address the diverse roles of music in films of the *sound era*. These sources attempt to define music's potential artistic contributions to the genre, prescribing theories and methods for its most creative and effective use. At the same time, reflecting the expansive growth of the film industry itself, these documents uncover a complex web of social, economic, and cultural cross-currents which shaped the development of music in film and television, and directed its increasing influence, both as an art and as a "by-product" of essentially commercial interests.

These sources reveal the way in which composers, directors, producers, technicians, theorists, and critics have grappled with the theorectical problems of musical *form and function*: how music both informs and responds to the filmic drama, character and plot development; how it best establishes, defines, or unifies a scene; how it relates to the dramatic/cinematographic whole; and, how it is (and should be) designed to best effect the goals thus defined for it.

Additional sub-headings identify sources which focus upon the *psychological perception* and subliminal influence of film music, and studies which further expand these basic questions to examine how film music may, in fact, have exerted a *social and cultural* impact by influencing our appreciation of specific musical styles, and shaping our conception of contemporary musical culture itself.

Section IV, SPECIAL TOPICS, presents a somewhat different view of the collaboration of the visual and musical arts. While sources cited elsewhere in the catalog have focused upon the way in which music contributes to the total experience of film, those cited here are concerned instead with the essential primacy of music, and address the many aesthetic, perceptual, technical, and cultural problems encountered where film art, in effect, plays a secondary role.

The first two "topics" concern the *performance of music on film and television*; that is, the use of film and television as a vehicle for the presentation of music originally composed for the stage, musical theater, or concert hall. Although many of these sources relate only tangentially to the historical and aesthetic issues raised earlier in the catalog, they nevertheless significantly inform our understanding of related topics presented in Sections I-III. The many problems associated with operatic performance on film and television, for example, provide a useful foundation for any discussion of "source music," and the surprisingly frequent occurrence of operatic and musical scenes specially composed for use in otherwise "non-musical" films. At the same time, discussions of jazz performance on film often reveal particular insights to the unique dramatic requirements and the broader cultural influence of jazz, both as a film genre and as a specialized technique of film scoring. Additionally, even critical analysis applied to such specific topics as the televised performances of Wagner operas holds potential both to encompass and inform theories of filmic *Gesamtkunstwerk* and the use of the *leitmotif* as a compositional and organizational device in film.

A third "topic" deals with *film musicals*. The history of this genre being well documented, a complete listing of available materials on the subject is not attempted here. Instead, *only* those sources that focus specifically on the role of the music in these films are listed, with special attention to the collaboration of composer and director in creating a musical/dramatic design for these films. It should be noted, however, that discussions of film and television adaptations of stage musicals are cited in the sections on "performance" noted above.

Finally, sources are cited which explain the experimental use of the film soundtrack itself as a generator of musical sounds, together with discussions concerning innovations in the use of computers and advanced film and video technology to create visual "realizations" of music and sound. *Animated sound and musical graphics*, highly specialized branches of the film music art, perhaps reflect the ultimate collaboration of music and media, as these processes function literally to transform sound into visual images and visual images into sound.

It is important to note that two very important special topics have been *excluded* from the catalog, since their inclusion would have greatly expanded its size and generally weakened its focus. Sources which deal with the use of film as a resource for *music education* and as a tool for *ethnomusicological research* appear in this volume *only* when they provide information which is relevant to other categories of film music research. For information on these topics, the user is again referred to appropriate headings in *Music Index* (#6242), *RILM Abstracts* (#6245), and to related subjects in the index to this volume.

Section V, RESEARCH, is a listing of resources, guides, catalogs, and reference works currently available to assist the film music scholar in continuing research. Sources are cited which survey the history and the literature of film music research, followed by a listing of the few guidebooks which catalog primary and secondary source materials held in the major archives and libraries for film research.

Additional sub-categories note compilations of resource materials and factual data, including general film music bibliographies, filmographies, and discographies. Note that materials of this kind that pertain to the work of a specific composer or topic listed elsewhere in this volume are indicated by annotations which accompany citations under those subject headings, and are *not* cross-referenced here. To locate these citations, the user should first consult the INDEX — Section VI.

Finally, a number of broadly general film and music reference works are cited. These directories, catalogs, and other lexicographical resources, though widely diverse and occasionally unreliable, may nevertheless provide the careful and cautious researcher with valuable information concerning film credits and additional, useful biographical data for film music composers, arrangers, conductors, orchestrators, editors, directors, producers, critics, and the like.

*　　　*　　　*

This rather weighty volume, born out of a need to discover source materials pertinent only to a very small and specific film music topic, thus now represents nearly three years of careful and "patient labor" (as Morton might have characterized it) spent in collecting, verifying, annotating, and organizing a wide range of materials fundamental to the study of film music history.

Even the most cursory review of these documents must reveal their inestimable potential for informing many of the most vital and critical issues of 20th-century music and culture. It is hoped that the broadly inclusive overview of the literature presented here may, therefore, serve as a useful and insightful guide to these essential materials, facilitating their acquisition and encouraging their use. At the same time, it may profitably direct the attention of film and music scholars to the evident *lacunae* which have been previously clouded by an apparent abundance of critical commentary on all aspects of film music theory and history. By establishing a single reliable and accurate reference, it may also benefit students of film music by abbreviating the time and effort required to unearth necessary sources, thus allaying at least some of the burden of basic, preliminary research.

In this way, it is hoped that this *Comprehensive Bibliography of Music for Film and Television* may serve not only to encourage, but to significantly enable continuing research in this important and highly rewarding field of musicological study.

ACKNOWLEDGMENTS

Although any research project of such a depth and dimension as this may at times seem an intolerably solitary endeavor, I nevertheless acknowledge my considerable indebtedness to many who have offered their assistance in the preparation of this volume.

I express thanks first to the librarians and staff of both the Walter Library and the Wilson Library at the University of Minnesota; the Minneapolis Public Library and Hennepin County Branch Libraries; the Cinema Arts Library at U.C.L.A.; and the Powell Library at Dartmouth College.

I am especially thankful for the kind assistance provided by Dr. Robert Knutson at the Archives for Performing Arts, and his staff at the Doheny Library at the University of Southern California; Maxine Fleckner at the Wisconsin Center for Film and Theater Research at the University of Wisconsin-Madison; John Ahouse at California State University-Long Beach; Stephen Fry at the Rubsamen Music Library at U.C.L.A.; and Carolyn Davis and the staff of the George Arents Research Library at Syracuse University.

My continuing gratitude is extended to Dr. Johannes Riedel, Professor Emeritus at the University of Minnesota, for his support and encouragement in this and many other projects, and to Dr. Donna Cardamone-Jackson and Dr. Susan McClary for their valued guidance.

I express my appreciation for the generous financial assistance provided by the Graduate School Film Study Fund and the Harold Leonard Film Study Fellowship at the University of Minnesota. Without this very welcome support, this work would never have been possible.

I am also immeasurably indebted to Susan Brown Kathmann, whose quiet reassurance urged me to continue my work on this project day after day; and to Joyce Batson, whose seemingly effortless generosity allowed me to see its finish. Ultimately, this volume and the energy expended in its realization, are dedicated with sincere gratitude to my parents, Grant and Irma Wescott, who showed me both the virtue and the folly of sturdy construction, the rewards of tenacity, and an altogether abundant vision of the patience of Job.

STEVEN D. WESCOTT

Hopkins, Minnesota
May 1985

A

COMPREHENSIVE BIBLIOGRAPHY

of

MUSIC for FILM and TELEVISION

I. HISTORY

Surveys

History (and Compositional Technique)

1. Acosta, Leonardo. "La musica, el cine y la experiencia cubana." Cine Cubano (Havana), No. 95 (1980), 72-86.

2. Akiyama, Kuniharu. Nihon no eiga ongaku shi. Tokyo: Tabata, 1974.

    A history of Japanese film music.

3. Amfitheatrof, Daniele. "La musica per film negli Stati Uniti." In La musica per film. Ed. Luigi Chiarini. Rome: Bianco e nero editore, 1950, pp. 118-28.

    A paper presented at the 1950 Venice conference. See Chiarini (#1627).

4. Arnshtam, Lev Oskarovich. Muzyka geroicheskogo. Moscow: Iskusstvo, 1977.

    (Music of the Heroic.) Soviet film makers, and the role of music in their films.

    -- Rev. in Iskusstvo kino, No. 8 (1978), 123-27.

5. The Art of Film: Music and Sound. Chicago: Perspective Films, n.d.

    A filmed documentary. Available through Perspective Films, 65 East South Water St., Chicago, Illinois, 60601.

6. Bal'ozov, Rumen. "Bălgarska filmova muzika." Bălgarska Muzika (Sofia), 25, No. 8 (October 1974), 34-37.

7. Barnouw, Erik, and S. Krishnaswamy. Indian Film. New York: Columbia University Press, 1963. (Second edition, 1980.)

    Chapters: "Mighty River of Music," pp. 70-73, "A Star, Six Songs, Three Dances," pp. 155-67, "There Are Other Kinds of Music," pp. 207-13, and many other references to film music. Includes bibliography, pp. 309-16.

8. Baudrier, Yves. Cinéma et musique. Lyon: Bureau Internationale du Film, 1953.

9. Bazelon, Irwin A. Knowing the Score: Notes on Film Music. New York: Van Nostrand Reinhold, 1975.

    Includes bibliographic references, musical examples, and interviews with composers John Barry, R. R. Bennett, Bernstein, Paul Glass, Goldsmith, Herrmann, Kubik, Johnny Mandel, North, Raksin, Rosenman, Laurence Rosenthal, Schifrin, Bernardo Segáll, and John Williams.

    -- Rev. in Composer (London), No. 61 (Summer 1977), 25-27.

    -- Rev. in Music in Education, 41, No. 385 (1977), 141-42.

    -- Rev. in Quarterly Review of Film Studies, 3, No. 1 (1978), 105-13.

    -- Rev. in Music Review, 39, No. 2 (1978), 141-42.

10. Bhanja, Manujendra, and N. K. Ghosh. "From 'Jamai Sashti' to 'Pather Panchali.'" In Indian Talkie, 1931-56. Bombay: Film Federation of India, 1956.

11. "BMI Presents 'The Score,' a Film Documentary Which Explores the Process of Composing Music for T.V. and the Motion Picture Screen." BMI: The Many Worlds of Music, No. 1 (1974), 4-13.

Accompanies the documentary film "The Score." See #114.

12. Bor, Vladimír. O filmové hudebností: se statěmi J. Kalaše et al. Prague: Československé filmové nakladelství. 1946.

13. Canadian Film Museum. La Cinémathèque canadienne, à l'occasion d'un hommage aux compositeurs Eldon Rathburn et Maurice Blackburn, présente: Musique et cinéma. Montréal: La Cinémathèque canadienne, 1965.

   Includes filmographies for Canadian composers.

14. Carcassonne, Philippe. "Dossier -- La Musique de film: Une politique des auteurs." Cinematographe (Paris), No. 62 (Nov. 1980), 16-24.

   A survey of major film music composers by geographic region.

15. Chamfray, Claude. "La Musique de film en France." Le Courrier musical de France, No. 16 (1966), 187-99. .

16. Chandavarkar, Bhaskar. "Film Music." Indian Cinema 82/83 (New Delhi), (1982-83), 35-39.

17. Cheremukhin, M. Muzyka zvukovogo filma. Moscow: Goskinoizdat, 1939.

18. Chrennikov, T. N. "La musica per film nell'U.R.S.S." In La musica nel film. Ed. Luigi Chiarini. Rome: Bianco e nero editore, 1950, pp. 129-34.

   A paper presented at the 1950 Venice conference. See Chiarini (#1627).

19. Cockshott, Gerald. Incidental Music in the Sound Film. (Pamphlet.) London: British Film Institute, 1946.

   -- Rev. by Lawrence Morton: "Rule, Britannia!" In Hollywood Quarterly, 3, No. 2 (Winter 1948), 211-14. See #1442.

20. Comuzio, Ermanno. Colonna sonora: dialoghi, musiche, rumori dietro lo schermo. Milan: Edizioni il Formichiere, 1980.

   Detailed study of compositional techniques. Includes composer lists and bibliography, pp. 359-65.

   -- Rev. by Nemesio Ala in Ikon (Milan), No. 8-9 (Summer-Autumn 1980), 38-39.

   -- Rev. by Mario Guidorizzi in Filmcritica (Rome), 31, Nos. 305-306 (May-June 1980), 247.

   -- Rev. by Marco Vecchi in Cineforum, No. 204 (May 1981), 74.

21. ----------. "Colonne sonore del dopoguerra -- II: Le nuove leve dei musicisti cinematografici francesi." Bianco e nero, 25, No. 10 (Oct. 1964), 1-30.

22. ----------. "Colonne sonore del dopoguerra -- III: Il peso tradizione nei musicisti cinematografici inglesi." Bianco e nero, 27, No. 12 (Dec. 1966), 1-44.

23. ----------. "Colonne sonore del dopoguerra -- IV: Drammatico nei musicisti cinematografici russi il contrasto fra il vecchio e il nuovo." Bianco e nero, 31, Nos. 7-8 (July-Aug. 1970); and 31, Nos. 9-10 (Sept.-Oct. 1970).

24. ----------. "Colonne sonore USA del dopoguerra -- I: La nuova scuola dei musicisti cinematografici americani." Bianco e nero, 24, No. 5 (May 1963), 1-15.

25. ----------. "L'evoluzione della musica cinematografica italiana attraverso la trasmissione t v: Colonna sonora." Bianco e nero, 28, Nos. 3-4 (Mar.-Apr. 1967), 79ff.

26. ----------. "La musica." In Venti anni di cinema italiano. Rome: Edizioni Sindacato Nazionale Critici Cinematografici Italiani, 1965.

27. ----------. "La musica per film in Russia nel contraddittorio clima del disgelo." Cineforum, No. 45 (May 1965).

28. Corper, Gerald. "Our Musical Heritage." The Max Steiner Music Society News Letter, No. 45 (Winter 1975), 5-7.

   With references to the music of Steiner.

29. ----------. "The Sound of Music." The Max Steiner Annual, No. 9 (1975), 12.

30. Elley, Derek. The Film Music Book. London: Talisman Books.

   Work in progress, 1982. Includes biographies and filmographies for 200 major film music composers.

31. Engmann, Hartmut. Filmmusik: Eine Dokumentation. Herausgezogen von Landesarbeitsgemeinschaft der Filmclubs von Nordrhein-Westfalen anlässlich einer filmkundlichen Arbeitstagung am 14. und 15. Sept. 1968 in Moers/Nordrhein. Munich: Wolfgang Gielow, 1968.

   An anthology containing articles by Eisenstein, Prokofiev, Copland, Zofia Lissa, and others.

32. Evans, Mark. Soundtrack: The Music of the Movies. Cinema Studies Series, ed. Lewis Jacobs. New York: Hopkinson and Blake, 1975.

   A useful, readable survey of film music history and technique, with an introduction by Miklos Rozsa.

   Reprint, New York: DaCapo, 1979. (Paperback.)

   -- Rev. in Audience, 8 (Dec. 1975), 9-10.

   -- Rev. in Music Educators Journal, 62, No. 6 (Feb. 1976), 127.

   -- Rev. in Music Educators Journal, 63, No. 4 (Dec. 1976), 69ff.

   -- Rev. in Fontes Artis Musicae, 25, No. 2 (1978), 199.

   -- Rev. in Quarterly Review of Film Studies, 3, No. 1 (1978), 105-13.

33. Fil'kevič, G. N. "Muzyka v ukrainskich chudožestvennych kinofil'mach." Ph.D. Diss., Kiev 1970.

   Music in Ukrainian feature films.

34. "Filmmusik." In Riemann Musik Lexicon. Ed. Wilibald Gurlitt and Hans Heinrich Eggebrecht. Mainz: B. Schotts Söhne, 1967, III, p. 288.

   Includes bibliography.

35. Frid, Emiliia Lazarevna. Muzyka v sovetskom kino. Leningrad: Muzyka Leningrad. otd-nie, 1967.

36. Gaillard, Marius François. "La musica per film in Francia." In La musica nel film. Ed. Luigi Chiarini. Rome: Bianco e nero editore, 1950, pp. 107-13.

   A paper presented at the 1950 Venice conference. See Chiarini (#1627).

37. Gillett, John, and Roger Manvell. "Music and Film." In The International Encyclopedia of Film. Ed. Roger Manvell et al. New York: Crown; London: Joseph, 1972, pp. 371-74.

   Includes bibliography, pp. 514-28.

38. Green, Christopher. "Composers for the Silver Screen." Music Teacher (Gt. Brit.), 60 (June 1981), 20-21.

39. Grigoriu, Theodor. "Muzica şi cea de a şaptea artă." Muzica, 15, No. 3 (March 1965), 1-10.

   Music and the "seventh art."

40. Grützner, Vera. "Traditionen, Stationen und Tendenzen der Filmmusikdramaturgie: aufgezeigt anhand von Spielfilmen des DEFA-Studios fur Spiel-

filme. Ein Beitrage zum Filmmusikschaffen in der DDR." Ph.D. Diss. Universität Halle 1975.

> Concerning the development of music in the German social-
> ist feature film, with references to the films of Eisen-
> stein and Balázs, and film music theories of Eisler and
> Zofia Lissa.

41. ----------. "Zum Filmmusikschaffen in der DDR." In Sammelbände zur Musikgeschichte der DDR. Vol. IV. Berlin: Neue Musik, 1975, pp. 170-200.

> Survey of the period 1946-1972. Applying the aesthetic
> theories of Hanns Eisler.

42. Hacquard, Georges. La Musique et le cinéma. Bibliothèque internationale
de musicologie. Paris: Presses Universitaires de France, 1959.

> Includes a bibliography, pp. 101-104.

43. Hagen, Earle. "The Score." BMI: The Many Worlds of Music, No. 1 (1974),
14-33.

> Transcript of the film documentary "The Score." See #114.
> Includes references to the music of Axt, David Mendoza,
> Steiner, and Bernstein.

43a. Excerpts appear as: "Composing for Films." Music Educators Journal,
64, No. 1 (Sept. 1977), 29-35.

> Includes a brief bibliography and discography.

44. ----------. Scoring for Films: A Complete Text. New York and Hollywood:
EDJ Music, 1971. (Sole selling agent: Criterion Music Corp., New York,
N.Y.)

> Includes: 1) "The Mechanics and Vocabulary of Film Composition,"
> 2) "The Psychology of Creating Music for Films" (a symposium
> with composers Friedhofer, Goldsmith, Newman, Schifrin, and
> Quincy Jones), and 3) "The Responsibilities of the Composer."

> References to scores for the T.V. series "I Spy," composed by
> Hagen and Friedhofer.

> -- Rev. in Billboard, 83 (Dec. 11, 1971), 12.

> -- Rev. in BMI: The Many Worlds of Music (April 1972), 17-18.

> -- Rev. in Crescendo International, 10 (Feb. 1972), 4.

> -- Rev. in International Musician, 71 (July 1972), 22.

> -- Rev. in Music Educators Journal, 58 (April 1972), 100.

45. Hamilton, Arthur. "Changes: Forty Years of Music and Film." Academy of
Motion Picture Arts and Sciences Bulletin, No. 5 (Spring 1974), 6ff.

46. Helman, Alicja. Dźwięczący ekran. Warsaw: Wydawnictwa Artystyczne i
Filmowe, 1968.

47. ----------. Na ściezce dźwiękowej: O muzyce w filmie. Kraków: Polskie
Wydawnictwo Muzyczne, 1968.

> An anthology.

48. Hickman, C. Sharpless. "Heard While Seeing." Music Journal, 9, No. 7
(Nov. 1951), 19.

> The first in a series of articles by Hickman, this intro-
> duction includes references to music by George Antheil.

49. Hoérée, Arthur. "Historie et fonction de la musique de film." Polyphonie,
Series 2, No. 6 (1950), 59-66.

50. Hrabal, František. Film a hudba. Brünn: Diplomarbeit, 1953.

51. Huntley, John. British Film Music. London: Skelton Robinson, 1947.

> A thorough study of film music in Great Britain, with an
> introduction by Muir Mathieson. Includes discography and
> a selected bibliography, pp. 244-46.

Reprinted as part of the series "The Literature of Cinema,"
New York: Arno Press, 1972.

-- Rev. by Lawrence Morton: "Rule, Britannia!" In Hollywood Quarterly, 3, No. 2 (Winter 1948), 211-14. See
#1442.

-- Rev. by Stuart Keen: "British Film Music." In Sight and
Sound, 16, No. 63 (Autumn 1947), 111.

52. ----------. "Film Music." Sight and Sound, 12, No. 48 (Jan. 1944), 90-93.

See the response to this article by Darrel Catling, #1227.

53. ÍAnov-ÍAnovskaía, N. S. Muzyka uzbekskogo kino. Tashkent: Fan, 1969.

Survey of film music in the Uzbek region of the U.S.S.R.

54. ----------. "Muzyka v kino i kinomuzyka." Sovetskaya muzyka, 33, No. 11
(Nov. 1969), 62-66.

55. "Introduction to Film and Music." Motion (Toronto), 4, No. 2 (1975), 6.

56. Irving, Ernest. Cue for Music: An Autobiography. With a Prologue and
Epilogue by Derek Hudson. London: Dennis Dobson, 1959.

Especially for Chapter 32: "Music in Films," and Chapter
34: "Rawsthorne, Walton and Vaughan-Williams."

57. ----------. "Film Music." Proceedings of the Royal Music Association, 76
(1949-1950), 35-45.

58. ----------. "La musica per film in Inghilterra." In La musica nel film.
Ed. Luigi Chiarini. Rome: Bianco e nero editore, 1950, pp. 114-17.

A paper presented at the 1950 Venice conference. See
Chiarini (#1627).

59. ----------, Hans Keller, and Wilfred H. Mellers. "Film Music." In Grove's
Dictionary of Music and Musicians. 5th ed. Ed. Eric Blom. London:
Macmillan; and New York: St. Martin's Press, 1954, III, pp. 93-110.

Includes sections on history and compositional techniques
(Keller), recording techniques (Irving), and film music
aesthetics (Mellers).

60. Joffe, Judah A. Muzyka sovetskogo kino: Osnovy muzykal'noi dramaturgii.
Leningrad, 1938.

61. Kak, Siddarth. "Editorial." Cinema Vision India, 1, No. 4 (Oct. 1980), 2.

Introduction to a special issue devoted to the music of
India's film industry. Includes articles by Chandavarkar
(#2744, 4233, 4496), Chatterjee (#2745), Ghatak (#4608),
Joshi (#5091), Kaushal (#2826), Mohan (#271), Ranade (#283),
Seth (#291), and Sharma (#116).

62. Kleiner, Arthur, and Christian Blackwood. Hollywood's Musical Moods.
New York: Blackwood Productions, n.d.

A filmed documentary. Available through Blackwood Productions, Inc., 58 West 58th St., New York, N.Y., 10019.

63. Kofin, Ewa. Muzyka telewizyjna. Warsaw: Wydawnictwa Radia i Telewizji,
1980.

-- Rev. in Ruch muzyczny (Warsaw), 25, No. 4 (1981), 18.

64. Kolodin, Irving. "Sounds for the Silver Screen." Saturday Review, 5,
No. 4 (Nov. 12, 1977), 44-46.

65. Korganov, Tomas Iosifovich, and Ivan Dmitrievich Frolov. Kino i muzyka:
muzyka v dramaturgii fil'ma. Moscow: Iskusstvo, 1964.

Includes an extensive and useful filmography noting composers and sound editors for Russian films, pp. 332-46.

66. Kreis, Robert B. "The Sound Track." Films in Review, 10, No. 2 (Feb.
1959), 114-15.

67. Kresh, Paul. "Is There Any Music at the Movies?" Stereo Review (Boulder, Colo.), 23, No. 3 (Sept. 1969), 75-80

    Reprinted in Limbacher, pp. 32-41. See #75.

68. Kułakowska, Zofia. "La musique de film en Pologne." Image et son, Nos. 136-137 (1960).

69. Kuna, Milan. Zvuk a hudba ve filmu: K analýze zvukové dramaturgie filmu. Hudební vědy, Series A, Vol. 7. Prague: Panton, 1969.

    Includes summaries in English and German.

70. Lacombe, Alain, and Claude Rocle. La musique du film. Paris: Éditions Francis Van de Velde, 1979.

    A valuable survey of European and American composers, with brief biographical information and filmographies, pp. 143-410. Includes a selected discography, pp. 437-56.

    -- Rev. in Cinéma 79, No. 250 (Oct. 1979), 96.

    -- Rev. in Ecran, No. 86 (Dec. 15, 1979), 74.

    -- Rev. in Harmonie (Paris), No. 153 (Dec. 1979), 138-39.

    -- Rev. by Renaud Bezombes: "Pianos mecaniques." In Cinematographe (Paris), No. 54 (Jan. 1980), 68-69.

    -- Rev. by Hubert Niogret in Positif (Paris), No. 228 (March 1980), 78-79.

    -- Rev. by Serge Champenier in Revue du cinema/Image et son, No. 349 (April 1980), 140.

    -- Rev. in Jazz Magazine (Paris), No. 291 (Nov. 1980), 8.

    -- Rev. by Ermanno Comuzio in Cineforum, No. 201 (Jan. 1981), 78-79.

71. la Motte-Haber, Helga de, and Hans Emons. Filmmusik: eine systematische Beschreibung. Munich: Carl Hanser Verlag, 1980.

    -- Rev. in Neue Zeitschrift für Musik, No. 3 (May-June 1981), 299-300.

    -- Rev. in Musik und Bildung, 14 (April 1982), 251-52+.

    -- Rev. in Musikforschung, 35, No. 3 (1982), 326-27.

    -- Rev. in Schweizerische Musikzeitung, 122, No. 2 (1982), 99ff.

72. Larson, Randall D. A Survey of Film Music in the Fantastic Cinema. (Mimeograph.) Los Altos, Calif.: Fandom, 1980.

    Includes discography.

73. Lavagnino, Angelo Francesco, and Gaetano Carancini. "La musica per film." In Enciclopedia della musica. Ed. Claudio Sartori et al. Milan: G. Ricordi, 1964, III, pp. 241-43.

    Includes bibliography.

74. Levy, Louis. Music for the Movies. London: Sampson Low, Marston, 1948.

    An autobiographical account by the British film music composer.

75. Limbacher, James L., comp. and ed. Film Music: From Violins to Video. Metuchen, N. J.: Scarecrow Press, 1974.

    Part I is an anthology of historical and theoretical material, including two articles by Limbacher: "How It All Began," pp. 13-14, and "Classical Composers on the Screen," p. 158. Contributions by 34 authors, including Buchanan, M.E. Bute, P. Cook, Eisenstein, J. Embler, G. Forrell, O.L. Guernsey, W. Hamilton, and composers Applebaum, E. Bernstein, Bliss, Dahl, Duning, J. Green, Mathieson, Raksin, Rosenman, Rozsa, Stevens, Tiomkin, Walton, and others, pp. 13-191.

    Part II is a listing of films and composers, including discography, pp. 193-835.

-- Rev. in <u>High Fidelity and Musical America</u>, 24, No. 11 (Nov. 1974), MA38-39.

-- Rev. in <u>Symphony News</u> (American Symphony Orchestra League), 25, No. 5 (1974), 24.

-- Rev. by Clifford McCarty in <u>MLA Notes</u>, 31, No. 1 (1974-75), 48-50.

-- Rev. in <u>Film Heritage</u>, 10, No. 3 (1975), 29-30.

76. ----------. <u>Four Aspects of the Film</u>. New York: Brussel and Brussel, 1969.

Part IV: "Sound," pp. 197-229, and "Appendix: Pioneer Sound Films," pp. 363-72. Includes bibliography, pp. 255-56.

77. Lindgren, Ernest. <u>The Art of the Film: An Introduction to Film Appreciation</u>. London: George Allen and Unwin, 1948.

Chapters: "The Use of Sound," pp. 97-116, and "Film Music," pp. 141-54, and many other references to music.

77a. Reprint, New York: Macmillan, 1963.

77b. Published in Russian translation, Moscow: Iskusstvo, 1956.

78. Lindlar, Heinrich, and Reinhold Schubert, eds. <u>Die drei grossen "F": Film--Funk--Fernsehen</u>. Musik der Zeit: eine Schriftenreihe zu Musik und Gegenwart, Neue Folge, II. Bonn: Boosey and Hawkes, 1958.

An anthology of 14 articles. See especially those by Edmund Nick (#767) and Fred K. Prieberg (#4825).

<u>79</u>. London, Kurt. <u>Film Music: A Summary of the Characteristic Features of Its History, Aesthetics, Technique, and Possible Developments</u>. London: Faber and Faber, 1936.

Includes an introduction by Constant Lambert, and a section "Silent Films and Musical Synchronization," pp. 66-70.

-- Rev. by M. D. Calvocoressi in <u>Sight and Sound</u>, 5, No. 9 (Autumn 1936), 92-93

See comments by George Antheil in <u>Modern Music</u>, 14, No. 2 (Jan.-Feb. 1937), 105-07. See #2976.

Reprinted as part of the series "The Literature of Cinema," New York: Arno Press, 1970.

79a. Published in Russian translation: <u>Muzyka fil'ma</u>. Moscow and Leningrad, 1937.

<u>80</u>. Māheśvarī, Oṅkāraprasāda. <u>Hindi-citrapaṭa kā gīti-sāhitya</u>, 1978.

History and criticism of motion picture music in India. Includes bibliography, pp. 346-50.

81. Manvell, Roger. <u>The Film and the Public</u>. Harmondsworth, Middlesex: Pelican Books, 1955.

Includes chapters: "Music and the Silent Film," pp. 50-53, "Music and the Sound Film," pp. 57-68, "Sound: The Great Revolution," pp. 54-56, "Counterpointing Sound and Image," pp. 73-74, along with references to Eisenstein's <u>The Film Sense</u> (see #4562), and other references to film music.

<u>82</u>. ----------, and John Huntley. <u>The Technique of Film Music</u>. Written and compiled with the guidance of the following committee appointed by the British Film Academy: William Alwyn (chairman), Ken Cameron, Muir Mathieson, and Basil Wright. The Library of Communication Techniques. London and New York: Focal Press, 1957. (Reprints, 1967, 1969, 1971.)

An important history of film music. Includes detailed analysis of scores by Walton, Thomson, Rozsa, and Alwyn, a section which deals with experiments in "animated sound" written by Norman McLaren, discography, pp. 225-280, and bibliography, pp. 285-91.

-- Rev. by Zofia Lissa in <u>Muzyka</u>, No. 4 (1957), 129-32.

82a. Published also as: Tecnica della musica nel film. Trans. Gioia Angiolillo Zannino. Collana di studi critici e scientifici del Centro sperimentale di cinematografia, VI. Rome: Edizioni di Bianco e Nero, 1959.

82b. Revised and enlarged edition by Richard Arnell and Peter Day. London and New York: Focal Press, 1975.

Includes a section "Four Films Since 1955," pp. 245-64, a discussion of The Devils (Peter Maxwell Davies), Kubrick's 2001 (music by Johann Strauss, Richard Strauss, György Ligeti, and Aram Khatchaturian), Second Best (Arnell), and Zabriskie Point (Pink Floyd, The Rolling Stones et al.).

Also includes reprints of articles by Gerald Pratley (see #4822) and Hans Keller (see #2953), and updated filmography, pp. 165-86, and bibliography, pp. 291-302.

-- Rev. in The School Musician, 46 (April 1975), 40.

-- Rev. in Quarterly Review of Film Studies, 3, No. 1 (1978), 105-11.

83. Mathieson, Muir. "The Movie Scene -- Film Music Series: Introductory Programme." Film Music Notes, 8, No. 4 (Mar.-Apr. 1949), 5-6.

The first in a series of six programs recorded for CBC."

84. Miceli, Sergio. "Musica e film: La colonna sonora ha cinquant'anni. E possibile un bilancio?" Nuova rivista musicale italiana, 11, No. 3 (July-Sept. 1977), 349-63.

Includes bibliography.

85. ----------. La musica nel film: Arte e artigianato. Rome, 1981.

-- Rev. by Ermanno Comuzio in Cineforum (Bergamo), No. 217 (Sept. 1982), 78.

86. Moser, Hans Joachim. "Tonfilm." In Musik Lexicon. 4th ed. Hamburg: Musikverlag Hans Sikorski, 1955, II, pp. 1300-02.

Includes bibliography.

87. Music for the Movies. New York: Canadian Broadcasting Corporation, n.d.

A filmed documentary available through CBC-TV, 245 Park Ave., New York, N. Y., 10017.

A symposium with contributions by Copland, Walton, Raksin, and Applebaum.

88. Newlin, Dika. "American Film Scores: Yesterday and Today." Pan Pipes of SAI (Des Moines, Iowa), 70, No. 2 (1978), 3-4.

89. Nick, Edmund, and Martin Ulner. "Filmmusik." In Die Musik in Geschichte und Gegenwart. Ed. Friedrich Blume. Kassel: Bärenreiter, 1955, IV, pp. 187-202.

Sections on silent and sound history and technique (Nick), and problems of sound recording (Ulner). Includes bibliography.

90. O'Toole, Lawrence. "Moving Music." Film Comment, 17, No. 5 (Sept.-Oct. (1981), 13-16, 18-20.

91. Paiva, Salviano Cavalcanti de. "Cinema Brasileiro e Música Popular." Chuvisco (Rio de Janeiro), (Oct. 1963), 60-63.

92. Palmer, Christopher. The Composer in Hollywood. Berkeley, Calif., 1975.

Work in progress, 1975.

93. ----------, and John Gillett. "Film Music." In The New Grove Dictionary of Music and Musicians. Ed. Stanley Sadie. London: Macmillan, 1980, VI, pp. 549-56.

A summary of film music function and technique, and a survey of its history in America (Palmer), Europe, and the Far East (Gillett).

Includes bibliography.

94. Pasinetti, Francesco. "Cenno storico sulla collaborazione della musica col film dalla nascita del cinema a oggi nei diversi paesi europei: Italia." In Atti del secondo congresso internazionale di musica, Firenze-Cremona, 11-26 maggio, 1937. Florence: F. Le Monnier, 1940, pp. 239-43.

> A paper presented at the 1937 Florence conference. Includes synopses in French and German, pp. 243-44. See #1186.

95. Patachich, Iván. Filmhang, filmzene. Filmamatörök kiskönyvtara, VI. Budapest: NPI, 1973

> Sound-film and film music.

96. Pauli, Hansjörg. Filmmusik: Geshichte, Funktion und Asthetik. Fünfteiliges Rundfunkmanuskript WDR, III, 1975.

97. ----------. "Filmmusik: Ein historisch-kritischer Abriss." In Musik in den Massenmedien, Rundfunk und Fernsehen: Perspektiven und Materialien. Ed. Hans-Christian Schmidt. Mainz: B. Schotts Söhne, 1976, pp. 91-119.

98. ----------. "Musik im Film." Schweizerische Musikzeitung (Revue musicale Suisse), 114, No. 6 (1974), 326-31.

99. Pellegrini, Glauco. "La musica del film." In La storia del cinema, III. Ed. Lorenzo Camusso and Riccardo Mezzanotte. Milan: Vallardi edizioni periodiche, 1966.

100. Petrova, Inna Fedorovna. Muzyka sovetskogo kino. Narodnii Universitet Fakultet literatury i iskusstva, No. 5. Moscow: Znaniye, 1964.

> Includes bibliography.

101. Pilka, Jiří. Tajemství filmové hudby. Knižnice Film a doba. Prague: Orbis, 1960.

102. ----------. "Tradice české filmové hudby." Dějiny a současnost, 2 (1960), 19-21.

> A brief survey of music in Czechoslovakian film.

103. Porcile, François. Présence de la musique à l'écran. 7ème art. Paris: Les Éditions du Cerf, 1969.

> Includes a useful listing of European and American composers with biographical information, listing of film and concert scores (and borrowings), and collaborations, pp. 207-328. Also a bibliography, pp. 329-31, and discography, pp. 333-35.
>
> > -- Rev. by Jean Matter in Schweizerische Musikzeitung (Revue musicale suisse), 110, No. 6 (Nov.-Dec. 1970). 367-70.

104. Prendergast, Roy M. A Neglected Art: A Critical Study of Music in Films. With a Foreword by William Kraft. New York: New York University Press, 1977.

104a. Reprinted in paperback with the title Film Music: A Neglected Art. New York: W. W. Norton, 1977.

> -- Rev. in American Record Guide (Washington, D.C.), 41 (April 1978), 42-43.
>
> -- Rev. in Music Educators Journal, 64 (April 1978), 8ff.
>
> -- Rev. by Martin Marks: "Focus." In Pro Musica Sana, 6, No. 4 (Fall 1978), 14-17.
>
> -- Rev. in Cantrill's Filmnotes (Melbourne), Nos. 31-32 (Nov. 1979), 19ff.

> Includes bibliography, pp. 254-60.

105. Prieberg, Fred K. "Filmmusik." In Lexicon der Neuen Musik. Freiburg/Munich: Karl Alber Verlag, 1958, p. 131ff.

106. Ranade, Ashok. "Music and Music Films." Journal of the Sangeet Natak

Akademi, 39 (Jan.-Mar. 1976), 23-29.

107. Rubsamen, Walter H. Descriptive Music for Stage and Screen. (Pamphlet.)
Los Angeles: the author (University of California), 1947.

    Reprinted from the Volume of Proceedings of the Music
Teachers National Association for 1946.

  107a. Reprinted in Hinrichsen's Musical Yearbook, 7 (1952), 559-69.

108. ----------. Music in the Dramatic Film. (Pamphlet.) Washington, D.C.:
United States Information Service, 1956.

  108a. Reprinted as: "Music in the American Dramatic Film." The
Juilliard Review, 4, No. 2 (Spring 1957), 20-28.

109. Ruiz de Luna, Salvador. La música en el cine y la música para el cine.
(Pamphlet.) Madrid: Pérez Galdós, 1960.

110. Sabaneev, Leonid Leonidovich. Music for the Films: A Handbook for Composers and Conductors. Translated from the Russian by S. W. Pring. London: Sir Isaac Pitman and Sons, 1935.

    Perhaps the earliest overview and guidebook for film mu-
sic composition.

    Reprinted as part of the series "The Literature of Cinema,"
New York: Arno Press, 1978.

    See comments by George Antheil in "Good Russian Advice...,"
#2965.

111. Schmidt, Hans-Christian. Filmmusik. Kassel: Bärenreiter, 1982.

    -- Rev. in Musik und Bildung, 15 (March 1983), 51.

112. Scholes, Percy A. The Oxford Companion to Music. 9th ed. London: Oxford
University Press, 1955.

    Entries: "Cinematograph and Music," pp. 186-87, "Gramo-
phone," pp. 421-25, and some composer entries.

113. Schwimmer, Helmut. "Film und Musik." Melos, 34, Nos. 7-8 (July-Aug. 1967),
249-58.

114. The Score. New York: Broadcast Music Inc., 1974.

    A filmed documentary. Available through BMI, 40 West 57th
St., New York, N.Y., 10019.

    For transcriptions of the film, see #43 and #115.

    Additional information accompanying the film may be found
at #11, #2345, and #6294.

115. "The Score: The Writers in Profile." BMI: The Many Worlds of Music, 1
(1974), 14-33.

    Transcript of the film documentary "The Score." See #43
and #114. Includes references to the music of Axt, E.
Bernstein, David Mendoza, and Max Steiner.

116. Sharma, Narendra. "Half a Century of Song." Cinema Vision India, 1,
No. 4 (October 1980), 56-61.

    See #61.

117. Shilova, Irina Mikailovna. Film i iego muzyka. Moscow: Vsesoiuznoi iz-
datel'stvo sovetskii kompozitor, 1973.

    Includes an introduction by M. Tapakanova, pp. 3-20,
filmography, pp. 220-26, and bibliography, pp. 227-28.

118. ----------. Muzyka v kino: Novoe v žizni, nauke, technike. Iskusstvo, I.
Moscow: Znanie, 1973.

119. Skiles, Marlin. Music Scoring for T.V. and Motion Pictures. Blue Ridge
Summit, Pa.: Tab Books, 1976.

    Includes interviews with Friedhofer, Green, Grusin, Jones,
North, and Lawrence Morton.

120. Skinner, Frank. _Underscore_. Hollywood, Calif.: Skinner Music Co., 1950.

> The composer traces, step by step, the creation of his score for "The Irishman."
>
> -- Rev. in _The Music Dealer_, 5 (Jan. 1951), 33.
>
> -- Rev. in _Etude_, 69 (March 1951), 9.
>
> -- Rev. in _The Instrumentalist_ (Evanston, Ill.), 6 (Sept. 1951), 30.
>
> Reprint, New York: Criterion Music Corp., 1960.

121. Steen, T. M. F. "The Sound Track." _Films in Review_, 11, No. 4 (April 1960), 242-44.

> A survey of French film music composers.

122. Sternfeld, Frederick W. "Film Music." In _Harvard Dictionary of Music_. 2nd rev. ed. Ed. Willi Apel. Cambridge, Mass.: Belknap/Harvard University Press, 1969, pp. 314-15.

> Includes bibliography.

123. ----------. "Music and the Cinema." In _Twentieth Century Music_. Ed. Rollo H. Myers. London: John Calder Ltd., 1960, pp. 95-111.

> Article also appears in the 2nd revised and enlarged edition, London: Calder, 1968, pp. 123-39.

124. Tarp, Svend Erik. "Film og musik (Part 1)." _Dansk Musiktidsskrift_ (Copenhagen), 24, No. 1 (1949), 5-12.

125. Taylor, Theodore. _People Who Make Movies_. Illustrated with Photographs. New York: Avon Camelot Books, 1967.

> Chapter: "Music and the Musical," p. 121ff.

126. Thiel, Wolfgang. "Filmmusik in der DDR: Ein historisch-kritischer Abriss." _Bulletin: Berlin DDR_, 16, No. 3 (1979), 3-13.

127. ----------. _Filmmusik in Geschichte und Gegenwart_. Berlin: Henschelverlag Kunst und Gesellschaft, 1981.

> A valuable recent work, with extensive bibliographic references.
>
> -- Rev. in _Schweizerische Musikzeitung_, 122, No. 3 (1982), 179ff.
>
> -- Rev. in _Musik und Gesellschaft_, 32 (Feb. 1982), 116-17.
>
> -- Rev. in _Musikforum_ (Leipzig), 28, No. 2 (1983), 31.

128. Thiery, Herman. _Lantarenmuziek: een nieuwe bundel filmatiek, ter gelegenheid van het 60ste jaarfest van de bioscoop_. Antwerp: Nederlandsche Boekhandel, 1957.

129. Thomas, Hans Alex. "Die deutsche Tonfilmmusik." Ph.D. Diss., Marpurg 1957.

130. ----------. _Die deutsche Tonfilmmusik: Von den Anfängen bis 1956_. Neue Beiträge zur Film- und Fernsehforschung, III. Gütersloh: Bertelsmann Verlag, 1962.

> Essays. Also includes a detailed listing of composers.
>
> -- Rev. by Gerhard Maletzke in _Rundfunk und Fernsehen_, 11 (1963), 312.

131. Thomas, Tony. _Film Score: The View from the Podium_. South Brunswick, N.J.: A. S. Barnes and Co., 1979.

> Biographies and comments by 20 major film music composers. Includes a discography by Page Cook (see #6275), and selective bibliography by Win Sharples, Jr. (see #6253).
>
> -- Rev. by Claudia Gorbman in _Film Quarterly_, 33, No. 4 (1980), 44-45.
>
> -- Rev. by David Meeker in _Film_ (London), No. 87 (1980), 12.

-- Rev. by A. Auster in Cineaste, 10, No. 4 (1980), 44.

-- Rev. by A. C. Robbins: "Film Smorgasbord." In Pro Musica Sana, 8, No. 3 (Summer 1980), 15-16.

-- Rev. in MLA Notes, 37, No. 3 (1981), 592-93.

-- Rev. by Page Cook in Films in Review, 32 (May 1981), 307.

132. ----------. Music for the Movies. South Brunswick, N.J.: A. S. Barnes; London: Tantivy Press, 1973.

A useful introductory survey. Includes discography, pp. 221-35, and filmography, compiled by Clifford McCarty, pp. 236-64.

-- Rev. in Kosmorama (Copenhagen), 22, No. 130 (1976), 167.

-- Rev. in Films in Review, 25 (Jan. 1974), 45-46.

-- Rev. in Variety, No. 275 (June 12, 1974), 20.

-- Rev. in Crescendo International, 12 (Dec. 1973), 24.

-- Rev. by Konrad Vogelsang in Die Musikforschung, 30, No. 1 (1977), 98-99.

133. Tinhorão, José Ramos. Música popular: teatro & cinema. Petrópolis (Brazil): Editôra Vozes, 1972.

Part 2: "A música popular no cinema," pp. 227-72. A survey of music in Brazilian feature films and documentaries. Includes bibliographic references and a selected filmography of silent and early sound films, 1899-1933.

134. Tonnerre, J. "Dossier: 44 noms pour memoire." Cinematographe (Paris), No. 50 (July-August 1980), 4-12.

135. Tuxen, Erik. "Film og musik (Part 3)." Dansk Musiktidsskrift (Copenhagen), 24, No. 3 (1949), 60-64.

136. van de Ven, Luc. Motion Picture Music. Mechelen, Belgium: Soundtrack, 1980.

Twenty four articles which originally appeared in Soundtrack (SCN). Includes discography and filmography.

137. Van Parys, Georges. "Film (Musique de)." In Encyclopédie de la musique. Ed. François Michel et al. Paris: Fasquelle éditeurs, 1959, II, pp. 58-62.

138. Vasina-Grossman, Vera Andreevna. Zametki o muzyke frantsuzskich fil'mov. Frantsuzskoe kinoiskusstvo. Moscow: Gos. muzykal'noe izd-vo, 1960.

139. Vlad, Roman. "Musica per film." In La musica, I: Enciclopedia storica. Ed. Alberto Basso and Guido Maria Gatti. Turin: Unione tipografico-editrice torinese, 1966.

140. Weber, Horst. "Filmmusik." In Das grosse Lexicon der Musik. Ed. Marc Honegger and Günther Massenkeil. Freiburg: Verlag Herder, 1980, III, pp. 92-95.

Includes bibliography.

SEE ALSO:
#338(Atkins), #473(Bruyr), #4423(Ariscarco), #4460(Boilès), #4515(Colpi), #4573(Eisler/Adorno), #4606(Germain), #4638(Helman), #4657(W. Johnson), #4663(Jungk), #4733(Lissa), #4819(Piva), #4836(Ringger), #4913(W. Thiel), #4915(W. Thiel), #6264(Hippenmeyer), #6301(ASCAP).

Film and Music Histories
(with references to Film Music)

141. Anderson, Joseph L., and Donald Richie. The Japanese Film: Art and Indus-
     try. Rutland, Vt., and Tokyo: Charles E. Tuttle, 1959.

>   Chapter: "The Talkies; Exterior: 1931-39," pp. 72-125,
>   and many other references to music in Japanese film.
>   Includes bibliography.

   141a. Expanded edition, with a foreword by Akira Kurosawa, Prince-
        ton, N.J.: Princeton University Press, 1982.

142. Austin, William V. Music in the Twentieth Century. New York: W. W. Norton,
     1966.

>   Brief references to theories espoused by Jean Cocteau and
>   Igor Stravinsky, and to the music of Auric, Chaplin, Cop-
>   land, Eisler, Hindemith, Honegger, Milhaud, Prokofiev, and
>   Shostakovich.

143. Bährens, Kurt. Der Schallfilm: Geschichte, Technik, Einsatz -- eine erste
     Darstellung, mit 13 Abbildungen und 1 Zeichnung im Text. Berlin: Verlag
     für Recht und Verwaltung, 1939.

144. Balcon, Michael, Ernest Lindgren, Forsyth Hardy, and Roger Manvell.
     Twenty Years of British Film, 1925-45. London: Focal Press, 1947.

>   Includes articles on early sound film (Lindgren), docu-
>   mentary (Hardy) and feature films (Manvell), with an in-
>   troduction by Balcon.

145. Baxter, John. The Australian Cinema. Sydney: Pacific Books, 1970.

146. Booch, S. H. Film Industry in India. New Delhi: India Information Ser-
     vices, 1953.

147. Brockhaus, Heinz Alfred, and Konrad Niemann. Sammelbände zur Musikge-
     schichte der Deutschen Demokratischen Republik, V. Berlin: Verlag
     Neue Musik, 1975.

>   -- Rev. in Medien und Erziehung (Munich), 22, No. 1
>   (1978), 63-65.

148. Cantacuzino, Ion. "L'evolution historique du cinéma roumain." Revue Rou-
     maine d'Histoire de l'Art (Bucarest), 5 (1968), 189-208.

149. Descaves, Pierre, and A. V. J. Martin. Un siècle de radio et de télévision.
     Paris: Office de Radiodiffusion-Télévision Française, and Les Productions
     de Paris, 1965.

>   Survey and an anthology. Includes articles by P. de Bois-
>   deffre (#5050), G. Clancier (#4509), J. Cocteau (#4510),
>   C. Contamine (#4526), P. Deharme (#2048), G. Desson (#4543),
>   E. Girardeau (#2061), and M. Philippot (#280).

150. Developing Mass Media in Asia. Paris: UNESCO, 1960.

151. Eames, J. D. The MGM Story: The Complete History of Fifty Roaring Years,
     1924-1974. New York: Crown; London: Octopus, Sundial, 1975.

>   -- Rev. in Variety, 281 (Dec. 10, 1975), 6.

152. Ewen, David. All the Years of American Popular Music. Englewood Cliffs,
     N.J.: Prentice-Hall, 1977.

>   Chapters: "The Silent Screen Erupts into Sound," pp. 380-
>   408, and "The Movies, the Radio, and Now Television,"
>   pp. 495-508. Many other references to music in film and
>   film musicals.

153. ----------. American Popular Songs from the Revolutionary War to the Pre-
     sent. New York: Random House, 1966.

References to the major song composers and their music for film and film musicals.

154. ----------. Great Men of American Popular Song. Englewood Cliffs, N.J.: Prentice-Hall, 1970.

Biographical sketches of the major song composers, many of whom have composed for film. References to the work of Henry Mancini, Victor Herbert, and others.

155. Fielding, Raymond, ed. A Technological History of Motion Pictures and Television. Berkeley and Los Angeles: University of California Press, 1967. (Second edition, 1979.)

Includes a history of sound and music recording. Special attention to the achievements of Augustin Lauste and Joseph T. Tykociner. See also Kellogg (#254).

156. Gaur, Madan. Other Side of the Coin: An Intimate Study of the Indian Film Industry. Bombay: Trimurti Prakashan, 1973.

157. Geduld, Harry M., comp. Film Makers on Film Making: Statements on Their Art by Thirty Directors. Bloomington, Ind.: Indiana University Press, 1975.

Valuable insight into their philosophies of film making, with only a few references to their views on sound and music.

158. Geiger, Franz. Zauberei in Zelluloid: das Buch vom Film. Munich: Verlag Paul Müller, 1952.

159. Gregor, Ulrich, and Enno Patalas. Geschichte des Films. Gütersloh: S. Mohn, 1962.

160. Griffith, Richard, and Arthur Mayer. The Movies: The Sixty-Year Story of the World of Hollywood and Its Effect on America, from Pre-Nickelodeon Days to the Present. New York: Simon and Schuster, 1957.

A general survey, with only a few comments concerning sound and music.

161. Häusler, Josef. Musik im XX. Jahrhundert: von Schönberg zu Penderecki. Bremen: Schünemann, 1969.

162. Hazumi Tsuneo. Eiga gojūnen shi. Tokyo: Masu Shobō, 1942.

Fifty years of Japanese film history.

163. Holmes, Winifred. Orient: A Survey of Films Produced in Countries of Arab and Asian Culture. London: British Film Institute, 1959.

164. Iijima Tadashi. Nihon eiga shi. 2 vols. Tokyo: Hakusuisha, 1955.

Many references to the use of music in Japanese films.

165. Jacobs, Lewis. The Rise of the American Film: A Critical History. New York: Harcourt, Brace, 1939. (Second edition, 1944.)

Only a few references to film music in the chapter "Refinements of Technique," pp. 433-45. Includes bibliography, pp. 541-64.

165a. Expanded edition, New York: Columbia University/ Teachers College Press, 1968.

Includes an additional article by Jacobs: "Experimental Cinema in America, 1921-1947," including comments on the work of James and John Whitney.

166. Joffe, Judah A. Sinteticheskoe izuchenie iskusstva i zvukovoe kino. Leningrad, 1937.

167. Kingman, Daniel. American Music: A Panorama. New York: Schirmer Books, 1979.

Chapter 10: "Broadway, Hollywood, and Tin Pan Alley," pp. 239-84; Chapter 14: "Music with Film, Dance, Drama, and Poetry," pp. 382-427 (including a section "Music with Film," pp. 387-95).

Includes a discussion of scores by L. Bernstein, Copland, and Thomson, and bibliographic references.

168. Knight, Arthur. <u>The Liveliest Art: A Panoramic History of the Movies</u>. New York: New American Library, 1957.

169. Koch, Heinrich, and Heinrich Braune. <u>Von deutscher Filmkunst: Gehalt und Gestalt</u>. Berlin: H. Scherping, 1943.

170. Lapierre, Marcel. <u>Anthologie du cinéma, rétrospective pas les textes de l'art muet qui devint parlant</u>. Paris: La nouvelle édition, 1946.

171. Lebedev, Nikolaĭ Alekseevich. <u>Otscherki istorii kino SSSR</u>. Moscow: Goskinoisdat, 1947.

Reprint, Moscow: Iskusstvo, 1965.

172. ----------, Jurij Sergeevich Kalšnikov, Rostislav Jurenev, and L. Pogosheva, eds. <u>Otscherki istorii sovetskogo kino</u>. 3 vols. Moscow: Iskusstvo, 1956.

An anthology.

173. Leyda, Jay. <u>Dianying: Electric Shadows, An Account of Films and the Film Audience in China</u>. Cambridge, Mass.: MIT Press, 1972.

174. Mahmood, Hameemuddm. <u>The Kaleidoscope of Indian Cinema</u>. New Delhi: Affiliated East-West Press, 1975.

Many references to music in Indian films.

175. Manvell, Roger. <u>The Animated Film</u>. London: Sylvan Press, 1954.

176. ----------, and John Halas, eds. <u>The Technique of Film Animation</u>. London and New York: Focal Press, 1959.

Chapter: "The Sound Track," pp. 69-83, and other sections dealing with the work of Norman McLaren. See #3569. Also includes an article by Francis Chagrin and Matyas Seiber. See #1622.

177. Mast, Gerald. <u>A Short History of the Movies</u>. New York: Bobbs-Merrill, 1971.

178. Mussulman, Joseph Agee. <u>The Uses of Music: An Introduction to Music in Contemporary American Life</u>. Englewood Cliffs, N.J.: Prentice-Hall, 1974.

179. Okada Susumu. <u>Nihon eiga no rekishi: sono kigyō gijutsu geijutsu</u>. Tokyo: Daviddosha, 1967.

A history of Japanese film, its commerce, technology, and art. Includes references to the use of music and sound.

180. Płażewski, Jerzy. <u>Język filmu</u>. Warsaw: Widawnictwo Artystyczne i Filmowe, 1961.

Includes bibliography.

181. Rangoonwalla, Firoze. <u>Seventy-Five Years of Indian Cinema</u>. New Delhi: India Library, 1975.

Many references to music in Indian films.

182. Ray, Satyajit. <u>Our Films, Their Films</u>. Calcutta: Orient Longmans, 1976.

183. Richie, Donald. <u>Japanese Cinema: Film Style and National Character</u>. New York: Doubleday; London: Secker and Warburg, 1971.

An expanded and revised version of <u>Japanese Movies</u>, Tokyo: Japanese Travel Bureau, 1961, which includes many references to the music in Japanese films.

184. Richter, Erika. <u>Realistischer Film in Ägypten</u>. Berlin: Henschel, 1974.

Includes filmography.

185. Rotha, Paul. Rotha on the Film: A Selection of Writings About the Cinema. Fair Lawn, N.J.: Essential Books; London: Faber and Faber, 1958.

Reprint, New York: Garland Publ., 1978.

A collection of essays by Rotha, with some references to the role of music in his films.

186. Sadoul, Georges. Histoire d'un art: Le Cinéma des origines à nos jours. Paris: Ernest Flammarion, 1949. (Reprints, 1953 and 1955.)

186a. Reprinted with the title Histoire mondiale du cinéma. Paris: Flammarion, 1959.

Historical developments in music and sound, with a geographical focus. Includes a listing of directors and major films (1892-1948). General bibliography, pp. 447-55.

187. ----------. Histoire générale du cinema. 6 vols. Paris: Éditions Denoël, 1946-1954.

See especially Vol. 3: "Le cinéma devient un art (1909-1920)," and Vol. 4: "L'époque contemporaine (1939-1954)." Many references to film music.

187a. Also published in German translation as: Geschichte der Filmkunst. Ed. Hans Winge. Vienna: Schönbrunn-Verlag, 1957.

188. Scheugl, Hans, and Ernst Schmidt, Jr. Eine Subgeschichte des Films: Lexikon des Avantgarde-, Experimental- und Undergroundfilms. 2 vols. Frankfurt: Suhrkamp, 1974.

References to "experimental" film music and experiments in "animated sound."

189. Sowjetischer Dokumentarfilm. Staatliches Filmarchiv der DDR. Berlin: Henschelverlag, 1967.

190. Stanley, Robert H. The Celluloid Empire. New York: Hastings House, 1978.

References to music and developments in sound technology.

191. Tanaka Jun'ichirō. Nihon eiga hattatsu shi. 4 vols. Tokyo: Chūō Kōronsha, 1957.

Development of the Japanese film.

192. Toeplitz, Jerzy. Historia sztuki filmowej, Vols. I-III. Instytut Sztuki Polskiej Akademii Nauk. Warsaw: Filmowa Agencja Wydawnicza, 1955-59; and Vol. IV. Warsaw: Wydawnictwa Artystyczne i Filmowe, 1967.

A chronological survey, 1895-1939. Includes bibliographies in Vol. I (pp. 207-11), and Vol. IV (pp. 422-32).

193. Vallet, Antoine, in collaboration with Charles Rambaud and F. Louis. Les genres du cinéma. 2nd rev. ed. Paris: Ligel, 1958.

Includes bibliography, p. 113.

194. Viviani, Almiro. (Pseud., Alex Viany.) Introdução ao Cinema Brasileiro. Rio de Janeiro: Ministério da Educação e Cultura, Instituto Nacional do Livro, 1959.

Survey of Brazilian film, with some references to film music.

195. Yahiro Fuji. Jidai eiga to gojūnen. Tokyo: Gakugei Shorin, 1974.

References to music in Japanese films.

196. Yamada Kazuo. Nihon eiga no hachijūnen. Tokyo: Isseisha, 1976.

Eighty years of Japanese film.

197. Zglinicki, Friedrich Pruss von. Der Weg des Films: die Geschichte der Kinematographie und ihrer Vorläufer. Berlin: Rembrandt-Verlag, 1956.

Survey of film history, with only a few references to film music. Includes bibliography, pp. 964-77.

Special Film Music Topics

198. Archibald, John B. "Reunion with Old Friends." _Pro Musica Sana_, 10,
     Nos. 3-4 (Fall 1983), 3-9.

     > Concerning composers' reuse of musical materials in later
     > films. References to the music of Herrmann, Newman, Rozsa,
     > and a few others.

199. Atkins, Irene Kahn. Interview with George R. Groves. Transcript is part
     of the _American Film Institute/ Louis B. Mayer Foundation Oral History
     Program_. Beverly Hills, Calif.: AFI, 1975.

     > Concerning Groves long career as a sound engineer with
     > Vitaphone and Warner Bros. Includes filmography, pp. 445-
     > 75.

200. ----------. "The Melody Lingers On: Source Music in Films of the American
     Past." _Focus on Film_, No. 26 (1977), 29-37.

     > Partially reprinted in Atkin's _Source Music..._ (#201).

201. ----------. _Source Music in Motion Pictures_. East Brunswick, N.J., Lon-
     don, and Toronto: Associated University Presses, 1983.

     > Includes several unique topical studies: "Songs in Films
     > of the American Past," pp. 50-72 (see #200), "Opera and
     > Concert Music Composed for Specific Films," pp. 73-107,
     > and "Ethnic Source Music," pp. 108-120.

     > Also includes a helpful annotated bibliography, pp. 128-
     > 185.

     > -- Rev. by Clifford McCarty in _The Cue Sheet_ (Los Angeles),
     >   1, No. 1 (January 1984), 9.

202. Badeaux, E. "Folksongs in Films." _Sing Out_ (New York), 10, No. 2 (1960),
     30-31.

203. Baxter, John. _The Hollywood Exiles_. London: Macdonald and Jane's Publish-
     ers, 1976.

     > References to several film music composers and other film
     > and music personalities, with special attention to Hanns
     > Eisler.

204. Beckley, Paul V. "Divas in Movieland." _Opera News_, 29 (Dec. 19, 1964),
     8-13.

     > A history of opera stars in Hollywood productions.

205. Bergman, Marilyn, and Alan Bergman. Seminar on "Producing the Film": AFI/
     CAFS, Nov. 1, 1976 (9:30 a.m.). Transcript of the seminar is held at the
     AFI/ Louis B. Mayer Library (Los Angeles).

206. Biswas, Anil. "The 'ghazal' in Indian Films." _Journal of the Sangeet na-
     tak Akademi_, 37 (July-Sept. 1975), 12-15.

207. Blaukopf, Kurt, Siegfried Goslich, and Wilfried Scheib, eds. _50 Jahre Mu-
     sik im Hörfunk: Beiträge und Berichte_. Herausgegeben aus Anlass des 9.
     internationalen IMZ-Kongresses. Vienna and Munich: Jugend und Volk Ver-
     lagsgesellschaft, 1973.

     > A collection of articles by S. Goslich (#244), M. Philip-
     > pot (#4816), L. Salter (#287), E. Schulze (#2545), R. Wan-
     > germée (#4952), and many others.

     > Includes bibliography, pp. 141-43.

208. Bradley, Scott. "Evoluzione della musica nei disegni animati." In _Musica
     e film_. Ed. S. G. Biamonte. Rome: Edizioni dell'Ateneo, 1959, pp. 217-
     221.

     > See Biamonte, #1606.

209. Bruce, Graham. "Music in Glauber Rocha's Films." _Jump Cut_, No. 22 (May

1980), 15-18.

> Music in works by the Brazilian film maker.

210. Bujacz, Janusz. "Muzyka w filmie animowanym." *Acta universitatis lodziensis*, 50 (1979), 191-200.

> In Polish, with a summary in French.

211. Care, Ross. "Cinesymphony: Music and Animation at the Disney Studio, 1928-42." *Sight and Sound*, 46, No. 1 (Winter 1976-77), 40-44.

212. ----------. "Symphonists for the Sillies: The Composers for Disney's Shorts." *Funnyworld*, No. 18 (Summer 1978), 38-48.

> Concerning the work of Frank Churchill, Leigh Harline, and Carl Stalling.

213. Ciment, Michel. *Kubrick*. Paris: Calmann-Lévy, 1980.

> References to the director's integral use of music and sound. Includes bibliography, pp. 233-35, and discography, p. 235.

> -- Rev. by Jacques Fieschi: "Kubrick de Michel Ciment." In *Cinematographe*, No. 64 (January 1981), 67.

> -- Rev. by Christian Descamps: "Le livre de Kubrick." In *Cahiers du cinéma*, No. 319 (Jan. 1981), xv-xvi.

> -- Rev. by Jean-Philippe Domecq: "Un voyage dans l'espace de Kubrick." In *Positif*, No. 239 (Feb. 1981), 45-46.

214. Comuzio, Ermanno. "Il cinema dei fratelli Taviani attraverso le colonne sonore dei loro film." *Bianco e nero*, 39, No. 4 (April 1978).

215. ----------. "Musica e suoni dei film di Visconti." *Cineforum*, 26 (June 1963).

216. ----------. "Musica, suoni e silenzi nei film di Ingmar Bergman." *Cineforum*, 32 (February 1964).

217. Connor, Edward, and Edward Jablonski. "The Sound Track." *Films in Review*, 8, No. 9 (Nov. 1957), 471-73.

> A brief survey of music for "horror" films.

218. ----------, and Gerald Pratley. "The Sound Track." *Films in Review*, 7, No. 1 (Jan. 1956), 37-39.

> Concerning the use of "classical music" for film background.

219. ----------, and Gerald Pratley. "The Sound Track." *Films in Review*, 7, No. 4 (April 1956), 181-83.

> Concerning source music in films.

220. Considine, Shaun. "The Music Behind the Dialogue Steps Out." *After Dark* (October 1973), 45-47.

> Concerning the use of records in film scenes.

221. Cook, Page. "The Sound Track." *Films in Review*, 14, No. 10 (Dec. 1963), 622-23.

> A survey of music for film "spectacles," with references to music by Bernstein, North, Rozsa, Steiner, and Tiomkin.

222. ----------. "The Sound Track," *Films in Review*, 15, No. 1 (Jan. 1964), 42-43.

> Music scoring for comedy films.

223. ----------. "The Sound Track." *Films in Review*, 21, No. 9 (Nov. 1970), 564-66.

> Concerning the technical difficulties of synchronizing sound and picture. A historical view.

224. ----------. "The Sound Track." *Films in Review*, 23, No. 6 (June-July 1972), 362-66.

Concerning film scores begun by one composer and completed or replaced by another.

225. ----------. "The Sound Track." Films in Review, 24, No. 6 (June-July 1973), 365-68.

A brief history of soundtrack record albums.

226. ----------. "The Sound Track." Films in Review, 29, No. 1 (Jan. 1978), 37-39, 42.

A brief survey of developments in sound recording, from Vitaphone to Dolby.

227. ----------. "The Sound Track." Films in Review, 29, No. 8 (Oct. 1978), 489-90.

A brief survey of film music "sequels."

228. ----------. "The Sound Track." Films in Review, 33, No. 9 (Nov. 1982), 561-66.

Scores for films starring Grace Kelly and Ingrid Bergman.

229. Craig, Warren. The Great Songwriters of Hollywood. San Diego: A. S. Barnes; London: Tantivy, 1980.

230. Darter, Tom. "Keyboards in the Movies." Contemporary Keyboard (San Diego, Calif.), 6 (April 1980), 46-57.

231. Daugherty, F. J. "Twenty Years of Sound." Christian Science Monitor Magazine, 3 (August 1946), 8-9.

232. Domarchi, Jean. George Cukor. Cinéma d'aujourd'hui, No. 33. Paris: Seghers, 1965.

Many references to music in Cukor's films and musicals.

233. Dumont, L. "Historical Tape Recordings: 'Hollywood on the Air.'" Hobbies (Chicago), 84 (Feb. 1980), 94-96.

234. Ehrenstein, David, and Bill Reed. Rock on Film. New York: Delilah, 1982.

-- Rev. in Stereo Review (Boulder, Colo.), 47 (April 1982), 67.

235. Fano, Nichel. "L'Ordre musical chez Alain Robbe-Grillet. Le discours sonore dans ses films. Communication au Colloque Robbe-Grillet de Cerisy." In Robbe-Grillet: Colloque de Cerisy, I. Paris, 1976, pp. 173-213.

236. Farren, Jonathan. "La taverne des revoltes." Cinéma 75, No. 200 (July-August 1975), 34-39.

A survey of "popular music" in films.

237. Fiedel, Robert D. "Sound Track: The Cornerstone Collection." American Film, 2, No. 9 (July-August 1977), 62-64.

A listing of 25 essential film score albums.

238. Ford, Peter. "History of Sound Recording. IV: Motion Picture and Television Sound Recording." Recorded Sound (London), 2, No. 12 (Oct. 1963) 146-54.

239. Foss, Hubert, and Noël Goodwin. London Symphony: Portrait of an Orchestra, 1904-1954. London, 1954.

240. Francis, Harry. "As I Was Playing." Crescendo International, 12 (Dec. 1973), 10.

Filmed biographies of composers a la Hollywood.

241. Frayne, John G., A.-C. Blaney, George R. Groves, and Harry F. Olson. "A Short History of Motion Picture Sound Recording in the United States." Journal of the Society of Motion Picture and Television Engineers, 85, No. 7 (July 1976), 515-28.

Survey of technical developments, with implications for film music.

242. Garland, Phyl. "Early Jazz in Film Shorts." Stereo Review, 45 (Oct. 1980), 104.

With implications for T.V. "Video" in the 1980's.

243. "The Golden Oscar." The Instrumentalist (Evanston, Ill.), 17 (Oct. 1962), 49.

A listing of Academy Award winning songs, 1935-61.

244. Goslich, Siegfried. "Daten und Tendenzen -- Eine Bilanz uber 50 Jahre Radiomusik." In 50 Jahre Musik im Hörfunk: Beiträge und Berichte. Ed. Kurt Blaukopf et al. Vienna: Jugend und Volk, 1973, pp. 7-18.

See Blaukopf (#207).

245. Hannemann, Volker, and Wolfram Hannemann. "Overtures: A Checklist and Commentary." Pro Musica Sana, 7, No. 2 (Spring 1979), 4-8.

246. Heckman, Don. "Sound Tracks: How Hollywood Buried Jazz." Jazz Magazine (New York), 1, No. 2 (Fall 1976), 41-43.

247. Heilbut, Anthony. Exiled in Paradise: German Refugee Artists and Intellectuals in America, from the 1930's to the Present. New York: Viking Press, 1983.

References to several film composers and musical personalities, with special attention to Hanns Eisler.

-- Rev. by Marcel Ophuls: "Winter's Tales: Strange Invaders." In American Film, 9, No. 3 (Dec. 1983), 60-62.

248. Hurtgen, Charles. "The Operatic Character of Background Music in Film Adaptations of Shakespeare." Shakespeare Quarterly, 20, No. 1 (Winter 1969), 53-64.

249. "It All Started with 'Ramona.'" ASCAP Today, No. 1 (1971), 32-33.

A brief history of movie "theme songs."

250. Jacobs, Arthur D. "Mathieson, Muir." In The New Groves Dictionary of Music and Musicians. Ed. Stanley Sadie. London: Macmillan, 1980, XI, p. 822.

251. Jenkinson, Philip, and Alan Warner. Celluloid Rock: Twenty Years of Movie Rock. London: Lorrimer Publ., 1974.

Includes filmography, pp. 127-32.

-- Rev. in Film (England), No. 25 (April 1975), 16.

-- Rev. in The Thousand Eyes Magazine, No. 9 (April 1976), 14.

252. Jomy, Alain, and Dominique Rabourdin. "Hommage à Max Deutsch." Cinéma 83, No. 290 (Feb. 1983), 26-29.

253. Jones, Chuck. "Music and the Animated Cartoon." Hollywood Quarterly, 1, No. 4 (July 1946), 364-70.

254. Kellogg, Edward W. "History of Sound Motion Pictures." Journal of the Society of Motion Picture and Television Engineers. Part I: 64, No. 6 (June 1955), 291-302; Part II: 64, No. 7 (July 1955), 356-74; Part III: 64, No. 8 (Aug. 1955), 422-37.

A supplement to an earlier series by E. I. Sponable. See #295. Includes a bibliography of technical articles which detail problems of recording and equipment: Part I, p. 302, and Part II, pp. 372-74.

Reprinted in Fielding (#155), pp. 174-220.

255. Kennington, Donald. The Literature of Jazz. London: Library Assoc., 1970.

See especially "Appendix," a survey of jazz on film.

Reprint, Chicago: American Library Association, 1971.

256. Knopf, Bill. Songs from the Stage and Screen. Bryn Mawr, Pa.: Theodore Presser, 1980.

-- Rev. in Bluegrass Unlimited (Burke, Va.), 14 (June 1980), 54.

257. Knudson, Carroll. Project Tempo. Los Angeles: the author, 1965.

A guidebook for the use of click tracks.

258. Kreuger, Miles. "In the Limelight." American Record Guide (Washington, D.C.), 34 (Dec. 1967), 346-48.

References to the music in Disney cartoons.

259. Kułakowska, Zofia. "Problemy instrumentacji w muzyce filmowej Andrzeja Markowskiego." Kwartalnik Filmowy, 11, No. 2 (1961).

260. LaBalbo, Anthony C. "Solo Concerto in Film Music." School Music News (New York), (Jan. 1983), 31.

261. Lippert, Robert L. "Film Music in the Main-Stream." Music Journal, 25, No. 9 (Nov. 1967), 40.

Concerning the use of popular music in films.

262. Lissa, Zofia. "Muzyka w polskich filmach eksperymentalniych." Kwartalnik Filmowy, 11, No. 2 (1961), 3-24.

Music in experimental Polish films.

263. "The Magical Music of Walt Disney: Fifty Years of Original Motion-Picture Soundtracks." High Fidelity and Musical America, 29 (March 1979), 130.

Soundtrack album review.

264. Mapp, Edward. Blacks in American Films: Today and Yesterday. Metuchen, N.J.: Scarecrow Press, 1972.

Includes bibliography, pp. 255-67

-- Rev. by Eileen Southern in The Black Perspective in Music, 2, No. 1 (Spring 1974), 88-89.

265. Mariani, John. "Music to Cry to Movies By." Film Comment, 15 (Sept.-Oct. 1979), 37-39.

266. Massimo, Leone. Breve storia della musica occidentale: corso di storia della musica per gli allievi dei corsi di regia, scenografia, costume e direzione di produzione. Centro sperimentale di cinematografia. Collana di testi per l'insegnamento, VI. Rome, 1957.

267. Matejka, Wilhelm. Musik im Radio. Vienna: Doblinger, 1982.

-- Rev. in Neue Zeitschrift für Musik, 144, No. 5 (May 1983), 42.

268. McClelland, Paul. The Unkindest Cuts. New York: A. S. Barnes, 1972.

Film editing. Includes a section on musical omissions and additions, pp. 157-73.

269. Milne, Tom. "Jazz in the Movies." Sight and Sound, 51, No. 2 (Spring 1982), 130-31.

References to Meeker's Jazz in the Movies. See #6328.

270. Milner, Anthony. "Music and the Radio." In Twentieth Century Music. Ed. Rollo H. Myers. London: John Calder Ltd., 1960.

The article also appears in the second revised and enlarged edition, London: Calder, 1968, pp. 115-22.

271. Mohan, Ram. "Stop the Action, Start the Song!" Cinema Vision India, 1, No. 4 (Oct. 1980), 30-39.

An interview with Vanraj Bhatia, with reflections on the history of Indian cinema. See also #61.

272. Nagy, Magda K. Balázs Béla világa. Budapest: Kussuth Könyv, 1973.

-- Rev. by János Breuer in Magyar zene, 16, No. 4 (Dec. 1975), 429-30.

273. Narducy, Raymond Don. "The Films of the Beatles: A Study in Star Images." Ph.D. Diss. Northwestern University 1981.

> Abstract: DAI 42:3793A (order #DA 8204945).

274. Newsom, Jon. "'A Sound Idea': Music for Animated Films." Quarterly Journal of the Library of Congress, 37, Nos. 3-4 (Summer-Fall 1980), 279-309.

> References to music by Antheil, Bradley, Herbert Fleischer, Tibor Harsányi, Riesenfeld, Carl Stalling, Raksin, and Oliver G. Wallace. Includes a phono recording of musical examples.

275. Osborne, Robert. 50 Golden Years of Oscar: The Official History of the Academy of Motion Picture Arts and Sciences. La Habra, Calif.: ESE California, 1979.

276. Palmer, Christopher. "Christopher Palmer Continues His Survey of Hollywood Music." Crescendo International, 13 (Oct. 1974), 26-27.

> Concerning Hollywood orchestrators.

277. ----------. "Focus on Films." Film Music Notebook, 1, No. 4 (Summer 1975), 23-30.

> Concerning the use of "classical music" in film.

278. ----------. "Music in the Hollywood Biblical Spectacular." Church Music (London), 3, No. 18 (1972), 5-9.

279. Parker, David L. "Golden Voices, Silver Screen: Opera Singers as Movie Stars." Quarterly Journal of the Library of Congress, 37, Nos. 3-4 (Summer-Fall 1980), 370-86.

280. Philippot, Michel P. "La Musique et la radiodiffusion." In Un siècle de radio et de télévision. Ed. Pierre Descaves and A. V. J. Martin. Paris: ORTF, 1965, pp. 343-64.

> See Descaves (#149).

281. Porfirio, Robert Gerald. "The Dark Age of American Film: A Study of the American Film Noir (1940-1960)." Ph.D. Diss. Yale University 1979.

> Vol. I, Chapter 8: "The 'Sound' of Noir: Dialogue, Narration, Effects and Music," pp. 191-234. Emphasis on the music of Miklos Rozsa.

> Vol. II includes several brief essays (as footnotes): "The Sound of Violence: Auditory Masking -- Off Screen Space," pp. 100-02, "Noir Sound Effects: Structuring Silence -- Dissonance, " pp. 102-03, "Ironic Juxtapositions: Visual and Aural," pp. 104-06, "Jazz and Expressionism: Violence, Death and Sexuality," pp. 110-11, "Jazz -- Expressionism -- The Libido," pp. 112-13, "Sequence from 'The Dark Corner': Aural Structure -- Music and Effects" (with musical examples by J. McHugh, Duke Ellington, and Harry Ruby), pp. 114-23. Also includes bibliography, pp. 269-80.

282. Ramin, Jordan. "Oscar's Songs." High Fidelity and Musical America, 25, No. 4 (April 1975), 54-57, 60.

> A listing of Academy Award winners and nominees.

283. Ranade, Ashok. "The Extraordinary Importance of the Indian Folk Song." Cinema Vision India, 1, No. 4 (Oct. 1980), 4-11.

> See #61.

284. Ranson, P., comp. By Any Other Name: A Guide to the Popular Names and Nicknames of Classical Music, and to the Theme Music in Films, Radio, Television and Broadcast Advertisements. North Shields: North Tyneside Libraries and Arts Department, 1978.

> -- Rev. by Julian Hodgson in Brio, 14, No. 2 (1977), 57.

285. Rizzo, Francis. "Shadow Opera." Opera News, 32, No. 14 (Feb. 3, 1968), 8-12.

> A survey of operas composed for use in films.

> Reprinted in Limbacher, pp. 166-72. See #75.

286. Routley, E. "Hymns by Accident." The Hymn Society of Great Britain and
     Ireland Bulletin, 10, No. 3 (1982), 79-81.

     The use and mis-use of hymntunes in film and T.V.

287. Salter, Lionel. "Musik im Hörspiel." In 50 Jahre Musik im Hörfunk: Bei-
     träge und Berichte. Ed. Kurt Blaukopf et al. Vienna: Jugend und Volk,
     1973, pp. 40-49.

     Translated by E. Obermayer and G. Rindauer.

     See Blaukopf (#207).

288. Schmidt, Edward A. "The Academy Awards for Music -- 1934 to 1969." The
     Max Steiner Annual, No. 4 (1970), 7-10.

289. Schmuckher, Aidano. Danza, folklore ed etnografia nel cinema. Genoa: Cine-
     club Luigi Boggiano, 1965.

290. Schneider, Anneliese. "Einsteins (sic) Gabe der Musikalität." Kunst und
     Literatur (Berlin), 28 (July 1980), 766-72.

     Concerning the films of Sergei Eisenstein.

291. Seth, Ragunath. "The Sound of Magic: A Survey of the Singing Voice in Hindi
     Films." Trans. from the Hindi by Shama Zaidi. Cinema Vision India, 1,
     No. 4 (Oct. 1980), 50-55.

     See #61.

292. Sineux, Michel. "Maestro, musique!: Image et son dans le cinéma de Stanley
     Kubrick." Positif (Paris), No. 186 (Oct. 1976), 36-41.

293. "16 mm Films." Film Music Notes, 9, No. 3 (Jan.- Feb. 1950), 21-22.

     Film scores by composers of "international note."

294. Snell, Mike. "Rambling with Snell: Of Oscars and Ostracism." The Max
     Steiner Journal, No. 4 (1979), 12-16.

     Concerning a trend toward greater use of pop and rock mu-
     sic in films.

295. Sponable, E. I. "Historical Development of Sound Films." Journal of the
     Society of Motion Picture Engineers. Parts 1 and 2: 48, No. 4 (April
     1947), 275-303; Parts 3-7: 48, No. 5 (May 1947), 407-422.

     A history of the development of sound recording techniques,
     with implications for film music.

     See also the articles by Edward W. Kellogg which supple-
     ment this survey. See #254.

296. Steen, T. M. F. "The Sound Track." Films in Review, 12, No. 5 (May 1961),
     303-05.

     Concerning the composers at Zagreb Film Studios (Yugoslavia).

297. ----------. "The Sound Track." Films in Review, 12, No. 10 (Dec. 1961),
     629-31.

     Music for Disney films by Oliver G. Wallace and others.

298. Stelzer, Christian. "Popmusik und Film: Versuch zur Bestimmung und histor-
     ischen Einordnung eines Film-Genres." Medien und Pädagogik (Munich), 20,
     No. 2 (1976), 101-13.

299. Still, William Grant. "The Negro and His Music in Films." In Writer's
     Congress: Proceedings of the Conference Held in October 1943 (by the
     Hollywood Writer's Mobilization Committee). Berkeley and Los Angeles:
     University of California Press, 1944, pp. 277-79.

300. Struck, Jürgen. Rock Around the Cinema: die Geschichte des Rockfilms.
     Munich: M. Nuechtern, 1979.

     -- Rev. in Musik und Bildung, 14 (May 1982), 365-66.

301. Taylor, John Russell. Strangers in Paradise: The Hollywood Emigrés, 1933-
     1950. New York: Holt, Rinehart and Winston, 1983.

References to Hanns Eisler and other film composers and personalities.

302. Thiel, Wolfgang. "Musik im Science-fiction-Film." _Musik und Gesellschaft_, 27, No. 10 (Oct. 1977), 585-91.

303. ----------. "Musik im Trickfilm." _Musik und Gesellschaft_, 26, No. 11 (Nov. 1976), 663-69.

304. Troitskaya, Galina. "Muzyka v ital'anskom neorealističeskom kino." _Sovetskaya muzyka_, 23, No. 9 (Sept. 1959), 110-17.

Music in the Italian neorealist film.

305. ----------. "Muzyka v poslevoennom pol'skom kino." _Sovetskaya muzyka_, 35, No. 7 (July 1971), 128-37.

Music in Polish post-war cinema.

306. ----------. "Zametki o klassičeskoj muzyke v kino." _Sovetskaya muzyka_, 39, No. 9 (Sept. 1975), 45-51.

Concerning the use of "classical" music in films, with examples from Russian and foreign films.

307. Trommer, Fritz. _Tontechnik_. Halle: Fotokinoverlag Halle, 1959.

308. Uselton, Roi. "Opera Singers on the Screen." _Films in Review_, 18, No. 4 (April 1967), 193-206; 18, No. 5 (May 1967), 284-309; 18, No. 6 (June-July 1967), 345-59.

Biographies of opera stars who have appeared in silent and sound films.

309. Wagner, J. "Music in the Western: Variations on the Folksong." _Image et son_, No. 248 (1972), 41.

310. Wahlström, Sten. "Levande bilder paa gott och ont: 40 aar har gaatt sedan ljudfilmen kom till Sverige." _Musikern_ (Stockholm), Nos. 7-8 (July-Aug. 1969), 12-13.

311. Warner, Alan. "Six-Gun Scoring." _Films and Filming_, 16, No. 1 (October 1969), 72.

Music for Westerns.

312. Weiland, Frederik Christoffel. "Relationships between Sound and Image." In _Electronic Music Reports_. Utrecht: Institute of Sonology, 1974, IV, pp. 66-92.

References to the Bauhaus experiments, Russian "color music," early sound and video art, electronic music, and music films.

313. Westphal, Frederick W. "Music in Radio Broadcasting." Ph.D. Diss. University of Rochester 1948.

Abstract: DA W1948 (DDAAU, H. W. Wilson), #111.

SEE ALSO:

#1559(Cameron), #2211(Walter), #2538(Roller), #2648(Overman), #2650(Rosenbaum), #2917(Lustig), #4417(Altman), #4753(Lucchesi), #5962(Ferrini), #5963(Feuer), #5977(Freed), #6000(Hertel), #6003(Hirschhorn), #6026(Kehr), #6031(Kobal), #6039(Lacombe/Rocle), #6045(Levy), #6066(McVay), #6073(Mordden), #6088(Piper), #6090(Powell), #6106(Sennett), #6108(Sidney), #6123(Stern), #6127(Taylor/Jackson), #6152(Wilder), #6153(Wilk), and #6328-6329(Meeker).

Silent and Early Sound Era

History

314. Abbiati, Franco. "Verso il cinesinfonismo?" La rivista di Bergamo (March 1930).

315. Abendroth, W. "Kompromisse und Schlimmeres." Allgemeine Musikzeitung, 56 (1929), 659-61.

316. Adam, M. "Hilfsapparate des Musikchronometers." Filmtechnik (1929), 31.

317. ----------. "Hilfsgeräte für den Blum'sche Musik-Chronometer." Kinotechnik (1927), 479.
    Concerning the work of Karl Robert Blum.

318. ----------. "Das Musikchronometer von Carl Robert Blum im Dienste der Filmkunst." Kinotechnik (1927), 94.

319. ----------. "Neues über das Blum'sche Musik-Chronometer." Kinotechnik (1927), 402.

320. ----------. "Die Technik des Musikchronometers." Filmtechnik (1929), 13.

321. ----------, and Hans Erdmann. "Die Verwendung des Musikchronometers." Filmtechnik (1927), 46.

322. Ahern, Eugene A. What and How to Play for Pictures. Twin Falls, Idaho: newsprint, 1913.
    Possibly the first book wholly devoted to the subject of music for films.

323. "Allegro, Presto, Whee!" Newsweek, 60 (Aug. 13, 1962), 83.
    A profile of pianist Arthur Kleiner.

324. "Alte Übel, neue Wege." Der Kinematograph (Berlin), No. 804 (1922).

325. "Amerikanische Filmmusik." Der Kinematograph (Berlin), No. 889 (1924).

326. Amzoll, Stefan. "Nahtstellen musikalischer Komposition: Dsiga Wertows revolutionäre Neuerungen im frühen sowjetischen Tonfilm." Musik und Gesellschaft, 27, No. 11 (Nov. 1977), 642-49.

327. "An die Musikverbraucher Deutschlands." Reichsfilmblatt, No. 46 (1928), 8.

328. Andreevsky, Alexander von. Postrojenije svukovogo filma. Moscow and Leningrad, 1931.

329. Anoschtschenko, Nikolai D. Svutschaschtschaya filma v SSSR i sagranitsche. Moscow, 1930.

330. Arnoux, Alexandre. Du Muet au parlant: mémoires d'un témoin. Paris: La Nouvelle Édition, 1946.

331. Aros, --. "Das missbrauchte Musikmonopol." Der Kinematograph (Berlin), No. 1074 (1927).

332. "Arranging Synchronized and Special Music Scores for Sound Pictures." Musician (Boston), 34 (June 1929), 32.

333. "The Art of Silent Film Accompaniment." Crescendo International, 12 (Nov. 1973), 18.

334. "Arthur and the Keystone Kops." American, 148 (Oct. 1949), 112.
    A profile of Arthur Kleiner, silent film pianist at the Museum of Modern Art.

335. Arvey, Verna. "How Music Has Helped the Stars." _Etude_, 50 (Oct. 1932), 693-94, 747.

> Concerning the musical background of the Hollywood stars, but with some useful information.

336. ----------. "Present Day Musical Films and How They are Made Possible." _Etude_ (Philadelphia), 49 (Jan. 1931), 16-17, 61-72.

337. Assum, Arthur L. "Cue-Sheet for 'The General.'" _Film Music_, 14, No. 2 (Nov.- Dec. 1954), 21-22.

> A film by Buster Keaton.

338. Atkins, Irene Kahn. Interviews with early sound and music editors: Milo Lory, Walter Elliott, Joseph Henrie, Evelyn Rutledge, Robert Tracy, George Adams, and June Edgerton, Sept. 9, 1974 - April 17, 1975. Transcripts are part of the _American Film Institute/ Louis B. Mayer Oral History Program_. Beverly Hills, Calif.: AFI, 1975.

> Includes filmographies, pp. 544-602.

339. _Atti del primo congresso internazionale di musica, Firenze, 30 aprile - 4 maggio 1933._ Ugo Ojetti, Presidente del Congresso. Florence: F. Le Monnier, 1935.

> Proceedings of the 1933 Florence Conference. Includes articles by A. Coeuroy (#4308), L. Colacicchi (#492), H. Fleischer (#558), L. Fürst (#4331), L. Koch (#5097), A. Lualdi (#708), B. Maine (#715), M. Mila (#4374), R.-A. Mooser (#746), H. Rosbaud (#4845), and E. Vuillermoz (#5097).

340. "Auf dem Wege zur Selbsthilfe." _Lichtbildbühne_, No. 283 (1927), 20.

341. "Das Aufführungsrecht an Musik: Werken in Deutschland." _Reichsfilmblatt_, No. 29 (1923), 11.

> Concerning problems of performing rights.

342. Aussig, --. "Von des Landesverbandes des deutsches Kinematographenbesitzungen in der Tschechoslowakei: Beilage -- Kinokapellmeister und Kinooperateur." _Die Lichtspielbühne_, 1 (June 1927).

343. Austin, Cecil. "Cinema Music." _Music and Letters_, 5, No. 2 (April 1924), 177-91.

> References to scores by Ernst Luz and Louis Silvers.

344. Azevedo, Artur. "Comovido por um Cinematógrafo." _O Pais_ (Dec. 3, 1906).

> 344a. Reprinted in "Arturo Azevedo, o 1º Cronista Cinematográfico da Cidade." _Revista de Teatro SBAT_, No. 320 (March-April 1961), 6ff.

345. Bagier, Guido R. G. _Der kommende Film: eine Abrechnung und eine Hoffnung. Was war? Was ist? Was wird?_ Stuttgart: Deutsche Verlags-Anstalt, 1928.

> Includes a brief bibliography, and references to the role of music in early sound and silent films.

346. Bakshy, Alexander. "The Movie Scene: Notes on Sound and Silence." _Theater Arts Monthly_ (February 1929), 97-107.

347. ----------. "With Benefit of Music." _Nation_, 132 (Apr. 1, 1931), 359-60.

348. Baldwin, Ruth Ann. "Motion Pictures Fertile Field for Composers." _Musical America_ (July 1917), 3.

349. Band, Lothar. "Der sprechende Film und seine Bedeutung für die Musik." _Hellweg_ (Essen), 3 (1923), 820.

350. ----------. "Wie entsteht Filmmusik?" _Hellweg_ (Essen), 7 (1928), 162.

351. Barbaro, Umberto. "Film e fonofilm." _L'Italia Letteraria_ (Rome), 20, No. 4 (1935).

352. Baresel, Alfred. "Grenzen des Rundfunks." Melos, 8, Nos. 5-6 (May-June 1929), 247-49.

353. Barry, Iris. The Talkies. Museum of Modern Art Film Library, Series I, Program 5. New York: Museum of Modern Art, n.d.

    Concerning the film "The Jazz Singer" (1927).

354. Bauer, --. "Herr Kapellmeister, warum dann all unsere Mühe?" Reichsfilmblatt, No. 34 (1923), 14.

355. ----------. "Nochmals Film und Musik." Reichsfilmblatt, No. 30 (1923), 15.

356. Baughan, E. A. "Moving Pictures and Music." Saturday Review (London), 133 (Jan. 14, 1922), 33-34.

    Defending the use of "classical music" for film accompaniment.

357. Beaton, Welford. Know Your Movies. Hollywood: Howard Hill, 1932.

    Chapters: "Music," pp. 81-95, and "Musical,", pp. 100-06. References to Steiner's score for "Bird of Paradise" (1932).

358. Becce, Giuseppe. "Revolution?" Reichsfilmblatt, No. 10 (1929), 9.

359. Beck, C. "Bänkelsänger und Kino." Heimatland, No. 1 (1922), 89.

360. Beiblatt, --. "Filmmusik." Reichsfilmblatt, No. 34 (1924).

    The first in a series of film music articles by Beiblatt.

361. Beijerinck, Frits Hendrick. "Die Entwicklung der Tonfilmindustrie." Ph.D. Diss., Bern 1933.

362. Bennett, Robert Russell. "Orchestrating for Broadway." Modern Music, 9, No. 4 (May-June 1932), 148-52.

363. Berg, Charles Merrell. "The Human Voice and the Silent Cinema." Journal of Popular Film, 4, No. 2 (1975), 165-77.

364. ----------. "An Investigation of the Motives for and Realization of Music to Accompany the American Silent Film, 1896-1927." Ph.D. Diss. (Mass Communications), University of Iowa 1973.

    An accurate and thorough study. A basic text. Abstract: DAI 35:490A.

   364a. Published as part of the Arno Press Cinema Program: Dissertations on Film Series. New York: Arno Press, 1976.

365. Berg, S. M. "Music for the Picture." The Moving Picture World, 26 (Dec. 11, 1915), 2018-19.

    This article, and those which follow (#365-394), include information for the silent film accompanist, including suggestions for music to accompany selected current films.

366. ----------. "-----." Moving Picture World, 26 (Dec. 25, 1915), 2367-68.

367. ----------. "-----." Moving Picture World, 27 (Jan. 15, 1916), 427-28.

368. ----------. "-----." Moving Picture World, 27 (Jan. 22, 1916), 599-600.

    Includes an article, "How to Play Themes."

369. ----------. "-----." Moving Picture World, 27 (Feb. 26, 1916), 1301-02.

370. ----------. "-----." Moving Picture World, 27 (March 4, 1916), 1475-76.

371. ----------. "-----." Moving Picture World, 27 (March 11, 1916), 1655.

372. ----------. "-----." Moving Picture World, 27 (March 18, 1916), 1827-28.

373. ----------. "-----." Moving Picture World, 28 (April 1, 1916), 83-84.

    Concerning opera and the silent film.

374. ----------. "-----." Moving Picture World, 28 (April 8, 1916), 263-64.

375. ----------. "Music for the Picture." The Moving Picture World, 28 (April 22, 1916), 623-24.
    See annotation for #365.
    Includes comments concerning the "Intermezzo."

376. ----------. "-----." Moving Picture World, 28 (May 13, 1916), 1171.

377. ----------. "-----." Moving Picture World, 28 (May 20, 1916), 1337-38.
    Includes guidelines for piano accompaniment of films.

378. ----------. "-----." Moving Picture World, 28 (May 27, 1916), 1511-12.
    Includes an original composition by Walter C. Simon.

379. ----------. "-----." Moving Picture World, 28 (June 10, 1916), 1884.

380. ----------. "-----." Moving Picture World, 28 (June 17, 1916), 2033-34.

381. ----------. "-----." Moving Picture World, 28 (June 24, 1916), 2237-39.
    Includes more guidelines for movie pianists.

382. ----------. "-----." Moving Picture World, 29 (July 1, 1916), 97-98.

383. ----------. "-----." Moving Picture World, 29 (July 22, 1916), 637-38.

384. ----------. "-----." Moving Picture World, 29 (July 29, 1916), 792-93.

385. ----------. "-----." Moving Picture World, 29 (Sept. 23, 1916), 1972-73.

386. ----------. "-----." Moving Picture World, 29 (Sept. 30, 1916), 2113-14.
    Includes an article, "Questions about the Organ."

387. ----------. "-----." Moving Picture World, 30 (Oct. 7, 1916), 76.

388. ----------. "-----." Moving Picture World, 30 (Oct. 14, 1916), 236-37.
    Includes an article, "Musical Conditions in New York."

389. ----------. "-----." Moving Picture World, 30 (Oct. 21, 1916), 393-94.
    Includes an article, "A Plea of an Organist."

390. ----------. "-----." Moving Picture World, 30 (Oct. 28, 1916), 548-49.

391. ----------. "-----." Moving Picture World, 30 (Nov. 4, 1916), 704-05.
    Includes an article, "Pictures vs. Vaudeville."

392. ----------. "-----." Moving Picture World, 30 (Nov. 11, 1916), 856-57.
    Includes an article, "Acoustics."

393. ----------. "-----." Moving Picture World, 30 (Nov. 18, 1916), 1011-12.
    Concerning the question of "tempo."

394. ----------. "-----." Moving Picture World, 30 (Nov. 25, 1916), 1159.
    Includes an article, "Music Must Be Subordinated to the Picture."

395. ----------, and Norman Stuckey. "Music for the Picture." The Moving Picture World, 29 (Aug. 5, 1916), 960-61.
    Concerning organ technique, with suggestions for music.

396. ----------, and Norman Stuckey. "Music for the Picture." The Moving Picture World, 29 (Aug. 26, 1916), 1405-06.
    Concerning pipe organ specifications, with suggestions for music.

397. ----------, and Norman Stuckey. "Music for the Picture." The Moving Picture World, 29 (Sept. 2, 1916), 1544-45.
    Concerning organ technique, with suggestions for music.

398. ----------, and Norman Stuckey. "Music for the Picture." The Moving Picture World, 29 (Sept. 9, 1916), 1700-01.
      Concerning organ technique, with suggestions for music.

399. ----------, and Norman Stuckey. "Music for the Picture." The Moving Picture World, 29 (Sept. 16, 1916), 1833-34.
      "How the Church Organist Can Become a Picture Player."
      Includes suggestions for music.

400. ----------, and Walter C. Simon. "Music for the Picture." The Moving Picture World, 29 (July 8, 1916), 253-54.
      Suggestions for music, along with an original composition by Simon.

401. Bernard, Gabriel. "La Musique et le cinéma." Le Courrier musical et théâtral (Paris), 20 (Jan. 1918), 2-5.
      Concerning "improvised" film accompaniments.

   401a. Partially reprinted in "The Movies as a Source of Musical Inspiration." Current Opinion, 65 (Aug. 1918), 95-96.

402. Bernhard, P. "Probleme der Filmmusik." Auftakt, 9 (1929), 174.

403. ----------. "Probleme der Filmmusik." Deutsche Tonkünstlerzeitung, 27 (1929), 514-16.

404. ----------. "Probleme der Filmmusik." Sozialistische Monatshefte (Berlin), 26, No. 1 (1928), 506-10.

405. Beyer, --. "Musik und Film." Die Musik, 21 (1929), 447-49.

406. Beyfuss, Edgar. "Der Film vor hundert Jahren." Lichtbildbühne, No. 89 (1924), 23.

407. Beynon, George W. Musical Presentation of Motion Pictures. New York and Boston: G. Schirmer, 1921.
      Music for silent films, 1903-1921. References to musical scores by Robert Hood Bowers, Carl Elinor, and George M. Rubinstein. Also concerning the film music activities of John Arthur, S. M. Berg, Carl Edouarde, Nat W. Finston, Erno Rapée, Alois Reiser, Hugo Riesenfeld, and Francis J. Sutherland. Classic scores by J. C. Breil.

408. ----------. "Music for the Picture." The Moving Picture World, 35 (Feb. 2, 1918), 675-76.
      A profile of George Beynon.

      This article, and those which follow (#408-430), include information for the silent film accompanist, including suggestions for music to accompany selected current film releases. Later in the series, Beynon's articles are accompanied by more detailed cue sheets prepared by various composers and compilers. See #431-452.

409. ----------. "-----." Moving Picture World, 35 (Feb. 9, 1918), 823-24.
      Includes a listing of "royalty free" compositions for use by silent film accompanists.

410. ----------. "-----." Moving Picture World, 35 (Feb. 16, 1918), 969-70.
      More "royalty free" compositions.

411. ----------. "-----." Moving Picture World, 35 (March 16, 1918), 1513-14.
      Concerning the preparation of cue sheets.

412. ----------. "-----." Moving Picture World, 35 (March 23, 1918), 1661-62.
      Concerning a new music service for exhibitors.

413. ----------. "-----." Moving Picture World, 35 (March 30, 1918), 1817-18.
      Includes an article, "Musical Library at the New York Strand,"

with references to the work of Carl Edouarde.

414. ----------. "Music for the Picture." <u>The Moving Picture World</u>, 36 (April 13, 1918), 245-46.

 See annotation for #408.

 Debates the merits of organ vs. orchestral accompaniment.

415. ----------. "-----." <u>Moving Picture World</u>, 36 (April 27, 1918), 541-42.

 Concerning the preparation of cue sheets.

416. ----------. "-----." <u>Moving Picture World</u>, 36 (May 4, 1918), 697-98.

 Concerning the appropriate use of the theater organ.

417. ----------. "-----." <u>Moving Picture World</u>, 36 (May 18, 1918), 1001-02.

 Concerning efforts to fit the music to the action.

418. ----------. "-----." <u>Moving Picture World</u>, 36 (May 25, 1918), 1141-42.

419. ----------. "-----." <u>Moving Picture World</u>, 36 (June 1, 1918), 1289-90.

420. ----------. "-----." <u>Moving Picture World</u>, 36 (June 8, 1918), 1435-36.

 Concerning the role of the Musical Director.

421. ----------. "-----." <u>Moving Picture World</u>, 36 (June 15, 1918), 1567-68.

 References to Hugo Riesenfeld and S. L. Rothapfel.

422. ----------. "-----." <u>Moving Picture World</u>, 36 (June 22, 1918), 1717-18.

423. ----------. "-----." <u>Moving Picture World</u>, 36 (June 29, 1918), 1841-42.

 A call for greater cooperation between the Musical Director and the Film Director.

424. ----------. "-----." <u>Moving Picture World</u>, 37 (July 6, 1918), 72-73.

 Includes an article, "Proper Presentation of Pictures Musically: Orchestral Balance."

425. ----------. "-----." <u>Moving Picture World</u>, 37 (July 20, 1918), 399-400.

426. ----------. "-----." <u>Moving Picture World</u>, 37 (July 27, 1918), 553-54.

 Includes an article, "Proper Presentation of Pictures Musically: Natural and Unnatural Endings."

427. ----------. "-----." <u>Moving Picture World</u>, 37 (Aug. 3, 1918), 677-78.

 A proposal for instituting the practice of community singing in movie theaters.

428. ----------. "-----." <u>Moving Picture World</u>, 37 (Aug, 10, 1918), 842-43.

 Includes an article, "Proper Presentation of Pictures Musically: Songs as Themes."

429. ----------. "-----." <u>Moving Picture World</u>, 37 (Aug. 17, 1918), 987.

430. ----------. "-----." <u>Moving Picture World</u>, 37 (Aug. 24, 1918), 1120-21.

 Includes an article, "Picture Playing a Dignified Profession."

431. ----------. "-----." <u>Moving Picture World</u>, 37 (Aug. 31, 1918), 1267-76.

 This article, and those which follow (#431-452), include cue sheets for current film releases. Here, they are prepared by George W. Beynon, James C. Bradford, Louis F. Gottschalk, and S. M. Berg. Beginning with #432, Harley Hamilton joins this group of composer/compilers, with regular contributions to the series.

432. ----------. "-----." <u>Moving Picture World</u>, 37 (Sept. 7, 1918), 1425-33.

 Again, concerning the practice of community singing in movie theaters.

433. ----------. "Music for the Picture." The Moving Picture World, 37 (Sept. 14, 1918), 1575-83.

    See annotation for #431.

    Includes an article, "Synchronizing the Music Score," and an additional cue sheet by J. C. Sullivan.

434. ----------. "-----." Moving Picture World, 37 (Sept. 21, 1918), 1753-61.

    Includes an article, "The Secret of Synchronized Scores."

435. ----------. "-----." Moving Picture World, 37 (Sept. 28, 1918), 1887-95.

436. ----------. "-----." Moving Picture World, 38 (Oct. 5, 1918), 81-89.

    Includes an article, "Musical Directors Should Take Artistic Responsibilities Seriously."

437. ----------. "-----." Moving Picture World, 38 (Nov. 9, 1918), 663-67.

    Includes an article, "The Evolution of Picture Music."

438. ----------. "-----." Moving Picture World, 38 (Nov. 16, 1918), 741-44.

    Includes "The Evolution of Picture Music, Part 2."

439. ----------. "-----." Moving Picture World, 38 (Nov. 23, 1918), 835-38.

    Includes "The Evolution of Picture Music, Part 3."

440. ----------. "-----." Moving Picture World, 38 (Nov. 30, 1918), 957-62.

    Speculation concerning the future of film music after the war.

441. ----------. "-----." Moving Picture World, 38 (Dec. 7, 1918), 1081-86.

    Concerning the preparation of cue sheets.

442. ----------. "-----." Moving Picture World, 38, (Dec. 14, 1918), 1213-18.

    Concerning the problem of fitting the music to the film.

443. ----------. "-----." Moving Picture World, 38 (Dec. 21, 1918), 1345-51.

444. ----------. "-----." Moving Picture World, 38 (Dec. 28, 1918), 1521-26.

    The influence of World War I on music and music for films.

445. ----------. "-----." Moving Picture World, 39 (Jan. 4, 1919), 85-92.

    Concerning organs and Fotoplayers.

446. ----------. "-----." Moving Picture World, 39 (Jan. 11, 1919), 215-21.

    Concerning problems of tempo and timing.

447. ----------. "-----." Moving Picture World, 39 (Jan. 18, 1919), 353-58.

    Concerning the work of the Musical Director.

448. ----------. "-----." Moving Picture World, 39 (Feb. 1, 1919), 639-44.

    The use of popular music for film accompaniments.

449. ----------. "-----." Moving Picture World, 39 (Feb. 8, 1919), 775-80.

450. ----------. "-----." Moving Picture World, 39 (Feb. 22, 1919), 1041-46.

    References to the work of Herbert Lubin, and the music of Hugo Riesenfeld and George Drumm. Includes an additional cue sheet by Joseph O'Sullivan.

451. ----------. "-----." Moving Picture World, 39 (March 1, 1919), 1215-19.

452. ----------. "-----." Moving Picture World, 39 (March 8, 1919), 1359-63.

    Beynon's last article in the regular series. Includes additional cue sheets by Joseph O'Sullivan and Max Winkler.

453. Bharatan, Raju. "The Final Touch Made All the Difference." Cinema Vision

<u>India</u>, 2, No. 2 (Jan. 1983), 66-67.

Concerning the work of composer S. D. Burman.

See #645.

454. Bingham, W. V. <u>Mood Music: A Compilation of 112 Edison Re-creations Ac-cording to "What They Will Do for You." Based on Psychological Experi-ments Conducted Under the Direction of W. V. Bingham</u>. Orange, N.J.: The Thomas A. Edison Co., 1921.

Includes "Research on Moods and Music," pp. 28-31.

455. Blaisdell, George. "Dramatizing the Song." <u>The Moving Picture World</u>, 20 (June 13, 1914), 1523.

456. Bloch, Ernst. "Über die Melodie im Kino." <u>Der neue Merkur</u>, 5 (1922), 812-19.

456a. Also published as: "La nascita della musica dallo spirito del cinema." Trans. F. Porcarelli. In <u>Filmcritica</u> (Rome), 28, Nos. 279-280 (Dec. 1977), 391-92.

457. Blum, Karl Robert. "Film und Musik." <u>Tägliche Rundschau</u> (Nov. 6, 1921).

458. ----------. "Musik-Chronometer im Dienste des Films." <u>Deutsche Tonkünst-lerzeitung</u>, 27 (1929), 517-19.

459. ----------. <u>Das Musik-Chronometer und seine Bedeutung für Filmtheater und die allgemeine Musikkultur</u>. Leipzig: F.E.C. Leuckart, 1926.

460. "Das Blum'sche Musikchronometer." <u>Lichtbildbühne</u>, No. 307 (1926), 28.

461. Boblitz, K. Sherwood. "Where 'Movie Playing' Needs Reform." <u>Musician</u> (Bos-ton), 25 (June 1920), 8, 29.

Favoring the use of "classical music" because of its po-tential for educating the public.

462. Bogoslavskij, S., and V. Messma. <u>Muzyka v kino</u>. Moscow: Kinoisdatelstvo RSFSR, Kinopeciat, 1926.

463. Borie, Bertrand. "Dossier -- La Musique de film: Le Piano des origines." <u>Cinematographe</u> (Paris), No. 62 (Nov. 1980), 14-15.

464. Bowen, Arthur Lloyd. "Music in Films." <u>Musical Standard</u> (London), 38 (July 1932), 121.

Films by S. Eisenstein, with scores by Edmund Meisel.

465. Bower, Dallas. <u>Plan for Cinema</u>. London: J. M. Dent and Sons, 1935.

Includes a section on music.

466. Bowers, Q. David. "Theatre Photoplayers." <u>Musical Box Society Internation-al</u>, 16, No. 5 (1970), 202-14.

467. Bradlet, John M. "Music for the Picture: Introductory." <u>The Moving Picture World</u>, 7 (Nov. 26, 1910), 1227.

An introduction to a new film music column by Clarence E. Sinn, which began in the next issue of <u>MPW</u>. See #888.

468. ----------. "The Pipe Organ." <u>The Moving Picture World</u>, 7 (Sept. 3, 1910), 526-27.

A statement against the use of organ for film accompaniments.

469. Bragaglia, Anton Giulio. <u>Il film sonoro: Nuovi orizzonti della cinemato-grafia</u>. Milan: Edizioni "Corbaccio," 1929.

470. Brav, Ludwig. <u>Die Praxis der Bearbeitung und Besetzung für kleines Orches-ter</u>. Berlin: Bote & Bock, 1927.

471. "BRD: Symposium zu Fragen der Stummfilmmusik." <u>Musik und Gesellschaft</u>, 30, No. 7 (July 1980), 440-41.

472. Brownlow, Kevin. <u>The Parade's Gone By</u>. New York: Knopf, 1968.

Chapter 30: "The Silents Were Never Silent," pp. 337-41.

Reprint, New York: Ballentine Books, 1969. (Chap. 30 is pp. 384-88.)

473. Bruyr, José. L'Écran des musiciens. With a Preface by André Coeuroy. Paris: Des Cahiers de France, 1930.

A collection of articles by leading French composers.

474. Buchanan, Charles L. "Music and the Movies." Outlook, 144 (Nov. 3, 1926), 307-08.

Concerning opera on film. Also includes references to scores by William Axt and David Mendoza.

475. Buchstab, M. "Klangfarbe im Kino-Orchester." Reichsfilmblatt, No. 34 (1929), 8.

476. Burman, S. D. "Far Away from the World of Music." Cinema Vision India, 2, No. 2 (Jan. 1983), 68-69.

See #645.

477. Burroughs, Wesley Ray. "With the Movie Organist." Diapason (Chicago), 7 (Feb. 1916), 3.

478. Bush, W. Stephen. "Possibilities of Musical Synchronization." The Moving Picture World (Sept. 2, 1911), 608.

479. Butting, Max. "Music of and for the Radio." Modern Music, 8, No. 3 (Mar.-Apr. 1931), 15-19.

480. Calvocoressi, M. D. "Music and the Film: A Problem of Adjustment." Sight and Sound, 4, No. 14 (Summer 1935), 57-58.

References to the music of Henri Rabaud, Florent Schmitt, and Arthur Honegger.

481. Cantacuzino, Ion. "De la naissance à Bucarest d'une branche du septième art, le cinema de recherche scientifique, en 1898." Revue Roumaine d' Histoire de l'Art (Bucarest), 7 (1970), 53-55.

482. Cavello, C. "Die Kinoorgel und ihre Propheten, I." Reichsfilmblatt, No. 2 (1929), 9.

483. ----------. "Die Kinoorgel und ihre Propheten, II." Reichsfilmblatt, No. 3 (1929), 9.

484. ----------. "Welche Ansprüche soll man an eine moderne Kino-Orgel stellen?" Reichsfilmblatt, No. 37 (1928), 19.

485. Chandavarkar, Bhaskar. "Sound in a Silent Era." Cinema Vision India, 1, No. 1 (Jan. 1980), 117-19.

486. Channing, Leroy L. "Are We Downhearted?: A Survey of Conditions After Three Years of Talkies." Metronome (Sept. 1929), 47-48.

487. Chaplin, Charles S. "The Future of the Silent Picture." Windsor Magazine (London), (Sept. 1936).

488. Charent, Brian. "The Silents with Charles Hofmann and Horace Lapp." Motion (Toronto), 4, No. 2 (1975), 10-12.

489. Chatterton, Julia. "The Liason of Music and Cinema." Musical Standard (Feb. 25, 1922), 65.

490. "A Cheerful Idiot." The Moving Picture World, 7 (Dec. 24, 1910), 1465.

491. Cinema Music as a Profession. Issued by the Educational Section of the Screen Music Society. London: Torquay, 1925.

492. Colacicchi, Luigi. "Il disco e la musica." In Atti del primo congresso internazionale di musica, Firenze, 30 aprile - 4 maggio 1933. Florence: F. Le Monnier, 1935, pp. 76-83.

A paper presented at the 1933 Florence conference. See #339.

493. Connor, Edward, and Don Miller. "The Sound Track." Films in Review, 10, No. 3 (March 1959), 172-75.

Also deals with musicals and soundtrack albums of 1959.

494. ----------, and Gerald Pratley. "The Sound Track." Films in Review, 7, No. 2 (Feb. 1956), 87-89.

Concerning the earliest composed scores for silents.

495. Converse, Frederick S. "Music and the Motion Picture." Arts, 4 (Oct. 1923), 210-12.

An analysis of his score for "Puritan Passions" (1923).

496. Cook, Burr C. "Fitting Music to the Movie Scenes: Screen Opera the Latest Thing in Filmdom." Motion Picture Magazine, 12 (Oct. 1916), 111-14.

Concerning Breil's score for "Birth of a Nation." Also, references to music by Victor Herbert and Engelbert Humperdinck.

497. Cooke, James Francis. "New Musical Marvels in the Movies." Etude (Philadelphia), 44 (Oct. 1926), 781.

An editorial response to the New York City exhibition of Vitaphone: Warner's "Don Juan" (1926).

498. Coppola, Carlo. "Songs of Injustice." Cinema Vision India, 2, No. 2 (Jan. 1983), 79-81.

Concerning the works of Sahir Ludhianvi. See #645.

499. Corradini, Bruno. "Cinéma abstrait, musique chromatique (1912)." In Cinéma: theorie, lectures. Comp. Dominique Noguez. A special issue of Revue d'esthetique, 26, Nos. 2-4 (1973), 267-74.

500. Courtnay, Jack. Theatre Organ World: Cinema Organists and Their Instruments "Spotted" for Your Information by Famous Writers, Artists and Musicians. London: Theatre Organ World Publications, 1946.

501. Cousins, Edmund George. Filmland in Ferment. London: Archer, 1932.

Chapter: "The Savage Breast," pp. 117-22. Concerning the use of "theme songs," with references to the music of Herbert Stothart.

502. "A Criticism of Picture Music." The Moving Picture World, 13 (Aug. 17, 1912), 639.

503. Czerny, L. "Film-Musik." Der Film, No. 35 (1922), 34.

504. Daussig, F. "Filmmusik." Velhagen und Klasing's Monatshefte, 40, No. 1 (1925-1926), 342-45.

505. Dautun, --. "Musique et cinéma." Almanach Ciné-Miroir (Paris), (1933).

506. Delong, Thomas A. The Mighty Music Box: The Golden Age of Musical Radio. Los Angeles: Amber Crest Books, 1980.

507. Deming, Wilford. "Talking Picture in India." Cinema Vision India, 1, No. 2 (April 1980), 19-22.

Reprinted from the American Cinematographer.

508. Dench, Ernest Alfred. Making the Movies. New York: Macmillan, 1915.

Chapter: "Musical Matters in Motion Pictures," pp. 95-99.

509. Deneke, Hans. "Film und Musik." Süddeutsche Monatshefte (Munich), 30 (Feb. 1933), 286-88.

510. De Profundis (pseud.). "Choir and Organ: In Which We Forsake the Choir Loft Temporarily to Investigate the Duties of the Moving Picture Organist." Musician (Boston), 29 (Dec. 1924), 41.

511. ----------. "What Chance Has the Church Organist to Make Good in the Moving Picture Theatre?" Musician (Boston), 29 (Nov. 1924), 41.

512. Diedrich, Paulheinz. "Musik im Lichtspieltheater: Richtlinien für den Theaterbesitzer." Reichsfilmblatt, No. 20 (1929), 29.

513. Dransmann, --. "Musik und Film." Reichsfilmblatt, No. 50 (1925).

514. Droop, A. "Die Kinematographie im Unterricht der technischen Fächer." Lichtbildkunst, 3 (1914), 143.

515. Droop, F. "Kino-Musik." Der Türmer, 16, No. 1 (1914), 971-73.

516. du Fais, H. "Film und Musik." Tägliche Rundschau (March 5, 1922).

517. "Durchkomponierte Begleitmusik." Der Kinematograph (Berlin), No. 882 (1924).

518. Dykema, P. W. Music as Presented by the Radio. New York: Radio Institute of the Audible Arts, 1935.

519. Eckert, Gerhard. "Der Ton im Film." Die Literatur, 36 (1933-1934), 151-52.

520. Einstein, Alfred. "Schönberg's Super-Film Music." Modern Music, 8, No. 3 (March-April 1931), 45-46.
       Concerning the "Begleitmusik zu einer Lichtbildszene."

521. "Das Elend der heutigen Filmmusik." Der Kinematograph (Berlin), No. 793 (1922).

522. Engl, Jo. Der tönende Film. Braunschweig: Verlag Vierweg & Sohn, 1927.

523. Epstein, Dave A. "Flicker Flashback: Music Still Hath Charm." Music Journal, 23, No. 4 (April 1965), 42-43, 99.

524. Epstein, Jean. Cinéma: Collection des Tracts. Paris: Éditions de la Siréne, 1921.

525. Erdmann, Hans. "Aufnahmeapparat und Musik." Kinotechnik (1925), 455.
       See Barsy's response to this article, #1137.

526. ----------. "Filmmusik 1927/28." Reichsfilmblatt, No. 25 (1928), 8.

527. ----------. "Film und Musikpraxis." Reichsfilmblatt, No. 30 (1926), 114.

528. ----------. "Gedanken bei Eröffnung eines Theaters." Reichsfilmblatt, No. 4 (1928), 29.

529. ----------. "Kampf oder Einigung? Das GEMA-Problem." Reichsfilmblatt, No. 43 (1927), 9.

530. ----------. "Musikautorenschutz." Reichsfilmblatt, No. 1 (1927), 16.

531. ----------. "Musiker-Organisationen und Musiker-Tarif." Reichsfilmblatt, No. 33 (1925), 16.

532. ----------. "Musikpraktikum." Filmtechnik (1926), 528.

533. ----------. "Der Musikrhythmus im Filmatelier." Filmtechnik (1926), 438.

534. ----------. "Rund um das Aufführungsrecht." Reichsfilmblatt, No. 50 (1927), 9.
       Concerning problems of performing rights.

535. ----------. "Eine Schule für die Filmmusik." Filmtechnik (1929), 63.

536. ----------. "Die Technik des Orchesterraumes." Filmtechnik (1928), 508.

537. ----------. "Um die Kino-Orgel." Reichsfilmblatt, No. 24 (1928), 32.
       See Frerk's response to this article, #565.

538. ----------. "Eine Unterhaltung mit E. Rappée." Reichsfilmblatt, No. 13 (1926), 17.

539. "Erno Rapée, Conductor at Capitol, Joins Synchronized Music Company." The Moving Picture World (June 4, 1921), 526.

540. L'Estrange, F. Die Welt des Films. Zurich, 1932.

541. Etthofen, --. "Musikaufstellungen." Film-Kurier, No. 39 (1930).

542. Evans, Edwin. "Music and the Cinema." Music and Letters, 10, No. 1 (Jan. 1929), 65-69.

543. Ewen, David. "Welcome to a Beloved Composer." American Hebrew, 126 (Jan. 24, 1930), 399.

        Welcoming Oscar Straus to Warner Bros.

544. Fazalbhoy, Y. A. The Indian Film: A Review. Bombay: Bombay Radio Press, 1939.

545. "Feature Films for Feature Music." The Moving Picture World, 6 (April 16, 1910), 591.

        A call for special musical programs which will fit the action of the film.

546. Ferguson, Stanley. "Gone with the Sound Track." New Republic, 106, No. 13 (March 30, 1942), 426-27.

        Concerning the demise of the pit orchestra. Includes references to the work of Erno Rapée and Maurice Borodkin.

547. Ferrell, MacCullum. "Playing Tunes for the Cutting Room." The Moving Picture World, 85 (March 26, 1927), 361, 440.

548. Field, Mary, and Percy Smith. The Secrets of Nature. With a Preface by H. Bruce Woolfe. London: Faber and Faber, 1934.

        Includes comments on the music for the film series.

549. "Der Film im Klavierunterricht." Zeitschrift für Instrumentenbau, 37 (1916-1917), 215.

550. "Filmmusikalische Kurse am Stern'schen Konservatorium." Lichtbildbühne, No. 292 (1929).

551. "Filmmusikarbeit an der Hochschule." Film-Kurier, No. 28 (1930).

552. "Filmmusik auf Schallplatten." Rhein-Main-Volkszeitung (July 11, 1929).

553. "Filmmusiknöte." Reichsfilmblatt, No. 21 (1927), 31.

554. "Ein Film über die Herstellung der Klaviermechanik." Deutsche Instrumentenbau-Zeitung (1928), 233.

555. Fischer, --. "Filmmusik." Der Kunstwart, 35 (Jan. 1922), 215-16.

556. Fischer, Lucy. "Rene Clair, 'Le Million,' and the Coming of Sound." Cinema Journal, 16, No. 2 (Spring 1977), 34-50.

        Concerning the very careful use of music and rhythm in Clair's films.

557. Fischer, René. "Ton Film und Film: Begleitmusik." Ed.D. Diss., Heidelberg 1932.

    557a. Published with the title Tonfilm und Filmbegleitmusik: ihre urheberrechtliche Stellung im geltenden deutschen Recht. Heidelberg: Vereinsdruckerei Heidelberg, 1932.

        Includes bibliography, pp. 6-7.

558. Fleischer, Herbert. "Neue Musik und Mechanische Musik." In Atti del primo congresso internazionale di musica, Firenze, 30 aprile - 4 maggio 1933. Florence: F. Le Monnier, 1935, pp. 68-75.

        A paper presented at the 1933 Florence conference, with a

synopsis in Italian: "Musica nuova e musica meccanica."
See #339.

559. Fletcher, Stuart. "Two Arts That Meet as One." Sackbut (June 1929), 374.

560. Forschneritsch, --. "Der Kapellmeister und die Filmkritik. Der Kinemato-graph (Berlin), No. 833 (1923).

561. Fourniols, --. "Le cinématographe parlant de M. Gaumont." Cosmos (1911), 38.

562. Fox, Joseph. "Interpretive Music for the Movies." Melody (Jan. 1922), 25.

563. Fraenkel, Heinrich. Unsterblicher Film: die grosse Chronik von der Laterna magica bis zum Tonfilm. Munich: Kindler, 1956.

564. Franke, C. W. "Die Kino-Orgel und der Bau von Orgelkammern." Reichsfilm-blatt, No. 33 (1928), 28.

565. Frerk, --. "Um die Kino-Orgel." Reichsfilmblatt, No. 30 (1928), 18.

    Response to an article by Erdmann. See #537.

566. Friedland, M. "Mozart und Beethoven als Kino-'Stimmungsmusiker.'" Allge-meine Musikzeitung, 53 (1926), 274.

567. Fülöp-Miller, René, and Joseph Gregor. Das amerikanische theater und kino: zwei kulturgeschichtliche Abhandlungen. Zurich and Vienna: Amalthea-Verlag, 1931.

    Actually two works: "Das amerikanische Theater," by Joseph Gregor (pp. 9-56), and "Das amerikanische Kino," by René Fülöp-Miller (pp. 59-96). An extensive collection of photo-graphs, with just a few references to film music.

568. Fürst, Leonhard. "Rundfunk Mechanische Musik: Musikkritik und Tonfilm." Melos, 12, No. 3 (March 1933), 92-97.

569. Gad, Urban. Filmen, dens midler og maal. Copenhagen and Christiania: Nordisk forlag, Gyldendalske Boghandel, 1919.

    569a. Published again as: Der Film, seine Mittel -- seine Ziele. Trans. from the Danish by Julia Koppel. Berlin: Schuster & Loeffler, 1921.

        Chapter: "Kinomusik," pp. 266-68.

570. Gandert, Gero. "Ein Kinoorchester-Dirigent erinnert sich." In Stummfilm-musik Gestern und Heute. Ed. Walther Seidler. Berlin: Verlag Volker Spiess, 1979, pp. 35-50.

    An interview with Werner Schmidt-Boelcke, and reprint of an article by Willy Schmidt-Gentner. See Seidler (#875).

571. Gatschov, D. "Muzyka v svukovom filme." Sovetskoe kino, No. 6 (1934).

572. Gaumont, Léon. "Les films parlants." Bulletin de Société Francaise de Photographie (1911), 111-18.

573. Geduld, Harry M. The Birth of the Talkies: From Edison to Jolson. Bloom-ington, Ind.: Indiana University Press, 1975.

    Includes bibliographic references.

    See also #784 (Parker and Shapiro), which supplements and offers corrections to this volume.

574. Gizycki, Arkadiev A. von. Keine Vogelstrausspolitik in der Frage der musik-alischen Aufführungsrechte. Berlin: Hans J. Richter, 1929.

575. Glatt, Dorothea. "Als 'Gegengift' ein Wirtshausklavier." Musik und Mede-zin, 5 (1975), 47-51.

576. "Good Music or None." New York Dramatic Mirror (March 4, 1915), 22.

577. Gordon, Karl. "Kinomusik -- einst und jetzt." Reichsfilmblatt, No. 5 (1929), 11.

578. ----------. "Kinomusik -- einst und jetzt, II." Reichsfilmblatt, No. 6 (1929), 15.

579. Götze, Hellmuth. "Kritische Umschau: Vier Tonfilme." Melos, 10, No. 11 (Nov. 1931), 371-72.

580. Gräff, Werner. Das Buch vom Film. Stuttgart: K. Thienemann, 1931.

581. Gran, A. Musykalnaja rabota w kino. Roskino, 1933.

582. Grau, Robert. The Theatre of Science. New York: Benjamin Blom, 1969.
    Originally published in 1914.
    Includes a section on theater orchestras, organs, and sound paraphernalia, pp. 331-32.

583. Green, Alice. "Picture-House Beethoven -- and Then the Gramophone." The Gramophone, 6, No. 63 (Aug. 1928), 101-02.

584. Green, Fitzhugh. The Film Finds Its Tongue. New York and London: G. P. Putnam's Sons, 1929.

585. Gregor, Joseph. Das Zeitalter des Films. Kleine historische Monographien, 37. Vienna: Reinhold, 1932.

586. Grempe, F. M. "Kino-Musikwerke und -Automaten auf der Leipziger Messe." Der Kinematograph (Berlin), No. 377 (1914).

587. Grierson, John. "Introduction to a New Art." Sight and Sound, 3, No. 11 (Autumn 1934), 101-04.
    Concerning the role of sound and music in film.

    587a. Reprinted as "Creative Use of Sound." In Grierson on Documentary. Ed. and comp. Forsyth Hardy, with American notes by Richard Griffith and Mary Losey. New York: Harcourt, Brace and Co., 1947, pp. 112-18.
        Revised edition, Berkeley and Los Angeles: University of California Press, 1966. (Rpt. New York: Praeger, 1971.)

    587b. Reprinted as "Uso creativo del suono." Cinema (Rome), 10 (April 4, 1949).

588. Griggs, John. "The Music Master: The Days of the Piano and the Grand Organ Are Recalled by One Who Played Them." Films in Review, 5, No. 7 (Aug.-Sept. 1954), 338-42.

589. Groepler, Rudolf. "Das Recht der Bearbeitung im literatisch-musikalischen Urheberrecht unter besonderer Berücksichtigung des Filmrechts." Ph.D. Diss., Halle, May 24, 1923.

    589a. Published, Berlin: Möller, 1922.

590. Gruner, --. "Kinomusik." Der Kinematograph (Berlin), No. 255 (1911).

591. Guckel, --. "Filmlänge als Zeitgrösse." Filmtechnik (1927), 307.

592. Günther, F. "Film und Musik." Der Film, No. 33 (1922), 36.

593. Gutman, Hanns. "Der Musiker und der Tonfilm." Die Musik, 22, No. 3 (Dec. 1929), 192-94.

594. Guttmann, O. "Filmmusik." Bühne und Film, No. 4 (1920), 24.

595. ----------. "Filmmusik." Grazer Tageblatt (Nov. 21, 1919).

596. Güttinger, --. "Der Stummfilm im Zeugnis namhafter Zeitgenossen." Filmblätter (Frankfurt), No. 8 (n.d.).

597. H...Ki. "Muzyka w kinie." Ekran i Scena, Nos. 16, 17, 18, 19 (1924).

598. Haas, H. "Musik und Film." Deutsche Tonkünstlerzeitung, 27 (1929), 511-13.

599. Hafner, John. "Automatic Special Music." The Moving Picture World, 8 (Jan. 14, 1911), 76.

A suggestion for the use of player pianos for film accompaniments.

600. Hake, --. "Filmbegleitmusik." Reichsfilmblatt, No. 12 (1924), 10.

601. Haletzki, Paul. "Pionier der Filmmusik: der Komponist Gottfried Huppertz."
Film und Ton Magazin (Munich), 25 (Dec. 1979), 59-62.

602. Hall, Ben M. The Best Remaining Seats: The Story of the Golden Age of the
Movie Palace. New York: Clarkson N. Potter, 1961. (Reprint, 1975.)

Chapters: "... The Peal of the Grand Organ, the Flourish
of Golden Trumpets," pp. 175-81, and "The Apotheosis of
the Mighty Wurlitzer," pp. 183-99.

603. Hammond, Richard. "Pioneers of Movie Music." In Music and the Machine, a
special issue of Modern Music, 8, No. 3 (March-April 1931), 35-38.

Concerning "experimental" scores by Blitzstein, Milhaud,
and Colin McPhee.

604. Hanlon, Esther S. "Improvisation: Theory and Application for Theatrical
Music and Silent Film." Ph.D. Diss. (Musicology), University of Cincin-
ati 1975.

Abstract: UM 76-5992, and DAI 36:5626A (order #76-5992).

605. Hansford, Montiville Morris. "Preparing Music for Photoplay Accompaniment."
Dramatic Mirror (Aug. 11, 1917), 10.

606. ----------. "Preparing Music for Photoplay Accompaniments." Dramatic
Mirror (Aug. 25, 1917), 14.

607. ----------. "Preparing Programs for Photoplay Accompaniment." Dramatic
Mirror (July 21, 1917), 11.

608. ----------. "Preparing Programs for Photoplay Accompaniments." Dramatic
Mirror (July 28, 1917), 10.

609. Harding, Henry J. "The Evolution of the Picture House." Cadenza (Jan.
1915), 3-4.

610. Harrison, Louis Reeves. "Jackass Music." The Moving Picture World, 8
(Jan. 21, 1911), 124-25.

See the reply to this article by Wm. H. McCracken (#727).

611. Hatschek, P. "Das Orchester ohne Musiker." Filmtechnik, No. 21 (1930), 8.

612. Hausdorff, Max M. "Sonar, der lebende tönende Film." Der Kinematograph
(Berlin), No. 637 (1919).

613. Heller, Berndt. "Aus der Praxis junger Stummfilmpianisten." In Stummfilmmusik Gestern und Heute. Ed. Walther Seidler. Berlin: Verlag Volker
Spiess, 1979, pp. 83-94.

Interview with the contemporary pianist Albert Lévy. See #875.

614. Hensel, Paul R. "Musik und Film." Reichsfilmblatt, No. 13 (1929), 9.

615. Hermann, H. "Film und Filmmusik." Der Kinematograph (Berlin), No. 1065
(1927).

616. Hildebrandt, A. "Der Film als Werbemittel in der Pianoforte-Industrie."
Zeitschrift fur Instrumentenbau, 43 (1922-1922), 686.

616a. Reprinted in Deutsche Instrumentenbau-Zeitung (1923), 117.

617. Hitchcock, Alfred. "Music in Films." Cinema Quarterly (Edinburgh), 2,
No. 2 (1933).

618. Hofmann, Charles. Sounds for Silents. New York: Drama Books Specialists,
1970.

A basic text, includes bibliography. Foreword by Lillian
Gish.

619. ----------. "Sounds for Silents." Film Library Quarterly, 2, No. 1 (Win-

ter 1968-1969), 40-43.

> References to J. C. Breil's "Birth of a Nation" score, and a few others.

620. Holt, Richard. "Music and the Cinema." Musical Times, 65 (1924), 426-27.

> Concerning the current state of film music, with references to a score by Eugene Goosens.

621. Homola, B. "Filmproduktion und -musik." Der Führer: Fachzeitschrift des Kapellmeisters, 2, No. 2 (1929), 3.

622. Howard, Clifford. "Symphonic Cinema." Close Up (London), 10 (Dec. 1933), 347-50.

> References to the work of Louis De Francesco.

623. "How Music is Made to Fit the Films." Literary Digest, 56 (Jan. 26, 1918), 58.

> Excerpts from an article which originally appeared in the Cleveland Plain Dealer.

624. "How to Play a Movie." BMI: The Many Worlds of Music (April 1970), 14-15.

625. Hummel, F. "Die Filmmusik." Der Film, No. 36 (1922), 28.

626. Hunsberger, Donald R. "Orchestral Accompaniment for Silent Films." Image, 25, No. 1 (1982), 7-16.

> Includes bibliography.

627. Hyman, Dick. "Synchronizing Piano Music to Films." Contemporary Keyboard (San Diego, Calif.), 7 (March 1981), 53.

628. ----------. "Synchronizing with Films." Contemporary Keyboard (San Diego, Calif.), 7 (Feb. 1981), 64.

629. Hynes, Charles F. "The Onrush of Sound." The Film Daily Year Book (1929), 484-503.

630. Icart, Roger. "L'Avenement du film parlant." In La Révolution du parlant, a special issue of Cahiers de la cinémathèque, Nos. 13-14-15 (1975).

631. Iger, A. "Kinoorgel." Filmtechnik (1926), 288.

632. ----------. "Musikindustrielle Lehr- und Kulturfilme." Zeitschrift für Instrumentenbau, 47 (1926-1927), 275.

633. Ital, L. "Vom Podium des Musiklokals zum Pult des Kinokapellmeisters." Der Führer: Fachzeitschrift des Kapellmeisters, 1, No. 6 (1928), 1.

634. Jakob, Walter. "Mechanische Musik." Deutsche Tonkünstlerzeitung, 27 (1929), 551-52.

635. James, Leslie W. "The Organ in the Cinema." Musical Standard, 10 (Aug. 18, 1917), 109-10.

636. James, Neville. "Silent-Movie Orchestras Thrilled Fans in Early Flicker Days." Classic Film Collector, No. 56 (Fall 1977), x.-8.

637. Jason, Alexander. Handbuch für Filmschaffende. Berlin, 1933.

638. ----------. Handbuch der Filmwirtschaft. Jahrgang. Berlin: Verlag für Presse, Wirtschaft und Politik, 1930.

639. Jellenta, C. "Maximum i minimum w muzyce kinowej." Kinema, Nos. 47, 48, 49 (1925).

640. Johnson, Julian. "Pandora's Chatterbox." Saturday Evening Post (Jan. 23, 1932), 10-11ff.

> Concerning the operation of an early sound department.

641. Jokus, H. "Wenn man in den Film singt." Allgemeine Musikzeitung, 53 (1926), 266.

642. Josephson, Matthew. "Modern Music for the Films." New Republic, 66 (April 1, 1931), 183.

> A review of an evening of music by Copland, Sessions, Milhaud, Blitzstein, and McPhee.

643. Kahan, Hans. Dramaturgie des Tonfilms. Berlin: M. Mattisson, 1930.

644. Kahn, H. "Die Film-Symphonie." Weltbühne, 23, No. 2 (1927), 524-26.

645. Kak, Siddharth. "Editorial." Cinema Vision India, 2, No. 2 (Jan. 1983), 2.

> Introduction to a special issue which deals primarily with music in early sound films in India. Includes articles by M. A. Aziz (#2717), R. Bharatan (#453), S. D. Burman (#476), C. Coppola (#498), W. Y. Gadgil (#2799), S. Kinikar (#654), H. Mahmood (#714), V. Padukone (#782), A. Ranade (#812), V. A. K. Ranga Rao (#813), and K. C. Sharma (#879).

646. Kautzenbach, George. "Columbia University and the Rivoli Theater." Journal of Popular Culture, 6, No. 2 (1972), 300-12.

647. Kayser, H. "Aus der Praxis der Filmmusik." Der Anbruch (Vienna), (1929), 139-40.

648. Keen, Stuart. "Music for Silent Classics." Sight and Sound, 13, No. 50 (July 1944), 43-44.

> Concerning the use of records for synchronized musical accompaniment for films.

649. Keiler, Walter. "Hamburger Musikbrief." Der Kinematograph (Berlin), No. 730 (1921).

650. Kellner, --. "Kino und Musik." Kinotechnik (1921), 294.

651. Kerr, Alfred. Russische Filmkunst. Berlin: Ernst Pollak, 1927.

652. Kilenyi, Edward. "Fitting Music to the Films an Exacting Task." Musical America (Sept. 15, 1923), 4.

653. Kindschi, Lowell. "Twilight Furioso." Atlantic, 181 (May 1948), 95-96.
> Reminiscences of a silent theater organist.

654. Kinikar, Shashikant. "Lasting Lady: Khurshid-Saraswati." Cinema Vision India, 2, No. 2 (Jan. 1983), 70-73.

> An interview with India's first woman film composer, Saraswati Devi. See #645.

655. Kino-Kalendar der Lichtbildbühne. Berlin: Verlag der Lichtbildbühne, 1912-1921.

656. "Kinomusikerbezahlung." Frankfurter Nachrichten (Oct. 18, 1921).

657. "Das Klavier im Film." Deutsche Instrumentenbau-Zeitung (1923), 271.

658. Kleefeld, W. J. "Ziel der Filmmusik." Daheim, No. 31 (1927), 16.

659. Kleiner, Arthur. "Die Aufzeichnung von Originalmusik für Stummfilme." Filmkunst (Vienna), No. 81 (1978), 10.

660. ----------. "Film Scores." Sight and Sound, 13, No. 52 (Jan. 1945), 103-04.
> A brief survey of silent film scores.

661. ----------. "Music by the Frame." New Yorker, 25, No. 24 (Aug. 6, 1949), 14-15.

> An interview with Kleiner, composer of silent scores, and pianist at the Museum of Modern Art.

662. Klemm, Gustav. "Music and the Movies." Musical Courier (March 15, 1923), 7.

663. Klemperer, Victor. "Das Lichtspiel." Velhagen und Klasings Monatshefte, 16 (1912), 617.

664. Knessl, L. "Avantgarde 1920: Film und Musik bei der Wiener 'Reihe.'" Melos, 31, No. 10 (Oct. 1964), 318-19.

665. Knight, Arthur. "All Singing! All Talking! All Laughing! 1929: The Year of Great Transition." Theatre Arts Magazine (Sept. 1949), 33-40.

666. ----------. "How the Silents Sounded." Saturday Review, 43 (May 28, 1960), 76.

    Record review, with references to the work of Arthur Kleiner.

667. Kobitzsch, A. "Musik im Lichtspielhaus." Filmtechnik (1927), 58.

668. Koch, Gerhard R. "Aus der Praxis junger Stummfilmpianisten." In Stummfilmmusik Gestern und Heute. Ed. Walther Seidler. Berlin: Verlag Volker Spiess, 1979, pp. 73-81.

    Interview with the contemporary pianist Joachim Bärenz. See Seidler (#875).

669. Köfinger, --. "Übereinstimmen der Musik mit dem Filmbild." Filmtechnik (1925), 383.

670. Kohss, --. "Drei Fehler: über Zustände bei Kinoorchestern." Illustrierte Kino-Woche, No. 15 (1914), 175.

671. Kopsch, Julius. "Gegen Spekulation und Ausbeutung." Reichsfilmblatt, No. 47 (1928), 8.

672. Kreiser, K. "Kinomusik." Hellweg (Essen), 4 (1924), 365.

673. Kshirsagar, Sridhar. "Sounding Off." Cinema Vision India, 1, No. 2 (Apr. 1980), 48-51.

674. Kühn, Gertraude, Karl Tümmler, and Walter Wimmer, eds. Film und revolutionäre Arbeiterbewegung in Deutschland 1918-1932, Vol. I: Dokumente und Materialien. Berlin: Henschelverlag Kunst und Gesellschaft, 1975.

    Includes filmography.

675. Kuhn-Foelix, A. "Kinomusik?" Filmtechnik (1926), 254.

676. Kuleschov, L. Article in Iskusstvo kino (1929).

677. Künneke, Eduard. "Filmmusik." Der Film, No. 33 (1922).

678. Lambert, Constant. Music Ho! A Study of Music in Decline. London: Faber and Faber; New York: Scribners, 1934. (Many reprints.)

    Chapter: "Mechanical Music and the Cinema," pp. 256-68. Includes references to Eisenstein's "Potemkin," and a view of the future of the "surrealist" film.

679. ----------. "Music in the Kinema." Saturday Review (London), 147 (Apr. 13, 1929), 498-99.

680. Landon, John W. "Long Live the Mighty Wurlitzer." Journal of Popular Film, 2, No. 1 (Winter 1973), 3-13.

    A history of the use of organs in movie theaters, with references to the career of organist Jess Crawford.

681. Landsberger, H. "Die Filmbegleitmusik." Der Film, No. 36 (1922), 31.

682. Lane, Jerry. "Voice of the Film." Saturday Evening Post (March 11, 1933), 10-11ff.

    Concerning the use of sound effects in early sound films.

683. Latzko, Ernst. "Rundfunk und neue Musik." Melos, 7, No. 4 (April 1928), 191-94.

684. ----------. "Rundfunk -- Umschau." Melos, 8, Nos. 5-6 (May-June 1929), 244-47.

685. "Der Lautfilm: Der Tod der Unterhaltungsmusik." Kölner Zeitung (Jan. 6, 1930).

686. Lawrence, Harold. "Silent Film Music-Making." Audio (Boulder, Colo.), 45 (Jan. 1961), 58-59.

687. Leigh, Walter. "The Musician and the Film." Cinema Quarterly (Edinburgh), 3, No. 2 (Winter 1935), 70-74.

> Includes references to Leigh's score for "Song of Ceylon" (1934).

687a. Reprinted in Revue Musical, No. 276 (1957).

688. Lenvoc, L. "Von den Löhnen der Kinomusiker." Der Kinematograph (Berlin), No. 817 (1922); and No 818 (1922).

689. Leonhard, Hugo. "Neue Filmmusik." Der Kinematograph (Berlin), New Series, Nos. 136, 146, 171, 175, 236, 241, 276, 284 (1929).

690. ----------. "Zurück zur Melodie." Der Kinematograph (Berlin), New Series, No. 112 (1929).

691. Levy, Louis. "Background Music is a Help." Flickers Magazine (London), (1935).

692. Lich, M. "Betrachtungen über Kinomusik." Zeitschrift für Instrumentenbau, 47 (1926-1927), 362.

693. "Lichtbild und Musik." Illustrierte Kino-Woche, No. 4 (1915), 13.

694. Lindner, --. "Vorgeiger oder Klavierdirektion im Kino." Deutsche Musiker-zeitung, No. 2 (1927).

695. Lindsay, Vachel. The Art of the Moving Picture. New York: Macmillan, 1915.

> Chapter: "The Orchestra, Conversations and the Censorship," pp. 189-206.
>
> Reprint, New York: Liveright, 1970.

696. Lindworth, Erwin. "Filmbegleitmusik." Reichsfilmblatt, No. 18 (1927), 22.

697. Litolf, --. "Kinomusik in Amerika." Neue Zeitschrift für Musik, 88 (1921), 479-80.

698. London, Kurt. "Ausbildungs- und Berufsfragen für Filmmusiker." Die Musik-pflege, 1, No. 6 (1925).

> Also published separately as a pamphlet, 1925.

699. ----------. "Filmmusik als Lehrfach." Weser Zeitung (Bremen), (Jan. 27, 1930).

700. ----------. "Mechanische Filmmusik." Allgemeine Musikzeitung, 56 (1929), 771-73.

701. ----------. "Music and Film." International Review of Educational Cinema-tography (Rome), 6 (Apr. 1934), 289-91.

> References to the work of Hanns Eisler.

702. ----------. "Neue Wege der musikalischen Filmillustration." Der Film, No. 13 (1929), 6.

703. ----------. "Richard Strauss und die Filmmusik." Allgemeine Musikzeitung (Sept. 1926), 180.

704. Long, Barbara. "Saturday's Movies, Sunday's Miracles." Village Voice, 15, No. 29 (July 16, 1970), 25.

> Resurrecting organs and organ music for silent films.

705. Low, Rachael. The History of the British Film, 1906-1914. London: George Allen and Unwin, 1949.

> Includes a section on music and sound effects in silent films.

706. ----------. History of the British Film, 1914-1918. London: George Allen
    and Unwin, 1971.

    Includes a section on musical accompaniment, and the ac-
    companiment of filmed musicals.

707. ----------. History of the British Film, 1918-1929. London: George Allen
    and Unwin, 1973.

    Includes sections on musical accompaniment, and early
    film musicals with sound.

708. Lualdi, Adriano. "Due nuove vie per la musica: Radio e Film sonoro." In
    Atti del primo congresso internazionale di musica, Firenze, 30 aprile -
    4 maggio 1933. Florence: Le Monnier, 1935, pp. 43-51.

    A paper presented at the 1933 Florence conference. See #339.

709. Luedtke, Hans. "Kinoorgel und Raumgestaltung." Filmtechnik (1928), 508.

710. Luz, Ernst. "Picture Music." Moving Picture News (Oct. 26, 1911), 29.

711. Lydor, Waldemar. "Kann man mit der GDT-Musik auskommen?" Reichsfilmblatt,
    No. 40 (1929), 12.

712. ----------. "Praxis des Musikbetriebes: Der Kapellmeister äussert sich."
    Reichsfilmblatt, No. 38 (1928), 16.

    Concerning the work of M. Buchstab.

713. MacGowan, Kenneth. "When the Talkies Came to Hollywood." Quarterly of
    Film, Radio, and Television, 10, No. 3 (Spring 1956), 288-301.

714. Mahmood, Hameemuddm. "Music by Naushad." Cinema Vision India, 2, No. 2
    (Jan. 1983), 74-78.

    See #645.

715. Maine, Basil. "Some Effects of Mechanized Music." In Atti del primo con-
    gresso internazionale di musica, Firenze, 30 aprile - 4 maggio 1933.
    Florence: F. Le Monnier, 1935, pp. 84-92.

    A paper presented at the 1933 Florence conference, with a
    synopsis in Italian: "Alcuni effetti della musica meccani-
    ca." See #339.

716. Mamontowicz-Łojek, Bożena. Terpsychora i lekkie muzy. Taniec widowiskowy
    w Polsce w okresie międzywojennym (1918-1939). Krakow: Polskie Wydawn-
    ictwa Muzyczne, 1972.

    The "dance spectacle" in Poland between the wars. Includes
    bibliography.

717. Mann, Margery. "What's a Film Classic Without the Mighty Wurlitzer?" Pop-
    ular Photography, 66 (Jan. 1970), 27-28ff.

    Concerning the activities of the Avenue Photoplay Society
    of San Francisco.

718. Manning, Clifford S. "Organs in Walthamstow Cinemas." In Supplement to
    Showtime in Walthamstow. Ed. W. C. S. Tonkin, 1967, pp. 1-12.

719. Margadonna, E. M. "Orchestrina in film." Il Convegno (Milan), 10 (1929),
    209-18.

720. Marks, Martin. "Music for Silent Films." Ph.D. Diss. Harvard University.

    Work in progress, 1979.

721. Marsop, Paul. "Lichtspiel und Lichtspielmusik." Die Musik, 16, No. 5
    (Feb. 1924), 328-39.

722. Martini, W. "Filmmusik." Die Musikpflege, 1, No. 6 (1925), 68-73.

723. Massolle, Joseph, Hans Vogt, and Jo Engl. Der sprechende Film. Berlin:
    Selbstverlag, 1924.

724. Matzke, Hermann Karl Anton. Grundzüge einer musikalischen Technologie.

Breslau: Quader Druckerei und Verlagsanstalt GmbH., 1931.

725. McAndrew, J. "Star Studded Shellac." Record Research (New York), No. 74 (March 1966), 5.

726. McCarty, Clifford. "Filmusic for Silents." Films in Review, 8, No. 3 (March 1957), 117-18, 123.

> "Silent" film scores, 1908-1927, with references to music of Saint-Saens, Herbert, Romberg, and Deems Taylor.

727. McCracken, William H. "Jackass Music." The Moving Picture World, 8 (Jan. 28, 1911), 176.

> A reply to comments by Louis Reeves Harrison. See #610.

728. McDonald, Gerald D., comp. "A Bibliography of Song Sheets. Sports and Recreations in American Popular Songs, Part IV: Songs of the Silent Film." MLA Notes, 14, No. 3 (June 1957), 325-52; and 14, No. 4 (Sept. 1957), 507-33.

> Includes an index of stars, directors, producers, and films.

729. McLarty, James. "Silence Really is Golden." Motion (Toronto), 4, No. 2 (1975), 8-10.

730. McNulty, John. "Come Quick, Indians!" Holiday, 13 (Jan. 1953), 22-23ff.

> Recollections of the silent movie pianist.

731. McQuade, James S. "The Belasco of Motion Picture Presentations." The Moving Picture World, 10 (1911), 796-98.

> Concerning film music and the work of entrepreneur Samuel L. ("Roxie") Rothapfel.

732. "Mechanische Kinomusik." Deutsche Instrumentenbau-Zeitung (1929), 219.

733. "Mechanische Musikwerke," and "Projektion." Supplement to Internationale Film- und Kinematographen-Industrie. Berlin: Verlag Internationale Film- und Kinematographen-Industrie, 1907, I.

> The first of a series of supplements which accompanied the publication from Vol. 1 (1907) through Vols. 30-31 (1915).

734. "Mechanische oder wirkliche Musikbegleitung." Der Kinematograph (Berlin), No. 234 (1929).

735. Mermey, Maurice. "The Vanishing Fiddler: The Talkies Threaten Calamity." North American Review, 227 (March 1929), 301-07.

> Concerning the plight of "live" musicians in the era of sound films.

736. Mersmann, Hans. "Bühnenmusik auf Schallplatten." Melos, 8, Nos. 5-6 (May-June 1929), 251-53.

737. Mihály, Dénes von. Der sprechende Film. Berlin: M. Krayn, 1928.

738. Mila, Massimo. "Florence Music Congress." The New York Times (June 4, 1933), Section 9, p. 4.

> Comments on film music by a musicologist. See also Mila's paper presented at the conference, #4374.

739. ----------. "Musica e cinematografo." Pegaso: Ressegna di lettere e arti (Milan), 5, No. 2 (Feb. 1933), 152-60.

740. Miller, Channing T. "Scoring Silent Films." Films in Review, 8, No. 5 (May 1957), 228-29, 233.

741. Miller, Patrick. "Music and the Silent Film." Perspectives of New Music, 21, Nos. 1-2 (1982-1983), 582-84.

742. "Moderne Kinomusik." Lichtbildbühne, No. 171 (1925), 43.

743. Modern, Klara. "The Vienna of the Films." Close Up (London), 9, No. 2 (June 1932), 129-31.

744. Mohan, Ram. "The Sound Trackers." Cinema Vision India, 1, No. 2 (April 1980), 42-43.

745. Moore, Douglas. "The Motion Picture and Music." National Board of Review Magazine, 10 (Nov. 1935), 4-9.

    Survey of film music to 1935.

746. Mooser, R.-Aloys. "Le contrôle de la critique musicale sur les auditions radiophoniques." In Atti del primo congresso internazionale di musica, Firenze, 30 aprile - 4 maggio 1933. Florence: F. Le Monnier, 1935.

    A paper presented at the 1933 Florence conference, with a synopsis in Italian: "Il controllo della critica musicale sulle audizioni radiofoniche." See #339.

747. Moussinac, Léon. Rozhdenie kino. Leningrad, 1926.

   747a. Reprinted as Le Cinéma Soviétique. Paris, 1928.

748. "Movie Music." National Board of Review Magazine, 3 (May 6, 1928), 3.

    A plea for original scores.

749. Müller-Endenthum, H. "Film-Dirigenten und Film-Orchester." Der Kinematograph (Berlin), No. 957 (1925).

750. "Musical Accompaniments for Moving Pictures." The Moving Picture World, 5 (1909), 559.

751. "The Musical End." The Moving Picture World, 5 (July 3, 1909), 7-8.

    An editorial, one of the earliest devoted to film music.

752. "Musical Mechanisms in the Movies." Musical Box Society International, 22, No. 2 (1976), 146; and 22, No. 3 (1976), 211.

753. "Music and the Film." Sight and Sound, 3, No. 11 (Autumn 1934), 98-99.

    Concerning the music of Clarence Raybould.

754. "Music and the Movies." Outlook, 108 (Sept. 16, 1914), 158-59.

755. "Music for the Picture." The Moving Picture World, 5 (1909), 879.

    Concerning the work of pianist Gregg A. Frelinger.

756. "Music for the Picture: The Photoplayer, Its Inventors and the Manufacturing Plant." The Moving Picture World, 25 (July 10, 1915), 267.

757. "Musikalische Rundschau." Der Kinematograph (Berlin), No. 855 (1923).

758. "Musicalische Rundschau." Der Kinematograph (Berlin), No. 857 (1923).

759. "Musikalische Überillustration." Der Kinematograph (Berlin), No. 961 (1925).

760. "Musik bei Aussenaufnahmen." Der Kinematograph (Berlin), No. 913 (1924).

761. "Das Musikchronometer." Filmtechnik (1926), 531.

762. "Die Musik-Wirrnis." Reichsfilmblatt, No. 37 (1928), 10.

763. "Die neue Richtung in der Filmmusik." Der Kinematograph (Berlin), No. 485 (1916).

764. "Ein neues kinomusikalisches Problem." Der Kinematograph (Berlin), No. 799 (1922).

    Concerning the problem of music and advertisements.

765. "New Musical Wonder: A One-Man Orchestra Combination." The Moving Picture World, 3 (Dec. 19, 1908), 498.

766. "New Yorker Brief." Deutsche Instrumentenbau-Zeitung (1929), 97.

767. Nick, Edmund. "Musik der Stummfilmzeit." In Die drei grossen 'F': Film, Funk, Fernsehen. Ed. Heinrich Lindlar and Reinhold Schubert. Musik der Zeit, Neue Folge, Vol. II. Bonn: Boosey and Hawkes, 1958, pp. 33-37.

See Lindlar (#78).

768. Nick, Edmund. "Vom Orchestrion zur Kinothek: Die Musik zum Stummfilm." Musica, 8 (Sept. 1954), 390-93.

769. North, Joseph H. "The Early Development of the Motion Picture (1887-1909)." Ph.D. Diss. Cornell University 1949.

    769a. Published as part of the Arno Press Cinema Program: Dissertations on Film Series. New York: Arno Press, 1973.

    Concerning "performance practice" and the role of music in film. See especially "The Exhibitor and His Problems," pp. 67-98.

770. Noxon, Gerald F. "The European Influence on the Coming of Sound to the American Film, 1925-1940: A Survey." In Sound and the Cinema: The Coming of Sound to American Film. Ed. Evan William Cameron. Pleasantville, N.Y.: Redgrave Publishing, 1980, pp. 136-80.

    Cinemagraphic and musical influences. See Cameron (#1139).

771. O., D. "Egon berichtet über Zustände bei Kinoorchestern." Illustrierte Film-Woche, No. 38 (1918), 276.

772. Oderman, Stuart. "The Next Tremolo You Hear." Film Library Quarterly, 4, No. 1 (Winter 1970-1971), 54-56.

    Observations of a contemporary pianist for silents.

773. Ogden, Ronald. "Art of René Clair." Bookman, 82, No. 487 (April 1932), 64-67.

774. Orme, Michael. "Music and the Talking Pictures." Illustrated London News (London), 176 (March 29, 1930), 514.

    Advocates the composition of original cinematic operas.

775. ----------. "Music -- The Screen's Natural Ally." Illustrated London News (London), 180 (April 9, 1932), 540.

    An appeal for the use of music -- even in the "talkies."

776. O'Sullivan, Joseph. "Shooting the Music." Photoplay, 13 (March 1918), 41.

    Comments by the Musical Director of the Mutual Film Co.

777. Ott, --. "Musik und Film." Reichsfilmblatt, No. 43 (1923), 10.

778. Ottenheym, Konrad. "Film und Musik bis zur Einführung des Tonfilms: Beiträge zu einer Geschichte der Filmmusik." Ph.D. Diss. Berlin Friedrich-Wilhelm 1944.

    Includes bibliography.

779. "Our Music Column." Moving Picture News (June 24, 1911), 9.

    A call for better conditions for theater musicians.

780. "Our Music Column." Moving Picture News (July 8, 1911), 8.

    Continued.

781. "Die Ouverture im Kino." Der Kinematograph (Berlin), No. 857 (1923).

782. Padukone, Vijay. "A Commitment to Singing." Cinema Vision India, 2, No. 2 (Jan. 1983), 22-23.

    Concerning the works of Ghulam Mustafa Durrani. See #645.

783. Panovsky, Walter. Die Geburt des Films: Ein Stück Kulturgeschichte. Würzburg: Konrad Triltsch Verlag, 1944.

784. Parker, David L., and Burton J. Shapiro. "The Phonograph Movies." Journal of the Association for Recorded Sound Collections, 7, Nos. 1-2 (July 1975), 6-20.

    A supplement to Geduld's The Birth of the Talkies. See #573.

785. Pasche, H. "Filmmusik und Musikfilm, Part I: Original-Filmmusik." Signale für die musikalische Welt, 86-A (1928), 465-67.

786. ----------. "Musik-Lehrfilme." Signale für die musikalische Welt, 85-A (1927), 213-14.

787. Paschke, Gerhard. "Der deutsche Tonfilmmarkt." Ph.D. Diss., Berlin 1935.
    787a. Published, with the same title, Berlin-Charlottenburg: Gebrüder Hoffmann, 1935.

788. Pasquella, George Donald. "An Investigation in the Use of Sound in the American Motion Picture Exhibition, 1908-1919." M.A. Thesis, University of Iowa 1968.

789. Pauli, Hansjörg. Filmmusik: Stummfilm. Stuttgart: Klett-Cotta, 1981.

    Basic text. Includes bibliographic references.

    -- Rev. by Peter Neugart: "Stummfilm mit Musik." Medien und Erziehung (Munich), 25, No. 5 (1981), 297-98.

    -- Rev. in Nutida Musik (Stockholm), 25, No. 1 (1981), 70-71.

    -- Rev. by Helmut H. Diederichs: "Zur Geschichte des Stummfilms: und dem Anteil der Frauen das Westberliner Symposium und etliche Bücher." Medium (Frankfurt am Main), 11 (Sept. 1981), 38-43.

    -- Rev. by Thomas Brandlmeier: "Musik zum Stummfilm." Film und Ton, 27 (Nov. 1981), 10.

    -- Rev. in Neue Zeitschrift für Musik, No. 1 (Jan. 1982), 76.

    -- Rev. in Musik und Bildung, 14, No. 4 (May 1982), 363-64.

    -- Rev. in Schweizerische Musikzeitung, 122, No. 6 (1982), 377-78.

790. ----------. "Webers Wolfsschlucht-Musik für Frankenstein.". Neue Musikzeitung, 27, No. 6 (Dec. 1978-Jan. 1979), 3.

791. Peeples, Samuel A. "Films on 8 and 16." Films in Review, 27, No. 8 (Oct. 1976), 493-94, 499.

    Includes bibliography.

792. ----------. "The Mechanical Music Makers Brought Sound to the Silents." Films in Review, 24, No. 4 (April 1973), 193-200.

793. Petit, Raymond. "Music Written for French Films." Modern Music, 3, No. 3 (Mar.-Apr. 1926), 32-36.

    References to music by Satie, Milhaud, Honegger, and others.

794. Petric, Vlada. "Silence Was Golden: New Scores Have Been Added to Old Silents -- But the Sound Gain Represents a Loss." American Film, 2, No. 10 (Sept. 1977), 6-19.

    Concerning recent postsynchronization of a Chaplin film.

795. Petrovski, A. Kinofikazia iskusstv. Leningrad, 1929.

796. Pilar-Morin, Mme. "Silent Drama Music." The Moving Picture World, 6 (April 30, 1910), 676.

    A call for original compositions to accompany the silents.

797. Plugge, W. "Die internationale Verflochtenheit der Tonfilmindustrie." Die Musik, 24 (1931).

798. Pordes, V. "Theorien über das Kinodrama." Der Kinematograph (Berlin), No. 511 (1916).

799. Porten, Henny. Vom "Kintopp" zum Tonfilm: ein Stück miterlebter Filmgeschichte. Mit einer Einleitung von Hansjürgen Wille. Dresden: C. Reissner, 1932.

800. Potamkin, Harry Alan. "Music and the Movies." Musical Quarterly, 15, No. 2 (April 1929), 281-96.

Historical view. Advocates the continued use of live orchestras, rather than synchronized sound.

See Frankenstein's response to this article, #4329.

801. Pratt, George C. "Cue Sheets for Silent Films." Image, 25, No. 1 (1982), 17-24.

802. Preussner, Eberhard. "Der Musik -- 'Tonfilm' war da!" Melos, 9, No. 10 (Oct. 1930), 428-30.

803. ----------. "Tonfilm -- Notiz." Melos, 9, No. 3 (March 1930), 136-37.

804. ----------. "Der Tonfilm -- von der Musik aus gesehen." Melos, 10, No. 7 (July 1931), 230-32.

805. Pringsheim, Klaus. "Filmmusik." Weltbühne, 22, No. 1 (1926), 667-70.

806. ----------. "Künstlerische Filmmusik." Der Kinematograph (Berlin), No. 847 (1923).

807. ----------. "Schlechte Zeiten für Filmmusik." Filmtechnik, No. 2 (1930), 15.

808. ----------. "Stellung der Musik zum Kulturfilm." In Kulturfilmbuch. Ed. Edgar Beyfuss and A. Kossowsky. Berlin: Chryselius, 1924, pp. 328-32.

809. R., K. H. "Vom Tonfilm: 'Walzerkrieg.'" Melos, 12, No. 11 (Nov. 1933), 391-92.

810. Raida, C. A. "Eigene Filmmusik." Der Film, No. 35 (1919), 32.

811. Ramsaye, Terry. A Million and One Nights: A History of the Motion Picture. 2 vols. New York: Simon and Schuster, 1926.

Reprint, London: Frank Cass, 1964.

An extensive history, with a valuable historical viewpoint. Unfortunately, very few references to music.

812. Ranade, Ashok. "When a Song Paid Fifty and Petrol Was Six Annas a Gallon." Cinema Vision India, 2, No. 2 (Jan. 1983), 15-19.

An interview with Rajkumari, translated by Hilla Sethna. See #645.

813. Ranga Rao, V. A. K. "The Sound of Music: Too Late by Two Years." Screen (May 19, 1982).

813a. Reprinted in Cinema Vision India, ?, No. 2 (Jan. 1983), 88-90.

See #645.

814. Rapée, Erno. "Future of Music in Moviedom." Etude, 47 (Sept. 1929), 649-50, 699.

An interview with Rapee, a composer, and conductor of the Roxy Theatre Symphony Orchestra and at New York City's Capitol Theatre. Concerning the use of "classical" music for film accompaniments.

815. Raybould, Clarence. "Music and the Synchronized Film." Sight and Sound, 2, No. 7 (Autumn 1933), 80-81.

References to music in documentary films.

816. Redewill, Helena Munn. "Laugh and the World Laughs." The Triangle (Feb. 1932).

Concerning music for Disney cartoons.

816a. Reprinted in The Triangle of MPE (Campbell, Calif.), 73, No. 3 (1979), 20-21.

817. Reichenbach, Hermann. Denkschrift über die Sonderzahlung von Musikantiemen für musikalische Filmbegleitung. Dresden: Selbstverlag, 1927.

Concerning legal matters: copyright, royalties, wages, etc.

818. ----------. "Das Tantiemen-Unrecht." Lichtbildbühne, No. 235 (1927), 14.

819. Renaud, Tristan. "Requiem et fugue pour grandes orgues." Cinéma 73, No. 172 (Jan. 1973), 18-20.

820. Richardson, Dorothy M. "Continuous Performance: Musical Accompaniment." Close Up (London), 1 (Aug. 1927), 58-62.

821. Rogers, Bernard. "Is the Screen a Sesame to Opportunity for Our Composers?" Musical America, 40, No. 7 (June 7, 1924), 5, 32.

        References to the work of Hugo Riesenfeld and others.

822. Roland, Marc. "Gleichlaufsysteme." Filmtechnik (1926), 348.

823. ----------. "Kapellmeister und Vorführer." Filmtechnik (1926), 307.

824. ----------. "Schwierigkeiten." Filmtechnik (1926), 285.

        Concerning problems of sound synchronization.

825. Rolle, --. "Zusammenspiel von Film und Musik." Kinotechnik (1926), 102.

826. Rose, Donald. "Silence is Requested." North American Review (July 1930), 127-28.

827. Rothapfel, Samuel L. ("Roxy"). "Music and Motion Pictures." The Moving Picture World, 6 (April 16, 1910), 593.

        Concerning the repertoire and technique of the film pianist.

828. Rothstein, Edward. "Silent Films Had a Musical Voice." New York Times, 130 (Feb. 8, 1981), Section 2, p.1ff.

829. Rudnicki, M. "Ilustracja muzyczna filmu." Ekran, No. 4 (1919).

830. Ruhemann, K. "Kinomusik." Die Weltbrille, 2 (1930), 41.

831. Ruttmann, Walter. "Révélation du monde audible." Pour Vous (Paris), 12 (1929).

    831a. Reprinted in Anthologie du cinéma: rétrospective par les textes de l'art muet qui devint parlant. Paris: La Nouvelle édition, 1946, pp. 247-48.

832. Sabaneev, Leonid. "Music and the Sound Film." Music and Letters, 15 (Apr. 1934), 147-52.

        Includes references to early experiments in animated sound.

833. ----------. "Music in the Cinema." Musical Times (Feb. 1, 1929), 115.

834. Salotti, Marco. "Orson Welles: in principio era la radio." Filmcritica (Rome), 30, Nos. 296-297 (Aug. 1979), 270-74.

835. Sarnette, Eric. "Musique et electricité." In Le Film sonore: l'écran et la musique en 1935, a special issue of La Revue musicale, 15, No. 151 (Dec. 1934), 401-07 (i.e., pp. 80-87).

836. "Schallplattenmusik zum stummen Film." Der Kinematograph (Berlin), New Series, No. 138 (1929).

837. Scheer, Ludwig. "Ludwig Scheer über die Filmmusik." Reichsfilmblatt, No. 4 (1926), 27.

838. Schinke, --. "Ein neues Kino-Musikinstrument." Reichsfilmblatt, No. 30 (1924), 9.

839. Schirmann, Alexander. "Mehr klassische Kinomusik!" Reichsfilmblatt, No. 16 (1929), 9.

840. Schliepe, E. "Musiknot durch den Tonfilm." Deutsche Allgemeine Zeitung (July 4, 1930).

841. Schloezer, Boris de. "Man, Music and the Machine." Modern Music, 8, No. 3

(Mar.-Apr. 1931), 3-9.

842. Schmidl, Poldi. "Ein Ausweg aus der Misere der Filmmusik." Der Kinematograph (Berlin), No. 700 (1920).

843. ----------. "Bunte Verhältnisse in der bunten Kinokunst." Der Kinematograph, No. 818 (1922).

844. ----------. "Die Ergänzung des Kino-Orchester-Archives." Der Kinematograph, No. 853 (1923).

845. ----------. "Ernö Rappées Abschiedsfeier im Gloria-Palast." Lichtbildbühne, No. 178 (1926), 11.

846. ----------. "Die erste filmdramatische Komposition." Der Kinematograph,
No. 350 (1913).

847. ----------. "Filmdramen mit eigener Musik." Der Kinematograph, Nos. 642-
643 (1919).

848. ----------. "Filmische Lösungen von Musikproblemen." Filmtechnik (1926),
151.

849. ----------. "Filmmusikalische Beiräte." Der Kinematograph, No. 803 (1922).

850. ----------. "Filmmusikalische Streifzüge." Der Kinematograph, No. 810
(1922).

851. ----------. "Filmmusikalische Streifzüge: Die moderne Kinomusikbibliothek."
Der Kinematograph, No. 816 (1922).

852. ----------. "Der Kinokapellmeister der Zukunft." Filmtechnik (1926), 55.

853. ----------. "Kinomusik in der Schweiz." Lichtbildbühne, No. 139 (1926),
26.

854. ----------. "Musikalische Geräusche im Kino." Der Kinematograph, No. 331
(1913).

855. ----------. "Musikalisches aus dem Kino der Gegenwart." Der Kinematograph, No. 219 (1911).

856. ----------. "Musikalische Stimmungstötung." Der Kinematograph, No. 287
(1912).

857. ----------. "Musikalische Taten und Experimente vom Tage." Filmtechnik
(1925), 99.

858. ----------. "Der musikalische Teil." Lichtbildbühne, No. 21 (1926), 3.

859. ----------. "Die Phantasie des Kinomusikers." Der Kinematograph, No. 300
(1912).

860. ----------. "Stilisierte Kinomusik." Filmtechnik (1925), 27.

861. ----------. "Tanzmusik im Film." Filmtechnik (1925), 152.

862. ----------. "Zwischen Parkett und weisser Wand." Der Kinematograph,
No. 354 (1913).

863. ----------. "Zwischen Parkett und weisser Wand." Der Kinematograph,
No. 358 (1913).

864. ----------. "Zwischen Parkett und weisser Wand." Der Kinematograph,
No. 369 (1914).

865. Schmidt, Georg F. "Voraussetzung für Originalmusik." Der Führer: Fachzeitschrift des Kapellmeisters, 1, No. 4 (1928), 7.

866. Schmidt, H. W. "Die Musikerfrage im Lichtspieltheater." Der Kinematograph (Berlin), No. 952 (1925).

867. ----------. "Musik und Film." Reichsfilmblatt, No. 12 (1923), 12.

868. Schmidt, Leopold. "Der Filmdirigent." *Der Merker* (Vienna), 10 (1919), 616-19.

869. ----------. "Film und Musik." *Der Kunstwart*, 27, No. 3 (June 1914), 294-97.

870. Schmidt-Gentner, Willy. "Die Zukunft den Kinomusik." *Reichsfilmblatt*, No. 10 (1929).

871. Schönfeldt, Kurt. "Etwas über Filmmusik." In *Film-Almanach 1921*. Ed. O. Skolnar. Berlin, 1921, pp. 63-65.

872. Schünemann, --. "Musikpädagogische Lehrfilme." *Die Musik*, 20 (1928), 524.

873. Schwers, P. "Filmmusik und Film-Orgel." *Allgemeine Musikzeitung*, 49 (1922), 337.

874. Sedding, --. "Film und Musik." *Reichsfilmblatt*, No. 27 (1923), 15.

875. Seidler, Walther, ed., in collaboration with Lothar Prox and Christa Schahbaz. *Stummfilmmusik Gestern und Heute: Beiträge und Interviews anlässlich eines Symposiums im Kino Arsenal am 9. Juni 1979 in Berlin*. Berlin: Verlag Volker Spiess, 1979.

   A program of the symposium, with a useful bibliography, pp. 101-15, drawn from Birett (see #6200).

   Includes an introduction by Heinz Rathsack, and articles by G. Gandert (#570), B. Heller (#613), F. Kahlenberg (#4349), G. Koch (#668), and Lothar Prox (#2527 and 2684).

876. Seldes, Gilbert. *An Hour with the Movies and the Talkies*. Philadelphia: J. P. Lippincott, 1929.

877. ----------. "Theory About Talkies." *New Republic* (Aug. 28, 1928), 305-06.

878. Shaindlin, Jack. "Don't Shoot the Piano Player." *Variety*, 241 (Jan. 5, 1966), 205.

   Reprinted in Limbacher (#75), pp. 25-28.

879. Sharma, K. C. "The Dentist Who Made Musical History." *Cinema Vision India*, 2, No. 2 (Jan. 1983), 34-38.

   Concerning the work of Ghulam Haider. See #645.

880. Sharp, Dennis. *The Picture Palace and Other Buildings for Movies*. London: Hugh Evelyn, 1969.

   References to silent film music and musicians.

881. Shavin, Norman. "Them Days Is Gone Forever." *Music Journal*, 12 (March 1954), 13, 74-75.

   Concerning piano accompaniments for silent films.

882. Shaw, L., Jr. "The Motion Picture Pianist." *Metronome*, 30, No. 11 (1914), 32.

883. Shepard, David. "Silent Music." *American Film Institute Report*, No. 1 (1972), 3.

   Includes an overview of books which deal with silent film.

884. "Silent Era Anything But Silent, Organist Recalls." *Boxoffice*, 113 (May 8, 1978), E-8.

885. "Silent Film Nostalgia Evokes Sounds of Music." *Boxoffice*, 113 (July 17, 1978), ME-4.

886. Sinn, Clarence E. "The Music and the Picture." *The Moving Picture World*, 6 (April 16, 1910), 590-91.

   This article, and the one which follows (#887), appeared as early editorials calling for the improvement of film accompaniments. They are a prelude to Sinn's regular film music column which begins with #888.

887. ----------. "The Music and the Picture: II." The Moving Picture World, 6 (May 14, 1910), 772.

    See annotation for #886.

888. ----------. "Music for the Picture." The Moving Picture World, 7 (Dec. 3, 1910), 1285.

    Sinn's first article in the regular column which ran in MPW for many years. This article deals with musical accompaniments for steriopticons, panoramas, and early motion pictures.

889. ----------. "-----." Moving Picture World, 8 (Jan. 14, 1911), 76.

890. ----------. "-----." Moving Picture World, 8 (Feb. 18, 1911), 353.

891. ----------. "-----." Moving Picture World, 8 (March 25, 1911), 642.

892. ----------. "-----." Moving Picture World, 8 (April 8, 1911), 766.

    Concerning the important contribution of the drummer.

893. ----------. "-----." Moving Picture World, 8 (April 22, 1911), 885-86.

    Concerning the use of popular songs -- and drums.

894. ----------. "-----." Moving Picture World, 10 (Oct. 7, 1911), 29-30.

    Suggestion for a detailed classification of music to facilitate film score arrangements.

895. ----------. "-----." Moving Picture World, 12 (April 6, 1912), 33.

896. ----------. "-----." Moving Picture World, 12 (May 25, 1912), 717.

897. ----------. "-----." Moving Picture World, 15, No. 3 (Jan. 19, 1913), 254.

    This article, and many of those which follow in the series, contains detailed suggestions for music to accompany films of current release.

898. ----------. "-----." Moving Picture World, 15, No. 4 (Jan. 25, 1913), 352.

    Suggestions for music.

899. ----------. "-----." Moving Picture World, 15, No. 5 (Feb. 1, 1913), 469-70.

    Concerning the problem of sound effects, and the role of the drummer. Suggestions for music.

900. ----------. "-----." Moving Picture World, 15, No. 9 (Mar. 1, 1913), 878.

    References to the work of Milton E. Schwarzwald and William E. King. More about drummers.

901. ----------. "-----." Moving Picture World, 15, No. 10 (Mar. 8, 1913), 985.

    References to Milton E. Schwarzwald, and suggestions for music.

902. ----------. "-----." Moving Picture World, 15, No. 13 (Mar. 28, 1913), 1325.

    Suggestions for music by F. Edgar Ray and H. R. Seeman.

903. ----------. "-----." Moving Picture World, 16, No. 1 (Apr. 5, 1913), 56.

    Suggestions for music by William E. King.

904. ----------. "-----." Moving Picture World, 16, No. 2 (Apr. 12, 1913), 169.

    More on the topic of sound effects, along with suggestions for music by Sinn.

905. ----------. "-----." Moving Picture World, 16 (May 17, 1913), 693-94.

    Suggestions for music by Sinn.

906. ----------. "-----." Moving Picture World, 16 (May 31, 1913), 908.

Suggestions for music by E. C. Zane. See annotation for
#897.

907. ----------. "Music for the Picture." The Moving Picture World, 16 (June 7,
1913), 1020-21.
Concerning the expanded use of percussion. Also, suggestions for music.

908. ----------. "-----." Moving Picture World, 16 (June 21, 1913), 1240-41.
Concerning the use of musical machines for film accompaniments.

909. ----------. "-----." Moving Picture World, 16 (June 28, 1913), 1362.
A call for the use of "good" pianos. Suggestions for music
by F. Edgar Ray.

910. ----------. "-----." Moving Picture World, 17 (July 19, 1913), 303.
Suggestions for music by Sinn.

911. ----------. "-----." Moving Picture World, 17 (Aug. 23, 1913), 833.
A call for better quality in piano playing.

912. ----------. "-----." Moving Picture World, 17 (Aug. 30, 1913), 948.
Suggestions for music by H. R. Seeman.

913. ----------. "-----." Moving Picture World, 17 (Sept. 13, 1913), 1180.
Concerning the use of the organ for film accompaniment.

914. ----------. "-----." Moving Picture World, 18 (Oct. 4, 1913), 38-39.
A call for music that will fit the action of the picture.

915. ----------. "-----." Moving Picture World, 18 (Oct. 11, 1913), 144.
Concerning organ music for pictures.

916. ----------. "-----." Moving Picture World, 18 (Nov. 8, 1913), 599.
More organ guidelines for pictures.

917. ----------. "-----." Moving Picture World, 18 (Nov. 15, 1913), 725-26.
Concerning "good music" for film accompaniment.

918. ----------. "-----." Moving Picture World, 18 (Oct. 13, 1913), 1267.
The question of performing concert music in movie houses.

919. ----------. "-----." Moving Picture World, 19 (Jan. 31, 1914), 534.

920. ----------. "-----." Moving Picture World, 19 (Feb. 14, 1914), 796.

921. ----------. "-----." Moving Picture World, 19 (Feb. 28, 1914), 1072-73.
Concerning the Style-M Photoplayer.

922. ----------. "-----." Moving Picture World, 19 (Mar. 28, 1914), 1671.

923. ----------. "-----." Moving Picture World, 20 (Apr. 4, 1914), 50.

924. ----------. "-----." Moving Picture World, 20 (Apr. 25, 1914), 505.
The problem of incidental music vs. concert music.

925. ----------. "-----." Moving Picture World, 20 (May 16, 1914), 952.
Concerning organs and orchestras.

926. ----------. "-----." Moving Picture World, 20 (June 13, 1914), 1528.
Suggestions for music by Claude R. Hartzell.

927. ----------. "-----." Moving Picture World, 21 (July 11, 1914), 292.
Concerning the film "Judith of Bethulia" (1913), with suggestions for music by George P. Montgomery.

928. ----------. "Music for the Picture." The Moving Picture World, 21
     (July 18, 1914), 422.
          Suggestions for music by Sinn. See annotation for #897.

929. ----------. "-----." Moving Picture World, 21 (July 25, 1914), 560.
          Suggestions for music by Will A. Bryant.

930. ----------. "-----." Moving Picture World, 21 (Aug. 8, 1914), 823.
          Suggestions for music by E. Russell Sanborn, Claude R.
          Hartzell, and George P. Montgomery.

931. ----------. "-----." Moving Picture World, 21 (Aug. 8, 1914), 1225.
          Concerning the organist E. Russell Sanborn.

932. ----------. "-----." Moving Picture World, 21 (Sept. 26, 1914), 1763.
          Suggestions for music by George P. Montgomery.

933. ----------. "-----." Moving Picture World, 22 (Oct. 17, 1914), 339-40.
          Suggestions for music by Carrie Hetherington.

934. ----------. "-----." Moving Picture World, 22 (Nov. 7, 1914), 776.
          Rules for movie house drummers.

935. ----------. "-----." Moving Picture World, 22 (Nov. 21, 1914), 1079-80.
          Article: "What to Play for Pictures?"

936. ----------. "-----." Moving Picture World, 23 (Jan. 2, 1915), 62-63.
          Suggestions for music by Nat E. Solomons.

937. ----------. "-----." Moving Picture World, 23 (Jan. 23, 1915), 505-06.
          Suggestions for music by Max Winkler.

938. ----------. "-----." Moving Picture World, 24 (May 1, 1915), 717-18.
          Suggestions for music by Carrie Hetherington.

939. ----------. "-----." Moving Picture World, 24 (May 15, 1915), 1077-78.
          In praise of organ accompaniment for silent films.

940. ----------. "-----." Moving Picture World, 25 (July 3, 1915), 53-54.
          Suggestions for music by Max Winkler and Dick Bertram.

941. ----------. "-----." Moving Picture World, 25 (July 31, 1915), 827.
          Suggestions for music by Max Winkler and William Wertsch.

942. ----------. "-----." Moving Picture World, 25 (Sept. 18, 1915), 1984-85.
          Suggestions for music by Frank H. Anderson and Adolph Ro-
          senthal.

943. ----------. "-----." Moving Picture World, 26 (Oct. 16, 1915), 458-59.
          Suggestions for music by Harry I. Garson and Carrie Heth-
          erington.

944. ----------. "-----." Moving Picture World, 26 (Nov. 13, 1915), 1295-96.
          Article: "Improvising," Part I, No. 1.

945. ----------. "-----." Moving Picture World, 26 (Dec. 4, 1915), 1823-24.
          Article: "Improvising," Part I, No. 2. Also, suggestions
          for music by S. M. Berg, and an original composition by
          Walter C. Simon.

946. ----------. "-----." Moving Picture World, 26 (Dec. 18, 1915), 2178-79.
          Article: "Improvising," Part I, No. 3. Also, suggestions
          for music by S. M. Berg, and a cue sheet for "Carmen" by
          Dick Bertram.

947. ----------. "Music for the Picture." The Moving Picture World, 30 (Dec. 16, 1916), 1643.

        Concerning the "Harmo-Electric Pipe Organ."

948. ----------. "-----." Moving Picture World, 32 (April 21, 1917), 426.

        Article: "Improvising," Part II, No. 4.

949. ----------. "-----." Moving Picture World, 32 (May 5, 1917), 798.

        Article: "Improvising," Part II, No. 5.

950. ----------. "-----." Moving Picture World, 32 (June 23, 1917), 1930.

        Article: "Improvising," Part II, No. 6.

951. ----------. "-----." Moving Picture World, 33 (July 7, 1917), 85.

        Article: "Improvising," Part II, No. 7.

952. ----------. "-----." Moving Picture World, 33 (July 28, 1917), 637.

        Article: "Improvising," Part II, No. 9.

953. ----------. "-----." Moving Picture World, 33 (Sept. 8, 1917), 1530.

        Concerning questions of copyright.

954. ----------. "-----." Moving Picture World, 33 (Sept. 22, 1917), 1842.

        Article: "Improvising," Part II, No. 10.

955. ----------. "-----." Moving Picture World, 34 (Oct. 13, 1917), 227.

        Concerning questions of copyright.

956. ----------. "-----." Moving Picture World, 34 (Nov. 10, 1917), 848-51.

        Part One of a listing of "royalty free, non-taxable" theater music available to the motion picture accompanist. Continues in #957-961.

957. ----------. "-----." Moving Picture World, 34 (Nov. 24, 1917), 1165-67.

958. ----------. "-----." Moving Picture World, 34 (Dec. 1, 1917), 1313-14.

959. ----------. "-----." Moving Picture World, 34 (Dec. 29, 1917), 1934-35.

960. ----------. "-----." Moving Picture World, 35 (Jan. 12, 1918), 223-26.

961. ----------. "-----." Moving Picture World, 35 (Jan. 26, 1918), 510.

962. ----------. "The Song and the Singer." The Moving Picture World, 10 (Nov. 4, 1911), 377.

        One of several articles devoted to the practice of the "song slide."

963. ----------, and C. C. Pettijohn. "Music for the Picture." The Moving Picture World, 33 (Sept. 29, 1917), 1972-73.

        Includes an article (by Pettijohn): "Music Copyright Question."

964. ----------, and Frank E. Kneeland. "Music for the Picture." The Moving Picture World, 32 (June 9, 1917), 1594.

965. ----------, ----------. "Music for the Picture." The Moving Picture World, 32 (June 16, 1917), 1774.

        Concerning conducting techniques. Also includes references to the music of Victor Herbert.

966. ----------, ----------. "Music for the Picture." The Moving Picture World, 32 (June 30, 1917), 2086.

967. ----------, ----------. "Music for the Picture." The Moving Picture World, 33 (July 14, 1917), 230.

        Includes the article "Improvising," Part II, No. 8.

968. ----------, and Norman Stuckey. "Music for the Picture." The Moving Picture World, 31 (Jan. 13, 1917), 232-33.

>Includes the article "Improvising," Part II, No. 1.

969. ----------, ----------. "Music for the Picture." The Moving Picture World, 31 (Jan. 20, 1917), 372.

>The "Victrola" as an accompaniment for pictures.

970. ----------, ----------. "Music for the Picture." The Moving Picture World, 31 (Jan. 27, 1917), 520-21.

>Concerning "appropriate" instruments for film accompaniment. Also a listing of "standard classical works."

971. ----------, ----------. "Music for the Picture." The Moving Picture World, 31 (Feb. 3, 1917), 684-85.

>References to the work of Samuel L. ("Roxy") Rothapfel.

972. ----------, ----------. "Music for the Picture." The Moving Picture World, 31 (Feb. 10, 1917), 840-41.

>A discussion of "tubular organs," an early original score by William Furst, and the article "Improvising," Part II, No. 2.

973. ----------, ----------. "Music for the Picture." The Moving Picture World, 31 (Feb. 24, 1917), 1177.

>References to the organist Clarence Eddy.

974. ----------, ----------. "Music for the Picture." The Moving Picture World, 31 (March 3, 1917), 1348.

>Concerning an original score by William Furst.

975. ----------, ----------. "Music for the Picture." The Moving Picture World, 31 (March 17, 1917), 1771.

>Includes the article "Improvising," Part II, No. 3.

976. ----------, ----------. "Music for the Picture." The Moving Picture World, 31 (March 24, 1917), 1919.

977. ----------, ----------. "Music for the Picture." The Moving Picture World, 31 (March 31, 1917), 2106.

>Concerning the activities of conductor Carl Edouarde.

978. ----------, ----------. "Music for the Picture." The Moving Picture World, 32 (April 14, 1917), 278.

>References to director Hugo Riesenfeld, and a discussion of appropriate organ registration.

979. ----------, Norman Stuckey, and Caroline I. Hibbard. "Music for the Picture." The Moving Picture World, 32 (May 19, 1917), 1118.

980. ----------, Norman Stuckey, and Samuel L. Rothapfel. "Music for the Picture." The Moving Picture World, 31 (March 10, 1917), 1568.

>Includes an article (by Rothapfel): "High Class Music a Feature."

981. ----------, and S. M. Berg. "Music for the Picture." The Moving Picture World, 27 (Jan. 1, 1916), 84-85.

>Article: "Improvising," Part I, No. 4, along with suggestions for music, and an original composition by Walter C. Simon.

982. ----------, ----------. "Music for the Picture." The Moving Picture World, 27 (Jan. 8, 1916), 247-48.

>Suggestions for music.

983. ----------, ----------. "Music for the Picture." The Moving Picture World, 27 (Feb. 5, 1916), 779-80.

Article: "Improvising," Part I, No. 5, along with an original composition by Walter C. Simon.

984. ----------, ----------. "Music for the Picture." The Moving Picture World, 27 (Feb. 19, 1916), 1131-32.

Article: "Improvising," Part I, No. 6. Also, suggestions for music.

985. ----------, ----------. "Music for the Picture." The Moving Picture World, 27 (March 25, 1916), 2007-08.

Article: "Improvising," Part I, No. 7. Also, suggestions for music, and an original composition by Walter C. Simon.

986. ----------, ----------. "Music for the Picture." The Moving Picture World, 28 (April 15, 1916), 443-44.

Article: "Improvising," Part I, No. 8. Also, suggestions for music, and an original composition by Walter C. Simon.

987. ----------, ----------. "Music for the Picture." The Moving Picture World, 28 (May 6, 1916), 975-76.

Article: "Improvising," Part I, No. 9. Also, suggestions for music.

988. ----------, ----------. "Music for the Picture." The Moving Picture World, 29 (July 15, 1916), 457-58.

A description of a new Wurlitzer instrument. Also, suggestions for music.

989. ----------, ----------. "Music for the Picture." The Moving Picture World, 29 (Aug. 12, 1916), 1117-18.

A description of the Seeburg Pipe-Organ Orchestra. Also, suggestions for music.

990. ----------, ----------, and Walter C. Simon. "Music for the Picture." The Moving Picture World, 29 (Aug. 19, 1916), 1248-49.

Suggestions for music, along with an original composition by Simon.

991. Skaupy, Franz, in collaboration with Max Wolff. Die Grundlagen des Tonfilms. Berlin: Union deutsche Verlagsgesellschaft, 1932.

992. Smith, Irma. "Cocteau's Collaborations with Musicians." Ph.D. Diss. Pennsylvania State University 1975.

993. Sorgenfrei, Paul. "Über Kino-Musik." Zeitschrift für Musik, 88 (1921), 469-70.

994. "Sound-Proof Studios for Talkies." Literary Digest (Jan. 12, 1929), 19.

995. Spivak, Morris Joseph. Broken Melody: A Drama for the Talking Screen. The Talking Picture Publishing Co., 1929.

996. Spoerl, H. "Filmmusik." Der Kinematograph (Berlin), No. 796 (1922).

997. "Der Standpunkt der Behörden der musikalischen Filmkunst gegenüber." Der Kinematograph (Berlin), No. 654 (1919).

998. Stang, Joanne. "Making Music: Silent Style." The New York Times Magazine, 110 (Oct. 23, 1960), 83-84.

Concerning the work of Arthur Kleiner.

999. Stearns, Theodore. "Music for the Movies." Musician, 21 (April 1916), 203.

1000. Stein, J. "Ilustracja muzyczna." Kino dlja wszystkich, No. 49 (1927).

1001. Stein, Richard H. "Vom Tonfilm." Die Musik, 24 (1931).

1002. Stepun, Fedor Avgustovich. Theater und Kino. Berlin: Bühnenvolksbundverlag, 1932.

1002a. Reprinted with the title _Theater und Film_. Munich: Carl Hanser Verlag, 1953.

1003. Stern, Dietrich. "Filmkomposition zu Beginn der Stummfilmzeit." Ph.D. Diss. (Musicology), Freie Universität, Berlin.

Work in progress, 1981.

1004. Stjerne, Harald. "Low Fidelity." _Chaplin_ (Stockholm), 17, No. 4 (#139), (1975), 178-79.

1005. Stokowski, Leopold. "Sound Recording -- from the Musician's Point of View." _Journal of the Society of Motion Picture Engineers_, 18, No. 2 (Feb. 1932), 164-71.

1006. Straus, Oscar. "And So to Hollywood: Notes on a Pilgrimage to the Sound Studios." _Theatre_, 51 (April 1930), 40, 62.

1007. Strobel, Heinrich. "Die Baden-Baden Kammermusik, 1929." _Melos_, 8, Nos. 8-9 (Aug.-Sept. 1929), 395-400.

Notes on the Baden-Baden Music Festival, 1929.

1008. ----------. "Film und Musik: Zu den Baden-Baden Versuchen." _Melos_, 7, No. 7 (July 1928), 343-47.

Notes on the Baden-Baden Music Festival, 1929.

1009. ----------. "Über Filmmusik." _Melos_, 12, No. 2 (Feb. 1933), 53-54.

1010. Stromenger, K. "Muzyka wzrokowa." _Wiadomości Literackie_, No. 577 (1934).

1011. Stuckenschmidt, Hans Heinz. "Machines: A Vision of the Future." _Modern Music_, 4, No. 3 (March-April 1927), 8-14.

1012. ----------. "Mechanische Musik." _Der Auftakt_, 6, No. 8 (1926), 170-73.

1013. ----------. "Die Musik zum Film." _Die Musik_, 18, No. 11 (Aug. 1926), 807-17.

1014. Swigart, Bill. "Studio Music." _Variety_ (Jan. 8, 1930), 121.

1015. "Tagung Deutsche Kinomusik Baden-Baden." _Frankfurter Zeitung_ (July 12, 1927).

Concerning the 1927 Baden-Baden conference.

1016. "Tarifvertrag für Kino und Musik, Berlin, Feb. 21, 1922." _Der Lichtbildtheater-Besitzer_, No. 6 (1922), 18.

1017. Teetor, Henry C., and Herbert S. Mikesell. _The Pipe Organ: Mechanics -- Maintenance -- Technic; Theatre and Church_. Richmond, Ind.: Teetor-Mikesell Extension Training School, 1928.

1018. Templiner, --. "Die Musikbegleitung des Lichtbildes und der Verband zum Schutze musikal: Aufführungsrechte." _Reichsfilmblatt_, No. 13 (1924), 14.

Concerning problems of performing rights.

1019. Tessner, H. "Film und Musik." _Leipziger Neueste Nachrichten_ (Oct. 30, 1926).

1020. Thakkar, S. B. "The Challenge of Sound." _Cinema Vision India_, 1, No. 2 (April 1980), 13-18.

1021. "Theorie und Praxis: Illustrations-Kinothek für den Kinokapellmeister." _Reichsfilmblatt_, No. 18 (1928), 36.

1022. Thiel, Wolfgang. "Gibt es eine Renaissance der Stummfilmmusik?" _Film und Fernsehen_ (Berlin, DDR), 9, No. 3 (1981), 22-26.

1023. ----------. "Musik für Stummfilme." _Film und Fernsehen_ (Berlin, DDR), 10, No. 6 (1982), 24-25.

1024. ----------. "Pariser Filmmusik-Premiere anno 1908." _Musik und Gesellschaft_, 28, No. 12 (Dec. 1978), 712-13.

Film music by Camille Saint-Saëns.

1025. Thielemann, W. "Der Filmdirigent." Umschau (Frankfurt am Main), (1919), 395.

1026. ----------. "Kinematographie des Gesanges." Schaffende Arbeit und Kunst in der Schule, 7 (1919), 257-58.

1027. Thomson, Oscar. "More Fun, Less Music." Modern Music, 6, No. 1 (Nov.-Dec. 1928), 38-40.
        Notes on the Baden-Baden Music Festival, 1928.

1028. "Der Tonfilm und die Opernbuhne im Reich." Allgemeine Zeitung (Chemnitz), (May 15, 1930).

1029. "Tonfilm und Kinoorchester." Deutsche Instrumentenbau-Zeitung (1929), 153.

1030. "Tonfilm und Musikintrumentenindustrie." Deutsche Instrumentenbau-Zeitung (1929), 245.

1031. Trebesius, Ernst. "Der sprechende Film." Der Kinematograph (Berlin), No. 635 (1919).

1032. Trystan, L. "Kino a muzyka." Kinema, No. 24 (1922).

1033. Turner, W. J. "Music in the Cinema." New Statesman (London), 18, No. 457 (Jan. 14, 1922), 419-20.

1034. Ulitzsch, Ernst. "Musik im Film." Der Kinematograph (Berlin), No. 899 (1924).

1035. "Um die Forderungen der Musikautoren." Reichsfilmblatt, No. 12 (1927), 11.

1036. "Unfug in der musikalischen Filmbegleitung." Der Kinematograph (Berlin), No. 963 (1925).

1037. "Unwirkliche Kinomusik." Der Kinematograph (Berlin), No. 859 (1923).

1038. Urgiss, Julius. "Musik und Film." Bild und Film, 4 (1914-1915), 7-8.

1039. ----------. "Warum ist die Begleitmusik zum Film notwendig?" Kinematograph (Düsseldorf), No. 468 (1915).

1040. Van Vechten, Carl. Music and Bad Manners. New York: Alfred A. Knopf, 1916.
        Chapter: "Music for the Movies," pp. 44-54.
        Includes references to "Carmen" (1915), and Victor Herbert's score for "The Fall of a Nation" (1916). A call for more new scores by prominent "serious" composers.

1041. ----------. "Music and the Electrical Theatre." Seven Arts, 2 (May 1917), 97-102.
        Concerning movie overtures and entr'actes.

1042. Verdone, Mario. "Il mondo sonoro del film muto: musica e sottotitoli." Bianco e nero, 28, Nos. 3-4 (Mar.-Apr. 1967), 3-17.

1043. Verity, Frank. "The Sound Track." Films in Review, 15, No. 5 (1964), 295-97, 300.
        Concerning the Academy Award for music.

1044. "Verzeichnis des Repertoires der GDT." Reichsfilmblatt, No. 27 (1929), 23.
        The listing continues in No. 28 (1929), 20; No. 29 (1929), 19; No. 31 (1929), 20; No. 34 (1929), 19; No. 36 (1929), 20; No. 37 (1929), 18; and No. 42 (1929), 23.

1045. Vieregg, --. "Kinomusik." Illustrierte Film-Woche, No. 5 (1919), 32.

1046. Viviani, Almiro. (Pseud., Alex Viany.) "Viagem em Torno do Filme Musical e de Carnaval." Jornal do Brasil (Feb. 15, 1969).

1047. Vogt, Hans. "Theater: stummer und sprechender Film." Berliner Tageblatt, 31 (Oct. 1922).

1048. Vuillermoz, Émile. "Musique et cinéma: 'Deux Mamelles' par André Obey." In Le Cinéma, a special issue of La Crapouillot (Mar. 16, 1923), 16-21.

1049. Wagner, Victor. "Scoring a Motion Picture." Society of Motion Picture Engineers: Transactions (Easton, Pa.), No. 25 (May 3-6, 1926), 40-43.

1050. Walsh, J. "Favorite Pioneer Recording Artists: 'Movie Songs' on Records." Hobbies (Chicago), 85 (June 1980), 35-36ff.

1051. ----------. "Favorite Pioneer Recording Artists: 'Movie Songs' on Records." Hobbies, 85 (July 1980), 35-36ff.

1052. ----------. "Favorite Pioneer Recording Artists: 'Movie Songs' on Records." Hobbies, 85 (Aug. 1980), 35-36ff.

1053. Warschauer, Frank. "Filmmusik." Der Anbruch (Vienna), (1929), 130-34.

1054. ----------. "Tonfilm in Frankreich." Melos, 9, No. 7 (July 1930), 314.

1055. Warshow, Paul. "More is Less: Comedy and Sound." Film Quarterly, 31, No. 1 (Fall 1977), 38-45.

     Concerning recent postsynchronization of silent films.

1056. "Was soll im Kino gespielt werden?" Reichsfilmblatt, No. 15 (1929), 10.

1057. Weil, Alfred R. "Between the Keys: Amarcord (I Remember)." Piano Quarterly, 24, No. 93 (Spring 1976), 23-24.

1058. Weinberg, Gretchen. "The Backroom Boys: Arthur Kleiner." Film Culture, No. 41 (Summer 1966), 83-87.

1059. Weisel, J. H. "The Moving Picture Organist: Ideal Usefulness of the Organ for Moving Pictures: Requirements of a Successful Organist: Selection and Timing of Numbers." Musical Observer, 13 (March 1916), 177-78.

1060. "Welche Kinomusik?" Deutsche Instrumentenbau-Zeitung (1929), 304.

1061. Weller, Alanson. "For the Movie Organist." Etude, 44 (July 1926), 538.

1062. ----------. "A Movie Player's Stock." Etude, 47 (May 1929), 380-81.

     Advice for the "small town" movie organist.

1063. Wesse, Curt. Grossmacht Film: das Geschöpf von Kunst und Technik. Berlin: Deutsche Buch-Gemeinschaft GmbH, 1928.

1064. White, Eric W. "The Music to 'Harlequin.'" Close Up (London), 9, No. 3 (Sept. 1932), 164-71.

     Score is by Eric White.

1065. Whithorne, Emerson. "Music and the Movies." Musical Courier (Aug. 5, 1926), 6.

1066. Whitworth, Reginald. The Cinema and Theatre Organ: A Comprehensive Description of This Instrument, Its Constituent Parts, and Its Uses. London: Musical Opinion, 1932.

1067. Wiegand, H. "Filmmusik und Tonfilm." Leipziger Volkszeitung (Oct. 7, 1930).

1068. Winkler, Max. "The Origin of Film Music." Films in Review, 2, No. 10 (Dec. 1951), 34-42.

     An excerpt from Winkler's autobiography Penny from Heaven. Presents an interesting, but falacious account of the "invention" of the cue sheet. See #1545.

     Reprinted in Limbacher (#75), pp. 15-24.

1069. Winnig, Walter. "GEMA - GDT." Reichsfilmblatt, No. 43 (1929), 9.

1070. Winterfeld, --. "Musik und Kino." <u>Musik Salon</u>, No. 5 (1913), 19-20.

1071. Wlaikow, W. <u>Hilfstabellen für den Kinokapellmeister</u>. Dresden: Salora Verlag, 1927.

1072. Wollenberg, Hans H., and Heinz Umbehr. <u>Der Tonfilm: Grundlagen und Praxis seiner aufnahme und wiedergabe</u>. Bücher der Praxis, IV. Berlin: Verlag der Lichtbildbühne, 1930.

1073. Wolpe, --. "Was ist Filmmusik?" <u>Das Kunstblatt</u>, 10 (1926), 309-13.

1074. Wyatt, Geoffrey. <u>At the Mighty Organ</u>. Oxford: Oxford Illustrated Press, 1974.

1075. Young, Robert R. "Music Makes the Difference in the Enjoyment of Silent Films." <u>Classic Film Collector</u>, No. 47 (Summer 1975), 29-31.

SEE ALSO:

#62(Kleiner/Blackwood), #76(Limbacher), #79(London), #91(Paiva), #128 (Thiery), #133(Tinhorão), #152(Ewen), #170(Lapierre), #199(Atkins), #249, #272(Nagy), #308(Uselton), #1227(Catling), #1231(Chavez), #1304 (Hellgren), #1495(Sadoul), #1544(Wilson), #2527(Prox), #2543(Schreger), #2684 (Prox), #2789(Ellis), #2857(Oderman), #2898-2899(Vedrilla), #2902 (Waggoner), #2930(Prox), #3000(Auric), #3018(Preussner), #3020(Branscombe), #3021(Mendoza), #3101-3102(Breil), #3103, #3104(Stern), #3130(Huff), #3139(Sokolsky), #3180(Dessau), #3181(Fanck), #3182(Hanisch), #3183(London), #3269(Atkins), #3352(Herbert), #3353(McCarty), #3354(Shirley), #3422-3423(Hindemith), #3424, #3440(Vuillermoz), #3478(Atkins), #3573 (Chowl), #3574(Ebert-Obermeier), #3575(Kriegsman), #3576-3578(Meisel), #3588-3589(Milhaud), #3758(Desilets), #3759, #3760-3762(Riesenfeld), #3763(Russell), #3764(Vila), #3908(Gallez), #4223(Atkins), #4256-4257 (Orledge), #4264 (Prox), #4754(Luciani), #4789(Moore), #4827(Prox), #4953 (Watts), #4987(Brillouin), #4988(Cantril/Allport), #4990(Dauriac), #5005 (Huber), #5018(Lissa), #5039(Washburn/Dickinson), #5067(Erdmann), #5079 (Goldsmith,A./Lescarboura), #5097(Koch), #5114(Sarris), #5118(Schopen), #5125(Smith), #5128(Spaeth), #5133, #5138(Vuillermoz), #5141(Westphal), #5192(London), #5440(Phraner), #5893(Bakshy), #5912(Brauner), #5924(Castle), #5930(Comuzio), #5947(Dale), #5970(Fischer,L.), #5980(Gerstein), #5996(Henderson), #5999(Herring), #6032(Kothes), #6034, 6037(Kreuger), #6042(Leonard/Parish), #6071(Milne), #6079, #6085(Parker), #6089(Pitts), #6103(Schmidl), #6115, #6136(Traubner), #6146(Vernhes), #6174(Popper), #6184(Winckel), #6185-6187(Diederichs), #6200(Birrett), #6272(Rangoonwalla), #6306(Burton), and #6331(Munden).

Also, see entries under the following categories: SILENT AND EARLY SOUND ERA -- Performance Manuals (#1076-1136), Sound Techniques and Technology (#1137-1171); AESTHETICS -- Form and Function: Silent and Early Sound Era (#4277-4412); SPECIAL TOPICS -- Musical Performance on Film: Silent and Early Sound Era (#5144-5178).

Performance Manuals

1076. <u>Ascherberg's Ideal Cinema Series</u>. London: Ascherberg, Hopwood & Crew, 1928-1929.

>8 vols., each containing works for piano and orchestra by a different composer: H. Baynton-Power, Philip Cathie, Walter R. Collins, Percy Elliot, Herman Finck, Walford Hyden, Reginald Somerville, and Arthur Wood.

1077. Baker, Lacey, comp. <u>Picture Music: A Collection of Classic and Modern Compositions for the Organ Especially Adapted for Moving Pictures with Practical Suggestions to the Organist</u>. 2 vols. New York: H. W. Gray, 1919.

1078. Barnes, Bernard. <u>From Piano to Theatre Pipe Organ: An Instruction Book Written for the Pianist Who Wishes to Become an Efficient Organist</u>. Educational Library for the Music Student, 17. New York: Belwin, 1928.

1079. Bastian, John L. The Theatre: Dramatic and Moving Picture Music. 2 vols. Chicago: Bastian Supply Co., 1913.

> A collection of "moods" and short pieces for piano.

1080. Bath, Hubert. Feldman's Film Fittings. London: B. Feldman, 1925.

> Eight works for piano. Also published separately arranged for orchestra.

1081. Becce, Giuseppe. Kinothek: Neue Filmmusik. 12 vols. Berlin: Schlesinger, 1920-27.

> An important collection of music for silent film accompaniment, includes works for orchestra with piano arrangements by Richard Tourbié.

> Vol. I (A and B): Tragisches Drama, Vol. II (A and B): Lyrisches Drama (Chopiniana), Vol III (A and B): Grosses Drama, Vol. IV (A and B): Hochdramatisches Agitatos, Vol. VA: Ernste Intermezzi, Vol. VB: Verschiedenes, Vol. VIA: Exotika, and Vol. VIB: Verschiedenes.

> -- Rev. (of Vol. III): "Neue Kinomusik." In Der Kinematograph (Berlin), No. 825 (1922).

1082. Bijok, Josef, ed. Handbuch der Film-Illustration. Leipzig: Otto Junne, 1921.

1083. Borodkin, Maurice M. Borodkin's Guide to Motion Picture Music. Los Angeles: the author, 1927.

> Thousands of musical titles arranged by "mood" and use.

1084. Brav, Ludwig. Thematischer Führer durch die Orchestermusik. Berlin: Bote und Bock, 1927.

1085. Breil, Joseph Carl. Joseph Carl Breil's Original Collection of Dramatic Music for Motion Picture Plays. London: Chappell, 1917.

> Twelve works for piano, organ, and orchestra.

1086. Brockton, Lester, comp. Carl Fischer's Loose Leaf Motion Picture Collection for Piano Solo, Vol. III. New York: Carl Fischer, Inc., 1918.

> Vols. I and II compiled by M. Lester Lake. See #1106.

1087. Buckley, P. Kevin. The Orchestral and Cinema Organist: A Popular Treatise on the Use of the Organ and Harmonium in Cinema, Hotel, and Other Bands, with a Simple Introduction to the Study of Harmony. London: Hawkes and Son, 1923.

1088. Carl Fischer Moving Picture Folio, Especially Designed for Moving Picture Theatres, Vaudeville Houses, Etc. New York: Carl Fischer, Inc., 1913.

> A collection of works by several composers, arranged by M. Lester Lake.

1089. Carter, G. Roy. Theatre Organist's Secrets: A Collection of Successful Imitations, Tricks and Effects for Motion Picture Accompaniment on the Pipe Organ. Los Angeles: the author, n.d.

1090. Classified Catalogue of Sam Fox Publishing Company Motion Picture Music. Cleveland, Ohio: Sam Fox Publishing Co., 1929.

> An index arranged by title and musical "type."

1091. Ditson's Music for the Photoplay. Boston: Oliver Ditson, 1918-1925.

> A series of five loose-leaf volumes, including works by the composers: Nicolas Amani, Gaston Borch, Lucius Hosmer, Otto Langey, Christopher O'Hare, T. H. Rollinson, and Berthold Tours.

1092. Erdmann, Hans, and Giuseppe Becce. Allgemeines Handbuch der Filmmusik. Unter Mitarbeit von Ludwig Brav. 2 vols. Berlin: Schlesinger'sche Buch- und Musikhandlung, 1927.

An extremely valuable collection, intricately organized, thorough, and useful.

Vol. I: Musik und Film: Verzeichnisse is a history of film music, with a listing of composers. Vol. II: Thematisches Skalenregister is a catalogue of film music arranged by category.

-- Rev. by Schuftan: "Was wir brauchen: Über das 'Allgemeine Handbuch der Filmmusik.'" Reichsfilmblatt, No. 35 (1927), 13.

1093. Fillustra: Führer für Film-Illustration: Roehr's Konzertmusik-Katalog in seiner Eigenschaft als Filmbegleitung. Berlin: Roehr, n.d.

1094. Der Filmillustrator: Führer durch die Filmmusik. Leipzig, Bosworth & Co., 1927.

1095. Foort, Reginald. The Cinema Organ: A Description in Non-Technical Language of a Fascinating Instrument and How It Is Played. London: Pitman, 1932.

1095a. Second revised edition, Vestal, N.Y.: Vestal Press, 1970.

-- Rev. in Hobbies (Chicago), 75 (Jan. 1971), 144.

1096. Fruttchey, Frank. Something New: 400 Self-Help Suggestions for Movie Organ Players. Detroit, n.d.

1097. George, W. Tyacke. Playing to Pictures: A Guide for Pianists and Conductors of Motion Picture Theaters. London: Kinematograph Weekly, 1912.

1097a. Second edition, London: E. T. Heron and Co., 1914.

1098. Gottschalk, Gustav. Katalog aufführungsfreier Musikstücke. Berlin: Selbstverlag, 1928.

1099. Gregory, Adam, comp. Denison's Descriptive Music Book for Plays, Festivals, Pageants, and Moving Pictures. Chicago: T. S. Denison, 1923.

Simplified arrangements of nearly 150 well-known works for piano, classified by form and "mood."

1100. Grelinger, Charles. Musical Cinéma Guide: Guide musical à l'usage du pianiste de cinéma. Paris: Édition A. de Smit, 1919.

1101. The Hawkes Photo-Play Series. 20 vols. London: Hawkes, 1922-1928.

An extensive collection. Each volume presents the works of one composer.

1102. Homocord: Filmton-Illustration. Berlin: Hermann Schmidts Buchdruckerei, 1930.

1103. Katalog aufführungsgebührenfreier Musikstücke. Berlin: Katalogverlag aufführungsgebührenfreier Musikstücke, 1928.

1104. Kinokapellmeister: Monatsschrift für unsere Kinoorchester. Aussig: Kinolitera, 1927.

The first of several volumes in the series.

1105. Kinoorchester: Filmbegleitmusik -- Kinokonzert -- Bühnenschau. Berlin: Verlag Lichtbildbühne, 1925.

Published in 14 parts, as supplements to issues of the periodical Lichtbildbühne.

1106. Lake, M. Lester, comp. Carl Fischer's Loose Leaf Motion Picture Collection for Piano Solo, Vols. I and II. New York: Carl Fischer, Inc., 1915-1916.

A third volume in the series was compiled by Lester Brockton. See #1086.

1107. Lang, Edith, and George West. Musical Accompaniment of Moving Pictures: A Practical Manual for Pianists and Organists and an Exposition of the Principles Underlying the Musical Interpretation of Moving Pictures. Boston: Boston Music Co.; New York: G. Schirmer, 1920.

Reprinted as part of the series "The Literature of Cinema,"

New York: Arno Press, 1970.

1108. Levy, Sol P. Gordon's Motion Picture Collection. 2 vols. New York: Hamilton S. Gordon, 1914.

1109. Luz, Ernst. Motion Picture Synchrony: For Motion Picture Exhibitors, Buyers and Orchestras. New York: Music Buyers' Corp., 1925.

    Describing the "Symphonic Color Guide," a new method for musical "cueing."

1110. Mapp, T. J. A. The Art of Accompanying the Photo-Play. New York: Photo-Play Musical Bureau, 1917.

1111. McGill, Maude Stolley. "A Ten-Lesson Course in Motion-Picture Playing." Melody (Feb. 1922), 7. (See #1126.)

1112. Meeker, May Shaw. The Art of Photoplaying ... In Operating Any Photoplayer or Double Tracker Piano Players for Theatres. St. Paul, Minn., 1916.

    Concerning the use of piano rolls and photoplayers.

1113. Mills, May Meskimen. The Pipe Organist's Complete Instruction and Reference Work on the Art of Photoplaying. Philadelphia: the author, 1922.

    Includes a section "Requirements of the Movie Organist," and an index of music classified by "mood." Also includes bibliography.

1114. Mühlenau, Max. (Pseud., Maximilian Müller.) Kinobrevier: Anleitung zur musikalischen Filmillustration. Berlin: Maximilian Müller, 1926.

1115. "Music Cue Sheets for Films of Current Release." The Moving Picture World, 40 (April 3, 1919).

    The first in a series of cue sheets published intermittently in MPW for several years. Cue sheets were prepared by S. M. Berg, Max Winkler, James C. Bradford, Harley Hamilton, Joseph O'Sullivan, Louis F. Gottschalk, and others.

1116. Orchester-Katalog für grosse und kleine Orchester, Salonorchester und Militärmusik mit Anregungen für den Filmillustration. Leipzig: Hofmeister, 1925.

1117. PianOrgan Film Books of Incidental Music, Extracted from the World Famous "Berg" and "Cinema" Incidental Series. 7 vols. New York: Belwin, 1925.

    A re-publication of short works by Morris Aborn, Gaston Borch, Charles K. Herbert, Sol P. Levy, Adolf Minot, and others.

1118. Rapée, Erno A. Erno Rapée's Encyclopedia of Music for Pictures: As Essential as the Picture. New York: Belwin, 1925.

    An extensive 480-page alphabetical listing of musical titles classified by mood, color and type. Also a listing by composer and publisher.

    Reprinted as part of the series "The Literature of Cinema," New York: Arno Press, 1970.

1119. ----------. Kinokatalog: Ratgeber zur musikalischen Filmillustration: Kinomusikal -- Klassifizierung der Orchesterwerke aus der Lyra-Edition. Leipzig: Benjamin, 1926.

1120. ----------. Motion Picture Moods for Pianists and Organists: A Rapid Reference Collection of Selected Pieces Arranged by Erno Rapee -- Adapted to Fifty-Two Moods and Situations. New York: G. Schirmer, 1924.

    An extensive and valuable collection. 678 pages.

    Reprinted as part of the series "The Literature of Cinema," New York: Arno Press, 1970.

1121. Reeves, Ernest, arr. Augener's Cinema Music for Piano, Violin and Violoncello, to Which May Be Added Violin II, Bass and Harmonium. 25 vols. London: Augener, 1921-1923.

1122. Savino, Domenico. Descriptive and Dramatic Photoplay Series for Piano and

Organ. New York: Robbins Music Corp., 1924.

1123. _Schirmer's Photoplay Series: A Loose Leaf Collection of Dramatic and De-_
scriptive Musical Numbers ... Arranged for Small or Full Orchestra and
Playable for Any Combination of Instruments Which Includes Violin and
Piano. 7 vols. New York: G. Schirmer, 1915-1929.

    Includes works by J. E. Andino, Irénée Bergé, W. W. Ber-
    gunker, Gaston Borch, Arcady Dubensky, Edward Falck, Wil-
    liam Lowitz, Otto Langey, Adolf Minot, Hugo Riesenfeld,
    Domenico Savino, and Walter C. Schad.

    Several of these pieces are reprinted in Rapée (#1120).

1124. Seredy, Julius S., comp. _Carl Fischer's Analytical Orchestra Guide: A_
Practical Handbook for the Profession. New York: Carl Fischer, Inc.,
1929.

    An extensive listing of musical titles, classified by
    mood, form, key, duration, and tempo.

1125. ----------, Charles J. Roberts, and M. Lester Lake, comps. _Motion Picture_
Music Guide to the Carl Fischer Modern Orchestra Catalogue: Indicating
All the Themes and Motives Suitable for Motion Pictures, and Showing
Their Practical Application to the Screen. New York: Carl Fischer, Inc.,
1922.

1126. Stolley-McGill, Maude. _The Stolley-McGill Ten Lesson Course in Moving Pic-_
ture Piano Playing. Portland, Ore.: Stolley-McGill Publ. Co., 1916.

    Later reprinted in several issues of the periodical _Melody_,
    beginning with the article cited at #1111.

1127. "Suggestions for Music," and "Incidental Music for Edison Pictures." In
The Edison Kinetogram (Sept. 15, 1909), 12-13.

    The first in a series of cue sheets which appeared with
    these titles in the weekly (and semi-monthly) publication
    of the Thomas A. Edison Co., Orange, N.J.

1128. Swinnen, Firmin. _Motion Picture Organist_. New York: G. Schirmer, 1928.

1129. ----------. _The Theater Organist: Original Compositions_. 5 vols. New
York: Fischer, 1921-1922.

    Volumes are entitled: _Dramatic Andantes_, _Dramatic Agitatos_,
    Themes, _Misteriosos_, and _Hurries_.

1130. Talmadge, William E. _How to Play Pictures_, 1914.

1131. _Thematischer Führer durch die klassische und moderne Orchestermusik zum be-_
sonderen Gebrauch für die musikalische Film-Illustration. 4 vols. Berlin: Bote und Bock, 1927.

    Includes an essay by Ludwig Brav: "Die Praxis der Bear-
    beitung."

1132. Tootell, George. _How to Play the Cinema Organ: A Practical Book by a Prac-_
tical Player. With a Foreword by Herbert Snow. London: W. Paxton, 1927.

    A handbook prepared by the well-known English organist.

1133. True, Lyle C. _How and What to Play for Moving Pictures: A Manual and Guide_
for Pianists. San Francisco: Music Supply Co., 1914.

1134. _Universal-Film-Musik: Generalkatalog der berühmtesten Serien von Original-_
Film-Kompositionen. Berlin: Schlesinger, n.d.

1135. _What to Play for the Movies: A Complete Motion Picture Music Guide for Pian-_
ists and Conductors. New York: Carl Fischer, Inc., n.d.

1136. Zamecnik, John S. _Sam Fox Moving Picture Music_. 3 vols. Cleveland: Sam
Fox Music Co., 1913-14.

    Short compositions for piano, most written or arranged
    by Zamecnik. A fourth volume appeared in 1923.

1137. Frelinger, Gregg A. Motion Picture Piano Music: Descriptive Music to Fit the Action, Character or Scene of Moving Pictures. Lafayette, Ind.: G. A. Frelinger, 1909.

> One of the earliest anthologies of music for motion picture accompaniment.

SEE ALSO:

> #322(Ahern), #365-394(Berg), #395-399(Berg/Stuckey), #400(Berg/Simon), #407-430(Beynon), #431-452(Beynon et al.), #454(Bingham), #470(Brav), #897-912, 926-946(Sinn), #981, 983-990(Sinn/Berg), #1017(Teetor/Mikesell), #1066(Whitworth), and #4290-4300(Beynon).

Sound Techniques and Technology

1138. Barsy, --. "Aufnahmeapparat und Musik." Kinotechnik (1925), 489.

> Response to an article by Erdmann. See #525.

1139. Cameron, Evan William, William F. Wilbert, and Joan Evans-Cameron. Sound and the Cinema: The Coming of Sound to American Cinema, 1925-1940. Pleasantville, N.Y.: Redgrave Publishing, 1980.

> Proceedings of the 1973 International Museum of Photography Symposium held in Rochester, N.Y.

> Includes articles by E. W. Cameron (#4480), R. Fielding (#1147), L. Fischer (#5970), D. Gomery (#1153), B. Herrmann (#3393), G. Noxon (#770), and J. Steward (#1169). Also includes bibliography, pp. 220-223.

1140. Cameron, James Ross. Motion Pictures with Sound. Manhattan Beach, N.Y.: Cameron Publ. Co., 1929.

1141. Cass, John L. "The Illusion of Sound and Picture." Journal of the Society of Motion Picture Engineers, 14, No. 3 (March 1930), 323-26.

> Concerning developments in sound technology with implications for film music.

1142. Chapple, Stanley. "Film Synchronization." The Gramophone, 11, No. 97 (June 1931), 8-9.

1143. Clarke, Eric T. "An Exhibitor's Problems in 1925," Transactions of the Society of Motion Picture Engineers (Oct. 1925).

1144. Cowan, Lester, ed. Recording Sound for Motion Pictures. New York and London: McGraw-Hill, 1931.

> A collection of articles by experts in the field of sound recording, prepared by Cowan for the Academy of Motion Picture Arts and Sciences School in Sound Fundamentals.

> Updated by the volume edited by A. P. Hill et al. in 1938. See #1567.

1145. Dickson, W. K. L. "A Brief History of the Kinetograph, the Kinetoscope, and the Kineto-Phonograph." Journal of the Society of Motion Picture Engineers, 21, No. 6 (Dec. 1933), 435-55.

1146. ----------, and Antonia Dickson. History of the Kinetograph, Kinetoscope and Kineto-Phonograph. New York: Albert Bunn, 1895.

> Reprint, New York: Arno Press, 1970.

1147. Fielding, Raymond. "The Technological Antecedents of the Coming of Sound: An Introduction." In Sound and the Cinema: The Coming of Sound to American Film. Ed. Evan William Cameron et al. Pleasantville, N.Y.: Redgrave Publishing, 1980, pp. 2-23.

See Cameron (#1139).

1148. Franklin, Harold B. Sound Motion Pictures: From the Lab to Their Presentation. Garden City, N.Y.: Doubleday, Doran and Co., 1929.

Concerning sound and music recording.

1149. Gomery, Douglas. "The Coming of Sound to Hollywood." In The Cinematic Apparatus: Technology as Historical and Ideological Form. Ed. Stephen Heath and Teresa de Lauretis. London: Macmillan; New York: St. Martin's Press, 1980.

Includes papers and discussions from the Center for 20th Century Studies Conference, Feb. 1978, University of Wisconsin, Milwaukee.

1150. ----------. "The Coming of Sound to the American Cinema: A History of the Transformation of an Industry." Ph.D. Diss. University of Wisconsin (Madison) 1975.

Abstract: DAI 36:5617A (order #7526503).

1151. ----------. "The Coming of Sound to the German Cinema." Film Studies Annual (West Lafayette, Ind.: Purdue Research Foundation), No. 1 (Aug. 1976), 136-43.

1152. ----------. "The Coming of the Talkies: Invention, Innovation, and Diffusion." In The American Film Industry: An Historical Anthology. Ed. Tino Balio. Madison: University of Wisconsin Press, 1976, pp. 193-211.

1153. ----------. "Hollywood Converts to Sound: Chaos or Order?" In Sound and the Cinema: The Coming of Sound to American Film. Ed. Evan William Cameron et al. Pleasantville, N.Y.: Redgrave Publ., 1980, pp. 24-37.

See Cameron (#1139).

1154. ----------. "Problems in Film History: How Fox Innovated Sound." Quarterly Review of Film Studies, 1, No. 3 (Aug. 1976), 315-30.

1155. Hampton, Benjamin B. A History of the Movies. New York: Covici/Friede, 1931.

1155a. Reprinted as History of the American Film Industry from Its Beginnings to 1931. New York: Dover Publications, 1970.

Includes a section devoted to sound techniques, pp. 362-434.

1156. Horváth, Árpád. Muzsikáló Szerkezetek története. Budapest: Táncsics Könyvkiadó, 1967.

A history of "mechanical musical instruments." Includes bibliography.

1157. Hulfish, David S. Cyclopedia of Motion-Picture Work: A General Reference Work on the Optical Lantern, Motion Head, Specific Projecting Machines, Talking Pictures, Color Matography, Fixed Camera Photography, Motography, Photo-Plays, Motion Picture Theater Management and Operation, Audience, Program, Etc. 2 vols. Chicago: American School of Correspondence, 1911.

1158. Knox, H. G. "Ancestry of Sound Pictures." In Recording Sound for Motion Pictures. Ed. Lester Cowan. New York: McGraw-Hill, 1931.

A history of technical developments, with a few references to music recording.

1159. Lafferty, William Charles, Jr. "The Early Development of Magnetic Sound Recording in Braodcasting and Motion Pictures, 1928-1950." Ph.D. Diss. Northwestern University 1981.

Abstract: DAI 42:3792A (order #DA 8204930).

1160. Laura, Ernesto G. "Nascita del cinema sonoro negli Stati Uniti d'America (1926-32)." Bianco e nero, 23, Nos. 9-10 (Sept.-Oct. 1962), 55-95.

Concerning developments in sound technology with implications for film music.

1161. "Lautsprecher im Filmbetrieb." Reichsfilmblatt, No. 24 (1926), 16.

1162. Lega, Giuseppe. Il fonofilm: l'arte e la tecnica della cinematografia par-
    lata e sonora. Novissima enciclopedia monografica illustrata, 27. Flo-
    rence, 1932.

1163. MacGowan, Kenneth. "The Coming of Sound to the Screen." Quarterly of
    Film, Radio, and Television, 10, No. 2 (Winter 1955), 136-45.

1164. "Ein neuer Beruf: Der Phono-Mixer." Reichsfilmblatt, No. 37 (1929), 11.

1165. Pitkin, Walter Boughton, and William Moulton Marston. The Art of Sound
    Pictures. With an Introduction by Jesse L. Lasky. New York and London:
    D. Appleton, 1930.

    Chapters: "Sound Effects," pp. 194-208, and "Sound Tech-
    nique," pp. 215-40.

1166. Ramsaye, Terry. "Early History of Sound Pictures." Transactions of the
    Society of Motion Picture Engineers, No. 35 (1928), 597-602.

    Concerning developments in sound and music recording.

1167. Salt, Barry. "Film Style and Technology in the Thirties." Film Quarterly,
    30, No. 1 (Fall 1976), 19-32.

    Includes a section: "Sound Recording," pp. 30.

1168. Scotland, John. The Talkies. London: Crosby Lockwood, 1930.

    Concerning the problems and techniques of early sound re-
    cording and film synchronization.

1169. Stewart, James G. "The Evolution of Cinematic Sound: A Personal Report."
    In Sound and the Cinema: The Coming of Sound to American Film. Ed. Evan
    William Cameron et al. Pleasantville, N.Y.: Redgrave Publishing, 1980,
    pp. 38-67.

    Comments by a specialist in sound production and post-
    production editing.

1170. Thrasher, Frederic, ed. Okay for Sound: How the Screen Found Its Voice.
    New York: Duell Sloan and Pearce, 1946.

    A survey of technical developments, with implications for
    film music.

1171. Waley, H. D. "Sub-Standard Sound Film: A Summary of Systems in Use."
    Sight and Sound, 3, No. 10 (Summer 1934), 92-94.

    Concerning the advantages of optical printing, and other
    technical matters.

    SEE ALSO:

    #155(Fielding), #199(Atkins), #223, 226(Cook), #231(Daugherty), #238
    (Ford), #241(Frayne et al.), #254(Kellogg), #295(Sponable), #312(Weiland),
    #338(Atkins), #640(J. Johnson), #824(Roland), #1049(V. Wagner), and #4968.

1935-1949

History

1172. Abel, Victor. Wie screibt man einen Film? Vienna: Sensenverlag, 1937.

    Includes references to film music.

1173. Adomian, Lan. "The Great Glinka." Film Music Notes, 7, No. 3 (Jan.-Feb.
    1948), 13-14.

    Musical director for the film was Vissarion Shebalin.

1174. ----------. "The Pearl." <u>Film Music Notes</u>, 7, No. 4 (Mar.-Apr. 1948), 16-17.

       Film music by Antonio Diaz Conde.

1175. Alwyn, William. "The Composer and Crown." <u>Sight and Sound</u>, 21, No. 4 (Apr.-June 1952), 176-77.

       Composing film scores for the Crown Film Unit (Gt. Brit.).

1176. Anschütz, Georg. "Musik und Farbe im Tonfilm." <u>Der Deutscher Film</u> (Berlin), 2 (1937), 103-04.

1177. Antheil, George. "Breaking into the Movies." <u>Modern Music</u>, 14, No. 2 (Jan.-Feb. 1937), 82-86.

1178. ----------. "On the Hollywood Front." <u>Modern Music</u>, 15, No. 1 (Nov.-Dec. 1937), 48-51.

       References to the music of Steiner and Thomson.

1179. ----------. "On the Hollywood Front." <u>Modern Music</u>, 15, No. 2 (Jan.-Feb. 1938), 117-18.

       References to Kurt Weill and others.

1180. ----------. "On the Hollywood Front." <u>Modern Music</u>, 16, No. 1 (Nov.-Dec. 1938), 62-65.

       References to the music of Weill and Steiner.

1181. ----------. "On the Hollywood Front." <u>Modern Music</u>, 16, No. 2 (Jan.-Feb. 1939), 130-33.

       Concerning the work of Boris Morros and Adolphe Borchard.

1182. ----------. "On the Hollywood Front." <u>Modern Music</u>, 16, No. 3 (Mar.-Apr. 1939), 194-96.

       A comparison of film music in Europe and America.

1183. ----------. "On the Hollywood Front." <u>Modern Music</u>, 16, No. 4 (May-June 1939), 278-80.

       References to music by Honegger, Auric, and Prokofiev.

1184. Applebaum, Louis. "Dreams That Money Can Buy." <u>Film Music Notes</u>, 8, No. 1 (Sept.-Oct. 1948), 19-20.

       References to works by John Cage, Paul Bowles, Darius Milhaud, and David Diamond.

1185. ----------. "Mourning Becomes Electra." <u>Film Music Notes</u>, 7, No. 3 (Jan.-Feb. 1948), 15.

       Film music by Richard Hageman.

1186. <u>Atti del secondo congresso internazionale di musica, Firenze-Cremona, 11-26 maggio, 1937</u>. Ugo Ojetti, Presidente del Congresso. Florence: F. Le Monnier, 1940.

       Proceedings of the 1937 Florence Conference. Includes articles by E. Bondeville (#1200), J. Brillouin (#4986), A. Cavalcanti (#4490), P. Collaer (#5062), P. Coppola (#5064), G. Debenedetti (#4538), S. de Feo (#1253), L. Innamorati (#1569), D. Milhaud (#3593), R.-A. Mooser (#5107), F. Pasinetti (#94), G. Razzi (#1478), W. Reich (#5110), Roland Manuel (#4841), H. Rosbaud (#5113), A. Schaffner (#5115), and A. Veretti (#4946).

1187. Bagier, Guido Rudolf Georg. <u>Das tönende Licht: die schilderung einiger seltsamer begebenheiten seit der erfindung der kinematographie, unter verwendung wichtiger und unbekannter dokumente</u>. Berlin and Wilmersdorf: A. Gross, 1943.

       Includes a section on music in film.

1188. Bailey, Gordon. "Teaching Possibilities in Current Films." <u>Film Music Notes</u>, 6, No. 3 (Dec. 1946-Jan. 1947), 15-16.

1189. Bakaleinikoff, Constantin. "Select for Yourself." In Music and Dance in California and the West. Ed. Richard Drake Saunders. Hollywood: Bureau of Musical Research, 1948, pp. 81, 143.

      See Saunders (#1496).

1190. Barilli, Bruno. "Musiche di film." Omnibus (Rome), (Oct. 1937).

1190a. Reprinted in Sequence, No. 9 (1937).

1191. Baxter, John. Hollywood in the Thirties. New York: A. S. Barnes, 1975.

1192. Belviso, Thomas H. "Music Rights in Radio." In Music in Radio Broadcasting. Ed. Gilbert Chase. New York: McGraw-Hill, 1946, pp. 105-24.

1193. Bennett, Tom. "Arranging Music for Radio." In Music in Radio Broadcasting. Ed. Gilbert Chase. New York: McGraw-Hill, 1946, pp. 76-90.

1194. Berman, Z. "Komizm muzyczny w operze i filmie." Wiadomości Filmowe (Warsaw), No. 24 (1938).

1195. Bernard, Guy. "Ciné-Musique." L'Écran français (Paris), 4, No. 20 (1948).

1196. ----------. "Hollywood et les musiciens." In Formes et couleurs, a special issue of Cinéma (1946).

1197. Bernier, --. "Les grands musiciens dans le film." Almanach Ciné-Miroir (Paris), (1936).

1198. Beydts, Louis. La musica: Kermesse eroica. Rome: Edizioni Bianco e nero, 1937.

1199. Black, Frank J. "Conducting for Radio." In Music in Radio Broadcasting. Ed. Gilbert Chase. New York: McGraw-Hill, 1946, pp. 66-75.

1200. Bondeville, Émmanuel. "La radiophonie et la musique contemporaine." In Atti del secondo congresso internazionale di musica, Firenze-Cremona, 11-26 maggio, 1937. Florence: F. Le Monnier, 1940, pp. 125-27.

      A paper presented at the 1937 Florence conference, with synopses in Italian and German, p. 128. See #1186.

1201. Bonito, Rebelo. Notas Explicativas (Clube Português de Cinematografia: Sarau Musical.) Porto, June 30, 1949.

1202. Böttner, Bernhard. "Film und Filmmusik." Theater der Zeit, 3, No. 8 (Aug. 1948), 22-24.

1203. Bowles, Paul. "Films and Theatre." Modern Music, 20, No. 1 (Nov.-Dec. 1942), 57-61.

      References to music by Rozsa, Kubik, Stothart, and Sol Kaplan.

1204. ----------. "Films and Theatre." Modern Music, 20, No. 2 (Jan.-Feb. 1943), 129-32.

      References to music by Skinner and Kubik.

1205. ----------. "On the Film Front." Modern Music, 17, No. 2 (Jan.-Feb. 1940), 113-15.

      Music by Walter Leigh, Sylvestre Revueltas, Ernst Toch, and Dimitri Kabalevsky.

1206. ----------. "On the Film Front." Modern Music, 17, No. 3 (Mar.-Apr. 1940), 184-87.

      References to music by Louis Gruenberg and Alfred Newman.

1207. ----------. "On the Film Front." Modern Music, 17, No. 4 (May-June 1940), 265-67.

      Music by Milhaud, Waxman, and Werner Janssen.

1208. ----------. "On the Film Front." Modern Music, 18, No. 1 (Nov.-Dec. 1940), 58-61.

      Scores by Copland, Blitzstein, Douglas Moore, Richard

Hageman, and Herbert Windt.

1209. ----------. "On the Film Front." Modern Music, 18, No. 2 (Jan.-Feb. 1941), 133-34.

References to Disney's "Fantasia," and music by George Antheil, Roy Harris, and others.

1210. ----------. "On the Film Front." Modern Music, 18, No. 3 (Mar.-Apr. 1941), 193-95.

Music by Rozsa, Gruenberg, and Lev Schwartz.

1211. Brodmann, R. "Filmmusik und Musikfilme." Musica Aeterna (Zurich), (1948).

1212. Broekman, David. The Shoestring Symphony. New York: Simon and Schuster, 1948.

A fictional "autobiography."

1213. Brown, Harold. "Current Films." Film Music Notes, 8, No. 4 (Mar.-Apr. 1949), 18-19.

Music in British films by Brady, Jacobs, and Harry Warren. References to music by Steiner and Victor Young.

1214. Buchanan, Andrew. Film Making: From Script to Screen. London: Faber and Faber, 1937. (Reprint, 1947.)

Includes articles reprinted from the Amateur ciné world and World Film News.

1214a. Revised edition, London: Phoenix House, 1951.

Includes many references to music in films.

1215. Burke, Johnny. "The Quiet Life of Film Song Writers." Music Publishers Journal, 3, No. 5 (Sept.-Oct. 1945), 19.

1216. Cameron, Ken, and Muir Mathieson. "Film Music." Piping Times, 4, No. 2 (1944).

1217. Capell, Richard. "'Fantasia' or the New Barbarism." Musical Opinion (London), 67 (Nov. 1943).

1218. Capitani, Ugo. Il film nel diritto d'autore. Rome: Edizioni Italiane, 1943.

1219. Carbonara, Gerard. "Leitmotif in Film Scoring." In Music and Dance in California. Comp. William J. Perlman. Hollywood: Bureau of Musical Research, pp. 133-36.

See Perlman (#1467).

1220. Care, Ross B. "Threads of Melody." Quarterly Journal of the Library of Congress, 40, No. 2 (Spring 1983), 76-97.

Concerning Disney's "Bambi" (1942), with music by Frank Churchill and Edward Plumb.

1221. Carpenter, Paul S. Music: An Art and a Business. Norman, Okla.: University of Oklahoma Press, 1950.

Chapter: "Hollywood Carrousel," pp. 40-68.

1222. Carter, Elliott. "Films and Theatre." Modern Music, 20, No. 3 (Mar.-Apr. 1943), 205-07.

References to music by Louis Gruenberg.

1223. ----------. "Theatre and Films." Modern Music, 20, No. 4 (May-June 1943), 282-84.

Music by Roy Webb and Max Steiner.

1224. ----------. "Theatre and Films." Modern Music, 21, No. 1 (Nov.-Dec. 1943), 50-53.

Concerning scores by Aaron Copland and Alexandre Tansman.

1225. Carter, Everett. "A Short Inquiry into a Form of Popular Poetry." Hollywood Quarterly, 1, No. 4 (July 1946), 396-404.

Concerning lyric for commercial songs.

1226. Casella, Alfredo. "Il cinema arte e gli artisti delle altri arti." Cinema (Rome), (Feb. 10, 1937), 91.

1227. Catling, Darrel. "Film Music: A Letter from Darrel Catling." Sight and Sound, 13, No. 49 (May 1944), 19.

A reply to an article by John Huntley. See #52.

1228. Cavalcanti, Alberto. "Sound in Films." Films: A Quarterly of Discussion and Analysis, 1, No. 1 (Nov. 1939), 25-39.

Concerning the interaction of dialogue, music, and noise.

Reprinted in Kirstein (#1362).

1229. Chandshokow, A. Perwyje gody russkoi kinopromyschlennosti. Leningrad, 1937.

1230. Chavez, Carlos. "Music for the Radio." Modern Music, 17, No. 2 (Jan.-Feb. 1940), 86-92.

1231. ----------. Toward a New Music: Music and Electricity. Trans. from the Spanish by Herbert Weinstock. New York: W. W. Norton, 1937.

Chapters: V:"The Sound Film," pp. 89-121, VI:"The Radio," pp. 122-37, VIII:"Toward a New Music," pp. 166-80.

1232. Cheremukhin, M. "Muzyka 'Aërograda.'" Iskusstvo kino (Moscow), No. 1 (Jan. 1936).

1233. ----------. "Muzyka v kinokomedii." Iskusstvo kino (Moscow), No. 10 (Oct. 1940), 60-62.

1234. Chiarini, Luigi. "La musica nel film." Bianco e nero, 3, No. 6 (June 1939).

1235. Chotzinoff, Samuel. "Music in Radio." In Music in Radio Broadcasting. Ed. Gilbert Chase. New York: McGraw-Hill, 1946, pp. 1-17.

1236. Churchill, Douglas W. "Baghdad at Hollywood and Vine." The New York Times (Aug. 1, 1937).

1237. ----------. "Music in the Cinema: Hollywood Has Discovered How the Score Improves the Photoplay." The New York Times (Sept. 29, 1935), Section 10, p. 4.

1238. Churchill, Winston. "Everybody's Language." Collier's, 26 (Oct. 1935), 24ff.

Concerning the use of sound and music in the films of Charlie Chaplin.

1239. "Classical Music in Films." Picture Show (1945).

1240. Clifford, Hubert. "British Film Music." Tempo (London), No. 12 (Sept. 1944).

1241. ----------. "Music for the Films." Tempo (London), (March 1945).

1242. ----------. "Music for the Films." Tempo (London), (June 1945).

1243. ----------. "Music for the Films." Tempo (London), (Dec. 1945).

1244. Cockshott, Gerald. "Comments on a Review." Hollywood Quarterly, 3, No. 3 (Spring 1948), 326-27.

A response to Lawrence Morton's negative review of Incidental Music in the Sound Film. See #19 and #1442.

1245. Colacicchi, Luigi. "Musica e film al Congresso di Firenze." Cinema (Rome), No. 22 (1937).

Concerning the 1937 Florence conference.

1246. Connor, Edward. "The Sound Track." _Films in Review_, 8, No. 6 (June-July 1957), 291-93.

> A survey of early soundtrack recordings.

1247. Crews, Albert. _Radio Production Directing_. Boston: Houghton Mifflin, 1944.

> Chapter 6: a discussion of music as an important aspect of radio productions, pp. 147-61, and Chapter 10: an analysis of procedures in planning musical programs, pp. 264-324.

1248. Culshaw, John. "Film Music and the Gramophone." _The Gramophone_, 24, No. 280 (Sept. 1946), 45.

1249. Dahl, Ingolf. "Notes on Cartoon Music." _Film Music Notes_, 8, No. 5 (May-June 1949), 3-13.

> An important article, with excerpts from scores by Scott Bradley.
>
> Reprinted in Limbacher (#75).

1250. Dale, Edgar. _How to Appreciate Motion Pictures_. New York: Macmillan, 1935.

> Chapter: "Sound and Music," pp. 171-79.

1251. Daugherty, F. J. "Music for the Millions." _Christian Science Monitor Magazine_ (April 27, 1938), 8-9.

1252. Davis, George. _Music-Cueing for Radio-Drama_. New York: Boosey and Hawkes, 1947.

1253. de Feo, Sandro. "La musica nel cinematografo." In _Atti del secondo congresso internazionale di musica, Firenze-Cremona, 11-26 maggio, 1937_. Florence: F. Le Monnier, 1940, 232-37.

> A paper presented at the 1937 Florence conference, with synopses in French and German, p. 238. See #1186.

1254. Delapierre, --. "Ciné-musique." _L'Écran français_ (Paris), 4 (April 1948).

1255. Deleplace, G. "La musique dans le film." _Film et famille_ (Paris), No. 31 (Sept. 1946).

1256. de Saxe, Rudy. "Drastic Decade." In _Music and Dance in California and the West_. Ed. Richard Drake Saunders. Hollywood: Bureau of Musical Research, 1948, pp. 80, 132.

1257. De Vore, Nicolas. "Film Music Attains Artistic Stature." _Musician_, 51 (Nov. 1946), 150-51.

> References to the music of Korngold, Alexandre Tansman, and others.

1258. Dickinson, Thorold. "Search for Music." _Penguin Film Review_, No. 2 (Jan. 1947), 9-15.

> Collecting music in Africa for the score of "Men of Two Worlds," directed by Dickinson, with music by Arthur Bliss and William Walton.

1259. Doniol-Walçroze, Jacques, and Jacques Bourgeois. "Tous les oiseaux sont morts: Sujet de film dansé." _La Revue du Cinéma_ (Paris), New series, 3, No. 14 (1949), 39-47.

1260. Eckert, Gerhard. _Hörspiel und Schallfilm: von Werden, Wesen und Zukunft des Hörspiels_. Reihe Wort und Ton, III. Berlin: Verlag für Recht und Verwaltung, 1939.

> Includes a section on music in radio drama.

1261. Eremin, Dmitri Ivanovich, ed. _Tridtsat' let sovietskoii kinematografii_. Moscow: Goskinoizdat, 1950.

> Includes articles by D. Shostakovich, Isaak Dunajewski, N. Krjukov, and others.

1262. Ericsson, Peter. "The Films of Walt Disney." _Sequence_ (New Year 1950).

1263. Evans, Lawrence. "Motion Picture Roles and Careers of Concert Artists." _Music Publishers Journal_, 3, No. 5 (Sept.-Oct. 1945), 21, 72.

1264. Farkas, Ferenc. "Magyar filmek zenéje." _Tükör Jahrgang_ (Budapest), No. 1 (Jan. 1937).

1265. Ferguson, Otis. "Love Me Some Other Time." _New Republic_, 83, No. 1077 (July 24, 1935), 308.

     Concerning the use of "serious" music in films.

1266. Field, Robert. _The Art of Walt Disney_. New York and London: Collins, 1944.

     References to music in Disney films.

1267. "Film Music and No Film Music." _Music Review_, 10 (Feb. 1949), 50-51.

1268. "Film Music: A Teacher's Attitude." _Music in Education_ (July 1946).

1269. "Film Music Courses." _Film Music Notes_, 8, No. 3 (Jan.-Feb. 1949), 4-5.

1270. "Film Music: Nine Swiss Shorts." _Music Review_, 10 (Aug 1949), 225-26.

1271. _Films for Music Education_. A booklet prepared by the Films in Music Education Committee of M. E. N. C. and the Audio-Visual Education Association of California, 1949.

1272. _Le Film sonore: l'écran et la musique en 1935_. A special issue of _La Revue Musicale_, 15, No. 151 (Dec. 1934).

     Includes articles by J. Brillouin (#4987), A. Hoerée (#4343, 4344), A. Hoerée and A. Honegger (#3431), J. Ibert (#3446), C. Koechlin (#4353), L. Landry (#4715), and E. Sarnette (#835).

1273. Finston, Nathaniel W. "The Screen's Influence in Music." In _Music and Dance in California_. Comp. William J. Perlman. Hollywood: Bureau of Musical Research, 1940, pp. 123-25.

     Comments by the Music Director at M.G.M. See Perlman (#1467).

1274. ----------. "Time Tells the Tale." In _Music and Dance in California and the West_. Ed. Richard Drake Saunders. Hollywood: Bureau of Musical Research, 1948, p. 78.

     See Saunders (#1496).

1275. Forrell, Gene. "Teaching Film Music." _Film Music Notes_, 9, No. 1 (Sept.-Oct. 1949), 16.

1276. ----------, John B. Currie et al. "Current Films Reviewed and Recommended." _Film Music Notes_, 6, No. 5 (April-May 1947), 19-20.

     References to the music of Milhaud, Alwyn, Steiner, Rozsa, Tiomkin, and Adolph Deutsch.

1277. ----------, and William Hamilton. "Current Films." _Film Music Notes_, 8, No. 5 (May-June 1949), 16.

     Music by John Greenwood and Alfred Newman.

1278. Frangolc, D. "Chudoshniki svuka." _Iskusstvo kino_ (Moscow), No. 4 (April 1948).

1279. Frank, Alan. "Music and the 'Cellulose Nit-Wit.'" _The Listener_, 18, No. 468 (Dec. 29, 1937), 1444-45.

1280. Freund, --. "Filmmusik." _Die Literatur_ (Stuttgart), 39 (1937), 232-33.

1281. Furmanik, S. "Muzyka w filmie." _Muzyka Polska_, 5 (1936).

1282. Garden, Mary. "Music Comes to Hollywood." _Cinema Arts_, 1, No. 1 (June 1937), 19.

1283. Geduld, Harry M., and Ronald Gottesman, eds. _Sergei Eisenstein and Upton_

Sinclair: The Making and Unmaking of "Que Viva Mexico!" London: Thames & Hudson; Bloomington, Ind.: Indiana University Press, 1970.

A history of the production, assembled from correspondence held at the Lilly Library at Indiana University, with references to plans for the musical score by Riesenfeld.

Includes bibliography, pp. 429-43.

1284. Glinski, M.. "Muzyka w filmie polskim." Wiadomości Filmowe (Warsaw), No. 4 (1935).

1285. Gorodinski, V. "Glinka." Iskusstvo kino (Moscow), No. 2 (Feb. 1947).

Concerning the filmed life of Glinka.

1286. Granich, Tom. "Cinema e jazz." Bianco e nero, 9, No. 8 (Aug. 1948).

1287. Groll, Gunter. "Das Gesetz des Films." Ph.D. Diss., Munich 1937.
1287a. Published with the title Film, die unentdeckte Kunst. Mit einem Geleitwort von Mathias Wieman. Munich: Beck, 1937.

Includes a section "Film und Musik," pp. 99-111.

1288. ----------. "I mezzi d'espressione del film." Cinema (Rome), 7 (1943).

1289. Gronostay, Walter. "Der Film im Strome des Geistesgeschichte." Jahrbuch der Reichsfilmkammer 1937 (1937), 22-29.

1290. ----------. "Wo steht die deutsche Filmmusik?" Der deutscher Film (Berlin), 2 (1937), 22.

1291. Gutman, John A. "Casting the Film Composer." Modern Music, 15, No. 4 (May-June 1938), 216-21.

References to many European film composers.

1292. Haggin, B. H. "Music for Documentary Films." Nation, 152 (Feb. 15, 1941), 194.

References to music by Biltzstein and Copland.

1293. Hall, David. "Musical Continuity for Radio." In Music in Radio Broadcasting. Ed. Gilbert Chase. New York: McGraw-Hill, 1946, pp. 91-104.

1294. Hamilton, Marie L. "Lighter Films." Film Music Notes, 8, No. 2 (Nov.-Dec. 1948).

References to scores by Newman, Friedhofer, Young, and others.

1295. Hamilton, William. "Current Film Reviews." Film Music Notes, 9, No. 1 (Sept.-Oct. 1949), 19-21.

Concerning music by Richard Hageman, and Musical Director Charles Previn.

1296. ----------. "Current Films." Film Music Notes, 7, No. 3 (Jan.-Feb. 1948), 16-17.

Music by Newman, Waxman, Rozsa, Skinner, Allan Gray, and David Tamkin.

1297. ----------. "Current Films." Film Music Notes, 7, No. 4 (Mar.-Apr. 1948), 18-21.

Music by Newman, Steiner, and Robert Blum.

1298. ----------, Harold Brown et al. "Current Films." Film Music Notes, 7, No. 5 (May-June 1948), 8-11.

References to music by Auric, Gruenberg, Steiner, and Cedric Thorpe Davie.

1299. Hartwell, D. "Masses Go for Music." Collier's, 119 (May 24, 1947), 14-15ff.

Concerning the use of "classical" music in films.

1300. Haver, Ursula. "Musikübertragung, Musikausübung und Komposition funkeigener Werke unter Beachtung der technischen und akustischen Grenzen des Rundfunks." Ph.D. Diss, Munich 1942.

    1300a. Published with same title, Würzburg: Triltsch, 1942.

1301. Heindorf, Ray. "Screen Recording." In Music and Dance in California. Comp. William J. Perlman. Hollywood: Bureau of Musical Research, 1940, pp. 140-42.

    See Perlman (#1467).

1302. Heinsheimer, Hans W. "Hollywood's Music Doctors." Science Digest (Aug. 1947), 52-56.

1303. ----------. Menagerie in F-Sharp. Garden City, N.Y.: Doubleday, 1947.

    Chapter 13: "An Old Friendship" (with George Antheil), pp. 201-08; Chapter 14: "Hollywood; or the Bases are Loaded," pp. 209-35; and Chapter 15: "Deadlines, Click Tracks, and Stop Watches," pp. 236-56.

    1303a. Portions (condensed) appear as "Music Out of Hollywood." In Music Digest, No. 7 (1950), 140-43.

    1303b. Also published as Menagerie in fis-dur. Zurich: Pan, 1953.

1304. Hellgren, Dick. "Musik i svenska ljudfilmer 1929-1939." Filmrutan (Sweden), 24, No. 3 (1981), 34.

1305. Henrichsen, Borge Roger. "Film og musik (Part 6)." Dansk Musiktidsskrift (Copenhagen), 24, No. 6 (1949), 135-37.

1306. Hensel, Paul Richard. "Da gibt es einen guten Klang ... Der Tonmeister." Die illustrierte Zeitung (Leipzig), No. 4762 (1936), 820.

1307. Heppner, Sam. "Background Music to the Fore." Sound Illustrated (London), (Dec. 1944).

1308. Higham, Charles, and Joel Greenberg. Hollywood in the Forties. London: Tantivy Press; New York: A. S. Barnes, 1968.

1309. Hill, Ralph. "The Story of British Film Music." Radio Times: Journal of the British Broadcasting Corporation (London), (Dec. 31, 1937).

1310. Hine, A. "Movie Music Has Plenty of Listeners." Holiday, 6 (July 1949), 22.

1311. "Hollywood's Boy Choirs." Film Music Notes, 7, No. 2 (Nov.-Dec. 1947), 15.

1312. Hopkins, Antony. "Music." Sight and Sound, 19 (New Series), (Dec. 1949), 23.

1313. Huntley, John. "Arthur Wilkinson." Music Parade, 1, No. 13 (1949), 15-16ff.

1314. ----------. "British Film Music." Film Music Notes, 4 (April 1944).

1315. ----------. "British Film Music." Penguin Film Review, No. 6 (Apr. 1948), 91-96.

    References to music by Korngold and Walton.

    1315a. Reprinted in The Penguin Film Review, 1946-1949. Yorkshire: Scolar Press; Totowa, N.J.: Rowman and Littlefield, 1978.

    A two volume reprint of all 9 issues of the periodical which was edited by Roger Manvell.

1316. ----------. "British Film Music and World Markets." Sight and Sound, 15, No. 60 (Winter 1946-1947), 135.

1317. ----------. "Criticism from London." Film Music Notes, 5 (Sept. 1945).

1318. ----------. "Film Music." Hinrichsen's Musical Year Book (London), 4-5 (1947-1948), 382-88.

1319. ----------. "Film Music in England." Film Music Notes, 4 (Dec. 1944).

1320. ----------. "Film Music News from England." Film Music Notes, 5 (Nov.

1945).

1321. ----------. "Film-Music Orchestras." Penguin Film Review, No. 5 (Jan. 1948), 14-18.

    References to music for "The October Man" by William Alwyn, and a survey of conductors and orchestras in England.

    Reprinted in Manvell (#1315a).

1322. ----------. "Getting the Gen: A Course in Film Music." Film Music Notes, 5 (Oct. 1945).

1323. ----------. "Music and World News." Sound Illustrated (London), (Dec. 1944).

1324. ----------. "Music for All." Film Music Notes, 5 (Sept. 1945).

1325. ----------. "Music for the Olympic Games Film." Sound Illustrated (London), (Sept. 1948).

1326. ----------. "Music in Current British Films." Film Music Notes, 8, No. 3 (Jan.-Feb. 1949), 15-16.

    Music by Alwyn, Easdale, Walton, and Clifton Parker.

1327. ----------. "Music in New British Films." Cinema and Theatre, 15, No. 1 (1947).

1328. ----------. "Newsreel Music." Film Music Notes, 5 (April 1946).

1329. ----------. "Notes on Film Music." Penguin Film Review, No. 1 (Aug. 1946), 35-37.

    A survey of music in current films.

    Reprinted in Manvell (#1315a).

1330. ----------. "Notes on Film Music." Penguin Film Review, No. 3 (Aug. 1947), 15-17.

    Reprinted in Manvell (#1315a).

1331. ----------. "Stage One Music Theatre, Denham." Film Industry, 2, No. 2 (1947).

1332. ----------. "The Year in Film Music." Film Industry (Dec. 30, 1948).

1333. "Information on Film Music in the United States." Film Music Notes, 8, No. 4 (Mar.-Apr. 1949), 12-14.

    Includes a limited discography.

1334. Inglis, Ruth A. Freedom of the Movies: A Report on Self-Regulation from the Commission on Freedom of the Press. Chicago: University of Chicago Press, 1947.

    An interesting document concerning the role of film, media, and music in contemporary America.

    1334a. Also published as Der amerikanische Film. Nürnberg: Nest-Verlag, 1951.

1335. "Introduzione alla 'Musica d'Accompagnamento per una Scena di Film' di Arnold Schoenberg." Filmcritica, 24 (Jan.-Feb. 1973), 34-40.

1336. Iros, Ernst. Wesen und Dramaturgie des Films. Zurich and Leipzig: Max Niehaus Verlag, 1939. (Reprint, 1957.)

    Second edition, with a supplement and Foreword by Martin Schlappner, Zurich: Die Arche, 1962.

    Includes a section "Die Musik im Film," pp. 123-29, with subheadings "Musik im Operettenfilm," p. 128, and "Film und Oper," p. 129.

1337. Irving, Ernest. "British Film Music." Kinematograph Weekly (London), (Dec. 19, 1946).

1338. ----------. "Film Music." Tempo, New Series, No. 1 (Sept. 1946), 31-32.
    References to music by Georges Auric and Arthur Bliss.

1339. ----------. "Film Music." Tempo, New Series, No. 2 (No. 17), (Dec. 1946),
    26-27.
        Concerning music by Tiomkin, with references to the auto-
        biography of Oscar Levant (#3540).

1340. ----------. "Film Music." Tempo, New Series, No. 3 (No. 18), (Mar. 1947),
    26-27.
        Concerning the "quality" of music in films.

1341. ----------. "Music and the Film Script." In British Film Yearbook, 1947-
    1948. Ed. Peter Noble. London: Skelton Robinson British Yearbooks, 1948,
    pp. 47-52.
        An address delivered to the British Screenwriters Assn.
    1341a. Reprinted in Film Music Notebook, 1, No. 4 (Summer 1975),
        10-13.

1342. ----------. "Music from the Films." Tempo (London), (June 1946).

1343. Isaacs, Hermine Rich. "Face the Music: The Films in Review." Theatre Arts,
    28 (Dec. 1944), 718-27.

1344. ----------. "New Horizons: 'Fantasia' and Fantasound." Theatre Arts, 25
    (Jan. 1941), 55-61.

1345. Janssen, Werner. "Scoring for the Screen." New York Times (Aug. 23,
    1936), Section 9, p. 4.

1346. ----------. "Visualization of Music on the Screen." Music Publishers
    Journal, 3, No. 5 (Sept.-Oct. 1945), 29, 70.

1347. Jay, Martin. "The Frankfurt School: An Intellectual History of the Insti-
    tut für Sozialforschung, 1923-1950." Ph.D. Diss. Harvard 1971.
    1347a. Published with the title The Dialectical Imagination: A
        History of the Frankfurt School and the Institute of So-
        cial Research 1923-1950. Boston: Little, Brown, 1973.
            Includes bibliography, pp. 355-70.

1348. Jerry, --. "Czym jest dźwiek dlja filmu." Film, No. 22 (1936).

1349. ----------. "Piosenka francuska." Film, Nos. 15, 17, and 21 (1936).

1350. Jones, Emily S. "Film Councils in America." Film Music Notes, 7, No. 5
    (May-June 1948), 12-13.

1351. Jungk, Klaus. "Musik im Film." Theater der Zeit, 2, No. 11 (Nov. 1947),
    28-32.

1352. Katz, Bernard. "The Speeding Hour." In Music and Dance in California and
    the West. Ed. Richard Drake Saunders. Hollywood: Bureau of Musical Re-
    search, 1948, pp. 86-87, 145.
        See Saunders (#1496).

1353. Keen, Stuart. "Must We Always Have Dialogue?" Sight and Sound, 15, No. 60
    (Winter 1946-1947), 145.

1354. Keim, Jean Alphonse. Un nouvel art: Le Cinéma sonore. Paris: A. Michel,
    1947.

1355. Keller, Hans. "Film Music." Music Review, 9 (1948), 304-05.
        References to music by Alwyn, Stevens, and Benjamin Frankel.

1356. ----------. "Film Music." Music Review, 10, No. 4 (1949), 303.
        References to music by Bliss, Frankel, Larsson, and Berg.

1357. ----------. "Film Music." Music Survey (London), 1, No. 6 (1949), 196-97.

1358. ----------. "Film Music: The Question of Quotation." _Music Survey_, 2,
No. 2 (Autumn 1949), 25-27.

1359. ----------. "Hollywood Music: Another View." _Sight and Sound_, 16, No. 64
(Winter 1947-1948), 168-69.

> Response to an article by Anthony Thomas. See #1522.

1360. Kiesling, Barrett C. _Talking Pictures: How They Are Made, How to Appreciate
Them_. Richmond, Va.: Johnson Publishing Co., 1937.

> Chapter: "Music in Pictures," pp. 209-15, is a view of
> the Music Department at M.G.M.

> Reprint, London and New York: Spon, 1939.

1361. King, William G. "Music and Musicians: Samuel Goldwyn, Producer and Trend-
starter, Talks of Music in the Movies." _New York Sun_ (July 9, 1938),
p. 8.

1362. Kirstein, Lincoln, Jay Leyda, Mary Losey, Robert Stebbins, and Lee Stras-
berg. _Films: A Quarterly of Discussion and Analysis: Nos. 1-4 (1939-40)_.
New York: Arno Press, 1968.

> A reprint, in book form, of the four issues of this im-
> portant by short-lived periodical. Includes many arti-
> cles on film music.

1363. Kitschman, A. "Muzyka czy parodia muzyki w filmach polskich." _Ekran_,
No. 1 (1935).

1364. Klein, John W. "Recent Film Music." _Musical Opinion_ (London), 66 (June
1943).

1365. Knight, Arthur. "Planning a Film Music Program." _Film Music Notes_, 7,
No. 1 (Sept.-Oct. 1947), 20-21.

1366. Knipper, Lev. "Kino i muzyka." _Iskusstvo kino_ (Moscow), No. 4 (April
1936), 39-42.

1367. Kochnitzky, Léon. "On the Film Front." _Modern Music_, 19, No. 2 (Jan.-
Feb. 1942), 132-34.

> References to music by Adolph Deutsch and Hanns Eisler.

1368. ----------. "On the Film Front." _Modern Music_, 19, No. 4 (May-June 1942),
275-78.

> Music by Blitzstein, Chaplin, Rozsa, and Richard Arnell.

1369. ----------. "On the Film Front -- 'War Shorts.'" _Modern Music_, 19, No. 3
(Mar.-Apr. 1942), 192-94.

> Music by Antheil, Copland, and Gail Kubik.

1370. Kopp, Rudolph. "The Mood Comes First." In _Music and Dance in California
and the West_. Ed. Richard Drake Saunders. Hollywood: Bureau of Musical
Research, 1948, p. 82.

> See Saunders (#1496).

1371. Kortwich, Werner. _Filmbrevier_. Textzeichnungen von Kurt Wolfes. Berlin:
F. A. Herbig, 1940.

> Concerning the "practical" problems of film production,
> with a few references to music.

1372. Krjukov, N. "Muzyka i obras (w kino)." _Iskusstvo kino_ (Moscow), Nos. 1-2
(Jan.-Feb. 1940), 68-69.

1373. Kubik, Gail, Gene Forrell, and William Hamilton. "Current Films." _Film
Music Notes_, 8, No. 3 (Jan.-Feb. 1949), 19-21.

> Music by Friedhofer, Newman, and Steiner.

1374. Lacombe, Alain. "Concertos en 6,35: la musique dans le film noir."
Ecran 75, No. 32 (Jan. 1975), 42-45.

1375. Larsen (Lehrburger), Egon. _Spotlight on Films: A Primer for Film-Lovers_.

With a Foreword by Michael Balcon. London: Max Parish, 1950.

Includes a section on film music.

1376. Latouche, John. "On the Film Front." Modern Music, 19, No. 1 (Nov.-Dec. 1941), 58-59.

Includes references to the music of Bernard Herrmann.

1377. Lava, William. "Music by the Yard." In Music and Dance in California and the West. Ed. Richard Drake Saunders. Hollywood: Bureau of Musical Research, 1948, pp. 76-77, 128.

See Saunders (#1496).

1378. Lawson, John Howard. Theory and Technique of Playwriting and Screenwriting. New York: G. P. Putnam's Sons, 1949.

A revision of Lawson's earlier Theory and Technique of Playwriting, with a new section on film techniques. Includes filmography, pp. 439-50.

1379. Leigh, Walter. "Music and Microphones." World Film News (Aug. 1936), 40.

1380. Leinsdorf, Erich. "Some Views on Film Music." Music Publishers Journal, 3, No. 5 (Sept.-Oct. 1945), 15, 53-54.

See reply by Bernard Herrmann in the same volume, #3391.

1381. Levy, Louis. "Music from the Movies Radio Programme." Radio Pictorial (London), (Jan. 21, 1938).

1382. Lewicki, B. "Muzyka w filmie." Film, Nos. 9-10 (1939).

1383. ----------. "O budowie dziela filmowego." Zycie Sztuki (Warsaw), 1 (1936).

1384. Lissa, Zofia. "Muzyka i film." Sygnaly, No. 37 (1938).

1385. ----------. "O komizmie muzycznym." Kwartalnik Filozoficzny (Krakow), No. 1 (1938), 23-73; and No. 2 (1938), 95-107.

Includes references to music in film.

1386. ----------. "Z zagadnień muzyki w filmach dziesięciolecia." Kwartalnik Filmowy, 6, Nos. 2-3 (1956), 26-44.

Concerning the problem of music in Polish films following the war.

1387. Lo Duca, Giuseppe. Le Dessin animé: histoire, esthétique, technique. Paris: Prisma, 1948.

Includes bibliography, pp. 170-72.

Concerns the work of Walt Disney.

1388. London, Kurt. "Film Music of the Quarter." Films: A Quarterly of Discussion and Analysis, 1, No. 1 (Nov. 1939), 76-80.

References to music of Copland, Honegger, Korngold, and Prokofiev.

Reprinted in Kirstein (#1362).

1389. ----------. "Film Music of the Quarter." Films: A Quarterly of Discussion and Analysis, 1, No. 2 (Spring 1940), 43-48.

Concert and documentary films with music by Jaubert, Thomson, Sylvestre Revueltas, and Walter Leigh.

Reprinted in Kirstein (#1362).

1390. ----------. "Film Music of the Quarter." Films: A Quarterly of Discussion and Analysis, 1, No. 4 (Winter 1940), 25-29.

Music by Copland and Gruenberg, with references to Leopold Stokowski and Disney's "Fantasia."

1391. ----------. "Les Problèmes d'orchestration du film sonore." Musique et instruments, 28 (1937), 321-23.

1392. Lubitsch, Ernst. "Ernst Lubitsch ha fede nell'avvenire del nostro cinema." Lo Schermo (Rome), No. 10 (1936).

1393. ----------. "La pantomima moderna." Lo Schermo (Rome), No. 1 (1935).

1394. Mabee, Grace Widney. "Work and Purposes of the National Film Music Council." Music Publishers Journal, 3, No. 5 (Sept.-Oct. 1945), 31, 67.

1395. MacDougall, Ronald. "Sound -- and Fury." Screen Writer, 1 (Sept. 1945), 1-7.

1396. Maffery, George. "This Concerto Business." Keynote (1947).

1397. Malotte, Albert Hay. "Film Cartoon Music." In Music and Dance in California. Comp. William J. Perlman. Hollywood: Bureau of Musical Research, 1940, pp. 128-32.

   See Perlman (#1467).

1398. Mamorsky, Morris. "Composing for Radio." In Music in Radio Broadcasting. Ed. Gilbert Chase. New York: McGraw-Hill, 1946, pp. 47-65.

1399. Manvell, Roger. Film. Harmondsworth, Engl., and New York: Pelican Books, 1944.

   1399a. Revised and enlarged edition, 1946. (Reprint 1950.)

        Includes the chapter "Essentials of Film Art: Sound," pp. 58-76, a bibliography, pp. 174-78, and many references to film music.

   1399b. Also published in a Polish edition, Warsaw, 1960.

1400. Marshall, James. "Off the Beaten Track: 'Der Ewige Jude.'" Pro Musica Sana, 7, No. 4 (Fall 1979), 20.

        Music by composer F. R. Friedl.

1401. Mathieson, Muir. "Aspects of Film Music." Tempo (London), No. 9 (Dec. 1944), 7.

1402. ----------. "Background for British Pictures." Musical Express (London), (Jan. 3, 1947).

1403. ----------. "Developments in Film Music." Penguin Film Review, No. 4 (Oct. 1947), 41-46.

        An overview of Mathieson's career.

        Reprinted in Manvell (#1315a.)

1404. ----------. "Documentary Film Music." Film Music Notes, 7, No. 4 (Mar.-Apr. 1948), 14-15.

1405. ----------. "Dramatists in Music." Talkabout (London), (1945).

1406. ----------. "Film Music." Documentary News Letter (London), (Sept. 1940).

1407. ----------. "Film Music." Royal College of Music Magazine (London), 32, No. 3 (1936).

1408. ----------. Music for Crown. New York: British Information Services, 1948.

        A pamphlet concerning music for British documentaries produced by the Crown Film Unit. References to music by Addinsell, Britten, Leigh, Milhaud, Jaubert, Vaughan-Williams, and others.

   1408a. Also published as "Music for Crown." In Hollywood Quarterly, 3, No. 3 (Spring 1948), 323-26.

1409. Maxwell, Charles. "A Score is Born." Music Publishers Journal, 3, No. 5 (Sept.-Oct. 1945), 25, 50-53.

1410. May, Renato. "Colonne sonore." Bianco e nero, 10, No. 12 (Oct. 1949).

1411. McConnell, Stanlie. "Teaching Possibilities in Current Films." Film Music Notes, 7, No. 2 (Nov.-Dec. 1947), 17-18.

1412. ----------. "Teaching Possibilities in Current Films: 'Till the Clouds
      Roll By.'" Film Music Notes, 6, No. 4 (Feb.-Mar. 1947), 14-15.

      Musical direction by Lennie Hayton.

1413. Meakin, Jack. "Ethereal Substance." In Music and Dance in California and
      the West. Ed. Richard Drake Saunders. Hollywood: Bureau of Musical Re-
      search, 1948, p. 90.

      See Saunders (#1496).

1414. Melichar, Alois. "Musikfilm und Film-Musik." Deutsches Musikjahrbuch
      (1937), 138-49.

1415. Melson, S. "Film og musik (Part 2)." Dansk Musiktidsskrift (Copenhagen),
      24, No. 2 (1949), 32-35.

1416. Mendez, Ramon, and William Hamilton. "Current Film Reviews." Film Music
      Notes, 8, No. 2 (Nov.-Dec. 1948).

      References to scores by Brian Easdale and Alfred Newman.

1417. ----------, William Hamilton, and Harold Brown. "Current Films." Film Mu-
      sic Notes, 8, No. 1 (Sept.-Oct. 1948), 21-24.

      Music by Georges Auric, Mario Castelnuovo-Tedesco, Paul
      Schierbeck, and Roy Webb.

1418. The Men Who Write the Music Scores. (Pamphlet.) Hollywood: Motion Picture
      Producers and Distributors of America, 1943.

1419. Miller, Maud M., ed. Winchester's Screen Encyclopedia. London: Winchester
      Publications, 1948.

      Includes articles and checklists by John Huntley and Muir
      Mathieson.

1420. Minor, Monachus. "Music Library in the Film Studio." Music Publishers
      Journal, 3, No. 5 (Sept.-Oct. 1945), 35, 67-69.

1421. Möbius, M. R. "'Musik, der Liebe Nahrung ...' Bemerkungen zum gegenwärtig-
      en Filmmusik." Die Musik (Berlin), 30 (1937), 47-48.

1422. Moor, Paul. "Composers and the Music Track." Theater Arts, 33 (July 1949),
      49.

1423. Morelli, Giulio. "La musica nel cinematografo." Bianco e nero, 2, No. 7
      (July 1938).

1424. Moross, Jerome. "Hollywood Music Without Movies." Modern Music, 18, No. 4
      (May-June 1941), 261-63.

      Concerning the performance of "non-film" scores written
      by "film composers."

1425. Morrison, Margery. "Getting Acquainted with Some Film Music Scores." Mu-
      sic Publishers Journal, 3, No. 5 (Sept.-Oct. 1945), 38, 49.

      Concerning the policies and goals of the periodical Film
      Music Notes, written by one of its editors.

1426. Morros, Boris. "Motion Pictures Turn to Music." Musician, 43 (Sept. 1938),
      154.

1427. Morton, Lawrence. "Chopin's New Audience." Hollywood Quarterly, 1, No. 1
      (Oct. 1945), 31-33.

      Morton's first article in the new and important periodical,
      Hollywood Quarterly. Concerns Rozsa's score for "A Song to
      Remember."

      Morton was an orchestrator and composer, and at this time,
      was also the music editor for Script, and the L.A. corres-
      pondent for Modern Music.

1428. ----------. "Film Music of the Quarter." Hollywood Quarterly, 3, No. 1
      (Fall 1947), 79-81.

      Morton's first article in the regular film music column.

References to music by Eisler, Kaper, Stothart, and Waxman.

1429. ----------. "Jerome Moross: Young Man Goes Native." Modern Music, 22 No. 2 (Jan.-Feb. 1945), 111-14.

Deals with his First Symphony in some detail.

1430. ----------. "The Music Makers." Film Music Notes, 7, No. 1 (Sept.-Oct. 1947), 14-19.

Concerning musicians and orchestras at the major studios.

1431. ----------. "The Music Makers." Film Music Notes, 7, No. 2 (Nov.-Dec. 1947), 10-14.

1432. ----------. "The Music Makers." Film Music Notes, 7, No. 3 (Jan.-Feb. 1948), 12-16.

1433. ----------. "On the Hollywood Front." Modern Music, 21, No. 2 (Jan.-Feb. 1944), 116-18.

References to music by Deutsch, Newman, and Stothart.

1434. ----------. "On the Hollywood Front." Modern Music, 21, No. 3 (Mar.-Apr. 1944), 184-86.

Concerning Bernard Herrmann's score for "Jane Eyre."

1435. ----------. "On the Hollywood Front." Modern Music, 21, No. 4 (May-June 1944), 264-66.

References to music by Gail Kubik.

1436. ----------. "On the Hollywood Front." Modern Music, 22, No. 1 (Nov.-Dec. 1944), 63-65.

References to music by Leigh Harline and Hanns Eisler.

1437. ----------. "On the Hollywood Front." Modern Music, 22, No. 2 (Jan.-Feb. 1945), 135-37.

Concerning the current state of film music, with references to music by George Antheil.

1438. ----------. "On the Hollywood Front." Modern Music, 22, No. 3 (Mar.-Apr. 1945), 205-06.

References to music by Miklos Rozsa and Franz Waxman.

1439. ----------. "On the Hollywood Front." Modern Music, 23, No. 1 (Winter 1946), 75-76.

Music by Eisler, Friedhofer, Steiner, and Werner Janssen.

1440. ----------. "On the Hollywood Front." Modern Music, 23, No. 2 (Spring 1946), 141-43.

Concerning the use of folk music in films.

1441. ----------. "On the Hollywood Front." Modern Music, 23, No. 3 (Summer 1946), 220-22.

References to music by George Antheil and William Walton.

1442. ----------. "Rule, Britannia!" Hollywood Quarterly, 3, No. 2 (Winter 1948), 211-14.

A review of John Huntley's British Film Music (#51), and Gerald Cockshott's Incidental Music in the Sound Film (#19).

See also Cockshott's response, #1244.

1443. Moser, Hans Joachim. "Verfilmte Musikerbiographien." Das Musikleben, 3 (1950).

1444. "Movies and Music." Music News, 41 (Jan. 1949), 36.

1445. "Music and the War." In Writer's Congress: Proceedings of the Conference Held in October 1943 (by the Hollywood Writer's Mobilization Committee). Berkeley and Los Angeles: University of California Press, 1944, pp. 241-79.

A collection of articles, with contributions by A. Deutsch (#3188), H. Eisler (#3221), D. Milhaud (#3591), W. G. Still (#299), G. Kubik (#3526), and D. Raksin.

See also, sections in the same volume entitled "Song Writing and the War," pp. 280-304, and "Writers in Exile," pp. 329-58.

1446. "Music in Films: A Symposium of Composers." <u>Films: A Quarterly of Discussion and Analysis</u>, 1, No. 4 (Winter 1940), <u>5-20</u>.

Includes contributions by Blitzstein, Bowles, Britten, Copland, Cowell, Eisler, Rathaus, Schwartz, Shostakovich, Still, and Thomson.

Reprinted in Kirstein (#1362).

Accompanied by a bibliography. See #6226.

1447. "Music in the Movies Wins New Place." <u>Musician</u>, 40, No. 1 (Jan. 1935), 14.

Concerning the establishment of the Academy Award for music.

1448. "Music on the Films." <u>Etude</u> (Nov. 1935).

1449. "Music's Status on Video and Radio." <u>Musical Courier</u>, 140 (July 1949), 12-13.

1450. "La musique et le cinéma peuvent-ils s'accorder." <u>Journal musicale français</u> (Paris), (Dec. 1, 1949).

Interviews with film composers.

1451. "La musique et le cinéma peuvent-ils s'accorder." <u>Journal musicale français</u> (Paris), (Feb. 7, 1950).

Interviews with composers.

1452. Myers, Kurtz. "Audio-Visual Matters." <u>M. L. A. Notes</u>, 4, No. 2 (March 1947), 244-50.

A survey of 16-mm. sound films which deal with music, or use "classical" music as a structural feature of the film.

1453. Myers, Rollo H. <u>Music in the Modern World</u>. London: Edward Arnold, 1939. (Many reprints.)

Includes comments on film music in the chapter "The Music of the Future?," pp. 194-205.

1454. "National Film Music Council Conference." <u>Film Music Notes</u>, 8, No. 1 (Sept.-Oct. 1948), 15.

1455. Nelson, Robert U. "The Craft of the Film Score." <u>Pacific Spectator</u>, 1, No. 4 (Autumn 1947), 435-46.

References to music by Miklos Rozsa.

1456. Neuteich, M. "Muzyka w filmie dźwiekowym." <u>Film Artystyczny</u>, No. 2 (1937).

1457. Noble, Peter. <u>Transatlantic Jazz: A Short History of American Jazz and a Study of Its Leading Exponents and Personalities, Including a Guide to Classical Jazz Records and a Complete Bibliography</u>. London: The Citizen Press, 1945.

Includes references to the use of jazz in films, with a bibliography, pp. 95-96.

1457a. Reprint, London: Skelton Robinson British Yearbooks, 1946.

1458. Oboler, Arch. "Look -- Then Listen!" <u>Screen Writer</u>, 1 (Dec. 1945), 26-30.

1459. Oertel, Rudolf. <u>Filmspiegel: Ein Brevier aus der Welt des Films</u>. Vienna: W. Frick, 1942.

1460. "Opera and Concert Activities." <u>New York Times</u> (Nov. 8, 1936), Section 10, p. 7.

1461. Paeschke, Hans. "Musik und Film." <u>Deutsches Zukunft</u> (Berlin), 5, No. 13 (1937), 8.

1462. Palmer, Christopher. "Music from the Golden Age." _Crescendo International_, 12 (March 1974), 26-27.

1463. Parente, Alfredo. "Colori e suoni in 'Fantasia' di Walt Disney." _Rassegna musicale_, 17, No. 4 (Oct. 1947), 293-301.

1464. Pasinetti, Francesco. "Canzoni dall'America." _Cinema_ (Rome), No. 73 (1939).

1465. Perkoff, (Hugh) Leslie. "Music in Films." _World Film News_ (London), (Apr. 1937).

1466. ----------. "Music: Notes and Theories." _World Film News_, 2, No. 1 (Apr. 1937), 41.

1467. Perlman, William J., comp. _Music and Dance in California._ Ed. José Rodriguez. Hollywood: Bureau of Musical Research, 1940.

   A collection of articles, including contributions by G. Carbonara (#1219), N. Finston (#1273), R. Heindorf (#1301), E. W. Korngold (#3511), A. Malotte (#1397), J. Rodriguez (#1482), and Roy Webb (#1467).

   This volume was followed by another, edited by Richard Drake Saunders, in 1948. See #1496.

1468. Pestalozza, Luigi. "Folklore esotico: ricostruzioni feteli e arbitrarie." In _Musica e film_. Ed. S. G. Biamonte. Rome: Edizioni dell'Ateneo, 1959, pp. 113-38.

   See Biamonte (#1468).

1469. ----------. "Musica applicata." _Musica d'Oggi_ (Milan), 2 (Dec. 1959), pp. 465-67.

1470. Petsch, Robert. _Drama und Spielfilm_. Berlin: Olten Walter, 1942.

1471. Pizzetti, Ildebrando. "Significato della musica di 'Scipione l'Africano.'" _Bianco e nero_, 1, Nos. 7-8 (July-Aug. 1937).

1472. Poirier, Pierre. _Musique cinématographique_. Traité doctrinal et jurisprudentiel au droit d'auteurs. Brussels: F. Larcier, 1941.

   A report on the legal rights of composers, presented to the Société Nationale de Droits d'Auteur - NAVEA.

1473. Pollak, Robert. "Hollywood's Music." _Magazine of Art_, 31 (Sept. 1938), 512-13.

1474. Raiguel, Denise. _La Cinématographie et le droit d'auteur_. Montreux, Switz.: Imprimeur Corbaz, 1940.

1475. Rambaud, M. "Musique française." In _Le livre d'or du cinéma français_. Paris: Agence d'information cinématographique, 1945.

1476. Rasmussen, B. "Film og musik (Part 4)." _Dansk Musiktidsskrift_ (Copenhagen), 24, No. 4 (1949), 87-91.

1477. Rawlinson, Harold. "Music and the Film." _British Journal of Photography_ (March 16, 1945).

1478. Razzi, Giulio. "La musica lirica e sinfonica nella sua diffusione attraverso la radio." In _Atti del secondo congresso internazionale di musica, Firenze-Cremona, 11-26 maggio, 1937_. Florence: F. Le Monnier, 1940, 118-23.

   A paper presented at the 1937 Florence conference, with synopses in French and German, pp. 124-25. See #1186.

1479. Reis, Claire R. _Composers in America: Biographical Sketches of Contemporary Composers with a Record of Their Works_. New York: Macmillan, 1930.

   Revised and enlarged edition, 1947.

   Includes a listing of concert works and film scores for many film composers.

   See comments by Lawrence Morton: "Film Music in the Mainstream" (#4790).

1480. Rideout, Eric Hardwicke. _The American Film_. London: The Mitre Press, 1937.

Chapter: "Sound," pp. 90-98. Concerns the characteristic uses of sound and music in the works of various directors.

1481. Ripley, John. "Song-Slides." _Films in Review_, 22, No. 3 (Mar. 1971), 147-52.

1482. Rodriguez, José. "Ears, Antennas and Sales." In _Music and Dance in California_. Comp. William J. Perlman. Hollywood: Bureau of Musical Research, 1940, pp. 165-69.

See Perlman (#1467).

1483. ----------. "Music of the Animated Pictures." _Music Educators Journal_, 32, No. 5 (Apr. 1946), 18-19.

1484. Rosar, William H. "Music for the Monsters: Universal Pictures' Horror Film Scores of the Thirties." _Quarterly Journal of the Library of Congress_, 40, No. 4 (Fall 1983).

1485. Rosenheimer, Arthur, Jr. "Fanfare for 'Fantasia.'" _Films: A Quarterly of Discussion and Analysis_, 1, No. 4 (Winter 1940), 34-39.

A discussion of the film, with music supervision by Leopold Stokowski.

1486. Rotha, Paul, and Richard Griffith. _The Film Till Now: A Survey of the Cinema_. London: J. Cape, 1930.

Includes bibliography, pp. 344-45.

1486a. Revised and enlarged edition, London: Vision Press; New York: Funk and Wagnalls, 1949. (Second edition, 1951.)

Includes the section "The Visual and the Audible Cinema," pp. 403-14, and many references to film music and filmed musicals. Includes bibliography, pp. 706-08.

1487. ----------, and Roger Manvell. _Movie Parade_. London and New York: The Studio Publications, 1936.

A pictorial history, includes a chapter "Musicals," pp. 60-62.

1487a. Revised edition, published with the title _Movie Parade, 1888-1949: A Pictorial Survey of World Cinema_. Prepared in collaboration with the British Film Academy. London and New York: Studio Publications, 1950.

1488. Rubsamen, Walter H. "Fortunes in Movie Music." _Etude_, 65 (July 1947), 420.

1489. ----------. "La musica moderna nel film." _Rassegna Musicale_ (Rome), 18, No. 1 (Jan. 1948), 38-46.

1490. ----------. "Music in the Cinema." _Arts and Architecture_, 61, No. 8 (Aug. 1944), 14, 38.

Concerning current scores, with references to music by Miklos Rozsa.

1491. ----------. "Music in the Cinema." _Arts and Architecture_, 62, No. 2 (Feb. 1945), 20, 24-25.

Concerning Disney's "Fantasia."

1492. ----------. "Music in the Cinema." _Arts and Architecture_, 62, No. 9 (Sept. 1945), 20-21, 45.

Concerning a biographical film: George Gershwin.

1493. ----------. "Music in the Cinema." _Arts and Architecture_, 62, No. 12 (Dec. 1945), 26, 60.

Concerning current scores, with references to music by Kaper and Newman.

1494. ----------. "Music in the Cinema: Disney and Prokofiev." _Arts and Architecture_, 63, No. 7 (July 1946), 18, 32, 34, 38.

Concerning the "Peter and the Wolf" episode in Disney's "Make Mine Music."

1495. Sadoul, Georges. British Creators of Film Technique: British Scenario Writers, the Creators of the Language of D. W. Griffith, G. A. Smith, Alfred Collins, and Some Others. London: British Film Institute, 1948.

1496. Saunders, Richard Drake, ed. Music and Dance in California and the West. Hollywood: Bureau of Musical Research, 1948.

An anthology of essays. Includes chapters: "Films," pp. 76-85, and "Radio," pp. 86-93, along with a geographical survey of current musical activities, and a directory of musical personalities.

Includes articles by C. Bakaleinkoff (#1189), N. Finston (#1274), B. Katz (#1352), R. Kopp (#1370), W. Lava (#1377), J. Meakin (#1413), A. Sendrey (#1502), I. Talbot (#1520), E. Truman (#1527), R. Van Eps (#1532), M. Warnow (#1541), J. Weber (#1542), and M. Willson (#1543), and M. Rozsa (#3878).

1497. Scherchen, Herman. "La musique dans les programmes radiophoniques." In Bulletin de Documentation et d'Information (Organisation Internationale de Radiodiffusion et Télévision). Brussels and Prague, n.d.

1498. Schoenberg, Arnold. "Driven into Paradise." Stenographic record of an address delivered Oct. 9, 1935.

1499. Schürmann, Gerbrand. "The Composer." In Working for the Film. Ed. Oswell Blakeston. London: Focal Press, 1947, pp. 169-77.

1500. Schwartz, Lev. "(On the Scoring of 'New Gulliver.')" Sovietskoye kino (March 1935), 59.

In Russian.

1501. ----------. "O sovietskoi kinomuzyke." Iskusstvo kino (Moscow), No. 3 (March 1949), 4-6.

1502. Sendrey, Albert. "Where Seldom is Heard an Encouraging Word." In Music and Dance in California and the West. Ed. Richard Drake Saunders. Hollywood: Bureau of Musical Research, 1948, pp. 83, 143.

See Saunders (#1496).

1503. Shaindlin, Jack. "Stay East, Young Man! Stay East!" Film Music Notes, 8, No. 5 (May-June 1949), 14-15.

1504. Shcherbachev, Vladimir. "Muzyka v kino." Iskusstvo kino (Moscow), No. 3 (March 1936), 22-23.

1505. Smith, Alexander Brent. "Music and the Cinema." Piping Times, 4, No. 3 (1944).

1506. Sobel, Bernard. "Seeing Things: Let the Audience Think." Saturday Review of Literature, 28, No. 45 (Nov. 10, 1945), pp. 30, 32.

Includes a brief history of music for the stage and screen.

1507. Sokolov, I. "O dramaturgii muzyki 'Velikogo valca.'" Iskusstvo kino (Moscow), No. 10 (Oct. 1940).

1508. Spaeth, Sigmund. "Afterthoughts." Film Music Notes, 1946-1955.

A column of information and current events notes appended to many volumes of Film Music Notes. Often includes useful information of interest to scholars, educators and fans.

1509. ----------. "Spaeth on Popular Music." Film Music Notes, 8, No. 2 (Nov.-Dec. 1948).

1510. Stanley, Fred. "Film Tune Sleuths." Film Music Notes, 8, No. 3 (Jan.-Feb. 1949), 17-18.

Originally appeared in The New York Times.

1511. Sternfeld, Frederick W. "Film Music Session at M.T.N.A. in Boston." Film

<u>Music Notes</u>, 7, No. 4 (Mar.-Apr. 1948), 5-6.

1512. ----------. "Preliminary Report on Film Music." <u>Hollywood Quarterly</u>, 2, No. 3 (April 1947), 299-303.

> A report by Sternfeld, Assistant Professor at Dartmouth College, on the desirability of maintaining university collections of film music materials for scholarly study.

1513. Stevens, Bernard. "Film Music." <u>Music Survey</u>, 2, No. 3 (Winter 1950).

1514. Stokowski, Leopold. <u>Music for All of Us</u>. New York: Simon and Schuster, 1943.

> Chapters: "Recorded Music," pp. 221-29, "Broadcast Music," pp. 230-35, "Music and Motion Pictures," pp. 241-47, "Music and Television," pp. 248-51, and "Reproduction of Recorded and Broadcast Music, pp. 252-61.

1514a. Also published as <u>Músico para todos nosotros</u>. Trans. Francisco Serrano Méndez and Cynthia Boissevain. Buenos Aires: Espasa-Calpe Argentina, 1945.

1514b. Also published as <u>Musik för oss alla</u>. Trans. Folke H. Törnblom. Stockholm: Bonnier, 1947.

1514c. Also published as <u>Música para todos nosotros</u>. Trans. Antonio Iglesias. Madrid: Espasa-Calpe España, 1954.

1515. ----------. "My Symphonic Debut in the Films." <u>Etude</u> (Nov. 1936), 685-86.

1516. Stravinsky, Igor. "La musique de film? -- du papier peint!" <u>L'Écran français</u>, 4, No. 18 (Nov. 1947).

1516a. Reprinted in <u>Musik und Film</u> (Berlin), (1973), 1.

1517. ----------, and Ingolf Dahl. "Igor Stravinsky on Film Music." <u>Cinema</u>, 1, No. 1 (June 1947), 18ff.

> An interview.

1518. Stuckenschmidt, Hans Heinz. <u>Neue Musik: Zwischen den beiden Kriegen</u>. Berlin: Suhrkamp Verlag, 1951.

> Includes many references to film music and film composers.

1518a. Also published as <u>La musica moderna</u>. Trans. Mariangela Donà. Torino: Edizioni G. Einaudi, 1960.

> Includes bibliography, pp. 435-37.

1519. Taddei, Nazareno. "Musica in fotogrammi." <u>Civiltà cattolica</u> (Rome), No. 2349 (May 1948).

1520. Talbot, Irvin. "Conducting on Cue." In <u>Music and Dance in California and the West</u>. Ed. Richard Drake Saunders. Hollywood: Bureau of Musical Research, 1948, pp. 84, 142.

> See Saunders (#1496).

1521. Taylor, Davidson. "To Order, for Radio." <u>Modern Music</u>, 14, No. 1 (Nov.-Dec. 1936), 12-17.

1522. Thomas, Anthony. "Hollywood Music." <u>Sight and Sound</u>, 16, No. 63 (Autumn 1947), 97-98.

> References to music by Rozsa, Steiner, and others.

> See response to this article by Hans Keller, #1359.

1523. Thun, Rudolph. <u>Entwicklung der Kinotechnik</u>. Berlin: VDI-Verlag, 1936.

1524. Toch, Ernst. "The Cinema Wields the Baton." <u>New York Times</u> (Apr. 11, 1937), Section 11, p. 3.

1525. ----------. "Sound-Film and Music Theatre." <u>Modern Music</u>, 13, No. 2 (Jan.-Feb. 1936), 15-18.

1526. Towers, Harry, and Leslie Mitchell. <u>The March of the Movies</u>. London: Sampson Low, Marston, 1947.

Chapter: "Music: Introducing Muir Mathieson," pp. 54-62.

1527. Truman, Edward. "Heard But Not Seen." In Music and Dance in California and the West. Ed. Richard Drake Saunders. Hollywood: Bureau of Musical Research, 1948, pp. 92, 144.

See Saunders (#1496).

1528. Turner, W. J. "Music for the Films." New Statesman and Nation (London), 19, No. 477 (April 13, 1940), 490.

Concerning film scores by "serious" composers.

1529. Tyler, Parker. The Hollywood Hallucination. New York: Creative Age Press, 1944.

Chapter: "Orpheus à la Hollywood," pp. 155-67.

Reprint, New York: Simon and Schuster, 1970.

1530. Unwin, Arthur. "Music of the Cinema." Music Parade (London), (1945).

1531. Ussher, Bruno David. "Composing for the Films." New York Times (Jan. 28, 1940), Section 9, p. 6.

1532. Van Eps, Robert. "The Commercial Scarecrow." In Music and Dance in California and the West. Ed. Richard Drake Saunders. Hollywood: Bureau of Musical Research, 1948, pp. 91, 147.

See Saunders (#1496).

1533. Vellard, R. Le Cinéma sonore: théorie et pratique. Paris: Dunod, 1936.

1534. Verdone, Mario. "Un breve scenario cinematografico di Alban Berg." In La musica nel film. Ed. Luigi Chiarini. Rome: Bianco e nero editore, 1950, pp. 135-38.

See Chiarini (#1627).

1535. Voigt, Hans Otto. "Musik im Film." Der Österreichischer Musiker (1937), 14-15.

1536. Volk, I. "Svuk v kino." Iskusstvo kino (Moscow), No. 4 (April 1948).

1537. Volkov, V. "Svukovyie protivoretschiia v 'Peterburgskich notschach.'" Iskusstvo kino (Moscow), No. 3 (Mar. 1934), 36-40.

1538. Wanderscheck, Hermann. "Musik" and "Filmmusik." Articles in Der Filmkurier (1938-1942).

1539. ----------. "Musik im Film und ihre Schöpfer." Deutsches Filmschaffen (1943).

1540. "Warner Brothers Rode to Success on Wave of Sound." Newsweek (Dec. 26, 1936), 23-26.

1541. Warnow, Mark. "New Sounds on the Air." In Music and Dance in California and the West. Ed. Richard Drake Saunders. Hollywood: Bureau of Musical Research, 1948, pp. 88, 129.

See Saunders (#1496).

1542. Weber, John Roy. "Every Trick Is Needed." In Music and Dance in California and the West. Ed. Richard Drake Saunders. Hollywood: Bureau of Musical Research, 1948, pp. 93, 147.

See Saunders (#1496).

1543. Willson, Meredith. "Mozart vs. Mayhem." In Music and Dance in California and the West. Ed. Richard Drake Saunders. Hollywood: Bureau of Musical Research, 1948, pp. 89, 145.

See Saunders (#1496).

1544. Wilson, Sandy. "From Broadway to Hollywood: A Revaluation of the Light Composers of the 1930's." Twentieth Century (London), 177, No. 1042 (1969), 35-38.

1545. Winkler, Max. <u>A Penny from Heaven</u>. New York: Appleton-Century-Crofts, 1951.

>Winkler's autobiography. Excerpts also appeared in <u>Films in Review</u>. See #1068.

1546. Winter, Marian Hannah. "The Function of Music in Sound Film." <u>Musical Quarterly</u>, 27, No. 2 (April 1941), 146-64.

1547. Woll, Allen L. "From 'Blues in the Night' to 'Ac-cent-tchu-ate the Positive': Film Music Goes to War, 1939-1945." <u>Popular Music and Society</u>, 4, No. 2 (1975), 66-76.

1548. Yamada, Koscak. "Music and the Motion Picture." <u>Cinema Year Book of Japan, 1936-1937</u>. Tokyo: Sanseido Co., 1937, pp. 36-39.

>A brief statement by the composer.

1549. "Young Veteran of Film Music: Muir Mathieson." <u>Music Parade</u>, 2, No. 1 (1949), 1.

1550. Yunkers, Adja M. <u>Film och jazz</u>. Stockholm: Universal Press, 1936.

1551. Yutkevich, S. "Vysokoye iskusstvo smeschnogo." <u>Iskusstvo kino</u> (Moscow), No. 3 (March 1940).

1552. Zissu, Leonard. "The Copyright Dilemma of the Screen Composer." <u>Hollywood Quarterly</u>, 1, No. 3 (April 1946), 317-20.

>SEE ALSO:

>#17(Cheremukhin), #110(Sabaneev), #141(Anderson/Richie), #272(Nagy), #299 (Still), #778(Ottenheym), #1802(Lissa), #2975, 2978(Antheil), #2986(Applebaum), #3000(Auric), #3027(Baudrier), #3151(Copland), #3217, 3221, 3223 (Eisler), #3592(Milhaud), #3886, 3888(Rozsa), #4009(Stevens), #4015(Harmetz), #4039(Thomson), #4099(Vlad), #4139(Morton), #4159(Whitney/Whitney), #4265(Prox), #4279(Arnheim), #4431(Bächlin), #4436, 4437(Balázs), #4583 (Fey), #4635(Hazumi), #4644(Huntley), #4648(Imamura), #4682, 4683(Kishi), #4695(Kracauer), #4787(Moholy-Nagy), #4959(Wiese), #4982(Arnheim), #5021 (Meyerhoff), #5042(Williams), #5110(Reich), #5127(Spaeth), #5236(Franks), #5930(Comuzio), #6006(Hodgkinson), #6032(Kothes), #6036(Kreuger), #6042 (Leonard/Parish), #6076, 6078, #6083(Ortman), #6087(Perez), #6096(Roth), #6137, 6138(Traubner), #6162, #6172(Leyda), #6175(Potter), #6180, 6181 (Whitney/Whitney), #6194(Huntley), #6226, #6248, 6249(Rubsamen/Nelson), #6290(Raymond), #6295(Smolian), #6291(Ried), #6302(ASCAP), #6315, and #6333(Noble).

Sound Techniques and Technology

1553. Batsel, M. C. "Recording Music for Motion Pictures." <u>Journal of the Society of Motion Picture Engineers</u>, 25, No. 8 (Aug. 1935), 103-08.

1554. Beatty, Jerome. "Norma Shearer's Noisy Brother." <u>American Magazine</u>, 123 (May 1937), 26-27ff.

>Concerning the work of sound engineer Douglas Shearer.

1555. Bernhart, José. <u>Traité de prise de son</u>. Paris: Édition Eyrolles, 1949.

>Concerning techniques of sound recording, with implications for music in films.

1556. "Bringing the Symphony Orchestra to Movie Patrons: Multiple Channel Recordings." <u>Etude</u>, 55 (Nov. 1937), 710.

1557. Brown, Bernard. "Pre-Scoring and Scoring." In <u>The Technique of Motion Picture Production: Papers Presented at a Symposium at the 51st Semi-Annual Convention of the Society of Motion Picture Engineers, Hollywood,</u>

California. New York: Interscience Publishers, 1944, p. 65ff.

1558. Cameron, James Ross. Cameron's Sound Motion Pictures, Recording and Repro-
ducing. Woodmont, Conn.: Cameron Publ. Co., 1935. (Many reprints: 1937,
1939, 1941.)

> The first of several editions (mimeographed) by the author
> of many manuals and textbooks which deal with sound prob-
> lems in film, radio, and television. Includes a section on
> music recording and reproduction.

1559. Cameron, Ken. Sound and the Documentary Film. London: Isaac Pitman and
Sons, 1947.

> Includes a chapter "Music," pp. 46-73, by sound technician
> Ken Cameron, and a foreword by Alberto Cavalcanti.

1560. ----------. Sound in Films: A Speech Delivered at the British Film Institute's Summer School at Bangor, August 1944. London: Coombelands, 1944.

1561. ----------. "Sound Recordist Ken Cameron Protests." Sight and Sound, 10,
No. 40 (Spring 1942), 75-76.

> Cameron's reaction to an article by Elizabeth Cross. See
> #1562.

1562. Cross, Elizabeth. "Plain Words to the Exhibitor." Sight and Sound, 10,
No. 39 (Autumn 1941), 44-45.

> See response to this article by Ken Cameron of the Crown
> Film Unit (#1561).

1563. Crowhurst, Cyril. "How a Music Recording Theatre Was Made from a Sound
Stage." Kinematograph Weekly (London), (Sept. 26, 1946).

1564. Elliott, William Francis. Sound Recording for Films: A Review of Modern
Methods. London: Sir Isaac Pitman, 1937.

1565. Forrest, David. "From Score to Screen." Hollywood Quarterly, 1, No. 2
(Jan. 1946), 224-29.

> Comments on sound technique by a sound mixer at Warner
> Bros. Studios in the late 1920's and 1930's.

1566. Goehr, Walter. "Fitting the Music to the Picture." Sound Illustrated (London), (Oct. 1946).

1567. Hill, A. P., Fred Albin, L. E. Clark, John Hilliard, and Harry Kimball.
Motion Picture Sound Engineering: A Series of Lectures. New York: D.
van Nostrand, 1938.

> A collection of lectures prepared for the Research Council
> of the Academy of Motion Picture Arts and Sciences.
>
> Updates the 1931 anthology edited by Cowan. See #1144.

1568. Huntley, John. "The Music Mixer." Film Music Notes, 9, No. 3 (Jan.-Feb.
1950), 12-13.

> Reprinted in Limbacher, pp. 72-75. See #75.

1569. Innamorati, Libero. "I problemi della registrazione musicale." In Atti
del secondo congresso internazionale di musica, Firenze-Cremona, 11-26
maggio, 1937. Florence: Le Monnier, 1940, pp. 261-64.

> A paper presented at the 1937 Florence conference, with
> synopses in French and German, pp. 264-65. See #1186.

1570. Kellog, Edward W. "The ABC of Photographic Sound Recording." Journal of
the Society of Motion Picture and Television Engineers, 44, No. 3 (Mar.
1945).

1571. "Latest in Music Add Thrills to Movies." Popular Mechanics, 68 (Dec.
1937), 830-31ff.

> A discussion of sound mixing techniques, with references
> to performances by Leopold Stokowski.

1572. Levinson, Nathan. "What Sound Hath Wrought." Scientific American (Aug.

1946), 101-09; and (Sept. 1946), 176-90.

1573. Lichte, Hugo, and Albert Narath. Physik und Technik des Tonfilms. Leipzig: S. Hirzel Verlag, 1943.

Includes bibliography, pp. 372-401.

Reprint, Ann Arbor, Mich.: Edwards Bros., 1945.

1574. Mertz, Paul. "Recording a Musical Performance: The 'How' and 'Why' of
Different Methods of Recording Music for Motion Pictures." Tempo (London), (Aug.-Nov. 1938).

1575. Moser, Hans Joachim. "Die Erfahrungswelt der Tonmeister." Die Musikwoche,
5, No. 32 (1937), 1-3.

1576. Peck, A. P. "What Makes 'Fantasia' Click: Multiple Sound Tracks and Loud-
Speakers Give Auditory Perspective to Sound Movie Screen." Scientific
American, 164, No. 1 (Jan. 1941), 28-30.

1577. Rettinger, M. "Scoring-Stage Design." Journal of the Society of Motion
Picture Engineers, 30, No. 5 (May 1938), 519-34.

Concerning technical problems of film music recording.

1578. Shearer, Douglas. "Hollywood's Tin Ear: An ABC of Sound." Cinema Arts, 1,
No. 3 (Sept. 1937), 32-35.

Comments by a sound recordist at M.G.M. Studios.

1578a. Reprinted in Behind the Screen: How Films Are Made. Ed.
Stephen Watts. London: Barker, 1938.

1579. Silverman, Edward. "Putting in the Sound Track." Our Time (London), (Oct.
1946).

1580. Townsend, R. H. "Some Technical Aspects of Recording Music." Journal of
the Society of Motion Picture Engineers, 25, No. 9 (Sept. 1935), 259-68.

SEE ALSO:

#59(Irving/Keller/Mellers), #155(Fielding), #199(Atkins), #223, 226(Cook),
#231(Daugherty), #238(Ford), #241(Frayne et al.), #254(Kellogg), #295
(Sponable), #307(Trommer), #312(Weiland), #1139(E.W. Cameron), #1159(Laf-
ferty), #1167(Salt), #1300(Haver), #1523(Thun), #4503(Chiarini), #4650
(Irving), and #6178(Solev).

Music for T.V.

1581. Bowman, Roger. "Music for Films in Television." Film Music Notes, 8,
No. 5 (May-June 1949), 20.

1582. ----------. "Music in Television and Its Problems." Film Music Notes, 8,
No. 4 (Mar.-Apr. 1949), 10-11.

1583. ----------. "New Regulations Proposed for Music in T.V. Films." Film Music Notes, 9, No. 2 (Nov.-Dec. 1949), 6.

1584. Chotzinoff, Samuel. "Music in Television." Variety, 173 (Jan. 5, 1949),
170.

1585. Cooke, James Francis. "The New World of Television: A Conference with
Paul Whiteman." Etude, 67 (June 1949), 341-42.

1586. Heylbut, Rose. "Background of Background Music: How NBC's Experts Fit Music to Dramatic Shows." Etude, 63 (Sept. 1945), 493-94.

1587. "Menotti Tells About His Video Opera Commissioned by NBC-TV." Musical
Courier (New York), 139 (May 1, 1949), 8.

1588. Sosnik, Harry. "Scoring for Television." Variety, 173 (Jan. 5, 1949), 95.

1950's

History

1589. "African Music for a Film." African Music, 1, No. 1 (1954), 86.

1590. Algar, James. "Film Music and Its Use in 'Beaver Valley.'" Film Music Notes, 10, No. 2 (Nov.-Dec. 1950), 17-19.

> Concerning the score by Paul Smith.

1591. "Allgemeine Bedingungen zum Filmmusikvertrag (Fassung 1958)." Archiv für Urheber-, Film-, Funk- und Theaterrecht (Baden-Baden), 28 (1959), 92-96.

1592. Anderson, Lindsay. Making a Film: "The Secret People." Together with the Shooting Script of the Film by Thorold Dickinson and Wolfgang Wilhelm. London: George Allen and Unwin, 1952.

> Includes references to music for the film.

1593. Asklund, Gunnar, and Kathryn Grayson. "Singing in the Movies." Etude, 70, (Nov. 1952), 16, 59.

1594. Bachmann, Gideon. "8x8: An Interview with Hans Richter." Film and TV Music, 16, No. 2 (Winter 1956), 19-20.

1595. Barrett, John Townsend. "A Descriptive Study of Selected Uses of Dance on Television: 1948-1958." Ph.D. Diss. University of Michigan 1968.

> Abstract: DAI 29:2732A (order #DA 69-2281).

1596. Barron, Lewis, and Bebe Barron. "Forbidden Planet." Film Music, 15, No. 5 (Summer 1956), 18.

> Concerning the electronic music score for the film, by Lewis and Bebe Barron.

1597. Bauer, Rudolf. "Der Ton zum Bild." Melos, 18 (April 1951), 102-05.

1598. ----------. "Der Ton zum Bild." Melos, 18 (May 1951), 136-38.

1599. Beams, David. "Soviet Filmusic." Films in Review, 10, No. 5 (May 1959), 306-08.

1600. Becker, Paul, Hans Rutz, and Jack Bornoff. Cahiers d'Études de Radio-Télévision, No. 12: International Conference on Opera in Radio, TV and Film. Paris: Centre d'Études de la RTF, 1956.

1601. Beer, Otto F. "Neue Tendenzen des italienischen Films." Universitas (Stuttgart), 6 (1951), 649-54.

1602. Beguiristain, Mario Eugenio. "Theatrical Realism: An American Film Style of the Fifties." Ph.D. Diss. University of Southern California 1978.

> Abstract: DAI 1978: 6991A.

> References to music by Bernstein, North, Rosenman, and Kenyon Hopkins.

1603. Belinsky, Dmitri. "The Sound Track." Films in Review, 8, No. 8 (Oct. 1957), 418-19.

> References to the music of Boris Morros.

1604. Beyle, Claude. "Musique et cinéma." Radio-Cinéma-Télévision, 11, No. 462 (Nov. 23, 1958), 23.

1605. Biamonte, S. G. "Il jazz nel cinema." In Musica e film. Ed. S. G. Biamonte. Rome: Edizioni dell'Ateneo, 1959, pp. 139-54.

     See #1606.

1606. ----------, ed. Musica e film. Volume publicato a cura della Mostra d'
Arte Cinematografica di Venezia. Rome: Edizioni dell'Ateneo, 1959.

     An important collection of articles selected from papers
presented at the 1959 Congress of Music in Florence, and
the 1950 Florence conference. See the annotation which accompanies Chiarini (#1627).

     Includes a filmography, and contributions by S.G. Biamonte
(#1605), S. Bradley (#208), C. Casini (#4489), G. Castello
(#5922), A. Cicognini (#4506), G. Confalonieri (#4523), L.
Emmer (#1666), F. Ferrara (#1667), C. Gallone (#1678), A.
Hopkins (#4642), H. Keller (#1748), M. Labroca (#4706), F.
Lunghi (#5271), G. Nataletti (#1837), L. Pestalozza (#1468),
I. Pizzetti (#1848), B. Rondi (#5292), and Vlad (#4098).

     -- Rev. in Musica Jazz (Milan), 16 (Aug.-Sept 1960), 18.

     -- Rev. in La Rassegna Musicale (Rome), 29, No. 4 (1959),
366-67.

1607. Blasco, Ricardo. "Quando Vienna rideva, I: Operette senza musica." Cinema (Rome), New series, No. 104 (Feb. 28, 1953).

1608. ----------. "Quando Vienna rideva, II: L'euforia musicale." Cinema (Rome),
New series, No. 105 (Mar. 15, 1953).

1609. ----------. "Quando Vienna rideva, III: La musica alleata e non serva dell'
espressionismo." Cinema (Rome), New series, No. 106 (Apr. 15, 1953).

1610. ----------. "Quando Vienna rideva, IV: Ultima evoluzione." Cinema (Rome),
New series, No. 107 (Apr. 30, 1953).

1611. Blasetti, Alessandro, Mario Serandrei, and Sebastiano A. Luciani. "Il par-
ere del registra, del montatore e della critica." In La musica nel film.
Ed. Luigi Chiarini. Rome: Bianco e nero editore, 1950, pp. 91-96.

     Contributions to the 1950 Venice conference. See #1627.

1612. Blum, Karl. "Musik zu neuen Kulturfilmen." Melos, 23 (Apr. 1956), 116.

1613. Borneman, Ernest J. "Hollywood and Songs." Melody Maker, 29 (June 20,
1953), 4.

1614. Bowers, Faubion. Dance in India. New York: Columbia University Press,
1953.

     References to music and dance in Indian films.

     Reprint, New York: AMS Press, 1967.

1615. Broder, Nathan. "How American Composers Pay Their Rent." High Fidelity,
9, No. 7 (July 1959), 39ff.

1616. Brodianskaya, N., and G. Shiv. "Debiut S. Zinzadse v kino." Sovetskaya
muzyka, 19, No. 4 (Apr. 1955).

1617. Bute, Mary Ellen. "New Film Music for New Films." Film Music, 12, No. 4
(Mar.-Apr. 1953), 15-18.

     Reprinted in Limbacher, pp. 173-75. See #75.

1618. Cacia, Nino. "Il film, il compositore, il critico." Cinema (Rome), New
series, No. 153 (Oct. 1955).

1619. Candini, Pino. "Con la faccia pulita il jazz hollywoodiano." Schermi (Milan), 1, No. 1 (Apr. 1958).

1620. Celletti, V. "Il jazz nel cinema." Biblio-Cinema (Rome), Nos. 13-16
(1957).

1621. Cerulli, Dom. "Charivari." Down Beat, 26 (Feb. 19, 1959), 40-41.

     Views on the use of jazz in films by D. Tiomkin and J. Mandel.

1622. Chagrin, Francis, and Matyas Seiber. "The Composition and Recording of Music for Animated Films." In The Technique of Film Animation. Ed. John Halas and Roger Manvell. London and New York: Focal Press, 1959, pp. 237-53.

>   See #176.

1623. Chamberlain, Gladys E. "Film Music and the Library." Film Music, 13, No. 2 (Nov.-Dec. 1953), 23.

1624. Chamfray, Claude. "Musique de films." La Vie musicale, 2 (May 1952), 13.

1625. ----------. "Musique de films." La Vie musicale, 2 (Oct. 1952), 10.

1626. Chevassu, François. "La musique concrète." Image et son, No. 102 (1957).

1627. Chiarini, Luigi, ed., and Enzo Masetti, comp. La musica nel film: Quaderni della Mostra internazionale d'arte cinematografica di Venezia. Rome: Bianco e nero editore, 1950.

>   An important collection of 27 articles and papers delivered at the Venice conference in conjunction with the International Music Conference in Florence in the same year.
>
>   Includes the article "Nota dell'Editore," pp. 5-6, by Chiarini, and contributions by D. Amfitheatrof (#3), A. Blasetti, M. Serandrei, and S.A. Luciani (#1611), E. Cavazzuti (#4491), T. Chrennikov (#18), N. Costarelli (#4532), A. Cicognini (#5928), F. Ferrara (#1668), R. Gervasio (#1681), F. Lavagnino (#1785), F. Lunghi (#1805), M.F. Gaillard (#36), E. Irving (#58), A. Longo (#4752), G.-F. Malipiero, G. Petrassi, and I. Pizzetti (#1806), G. Marinuzzi (#4768), E. Masetti (#3565), G. Rosati (#4844), V. Tommasini (#4923), M. Verdone (#1534 and #6255), A. Veretti (#4945), R. Vlad (#1915), and A. Zecchi (#4978).
>
>   NOTE: Several sources cite this volume as a collection of papers presented at the 1950 Congress in Florence, yet the articles noted here in no way coincide with the reports by Hopkins and Keller of papers read at the Florence Congress (see # 1723 and #1774).
>   The same sources also suggest that this volume is a reprinting, in book form, of a special issue of the periodical Bianco e nero (Vol. 11, Nos. 5-6 (May-June 1950), see #1832). While the exact contents of the special issue are not known to this compiler, there is evidence to suggest that this may not be the case.
>   For further confusion on this issue, see the Proceedings of Congresso (#1864), and the collection of papers edited by S. G. Biamonte (#1606).

1628. Chumakova, I. "'Otchiy dom' i 'Mayskie zvezdy.'" Sovetskaya muzyka, 23, No. 7 (July 1959), 123-24.

1629. Comuzio, Ermanno. "Pentagramma." Rassegna del film (Turin), (Jan. 1954).

>   The first article in a regular film music column.

1630. ----------. "Strawinski e il cinema." Cineforum (Bergamo), (Apr. 1971).

1631. Connor, Edward. "The Composer on the Screen." Films in Review, 7, No. 4 (Apr. 1956), 164-70.

>   Concerning filmed biographies of composers.

1632. ----------. "The Sound Track." Films in Review, 7, No. 9 (Nov. 1956), 473-74.

>   Concerning Disney's "Fantasia."

1633. ----------. "The Sound Track." Films in Review, 9, No. 6 (June-July 1958), 339-40.

>   A survey of current scores.

1634. ----------. "The Sound Track." Films in Review, 9, No. 10 (Dec. 1958), 580.

Concerning current soundtrack recordings.

1635. ----------. "The Sound Track." Films in Review, 11, No. 6 (June-July 1960), 371-73.

1636. ----------, and Don Miller. "The Sound Track." Films in Review, 10, No. 7 (Aug.-Sept. 1959), 431-34.

Concerning the use of historical quotations.

1637. ----------, and Edward Jablonski. "The Sound Track." Films in Review, 8, No. 7 (Aug.-Sept. 1957), 340-41.

Film scores by Mischa Spoliansky and others.

1638. ----------, ----------. "The Sound Track." Films in Review, 9, No. 1 (Jan. 1958), 36-38.

A "ranking" of contemporary film composers.

1639. ----------, ----------. "The Sound Track." Films in Review, 9, No. 4 (April 1958), 211-13.

A survey of current film scores.

1640. ----------, ----------. "The Sound Track." Films in Review, 9, No. 5 (May 1958), 273-75.

A survey of current film scores.

1641. ----------, ----------. "The Sound Track." Films in Review, 9, No. 7 (Aug.-Sept. 1958), 392-93.

References to music by E. Bernstein and Mario Nascimbene.

1642. ----------, ----------. "The Sound Track." Films in Review, 9, No. 8 (Oct. 1958), 468-70.

Film scores by Jerome Moross and Mario Nascimbene.

1643. ----------, and Gerald Pratley. "The Sound Track." Films in Review, 5, No. 10 (Dec. 1954), 545-47.

1644. ----------, ----------. "The Sound Track." Films in Review, 6, No. 2 (Feb. 1955), 88-90.

Concerning the quotation of classical music in films.

1645. ----------, ----------. "The Sound Track." Films in Review, 6, No. 3 (Mar. 1955), 135-37.

Filmscores of 1954, with references to the work of Max Steiner.

1646. ----------, ----------. "The Sound Track." Films in Review, 6, No. 6 (June-July 1955), 292-94.

Concerning the use of jazz as film background music.

1647. ----------, ----------. "The Sound Track." Films in Review, 6, No. 7 (Aug.-Sept. 1955), 350-53.

Concerning the availability of film music scores and manuscripts.

1648. ----------, ----------. "The Sound Track." Films in Review, 6, No. 8 (Oct. 1955), 416-19.

Music for historical films, with references to the music department at Warner Bros., and the work of Ray Heindorf.

1649. ----------, ----------. "The Sound Track." Films in Review, 6, No. 9 (Nov. 1955), 469-71.

1650. ----------, ----------. "The Sound Track." Films in Review, 7, No. 3 (Mar. 1956), 134-36.

References to music by William Walton, the Indian composer Naushad, and others.

1651. ----------, ----------. "The Sound Track." Films in Review, 8, No. 1

(Jan. 1957), 38-40.

    Comments on a film score by Philip Sainton.

1652. ----------, Robert B. Kreis, and David Beams. "The Sound Track." <u>Films in Review</u>, 10, No. 6 (June-July 1959), 365.

    A survey of contemporary scores and new soundtrack albums.

1653. ----------, and T. M. F. Steen. "The Sound Track." <u>Films in Review</u>, 10, No. 10 (Dec. 1959), 626-27.

    References to music by Edwin Astley.

1654. Czapski, Georg. "Die Rechtsstellung des Komponisten eines Tonfilms nach der niederländischen Rechtsprechung." <u>Gewerblicher Rechtsschutz und Urheberrecht</u>, 53 (1951), 149-51.

1655. D., A. "Filmmusik gewinnt an Wert." <u>Vier Viertel</u>, 8, No. 11 (1954), 8-9.

1656. Daragan, D. "Sud'va cheloveka." <u>Sovetskaya muzyka</u>, 23, No. 7 (July 1959), 122-23.

1657. De Blasio, A. "Effetti musicali, musica concreta, musica elettronica." <u>Biblio-cinema</u> (Rome), Nos. 10-12 (1957).

1658. Debnam, Richard. "Celluloid to Vinylite: The Hollywood LP's." <u>Saturday Review</u>, 39, No. 24 (June 16, 1956), 43-44.

    Includes a discography.

1659. Dickson, James P. "Film Music in a Public Library." <u>Film Music</u>, 13, No. 5 (May-June 1954), 19.

1660. Dill, Helen C. "Film Music on the Western Campus (U.C.L.A.)." <u>Film Music Notes</u>, 10, No. 5 (May-June 1951), 15-16.

1661. "Disney's 'Lady, Tramp' Uses Music Adroitly -- and Uses Good Music." <u>Down Beat</u>, 22 (June 1, 1955), 31.

1662. Doflein, Erich. "Das Filmkonzert." <u>Das Musikleben</u>, 3 (1950), 173-74.

1663. Dubin, Joseph S. "20,000 Leagues Under the Sea." <u>Film Music</u>, 14, No. 3 (Jan.-Feb. 1955), 6-15.

    Musical score by Paul Smith, with orchestration by Dubin.

1664. Elian, Edgar. "Muzica filmelor documentare românesti." <u>Muzica</u>, 2 (1951), 25-28.

1665. Emge, C. "Some Real Progress in Film Music During 1953." <u>Down Beat</u>, 21 (Feb. 10, 1954), 5.

1666. Emmer, Luciano. "La musica nel cortometraggio cinematografico." In <u>Musica e film</u>. Ed. S. G. Biamonte. Rome: Edizioni dell'Ateneo, 1959, pp. 213-15.

    A paper presented at the 1950 Florence Congress. See #1606 and #1864.

1667. Ferrara, Franco. "La direzione dell'orchestra e la colonna sonora." In <u>Musica e film</u>. Ed. S. G. Biamonte. Rome: Edizioni dell'Ateneo, 1959, pp. 171-78.

    See #1606.

1668. ----------. "La direzione dell'orchestra e la musica cinematografica." In <u>La musica nel film</u>. Ed. Luigi Chiarini. Rome: Bianco e nero editore, 1950, pp. 78-79.

    A paper presented at the 1950 Venice conference. See #1627.

1669. "Film Music." <u>Musical Denmark</u> (Copenhagen), No. 7 (May 1955), 7.

1670. "Film Music's Coming of Age." <u>Variety</u>, 209 (Feb. 12, 1958), 56.

1671. <u>Filmmusik</u>. A special issue of <u>Das Musikleben</u>, 3 (1950).

Includes an article by E. Doflein (#1662), and contributions by A. Copland, Werner Egk, Wolfgang Fortner, Theo
Mackeben, D. Milhaud, I Stravinsky, and K. Weill.

1672. Fischer, Hans. "Musik im Film." Die Musik-Woche, 14 (1954), 356-59.

1673. Fremer, Björn. "Stark film med jazzbakgrund." Orkester Journalen (Stockholm), 27 (Mar. 1959), 18.

1674. Frielinghaus, Karl-Otto. "Wie entsteht ein Tonfilm?" Bild und Ton, No. 4
(1955), 108.

1675. Fulchignoni, Enrico. "Musica e film." La rivista del cinema italiano (Milan and Rome), No. 2 (Feb. 1954).

1676. ----------. "Son et image." La Revue musicale, Numero special, No. 236
(1957), 77-93.

Includes bibliography, pp. 89-93, which, though here attributed to Fulchignoni, was actually compiled by Mario
Verdone, and first published in Chiarini (see #6255). This
reprint introduces no new bibliographic information, but
unfortunately introduces many errors and a few omissions
are noted from Verdone's original listing.

1677. Gallez, Douglas W. "The Music for 'The Black Cat.'" Film and TV Music,
17, No. 1 (Fall 1957-Winter 1958), 16-18.

Concerning Gallez's original score for a production at
U.S.C. See also the article by Wagner, #1921.

1678. Gallone, Carmine. "Il valore della musica nel film e l'evoluzione dello
spettacolo lirico sullo schermo." In Musica e film. Ed. S. G. Biamonte.
Rome: Edizioni dell'Ateneo, 1959, pp. 203-06.

A paper presented at the 1950 Florence Congress. See #1606
and #1864.

1679. Garcia, P. "Music and the Cinema." Image et son, Nos. 88-90 (1956), 5.

1680. Genina, L. "O muzyke k kartine 'Idiot.'" Sovetskaya muzyka, 22, No. 9
(Sept. 1958).

1681. Gervasio, Raffaele. "La musica nel documentario." In La musica nel film.
Ed. Luigi Chiarini. Rome: Bianco e nero editore, 1950, pp. 69-71.

A paper presented at the 1950 Venice conference. See #1627.

1682. Geviksman, V. "Muzyka v dokumentarnom kino." Iskusstvo kino (Moscow),
No. 11 (Nov. 1958), 100-02.

1683. Gieure, R. "Song in the Cinema." Image et son, Nos. 117-121, 125-127
(1958-1960).

1684. Gilbert, Herschel Burke. "The Thief." Film Music, 12, No. 2 (Nov.-Dec.
1952), 4-12.

Including extensive excerpts from Gilbert's score.

Text of the article reprinted in Limbacher, pp. 106-08.
See #75.

1685. Gilson, R. "Jazz on the Soundtrack." Cinema, 58 (Nov. 1958), 25.

1686. Glazer, Tom. "Notes on the Score of 'A Face in the Crowd.'" Film and TV
Music, 16, No. 4 (Summer 1957), 13-19.

Includes musical excerpts from Glazer's score.

1687. Golovinskii, G., and V. Zato. "O muzyke v kino." Sovetskaya muzyka, 22,
No. 7 (July 1958), 49-58.

1688. Gray, Allan. "The Music of 'The African Queen.'" Film Music, 11, No. 4
(Mar.-Apr. 1952), 19-21.

Description of the score, by the composer.

1689. Gray, Hugh. "Neue Dimensionen in Bild und Ton." Melos, 24 (July-Aug.

1957), 217-21.

      Translated by G. Voellmer.

1690. Green, Philip. "The Music Director." <u>Films and Filming</u>, 3, No. 9 (June 1957), 12-13.

1691. Griffith, Richard. <u>Anatomy of a Motion Picture</u>. New York: St. Martin's Press, 1959.

      An analysis of the film "Anatomy of a Murder," includes a section on the musical score by Duke Ellington, pp. 105-08.

1692. Grimm, Friedrich Karl. "Vom Stande der europäischen Filmmusik." <u>Die Bühnengenossenschaft</u>, 8 (1956), 141-42.

1693. Guernsey, Otis L., Jr. "The Movie Cartoon is Coming of Age." <u>Film Music</u>, 13, No. 2 (Nov.-Dec. 1953), 21-22.

      Originally appeared in the <u>New York Herald Tribune</u>.

      Reprinted in Limbacher, p. 182. See #75.

1694. Haentjes, W. "Musik und Film." <u>Musica</u>, 4 (Sept. 1950), 359.

1695. Hall, Barrie. "Musical Roundabout." <u>Music Teacher</u> (London), 38 (Feb. 1959), 75.

      Concerning the difficulties posed by inadequate time and planning in the preparation of film scores.

1696. Hamraaz, Har Mandir Singh. <u>Hindi philma gita kosa 1951 se 1960, Vol. III</u>, 1980.

      An encyclopedia of Hindi film songs, includes a listing of films, with information about the film and composer. Also includes a discography.

1697. Hendricks, Gordon. "Hollywood Film Music." <u>Music Journal</u>, 8 (May-June 1950), 11-12.

1698. ----------. "The Sound Track." <u>Film Culture</u>, 1, No. 2 (Mar.-Apr. 1955), 45-47.

      Concerning Roman Vlad's music for "Romeo and Juliet," with references to "Gate of Hell," and other Japanese films.

1699. ----------. "The Sound Track." <u>Films in Review</u>, 4, No. 1 (Jan. 1953).

1700. ----------. "The Sound Track." <u>Films in Review</u>, 5, No. 2 (Feb. 1954), 99-100.

1701. Hentoff, Nat. "Movie Music Comes into Its Own." <u>Reporter</u>, 18 (June 12, 1958), 28-30.

      Concerning the "rise" of the soundtrack album.

1702. Heylbut, Rose. "Disney Fun with Music." <u>Etude</u>, 74 (Oct. 1956), 23ff.

1703. Hickman, C. Sharpless. "Heard While Seeing." <u>Music Journal</u>, 9, No. 8 (Dec. 1951), 32-33.

      Concerning recent "experiments" in film music.

1704. ----------. "Heard While Seeing." <u>Music Journal</u>, 10, No. 2 (Feb. 1952), 38-39.

      Filmscores of 1951.

1705. ----------. "Heard While Seeing." <u>Music Journal</u>, 10, No. 4 (Apr. 1952), 46-47.

      Concerning the music department and music library at M.G.M.

1706. ----------. "Heard While Seeing." <u>Music Journal</u>, 10, No. 5 (May 1952), 30-32.

      More on the music department at M.G.M.

1707. ----------. "Movies and Music." Film Music, 13, No. 1 (Sept.-Oct. 1953), 21-22.

       Originally appeared in an issue of Music Journal.
       Concerning the music department at Paramount Pictures.

1708. ----------. "Movies and Music." Music Journal, 10, No. 6 (Sept. 1952), 38.

       A survey of current scoring activities.

1709. ----------. "Movies and Music." Music Journal, 10, No. 7 (Oct. 1952), 36-37.

       A discussion of "dubbing" practices.

1710. ----------. "Movies and Music." Music Journal, 11, No. 3 (Mar. 1953), 34.
       A survey of current scores.

1711. ----------. "Movies and Music." Music Journal, 11, No. 4 (Apr. 1953), 38.
       A survey of current scores.

1712. ----------. "Movies and Music." Music Journal, 11, No. 11 (Nov. 1953), 26-27.
       Concerning animated films by United Productions of America.

1713. ----------. "Movies and Music." Music Journal, 11, No. 12 (Dec. 1953), 26-27.

       Music for Disney films, with references to the work of
       Paul Smith.

1714. ----------. "Movies and Music." Music Journal, 12, No. 3 (Mar. 1954), 60.
       Filmscores of 1953.

1715. ----------. "Movies and Music." Music Journal, 12, No. 4 (Apr. 1954), 21.
       Concerning film music courses at U.C.L.A. and U.S.C., with
       references to the work of Boris Kremenliev.

1716. ----------. "Movies and Music." Music Journal, 12, No. 9 (Sept. 1954), 46-47.

       Concerning the film recording activities of the Roger Wag-
       ner Chorale.

1717. ----------. "Movies and Music." Music Journal, 12, No. 11 (Nov. 1954), 45-46.

       Concerning film music composed for concert band, with refer-
       ences to the work of Leon Arnaud.

1718. ----------. "Musicians in Films." Musical Courier, 146 (Nov. 15, 1952), 17.

1719. ----------. "Musicians in Films." Musical Courier, 147 (Jan. 1, 1953), 15.

1720. ----------. "Music School for Movies." Music Journal, 12, No. 7 (July 1954), 18-19.

       Concerning film music opportunities at U.S.C., with refer-
       ences to the work of Miklos Rozsa.

1721. Hopkins, Antony. "Music." Sight and Sound, 19, No. 1 (Mar. 1950), 32-33.

1722. ----------. "Music." Sight and Sound, 19, No. 3 (May 1950), 127.

1723. ----------. "Music: Congress at Florence." Sight and Sound, 19, No. 6 (Aug. 1950), 243-44.

       A report on the International Congress of Music at Florence,
       which was devoted to the topic of film music. Includes a
       listing of papers presented at the Congress, and some ob-
       jections to Hollywood's film music.

NOTE: Hopkins' comments initiated a small debate. See a response to this article, by Lawrence Morton, in Hollywood Quarterly (#1821). Morton's comments were also partially reprinted in Sight and Sound (#1826).

1724. "How Songs Are Written to Fit Action in Movies." Down Beat, 21 (Jan. 13, 1954), 32.

1725. Huesmann, L. "Musik im Film." In Filmstudien: Beiträge des Filmseminars im Institut für Publizistik an der Universität Münster. Emsdetten: Lechte, 1952.

1726. Huntley, John. "'The African Queen': The Composer and the Film." Film Music Notes, 11, No. 4 (Mar.-Apr. 1952), 22.

Music for the film composed by Allan Gray.

Reprinted in Limbacher, p. 76. See #75.

1727. ----------. "The British Film Institute." Film Music, 13, No. 5 (May-June 1954), 11-12.

1728. ----------. "The Sound Track." Sight and Sound, 19, No. 9 (Jan. 1951), 381.

Concerning music in the films of Michael Powell.

1729. ----------. "The Sound Track." Sight and Sound, 19, No. 10 (Feb. 1951), 417, 422.

Concerning music and sound effects in film.

1730. ----------. "The Sound Track." Sight and Sound, 20, No. 1 (May 1951), 31.

Concerning current sound track albums.

1731. ----------. "The Sound Track." Sight and Sound, 21, No. 2 (Oct.-Dec. 1951), 95.

Concerning movie theme songs.

1732. ----------. "The Sound Track." Sight and Sound, 21, No. 3 (Jan.-Mar. 1952), 140.

Concerning the studio orchestra at M.G.M.

1733. ----------. "The Sound Track." Sight and Sound, 22, No. 2 (Oct.-Dec. 1952), 94.

Concerning music in John Ford films.

1734. ----------. "The Sound Track." Sight and Sound, 22, No. 4 (Apr.-June 1953), 202-03.

Concerning music for Ealing Studios' comedies.

1735. ----------. "The Sound Track." Sight and Sound, 24, No. 2 (Oct.-Dec. 1954), 107.

Concerning a proposed film: "London Symphony: Portrait of an Orchestra."

1736. ----------. "Syllabus of a Course of Nine Lectures on Music and the Cinema." Film Music Notes, 10, No. 4 (Mar.-Apr. 1951), 18-20.

Outline for a series of lectures delivered at the University of London, University Extension Courses.

1737. ----------. "The Telekinema in London." Film Music Notes, 10, No. 5 (May-June 1951), 13-14.

Concerning music for the Telekinema by William Alwyn and Louis Applebaum.

1738. Îârustovskiĭ, Boris M. "Muzykalny obras v filme." Iskusstvo kino (Moscow), No. 11 (Nov. 1952), 21-29.

1739. ----------. "O muzykalnom obrase." Sovetskaya muzyka (Moscow), 17, Nos. 7-9 (July-Sept. 1953).

1740. Inglese, Alberto M. "Cinema e musica." _Primi piani_, Nos. 3-4 (Mar.-Apr. 1957).

1741. Jablonski, Edward. "The Sound Track." _Films in Review_, 8, No. 10 (Dec. 1957), 534-35.

Concerning new soundtrack recordings.

1742. Jacobs, Lewis. "La musique de film en France." _Raccords_ (Paris), No. 5 (Oct. 1950).

1743. "Jazz is Heard at the Movies." _Music U.S.A._ (July 1959), 38ff.

1744. Jennings, Humphrey. _London Symphony_. London: Naldrett Press, 1954.

Concerning a proposed film about the orchestra and its role in recording music for films.

1745. Joachim, Robin Jon. "Music at the Cannes International Film Festival." _Film Music_, 14, No. 5 (May-June 1955), 20, 24.

1746. Jungk, Klaus. _Wie ein Tonfilm entsteht_. Filmbücher für alle, I. Dusseldorf: Verlag W. Knapp, 1952.

1747. Jurenev, Rostislav. "Volschebnik Glinka." _Iskusstvo kino_ (Moscow), No. 10 (Oct. 1952).

1748. Keller, Hans. "Citazioni di musica classica nel film." In _Musica e film_. Ed. S. G. Biamonte. Rome: Edizioni dell'Ateneo, 1959, pp. 223-26.

A paper presented at the 1950 Florence Congress. See #1606 and #1864.

1749. ----------. "Film Music." _Musical Times_, 96, No. 1350 (Aug. 1955), 435.

References to music by Arnold, Blomdahl, and Frankel.

1750. ----------. "Film Music." _Music Survey_, 3 (March 1951), 181-82.

1751. ----------. "Film Music and Beyond." _Music Review_, 11 (1950), 324.

Concerning the current state of film music.

1752. ----------. "Film Music and Beyond." _Music Review_, 12, No. 2 (1951), 147-49.

References to music by Roman Vlad.

1753. ----------. "Film Music and Beyond." _Music Review_, 14, No. 1 (1953), 59.

References to the work of Walter Scharf.

1754. ----------. "Film Music and Beyond." _Music Review_, 14, No. 4 (1953), 311-12.

1755. ----------. "Film Music and Beyond." _Music Review_, 17, No. 2 (1956), 154-56.

Music by Auric, Benjamin, Rawsthorne, and Walton.

1756. ----------. "Film Music and Beyond." _Music Review_, 17, No. 3 (1956), 254-55.

Music by William Alwyn and Arthur Benjamin.

1757. ----------. "Film Music and Beyond." _Music Review_, 17, No. 4 (1956), 337-40.

Music by Malcolm Arnold and Benjamin Frankel.

1758. ----------. "Film Music and Beyond." _Music Review_, 20, No. 4 (Nov. 1959), 301.

Concerning the work of Joseph Kosma.

1759. ----------. "Film Music and Beyond: From Auden to Hollywood." _Music Review_, 12, No. 4 (1951), 315-17.

Includes bibliographic references.

1760. ----------. "Film Music and Beyond: The Dragon Shows His Teeth." Music Review, 12, No. 3 (Aug. 1951), 221-25.

> Keller's contribution to the ongoing debate between Lawrence Morton and Antony Hopkins which began in Sight and Sound (#1723).
>
> See also a response to this article by L. Morton, #1817.
>
> Includes a brief bibliography.

1761. ----------. "Film Music and Beyond: Noisy Music and Musical Noise." Music Review, 13, No. 2 (1952), 138-40.

1762. ----------. "Film Music and Beyond: World Review." Music Review, 13, No. 4 (1952), 310-12.

1763. ----------. "Film Music and Not Beyond: LCMC-ICA Failure." Music Review, 13, No. 3 (1952), 209-11.

1764. ----------. "Film Music: Continental, British and American." Music Review, 13, No. 1 (1952), 54-56.

1765. ----------. "Film Music: Reply to Pizzetti." Music Survey, 3 (Summer 1951), 42-43.

1766. ----------. "Film Music: Some Objections." Sight and Sound, 15, No. 60 (Winter 1946-1947), 136.

> A call for "better" music in films.

1767. ----------. "The Half-Year's Film Music." Music Review, 14, No. 3 (1953), 222-23.

1768. ----------. "The Half-Year's Film Music." Music Review, 15, No. 1 (1954), 64-66.

1769. ----------. "The Half-Year's Film Music." Music Review, 15, No. 3 (1954), 220.

1770. ----------. "The Half-Year's Film Music." Music Review, 16, No. 1 (1955), 65-66.

1771. ----------. "The Half-Year's Film Music." Music Review, 16, No. 3 (1955), 234.

1772. ----------. "Music on Everest." Musical Opinion, 77 (Jan. 1954), 213ff.

> Concerning the film "Conquest of Everest."

1773. ----------. "Recent Film Music." Musical Times, 96, No. 1347 (May 1955), 265-66.

1774. ----------. "XIII (Tredicésimo) Maggio Musicale Fiorentino: VII Congresso Internazionale di musica." Music Review, 11 (Aug. 1950), 210-12.

> A report on the 1950 Florence Congress, including commentary on the papers presented there.
>
> See also the response to this article by Lawrence Morton in Hollywood Quarterly, #1821.

1775. ----------. "'West of Zanzibar': Some Problems of Film Music." Musical Opinion (London), 77 (July 1954), 585ff.

1776. Knight, Arthur. "Movie Music Goes On Record." Film Music, 11, No. 3 (Jan.-Feb. 1952), 21-23.

1777. Kögler, Horst. "Filmmusik und Musikfilm 1951." Das Musikleben, 5 (Feb. 1952), 41-44.

1778. Kont, Paul. "Filmmusik: Eine aggressive Plauderei." Österreichisches Musikzeitschrift, 7 (1952), 3-6.

1779. Kramskoj, A. "O boleznjach našej kinomuzyki." Sovetskaya muzyka, 22, No. 10 (Oct. 1958), 30-34.

1780. Kreis, Robert B. "The Sound Track." _Films in Review_, 10, No. 4 (Apr. 1959), 243-44.

    Concerning George Brun's "adaptation" of Tchaikovsky.

1781. Kremenliev, Boris A. "Can Film Composing Be Taught?" _Film Music_, 11, No. 5 (May-June 1952), 12-15.

1782. ----------. "The Tell-Tale Heart." _Film Music_, 13, No. 4 (Mar.-Apr. 1954), 11-15.

    Notes on the score, by the composer.

1783. Krjukov, N. "Film a hudba." _Hudební Rozhledy_ (Prague), 4, No. 1 (Jan. 1951), 28-29.

1784. Kuna, Milan. _Hudba v krátkém filmu: příručka pro filmové amatéry_. Prague: Orbis, 1961.

1785. Lavagnino, Angelo Francesco. "La musica nel disegno animato." In _La musica nel film_. Ed. Luigi Chiarini. Rome: Bianco e nero editore, 1950, pp. 63-68.

    A paper presented at the 1950 Venice conference. See #1627.

1786. Lavastida, Bert, Pete Stallings, Norman Phelps, and Glen Gould. "Music for Motion Pictures." _Journal of the University Film Producers Association_, 7, No. 2 (Winter 1954), 12-16.

    Transcript of a presentation to the conference of University Film Producers.

1787. Lawrence, Harold. "Baton and Stop Watch." _Audio_ (Boulder, Colo.), 42 (Feb. 1958), 56-57.

1788. Lebedev, Nikolaĭ A. "Roshdeniye svukovogo kino." _Voprosy kinoiskusstva_ (1955).

1789. Leibell, Vincent L. _Civil Action No. 13-95_. Entered on March 14, 1950.

    Judge Leibell's decision against ASCAP, prohibiting royalty income from individual theaters.

1790. Leirens, Jean. _Le Cinéma et le temps_. 7ème art. Paris: Éditions du Cerf, 1954.

1791. Lemaître, Henri. _Beaux-arts et cinéma_. 7ème art. Paris: Éditions du Cerf, 1956.

1792. Lewin, Frank. "'Fantasia' Revisited." _Film Music_, 15, No. 3 (Jan.-Feb. 1956), 20.

1793. ----------. "Martin Luther." _Film Music_, 13, No. 1 (Sept.-Oct. 1953), 5-6.

    Film score by Mark Lotar.

1794. ----------. "Pictura." _Film Music_, 11, No. 5 (May-June 1952), 4-6.

    A film score with contributions by Isaac Albeniz, Guy Bernard, Darius Milhaud, Lan Adomian, and Roman Vlad.

  1794a. Reprinted (complete) in _Film Music_, 12, No. 1 (Sept.-Oct. 1952), 23-24.

1795. ----------, and Willis Schaefer. "Current Scores." _Film and TV Music_, 16, No. 4 (Summer 1957), 12.

    References to the music of Hugo Friedhofer and Victor Young.

1796. Liaud-Sabiel, J. "Unfaithfully Yours ..." _Contrepoints_, No. 7 (1951), 87-93.

1797. Libik, A. "Die Musik im ungarischen Filmschaffen." _Studio_, No. 9 (1956).

1798. Limbacher, James L. "Film Music at the Stratford Film Festival." _Film and TV Music_, 17, No. 1 (Fall-Winter 1957-1958), 15.

1799. ----------. "Film Music in the Air." _Film Music_, 12, No. 3 (Jan.-Feb.

1953), 21-22.

1800. ----------. "What Film Music Means to Me." Film Music, 13, No. 5 (May-June 1954), 20.

1801. Linn, Robert. "The Story Tellers of the Canterbury Tales." Film Music, 14, No. 4 (Mar.-Apr. 1955), 12-15.

    Includes excerpts from the score by Robert Linn.

1802. Lissa, Zofia. "Muzyka filmowa." In Kultura muzyczna Polski Ludowej, 1944-1955. Krakow, 1957, pp. 245-62.

1803. Livingston, D. D. "Notes on a Dance Film Festival." Film Music, 12, No. 2 (Nov.-Dec. 1952), 20-21.

1804. Luft, Friedrich. "Vom grossen schönen Schweigen." Der Monat, No. 44 (1952), 184-92.

1805. Lunghi, Fernando Ludovico. "La musica e il neo-realismo." In La musica nel film. Ed. Luigi Chiarini. Rome: Bianco e nero editore, 1950, pp. 56-60.

    A paper presented at the 1950 Venice conference. See #1627.

1806. Malipiero, Gian-Francesco, Ildebrando Pizzetti, and Goffredo Petrassi. "Tre opinioni." In La musica nel film. Ed. Luigi Chiarini. Rome: Bianco e nero editore, 1950, pp. 80-85.

    Contributions to the 1950 Venice conference. See #1627.

1807. Manson, Eddy. "'Lovers and Lollipops': Operation New York." Film Music, 15, No. 4 (Spring 1956), 14-20.

    Notes on the score by Manson.

1808. ----------. "The Music for 'Little Fugitive.'" Film Music, 13, No. 3 (Jan.-Feb. 1954), 8-14.

    Notes on the score by Manson.

1809. Manvell, Roger, ed. Experiment in the Film. London: Grey Walls Press, 1949.

    A geographical survey, with references to music in film. Also includes a section on the work of John Whitney, and experiments in animated sound.

1810. Marcorelles, Louis. "Prélude à la danse." Cahiers du cinéma, 12, No. 70 (Apr. 1957), 32-33.

1811. Martin, Jan. "O hudbě ve filmu." Film a doba, 4 (1958), 713-15.

1812. Mathieson, Muir. "Documentary Film Music." Film Music, 11, No. 2 (Nov.-Dec. 1951), 22.

1813. McCarty, Clifford. "Filmusic Librarian." Films in Review, 8 (June-July 1957), 292-93.

    Concerning the duties and responsibilities of the film music librarian, with specific references to George G. Schneider, librarian at M.G.M.

1814. Miller, Don. "The Sound Track." Films in Review, 10, No. 9 (Nov. 1959), 549-50.

    References to the music of Gerald Fried.

1815. Mitchell, Donald. "Film Music." Music Survey, 3, No. 3 (1951).

1816. Morrison, Alen. "The Summoning of Everyman." Film and TV Music, 16, No. 5 (Late Summer 1957), 19-20.

    Music by David M. Epstein.

1817. Morton, Lawrence. "Composing, Orchestrating and Criticizing." Quarterly of Film, Radio, and Television, 6, No. 2 (Winter 1951), 191-206.

    References to the music of Duning, Friedhofer, and Raksin.

This is Morton's final word in the ongoing debate between
Antony Hopkins, Hans Keller, and himself, which began in
Sight and Sound. See #1723.

1818. ----------. "Control Room Maestros." Score, 4 (March 1950), 3-4.

1819. ----------. "Film Music Art or Industry." Film Music, 11, No. 1 (Sept.-
Oct. 1951), 4-6.

1820. ----------. "Film Music of the Quarter." Hollywood Quarterly, 5, No. 2
(Winter 1950), 178-81.

    References to music by Antheil, Friedhofer, and Waxman.

1821. ----------. "Film Music of the Quarter." Hollywood Quarterly, 5, No. 3
(Spring 1951), 282-88.

    Concerning the practice of orchestration and the use of
    orchestrators in Hollywood.

    A response to comments by Antony Hopkins in Sight and
    Sound. See #1723. Also, indirectly, a response to articles
    by Hans Keller (#1774) and Daniele Amfitheatrof (#2957).

    This article is also partially reprinted, along with a
    further rebuttal by Hopkins, in Sight and Sound. See #1826.

1822. ----------. "Film Music of the Quarter." Hollywood Quarterly, 5, No. 4
(Summer 1951), 412-16.

    References to music by Daniele Amfitheatrof, David Buttolph,
    Ernest Irving, Renzo Rossellini, and Victor Young.

1823. ----------. "Film Music of the Quarter." Quarterly of Film, Radio and
Television, 6, No. 1 (Fall 1951), 69-72.

    Concerning a film score by Werner Eisbrenner.

1824. ----------. "For God and Culture." Score, 4 (Jan. 1950), 4-5.

1825. ----------. "Los Angeles Letter." Counterpoint, 17 (Feb. 1952), 32-34.

1826. ----------, and Antony Hopkins. "Film Music: Orchestration Run Riot?"
Sight and Sound, 20, No. 1 (May 1951), 21-23, 30.

    Partial reprint of an article by Morton in Hollywood Quar-
    terly (#1821), with a rebuttal by Hopkins.

    And, the debate continues with a response by Hans Keller.
    See #1760.

1827. "Movie Background Music Available for All Moods." Popular Photography, 37,
No. 3 (Sept. 1955), 111.

    Notification of "pre-packaged" music for amateur films.

1828. Mullendore, J. "Problems of the Present-Day Arranger and Composer." Score,
4 (May 1950), 6-7.

1829. Müller, Fritz. "Schlager in Kinovorstellungen." Musik in der Schule (Berlin), 14, No. 5 (1963), 228.

1830. "La musica." Cinema nuovo, No. 1 (Dec. 1952).

1831. "La musica en la semana de cine italiano." Musica (Madrid), 2 (Jan.-June
1953), 273-75.

1832. La musica nel film. A special double issue of Bianco e nero, 11, Nos. 5-6
(May-June 1950).

    NOTE: The exact contents of this special issue is not known
    to this compiler. Several sources report that it is a collec-
    tion of papers presented at the 1950 Florence Congress, and
    was published again in that year in book form, edited by Luigi
    Chiarini. See #1627.
        The special issue apparently does contain articles by
    Enzo Masetti (#3565), Enrico Cavazzuti (#4491), and Roman Vlad
    (#1915), which also appear in Chiarini. None of these, however,
    were presented at the Florence Congress (as reported by Hans

Keller (see #1774) and Antony Hopkins (see #1723)).
The rest of the special issue may, therefore, contain additional articles from the Chiarini volume, or perhaps, may contain papers noted under the listing for the Proceedings of Congresso (#1864).

1833. "Musica y cine: a proposito de un documental del Greco." Musica (Madrid), 2 (Jan.-June 1953), 275-77.

1834. "Music and the Film." Music Teacher (Gt. Brit.), 30 (June 1951), 268.

1835. "Musique de films." La Vie Musicale, 1 (Dec. 1950), 9.

1836. "Musique de films." La Vie Musicale, 2 (Mar. 1952), 16.

1837. Nataletti, Giorgio. "La musica folklorica italiana nel cinema." In Musica e film. Ed. S. G. Biamonte. Rome: Edizioni dell'Ateneo, 1959, pp. 105-12.

See Biamonte (#1606).

1838. Neale, Denis Manktelow. How to Add Sound to Amateur Films. Focal Cinebooks. London and New York: Focal Press, 1954. (Reprints, 1958, 1969.)

1839. Neumann, Ede. "Muszorgszkij -- Eizenstein." Fejér Megyei Szemle (1967).

A comparison of Mussorgsky's "Boris Godunov" and Eisenstein's "Potemkin," with a score by Edmund Meisel.

1840. "New Employment Field Opens Up in Hollywood." Down Beat, 18 (June 1, 1951), 9.

1841. "NYU Offers Music Course for Radio and TV." Musical Courier, 150 (Sept. 1954), 38.

1842. Orling, Hans G. "Thema: Filmkomponisten." Vier Viertel, 7, No. 8 (1953), 4-5.

1843. Ottavi, A. "Musique Italienne." Positif (Paris), No. 28 (1958).

1844. Péché, Jean-Jacques. "La tentation de la musique." Script, 3, Nos. 10, 11, and 12 (1964).

1845. Pilka, Jiří. "Český hudební film." Film a doba (Prague), No. 10 (1957).

1846. ----------. "Elektronická i konkretní hudba a film." Film a doba (Prague), (1959), 427-28.

1847. ----------. "Hudba k filmům Jan Hus a Jan Žižka." Hudební Rozhledy, 9 (1956), 223-25, 269-70.

Concerning music by Jiří Srnka.

1848. Pizzetti, Ildebrando. "Discorso di chiusura del VII congresso internazionale di musica, Firenze, 19 maggio 1950." In Musica e film. Ed. S. G. Biamonte. Rome: Edizioni dell'Ateneo, 1959, 227-34.

An address, and comments on the closure of the Congress, by Pizzetti, who was the chairman of the conference. See #1606 and #1864.

1849. ----------. "La musica e il film." Rassegna Musicale, 20 (Oct. 1950), 291-97.

A paper presented at the 1950 Venice conference.

1850. Płażewski, Jerzy. "Dramaturgia muzyki w 'La Strada.'" Teatr i Film (Warsaw), No. 8 (1958).

1851. ----------. "Zwycięstwo muzyki narodowej: Analiza krytyczna filmu 'Warszawska premiera.'" Kwartalnik Filmowy, 1, No. 1 (1951).

1852. "Pop Records." Time, 71 (Feb. 24, 1958), 46ff.

Concerning the "rise" of soundtrack record albums.

1853. Potts, J. E. "European Radio Orchestras." Musical Times (London), 96

(1955).

1854. Poulenc, Francis. "Musique de film." Cahiers du cinéma, 9, No. 49 (July 1955), 27-28.

>References to the film "Carmen Jones" (Georges Bizet/Herschel Burke Gilbert), and to music by Auric, Prokofiev, Maurice Blackburn, and others.

1855. Pratley, Gerald. "Canadian Film News." Film Music, 13, No. 1 (Sept.-Oct. 1953), 19-20.

1856. ----------. "Composers At Work." Film Music, 15, No. 4 (Spring 1956), 23.

1857. ----------. "Corral." Film Music, 15, No. 2 (Winter 1955), 20-23.

>Film score by Eldon Rathburn.

1858. ----------. "Film Scores Considered Independent Art Form Aside from Plug Value." Variety, 208 (Sept. 4, 1957), 55.

1859. ----------. "Furthering Motion Picture Appreciation by Radio." Hollywood Quarterly, 5, No. 2 (Winter 1950), 127.

>Concerning radio broadcasting of film soundtracks.

1860. ----------. "High Tide in Newfoundland." Film Music, 14, No. 4 (Mar.-Apr. 1955), 16-18.

>Film score by Eldon Rathburn.

1861. ----------. "Music in the Films: Canada." Film Music, 11, No. 5 (May-June 1952), 16-17.

1862. ----------. "News from Canada." Film Music, 13, No. 4 (Mar.-Apr. 1954), 20-21.

1863. ----------. "The Romance of Transportation in Canada." Film and TV Music, 16, No. 1 (Fall 1956), 16-19.

>Film score by Eldon Rathburn.

1864. Proceedings of Congresso Internazionale di Musica. Florence, 1950.

>NOTE: This volume is cited by only one source (Grove's 5th ed.). Its exact contents are not known to this compiler.
>
>Reports of the proceedings of the 1950 Florence Congress, by Keller (see #1774) and Hopkins (see #1723), suggest that it may contain articles by Daniele Amfiteatrof, Yves Baudrier, Valentino Bucchi, Nicolas Castarelli, Alessandro Cicognini, Fred Goldbeck, Roland-Manuel, Enzo Masetti, Wilfred Mellers, Guido Pannain, -. Previtali, Andre Schaeffner, Hermann Scherchen, Boris de Schloezer, Hans Strobel, Maurice Thiriet, and Max Vredenburg.
>
>Additional papers from the Florence Congress which may appear in this volume are also published in a collection edited by S. G. Biamonte. See #1606. These include articles by Luciano Emmer (#1666), Carmine Gallone (#1678), Antony Hopkins (#4642), Hans Keller (#1748), Ildebrando Pizzetti (#1848), and Roman Vlad (#4098).
>
>Some (or all) of the Florence papers may also appear in a special issue of Bianco e nero. See #1832.

1865. Rath, M. "Film Music." Canon, 8 (June 1955), 426-29.

1866. Rattner, David S., and Quaintance Eaton. "Current Scores." Film and TV Music, 16, No. 3 (Spring 1957), 16-17.

>References to music by Auric, Newman, and Alec Wilder.

1867. Rawlings, F. How to Choose Music for Amateur Films. Focal Cinebooks. New York and London: Focal Press, 1955. (Second ed., 1961.)

1868. Rees, Clifford B. "Film Music in the Making." Musical Events, 15 (Feb. 1960), 32-33.

1869. Riesfeld, Bert. "Filmkomponist oder Musikzuschneider? Oder: Bei uns in

Hollywood." <u>Musica</u>, 8, No. 2 (Feb. 1954), 57-59.

1870. ----------. "Illustrierte Musik in Amerika." <u>Musica</u>, 13, No. 4 (Apr. 1959), 266-67.

1871. ----------. "Musik und Filmindustrie." <u>Musica</u>, 4, No. 11 (Nov. 1950), 438-39.

1872. "RKO First Major Studio to Drop Staff Orchestra." <u>Down Beat</u>, 21 (April 21, 1954), 1.

1873. Robin, Harry. "The Music Track for 'Ode on a Grecian Urn.'" <u>Film and TV Music</u>, 16, No. 1 (Fall 1956), 21.

    Musical score by Henry Brant.

1874. "'Rocketship X-M': Background Music Produced by a Theremin." <u>Melody Maker</u> (London), 26 (Aug. 19, 1950), 2.

1875. Rodetsky, S. "Music in Movies as a Career." <u>American Music Teacher</u> (Cincinnati), 1 (Sept.-Oct. 1951), 1ff.

1876. Roggensack, Delinda. "The Scope of Film Music Education." <u>Film Music Notes</u>, 10, No. 4 (Mar.-Apr. 1951), 15-16.

    NOTE: Roggensack also contributed several articles to <u>FMN</u> concerning the use of film for music education.

1877. Ronell, Ann. "'The Titan' and His Music." <u>Film Music Notes</u>, 9, No. 3 (Jan.-Feb. 1950), 14-15.

    Film score by Alois Melichar.

1878. Sainton, Philip. "The Music for 'Moby Dick.'" <u>Film Music</u>, 15, No. 5 (Summer 1956), 3-6.

    Comments on the score, by the composer.

1879. "Salzburg Congress." <u>Music Review</u>, 20 (Aug.-Nov. 1959), 309-10.

1880. Sargeant, Winthrop. "Music for Murder." <u>The New Yorker</u> (Oct. 30, 1954).

1881. "Scharf Defends Hollywood." <u>Musical Courier</u>, 147 (Feb. 15, 1953), 26.

    Comments by Walter Scharf.

1882. Schinsky, Karl. "Neue Versuche auf dem Gebiet der Filmmusik. Über die Musik zu den DEFA-Filmen 'Bärenburger Schnurre' und 'Tinko.'" <u>Deutsche Filmkunst</u>, 5 (1957), 172-74.

1883. Schumann, Walter. "The Night of the Hunter." <u>Film Music</u>, 15, No. 1 (Sept.-Oct. 1955), 13-17.

    Comments on the score, by the composer.

1884. Schwartz, Elwyn. "Teaching Film Music." <u>Film Music</u>, 11, No. 4 (Mar.-Apr. 1952), 23.

    Concerning a course in film music designed by Schwartz, a professor at the University of Idaho.

1885. "Scoreboard." <u>Score</u>, 5, Nos. 2-3 (1953), 8-10.

    A listing of composers and orchestrators for current films.

1886. Scott, Tom. "Summer Sequence." <u>Film Music</u>, 13, No. 5 (May-June 1954), 3-8.

    Comments on the score, by the composer.

1887. Sezenskij, H. "Sovetskaya muzyka po radio." <u>Sovetskaya muzyka</u>, 9 (1958).

1888. Shaindlin, Jack. "Re. 'Cinerama Holiday' Music Score." <u>Film Music</u>, 14, No. 3 (Jan.-Feb. 1955), 16-19.

    Film score by Morton Gould and Van Cleave.

    Reprinted in Limbacher, p. 124. See #75.

1889. Sheets, W. "Situation Now Confronting All Arrangers and Composers." <u>Score</u>,

4 (March 1950), 6-7.

1890. Shindo, Tak. "Japanese Music Today." <u>Film Music</u>, 12, No. 1 (Sept.-Oct. 1952), 21-22.

1891. Simon, Alfred E. "Strictly Dishonorable." <u>Film Music</u>, 11, No. 1 (Sept.-Oct. 1951), 12-13.

      Film score by Mario Castelnuovo-Tedesco, and musical direction by Lennie Hayton.

1892. Spaeth, Sigmund. "From the Reviewing Stand." <u>Music Clubs Magazine</u> (Indianapolis), 33 (Jan. 1954), 18.

1893. ----------. "Motion Pictures." <u>Music Clubs Magazine</u> (Indianapolis), 30 (Oct. 1950), 23-24.

1894. ----------. "New Trends in Motion Picture Music." <u>Music Clubs Magazine</u> (Indianapolis), 33 (Sept. 1953), 21-22ff.

1895. Spottiswoode, Raymond. <u>Film and Its Techniques</u>. London: Faber and Faber; Berkeley: University of California Press, 1951. (Reprint, 1964.)

      Chapters: "Sound: Getting It onto Film," pp. 275-322, "Sound: Getting It onto the Screen," pp. 323-35, and "The Liberation of Sound/Music without Instruments," pp. 381-87. Also includes bibliography, pp. 485-501.

1896. ----------. <u>A Grammar of the Film: An Analysis of Film Technique</u>. London: Faber and Faber, 1935.

   1896a. Second edition, Berkeley and Los Angeles: University of California Press, 1951. (Reprint, 1969.)

      Chapters: "Visual and Aural Material of the Cinema," pp. 114-16, "The Sound Factor," pp. 48-49, and a section on sound and music, pp. 173-92.

   1896b. Also published as <u>Una grammatica del film</u>. Trans. by Aldo Paolo Filippino. Rome: Edizioni di Bianco e nero, 1939.

1897. Starr, J. "Movie Music Makers." <u>Life with Music</u>, 3 (Feb. 1950), 14-15ff.

1898. ----------. "Movie Music Makers." <u>Life with Music</u>, 3 (Apr. 1950), 22-24.

1899. "Stravinsky on Music Reproduction." <u>Music Teacher</u> (Gt. Brit.), 29 (May 1950), 243.

1900. Sülwald, P. H. "Die Tantième der Filmkomponisten: Eine Warnung." <u>GEMA-Nachrichten</u>, No. 23 (1955), 48.

      Concerning legal aspects of film music.

1901. Sykes, Wanda. "Nature's Half Acre." <u>Film Music</u>, 11, No. 1 (Sept.-Oct. 1951), 16-19.

      Film score by Paul Smith.

1902. Talbert, Thomas, Alfred Simon, and Frank H. Smith. "Current Scores." <u>Film and TV Music</u>, 17, No. 1 (Fall-Winter 1957-1958), 13-15.

      References to music by Auric, Arnold, Deutsch, Duning, and Waxman.

1903. ----------, and Willis Schaefer. "Current Scores." <u>Film and TV Music</u>, 16, No. 5 (Late Summer 1957), 17-18.

      References to music by Bernstein, Friedhofer, Waxman, Jerry Ross, and Richard Adler.

1904. "Teater pa villspor." <u>Norsk Musikerblad</u> (Oslo), 48 (Feb. 1959), 1-2.

1905. Thiriet, Maurice. "Filmmusik." <u>Antares</u>, 4, No. 1 (1956), 32-37.

1906. Thompson, H. "Notes on a Music Maker." <u>New York Times</u>, 100 (Aug. 5, 1951), Section 2, p. 3.

1907. Tilton, Roger. "Jazz Dance." <u>Film Music</u>, 15, No. 2 (Winter 1955), 19.

1908. Toeplitz, Jerzy. "Młodość Chopina." Kwartalnik Filmowy, 2, Nos. 5-6 (1952).

1909. Torres, R. Martinez. "Memoria del curso de composicion de musica cinemato-grafica en el Real Conservatorio de Musica de Madrid, ano 1955." Musica (Madrid), 4, No. 14 (1955), 115-18.

1910. Tynan, John. "Film Flam." Down Beat, 25 (June 12, 1958), 35.
    Concerning the increasing use of jazz in film scoring.

1911. ----------. "Take Five: Jazz in Motion Pictures." Down Beat, 26 (Jan. 8, 1959), 42-43.

1912. Ulmann, H. von. "Elektronische Musik und Film." Musica, 10, No. 12 (Dec. 1956), 867.

1913. Várady, László. "Filmzenénk egyes kérdéseiröl." Uj zenei szemle, No. 3 (1951), 17-24.
    Concerning problems of music in Hungarian films.

1914. Veurman, B. W. E. "Modern en oud en radio." Neerlands volksleven, 10 (1959-1960), 23-25.

1915. Vlad, Roman. "La musica nel documentario." Bianco e nero, 11, No. 5-6 (May-June 1950).
    A paper presented at the 1950 Venice conference. See #1832.
    1915a. Also published in La musica nel film. Ed. Luigi Chiarini. Rome: Bianco e nero editore, 1950, pp. 72-76.
        See Chiarini (#1627).

1916. ----------. "La musica nel documentario d'arte." Bianco e nero, 11, Nos. 8-9 (Aug.-Sept. 1950).

1917. Vogel, Karl-Heinz. "Zum Leistungsschutzrecht des ausübenden Musikers beim Film." Gewerblicher Rechtsschutz und Urheberrecht, 55 (1953), 199-203.

1918. Volodin, V. "O filme s muzykoi i muzykalnom filme." Iskusstvo kino (Mos-cow), No. 10 (Oct. 1954), 52-59.

1919. Vredenburg, Max. "Muziek op het filmfestival te Cannes." Mens en Melodie (Utrecht), 7 (June 1952), 181-83.

1920. Wagner, K. "Musik im Zeichenfilm." Musica, 4 (May-June 1950), 212-13.

1921. Wagner, Robert W. "Original Music in College and University Film Produc-tion." Film and TV Music, 17, No. 1 (Fall-Winter 1957-1958), 16.
    See also comments by Douglas Gallez, #1677.

1922. Watson, Ernest C. "The Benny Goodman Story." Film Music, 15, No. 3 (Jan.-Feb. 1956), 18-19.
    Additional music for the film is by Henry Mancini.

1923. Weinert, Joachim. "Filmmusik ohne Echo." Musik und Gesellschaft, 4 (1954), 360-62.

1924. ----------. "Der Komponist als Filmgestalter. Neue DEFA-Filme und ihre Mu-sik." Musik und Gesellschaft, 7 (1957), 522-26.

1925. ----------. "Komposition -- nicht Konfektion: Musik zu DEFA-Filmen." Mu-sik und Gesellschaft, 7 (1957), 210-13.

1926. ----------. "Musik zu Filmen -- Film zur Musik." Musik und Gesellschaft, 5 (1955), 292-93.

1927. Werhahn, Jürgen W. "Urheberrecht am Tonfilm." Gewerblicher Rechtsschutz und Urheberrecht, 50, No. 1 (1954), 16-22.

1928. Witenson, S. "O pesne v filme." Iskusstvo kino (Moscow), No. 10 (Oct. 1955).

1929. Zurbach, W. "Tanz und Musik im Film." Studio, No. 2 (1956).

SEE ALSO:

#3(Amfitheatrof), #18(Chrennikov), #68(Kułakowska), #146(Booch), #251 (Jenkinson/Warner), #3025(Baudrier), #3334(Hickman), #3336, #3563(Masetti), #4479(Cage), #4489(Casini), #4516(Colpi), #4684, #4738(Lissa), #4867 (Schall), #4870(Schinsky), #5089(IMC/IMZ), #5105(Melichar), #5202(Arundell), #5206(Boll), #5222(Cuenca), #5251(Helm), #5255, 5256(IMC/IMZ), #5293(Rutz), #5523(Eaton), #5538, #5539(Helm), #5552(Koster), #5573(Podest), #5579(Robin), #5914, #5928(Cicognini), #6017(Jelot-Blanc), #6069 (Mellers), #6080(Newton), #6145(Vaughan), #6156, #6193(Hickman), #6261-6262(Farren), #6278-6281(Limbacher), #6282-6283(Morrison), #6284-6288 (Pratley), #6295(Smolian), #6296(Thomas), #6298(ASCAP), and #6318.

Sound Techniques and Technology

1930. Frayne, John G., and Halley Wolfe. Elements of Sound Recording. New York; John Wiley and Sons, 1949.

>   The standard technical manual for the 1950's.

1931. Fréchet, Étienne S., and L. Rodor. Comment sonoriser vos films 8-9, 15-16 millimetre. Paris: Éditions Photo-Cinéma Paul Montel, 1955.

>   Several reprints and revisions were also published by Paul Montel, with the titles: La sonorisation des films, 1957; La pratique de l'enregistrement magnétique et la sonorisation des films, 1957; La sonorisation des films d'amateurs et l'enregistrement magnétique (in collaboration with S. de Marchi), 1961; and Le cinéma sonore d'amateur et l'enregistrement magnétique, 1966.

1932. Geiseler, W. "Technische Entwicklung: Feind der Rundfunkmusik?" Melos, 17 (1950).

1933. Hickman, C. Sharpless. "Movies and Music." Music Journal, 11, No. 6 (June 1953), 30.

>   Concerning techniques of sound recording.

1934. Huntley, John. "The Sound Track." Sight and Sound, 23, No. 3 (Jan.-Mar. 1954), 166-67.

>   Concerning new developments in sound technology, and the use of sound in 3-D and CinemaScope.

1935. Leistner, E. Der Filmtonmeister und seine technisch-künstlerischen Aufgaben in der Filmproduktion. Detmold, 1951.

1936. Lewin, Frank. "The Soundtrack in Non-theatrical Motion Pictures." Journal of the Society of Motion Picture and Television Engineers, 68, No. 3 (Mar. 1959); 68, No. 6 (June 1959); and 68, No. 7 (July 1959).

1937. McCullum, Gordon. "The Sound Department." Films and Filming, 3, No. 11 (Aug. 1957), 30-31ff.

1938. Oringel, Robert S. Audio Control Handbook for Radio and Television Broadcasting. New York: Hastings House, 1956. (Revised edition, 1963.)

1939. Robson, Mark. "Why You Hear What You Hear at the Movies." Good Housekeeping (July 1955), 99-102.

1940. Stein, Fritz. "Auflösung von Filmverträgen." Österreichische Autorenzeitung, 2, No. 3 (1950).

1941. Winckel, Fritz Wilhelm. "Der Tonmeister." In Humanismus und Technik (Gesellschaft von Freunden der Technischen Universität Berlin-Charlottenburg, II), 25, No. 3 (Dec. 1954).

SEE ALSO:
#59(Irving/Keller/Mellers), #155(Fielding), #199(Atkins), #223, 226(Cook), #238(Ford), #241(Frayne et al.), #254(Kellogg), #307(Trommer), #312(Weiland), #1895-1896(Spottiswoode), #4489(Casini), and #4630(Guillot de Rode).

Music for T.V.

1942. "'Background' in TV Upbeat." _Variety_, 216 (Nov. 18, 1959), 59ff.

1943. Bowman, Roger. "New Radio and Television Prices and Conditions." _Film Music Notes_, 10, No. 5 (May-June 1951), 16-17.

> An overview of the film music business in 1951.

1944. ----------. "Notes on Music for Television." _Film Music Notes_, 10, No. 3 (Jan.-Feb. 1951), 20.

1945. ----------. "Television Notes." _Film Music_, 12, No. 4 (Mar.-Apr. 1953), 23-24.

1946. ----------. "Television Survey." _Film Music_, 11, No. 3 (Jan.-Feb. 1952), 24.

1947. Briggs, John. "Aiding the Composer: Original Musical Scores Are Obtained for 'Twentieth Century' Series." _New York Times_, 108 (Apr. 12, 1959), Section 2, p. 11.

1948. Broekman, David. "Music and the Wide Wide World." _Film and TV Music_, 16, No. 4 (Summer 1957), 20-21.

> Concerning music for the television series "Wide Wide World."

1949. "Coast Studio Musicians Are Getting TV Jitters." _Down Beat_, 19 (Dec. 31, 1952), 2.

1950. Dahlgren, C. "Jazz-drama i TV." _Orkester Journalen_ (Stockholm), 23 (Jan. 1955), 8-9ff.

1951. Daniel, O. "Modern Composers You Should Know." _Music at Home_, 1 (July-Aug. 1954), 37-39ff.

> Concerning the use of "contemporary" music for TV background.

1952. Elias, Albert J. "Background Music in Radio and TV." _Etude_, 73 (Nov. 1955), 18ff.

1953. ----------. "TV Music by Contemporary Composers." _Etude_, 74 (Nov. 1956), 22ff.

1954. Freedman, Lewis, and John McGiffert. "Music on Camera Three." _Film and TV Music_, 16, No. 2 (Winter 1956), 22.

1955. Harman, C. "Use of Music on Video: Ways in Which Programs Employ Live and Recorded Performances." _New York Times_, 100 (Feb. 11, 1951), Section 2, p. 7.

1956. Hijman, J. "Een televisie-opera van Menotti." _Mens en Melodie_ (Utrecht), 8 (Jan. 1953), 4-7.

1957. Hodder-Williams, C. "TV Music." _Melody Maker_ (London), 31 (June 23, 1956), 10; and 31 (June 30, 1956), 10.

1958. Holde, Artur. "Amahl und die nächtlichen Gäste." _Das Musikleben_, 5 (Dec. 1952), 374-75.

> Opera for television, by Gian Carlo Menotti.

1959. Keller, Hans. "Twelve-Note Music on Television." Musical Times, 95,
      No. 1332 (Feb. 1954), 92.
>   Concerning music for BBC-TV film productions, by Matyas
>   Seiber.

1960. Koster, Ernst. "Fernseh-Oper von Menotti im NWDR." Melos, 21 (Feb. 1954),
      52-53.

1961. ----------. "Musikalische Kulisse im Hörspiel." Das Musikleben, 8 (Jan.
      1955), 16-19.

1962. ----------. "Musik im Fernsehfunk." Musica, 7, No. 10 (Oct. 1953), 440-42.

1963. Lalou, Étienne. Regards neufs sur la télévision. Peuple et culture, 12.
      Paris: Éditions du Seuil, 1957.
>   Includes references to music and musical programing on TV.

1964. Land, B. "A Composer Serious About Television Music." New York Times, 106
      (Feb. 10, 1957), Section 2, p. 11.
>   Concerning the work of Stanley Hollingsworth.

1965. Rigault, J. de. "A Menotti rien d'impossible." La Revue musicale, No. 211
      (Feb. 1952), 33-35.

1966. Scott, Tom. "Music for Television." Film Music, 15, No. 5 (Summer 1956),
      19-23.

1967. Seymour, A. "Menotti's TV Opera: 'Amahl and the Night Visitors.'" The Ca-
      non (Australia), 11 (June 1958), 361-63.

1968. Sosnik, Harry. "Music's Vital to Films -- Why Not Television?" Variety,
      193 (Jan. 6, 1954), 97.

1969. Stadrucker, Ivan. "História jedného zvukového pracoviska." Slovenská Hu-
      debni, 13, Nos. 9-10 (Nov.-Dec. 1969), 342-49.
>   A brief history of the Czechoslovakian TV sound studio in
>   Bratislava, and a listing of TV studios around the world.

1970. Tanassy, Cornel. "Report on Music in Television." Film Music, 14, No. 4
      (Mar.-Apr. 1955), 23.

1971. Taubman, Howard. "Credit Overdue: Composers Whose Music Makes TV Back-
      ground." New York Times, 103 (May 2, 1954), Section 2, p. 7.
   1971a. Reprinted in Film Music, 13, No. 5 (May-June 1954), 13-14.

1972. "TV Needs New Composers." Down Beat, 26 (Oct. 29, 1959), 14-15.

1973. Tynan, John. "Down with Canning." Down Beat, 26 (Dec. 10, 1959), 15-16.
>   A criticism of the use of pre-recorded music on TV.

   SEE ALSO:

    #25(Comuzio), #4555(Eckert), #4913, 4915(Thiel), #5035(Tannenbaum), #5140
    (Weaver), #5230(Eisner), #5256 and 5654(IMC/IMZ).

1960's

History

1974. "Aboard the Bandwagon." Time, 87 (Jan. 14, 1966), 62ff.
>   References to the music of John Barry.

1975. Adams, Stanley. "Music and Motion Pictures." ASCAP in Action (New York), 1, No. 2 (June 1967), opp. p. 1-1.

1976. Amsden, Peter. "Composing for Films." Screen, 11, No. 2 (1970), 80-85.

    An interview with composer Michael J. Lewis.

1977. Arnold, Malcolm. "Film Music." Recorded Sound (London), No. 18 (Apr. 1965), 328-34.

1978. Arnshtam, Lev. "Dukhovnostta -- nai-silnoto ni oruzhie." Kinoiskusstvo, 30 (Aug. 1975), 33-35.

1979. Ascher, Felice. "An Interview with Teo Macero." Film Library Quarterly, 2, No. 2 (Spring 1969), 9-12.

1980. Assayas, Olivier. "Le rendez-vous d'Angers." Cahiers du cinéma, No. 310 (April 1980), xii.

    Concerning the 1980 Festival "Cinéma et Musique, Musique et Cinéma," with special reference to the music of Miklos Rozsa.

1981. Bach, Steven. "The Hollywood Idiom." Arts Magazine (Dec. 1967), 16-17.

1982. Baronijan, Vartkes. "Zabavno muzicki zivot Holivuda." Zvuk (Sarajevo), Nos. 104-105 (1970), 212-14.

1983. Bélai, István. "Gondolatok az elektronikus zenéról." Alföld, 18, No. 6 (June 1967), 66-67.

1984. Bergquist, Mats. "Johnny Mandel och filmjazzen." Orkester Journalen (Stockholm), 28 (Jan. 1960), 12.

1985. Bessy, Maurice, and Jean-Louis Chardans. Dictionaire du cinéma et de la télévision. Paris: Pauvert, 1966.

    See especially the article "Enregistrement sonore" in Vol. II.

1986. Bhatia, Vanraj. "Film Music." Seminar (New Delhi), (Dec. 1961).

1987. Bobker, Lee R. Elements of Film. New York: Harcourt, Brace and World, 1969.

    Includes discussions of sound and music, pp. 97-127 and pp. 143-53.

1988. Bock, Fred. "Motion Picture Music: A New Educational Tool." The School Musician (Chicago), 34 (June-July 1963), 40-43.

    Includes a Foreword by David Raksin.

1989. Borisov, A. "'Dusha poet ...'" Sovetskaya muzyka, 27, No. 3 (Mar. 1963), 89-93.

1990. Buck, H. "Butch Cassidy and the Sundance Kid." Jazz and Pop (New York), 8 (Dec. 1969), 54.

    Film score by Burt Bacharach.

1991. Canby, Vincent. "Music is Now Profit to the Ears of Filmmakers." New York Times (May 24, 1966).

1992. Carey, Gary. "The Music of Sound." Seventh Art, 1, No. 2 (Spring 1963), 6-7.

    A discussion of Antonioni's use of music and sound.

1993. Cary, Tristram. "Moving Pictures from an Exhibition." Composer, No. 25 (Autumn 1967), 10-12.

    Concerning Carey's collaboration with film producer James Archibald for an exhibition at the British Pavilion at Montreal's Expo 67.

1994. Castello, Giulio Cesare, and Mario Verdone. Article in Bianco e nero, 28, Nos. 3-4 (Mar.-Apr. 1967), 119.

1995. Cavalcanti: Alberto Cavalcanti. Staatlichen Filmarchiv der DDR und dem

Club der Filmschaffenden der DDR. Berlin, 1962.

1996. "The Cement of Films." BMI: The Many Worlds of Music (May 1968), 5.

1997. Chamfray, Claude. "Musique pour le cinéma." Le Courrier musical de France, No. 28 (1969), 249.

1998. Chevassu, François. "Musique de films." Revue du cinéma/Image et son, No. 290 (Nov. 1974), 15-16.

1999. ----------. "Musique et cinéma." Revue du cinéma/Image et son, No. 281 (Feb. 1974), 15.

2000. ----------. "Musique et cinéma." Revue du cinéma/Image et son, No. 346 (Jan. 1980), 138-40.

2001. Comolli, Jean Louis. "Jazz et cinéma: annee zero." Jazz Magazine (Paris), No. 113 (Dec. 1964), 84-87.

2002. Comuzio, Ermanno. "La colonna sonora spia della 'nouvelle vague.'" Cineforum, No. 22 (Feb. 1963).

2003. ----------. "Colonne sonore." Cineforum (Jan. 1968).
      The first article in a regular film music column by Comuzio.

2004. ----------. "Colonne sonore." Schermi (Milan), (Oct. 1960).
      The first article in a regular film music column by Comuzio.

2005. ----------. "Il sonoro di 'Persona.'" Cineforum, No. 61 (Jan. 1967).

2006. ----------. "L'uso della musica nei film amatoriali." Il cineamatore (Apr. 1968).

2007. Connor, Edward, and T. M. F. Steen. "The Sound Track." Films in Review, 12, No. 1 (Jan. 1961), 43-45.
      Concerning the use of "classical quotations" in film scores. Also includes references to music by Daniele Amfitheatrof and Adolph Deutsch.

2008. Cook, Page. "The Sound Track." Films in Review, 15, No. 3 (Mar. 1964), 169-70.
      References to music by Jerome Moross and Manos Hadjidakis.

2009. ----------. "-----." Films in Review, 15, No. 4 (Apr. 1964), 233-36.
      References to music by Previn, Rosenthal, and Tiomkin.

2010. ----------. "-----." Films in Review, 15, No. 6 (June-July 1964), 363-64, 367.
      Film scores of 1963, with references to music by Bernstein, Newman, North, Previn, and Rozsa.

2011. ----------. "-----." Films in Review, 15, No. 7 (Aug.-Sept. 1964), 433-35.
      References to music by E. Bernstein, Meredith Willson, and others.

2012. ----------. "-----." Films in Review, 16, No. 2 (Feb. 1965), 105-06.
      Film scores of 1964, with references to music by Herrmann, North, and others.

2013. ----------. "-----." Films in Review, 16, No. 3 (Mar. 1965), 170-72.
      A discussion of current musical films, with references to music by Max Steiner and Michel Legrand.

2014. ----------. "-----." Films in Review, 16, No. 10 (Dec. 1965), 636-37.
      References to music by Piero Piccioni.

2015. ----------. "-----." Films in Review, 17, No. 1 (Jan. 1966), 38-40.
      A survey of current film scores.

2016. ----------. "The Sound Track." <u>Films in Review</u>, 17, No. 2 (Feb. 1966), 111-12.
        Film scores of 1965, with references to music by Newman and others.

2017. ----------. "-----." <u>Films in Review</u>, 17, No. 3 (Mar. 1966), 177-78.
        References to music by Sol Kaplan.

2018. ----------. "-----." <u>Films in Review</u>, 17, No. 5 (May 1966), 306-08.
        References to music by Bernstein, Shostakovich, and Arnold.

2019. ----------. "-----." <u>Films in Review</u>, 17, No. 6 (June-July 1966), 371-73.
        References to music by Skinner, Waxman, and Satyajit Ray.

2020. ----------. "-----." <u>Films in Review</u>, 17, No. 7 (Aug.-Sept. 1966), 440-42.
        References to music by Bernstein, Newman, and North.

2021. ----------. "-----." <u>Films in Review</u>, 17, No. 8 (Oct. 1966), 509-11.
        References to music by John Addison and Toshiro Mayuzumi.

2022. ----------. "-----." <u>Films in Review</u>, 17, No. 9 (Nov. 1966), 577-79.
        References to music by Bernstein and Frank Skinner.

2023. ----------. "-----." <u>Films in Review</u>, 17, No. 10 (Dec. 1966), 658-59.
        References to music by Herrmann and Goldsmith.

2024. ----------. "-----." <u>Films in Review</u>, 18, No. 1 (Jan. 1967), 44-45, 47.
        A survey of current film scores.

2025. ----------. "-----." <u>Films in Review</u>, 18, No. 2 (Feb. 1967), 107-08, 111.
        Film scores of 1966.

2026. ----------. "-----." <u>Films in Review</u>, 18, No. 4 (Apr. 1967), 230-32.
        References to music by Delerue, Rota, and Francis Lai.

2027. ----------. "-----." <u>Films in Review</u>, 18, No. 5 (May 1967), 300-01.
        References to music by David Rose and Angelo Francesco Lavagnino.

2028. ----------. "-----." <u>Films in Review</u>, 18, No. 6 (June-July 1967), 360-61.
        A survey of current film scores.

2029. ----------. "-----." <u>Films in Review</u>, 18, No. 7 (Aug.-Sept. 1967), 437-38, 440.
        References to music by Addison, Kaper, and Frank De Vol.

2030. ----------. "-----." <u>Films in Review</u>, 18, No. 8 (Oct. 1967), 496-97.
        References to music by John Barry and Dimitri Tiomkin.

2031. ----------. "-----." <u>Films in Review</u>, 19, No. 1 (Jan. 1968), 38-40.
        References to music by Richard Rodney Bennett and John Williams.

2032. ----------. "-----." <u>Films in Review</u>, 19, No. 2 (Feb. 1968), 99-100.
        Film scores of 1967.

2033. ----------. "-----." <u>Films in Review</u>, 19, No. 3 (Mar. 1968), 162-63, 166.
        Comments on the "declining quality" of current film scores. References to music by Schifrin and Francis Lai.

2034. ----------. "-----." <u>Films in Review</u>, 19, No. 4 (Apr. 1968), 234-36.
        References to music by Goldsmith, Raksin, and Rozsa.

2035. ----------. "-----." <u>Films in Review</u>, 19, No. 5 (May 1968), 298-300.

Comments on the score for Kubrick's "2001." Also, music by Bernstein and Mario Nascimbene.

2036. ----------. "The Sound Track." Films in Review, 19, No. 6 (June-July 1968), 364-66.

References to music by Vyacheslav Ovchinnikov and Manos Hadjidakis.

2037. ----------. "-----." Films in Review, 19, No. 7 (Aug.-Sept. 1968), 447-49.

References to music by Delerue and Rozsa.

2038. ----------. "-----." Films in Review, 19, No. 8 (Oct. 1968), 508-09.

A survey of current scores.

2039. ----------. "-----." Films in Review, 19, No. 10 (Dec. 1968), 634-35, 638.

References to music by Phillip Lambro.

2040. ----------. "-----." Films in Review, 20, No. 1 (Jan. 1969), 46-48.

References to music by Kaper, North, and Ravi Shankar.

2041. ----------. "-----." Films in Review, 20, No. 2 (Feb. 1969), 110-11.

Film scores of 1968, with references to music by Herrmann, Newman, Raksin, and Rozsa.

2042. ----------. "-----." Films in Review, 20, No. 3 (Mar. 1969), 169-70.

Concerning the increased infusion of pop music, and the consequent "decline" of film music.

2043. ----------. "-----." Films in Review, 20, No. 5 (May 1969), 308-10.

References to music by Herrmann, Michel Legrand, and Rod McKuen.

2044. ----------. "-----." Films in Review, 20, No. 8 (Oct. 1969), 505-07.

References to music by Goldsmith, Herrmann, and Gerald Fried.

2045. ----------. "-----." Films in Review, 20, No. 9 (Nov. 1969), 561-63, 565.

References to music by Georges Delerue, Ronald Stein, and Ron Goodwin.

2046. ----------. "-----." Films in Review, 20, No. 10 (Dec. 1969), 627-29.

References to music by Ernest Gold and Michael J. Lewis.

2047. Cummings, Jack. "Music: Hollywood's Star Salesman." Music Journal, 23, No. 4 (Apr. 1965), 97.

2048. Deharme, Paul. "Pour un art radiophonique." In Un siècle de radio et de télévision. Ed. Pierre Descaves and A. V. J. Martin. Paris: ORTF, 1965, pp. 240-46.

See Descaves (#149).

2049. Delubac, Yves. "Hyeres et demain." Jazz Magazine (Paris), Nos. 156-157 (July-Aug. 1968), 13.

2050. Dolan, Robert Emmett. Music in Modern Media: Techniques in Tape, Disc and Film Recording, Motion Picture and Television Scoring and Electronic Music. New York: G. Schirmer, 1967.

Includes a large section on "Films," pp. 51-144, and the application of electronic music to films, pp. 164-73.

Provides analyses and examples of scores by Copland, Friedhofer, Newman, North, Raksin, and Van Cleave.

-- Rev. in Variety, 249 (Dec. 27, 1967), 38.

-- Rev. in Pan Pipes of SAI (Wisconsin), 60, No. 3 (1968), 39-40.

-- Rev. in The Strad, 78 (Jan. 1968), 363.

-- Rev. in Music Educators Journal, 54 (May 1968), 77-80.

2051. Eaton, Quaintance. "TV -- Radio -- Films." Showcase, 41, No. 2 (1961-1962), 23.

2052. Eswar, N. V. "In India Films Are 'Musicals' by Fixed Convention." Variety, 230 (May 8, 1963), 146.

2053. "Film: 'Ta nase pisnicka ceska.'" Hudební Rozhledy, 20, Nos. 21-22 (1967), 675.

2054. Fischer, E. Kurt. "Grenzen der Bildungsarbeit im Rundfunk." In Publizistik: Festschrift für Emil Dovifat. Ed. Günter Kieslich and Walter J. Schütz. Bremen: B. C. Heye, 1960, pp. 55-64.

2055. Fleuret, Maurice. "Musique et cinéma." Journal Musical Français, No. 153 (Jan. 1967), 48-49.

2056. "Floyd Write Major Film Score." Melody Maker, 44 (Dec. 13, 1969), 3.
    Concerning a film score by Pink Floyd.

2057. Galling, Dennis. "Arthur Freed." Films in Review, 15, No. 9 (Nov. 1964), 521-44.
    Includes filmography, and a discussion of Freed's musicals.

2058. Garel, Alain. "La musique de films: pour en finir (momentanément) avec le domaine extra-cinematographique." Revue du cinéma/Image et son, No. 372 (May 1982), 137-41.

2059. Gaspard, Jacques J. "Jazz et cinéma." Musica (Chaix, Fr.), No. 72 (Mar. 1960), 32-39.

2060. Gautier, Henri. "Jazz au cinéma." Premier plan (Lyon), No. 11 (1960).

2061. Girardeau, Émile. "La Radiodiffusion, sa puissance, ses faiblesses." In Un siècle de radio et de télévision. Ed. Pierre Descaves and A. V. J. Martin. Paris: ORTF, 1965, pp. 210-17.
    See Descaves (#149).

2062. Grosheva, Elena. "Rozy dlya vsekh." Sovetskaya muzyka, 29, No. 2 (Feb. 1965), 23-30.

2063. Grzelecki, Stanislaw. "Niezastapiona i nieoceniona." Ruch Muzyczny (Warsaw), 4 (Apr. 1, 1960), 33.

2064. Gudmundsen-Holmgreen, Pelle. "Film og Musik." Dansk Musiktidsskrift, 44, No. 1 (1969), 9-12.

2065. Gustafson, Dwight L. "Composing for a Celluloid Taskmaster." Music Journal, 21, No. 8 (Nov. 1963), 56-57ff.
    Concerning a student film produced at Bob Jones University.

2066. Hajdu, André. "Notes sur la musique du film 'Kriss Romani.'" Etudes tsiganes, 9, No. 4 (1963), 12-13.

2067. Hanson, Curtis Lee. "Three Screen Composers: Maurice Jarre, Dimitri Tiomkin and Henry Mancini." Cinema (Los Angeles), 3, No. 3 (July 1966), 8-10, 16, 33-34.
    Interviews with the composers.

2068. Haye, Abdul. Gătă ja'e banjără. 1964.

2069. Helman, Alicja. "Hauptrichtungen der Musikentwicklung im modernen Film." Filmwissenschaftliche Mitteilungen, No. 1 (1965), 103.

2070. ----------. "Jak sluchamy muzyki filmowej." Kino, 9 (May 1974), 32-35.

2071. Herrmann, Günter, comp. Rundfunkgesetze: Textsammlung. Cologne: C. Heymann, 1966.
    Concerning the legal problems, performing rights, etc., on radio. Including musical performance and original music.

2071a. Second edition, Rundfunkgesetze: Fernsehen und Hörfunk: Text-sammlung. Cologne: C. Heymann, 1977.

Includes bibliography, pp. 349-53.

-- Rev. in Musikhandel, 30, No. 1 (1979), 48.

2072. "Hudba a film." Hudební Rozhledy, 19, No. 10 (1966), 295-97.

Includes discography.

2073. Internationales Musikzentrum, Vienna. IMZ Report: Composition and Realization in the Technical Media. Munich: IMZ, 1969.

In English, French, and German.

2074. Jones, Kenneth V. "Music for Films." Royal College of Music Magazine (London), 63, No. 2 (1967), 55-56.

2075. Kaczynski, Tadeusz. "Pokaz filmow francuskich (z muzyka eksperymentalna)." Ruch Muzyczny (Warsaw), 8, No. 21 (1964), 11.

2076. Karanovich, A. "Rezhisser vstrechaetsya s kompozitorom." Sovetskaya muzyka, 26, No. 12 (Dec. 1962), 8-13.

2077. Kaufmann, Serge. "La Musique de film." Journal musical français, No. 158 (June 1967), 33-36.

2078. Kharon, Y. "Muzyka 'glubokogo' ekrana." Sovetskaya muzyka, 26, No. 12 (Dec. 1962), 5-8.

2079. ----------. "Za fil'm kompozitora." Sovetskaya muzyka, 28, No. 8 (Aug. 1964), 98-101.

2080. Khachaturian, Karen Surenovich. "Novye fil'my: Volnuyushchie kadry." Sovetskaya muzyka, 31, No. 10 (Oct. 1967), 150-51.

2081. Kofsky, Frank. "Jazz Mail Box." Jazz Magazine (New York), 6 (Apr. 1967), 7.

Reply to an article by Leonard Feather. See #5075.

2082. Komorowska, Malgorzata. "Muzyka v filmie." Ruch Muzyczny (Warsaw), 13, No. 18 (1969), 18-19.

2083. Korganov, Tomas I. "Zametki muzykanta." Sovetskaya muzyka, 26, No. 3 (Mar. 1962), 97-101.

2084. Kouwenhoven, John A. "Stone, Steel, and Jazz." In The Popular Arts: A Critical Reader. Ed. Irving Deer and Harriet A. Deer. New York: Scribner, 1967, pp. 21-48.

2085. Kraft, Günther. "'Das Lied hinter Sacheldraht': Ein Amateurfilm uber kulturelle Zeugnisse des antifaschistischen Widerstandskampfes." Musik und Gesellschaft, 12, No. 2 (Feb. 1962), 80-85.

2086. Krellmann, Hanspeter. "Mauricio Kagels 'Synchronstudie.'" Musica, 23, No. 6 (June 1969), 582.

2087. Kuna, Milan. "Hudba ve zvukove dramaturgii filmu." Hudební Rozhledy, 15, Nos. 23-24 (1962), 1018-19.

2088. ----------. "Tanecni hudba ve filmu." Hudební Rozhledy (Prague), 15, No. 11 (1962), 468-69.

2089. Lees, Gene. "The New Sound on the Soundtracks." High Fidelity and Musical America, 17 (Aug. 1967), 58-61.

2090. "Lights .. Camera ... Music!" Newsweek (July 24, 1967), 77-78.

2091. Limmert, E. "Experimentelle Filme: die Attraktion von Hannover." Melos, 28, No. 3 (Mar. 1961), 92.

2092. "Luminous Art of the Computer." Life, 65, No. 19 (Nov. 8, 1968), 52-58.

Includes references to the work of John Whitney.

2093. MacCann, Richard Dyer, ed. Film: A Montage of Theories. New York: E. P.
      Dutton, 1966.
            A collection of articles, including reprints of essays by
            René Clair (# 4508), Gavin Lambert (#4709), and Suzanne K.
            Langer (#4717).

2094. Malle, Louis. "Le probleme de la musique de film est un probleme horrible-
      ment complique." Jazz Hot (Paris), 26 (June 1960), 14-15.

2095. Mann, Anthony. "Music and the Cinema." Music Journal, 22, No. 3 (Mar.
      1964), 66.

2096. Mascott, Laurence E. "Documentary Film Music." Music Journal, 25, No. 3
      (Mar. 1967), 36, 77.

2097. Matejka, Wilhelm. "Erfolgreiche Musiktage in Donaueschingen." Österreich-
      ische Musikzeitschrift, 34 (Dec. 1979), 641.

2098. McCutcheon, Bill. "1960's Best Filmusic." Films in Review, 12, No. 3 (Mar.
      1961), 180-81.
            References to music by Herrmann, Tiomkin, and André Previn.

2099. ----------. "1961's Best Filmusic." Films in Review, 13, No. 3 (Mar.
      1962), 178-80.
            References to music by Mancini, Friedhofer, and Rozsa.

2100. ----------. "The Sound Track." Films in Review, 14, No. 3 (Mar. 1963),
      181-83.
            Filmscores of 1962, with references to music by Bernstein,
            Goldsmith, Previn, and Waxman.

2101. ----------. "The Sound Track." Films in Review, 14, No. 5 (May 1963),
      294-95.
            References to film scores by Newman, and Maurice Jarre.

2102. Medjuck, Joe. "Frank Zappa." Take One, 2, No. 2 (1968), 8-9.

2103. Menge, Rolf. "Musik im Amateurfilm." Film und Ton, 22 (Sept. 1976), 42ff.

2104. Meylan, Pierre. "Le Film 'Viridiana' de Luis Bunnel: a-t-il donne lieu a
      un scandale musical?" Revue Musicale de Suisse Romande, 17, No. 3 (1964),
      2.

2105. Miller, Bert. "Bakom filmens kulisser." Musikern (Stockholm), No. 4 (Apr.
      1960), 8-9.

2106. "The Motion Picture: A Sourcespring of Great Music." Billboard, 80
      (Mar. 30, 1968), UA-4.

2107. "Musique de film." Journal Musical Français, No. 153 (Jan. 1967), 31-32.

2108. "Muzikata kum 'Shibil.'" Bulgarska Muzika (Sofia), 19, No. 5 (1968), 79-80.

2109. Neale, Denis Manktelow. Des Schmalfilm Tönt. Dusseldorf: Wilhelm Knapp
      Verlag, 1960.

2110. "New Sounds in Film Music from India." High Fidelity and Musical America,
      16 (Oct. 1966), 68.

2111. Niekerk, Paul van. "Toekomst in de muziek." Skrien (Amsterdam), No. 123
      (Winter·1982-1983), 38-39.

2112. Olivemark, Gustaf, and Bertil Wendelborn. "Biografavtalet." Musikern
      (Stockholm), No. 1 (Jan. 1969), 4-5ff.; and No. 3 (Mar. 1969), 9ff.

2113. Paap, Wouter. "Films van musici." Mens en Melodie (Utrecht), 20 (Nov.
      1965), 336-38.

2114. Paiva, Salviano Cavalcanti de. "Cinema: A Noite do Meu Bem." Correio da
      Manhã (Rio de Janeiro), (Mar. 6, 1969), 3.

2115. Pellegrini, Glauco. "Colonna sonora: Viaggio attraverso il cinema italiano." _Bianco e nero_, 28, Nos. 3-4 (Mar.-Apr. 1967), 18-53.

> "Testi completi della omonima trasmissione televisiva-interventi di Giulietta Masina, L. Chiarini, Alberto Lattuada, G. F. Malipiero, P. P. Pasolini, F. Fellini, N. Rota, M. Camerini, M. Soldati, F. Sacchi, Renzo e Roberto Rossellini, G. De Sanctis, G. Petrassi, V. Marinucci, G. Fusco, V. De Sica, C. Zavattini, A. Cicognini, U. Tognazzi, F. Cristaldi, C. Rustichelli, Mario Verdone, F. Rosi, P. Piccioni, G. Visentini, Roman Vlad, V. Zurlini, M. Nascimbene, M. Ergas, A. F. Lavagnino, S. Milo."

2116. ----------, and Mario Verdone, eds. _Colonna sonora_. A special issue of _Bianco e nero_, 28, Nos. 3-4 (Mar.-Apr. 1967).

> Includes a filmography of Pellegrini, and articles by S. G. Biamonte (#4457), Anton Giulio Bragaglia (#4465), Luciano Chailly (#4494), Ermanno Comuzio (#25), S. M. Eisenstein et al. (#4314), Maurice Jaubert (#3466), S. A. Luciani (#4755), G. Pellegrini (#2115), Mario Verdone (#4943-#4944), and Dziga Vertov (#2191).

2116a. Also published as _Colonna sonora_. Collana di studi, ricerche e documentazioni del Centro sperimentale di cinematografia, 13. Rome: Edizioni di Bianco e nero, 1967.

2117. Pilka, Jiří. "'Hluboke platno' a nase filmova hudba." _Hudební Rozhledy_, 13, No. 8 (1960), 334-35.

2118. ----------. "Piate koleso pri filme?" _Slovenská hudba_, 9, No. 9 (1965), 415-16.

2119. Pinchard, Max. "La Musique et le cinéma." _Musica_ (Chaix, Fr.), No. 74 (May 1960), 6-9.

2120. ----------. "La Musique et le cinéma." _Musica_ (Chaix, Fr.), No. 82 (Jan. 1961), 10-13.

2121. ----------. "La Musique et le cinéma." _Musica-Disques_, No. 82 (1961), 10-13.

2122. Pleasants, Henry. "Jazz and the Movies." _The World of Music_ (UNESCO), 10, No. 3 (1968), 38-47.

> In English, French, and German.

2123. Porcile, François. "Collaborateurs de création du jeune cinéma français." _Cinéma 64_, No. 89 (Sept.-Oct. 1964), 50-66.

> Interviews with composers Pierre Barbaud, Georges Delerue, Maurice Jarre, Michel Legrand, Maurice Le Roux, and Francis Seyrig. Includes filmographies for each composer.

2124. Poullin, Jacques. "Les chaines électro-acoustiques." _Cahiers d'Études de Radio-Télévision_, Nos. 27-28 (1960), 229-39.

2125. "Protest gegen Mahler-Diffamierung." _Österreichische Musikzeitschrift_, 27 (June 1972), 356-57.

> Concerning Visconti's "Death in Venice."

2126. "Raskryvat' dukhovnoe bogatstvo cheloveka." _Sovetskaya muzyka_, 26, No. 12 (Dec. 1962), 3-5.

2127. Rauhut, Franz. "Die Filmmusik im Urteil der Komponisten." _Universitas_, 22 (1967), 1197-1204.

2128. Reisfeld, Bert. "Musik aus dem Werkzeugkasten." _Musica_, 21, No. 2 (1967), 80-81.

2129. ----------. "Musikdämmerung in Hollywood." _Musica_, 14, No. 3 (Mar. 1960), 180-81.

2130. ----------. "'Sound' disqualifiziert." _Musica_, 18, No. 2 (Feb. 1964), 82-83.

2131. ----------. "'Sound' statt Musik." Musica, 17, No. 5 (1963), 228-29.

2132. Reisner, Joel. "Cinema Music." Music Journal, 26, No. 7 (Sept. 1968), 12, 14, 85.

    Concerning the film "Laudate," based upon Stravinsky's Symphony of Psalms.

2133. ----------. "Cinema Music." Music Journal, 26, No. 10 (Dec. 1968), 102-03.

    A survey of current film scores.

2134. Renan, Sheldon. An Introduction to the American Underground Film. New York: E. P. Dutton, 1967.

    Many references to music in film, with special emphasis on the work of John Whitney. Includes bibliography, pp. 295-96.

2135. Resberg, Lars. "Svensk jazzelit skriver filmmusik." Orkester Journalen (Stockholm), 36 (Jan. 1968), 11.

2136. Roskosz, Christian Gilbert. Muzyka w filmie amatorskim. Warsaw: CPARA, 1970.

    -- Rev. in Ruch Muzyczny (Warsaw), 15, No. 10 (1971), 17.

2137. Rotondi, U., ed. Musica: Biennio di cinema 1965/67 diretto da Nazareno Taddei. Milan: Centro S. Fedele, 1967.

2138. Rubin, M. "Music for a Lover's Kiss." New York Times, 113 (June 14, 1964), Section 2, p. 17.

2139. Sanucci, Frank. "So You Want to Be a Film Music Director." Clavier (Evanston, Ill.), 6, No. 6 (1967), 54-55.

2140. Sargeant, Winthrop. "Musical Events." The New Yorker, 44 (Mar. 30, 1968), 120ff.

2141. Schelp, Arend. "'Pan': een film van Herman van der Horst." Mens en Melodie (Utrecht), 17 (Jan. 1962), 5-7.

2142. Schiffer, George. "The Law and the Use of Music in Film." Film Comment, 1, No. 6 (Fall 1963), 39-43.

2143. Schnee, Charles. "Hollywood Plots with Music." Music Journal, 21, No. 4 (Apr. 1963), 48, 92.

2144. Schoenecker, Hans. Der Ton zum Amateurfilm. Halle: VEB Fotokinoverlag, 1963.

2145. Schoenfeld, H. "Disney Quick to Exploit Music." Variety, 245 (Dec. 21, 1966), 4.

2146. Schonberg, Harold C. "Movie Musicians." New York Times, 112 (Nov. 25, 1962), Section 2, p. 11.

2147. Schumach, Murray. "Hollywood 'Music.'" New York Times, 112 (June 23, 1963), Section 2, p. 7.

2148. Seelmann-Eggebert, Ulrich. "Eindrücke bei den III. Schweizerischen Filmtagen in Solothum." Neue Zeitschrift für Musik, 129, No. 3 (Mar. 1968), 108-09.

2149. Šefl, Vladimir. "Film potřebuje hudbu." Hudební Rozhledy, 17, No. 9 (1964), 355-58.

2150. ----------. "Hudba a film." Hudební Rozhledy, 19 (1966), 295-97.

2151. Senior, Evan. "Hoffnung at Home." Music and Musicians, 16 (Mar. 1968), 48-49.

2152. Shemel, Sidney, and M. William Krasilovsky. This Business of Music. Ed. Paul Ackerman. New York: Billboard Publ. Co., 1964.

2153. Sierpinski, Z. "Polsky festival hudebnich filmu." Hudební Rozhledy, 16, No. 16 (1963), 674.

2154. Smolka, Jaroslav. "I hudba z archivu je hudba." Hudební Rozhledy, 14, No. 14 (1961), 590-91.

2155. Somma, Robert. "Movie Music and Manfred Mann." Crawdaddy, No. 18 (Sept. 1968), 46-48.

2156. Souris, André. "Entretien." Script, 3, Nos. 10, 11, and 12 (1964).

2157. Spaeth, Sigmund. "In and Out of Tune." Music Journal, 20, No. 4 (Apr. 1962), 72.

    Concerning the practice of "dubbing" in films.

2158. ----------. "The Year in Film Music." Music Journal Annual (1963), 60ff.

2159. ----------. "The Year in Film Music." Music Journal Annual (1964), 129-30.

2160. ----------. "The Year in Film Music." Music Journal Annual (1965), 76ff.

2161. "Spolutvurce filmu." Hudební Rozhledy, 15, No. 7 (1962), 280-84.

2162. Staehling, Richard. "The Truth About Teen Movies." Rolling Stone, No. 49 (Dec. 27, 1969), 34-42ff.

    Includes a filmography, p. 44ff.

2163. Steen, T. M. F. "The Sound Track." Films in Review, 11, No. 2 (Feb. 1960), 109-12.

    Concerning music in movie "mysteries" and "thrillers."

2164. ----------. "The Sound Track." Films in Review, 11, No. 8 (Oct. 1960), 497-99.

    Concerning music for film "shorts."

2165. ----------. "The Sound Track." Films in Review, 11, No. 9 (Nov. 1960), 560-62.

    Film scores by Herrmann, Jarre, Waxman, and Gyorgy Seiber.

2166. ----------. "The Sound Track." Films in Review, 12, No. 2 (Feb. 1961), 116-18.

    Concerning music for cartoons.

2167. ----------. "The Sound Track." Films in Review, 12, No. 3 (Mar. 1961), 178-79.

    Film scores by Herrmann, Van Parys, and Malcolm Arnold.

2168. ----------. "The Sound Track." Films in Review, 12, No. 7 (Aug.-Sept. 1961), 436-37.

    Concerning music for "La Francaise et l'Amour."

2169. ----------. "The Sound Track." Films in Review, 12, No. 8 (Oct. 1961), 492-94.

    Concerning music, etc., by Friedrich Feher.

2170. ----------. "The Sound Track." Films in Review, 12, No. 9 (Nov. 1961), 559-60.

    Film scores by Alec Wilder.

2171. ----------. "The Sound Track." Films in Review, 13, No. 6 (June-July 1962), 369-70.

    Film scores by Jean Prodromidès.

2172. ----------. "The Sound Track." Films in Review, 13, No. 8 (Oct. 1962), 495-96.

    A survey of current film scores.

2173. Stepanov, O. "Pamjat' serdca." Sovetskaya muzyka, 25, No. 8 (Aug. 1961), 20-22.

    Concerning film scores by A. N. Aleksandrov.

2174. Stockton, Ann Mason, and Dorothy Remsen. "Motion Picture Recording." The American Harp Journal (Englewood, N.J.), 1, No. 2 (1967), 8-9.

2175. Sullivan, Liam. "Hollywood's Wonderful World of Music." Music Journal, 22, No. 5 (May 1964), 38, 54.

2176. Sundin, Bertil. "Film om jazzmusikerproblem." Orkester Journalen (Stockholm), 30 (Sept. 1962), 19.

2177. Swimmer, Saul. "Music Boxes on Film." Music Journal, 19, No. 6 (Sept. 1961), 68-69.

2178. Terpilowski, Lech. "Co w filmie 'nie gra.'" Ruch Muzyczny (Warsaw), 5, No. 11 (1961), 20-21.

2179. Thiel, Jörn. "Musikdramaturgie für den Bildschirm: Autoren-, Producer- und Regieprobleme." Neue Zeitschrift für Musik, 126, No. 4 (April 1965), 138-42.

   2179a. Also published in Das Orchester (Hamburg), 13 (May 1965), 171-77.

2180. ----------. "Die technischen Mittler in der Akademie für Musik und darstellende Kunst." Musikerziehung, 13 (June 1960), 205-10.

2181. Thomas, Anthony, and Page Cook. "The Sound Track." Films in Review, 15, No. 9 (Nov. 1964), 567-69.

2182. "To Touch a Moment." Time, 83, No. 3 (Jan. 17, 1964), 70.
         A brief survey of current film scoring activities, with references to music by Henry Mancini and others.

2183. Trachtenberg, L. "Sametki o musyke kino." Iskusstvo kino (Moscow), No. 11 (Nov. 1960), 109-111.

2184. Troitskaya, Galina. "Dama s Sobachkov." Sovetskaya muzyka, 24, No. 6 (June 1960), 117-19.

2185. Turroni, Giuseppe. Il sonoro nel film d'amatore. Milan: Edizioni Il Castello, 1967.

2186. Tuslar, Adelaide. Interview with Lawrence Morton. Tapes and transcript (from the University of California) are part of the project Oral History: American Music. New Haven, Conn.: Yale University, 1966.

2187. Vajda, Igor. "Hornakuv film 'Dvanast.'" Hudební Rozhledy, 21, No. 9 (1968), 266-67.

2188. Van Gelder, Lawrence. "'Looking at Music' Through 46 Films." New York Times, 132 (Feb. 11, 1983), Section C, p. 15.

2189. Vasina-Grossman, Vera. "Iz bloknota kinolyubitelya." Sovetskaya muzyka, 25, No. 1 (Jan. 1961), 38-45.

2190. ----------. "Iz bloknota kinolyubitelya." Sovetskaya muzyka, 26, No. 5 (May 1962), 119-22.

2191. Vertov, Dziga. "Tre canzoni su Lenin." Bianco e nero, 28, Nos. 3-4 (Mar.-Apr. 1967), 94-95.
         See #2116.

2192. "Von der Kinomusik zur Filmmusik." Musikalische Jugend (Regensburg), 16, No. 6 (1967-1968), 5.

2193. Weiler, Harold D. "Sound and Sight." Audio (Boulder, Colo.), 49 (Oct. 1965), 78ff.

2194. Weisman, Ben. "The Melody Lingers On." Music Journal, 26, No. 2 (Feb. 1968), 79.

2195. "What's the Score?" BMI: The Many Worlds of Music (Oct. 1968), 5-6.

2196. Whittenberg, Charles. "Ussachevsky's Film Music." American Composers Alliance Bulletin (New York), 11, No. 1 (1963), 5.

2197. Williams, Martin T. "Jazz at the Movies." Saturday Review, 50, No. 28 (July 15, 1967), 49.

>   References to scores by Miles Davis, John Lewis, and Sonny Rollins.
>
>   Reprinted in Limbacher, pp. 42-44. See #75.

2198. Wilson, John S. "Jacques Belasco." BMI: The Many Worlds of Music (Oct. 1967), 17.

2199. Yakubov, Manashir Ya. "Nezvanye Gosti." Sovetskaya muzyka, 24, No. 6 (June 1960), 119-20.

2200. Yanov-Yanovskaya, N. S. "Muzyka v kino i kinomuzyka." Sovetskaya muzyka, 33, No. 11 (Nov. 1969), 62-66.

2201. "Za 'kruglym stolom' redaktsii." Sovetskaya muzyka, 27, No. 3 (Mar. 1963), 94-97.

2202. Zeljenka, Ilja. "Starosti filmoveho skladatela." Slovenska Hudba (Bratislava, Czech.), 4 (Oct. 1960), 493-94.

2203. Zhito, Lee. "Hollywood and High Fidelity." High Fidelity, 12, No. 1 (Jan. 1962), 46-48ff.

2204. Zhivov, L. "Pesnya o druzhbe." Sovetskaya muzyka, 27, No. 6 (June 1963), 112-13.

>   SEE ALSO:
>
>   #13, #251(Jenkinson/Warner), #273(Narducy), #323, #471, #686(Lawrence), #885, #998(Stang), #2464(Lacombe), #3665(North), #4160, 4161, 4179(Whitney), #4814(Petri), #4875(H.-C. Schmidt), #4909(Tariverdiev), #5075(Feather), #5083, 5084, 5087-5089(IMC/IMZ), #5108, #5120, #5121(Shank), #5135 (UNESCO), #5324(Bornoff), #5364(UNESCO), #5670(Pauli), #5696(Sittner), #5972(Fleuret), #6017(Jélot-Blanc), #6024(A. Jones), #6150(Wiener), #6170 (Langsner), #6261, 6262(Farren), #6295(Smolian), #6299(ASCAP), and #6317.

Sound Techniques and Technology

2205. Margargle, H. "Let's Talk About Tape Synchronization." Audio (Boulder, Colo.), 46 (Nov. 1962), 25-26ff.

>   Concerning procedures for the use of tape recorders in synchronization with motion picture film.

2206. Mikoyan, N. "V edinstve s rezhisserom." Sovetskaya muzyka, 27, No. 6 (June 1963), 110-12.

2207. Nisbett, Alex. The Technique of the Sound Studio. New York: Hastings House, 1962.

>   A basic text.

2207a. Reprinted as The Technique of the Sound Studio: For Radio, Television, and Film. London and New York: Focal Press, 1974.

2208. Raksin, Ruby. Mathematics of Motion Picture Synchronization. Hollywood, Calif.: Pacific Music Papers, 1966.

>   See #2209.

2209. ----------. Technical Handbook of Mathematics for Motion Picture Music Synchronization. Sherman Oaks, Calif.: R-Y Publishing Co., 1972.

>   A revised second edition of #2208.

2210. Reisz, Karel, and Gavin Millar. The Technique of Film Editing. Enlarged edition. New York: Hastings House, 1968.

Includes the chapter "Sound Editing," pp. 256-72.

2211. Walter, Ernest. The Technique of the Film Cutting Room. The Library of Communication Techniques. New York: Hastings House; New York and London: Focal Press, 1969.

    2211a. Second revised edition, New York: Hastings House, 1973.

Includes Chapter 9: "Sound Editing," pp. 171-84, Chapter 10: "Music Editing," pp. 185-205, and Chapter 11: "Sound Dubbing," pp. 207-36.

SEE ALSO:

#155(Fielding), #199(Atkins), #223, 226(Cook), #241(Frayne et al.), #257 (Knudson), #268(McClelland), #312(Weiland), #1931(Frechet et al.), #1938 (Oringel), #1985(Bessy/Chardons), #1987(Bobker), #2050(Dolan), #2136(Roskosz), #3978(Rosenberg/Silverstein), and #6163(Citron/Whitney).

Music for T.V.

2212. Breuer, Robert. "Menottis Weg ins Freie über den amerikanische Bildschirm." Melos, 30, No. 4 (Apr. 1963), 133-34.

2213. Callahan, J. P. "Music: Television's Other Dimension." New York Times, 113 (June 7, 1964), Section 2, p. 15.

2214. Candra, Zdenek. "Televizni drama s hudbou." Hudební Rozhledy (Prague), 15, No. 8 (1962), 320.

2215. Cook, Page. "The Sound Track." Films in Review, 20, No. 4 (Apr. 1969), 244-46.

2216. Eastwood, Thomas. "Writing an Opera for Television." Composer, No. 25 (Autumn 1967), 4-10.

    2216a. Also published as "Kak pisat' teleoperu," in Sovetskaya Muzyka, 32, No. 4 (Apr. 1968), 136-38.

2217. Jungheinrich, Hans-Klaus. "Hörmassage: Musik in der Werbung." Musica, 23, No. 6 (June 1969), 559-61.

2218. Kaltofen, Günter. "Der Fernsehfilm." In Jahrbuch des Films, 1960. Berlin: Henschelverlag, 1961.

2219. Kaplan, Sol. "Music for TV: Incidental But Important." New York Times, 109 (Apr. 17, 1960), Section 2, p. 13.

2220. Müller-Medek, Tilo. "Musik im Hörspiel." Musik und Gesellschaft, 17, No. 2 (Feb. 1967), 91-94.

Concerning music for radio dramas and its influence on musical "taste."

2221. Nalle, Billy. "Music for Television Drama." Music Journal, 20, No. 1 (Jan. 1962), 120-21.

2222. Novick, Honey. "Readers Letters: A Composer Comments on the Way Television Has Affected New Music." The Canadian Composer/Le Compositeur Canadien, No. 156 (Dec. 1980), 34-35.

Also in French.

2223. Rhotert, Bernt. "Das Fernsehspiel: Regie, Dramaturgie und Sendung als Ausgangspunkte für den Versuch einer wesensgemassen Einordnung in die Moglichkeiten schöpferischer Mitteilung." Ph.D. Diss., Munich 1961.

Includes a bibliography, pp. 125-30.

2224. Rinaldi, Mario. La musica nelle trasmissioni radiotelevisive. Lo Smeraldo, No. 12. Caltanisetta: Sciascia, 1960.

2225. Stern, Walter H. "Music on the Air: Commissions for TV." Music Leader, 94 (Aug. 1962), 6.

2226. "Television." BMI: The Many Worlds of Music (Mar. 1967), 15; (Apr. 1967), 5; (June 1967), 7; and (Nov. 1967), 6-9.

> Concerning music for current television series and special productions.

2227. "Television." BMI: The Many Worlds of Music (Jan. 1968), 14-15; (Feb. 1968), 15; (Apr. 1968), 8; (May 1968), 8; (June 1968), 21; and (Oct. 1968), 20.

2228. "Television." BMI: The Many Worlds of Music (Jan. 1969), 5-7; (Apr. 1969), 5; (Oct. 1969), 4-7; and (Nov. 1969), 12.

2229. La T.V. -- Source d'inspiration musicale: Report of the RTB. Brussels: Radiodiffusion-Television Belge, 1968.

SEE ALSO:

#25(Comuzio), #44(Hagen), #2179(J. Thiel), #2711(Addison), #2777(Cook), #4429(Auer-Sedak), #4446(Battenberg), #4448(Bauche), #4526(Contamine), #4543(Desson), #4913, 4915(W. Thiel), #4927(Troitskaya), #5654(IMZ), and #5726(Bertz-Dostal).

1970's

History

2230. Aldridge, Henry. "Film Music." Cinegram Magazine (Ann Arbor, Mich.), 3, No. 1 (1978), 32-34.

2231. Alexander, Patricia. "Close-Ups: Tony Asher." Millimeter, 9 (Mar. 1979), 92.

> An interview.

2232. Alion, Yves. "Breve rencontre ... avec Bernard Dauman." Ecran 77, No. 64 (Dec. 15, 1977), 19-20.

2233. Amzoll, Stefan. "Für das Gedeihen einer musikalischen Radiokunst: Tendenzen medienspezifischer Komposition im Rundfunk." Musik und Gesellschaft, 27, No. 2 (Feb. 1977), 65-73.

2234. ----------. "'Die Stimmen der toten Dichter' -- eine Radio-Komposition von Georg Katzer." Musik und Gesellschaft, 28, No. 12 (Dec. 1978), 720-21.

2235. Aquino, John. "Overtones." Music Educators Journal, 64, No. 1 (Sept. 1977), 5.

> An introduction to the special film music issue of MEJ.

2236. "Arsfilm a hudba." Hudební Rozhledy (Prague), 30, No. 1 (1977), 28.

2237. Ashley, Robert. "Studs Terkel of the Avant-Garde." American Film, 3 (Feb. 1978), 28.

2238. Atkins, Irene Kahn. Interviews with Bill Stinson, 10/12/77 and 10/13/77. Tapes and transcripts are part of the project Oral History: American Music. New Haven, Conn.: Yale University, 1977.

2239. ----------. Interview with Morris Stoloff, 3/17/78. Tapes and transcript are part of the project Oral History: American Music. New Haven, Conn.: Yale University, 1978.

2240. Bachmann, Claus Henning. "IMZ-Medienkongress in Salzburg." Österreich-

ische Musikzeitschrift, 32, No. 10 (Oct. 1977), 458-59.

2241. "Background-Musik zu ihrem Spanien-Film." _Film und Ton_, 19 (May 1973), 12.

2242. Baratta, Paul. "A Closeup on Film Scoring." _Songwriter Magazine_ (Hollywood, Calif.), 3 (Dec. 1977), 36-39.

    An interview with Al Bart.

2243. Baronijan, Vartkes. "Filmska muzika." _Zvuk_ (Sarajevo), 3 (Fall 1973), 263-70.

2244. Bartholomew, David. "The Wicker Man." _Cinefantastique_, 6, No. 3 (1977), 4-19ff.

    Concerning the work of Paul Giovanni.

2245. Bascone, Salvo. "Cinema e musica pop." _Filmcritica_, 30, Nos. 296-297 (Aug. 1979), 292-98.

2246. Baumgarten, Paul A., and Donald C. Farber. _Producing, Financing and Distributing Film_. New York: Drama Book Specialists, 1973.

    Includes a chapter "Music," pp. 161-76.

2247. Bayne, Joris. "Le cinopera: une nouvelle avant-garde." _Ecran 74_, No. 23 (Mar. 1974), 42-48.

    Concerning films by Carmelo Bene and Werner Schroeter. Includes filmographies.

2248. "Beethoven a l'ecran." _Avant-Scene du cinéma_ (Paris), No. 213 (Oct. 1, 1978), 6.

2249. Beilby, Peter, and A. Cameron. "Production Report 'Blue Fin': Michael Carlos, Composer." _Cinema Papers_ (Melbourne, Austr.), No. 19 (Jan.-Feb. 1979), 210-11ff.

2250. Berg, Charles M. "Cinema Sings the Blues." _Cinema Journal_, 17, No. 2 (Spring 1978), 1-12.

2251. Bernstein, Elmer. "Collection News." _Film Music Notebook_, 3, No. 1 (1977), 1.

2252. ----------. "Collection News." _Film Music Notebook_, 3, No. 2 (1977), 1-2.

2253. ----------. "Collection News." _Film Music Notebook_, 4, No. 1 (1978), 1-2.

2254. ----------. "A Conversation with Leo Shuken." _Film Music Notebook_, 1, No. 3 (Spring 1975), 14-26.

2255. Blaedel, Michael, et al. "England." _Kosmorama_ (Copenhagen), 24, No. 139 (1978), 185-204.

    Includes filmographies.

2256. Bohn, Ronald L. "Oscars for Dramatic Scores During the '70's," in "Film Music in the 1970's: A Symposium." _Pro Musica Sana_, 8, No. 2 (Spring 1980), 16-19.

2257. Borchert, Christian. "Das Fotoporträt: Karl-Ernst Sasse." _Film und Fernsehen_ (Berlin, DDR), 4, No. 9 (1976), 20-21.

2258. Borisova, S., and Irma P. Yaunzem. "Bez yasnoy tseli." _Sovetskaya muzyka_, 36, No. 10 (Oct. 1972), 53-57.

2259. Bosseur, Jean-Yves. "Dossier Kagel: L'Oeuvre de Kagel." _Musique en jeu_, No. 7 (May 1972), 92-126.

    Includes filmography and bibliography.

  2259a. Also includes a section by Juan Allende-Blin: "Les films d'un compositeur," pp. 117-23.

2260. Boujut, Michel. "Jazz et cinéma: les occasions manquees." In _Cinéma et musique, 1960-1975_, a special issue of _Ecran 75_, No. 39 (Sept. 15, 1975), 26-30.

See #2463.

2261. Bradley, Jim. "Electronic Composers in Collaboration." Australasia Performing Right Association Journal, No. 9 (July 1973), 5.

     Concerning the film "Tullamarine."

2262. Bronchain, Christian M. "Rubrique musicale." APEC-Revue Belge du Cinéma, 14, No. 1 (1976), 92.

2263. ----------. "Rubrique musicale." APEC-Revue Belge du Cinéma, 14, No. 2 (1976), 102-09.

2264. Broughton, William. "Studio Musicians in Hollywood." The Instrumentalist (Evanston, Ill.), 33, No. 2 (Sept. 1978), 43-45.

2265. Brouwer, Leo. "Musiikki kuubalaisessa elokuvassa." Trans. by M. Yrttiaho. Filmihullu (Helsinki), No. 5 (1977), 14-15.

2266. Brown, Royal S. "The Best Film Scores of the 1970's." Fanfare, 5, No. 1 (1981), 44-45.

2267. ----------. "Changing the Score: Today's Film Composers Find Small Is Beautiful." American Film, 2, No. 6 (Apr. 1977), 62-63.

2268. ----------. "A Poignant Backdrop for Cinematic Horrors." High Fidelity and Musical America, 27, No. 5 (May 1977), 80.

     A review of a soundtrack recording of Pino Donaggio's score for "Carrie."

2269. ----------. "Soundtrack Albums: Why?" High Fidelity and Musical America, 25, No. 7 (July 1975), 49-55.

2270. ----------. "Sound Track: Changing the Score." American Film, 2, No. 6 (April 1977), 62-63.

2271. ----------. "Theater and Film." High Fidelity and Musical America, 26, No. 6 (June 1976), 108-09.

     Concerning music scores by Constant Lambert, Johnny Green, and others.

2272. Butler, Ivan. The Making of Feature Films: A Guide. Harmondsworth, Engl.: Penguin Books, 1971.

     References to music by Barry, Bennett, and Tiomkin in Chap. 11, pp. 158-66, and Chap. 12, pp. 167-71.

2273. Buxbaum, E. "Disney's Magical Music." Stereo Review, 42 (June 1979), 112.

     Soundtrack recording review.

2274. Canham, Cleve. "Aural Fixations: Dietz and Schwartz Alone Together." Audience (New York), 9 (Apr. 1977), 14.

     Concerning the work of Howard Dietz and Arthur Schwartz.

2275. Carter, Jack. "So How Would You Like to Go?" Crescendo International, 14 (Nov. 1975), 18.

2276. Champenier, Serge. "Le cinéma experimental a Bourges." Revue du cinéma/ Image et son, No 342 (Sept. 1979), 22-25.

     Includes filmography.

2277. Chanan, Michael. "Kagel's Films." Tempo (London), No. 110 (Sept. 1974), 45-46.

2278. ----------. "Mahler in Venice?" Music and Musicians, 19 (June 1971), 26-28.

     Concerning Visconti's film, "Death in Venice."

2279. Charent, Brian. "In Conversation with Gerald Pratley." Motion (Toronto), 4, No. 2 (1975), 42-43.

2280. Clarisse, Patrick. "Cine-disques: Guido et Maurizio de Angelis." Amis du film, cinéma et télévision (Brussels), No. 249 (Feb. 1977), 18-19.

2281. Cleave, Alan. "Let's Make Music for Our Movies." Movie Maker, 9, No. 1 (Jan. 1975), 30-31.

2282. ----------. "Let's Make Music for Our Movies." Movie Maker, 9, No. 2 (Feb. 1975), 98-99.

2283. ----------. "Let's Make Music for Our Movies." Movie Maker, 9, No. 3 (Mar. 1975), 182-83.

2284. ----------. "Let's Make Music for Our Movies." Movie Maker, 9, No. 4 (Apr. 1975), 238-39.

2285. ----------. "Let's Make Music for Our Movies." Movie Maker, 9, No. 5 (May 1975), 332-33.

2286. ----------. "Let's Make Music for Our Movies." Movie Maker, 9, No. 6 (June 1975), 398-99.

2287. ----------. "Let's Make Music for Our Movies." Movie Maker, 9, No. 7 (July 1975), 473ff.

2288. ----------. "Other People's Pictures." Movie Maker, 7, No. 2 (Feb. 1973), 110-13.

2289. Comuzio, Ermanno. "Colonne sonore: Musica ex-machina al servizio del cinema." Cineforum (Bergamo), No. 151 (Jan.-Feb. 1976), 9-18.

2290. ----------. "Ludwig Van e gli altri." Cineforum, No. 119 (Jan. 1973), 75-78.

2291. ----------. "La musica per film: cenerentola al ballo di mezzanotte." Cineforum, No. 189 (Nov. 1979), 660-66.

2292. Cook, G. Richardson. "Scoring with Composer Michael Small." Millimeter, 3 (Sept. 1975), 18-20ff.

2293. Cook, Page. "The Sound Track." Films in Review, 21, No. 1 (Jan. 1970), 42-44.
    References to music by David Amram, and Raymond Leppard.

2294. ----------. "-----." Films in Review, 21, No. 2 (Feb. 1970), 110-12.
    Film scores of 1969, with references to music by Delerue, Bernstein, and others.

2295. ----------. "-----." Films in Review, 21, No. 3 (Mar. 1970), 168-71.
    References to music by Delerue and Jarre, along with a brief survey of current film musicals.

2296. ----------. "-----." Films in Review, 21, No. 5 (May 1970), 295-99.
    References to scores by Rosenman, Bernstein, and Mikis Theodorakis.

2297. ----------. "-----." Films in Review, 21, No. 7 (Aug.-Sept 1970), 429-32.
    References to scores by Bernstein, Mancini, and others.

2298. ----------. "-----." Films in Review, 21, No. 8 (Oct. 1970), 494-96.
    References to scores by Rosenman and Scott Lee Hart.

2299. ----------. "-----." Films in Review, 21, No. 10 (Dec. 1970), 633-36.
    References to scores by Rozsa and by Frank Cordell.

2300. ----------. "-----." Films in Review, 22, No. 1 (Jan. 1971), 35-37.
    References to scores by John Scott and James Bernard.

2301. ----------. "-----." Films in Review, 22, No. 2 (Feb. 1971), 98-99, 102.
    Film scores of 1970, with references to music by Rozsa, Newman, and others.

2302. ----------. "The Sound Track." Films in Review, 22, No. 3 (Mar. 1971), 167-70.

        A survey of current film scores, with references to music by Delerue, Phillip Lambro, and others.

2303. ----------. "-----." Films in Review, 22, No. 4 (Apr. 1971), 225-28.

        References to music by John Barry, Michel Legrand, and Michael J. Lewis.

2304. ----------. "-----." Films in Review, 22, No. 5 (May 1971), 304-06.

        References to music by Herrmann and John Williams.

2305. ----------. "-----." Films in Review, 22, No. 7 (Aug.-Sept. 1971), 425-28.

        References to music by Friedhofer, Bernstein, Legrand, and Gerald Fried.

2306. ----------. "-----." Films in Review, 22, No. 10 (Dec. 1971), 631-34.

        References to music by Bernstein and Delerue.

2307. ----------. "-----." Films in Review, 23, No. 2 (Feb. 1972), 102-04.

        Film scores of 1971, with references to music by Herrmann, Raksin, John Williams, and others.

2308. ----------. "-----." Films in Review, 23, No. 3 (Mar. 1972), 181-84.

2309. ----------. "-----." Films in Review, 23, No. 4 (Apr. 1972), 236-39.

        References to music by John Barry and Jerry Fielding.

2310. ----------. "-----." Films in Review, 23, No. 5 (May 1972), 307-10.

        References to music by Mancini, Phillip Lambro, and Stephen Cosgrove.

2311. ----------. "-----." Films in Review, 23, No. 9 (Nov. 1972), 554-56.

2312. ----------. "-----." Films in Review, 24, No. 2 (Feb. 1973), 107-10.

        Film scores of 1972, with references to music by Fielding, Goldsmith, Jarre, Williams, and Scott Lee Hart.

2313. ----------. "-----." Films in Review, 24, No. 5 (May 1973), 298-300.

        Film music by Phillip Lambro.

2314. ----------. "-----." Films in Review, 24, No. 7 (Aug.-Sept. 1973), 426-28.

        Concerning soundtrack albums of music by Steiner and Newman.

2315. ----------. "-----." Films in Review, 24, No. 8 (Oct. 1973), 488-91.

        Concerning film musicals. Also, references to music by Richard Rodney Bennett.

2316. ----------. "-----." Films in Review, 24, No. 9 (Nov. 1973), 557-59.

        Concerning soundtrack albums.

2317. ----------. "-----." Films in Review, 24, No. 10 (Dec. 1973), 615-18.

        References to music by Herrmann and Friedhofer.

2318. ----------. "-----." Films in Review, 25, No. 1 (Jan. 1974), 35-38.

2319. ----------. "-----." Films in Review, 25, No. 2 (Feb. 1974), 104-07.

        Film scores of 1973, with references to music by Herrmann, Friedhofer, Goldsmith, Richard Rodney Bennett, and others.

2320. ----------. "-----." Films in Review, 25, No. 3 (Mar. 1974), 171-74, 177.

        Concerning soundtrack albums.

2321. ----------. "-----." Films in Review, 25, No. 9 (Nov. 1974), 560-63.

        Film music by Phillip Lambro.

2322. ----------. "The Sound Track." Films in Review, 26, No. 2 (Feb. 1975), 113-15.
> Film scores of 1974, with references to music by Bernstein, North, Rozsa, Rota, and others.

2323. ----------. "-----." Films in Review, 26, No. 3 (Mar. 1975), 167-69, 172.
> References to music by Stephen Sondheim and Nino Rota.

2324. ----------. "-----." Films in Review, 26, No. 6 (June-July 1975), 359-61.
> Concerning new soundtrack albums of music by Rozsa and others.

2325. ----------. "-----." Films in Review, 27, No. 1 (Jan. 1976), 45-48.
> References to music by Rozsa and Herrmann.

2326. ----------. "-----." Films in Review, 27, No. 2 (Feb. 1976), 116-18.
> Film scores of 1975, with references to music by Herrmann, Friedhofer, Scott Lee Hart, and David Shire.

2327. ----------. "-----." Films in Review, 27, No. 5 (May 1976), 308-10.
> References to music by Herrmann, Barry, and Legrand.

2328. ----------. "-----." Films in Review, 27, No. 10 (Dec. 1976), 623-25.
> References to music and soundtrack recordings of Rozsa and John Addison.

2329. ----------. "-----." Films in Review, 28, No. 2 (Feb. 1977), 112-15.

2330. ----------. "-----." Films in Review, 28, No. 4 (Apr. 1977), 239-41, 244.
> Film music by Rennie Dawson.

2331. ----------. "-----." Films in Review, 28, No. 8 (Oct. 1977), 495-98.
> References to music by Barry, Morricone, and Schifrin.

2332. ----------. "-----." Films in Review, 28, No. 9 (Nov. 1977), 550-53.
> References to music by Goldsmith and Addison.

2333. ----------. "-----." Films in Review, 28, No. 10 (Dec. 1977), 616-20.
> References to music by Delerue, David Grusin, and Stephen Cosgrove.

2334. ----------. "-----." Films in Review, 29, No. 2 (Feb. 1978), 102-05, 114.
> Film scores of 1977, with references to music by Rozsa, John Williams, and others.

2335. ----------. "-----." Films in Review, 29, No. 3 (Mar. 1978), 181-84.
> Concerning "Un Seul Moment," a filmed biography of Bizet.

2336. ----------. "-----." Films in Review, 29, No. 4 (Apr. 1978), 229-32, 236.
> Concerning soundtrack albums of music by Rozsa and Williams.

2337. ----------. "-----." Films in Review, 29, No. 6 (June-July 1978), 363-66.
> References to music by Addison, Goldsmith, Rosenman, Williams, and David Shire.

2338. ----------. "-----." Films in Review, 30, No. 1 (Jan. 1979), 38-41.
> Concerning the increased interest in soundtrack recordings.

2339. ----------. "-----." Films in Review, 30, No. 2 (Feb. 1979), 105-07, 124.
> Film and television scores of 1978, with references to music by Goldsmith, Williams, and others.

2340. ----------. "-----." Films in Review, 30, No. 3 (Mar. 1979), 167-70.
> Concerning reissues of Varese soundtrack albums.

2341. ----------. "The Sound Track." Films in Review, 30, No. 4 (Apr. 1979), 225-28.

An interview with Rennie Dawson.

2342. ----------. "-----." Films in Review, 31, No. 2 (Feb. 1980), 99-101, 105.

Film scores of 1979, with references to music by Rozsa, Goldsmith, Williams, and others.

2343. Corneau, A. "Le cinéma et Paris." Positif (Paris), Nos. 200-201-202 (Dec. 1977-Jan. 1978), 27-28.

2344. Corwin, Norman. "Lyrics, yeah." Producers Guild of America, Journal, 19, No. 2 (1977), 10-13.

Originally published in the periodical Westways.

2345. "Crescendo Presents a Special Showing of 'The Score,' a Significant Film Documentary." Crescendo International, 14 (May 1976), 4.

See #114.

2346. Creston, Paul. "Music and Mass Media." Music Educators Journal, 56, No. 8 (Apr. 1970), 35-36ff.

2347. Crystal, Tamar. "The Men Who Make the Music that Makes Madison Avenue Move." Millimeter, 5 (Apr. 1977), 36-38ff.

Concerning the work of Steve Chapin, Lenny Hambro, Don Elliott, Bernie Hoffer, Steve Karmen, Richard Lavsky, Stephen Lawrence, Rich Look, and David Lucas.

2348. ----------. "The Men Who Make the Music that Makes Madison Avenue Move." Millimeter, 5 (May 1977), 46-48ff.

2349. Culshaw, John. "2001: A Space Oddity." High Fidelity and Musical America, 32, No. 2 (Feb. 1982), 57.

Concerning Kubrick's use of music in film.

2350. Curi, Giandomenico. "I ribelli del reggae (Da Londra cinque film sulla musica popolare della Giamaica)." L'altro cinema (Nov.-Dec. 1978).

2351. "Cyril J. Mockridge: Gli addii." Bianco e nero (Rome), 40 (May-June 1979), 141-43.

Obituary.

2352. Davis, Carl. "'The World at War': Composing the Music." Society of Film and Television Arts Journal, 2, Nos. 9-10 (1974), 24-26.

2353. De Fornari, Oreste. "Perché 'The Bandwagon' e un bel film." Filmcritica, 28, Nos. 279-280 (Dec. 1977), 371-78.

2354. De Marco, Mario. "Why Not Bob Nolan?" Classic Film Collector, No. 64 (July 1979), 54.

2355. DeMary, Tom. "A Conversation with David Shire." Soundtrack Collectors Newsletter, 2, No. 9 (1977), 3-10; and 2, No. 10 (1977), 17-22.

Includes filmography and discography.

2356. De Prez, Daniel. "Music: Scoring." Cinemonkey (Portland, Ore.), 5, No. 1 (No. 16), (1979), 59-61.

2357. ----------. "Music: 'Scoring' or 'Licensed to Sync.'" Cinemonkey (Portland, Ore.), 4, No. 4 (No. 15), (1978), 52-53.

2358. ----------. "Sound as Score: The Lack of Music in 'Interiors.'" Cinemonkey (Portland, Ore.), 5, No. 1 (No. 16), (1979), 49.

2359. Deschenne, H. "Portrait: Alain Pierre." APEC-Revue Belge du cinéma, 14, No. 1 (1976), 3-5.

2360. DeWald, Frank. "A Backward Glance," in "Film Music in the 1970's: A Symposium." Pro Musica Sana, 8, No. 2 (Spring 1980), 6-8.

2361. ----------. "Filmusic and Film Music." Pro Musica Sana, 1, No. 3 (Fall 1972), 2-5.

2362. DiVanni, Roberto. "Love Makes Sweet Music." Filmcritica (Rome), 28, Nos. 279-280 (Dec. 1977), 363-65.

2363. Doherty, Jim. "Music for Worlds to Come." Midnight Marquee (Baltimore), No. 29 (Oct. 1980), 21-25.

    References to music by Barry, Goldsmith, and Rozsa.

2364. ----------. "'The Night of the Hunter': A Musical Critique." Midnight Marquee (Baltimore), No. 26 (Sept. 1977), 13-15.

    1955 film score by Walter Schumann.

2365. Donner, Otto, and Kaj Chydenius. "Aania ilman kuvaa." Filmihullu (Helsinki), No. 5 (1977), 20-24.

2366. Dostie, Bruno, et al. "En premiere: 'Le soleil se leve en retard,' un film d'Andre Brassard." Cinéma Quebec (Montreal), 5, No. 6 (1977), insert following p. 26 (16 pages).

    Concerning the work of Pierre Huet and Robert Leger. Includes filmography.

2367. Duynslaegher, Patrick. "Filmmuziek." Film en Televisie (Brussels), Nos. 228-229 (May-June 1976), 18-19.

    References to music by Herrmann, Jaubert, and François de Roubaix.

2368. Eisenberg, Ursula. "Filmmusik im Unterricht." Musik und Bildung, 9 (Dec. 1977), 686-89.

2369. Elia, Maurice. "Un cinéma en perpetuel devenir." Cinéma 73, Nos. 178-179 (July-Aug. 1973), 200-206.

    References to films by Stanley Kubrick and others.

2370. Eliezer, Zheyna. "Muzikata v chetiri bulgarski filma." Bulgarska Muzika (Sofia), 26, No. 6 (June 1975), 62-63.

2371. Elley, Derek. "Pre-Renaissance?," in "Film Music in the 1970's: A Symposium." Pro Musica Sana, 8, No. 2 (Spring 1980), 13-14.

2372. ----------. "Versatility." Films and Filming, 22, No. 7 (Apr. 1976), 44-46.

    Concerning the work of Wilfred Josephs.

2373. Evans, Colin. "Sound Pictures." Times Educational Supplement (London), No. 3244 (Aug. 5, 1977), 16.

2374. Fabian, Imre. "Berichte aus Teheran." Opernwelt, 19, No. 8 (1978), 15.

    Concerning the Internationales Festival der Musikfilme in Teheran.

2375. Fano, Michel. "Film, partition sonore." Musique en jeu, No. 21 (Nov. 1975), 10-13.

2376. ----------. "Musica e film." Filmcritica, 30, Nos. 296-297 (Aug. 1979), 288-91.

2377. Farren, Jonathan. "Chantons sous les sunlights." Cinéma 75, No. 200 (July-Aug. 1975), 27-33.

    Includes bibliography.

2378. ----------. "Jazz et cinéma: variations sur une couleur." Cinéma 75, No. 203 (Nov. 1975), 36-38.

2379. ----------. "Les Rapports cinéma musique." Cinéma 75, No. 200 (July-Aug. 1975), 41-43.

    Concerning the use of popular music and rock music in films.

2380. Feather, Leonard. "Don Ellis and 'The French Connection.'" Melody Maker,

47 (Apr. 22, 1972), 30.

2381. ----------. "From Pen to Screen: Don Ellis." International Musician, 70 (June 1972), 3.

2382. ----------. "From Pen to Screen: Fred Karlin." International Musician, 70 (Dec. 1971), 5ff.

2383. ----------. "From Pen to Screen: Fred Werner." International Musician, 73, No. 4 (Oct. 1974), 7, 32.

2384. ----------. "From Pen to Screen: Tom McIntosh." International Musician, 72, No. 4 (Oct. 1973), 9, 22.

2385. Fezco, M. "Zabriskie and The Floyd." Jazz and Pop, 9 (June 1970), 8.
       Film music by Pink Floyd.

2386. Fichter, Gerald. "Filmharmonic '77." The Max Steiner Journal, No. 2 (1978), 17.

2387. Fiedel, Robert D. "Recordings: Mystic Romanticism and Tudor Pomp." Take One (Montreal), 5, No. 6 (Jan. 1977), 27-28.
       References to music by Bernard Herrmann and Miklos Rozsa.

2388. ----------. "Sound Track: The Filmharmonic." American Film, 3, No. 6 (Apr. 1978), 64-65.

2389. Filipova, Veselka. "Muzika kum filmi." Bulgarska Muzika (Sofia), 26, No. 8 (Oct. 1975), 47.

2390. "Films." BMI: The Many Worlds of Music (Jan. 1972), 20-23; (Mar. 1972), 22-23; (Apr. 1972), 2, 4-5.
       Concerning scores for current films and film musicals.

2391. "Film Scores Return to Lush Orchestral Sound Cheers Patrick Williams." Variety, 295 (July 25, 1979), 43.

2392. "Film Scoring Course Started at University of Miami." The School Musician, Director, and Teacher (Chicago), 44, No. 10 (June-July 1973), 36.

2393. "Film Scoring: Tough But Lucrative." The Music Scene (Ontario), No. 256 (Nov.-Dec. 1970), 10.

2394. "Der Film soll tönen: Musik für Amateurfilme." Film und Ton, 20 (Mar. 1974), 10.

2395. Finkhousen, George. "The New Sound: Non-Synchronized Sound Enhances Theatre's Showmanship Performance." Boxoffice, 113 (Aug. 21, 1978), MT4ff.

2396. Fitzpatrick, John. "Introduction" and "Afterward" to "Film Music in the 1970's: A Symposium." Pro Musica Sana, 8, No. 2 (Spring 1980), 4-6, 24-28.
       Fitzpatrick's comments are continued in Pro Musica Sana, 8, No. 4 (Fall 1980), 19-20.

2397. Fong-Torres, Ben, et al. "Doin' the Hollywood Hustle: Rock on Reels." Rolling Stone, No. 263 (Apr. 20, 1978), 46-47.
       Concerning music by The Beatles and others.

2398. Forrest, Rick. "Soundtracks and Original Cast Recordings: The Creative Dilemma." Billboard, 91 (Oct. 6, 1979), ST2ff.

2399. Fovez, J. E. "Musique de film." APEC-Revue Belge du cinéma (Brussels), 1 (1973-1974), 18-19.

2400. Fox, T. C. "Martin Scorsese's Elegy for a Big-Time Band." Village Voice, 23 (May 29, 1978), 41ff.
       Concerning music for the film "The Last Waltz."

2401. Fraccaro, Steven. "Close-Ups: Lenny Hambro." Millimeter, 7 (Dec. 1979), 142-43.

2402. ----------. "Close-Ups: Ron Lockhart." Millimeter, 7 (Dec. 1979), 143-44.

2403. Fränkel, Salomo. "Monsterschau der Experimente in München." Melos, 39, No. 6 (Nov.-Dec. 1972), 349-55.

2404. Freedland, Nat. "Film Scoring No Snap for Rock Talent." Billboard, 85 (Dec. 8, 1973), 38.

2405. Funk, Heinz. "Der Moog-Synthesizer." Fernseh- und Kino-Technik, 27 (Dec. 1973), 427-29.

2406. Gardiner, Bennit. "The Tchaikovsky Film." Musical Events (London), 26 (May 1971), 13-14.
       Musical score by Dimitri Tiomkin.

2407. Garel, Alain. "Music Lovers: La musique de films." Écran 79, No. 78 (Mar. 15, 1979), 83-84.
       References to music by Bernard Herrmann and John Williams.

2408. Gay, Ken. "Documentary." Films and Filming, 20, No. 1 (Oct. 1973), 72.

2409. Geduld, Carolyn. Filmguide to "2001: A Space Odyssey." Bloomington, Ind.: Indiana University Press, 1973.

2410. Genkov, Georgi. "Nyakoi misli vuv vruzka s 'Bashcha mi boiadziiiata.'" Kinoizkusstvo (Sofia), 29 (Mar. 1974), 35-36.

2411. Giusti, Marco. "Il cinema canta." Filmcritica (Rome), 28, Nos. 279-280 (Dec. 1977), 366-70.

2412. Goldovskaia, Marina. "Snimat' -- kak chuvstvovat'!" Iskusstvo kino, No. 7 (1979), 82-100.
       Concerning the work of composer Levan Paatshvili.

2413. Grant, Jacques. "Promoteur de 'Cinéma et Rock,' Bernard Dauman ou le feeling." Cinéma 75, No. 200 (July-Aug. 1975), 21-27.
       An interview.

2414. Green, Archie. "Commercial Music Graphics: Chulas Fronteras." The John Edwards Memorial Foundation Quarterly (U.C.L.A.), 12, No. 43 (1976), 138-46.

2415. Grein, Paul. "Wonder Score a Rarity in Films." Billboard, 91 (Dec. 15, 1979), 43.
       Concerning Stevie Wonder's "The Secret Life of Plants."

2416. Gronau, K. "How to Score." Songwriter Magazine (Hollywood, Calif.), 4 (May 1979), 16-19.

2417. Grützner, Verz. "Musik in neueren Gegenwartsfilmen der DEFA." Musik und Gesellschaft, 22, No. 4 (Apr. 1972), 193-204.

2418. ----------. "Von Bach bis Beat: Tendenzen in der Filmmusik der neueren DEFA-Spielfilmproduktion." Film und Fernsehen, 4, No. 8 (1976), 17-21.

2419. Guiod, Jacques. "Un compositeur français: Entretien avec François De Roubaix." In Cinéma et musique, 1960-1975, a special issue of Écran 75, No. 39 (Sept. 15, 1975), 17-22.
       See #2463.

2420. Gusev, Sergei. "'Chemu, chemu svideteli my byli ...'" Iskusstvo kino, No. 7 (1979), 21-32.

2421. Hamer, Alan. "Roll of Honour," in "Film Music in the 1970's: A Symposium." Pro Musica Sana, 8, No. 2 (Spring 1980), 19-21.

2422. Hamilton, Arthur. "It's a Whole New Scene for Film Cleffers: Arthur Hamilton." Variety (Apr. 7, 1971).
       An interview.

2423. Harmetz, Aljean. "A Movie Tunesmith is Rediscovered at 85." New York Times,

129 (Dec. 7, 1979), Section C, p. 3.

Concerning the work of Henry Warren.

2424. Harmon, Larry. "The Clown Needs Music." Music Journal, 28, No. 4 (Apr. 1970), 20.

2425. Harvey, Steven. "Eine Kleiser Rockmusik." Film Comment, 14, No. 4 (July-Aug. 1978), 15-16.

Concerning the work of director Randal Kleiser.

2426. Helman, Alicja. "Sonorystyka filmu 'Na wylot.'" Kino, 8 (Sept. 1973), 16-19.

2427. Herpel, Karlheinz. "Besser geht's nicht immer mit Musik." Film und Ton, 25 (Oct. 1979), 30-31.

2428. Hiemenz, Jack. "Music to Commit Violence By." High Fidelity and Musical America, 22 (May 1972), 76-77.

Concerning Kubrick's use of music in "Clockwork Orange."

2429. Higham, Charles. "You May Not Leave the Movie House Singing Their Songs, But ..." New York Times, 124 (May 25, 1975), Section 2, p. 11.

2430. Huet, Pierre. "Crazy Horse de Paris." Cinéma 77, No. 228 (Dec. 1977), 84.

2431. Hutchinson, Ivan. "Brian May." Cinema Papers (Melbourne, Austr.), No. 17 (Aug.-Sept. 1978), 32-33.

2432. ----------. "The British Soundtrack." Cinema Papers (Melbourne, Austr.), 3 (June-July 1976), 79.

2433. Ilieva, Bagryana. "Muzikata kum pet bulgarski filma." Bulgarska Muzika (Sofia), 24, No. 10 (Dec. 1973), 67-68.

2434. Internationales Musikzentrum, Vienna. IMZ Report: Musik und Medien: Ein kritischer Bericht über IMZ-Veranstaltungen in München, Wien, Lugano, Brüssel und Helsinki. Ed. Jörn Thiel. Vienna: IMZ, 1973.

In German, French, and English. Includes (in the English section) reports on "The Presentation of New Music on TV," pp. 86-91, "Concert Reportage on Television," pp. 92-154, and a composer index, p. 155.

-- Rev. in The World of Music (UNESCO), 16, No. 1 (1974), 53-57.

2435. Ivanick, Daniel. "Ideas: Music in Films." Today's Filmmaker (New York), 5 (Spring 1978), 8-9.

2436. Jacques, Arthur O. "Law and Music." Motion (Toronto), 4, No. 2 (1975), 13.

2437. Jeancolas, Jean-Pierre. "Deux entretiens sur 'Vitam et sanguinem.'" Positif (Paris), No. 218 (May 1979), 49-54.

Interviews with Gyula Hernadi and composer Janos Kende.

2438. "Les jeunes et la musique." Telecine (Paris), No. 228 (May 1978), 25.

2439. "John Cameron Says Faddish Music Ideas Can Be a Film Hazard." Variety, 275 (May 15, 1974), 59.

2440. Jones, M. "Bringing Jazz to the Screen." Melody Maker, 45 (June 13, 1970), 10.

2441. Jordan, Isabelle. "Les petales de muchkunda." Positif (Paris), No. 219 (June 1979), 26-28.

Concerning music in Indian films.

2442. Kagarlitskaya, Anna. "Composer Evgeny Doga: Music Is the Soul of a Film." Soviet Film (Moscow), No. 255 (1978), 40-41.

2443. Kasha, Al, with Joel Hirschhorn and Irwin Kostal. Seminar on film music: AFI/CAFS, Nov. 9, 1977 (3:30 p.m.). Transcript of the seminar is held at the AFI/Louis B. Mayer Library (Los Angeles).

Concerning the collaboration on music for Disney's "Pete's Dragon," and problems of scoring for animated films.

2444. Kaufer, Stefan. _A Journal of the Plague Years_. New York: Atheneum, 1973.

2445. Kemp, Jeffery. "Write What the Film Needs: An Interview with Elisabeth Lutyens." _Sight and Sound_, 43, No. 4 (Autumn 1974), 203-05, 248.

2446. Kent, Mike. "Mini Tests: More Mood Music." _Film Making_ (Cambridge), 15 (Nov. 1977), 45.

2447. ----------. "Sound Sense: Fit the Movie to the Music." _Film Making_ (Cambridge), 18 (Oct. 1980), 28-29.

2448. ----------. "Sound Sense: How to Cut to Music and Not Miss a Beat." _Film Making_ (Cambridge), 16 (Jan. 1978), 32-33.

2449. ----------. "Sound Sense: The Sound of Music." _Film Making_ (Cambridge), 17 (Sept. 1979), 49ff.

2450. Keogh, M. "Young Composers at Film Unit." _Australasian Performing Right Association Journal_, No. 8 (Jan. 1973), 9.

2451. Keremidčieva-Dudekova, Mariya. "Za muzikata v našija animacionen film." _Bulgarska Muzika_, 25, No. 3 (1974), 73-74.

2452. Kerouini, Joseph. "Musique et cinéma: L'Exemple de la musique bretonne." _Cinéma pratique_, No. 127 (Nov.-Dec. 1973), 246-47.

2453. Ketting, Otto. "Film Music: Finished One Day, Recorded the Next and Usually Forgotten the Day After." _Key Notes Donemus_ (Amsterdam), 10, No. 2 (1979), 20-27.

2454. Kirk, Cynthia. "Billy Goldenberg." _BMI: The Many Worlds of Music_ (Summer 1975), 32-33.

2455. ----------. "Kirk on Film Scoring." _BMI: The Many Worlds of Music_ (Jan. 1971), 11.

2456. Koldys, Mark. "Morton Gould -- Interviewed by Mark Koldys." _Pro Musica Sana_, 6, No. 4 (Fall 1978), 12-14.

Concerning music for the T.V. mini-series "The Holocaust."

2457. ----------. "The State of the Art," in "Film Music in the 1970's: A Symposium." _Pro Musica Sana_, 8, No. 2 (Spring 1980), 9-11.

References to music by Goldsmith, Rozsa, and Williams.

2458. Köppl, Georg. "'F+T': Filmprofi - Diplom." _Film und Ton_, 22 (Oct. 1976), 12ff.

2459. Korall, Burt. "Perspective: Jazz Captains of Cinema/Video." _Down Beat_, 43, No. 4 (Feb. 26, 1976), 42-44.

2460. Kozintsev, Grigorii M. "Lo spàzio della tragedia." Trans. E. Suran. _Filmcritica_, 24 (Aug. 1973), 216-18.

Originally published in _Iskusstvo kino_, No. 1 (Jan. 1973).

2461. Krellmann, Hanspeter. "Köln: Kurse für Neue Musik." _Schweizerische Musikzeitung_, 110, No. 1 (1970), 43-44.

2462. Kurčenko, Alexandr. "Zametki o muzyke v mnogoserijnych fil'mach." _Sovetskaya muzyka_, 38, No. 8 (Aug. 1974), 35-41.

2463. Lacombe, Alain, ed. _Cinéma et musique, 1960-1975_. A special issue of _Écran 75_, No. 39 (Sept. 15, 1975).

Includes a chronology, a biographical dictionary, and articles by M. Boujut (#2260), A. Garel et al. (#6311), J. Guiod (#2419), A. Lacombe (#2464, #2465, #2641), G. Lenne (#2473), and J. Morlot and D. Bellemain (#2497).

2464. ----------. "Quinze ans de musique de films (1960-1975)." In _Cinéma et musique, 1960-1975_, a special issue of _Écran 75_, No. 39 (Sept. 15, 1975),

4-10.

See #2463.

2465. ----------. "Table ronde: cineastes et musiciens, avec Michel Colombier, Georges Delerue et Jacques Demy." In Cinéma et musique, 1960-1975, a special issue of Écran 75, No. 39 (Sept. 15, 1975), 11-16.

See #2463.

2466. Landy, Elliot. "Experimente mit Film und Musik, Musik und Film." Film und Ton, 19 (Dec. 1973), 18ff.

2467. Lange, Wolfgang. "Über das Komponieren für den Film: Werkstattgespräch mit dem Komponisten Siegfried Matthus." Film und Fernsehen (Berlin, DDR), 6, No. 10 (1978), 16-21.

An interview. Includes filmography.

2468. Lasher, John Steven. "Film Music in the Concert Hall." Symphony News (Newsletter of the American Symphony Orchestra League), 25, No. 1 (Feb.-Mar. 1974), 9-13.

Program notes of a 1973 performance by the Buffalo Philharmonic Orchestra which included film music "highlights."

2469. Latham, Richard. "Film-n-music." Royal College of Music Magazine (London), 68, No. 2 (1972), 43.

2470. Lees, Gene. "Focus on Education: School for Scoring." American Film, 3, No. 2 (Nov. 1977), 68-69.

Concerning the film music curriculum at the University of Colorado, designed by Pat Williams.

2471. ----------. "The Music Director: Good Step Backwards." American Film, 2, No. 7 (May 1977), 72-73.

Concerning the work of Dominic Frontiere, music director at Paramount Studios.

2472. ----------. "When the Music Stopped." High Fidelity and Musical America, 22, No. 7 (July 1972), 20.

2473. Lenne, Gérard. "Pop music et cinéma: belles fêtes, folles fêtes." In Cinéma et musique, 1960-1975, a special issue of Écran 75, No. 39 (Sept. 15, 1975), 37-44.

See #2463.

2474. Lewin, Frank. "Motion Picture Music: New Ways of Viewing -- New Ways of Listening." Today's Film Maker (New York), 1 (May 1972), 43, 64.

2475. Lexman, Juraj. "Využitie Novej hudby vo filme." Slovenská hudba, 15, No. 5 (1971), 186-92.

2476. Lilienthal, Peter, and Joachim E. Berendt. "Jazz im Film: 'Noon in Tunisia.'" Jazz Podium (Stuttgart), 21 (Aug. 1972), 20-21.

2477. Littman, Bill. "Dracula: His Music." Photon (New York), No. 27 (1977), 42.

2478. Luckým, Štěpánem (Stepan Lucky). "O filmové hudbě se Štěpánem Luckým." Hudební Rozhledy (Prague), 25, No. 10 (Oct. 1972), 455-56.

An interview.

2479. Maasch, Erik. "Vertonen von Amateur-Filmen in der Schule." Film und Ton, 19, No. 4 (Apr. 1973), 8ff.

2480. MacBean, James Roy. Film and Revolution. Bloomington, Ind.: Indiana University Press, 1976.

Includes reprints of articles originally published in Film Quarterly.

2481. Macklin, F. Anthony. "Welcome to Lion's Gate: Interviews with Director Alan Rudolph and Composer Richard Baskin." Film Heritage, 12, No. 1 (Fall 1976), 1-17.

2482. Magliozzi, Ron. "Starting a Soundtrack Collection." The Thousand Eyes
Magazine, 2, No. 6 (Feb. 1977).

2483. Maltin, Leonard. "The Movies: Warner's First Fifty Years." Stereo Review,
33, No. 1 (July 1974), 86.

    Soundtrack album review.

2484. Mandelli, Alfredo. "Mahler, non Mahler." Rassegna Musicale Curci (Milan),
24, No. 2 (1971), 6-16.

    Concerning Visconti's "Death in Venice."

2485. Mann, John. "Music and the Heroic." The Max Steiner Music Society News
Letter, No. 48 (Autumn 1976), 6.

2486. Marcus, Greil. "A Little Grace to Move On Through." Take One, 2, No. 11
(June 1970), 21-22.

2487. Maremaa, Thomas. "The Sound of Movie Music." New York Times, 125 (Mar. 28,
1976), Section 6, pp. 40-41.

    References to music by Herrmann, Korngold, Rozsa, Marvin
    Hamlisch, Richard Baskin, and David Shire.

2488. Marsh, Dave. "Schlock Around the Rock." Film Comment, 14, No. 4 (July-
Aug. 1978), 7-13.

2489. Maurelli, Guido. "'Due pezzi di pane': linguaggio musicale, linguaggio
verbale." Filmcritica (Rome), 30, No. 292 (Feb. 1979), 76-78.

2490. Mayer, Michael F. The Film Industries. New York: Hastings House, 1973.

    Includes the chapter (13) "Music and Film," pp. 191-95,
    dealing with legal and business aspects of film music.

2491. Mayr, William. "Close-Ups: Norman Richards." Millimeter, 7 (July 1979),
89-90.

2492. Mazurelle, Julien. "Patrick Moraz." Amis du film: Cinéma et télévision
(Brussels), No. 282 (Nov. 1979), 39.

2493. Mérigeau, Pascal. "'Music Lovers': travellings en si bemol mineur." Revue du cinéma/Image et son, No. 297 (June/July 1975), 42-48.

2494. Moret, Henry. "Cyril J. Mockridge." Écran 79, No. 78 (Mar. 15, 1979), 85.

    Obituary.

2495. Morgan, John W. "A Survey of Film Music." The Max Steiner Music Society
News Letter, No. 43 (Summer 1975), 7-8.

    Concerning a proposed film music curriculum at San Diego
    State University.

2496. Morley, Glenn. "The Synthesizer: The Mockingbird of Instruments." Cinema
Canada (Montreal), Nos. 60-61 (Dec. 1979-Jan. 1980), 45-47.

2497. Morlot, Jean-Claude, and Daniel Bellemain. "Soul music et cinéma: une noire
vaut deux blanches." In Cinéma et musique, 1960-1975, a special issue of
Écran 75, No. 39 (Sept. 15, 1975), 31-36.

    See #2463.

2498. "Move to Preserve Film Music Series." Variety, No. 286 (Apr. 20, 1977),
107.

2499. "Movies Should Be Heard." Music Educators Journal, 56 (Apr. 1970), 89.

2500. "Music Scoring: Editing Library Music." Business Screen (July 1978), 21.

2501. "Musik zum Film." Film und Ton, 20 (Feb. 1974), 49.

2502. Nacheva, Milka. "Muzikata vuv filma 'Avtostop.'" Bulgarska Muzika (Sofia),
23, No. 3 (1972), 77.

2503. Nadasy, Laszlo. "Mit jelent onek a film?" Filmkultura (Budapest), 12

(Nov.-Dec. 1976), 74-80.

An interview with Andras Pernye.

2504. Nau, Peter. "Drohende Gefahr, Angst Katastrophe." Filmkritik (Munich), 22 (Mar. 1978), 138-45.

2505. ----------. "Hauptstädtisches Journal: Filmmusik Workshop." Filmkritik (Munich), 22 (Mar. 1978), 114-37.

Includes bibliography.

2506. ----------. "Werner Eisbrenner im Gespräch." Filmkritik (Munich), 19 (Oct. 1975), 449-54.

2507. Nemitz, Donald. "Film Music Has a New Course." The Max Steiner Music Society News Letter, No. 47 (Summer 1976), 3-4.

Concerning a new course at Westminster College, Salt Lake City, Utah.

2508. Netzeband, Gunter. "In Amerika: Interview mit Konrad Wolf." Film und Fernsehen (Berlin, DDR), 3, No. 4 (Sept. 1975), 34-42.

2509. Noguez, Dominique. "Enseigner le cinéma à l'universite." Revue d'esthétique, 24, No. 1 (1971), 61-74.

2510. Nolan, Jack Edmund. "Films on T.V." Films in Review, 24, No. 7 (Aug.-Sept. 1973), 429-31.

Concerning the use of music by Cole Porter in T.V. productions.

2511. Norquist, Patricia Alexander. "Close-Up: John Tartaglia." Millimeter, 6 (May 1978), 156-57.

2512. Oliva, Ljubomir. "Nova moda v USA: diskofilmy." Film a doba (Prague), 24 (Oct. 1978), 592.

2513. "Outer-Space Film Music Giving B. O. Lift-Off to Symphs." Variety, No. 290 (Feb. 8, 1978), 24.

2514. Palmer, Christopher. "British Composers for the Film: Frank Cordell." Performing Right (London), No. 58 (Dec. 1972), 13-19.

2515. ----------. "The Changing World of Film Music." Crescendo International, 10 (Apr. 1972), 8ff.

2516. ----------. "The Remembrance of Things Past." Crescendo International, 14 (Oct. 1975), 26-27.

2517. ----------. "Whatever Happened to Hollywood Music?" Crescendo International, 12 (Apr. 1974), 8-10.

2518. Pauli, Hansjörg J. "Auf der Jagd nach den zündenden Nummern." Neue Musikzeitung (Regensburg), 28, No. 2 (1979), 3.

2519. ----------. "Komponisten an Hollywoods Fliessbändern." Neue Musikzeitung (Regensburg), 28, No. 1 (1979), 3.

2520. Pavelek, James ("Pav"). "A Tribute to California Film Composers." The Max Steiner Music Society News Letter, No. 48 (Autumn 1976), 8-10; and No. 49 (Winter 1976), 8-10.

A symposium with Elmer Bernstein, Ernest Gold, Arthur Kleiner, David Raksin, and Fred Steiner, held at the Oakland Museum, March 12, 1976.

2521. Penn, William. "The Celluloid Image and Mixed Media." The Composer (Cleveland, Ohio), 1, No. 4 (1970), 179.

2522. "Perche ci occupiamo di musica e di animazione." Cineforum, No. 162 (Feb. 1977), 83-85.

2523. Pistagnesi, Patrizia, Adriano Aprà, and Gianni Menon, eds. Il melodramma nel cinema italiano: Quaderno degli Incontri Cinematografici di Monticelli

Terme, 1977.

Includes articles on film music by several contributors.

2524. Pratley, Gerald. "The Ups and Downs of Creating Music for Canadian Feature Films." The Canadian Composer (Toronto), No. 104 (Oct. 1975), 10-15.

2525. Predal, Rene. "François de Roubaix." Cinéma 76 (Paris), No. 205 (Jan. 1976), 146-47.

2526. "PRO-Canada on Music and Film Offensive." Cinemag, No. 27 (Nov. 26, 1979), 14.

2527. Prox, Lothar. "Perspektiven einer Wiederaufbereitung von Stummfilmmusik." In Stummfilmmusik Gestern und Heute. Ed. Walther Seidler. Berlin: Verlag Volker Spiess, 1979, pp. 9-22.

Includes bibliographic references.

See Seidler, #875.

2528. Quantrill, Jay Alan. "Current Assignments." Film Music Notebook, 3, No. 2 (1977), 3-5.

2529. ----------. "State of the Art." Film Music Notebook, 4, No. 1 (1978), 3-8.

2530. ----------. "State of the Art." Film Music Notebook, 4, No. 2 (1978), 3-11.

2531. Queroy, Jean-Claude. "Jazz on Movies." Revue du cinéma/Image et son, No. 315 (Mar. 1977), 10-11.

2532. Quigley, Michael. "Renaissance?," in "Film Music in the 1970's: A Symposium." Pro Musica Sana, 8, No. 2 (Spring 1980), 11-13.

2533. Rabinovici, Jean. "Les jeunes et la musique, 1954-1978: du rock au punk." Telecine, No. 228 (May 1978), 19-21.

2534. "Records: Fifty Years of Film Music (3 Record Set)." Rolling Stone, No. 160 (May 9, 1974), 61-62.

2535. Rickey, Carrie, and Jonathan Rosenbaum. "The Main Event: Sound Thinking." The Thousand Eyes Magazine, 2, No. 1 (1978), 6-7.

2536. Roberts, Kenneth H., and Win Sharples, Jr. A Primer for Film-Making: A Complete Guide to 16mm and 35mm Film Production. Indianapolis, Ind.: Bobbs-Merrill, 1971.

Includes a section "The Audial Image," with Chap. 10: "The Aesthetics of Film Sound," pp. 339-69, Chap. 11: "The Sound Cutting Room," pp. 371-427, and Chap. 12: "The Sound Mix," pp. 429-69.

2537. Robinson, Keith. "The Right Music for the Right Film." Making Films in New York (Dec. 1970).

2538. Roller, Howard. "Fifty Years of Warner Bros.: The King of Unpretentious Movies-as-Entertainment Celebrates with Two Soundtrack-Excerpt Anthologies." High Fidelity and Musical America, 24, No. 4 (Apr. 1974), 87.

Soundtrack album review.

2539. Rothman, Lynn. "Taking Note of Commercial Composers: California." Millimeter, 7 (Mar. 1979), 69ff.

Concerning composers for television.

2540. Rowe, Peter. "The Art Form of the 90's." Cinema Canada (Montreal), No. 12 (Feb.-Mar. 1974), 28-29.

2541. "Samnordisk resolusjon om film og fjernsyn." Norsk Musikerblad (Oslo), 62 (Apr. 1973), 4.

2542. Schild, Walter. "'Hifi 76': 3. Internationale Ausstellung mit Festival: Verbindung von Musik und Technik." Film und Ton, 22 (Nov. 1976), 34-35.

2543. Schreger, Charles. "The Second Coming of Sound." Film Comment, 14, No. 5

(Sept.-Oct. 1978), 34-37.

2544. Schulman, Michael. "Two Films, Two Music Scores, and Two Less-Than-Happy Composers." The Canadian Composer (Toronto), No. 138 (Feb. 1979), 10-17ff.

2545. Schulze, Erich. "Probleme des Urheberrechts." In 50 Jahre Musik im Hörfunk: Beiträge und Berichte. Ed. Kurt Blaukopf et al. Vienna: Jugend und Volk, 1973, pp. 113-15.

See Blaukopf, #207.

2546. Schurig, Erich. "Was kann ein Synthesizer für die Filmvertonung leisten?" Film und Ton, 22 (July 1976), 57-58.

2547. Shadduck, Jim. "The Ku-ku Song Man!" Pratfall, 1, No. 7 (1972), 6.

Reprinted in Limbacher, pp. 176-81. See #75.

2548. Shales, Tom. "Movie Music Rediscovered as Special American Art." The Max Steiner Music Society News Letter, No. 44 (Autumn 1975), 3-4.

2549. Sharples, Win, Jr. "Explorations: Love's Labours Found." American Film, 1, No. 5 (Mar. 1976), 68-70.

Concerning the activities of the Miklos Rozsa Society, the Bernstein Collection and the FMC soundtrack series.

2550. Sherman, Garry. "Close-Up: Garry Sherman." Millimeter, 4 (May 1976), 38-39.

An interview.

2551. Shipp, R. "Setting Hollywood to Music." Christian Science Monitor, 72 (Nov. 30, 1979), B8-B9.

2552. Shragge, Lawrence. "Sounds Behind the Scenes." Cinema Canada (Montreal), Nos. 60-61 (Dec. 1979-Jan. 1980), 18-19.

2553. Siders, Harvey. "The Jazz Composers in Hollywood." Down Beat, 39 (Mar. 2, 1972), 12-15ff.

2554. Silverman, Faye-Ellen. "Report from New York City: Computer Conference, June 1973." Current Musicology, 17 (1974), 77-80.

Concerning the use of computers in art, music, and film, with references to the "computerization" of musical sound tracks.

2555. Simmons, David. "London Music." Musical Opinion, 93 (Jan. 1970), 182.

Concerning the use of electronic music in films.

2556. Sippel, John. "Film Music Creators Finally Making a Buck." Billboard, 91 (Mar. 17, 1979), 14ff.

2557. Sitney, P. Adams. Visionary Film: The American Avant-Garde. New York: Oxford University Press, 1974. (Second edition, 1979.)

Includes some references to film music, and a discussion of the work of John Whitney.

2558. Snell, Mike. "Rambling with Snell ..." The Max Steiner Journal, No. 2 (1978), 33-34.

A survey of current scores and views on film scoring.

2559. Sobel, Robert. "Film Music's the Thing: RCA Conductor Gerhardt." Billboard, 85 (Nov. 24, 1973), 37.

2560. Sobel, Stanford. "Music and the Industrial Writer." Making Films in New York, 9 (Aug. 1975), 24ff.

2561. Soloviev-Sedoi, Vasilii. "Vasily Soloviev-Sedoi: No Picture Can Do Without Music." Soviet Film (Moscow), No. 241, No. 6 (1977), 16-17.

2562. Sokol'sky, Matias. "Informatsiya ili portret?" Sovetskaya muzyka, 40, No. 1 (Jan. 1976), 78-79.

2563. Sonnichsen, P. "Film Reviews." Western Folklore (U.C.L.A.), 36, No. 2 (1977), 183-87.

2564. Stamelman, Peter. "Film Composer David Shire Shuffling Off from Buffalo." Millimeter, 4, No. 4 (Apr. 1976), 20-22ff.
       An interview. Includes filmography.

2565. Steinhauer, Walter. "Musik in Film und Fernsehen." Film und Ton, 20 (Feb. 1974), 39-40.

2566. ----------. "Musik in Film und Fernsehen." Film und Ton, 20 (May 1974), 42-43.

2567. Sterritt, David. "The Turning Point." Christian Science Monitor, 69 (Nov. 16, 1977), 24.

2568. Stevens, Mark. "The Score." Cinefantastique, 2, No. 3 (1973), 40-41.

2569. Strazhenkova, I. "My 'uslyshali' Goyyu." Sovetskaya muzyka, 36, No. 10 (Oct. 1972), 49-53.

2570. Street, Brian Jeffrey. "Introducing Kevin Gillis: Ottawa Soundtracks." Cinema Canada (Montreal), No. 44 (Feb. 1978), 9.

2571. Sutak, Ken. "Categories," in "Film Music in the 1970's: A Symposium." Pro Musica Sana, 8, No. 2 (Spring 1980), 14-16.

2572. ----------. The Great Motion Picture Soundtrack Robbery: An Analysis of Copyright Protection. Hamden, Conn.: The Shoe String Press, 1976.
       An important, scholarly study of the legal issues associated with music in films.

2573. ----------. "The Investment Market in Movie Music Albums." High Fidelity and Musical America, 22, No. 7 (July 1972), 62-66.

2574. Sutherland, Donald. "How to Match the Music to the Film." Popular Photography, 72 (Apr. 1973), 103-05ff.

2575. ----------. "Movies and Music: The Happy Marriage." Popular Photography, 72 (Mar. 1973), 103ff.

2576. Sutherland, Sam. "Rock Soundtracks: 'American Hot Wax', 'The Last Waltz,' 'FM.'" High Fidelity and Musical America, 28, No. 7 (July 1978), 126.

2577. Sutherland, Sandy. "Filmusic Now More Important: Bogart." Billboard, 84 (Aug. 19, 1972), 1ff.

2578. "The Synthesizer Is an Added Plus." Making Films in New York, 9 (Aug. 1975), 21.

2579. "'Szerelmi almok?': Muzsikus szemmel egy zenesz-filmrol." Muzsika (Budapest), 14 (Jan. 1971), 35-38.

2580. Szilagyi, Gabor. "'Szabadsag': 'egyeniseg' es korszeruseg az operatori munkaban: beszelgetes Kende Janossal." Filmkultura (Budapest), 15 (May-June 1979), 58-66.
       An interview with composer Janos Kende.

2581. Tadman, Aubrey. "Interview! Aubrey Tadman." The Canadian Composer/Le Compositeur Canadien (Toronto), No. 95 (Nov. 1974), 24-29.
       In English and French.

2582. Taylor, Chris. "Sound Spectrum: Facing the Music." Movie Maker, 4 (Apr. 1976), 239.

2583. Teegarden, John. "Aural Fixations." Audience (New York), 9 (Oct. 1977), 21-22.

2584. ----------. "Aural Fixations." Audience (New York), 9 (Nov. 1977), 9-10.

2585. Theodor, Barbara. "Musik -- Audiovisuell." Deutsches Musikleben (1970).

Reprinted in _Musik und Bildung_, 2, No. 6 (June 1970), 280-81.

2586. Thiel, Wolfgang. "Kein Platz für neue Musik in DEFA-Filmen der 70er Jahre?" _Musik und Gesellschaft_, 28, No. 12 (Dec. 1978), 706-12.

2587. ----------. "Musik in Film und Hörspiel: Notizen aus der filmmusikalischen Praxis." _Musik und Gesellschaft_, 24, No. 10 (Oct. 1974), 609-12.

2588. ----------. "Resümee einer Rückschau: Gespräch mit Andre Asriel über kompositorische Arbeit für den Film." _Film und Fernsehen_ (Berlin, DDR), 7, No. 9 (1979), 33-37.

An interview. Includes filmography.

2589. Tolbert, Kathryn. "Innerview: Japanese Man is Full Orchestra When at his Moog Synthesizer." _Toledo Blade_ (Oct. 5, 1976).

Reprinted in _Japanese Fantasy Film Journal_, No. 12 (1979), 4-5.

2590. Tomkins, Les. "Filmharmonic '72 Reviewed." _Crescendo International_, 11 (Nov. 1972), 22.

2591. Ulrich, Allan. _The Art of Film Music: A Tribute to California's Film Composers: The Oakland Museum -- March 12, 13 and 14, 1976_. Oakland, Calif.: Oakland Museum, 1976.

A symposium. Includes filmographies, and interviews with composers Elmer Bernstein, Ernest Gold, Lyn Murray, David Raksin, and Fred Steiner.

2592. Valentino, Thomas, Jr. "Music for Films: The Music Library." _Filmmakers Newsletter_, 4, No. 6 (Apr. 1971), 42-43.

2593. van Dijk, Dave. "Muziekfilm: de topgangster met soulkleren." _Skoop_ (The Hague), 13 (Feb.-Mar. 1977), 31-32.

2594. Vartanov, Anri Surenovich. "Mir lichnosti i mir muzyki -- na ekrane." _Sovetskaya muzyka_, 43, No. 6 (June 1979), 48-57.

2595. Vercelli, Gary G. "Profile: Dave Grusin." _Down Beat_, 43 (Sept. 9, 1976), 38-39.

2596. Vertlieb, Steve. "Soundtrack." _Cinemacabre_ (Baltimore, Md.), No. 1 (1978), 48-54.

References to the music of Miklos Rozsa and John Williams.

2597. ----------. "Soundtrack." _Cinemacabre_ (Baltimore, Md.), No. 2 (1979), 54-62.

Soundtrack album review, with references to music by Rozsa and Goldsmith.

2598. Vialle, Gabriel. "Musique: la quatrieme dimension." _Revue du cinéma/Image et son_, No. 291 (Dec. 1974), 10-12.

2599. Viberti, Enrico. "Il valzer del rock." _Filmcritica_, 30, Nos. 296-297 (Aug. 1979), 299-300.

2600. Viertel, Salka. _The Kindness of Strangers_. New York: Holt, Rinehart, and Winston, 1969.

2600a. Also published as _Das unbelehrbar Herz: Ein Leben in die Welt des Theaters, der Literatur und des Films_. Trans. Helmut Degner. Hamburg and Dusseldorf: Claasen, 1970.

2600b. The section "Ich schreibe keine 'entzükkende' Musik," is reprinted in _Opern Welt_, No. 2 (Feb. 1971), 20-21.

2601. Warner, Alan. "Shopping for Soundtracks." _Films and Filming_, 21 (Aug. 1975), 29.

2602. Weissman, Dick. _The Music Business: Career Opportunities and Self Defense_. New York: Crown Publishers, 1979.

2603. Wesley-Smith, Martin. "Intermedia -- A Composer's View." _Cantrill's Film-_

notes (Melbourne, Austr.), Nos. 31-32 (Nov. 1979), 53-55.

2604. "Who Edits the Music?" Making Films in New York, 9 (Aug. 1975), 41.

2605. Wicke, G. "Filmmusik in der Diskussion." Musik und Gesellschaft, 28, No. 7 (July 1978), 425-26.

2606. Wilkening, Albert. "Musik und Sound." Bild und Ton, 26 (Sept. 1973), 259.

2607. Wimbush, Roger. "Conciertos de musica para el cine." Buenos Aires Musical, 26, No. 424 (1971), 5-6.

2608. Wiseman, R. "Charley Fox." Songwriter Magazine (Hollywood, Calif.), 4 (June 1979), 28-33.

　　　　An interview.

2609. Wolf, William. "Facing the Music: Why Movie Scores Are Usually So Awful." Cue (New York), 39 (Dec. 5, 1970), 7.

　　　　Reprinted in Limbacher, pp. 51-54. See #75.

2610. Wolthuis, Julius J. C. "Filmmuziek." Skoop (The Hague), 12 (Oct. 1976), 32.

2611. ----------. "Filmmuziek." Skoop (The Hague), 12 (Nov. 1976), 14.

2612. ----------. "Filmmuziek." Skoop (The Hague), 12 (Dec. 1976), 22.

2613. ----------. "Filmmuziek." Skoop (The Hague), 13 (Jan. 1977), 35.

2614. ----------. "Filmmuziek." Skoop (The Hague), 13 (June-July 1977), 32.

2615. ----------. "Filmmuziek." Skoop (The Hague), 13 (Aug. 1977), 22.

2616. ----------. "Filmmuziek." Skoop (The Hague), 13 (Sept. 1977), 36.

2617. ----------. "Filmmuziek." Skoop (Amsterdam), 15 (Feb. 1979), 18.

2618. ----------. "Interview met Rogier van Otterloo." Skoop (The Hague), 13 (Oct. 1977), 36-37.

2619. Young, Jean, and Jim Young. Succeeding in the Big World of Music. Boston: Little, Brown, 1977.

2620. Young, Robert R. "Let's Put 'America' to Music." Classic Film Collector, No. 51 (Summer 1976), 49-51ff.

2621. Zaderackij, V. "Obretenie zrelosti." Sovetskaya muzyka, 36, No. 10 (Oct. 1972), 32-40.

　　　　Concerning the film music of composer M. Skorik.

2622. Zimmerer, Teresa. "Close-Ups: Suzanne Ciani." Millimeter, 7 (Jan. 1979), 92.

2623. Zlotnik, Olga. "Arno Babajanian: The Cinema Is My First Love." Soviet Film (Moscow), No. 230 (1976), 27-28.

　　　　An interview.

2624. Zorkaya, Natal'ya, and Jurij Bogomolov, eds. Muzy XX veka: Hudožestvennye problemy sredstv massovoj kommunikacii. Moscow: Iskusstvo, 1978.

　　　　A collection of articles by E. Averbach (#5720), J. Bogomolov (#5727), V. Borev (#5380), V. Demin (#5393), S. Furceva (#5401), V. Kisun'ko (#5770), E. Korčegina (#5775), G. Lučaj (#5425), E. Prohorov (#4826), A. Vartanov (#4938), N. Venžer (#4940), and N. Zorkaya (#5143).

2625. Zulfikarov, Timur. "A Word About My Colleague: Rumil Vildanov -- Listening to the Singer's Voice." Soviet Film (Moscow), No. 261 (No. 2), (Feb. 1979), 7.

SEE ALSO:

#251(Jenkinson/Warner), #292(Sineaux), #294(Snell), #471, #704(Long), #717 (Mann), #794(Petric), #875(Seidler), #885, #1055(Warshow), #2097(Matejka), #3053, 3060(Bernstein), #3522(Vallance), #3740, 3749(Raksin), #3956(Fiedel), #4177(Whitney), #4495(Chanan), #4531(Cornelis/Zaagsma), #4627(Grützner), #4691(Kominek), #4699(Kühn), #4776(McKay), #4823(D. Previn), #4914 (Thiel), #4972(Youngblood), #5078(Gillett/Manvell), #5134(Troitskaya), #5815(Scheib), #5983(Gillette), #5998(Henriksson), #6018(Jélot-Blanc), #6121(Steinhauer), #6150, 6151(Wiener), #6182(Whitney), #6188(Fiedel), #6191(Gorbman), #6261, 6262(Farren), #6275(Cook), #6300(ASCAP), #6326, and #6329(Morley).

Sound Techniques and Technology

2626. Alkin, E. G. Sound with Vision: Sound Techniques for Television and Film. New York: Crane-Russak, 1972.

2627. Amarasingham, Indiram. "Film - Sound - Space: The OSS (Optical Sound Synthesizer)." Filmmakers Newsletter, 4, No. 6 (Apr. 1971), 35-38.

Concerning technical develpoments of interest to composers of "designed music."

2628. Avron, Dominique. "Remarques sur le travail du son dans la production cinématographique standardisée." Revue d'esthétique, Special Issue (1973).

2629. "Die Bedeutung der Raumfunktionen für die Vermittlung von Sprache und Musik." Fernseh- und Kino-Technik, 29 (Feb. 1975), 42.

2630. Bobrow, Andrew C. "The Art of the Soundman: An Interview with Chris Newman." Filmmakers Newsletter, 7, No. 7 (May 1974), 24-28.

2631. Bomba, Raymond. "What Does a Sound Editor Do?" Cinemeditor (Summer 1971), 9-11.

2632. Cameron, Evan William. "On Mathematics, Music, and Film." Cinema Studies, 3 (Spring 1970).

2633. Collins, W. H. The Amateur Filmmaker's Handbook of Sound Sync and Scoring. Blue Ridge Summit, Pa.: Tab Books, 1974.

2634. Frater, Charles B. Sound Recording for Motion Pictures. London: Tantivy Press; New York: A. S. Barnes, 1977.

2635. Gerhartz, Leo Karl. "Rundfunk, Musik und musikalische Produktion: Überlegungen eines Rundfunkredakteurs." In Musik in den Massenmedien, Rundfunk und Fernsehen: Perspektiven und Materialien. Ed. Hans-Christian Schmidt. Mainz: B. Schotts Söhne, 1976, pp. 18-23.

See Schmidt, #5117.

2636. Happe, L. Bernhard. Basic Motion Picture Technology. New York: Hastings House, 1970.

Significant sections include Chap. 5: "Sound Recording and Reproduction," pp. 146-78, and Chap. 6: "Studio Production," pp. 206-10.

2637. Hilliard, John K. "Movie Sound Reproduction." Audio (Boulder, Colo.), 61 (Mar. 1977), 44-46ff.

2638. Hübner, Heinz. "Elektronische Musikerzeugung mit Walshfunktionen." Fernseh- und Kino-Technik, 28 (Oct. 1974), 318.

2639. Kallis, Stephen. "Background Music by Computer." American Cinematographer, 52, No. 11 (Nov. 1971), 1148-49.

Concerning the "Muse," an electronic music generator.

2640. Koldys, Mark, and John Fitzpatrick. "Techniques of T.V. Taping." Pro Musica Sana, 5, No. 3 (1977), 25-29.

2641. Lacombe, Alain. "Qu'est-ce qu'un editeur de musique de films? Entretien avec Georges Bacri." In Cinéma et musique, 1960-1975, a special issue of Écran 75, No. 39 (Sept. 15, 1975), 23-25.

        See #2463.

2642. Lajeunesse, Jacqueline, and André Cornand. "Entretien avec Antoine Bonfanti." La Revue du cinéma/Image et son, No. 285 (June-July 1974).

2643. Leipp, Emile. "Le Problème de l'equilibre sonore entre parole et musique." Conférence des journées d'étude, 13 (1971), 32-47.

        Concerning the role of the sound engineer. Includes bibliography.

2644. Lustig, Milton. "The Music Editor." Cinemeditor (Winter 1970-1971), 11-12.

2645. Moore, Richard. "Music, Films, Computers." Filmmakers' Newsletter, 4, No. 6 (Apr. 1971), 26-30.

        Concerning the possibilities for the use of computers in creating and coordinating sound and picture.

2646. "Movie Dolby." Stereo Review (Boulder, Colo.), 42 (Jan. 1979), 34.

2647. Osborne, Robert. "Film Music Editor." Music Educator's Journal, 63, No. 7 (Mar. 1977), 71.

        Concerning the work of Evelyn Kennedy.

2648. Overman, Michael. Understanding Sound, Video, and Film Recording. Blue Ridge Summit, Pa.: Tab Books, 1978.

2649. Parent, Bob. "Quadrasonics and the Filmmaker." Filmmakers' Newsletter, 4, No. 6 (Apr. 1971), 31-34.

2650. Rosenbaum, Jonathan. "Sound Thinking." Film Comment, 14, No. 5 (Sept.-Oct. 1978), 38-41.

        Includes a brief bibliography of French and English articles on sound in film.

2651. Rothe, Ernst. "Anwendung der Quadrophonie bei der Übertragung ernster Musik." Fernseh- und Kino-Technik, 30 (Mar. 1976), 89-91.

2652. Sturhahn, Larry. "The Art of the Sound Editor: An Interview with Walter Murch." Filmmakers' Newsletter, 8, No. 2 (Dec. 1974), 22-25.

2653. "350S 'Stylophone' Synthesizer for Electronic Music and Sound Effects." American Cinematographer, 57 (Dec. 1976), 1354-55.

2654. Tonmeistertagung (10.) 19.-22. November 1975, Köln: Bericht. Verband Deutscher Tonmeister. Cologne: Welzel und Hardt, 1976.

        A collection of highly technical reports, with transcripts of discussions held at the 1975 Conference of Sound Engineers in Cologne. Includes contributions by M. Jenke (#5090) and H.-G. Daehn (#4535).

2655. Wysotsky, Michael Z. Wide-Screen Cinema and Stereophonic Sound. New York: Hastings House, 1971.

        Concerning technical problems and developments in sound technology, with implications for film music. Includes the chapter "The Technology of Stereo Sound for Film," pp. 88-151.

        SEE ALSO:
        #119(Skiles), #190(Stanley), #199(Atkins), #226(Cook), #241(Frayne et al.), #268(McClelland), #312(Weiland), #2207(Nisbett), #2211(Walter), #2357 (De Prez), #2395(Finkhousen), #2536(Roberts/Sharples), #2554(Silverman), #2604, #2686(Rocholl), #4728(Lexman), and #6171(Le Grice).

Music for T.V.

2656. Armstrong, David. "How to Win Contracts and Influence Directors." Composer (London), No. 34 (Winter 1969-1970), 33-35.

   2656a. Also published as "The Harassed TV Composer," in The World of Music (UNESCO), 12, No. 4 (1970), 37-44.

   In English, French, and German.

2657. Baronijan, Vartkes. "Muzika kao primenjena umetnost." Zvuk (Sarajevo), Nos. 119-120 (1971), 433-36.

2658. Breh, Karl. "Der Klang, Stiefkind des Fernsehens." HiFi-Stereophonie, 17, No. 6 (1978), 684-86.

2659. Crystal, Tamar. "Producing Commercial Music -- To the Beat of a Different Drum." Millimeter, 6 (May 1978), 86-88ff.

2660. Curley, Joseph. "Taking Note of Commercial Composers Throughout the Land: New York." Millimeter, 7 (Mar. 1979), 44-46ff.

2661. Dobroski, Bernie, and Elizabeth F. von Bergen. "Days of Glory for Kojak." Accent (Evanston, Ill.), 1, No. 2 (1976), 10-14.

2662. Evans, P. "Britten's Television Opera." Musical Times, 112 (May 1971), 425-28.

2663. Feather, Leonard. "From Pen to Screen: Earle Hagen." International Musician, 68 (May 1970), 9ff.

2664. ----------. "From Pen to Screen: J. J. Johnson." International Musician, 71 (July 1972), 9ff.

2665. ----------. "From Pen to Screen: 'Night Gallery.'" International Musician, 71 (Nov. 1972), 5ff.

2666. ----------. "From Pen to Screen: Pat Williams." International Musician, 69 (Feb. 1971), 9ff.

2667. ----------. "From Pen to Screen: Shelly Manne." International Musician, 69 (Nov. 1970), 4.

2668. ----------. "From Pen to Screen: Stanley Wilson." International Musician, 69 (Aug. 1970), 11ff.

2669. Fiedel, Robert D. "Sound Tracks: Trekking." Take One (Montreal), 5, No. 10 (July-Aug. 1977), 48, 50.

   References to music by Alexander Courage, Fred Steiner, and others.

2670. Gerlach, R. "Musik in der Fernsehserie: 'Für Freunde der russischen Sprache.'" Musik und Gesellschaft, 23 (Nov. 1973), 692-93.

2671. "Gibt es nicht -- gibt es doch: Antworten der Rundfunkanstalten und ihrer Werbetochter." Medium, 9 (Nov. 1979), 24-26.

2672. Gough, Hilton. "Music 1: Television. Carey Blyton: Writing to Order." Film (London), No. 25 (April 1975), 10-11.

2673. Gräter, Manfred. "Elektronik als Kompositionselement und Gestaltungsmittel im Fernsehen." Neue Zeitschrift für Musik, 133, No. 2 (Feb. 1972), 77-82.

2674. Irvine, M. "Henze schreibt für das amerikanische Fernsehen." Melos, 41, No. 4 (Apr. 1974), 228-30.

   Concerning Henze's "Rachel, La Cubana."

2675. King, Marshall. "On the Firing Line in Television Music." The Instrumentalist (Evanston, Ill.), 33 (Sept. 1978), 36-40ff.

   An interview with D'Vaughn Pershing.

2676. Kofin, Ewa. "Muzyka telewizyjna." Ruch Muzyczny (Warsaw), 23, No. 15 (1979), 7-8.

2677. Lindsey, Mort. "TV Music Director." Music Educator's Journal, 63 (Mar. 1977), 62-63.

2678. Marlow, Eugene. "Corporate Video Music and Sound Effects." Videography (New York), 4 (Sept. 1979), 76-77.

2679. Meissner, Roland. "Die Funktion der Musik in der Rundfunk- und Fernsehwerbung." M.A. Thesis (Musicology), Technische Universität-Berlin 1973.

2680. ----------. "Mendelssohns Söhnlein: Musik in der Fernsehwerbung." Musik und Bildung, 6, No. 6 (June 1974), 305-07.

2681. Misiak, T. "Jeszcze o muzyce telewizyjnej." Ruch Muzyczny (Warsaw), 23, No. 24 (1979), 17.

2682. Müller-Medek, Tilo. "Erfahrungen mit der Horspielmusik." In Sammelbände zur Musikgeschichte der DDR. Berlin: Neue Musik, 1975, IV, pp. 201-11.
    Concerning music composed for radio plays.

2683. Nordemann, Wilhelm. "Die Musik im Netz der rechtlichen Ansprüche." Das Orchester (Hamburg), 25 (Jan. 1977), 1-2.

2684. Prox, Lothar. "Stummfilmvertonungen deutscher Fernseh-Redaktionen: eine Aufstellung." In Stummfilmmusik Gestern und Heute. Ed. Walther Seidler. Berlin: Verlag Volker Spiess, 1979, pp. 27-34.
    Concerning contemporary scores for silent films.

2685. Riethmüller, Albrecht. "Das Tonsignet: Versuch einer Bestimmung seiner Eigenschaften und Aufgaben." Archiv für Musikwissenschaft, 30, No. 1 (1973), 69-79.

2686. Rocholl, Peter. "Musik im Fernsehen: Erfahrungen eines Musikredakteurs." Musik und Bildung, 7, No. 4 (Apr. 1975), 174-76.

2687. Schmidt, Hans-Christian. "Musikalische Titel von Serien -- Sendungen des Fernsehens. Überlegungen zu einer alltäglichen Erscheinung." In Musik in den Massenmedien, Rundfunk und Fernsehen: Perspektiven und Materialien. Ed. Hans-Christian Schmidt. Mainz: B. Schotts Söhne, 1976, pp. 296-318.
    See Schmidt, #5117.
    -- Rev. in Medien und Erziehung (Munich), 22, No. 1 (1978), 63-65.

2688. ----------. "Musik im Fernsehen. Musikalische Titel von Fernseh-Serienfilmen. Eine Unterrichtssequenz für die Sekundarstufe I." Musik und Bildung, 9, No. 1 (Jan. 1977), 23-28.

2689. Searl, Hanford. "Demand Rises for Talents of Vet Motion Picture Composers." Billboard, 91 (Apr. 28, 1979), 47.
    A call for better music in television productions.

2690. Seckel, Sherry. "Taking Note of Commercial Composers: Major Centers." Millimeter, 7 (Mar. 1979), 60ff.

2691. Siders, Harvey. "Meet Pat Williams." Down Beat, 38 (Mar. 4, 1971), 20ff.

2692. Stehr, Richard. "Commercial Composers: The West Coast Contingent." Millimeter, 5 (Nov. 1977), 64ff.

2693. Steiner, Fred. "Keeping Score of the Scores: Music for 'Star Trek.'" Quarterly Journal of the Library of Congress, 40, No. 1 (Winter 1983), 4ff.
    Concerning music for the T.V. series by Steiner and seven other composers.

2694. "Television." BMI: The Many Worlds of Music (Jan. 1970), 12-15; (Mar. 1970), 23; (June 1970), 4-5; and (Nov. 1970), 4-7.

2695. "Television." BMI: The Many Worlds of Music (Apr. 1971), 12-13; (Summer 1971), 17; and (Nov. 1971), 4-7.

2696. "Television." BMI: The Many Worlds of Music (Jan 1972), 4; and No. 6 (1972), 26-29.

2697. "Television." BMI: The Many Worlds of Music, No. 1 (1973), 36-39.

2698. "Television: BMI Music in the Current Season." BMI: The Many Worlds of Music, No. 1 (1977), 41-47.

2699. "Television: BMI Music in the New Season." BMI: The Many Worlds of Music, No. 4 (1973), 4-7.

2700. "Television: '77-'78 -- BMI Music on the Home Screen." BMI: The Many Worlds of Music, No. 1 (1978), 30-36.

2701. "Television 1978: BMI Music on the Home Screen." BMI: The Many Worlds of Music, No. 4 (1978), 23-26.

2702. "Television 1979: BMI Music on the Home Screen." BMI: The Many Worlds of Music, No. 4 (1979), 23-26.

2703. Thiel, Wolfgang. "Aufgaben und Möglichkeiten der Musik in Gegenwartsfilmen des Deutschen Fernsehfunks." Musik und Gesellschaft, 22, No. 10 (Oct. 1972), 592-98.

2704. Tibbe, Monika Klein. "Fernsehmusik." Musik und Bildung, 7, No. 4 (Apr. 1975), 185-87.

2705. Tiegel, E. "Frankly, Patrick Williams." Down Beat, 48 (Sept. 1981), 19-21.

2706. Topalovich, Maria. "Bob McMullin Keeps Composer's Role Low-Key in Film Work." The Music Scene (Ontario), No. 289 (May-June 1976), 4.

2707. Warrack, J. "Britten's Television Opera." Opera (Gt. Brit.), 22 (May 1971), 371-78.

SEE ALSO:

#11, #63(Kofin), #126(Thiel), #284(Ranson), #2339(Cook), #2352(Davis), #2434(IMZ), #2456(Koldys), #2459(Korall), #2510(Nolan), #2539(Rothman), #2565, 2566(Steinhauer), #3100(Thiel), #3119(Schiffer), #3442(Feather), #4446, 4447(Battenberg), #4640(Hengst), #4687, 4688, 4689(Kofin), #4905 (Tagg), #4913-4916, 4918, 4920(Thiel), #4940(Venžer), #4955(Well), #4970 (Wüsthoff), #5043(Wintle), #5051(Bornoff/Salter), #5726(Bertz-Dostal), #5834(Troitskaya), #5871(Penney), #5951(Dexter), and #6125(Stoyanova).

1980's

History

2708. Acher, Chris. "La Belgique festivaliere: Les Films musicaux a Gand." Amis du film et de la télévision, No. 308 (Jan. 1982), 39.

2709. ----------. "Lewis Furey." Amis du film: Cinéma et télévision, No. 285 (Feb. 1980), 12.

2710. ----------, et al. "Au pays de Lewis Furey et Carole Laure." Amis du film: Cinéma et télévision, No. 285 (Feb. 1980), 12-13.

2711. Addison, John, et al. "Getting Started in Film and TV Scoring." ASCAP in Action (New York), (Fall 1981), 36-38.

2712. Ala, Nemesio. "La scena rock: 'Rust Never Sleeps.'" Filmcritica, 31, Nos. 305-306 (May-June 1980), 200-211.

2713. Ales, Bernard. "Gilbert Becaud: L'Amerique a surmonte la crise du spectacle!" <u>Cine Revue</u> (Brussels), 61 (May 21, 1981), 40-43.

An interview.

2714. Alexeieff, Alexandre, and Claire Parker. "Cinema d'animazione: strategia e tattica." <u>Filmcritica</u> (Rome), 31, Nos. 305-306 (May-June 1980), 219-21.

An interview. Includes references to music by Mussorgsky.

2715. Amzoll, Stefan. "'Busch singt,' Filmzyklus von Konrad Wolf." <u>Musik und Gesellschaft</u>, 33, No. 2 (Feb. 1983), 105-07.

2716. Aude, Françoise. "Encyclopedie permanente du cinematographe." <u>Positif</u> (Paris), No. 247 (Oct. 1981), 60-61.

2717. Aziz, M. Ashraf. "Many Songs Left to Sing." <u>Cinema Vision India</u>, 2, No. 2 (Jan. 1983), 84-87.

Concerning the career of performer Kundan Lal Saigal.

See #645.

2718. Barbano, Nicolas. "Film og komponister." <u>Kosmorama</u> (Copenhagen), 27, Nos. 155-156 (Dec. 1981), 196-97.

2719. ----------. "Fuzzy og filmmusikken." <u>Levende Billeder</u> (Copenhagen), 6 (Feb. 1980), 7-9.

2720. ----------. "Musik." <u>Kosmorama</u> (Copenhagen), 26, No. 148 (Sept. 1980), 156.

References to music by Barry, Conti, Gershwin, Goldsmith, and Williams.

2721. ----------. "Musik." <u>Kosmorama</u> (Copenhagen), 26, No. 149 (Oct. 1980), 203.

References to music by Goldsmith, Lai, Rosenman, and Williams.

2722. Berg, Charles. "Tracking the Score." <u>American Classic Screen</u>, 4 (Winter 1980), 22.

2723. ----------. "Tracking the Score." <u>American Classic Screen</u>, 4 (Spring 1980), 21.

2724. Bernardet, Jean-Claude, et al. "O som os compositores." <u>Filme Cultura</u> (Rio de Janeiro), No. 37 (Jan.-Mar. 1981), 8-16.

Interviews.

2725. Bertolina, Gian Carlo. "Note sulla musica nel film di Nicholas Ray." <u>Filmcritica</u> (Rome), 32, No. 314 (May 1981), 204-07.

Includes filmography.

2726. Bitomsky, Hartmut. "Reisen." <u>Filmkritik</u> (Munich), 24 (Feb. 1980), 55-59.

2727. ----------. "Zwei Sachen." <u>Filmkritik</u> (Munich), 24 (Jan. 1980), 28-29.

Concerning contemporary song lyrics.

2728. Blumschein, Christine. "Dann lieber gleich ein Musikjournal: das 'Notizbuch': die Entschäfung eines 'Argernisses.'" <u>Medium</u> (Frankfurt am Main), 11 (Feb. 1981), 7-11.

2729. Brandlmeier, Thomas. "Filmliteratur im Hanser Verlag." <u>Film und Ton</u>, 27 (Mar. 1981), 7-10.

2730. Broughton, Bruce, James Horner, and Basil Poledouris. "The Music of the Movies." AFI Seminar, March 21, 1984 (8:00 p.m.). Tape recording of the seminar is held at the AFI/Louis B. Mayer Library (Los Angeles).

2731. Brown, Royal S. "Oscar's Tin Ear." <u>Fanfare</u>, 5, No. 6 (1982), 50-55ff.

2732. Buchman, Chris, Jr. "Cinema Omnibus." <u>Classic Film/Video Images</u>, No. 70 (July 1980), 24-25.

2733. ----------. "Cinema Omnibus." <u>Classic Film/Video Images</u>, No. 71 (Sept.

1980), 12.

2734. Burg, Vinzenz B. "Fast ein Standardwerk über Filmmusik." Medien und Erziehung (Munich), 25, No. 2 (1981), 111-12.

2735. Burkert, Erwin. "Ein Jahr und zwei Monate eines Lebens." Film und Fernsehen (Berlin, DDR), 8, No. 6 (1980), 7-11.

   Concerning the work of Ernst Busch.

2736. Caps, John. "Discovering Patrick Gowers." Pro Musica Sana, 10, Nos. 3-4
(Fall 1983), 9-10.

2737. Carcassonne, Philippe. "Dossier -- La Musique de film: Hollywood mode d'
emploi." Cinematographe (Paris), No. 62 (Nov. 1980), 26.

2738. ----------, and Bertrand Borie. "Dossier -- La Musique de film: Table ronde
sur la musique de film -- Vladimir Cosma, Pierre Jansen, Philippe Arthuys,
François Porcile." Cinematographe (Paris), No. 62 (Nov. 1980), 2-8.

2739. Carrera, Alessandro. "Attraverso la California, sulle tracce di Woody Guth-
rie." Cineforum, No. 200 (Dec. 1980), 856-61.

   An interview with Mario Casetta.

2740. Carson, T. "Zapped Again." Village Voice, 25 (Jan. 7, 1980), 39.

   Concerning Frank Zappa's score for "Baby Snakes."

2741. Carvalho, Vladimir, et al. "O som os diretores." Filme Cultura (Rio de
Janiero), No. 37 (Jan.-Mar. 1981), 18-23.

2742. Champenier, Serge. "Bourges." Revue du cinéma/Image et son, No. 375 (Sept.
1982), 128.

2743. ----------. "Bourges: les musiciens ouvrent l'oeil." Revue du cinéma/Im-
age et son, No. 355 (Nov. 1980), 137.

2744. Chandavarkar, Bhaskar. "The Man Who Went Beyond Stop." Cinema Vision India, 1, No. 4 (Oct. 1980), 22-24.

   See #61.

2745. Chatterjee, Dhritiman. "Towards an Invisible Soundtrack?" Cinema Vision
India, 1, No. 4 (Oct. 1980), 12-19.

   An interview with Satyajit Ray.

   See #61.

2746. Chevallier, Jacques. "Boby Lapointe." Revue du cinéma/Image et son,
No. 356 (Dec. 1980), 139.

2747. Ciment, Michel. "The Poetry of Precision." American Film, 9, No. 1 (Oct.
1983), 70-73.

   An interview with director Robert Bresson, translated by
   Sally Dian Rainey.

2748. "Cinque canzoni." Revista del Cinematografo, 54 (Aug. 1981), 418-19.

2749. Cocking, Loren. "Reports: Ode to a Composer." University Film Association
Journal, 33, No. 1 (1981), 49-57.

2750. Collura, Joe. "Dialogue with Gaylord Carter." Classic Film/Video Images,
No. 70 (July 1980), 54-55.

2751. "Des compositeurs pour l'image." Soundtrack Collector's Newsletter, 2 (June
1983), 27.

2752. Comuzio, Ermanno. "Colonna sonora: nella vocalita di 'Fontamara' reinventa-
ta la musica dei 'Cafoni.'" Rivista del cinematografo (Rome), 54 (Jan.
1981), 47.

2753. ----------. "Colonna sonora: Wojciech Kilar, musicista di 'Un paese lon-
tano.'" Rivista del cinematografo, 54 (Dec. 1981), 687.

2754. ----------. "Glauco Pellegrini: Il maestro Veneziano." Cineforum (Bergamo), No. 211 (Jan.-Feb. 1982), 79.

2755. ----------. "Il disco: e ancora musica da film?" _Rivista del Cinematografo_ (Rome), 54 (Apr. 1981), 54.

2756. ----------. "Un musicista nuovo per Alain Resnais." _Rivista del Cinematografo_, 54 (July 1981), 385.

2757. ----------. "Travolti dall'onda che avanza." _Rivista del Cinematografo_, 54 (May 1981), 241.

2758. Cook, Page. "The Sound Track." _Films in Review_, 31, No. 1 (Jan. 1980), 35-37, 44-45.
        An interview with John Steven Lasher of Entr'acte Records.

2759. ----------. "-----." _Films in Review_, 31, No. 3 (Mar. 1980), 163.

2760. ----------. "-----." _Films in Review_, 31, No. 4 (Apr. 1980), 230.

2761. ----------. "-----." _Films in Review_, 31, No. 9 (Nov. 1980), 551-52, 572-73.
        Film music by Edward David Zeliff.

2762. ----------. "-----." _Films in Review_, 32, No. 2 (Feb. 1981), 108-10, 115.
        Film scores of 1980, with references to music by Claude Bolling, Alex North, Philippe Sarde, Edward David Zeliff, John Scott, and others.

2763. ----------. "-----." _Films in Review_, 32, No. 3 (Mar. 1981), 165-70, 176.
        An interview with record producer Lesley Anderson-Snell.

2764. ----------. "-----." _Films in Review_, 32, No. 4 (Apr. 1981), 230-32.
        Concerning John Morris's score for "The Elephant Man," and other current record releases.

2765. ----------. "-----." _Films in Review_, 32, No. 9 (Nov. 1981), 567-69.
        Film music by Edward David Zeliff.

2766. ----------. "-----." _Films in Review_, 32, No. 10 (Dec. 1981), 625-27.
        Concerning current soundtrack album releases.

2767. ----------. "-----." _Films in Review_, 33, No. 2 (Feb. 1982), 115-19.
        Film scores of 1981, with references to music by Goldsmith, North, Rozsa, John Morris, Philippe Sarde, and others.

2768. ----------. "-----." _Films in Review_, 33, No. 4 (Apr. 1982), 249-51.
        References to music by Leonard Rosenman and Miklos Rozsa.

2769. ----------. "-----." _Films in Review_, 33, No. 6 (June-July 1982), 371-73, 383.
        Concerning music for films by composer Friedrich Brock.

2770. ----------. "-----." _Films in Review_, 33, No. 8 (Oct. 1982), 500.
        Concerning music by contemporary composers Wendy Carlos, Harry Manfredini, David Whitaker, and Chris Young.

2771. ----------. "-----." _Films in Review_, 34, No. 1 (Jan. 1983), 56-58, 60.
        References to music by Elmer Bernstein, George Fenton, Ravi Shankar, and John Williams.

2772. ----------. "-----." _Films in Review_, 34, No. 2 (Feb. 1983), 118-22.
        Film scores of 1982, with references to music by Goldsmith, Rozsa, Williams, Basil Poledouris, Philippe Sarde, and others.

2773. ----------. "-----." _Films in Review_, 34, No. 3 (Mar. 1983), 178-80.
        Concerning the work of composer Stephen Cosgrove.

2774. ----------. "-----." Films in Review, 34, No. 4 (Apr. 1983), 245-47, 249.

2775. ----------. "-----." Films in Review, 34, No. 5 (May 1983), 311-13, 318.
Concerning Fred Steiner's research on Alfred Newman, see #3652. Also includes references to music by Newman and Ken Darby, and current T.V. scores by Mancini and Robert Cobert.

2776. ----------. "-----." Films in Review, 34, No. 7 (Aug.-Sept. 1983), 436-38.
References to music by Goldsmith, Williams, John Barry, and others.

2777. ----------. "-----." Films in Review, 34, No. 9 (Nov. 1983), 559-65.
References to music by Charles Koechlin, and film scores by Rota and Williams. Also includes a discussion of music for "The Twilight Zone" (the T.V. series and the movie) by Herrmann and Goldsmith.

2778. ----------. "-----." Films in Review, 35, No. 1 (Jan. 1984), 48-50.
References to music by Goldsmith, Legrand, James Horner, and Jean Prodromides.

2779. ----------. "-----." Films in Review, 35, No. 4 (Apr. 1984), 246-48.
Concerning the work of composer John Morris.

2780. Costabile, J. Paul. "Different Schools Together." Cinema Canada (Montreal), Nos. 60-61 (Dec. 1979-Jan. 1980), 26-29.
Concerning the film music of Paul Zaza and Carl Zittrer. Includes filmography.

2781. "Cronache: Venezia -- i tre momenti della musica per film." Cineforum, No. 200 (Dec. 1980), 793-94.

2782. Dagneau, Gilles. "Ken Russell: au coeur des problemes de son temps." Cinéma 81, No. 274 (Oct. 1981), 8-22.

2783. Daney, Serge, and Jean-Paul Fargier. "John Cage: Concerto pour radio, télévision et orchestre." Cahiers du cinéma, Nos. 334-335 (Apr. 1982), V-VI.
An interview with Cage, translated by Serge Daney.

2784. Day, S. "Jiadev and the New Wave." Cinema Vision India, 2, No. 2 (Jan. 1983), 83.

2785. Delamater, M. "Richard and Robert Sherman: Walt Disney's Dynamic Duo." Songwriter Magazine (Hollywood, Calif.), 5 (Sept 1980), 34-36.
An interview.

2786. Dimova, Stefka. "Poeziia i zhivopis v zvutsi." Kinoizkustvo (Sofia), 38 (Feb. 1983), 45-49.
Concerning the music of Simeon Pironkov.

2787. Doherty, Jim. "Kostal and the New 'Fantasia': Desecration of the Temple." Soundtrack Collectors Newsletter, 1 (Sept. 1982), 23-24.

2788. Elliker, Edwin. "Totenmasken: dokumentarisches Material zu Fassbinder und 'Querelle.'" Medien und Erziehung, 27, No. 1 (1983), 35-38.

2789. Ellis, Mundy. "In the Picture: Crowd Music." Sight and Sound, 50, No. 4 (Autumn 1981), 224.
Concerning a new score for an old film: Carl Davis's music for King Vidor's "The Crowd" (1928).

2790. "Ernst Busch." Cinematographe, No. 60 (Sept. 1980), 71.
Obituary.

2791. Fano, Michel, Henri Colpi, Alain Lacombe, and Maurice Le Roux. "Dossier -- La Musique de film: quatre reponses." Cinematographe (Paris), No. 62 (Nov. 1980), 9-13.

2792. Fieschi, Jacques. "Dossier -- La Musique de film: Chansons a voir." Cinematographe (Paris), No. 62 (Nov. 1980), 42-44.

2793. "Film Music Workshops Given by P.R.O. Canada." The Music Scene (Ontario), No. 315 (Sept.-Oct. 1980), 8-9.

2794. Fliangol'ts, Dmitrii. "Zvukooperator i zvukovaia kul'tura." Iskusstvo kino, No. 3 (Mar. 1981), 80-85.

2795. Foll, Jan. "Netradiční muzikál o životě a smrti." Film a Doba (Prague), 27 (Oct. 1981), 590-92.

2796. Francis, Harry. "As I Heard It." Crescendo International, 20 (Oct. 1981), 14.

2797. Fried, Robin. "Close-Ups: Jeff Slevin." Millimeter, 8 (Dec. 1980), 184-85.

2798. Frolova, Galina. "Music Is My Profession: Composer Raymond Pauls." Soviet Film (Moscow), 6, No. 277 (1980), 40-41.

2799. Gadgil, W. Y. "As the Stations Went By." Cinema Vision India, 2, No. 2 (Jan. 1983), 82-83.

    See #645.

    Originally published in the Maharashtra Times (Aug. 1, 1971). Concerning the work of composer Jiadev.

2800. Ghezzi, Enrico. "Da ragazzo suonavo il violino ma non amo la musica nel film: conversazione con Michelangelo Antonioni." Filmcritica (Rome), 31, Nos. 305-306 (May-June 1980), 200-201.

2801. ----------. "Dirigere l'orchestra o inventare spartiti." Filmcritica (Rome), 31, Nos. 305-306 (May-June 1980), 186-88.

2802. ----------. "La musica e i miei film: conversazione con Bernardo Bertolucci." Filmcritica (Rome), 31, Nos. 305-306 (May-June 1980), 202-07.

2803. ----------. "Musica - thrilling." Filmcritica (Rome), 32, No. 312 (Feb. 1981), 118-19.

2804. Giusti, Marco. "Cinema e musica a Venezia." Filmcritica (Rome), 31, Nos. 305-306 (May-June 1980), 218.

2805. ----------. "Con Carlo Savina." Filmcritica (Rome), 31, Nos. 305-306 (May-June 1980), 236-39.

    An interview.

2806. ----------. "Musica -- animazione: intervista a Emmanuele Luzzati." Filmcritica (Rome), 31, Nos. 305-306 (May-June 1980), 222-29.

    Includes filmography.

2807. Godard, Jean-Luc. "Godard a Avignon: propos rompus." Cahiers du cinéma, No. 316 (Oct. 1980), 10-17.

    Includes a section "La Musique," pp. 15-17.

2808. Goldberg, M. "Synthesized 'Apocalypse' of Nature, Men at War." Down Beat, 47 (Jan. 1980), 13.

    An interview with Patrick Gleeson.

2809. Goodfriend, J. "Movies I Heard with You." Stereo Review, 44 (June 1980), 56.

2810. Grelier, Robert. "Cannes 80: musique dans la salle." Revue du cinéma/Image et son, No. 352 (July-Aug. 1980), 14-15.

2811. Grützner, Vera. "Musik in neueren Spielfilmen der DEFA." Musik und Gesellschaft, 30 (Oct. 1980), 578-83.

2812. Hahn, Bob. "It's Mainly Because of the Music." Cinema Canada (Montreal), Nos. 60-61 (Dec. 1979-Jan. 1980), 40-42.

    Concerning the "promotion" of soundtrack albums.

2813. Hahn, Richard, and Howard Knopf. "Film Music: Some Legal Notes." Cinema

Canada (Montreal), Nos. 60-61 (Dec. 1979-Jan. 1980), 20-25.

2814. Harslöf, Olav. "Fascismens musik - fascismens orkester." _Dansk Musiktids-skrift_ (Copenhagen), 55, No. 3 (1980), 115-19.

2815. Haupt, Arthur. "Kubrick's Canned Music." _Pro Musica Sana_, 11, No. 1 (Spring 1984), 13-18.

2816. Holthof, Marc. "Komponist Jürgen Knieper." _Andere Sinema_ (Antwerp), No. 17 (March 1980), 8.

2817. Honigmann, Heddy. "Godard: wat is dat voor muziek?" _Skrien_ (Amsterdam), No. 104 (Feb. 1981), 8-9.

2818. Hosman, Harry. "Ruud Bos had er graag nog een tuba bij gehad." _Skoop_ (Amsterdam), 16 (Dec. 1980-Jan. 1981), 16-17.

     An interview.

2819. Insdorf, Annette. "'Soñar con tus ojos': Carlos Saura's Melodic Cinema." In _New Spanish Cinema_, a special issue of _Quarterly Review of Film Studies_, 8, No. 2 (Spring 1983), 49-53.

2820. "Is There Music After Death?" _Fanfare_, 3, No. 3 (1980), 186-89.

     Concerning scores for recent "horror" films.

2821. Jacobsen, Wolfgang, and Klaus Nothnagel. "Schwieriges Genre." _Medium_ (Frankfort am Main), 11 (July 1981), 45.

2822. Jernewall, M. "Bion noejes -- och arbetsplats i foervandling." _Musikern_ (Stockholm), No. 1 (Jan. 1982), 4-7.

2823. Jomy, Alain, and Dominique Rabourdin. "Entretien avec Arie Dzierlatka." _Cinéma 80_ (Paris), No. 263 (Nov. 1980), 41-47.

     Includes discography.

2824. Jones, Jerene. "An Olympian Effort by Composer Vangelis Ends in an Oscar for 'Chariots.'" _People_, 17 (April 19, 1982), 121.

2825. Jones, R. T. "An Outburst of Minimalism." _High Fidelity and Musical America_, 33, No. 2 (Feb. 1983), MA26-27.

2826. Kaushal, J. N. "There's More to Sound Than Music." _Cinema Vision India_, 1, No. 4 (Oct. 1980), 27-29.

     See #61.

     An interview with composer B. V. Karanth.

2827. King, Marshall. "Getting Your Foot in the Door: A Talk with Artie Malvin." _International Musician_, 82 (Sept. 1983), 6ff.

2828. Kirk, Cynthia. "Young Composers Need Many Things, But Agent May Not Be Necessary." _Variety_, 297 (Jan. 16, 1980), 1ff.

2829. Kolker, Robert P., and Leo Braudy. "Robert Altman: An Interview, Part II." _Post Script_, 1, No. 2 (1982), 2-14.

2830. Kolodynski, Andrzej. "Echa dyskoteki." _Kino_ (Warsaw), 15 (Mar. 1980), 46-50.

2831. Kopp, G. "Soundtrack Specialists Proliferate." _Billboard_, 92 (July 19, 1980), 73.

2832. Kroons, Hans. "'Casta Diva': marginale musical." _Skrien_ (Amsterdam), No. 124 (Feb. 1983), 4-6.

2833. Kupsch, Horst. "Musik für die Filmvertonung." _Film und Ton_, 26 (Dec. 1980), 9-10.

2834. ----------. "Neue Filmvertonungs Platten." _Film und Ton_, 26 (May 1980), 9.

2835. Lafaye, Claude. "Le petit monde de Paul Colline." _Avant-Scene du Cinéma_ (Paris), No. 241 (Feb. 1, 1980), 21-32.

Includes filmography.

2836. Landry, Jacques. "More Film-Scoring Jobs Available When Conditions Change: A Look at Music for Films in Quebec." The Music Scene (Ontario), No. 312 (Mar.-Apr. 1980), 4-5.

2837. Lardeau, Yann. "Cinéma et musique -- Angers 81: a l'italienne." Cahiers du cinéma, No. 322 (Apr. 1981), VII.

Concerning the Festival "Cinéma et Musique, Musique et Cinéma." Includes references to music by Nino Rota.

2838. Larson, Randall D. "The Score: He's a Low-Budget One-Man Band." Cinefantastique, 13, No. 5 (1983), 14.

Concerning the career of Richard H. Band.

2839. Lendvay, Kamillo. "A filmzene: magasrendu alkalmazott muveszet." Film-kultura (Budapest), 16 (Jan.-Feb. 1980), 56-58.

2840. Leontjev, Konstantin L., and Natalia S. Solovjova. "Farbmusik in der Architektur." Bild und Ton, No. 32 (June 1979), 184-86.

2841. Linck, David. "Screen Stars a Fan Never Sees." Boxoffice, 117 (Apr. 1981), 16.

2842. Loupien, S. "Reggae ... Splash." Jazz Magazine (Paris), No. 283 (Feb. 1980), 16-17.

2843. Ludin, Malte. "Gehemmte Schaulust: eine Rezension." Medium (Frankfurt am Main), 10 (May 1980), 41-42.

2844. MacMillan, R. "Lively Canadian Film Scene Here to Stay: Composers." The Music Scene (Ontario), No. 312 (Mar.-Apr. 1980), 4-7.

2845. Macy, Tom. "Unrecorded Scores: 'Raggedy Man.'" Soundtrack Collectors Newsletter, 1 (Dec. 1982), 4-5.

2846. Matveyev, Evgenii. "Composer Evgeny Ptichkin." Soviet Film (Moscow), 5, No. 312 (1983), 31.

2847. McCarthy, Todd. "Schmidt's Score Doesn't Score in L.A. Reconstruct of Dreyer's 'Arc.'" Variety, 311 (June 1, 1983), 4ff.

Carl T. Dreyer's film, with a score by Ole Schmidt.

2848. Meurice, J. "La musique: 'The Shining.'" Amis du film et de la télévision, No. 294 (Nov. 1980), 9.

Concerning Stanley Kubrick's use of music and sound.

2849. "Musical Scores, Film and Video Media and the Canadian Composer: Facts to Consider." The Canadian Composer (May 1983), S1-S27.

A pull-out supplement.

2850. Myers, Edith D. "Sounding It Out." Datamation, 28 (Mar. 1982), 40.

Concerning the use of computers for movie sound and music.

2851. Myrow, Fredric. Seminar on film music: AFI/CAFS, Nov. 18, 1981 (3:30 p.m.). Tape recording of the seminar is held at the AFI/Louis B. Mayer Library (Los Angeles).

2852. Norden, Martin F. "Society for Cinema Studies Conference: April, 1981." Quarterly Review of Film Studies, 6, No. 4 (Fall 1981), 457-62.

Includes "Session: Bernard Herrmann -- Aspects of His Work," noting contributions by Kathryn Kalinak, James Ferentino, and Royal S. Brown.

2853. Norton, M. J. "Mickey Hart's Rhythmic 'Apocalypse.'" Creem Magazine, 12 (Nov. 1980), 15-16.

2854. Oatis, Greg. "The Score: Only Kubrick's Soundtrack Manages to Shine." Cinefantastique, 10, No. 3 (1980), 16.

2855. Occhiogrosso, Peter. "Reelin' and Rockin'." _American Film_, 9, No. 6 (Apr. 1984), 44-50.

2856. Ochs, Ed, et al. "Scripting the Hits: Music and the Movies." _Billboard_, 92 (Aug. 2, 1980), M6ff.

2857. Oderman, Stuart. "Arthur Kleiner." _Classic Film/Video Images_, No. 69 (May 1980), 49.

2858. Pareles, J. "Frank Zappa's 'Baby Snakes.'" _Rolling Stone_, No. 311 (Feb. 21, 1980), 14.

2859. Paton, Robert. "Soundscape in Concert." _Cinema Canada_ (Montreal), Nos. 60-61 (Dec. 1979-Jan. 1980), 34-38.

> Concerning music by Murray Schafer.

2860. ----------. "Thriving on Variety." _Cinema Canada_ (Montreal), Nos. 60-61 (Dec. 1979-Jan. 1980), 14-17.

> Concerning music by Paul Hoffert.

2861. Pecqueriaux, Jean-Pierre, and Luc van de Ven. "Filmography/Discography: Bruno Nicolai, Part 2." _Soundtrack Collectors Newsletter_, 2 (June 1983), 10-12.

2862. Pede, Ronnie. "Parker: geweld en muziek." _Film en Televisie_ (Brussels), Nos. 302-303 (July-Aug. 1982), 18-19.

> An interview.

2863. Peel, M. "Mark Knopfler's Beautiful, Powerfully Exciting Film Soundtrack for 'Local Hero.'" _Stereo Review_ (Boulder, Colo.), 48 (Sept. 1983), 82ff.

2864. Penchansky, Alan D. "Disney Recording Digital Soundtrack for 'Fantasia.'" _Billboard_, 94 (Jan. 30, 1982), 3ff.

2865. Perre, Paul van de. "Filmmuziek." _Skrien_ (Amsterdam), No. 121 (Sept. 1982), 43.

2866. Pipkin, Vicki. "Movie Composers Share Experiences at Workshop." _Billboard_, 93 (Feb. 7, 1981), 48.

> Concerning an ASCAP West Coast film scoring workshop.

2867. Poirier, Marie. "Les films 'reggae.'" _Sequences_ (Montreal), No. 109 (July 1982), 24-25.

2868. Quantrill, Jay Alan. "Opinion." _The Cue Sheet_ (Los Angeles), 1, No. 1 (Jan. 1984), 10-12.

> A survey of current scores, with references to music by Conti, Delerue, Raksin, Goldsmith, James Horner, and Arthur Rubenstein.

2869. Quigley, Michael. "The Return of the Folio." _Pro Musica Sana_, 11, No. 1 (Spring 1984), 18-19.

2870. Rabourdin, Dominique, and Alain Jomy. "Musique du film." _Cinéma 80_, No. 254 (Feb. 1980), 64-65; and No. 255 (Mar. 1980), 70-71.

2871. Ravasini, Marco. "Lo spettatore critico: musica e film." _Filmcritica_ (Rome), 32, No. 312 (Feb. 1981), 116-17.

> Part 2.

2872. ----------. "Lo spettatore critico: musica e film." _Filmcritica_ (Rome), 32, No. 313 (Mar.-Apr. 1981), 181-82.

> Part 3.

2873. ----------. "Musica e film: Lo spettatore critico." _Filmcritica_ (Rome), 32, No. 311 (Jan. 1981), 60-61.

2874. Rocle, Claude. "Entretien avec Alain Lacombe." _Cinéma 80_, No. 264 (Dec. 1980), 70-71.

2875. Rogge, Jan-Uwe. "Schlager, Beat, Urterhaltung und die Musikinteressen Jugendlicher in der DDR." <u>Medien und Erziehung</u>, 24, No. 5 (1980), 273-83.

2876. Roquefort, Georges. "Table ronde sur le cinéma des surrealites enregistrée pendant Confrontation XV." <u>Cahiers de la cinematheque</u>, No. 30-31 (Summer-Autumn 1980), 95-114.

2877. Rothstein, Edward. "'Music Plus Film' in Manhattan Plus Brooklyn." <u>New York Times</u>, 131 (Apr. 2, 1982), Section C, p. 4.

2878. Sartor, Freddy. "Francis Lai." <u>Film en Televisie</u> (Brussels), Nos. 276-277 (May-June 1980), 29-30.

2879. Satariano, Cecil. "This Way to Better Movies: Lesson Nine -- The Soundtrack." <u>Movie Maker</u>, 15 (Jan. 1981), 32-33.

2880. Schepelern, Peter. "Nye boeger om filmmusik." <u>Dansk Musiktidsskrift</u> (Copenhagen), 55, No. 3 (1980), 140-41.

2881. Schoenberger, E. "Just Like Real Music." <u>Vrij Nederland</u> (June 19, 1982).

Reprinted in <u>Key Notes Donemus</u> (Amsterdam), No. 16 (1982), 42-43.

2882. Schonberg, Harold C. "'The Competition' Stirs Memories of Music in Movies." <u>New York Times</u>, 130 (Jan. 4, 1981), Section 2, p. 15.

2883. "Scoring 'The Earthling.'" <u>Cinema Papers</u> (Melbourne, Austr.), No. 26 (Apr.-May 1980), 119.

2884. Seesslen, Georg. "Punk: verfälscht und verketzert, weil provokativ." <u>Medien und Erziehung</u>, 24, No. 5 (1980), 268-72.

2885. Seregina, N. "Khudozhestvennoe obobshchenie temy." <u>Sovetskaya muzyka</u>, 44, No. 6 (June 1980), 11-16.

2886. Siegel, Lois. "Furey Knows the Score." <u>Cinema Canada</u> (Montreal), Nos. 60-61 (Dec. 1979-Jan. 1980), 30-32.

Film music by Lewis Furey.

2887. Silber, Frederic. "America in the Movies: Soundtracks Lost and Found." <u>Fanfare</u>, 5, No. 4 (1982), 347-48.

2888. Sineux, Michel. "La Symphonie Kubrick." <u>Positif</u> (Paris), No. 239 (Feb. 1981), 34-36.

2889. Snell, Mike. "Rambling with Snell: Film Music Off the Record." <u>The Max Steiner Journal</u>, No. 5 (1980), 39-40.

2890. "Soundtracks and Shows." <u>Fanfare</u>, 4, No. 2 (1980), 231-35.

Concerning current soundtrack album releases.

2891. Spurgeon, C. P. "Musical Scores, Film and Video Media and the Canadian Composer: Facts to Consider." <u>The Canadian Composer</u> (Toronto), No. 181 (May 1983), S1-S27.

A special supplement bound with this issue. In English and French.

2892. Starr, Cecile. "Music for Documentaries." <u>Sightlines</u>, 14, No. 4 (1981), 13-14.

2893. Stetter, Elmar. "Sound Becoming More Important as Integral Part of Motion Pics." <u>Variety</u>, 309 (Jan. 12, 1983), 147-48.

2894. Stevens, James. "Letters to the Editor." <u>Key Notes Donemus</u> (Amsterdam), 11, No. 1 (1980), 1.

2895. "This London Composer Keeps Active." <u>The Canadian Composer</u> (Toronto), No. 181 (May 1983), 38.

Concerning the work of composer Ken Musch.

2896. Vallerand, François. "Accords parfaits et dissonnances." <u>Sequences</u> (Montreal), No. 111 (Jan. 1983), 96-97.

2897. ----------. "Un musicien: François Dompierre." Sequences (Montreal), No. 100 (Apr. 1980), 82-89.

2898. Vedrilla, Ronald. "Erinnerung an einen Stummfilmpianisten: zum Tode Arthur Kleiners." Film und Ton, 26 (June 1980), 62.

2899. ----------. "Musik und Stummfilm: Filmworkshop in Bonn." Film und Ton, 26 (July 1980), 10-11.

2900. Vertlieb, Steve. "Soundtrack." Cinemacabre (Baltimore, Md.), No. 3 (1980), 56-62.

    Soundtrack album reviews, with references to music by Barry, Bernstein, Goldsmith, Rozsa, and Charles Gerhardt.

2901. ----------. "Soundtrack." Cinemacabre (Baltimore, Md.), No. 5 (Fall 1982), 53-59.

2902. Waggoner, W. F. "Arthur Kleiner." New York Times, 129 (Apr. 2, 1980), Section D, p. 23.

    Obituary.

2903. Walsh, Michael. "Music: Through the Looking Glass." Time, 121 (Jan. 24, 1983), 84.

2904. Weidenaar, Reynold. "In Search of Visual Music." Independent Film Journal, 6 (June 1983), 10-12.

2905. Wells, Robyn. "Nashville Music Community Is Delving into Soundtrack Field." Billboard, 93 (Nov. 28, 1981), 90.

2906. Wiener, Thomas. "Rock of Ages: Remembering that Old-Time Rock'n'Roll -- On Cassette." American Film, 9, No. 4 (Jan.-Feb. 1984), 61-64.

2907. Wiesmeier, Peter. "Die Karriere zweier Frauen." Film und Ton, 27 (May 1981), 65-66.

2908. "Workshops East: Film and T.V." ASCAP Today (Fall 1980), 28.

2909. Zaza, Paul. "Recording: Music in Film." Canadian Musician (Toronto), 4, No. 1 (1982), 69.

2910. ----------. "Recording: Recording for Film." Canadian Musician (Toronto), 3, No. 4 (1981), 85.

2911. ----------. "Recording: Recording for Film." Canadian Musician (Toronto), 3, No. 5 (1981), 81.

2912. ----------. "Recording: Recording for Film." Canadian Musician (Toronto), 4, No. 2 (1982), 69.

    SEE ALSO:

    #471, #627, 628(Hyman), #1022, 1023(Thiel), #1980(Assayas), #2111(Niekerk), #2924(V. Gregor), #3483(Cook), #3850(Jouvet), #4886(Silber), #5462(Comuzio), #5879(Scheib), #5921(Castell), #5931(Comuzio), #6120(Squarini), #6300(ASCAP), and #6329(Morley).

Sound Techniques and Technology

2913. Burton, Geoff. "What Have They Done to My Song, Ma?" The Max Steiner Journal, No. 5 (1980), 35.

    Concerning the role of the sound mixer.

2914. "Computer Assisted Filmmaking: Musync -- Computerized Music Editing." American Cinematographer, 63 (Aug. 1982), 783-86.

2915. Kennedy, Evelyn. "Film Music Editor." Music Educator's Journal, 69, No. 2 (Oct. 1982), 54.

2916. Lockhart, Ron. Audio in Advertising: A Practical Guide to Producing and Recording Music, Voiceovers, and Sound Effects. New York: F. Ungar, 1982.

    Includes bibliography, pp. 87-88.

2917. Lustig, Milton. Music Editing for Motion Pictures. New York: Hastings House; Toronto: Copp Clark, 1980.

    -- Rev. in Music Educator's Journal, 67 (Feb. 1981), 77.

2918. Potter, Stephen, and Richard Patterson. "PAP: Post Audio Processing." American Cinematographer, 63, No. 3 (Mar. 1982), 273-80.

2919. Stone, Chris. "'Canned' Music: But Can You Tell?" Cinema Canada (Montreal), No. 60-61 (Dec. 1979-Jan. 1980), 43-44.

    SEE ALSO:

    #2850(Myers), and #2864(Penchansky).

Music for T.V.

2920. Bukhov, Leonard. "V poiskakh zvukovoi dostovernosti." Iskusstvo kino, No. 3 (Mar. 1981), 85-89.

2921. Curley, Joseph, and Ric Gentry. "Commercial Composers Choose Up Sides." Millimeter, 8, No. 7 (July 1980), 94-111.

    Concerning the use of music in television advertising.

2922. Doray, Henri-Paul. "Publicite et télévision: connaissez-vous la musique?" Film Echange, No. 17 (Winter 1982), 51-55.

2923. Filletti, Connie. "The T.V. Composer's Untapped Potential." Cinema Canada (Montreal), Nos. 60-61 (Dec. 1979-Jan. 1980), 48-50.

    References to the work of Ron Harrison and John Mills-Cockell.

2924. Gregor, Vladimir. "Hudba pro film a televizi." Hudební Rozhledy (Prague), 34, No. 12 (1981), 565ff.

2925. Honickel, Thomas. "Jeder Film braucht eine eigne Musik: Interview mit Peer Raben." Film und Ton (Munich), 26 (July 1980), 38-43.

    Includes filmography.

2926. King, Marshall. "Getting Your Foot in the Door: Preparing for Television Music -- A Look at John Rodby." International Musician, 81 (Mar. 1983), 6ff.

2927. ----------. "Preparing for a Commercial Music Career." The Instrumentalist (Evanston, Ill.), 36 (Nov. 1981), 124-27.

2928. Kopecka, M. "Z televizni obrazovky i filmoveho platna." Hudební Rozhledy (Prague), 33, No. 10 (1980), 442-45.

2929. Le Guay, Philippe. "La jungle du jingle." Cinematographe (Paris), No. 79 (June 1982), 38.

    An interview.

2930. Prox, Lothar. "Musik zu alten Filmen: Stummfilmvertonungen der Fernsehanstalten." Musica, 34, No. 1 (Jan. 1980), 25-31.

2931. Sosnik, Harry. "The Rise (Radio) and the Fall (TV) in the Importance of Composers." Variety, 305 (Jan. 20, 1982), 100.

2932. Taubman, Joseph. "Musique, Videogrammes et copyright aux Etats-Unis." Film Echange, No. 11 (Summer 1980), 25-33.

2933. Tedesco, T. "Studio Log: 'Twilight Zone' Mystery Solved." Guitar Player, 17 (July 1983), 133.

2934. "Television, 1981-1982: BMI Music on the Home Screen." BMI: The Many Worlds of Music, No. 2 (1982), 23-26.

2935. "Television 1982-83: BMI Music on the Home Screen." BMI: The Many Worlds of Music, No. 4 (1982), 29-32.

2936. Williamson, Jeff, and Samir Hachem. "Bucking the Trends and Facing New Opportunities." Millimeter, 8 (Dec. 1980), 83-84ff.

SEE ALSO:

#2222(Novick), #2711(Addison), #2775(Cook), #2916(Lockhart), and #3179 (Jomy/Rabourdin).

II. COMPOSERS

Richard Addinsell (1904-1977)

2937. Huntley, John. "Richard Addinsell." Music Parade, 2, No. 1 (1949), 19-21ff.

2938. Palmer, Christopher. "Addinsell, Richard." In The New Grove's Dictionary of Music and Musicians. Ed. Stanley Sadie. London: Macmillan, 1980, I, p. 103.

SEE ALSO:

#1408(Mathieson), and #4112(Huntley).

John Addison

2939. Bernstein, Elmer. "A Conversation with John Addison." Film Music Notebook, 3, No. 3 (1977), 18-32.

2940. Cook, Page. "The Sound Track." Films in Review, 16, No. 7 (Aug.-Sept. 1965), 438-39, 442.

Also includes references to music by E. Bernstein and Ron Goodwin.

2941. Eaton, Quaintance. "High Treason." Film Music, 11, No. 5 (May-June 1952), 7-8.

2942. Palmer, Christopher. "Addison, John." In The New Grove's Dictionary of Music and Musicians. Ed. Stanley Sadie. London: Macmillan, 1980, I, p. 104.

2943. ----------. "British Composers for the Screen: Ron Goodwin and John Addison." Performing Right, No. 56 (Nov. 1971), 20-28.

2944. Rubenstein, Lenny. "Composing for Films: An Interview with John Addison." Cinéaste, 8, No. 2 (Fall 1977), 36-37, 59.

SEE ALSO:

#131(Thomas), #2021, 2029, 2328, 2332, 2337(Cook), and #2711(Addison).

William Alwyn (1905-)

2945. Alwyn, William. "Composing for the Screen." Films and Filming, 5, No. 6 (Mar. 1959), 9, 34.

2946. ----------. "How Not to Write Film Music." British Film Academy Journal (Autumn 1954), 7.

2947. ----------. "The Music in the Background." Music Parade (London), (1947).

2948. ----------. "Odd Man Out." Film Music Notes, 7, No. 2 (Nov.-Dec. 1947), 16.

2949. Brown, Harold. "Daybreak in Udi." Film Music Notes, 9, No. 5 (May-June 1950), 14.

2950. Eaton, Quaintance. "The Magic Box." Film Music, 12, No. 1 (Sept.-Oct. 1952), 12.

2951. Huntley, John. "British Film Composers: William Alwyn." Music Parade (London), 1, No. 7 (1948).

2952. ----------. "The Music in 'The Mudlark.'" Film Music Notes, 10, No. 3 (Jan.-Feb. 1951), 10-11.

Reprinted in Limbacher, p. 96. See #75.

2953. Keller, Hans. "Film Music: Speech Rhythm." Musical Times, 96, No. 1351 (Sept. 1955), 486-87.

Reprinted in Manvell/Huntley, pp. 288-90. See #82.

2954. ----------. "William Alwyn: Bad and Great Work." The Music Review, 11 (May 1950), 145-46.

2955. Kowalski, Alfons A. "William Alwyn." Pro Musica Sana, 8, No. 3 (Summer 1980), 4-11.

Includes filmography and discography.

Additions and corrections to the filmography are offered by Clifford McCarty in Pro Musica Sana, 8, No. 4 (Fall 1980), 21.

2956. Lindgren, Ernest. "The Composer: William Alwyn." In Films in 1951: A Special Publication on British Films and Film-Makers, a special issue of Sight and Sound (July 1951), 19-20.

SEE ALSO:

#82(Manvell/Huntley), #131(Thomas), #1175(Alwyn), #1276(Forrell/Carrie), #1321, 1326(Huntley), #1355(Keller), #1737(Huntley), and #1756(Keller).

Daniele Amfitheatrof (1901-1983)

2957. Amfitheatrof, Daniele. Italy: Music and Films. (Pamphlet.) Los Angeles: Academy of Motion Picture Arts and Sciences, 1950.

Concerning the International Music Congress in Florence.

See comments by Lawrence Morton in Hollywood Quarterly, #1821. Also see Amfitheatrof's address to the Congress, #3.

2958. Bernstein, Elmer. "A Conversation with Daniele Amfitheatrof." Film Music Notebook, 1, No. 4 (Summer 1975), 14-22.

2959. "Daniele Amfitheatrof." Variety, 311 (June 15, 1983), 86.

Obituary.

SEE ALSO:

#3(Amfitheatrof), #1822(Morton), #1864, #2007(Connor/Steen), and #3199 (Duning).

George Antheil (1900-1959)

2960. Amirkhanian, Charles. "Antheil, George." In The New Grove's Dictionary of Music and Musicians. Ed. Stanley Sadie. London: Macmillan, 1980, I, pp. 453-54.

2961. Antheil, George. Bad Boy of Music. Garden City, N.Y.: Doubleday, 1945.

Antheil's autobiography. Includes Chapter 5: "Hollywood," pp. 281-368.

-- Rev. by Virgil Thomson: "Books About Music." In the New York Herald Tribune (Dec. 30, 1945).

-- Rev. by John Cage: "Recent Books: The Dreams and Dedications of George Antheil." Modern Music, 23, No. 1 (Winter 1946), 78-79.

-- Rev. by Mildred Norton in Hollywood Quarterly, 1, No. 3 (Apr. 1946), 337-38.

Reprints, London and New York: Hurst and Blackett, 1947; London: National Book Assn. (Hutchinson and Co.), 1947; and many others.

2962. ----------. "Composers in Movieland." Modern Music, 12, No. 2 (Jan.-Feb. 1935), 62-68.

2963. ----------. "The Face of American Music." In Music in Contemporary Life: A Collection of Essays on the Function and Influence of Music in Our Times, Vol. II. Ed. Walter H. Rubsamen and Lawrence Morton. Los Angeles (U.C.L.A.): Unpublished typescript, pp. 471-76.

2964. ----------. "George Antheil on Tom Scott." Bulletin of American Composers Alliance, 6, No. 2 (Winter 1957), 3.

2965. ----------. "Good Russian Advice About Movie Music." Modern Music, 13, No. 4 (May-June 1936), 53-56.

A reaction to Sabaneev's Music for the Films. See #110.

2966. ----------. "Hollywood and the New Music." Cinema Arts, 1, No. 2 (July 1937), 28-29.

2967. ----------. "Hollywood Composer." Atlantic Monthly, 165 (Feb. 1940), 160-67.

2967a. Also published in College Prose. Ed. Theodore J. Gates and Austin Wright. Boston: D. C. Heath, 1942, pp. 370-84.

2968. ----------. "The Juggler." Film Music, 12, No. 5 (May-June 1953), 10-13.

2969. ----------. "More Melody, Please!" Stage Magazine (Jan. 1, 1935), 21-22.

2970. ----------. "The Musical Score to 'The Pride and the Passion.'" Film and TV Music, 16, No. 4 (Summer 1957), 3-11.

2971. ----------. "Music in the Film." New Theatre, 2 (Oct. 1935), 14-15.

2972. ----------. "Music Takes a Screen Test." American Scholar, 6, No. 3 (Summer 1937), 354-64.

Concerning the impact of film music on the spread of "good" music.

2972a. Reprinted in Music Clubs Magazine, 18, No. 2 (Nov.-Dec. 1938), 7-10, 22.

2973. ----------. "New Tendencies in Composing for Motion Pictures." Film Culture, 1, No. 4 (Summer 1955), 16-17.

> Reprinted in Ross, pp. 238-43. See #4850.

2974. ----------. "Notes on Music: 'In a Lonely Place.'" Film Music Notes, 9,
No. 5 (May-June 1950), 11-13.

2975. ----------. "On the Hollywood Front." Modern Music, 14, No. 1 (Nov.-Dec.
1936), 46-49.

> The first article in a regular series by Antheil. Refer-
ences to the music of Werner Janssen.

2976. ----------. "On the Hollywood Front." Modern Music, 14, No. 2 (Jan.-Feb.
1937), 105-07.

> Antheil's views on the current state of film music. Includes
comments on Kurt London's Film Music (see #79), and references to music by Honegger, Walton, Werner Janssen, Boris
Morros, and Arnold Schoenberg.

2976a. Reprinted in "From 'Modern Music': Some Representative Pas-
sages." Perspectives of New Music, 2, No. 2 (Spring-Summer 1964), 26-27.

2977. ----------. "On the Hollywood Front." Modern Music, 15, No. 3 (Mar.-Apr.
1938), 187-89.

> References to the music of Kurt Weill.

2978. ----------. "On the Hollywood Front." Modern Music, 15, No. 4 (May-June
1938), 251-54.

> References to music by Blitzstein, Shostakovich, and Thomson.

2979. Hickman, C. Sharpless. "Movies and Music." Music Journal, 11, No. 8 (Aug.
1953), 26-27.

2980. Morton, Lawrence. "An Interview with George Antheil." Film Music Notes,
10, No. 2 (Nov.-Dec. 1950), 4-7.

> One of a series of interviews on film music conducted by
Morton for the Canadian Broadcasting Corporation.

2981. Post, Carl. "Musicians in Films: Antheil en Riposte." Musical Courier,
147, No. 4 (Feb. 15, 1953), 26.

2982. Pound, Ezra Loomis. Antheil and the Treatise of Harmony. Chicago: Pascal
Covici, 1927.

2983. Reisfeld, Bert. "Opern: Uraufführung in Hollywood." Musica, 3, No. 3 (Mar.
1953), 113.

2984. Whitesitt, Linda Marie. "The Life and Music of George Antheil, 1900-1959."
Ph.D. Diss., University of Maryland 1981.

> Abstract: DAI 43/06:1743A (order #DA 8214492).

2984a. Published as The Life and Music of George Antheil, 1900-1959.
Studies in Musicology, No. 70. Ann Arbor, Mich.: University Microfilms International Research Press, 1983.

>> Includes a catalogue of film, T.V., and radio scores,
pp. 250-60; a discography, pp. 263-70; and a bibliography, pp. 303-35.

> SEE ALSO:
>
> #48(Hickman), #79(London/Antheil), #132(Thomas), #274(Newsom), #1177-1183
(Antheil), #1209(Bowles), #1303(Heinsheimer), #1369(Kochnitzsky), #1437,
1441, and 1820(Morton).

Louis Applebaum

2985. Adomian, Lan. "Louis Applebaum's Score for 'Lost Boundaries.'" Film Music

Notes, 9, No. 1 (Sept.-Oct. 1949), 6-13.

Includes excerpts from the score.

2986. Applebaum, Louis. "Documentary Film Music." Film Music Notes, 6, No. 2 (Oct.-Nov. 1946), 13.

Reprinted in Limbacher, pp. 66-71. See #75.

2987. ----------. "Documentary Films." Film Music Notes, 8, No. 2 (Nov.-Dec. 1948).

2988. ----------. "Notes on the Music for 'The Whistle at Eaton Falls.'" Film Music, 11, No. 1 (Sept.-Oct. 1951), 7-11.

Includes excerpts from the score.

2989. ----------. "Some Comments on the Score for 'Lost Boundaries.'" Film Music Notes, 9, No. 1 (Sept.-Oct. 1949), 5-6.

2990. Epstein, David. "Teresa." Film Music Notes, 10, No. 4 (Mar.-Apr. 1951), 10-11.

2991. Flohil, Richard, and Michael Schulman. "Interview! Lou Applebaum." The Canadian Composer/Le Compositeur canadien (Toronto), No. 87 (Jan. 1974), 10-19.

In English and French.

2992. Pratley, Gerald. "The Stratford Adventure." Film Music, 14, No. 1 (Sept.-Oct. 1954), 15-17.

SEE ALSO:

#87, #1184, 1185(Applebaum), #1737(Huntley), #3268, 3566, 4129, and 5718 (Applebaum).

Harold Arlen

2993. Jablonski, Edward. "American Song Writer Harold Arlen." Stereo Review, 31, No. 5 (Nov. 1973), 54-65.

A survey of the songs, and the shows and motion pictures for which most were written.

2994. ----------, and William R. Sweigert. "Harold Arlen." Films in Review, 13, No. 10 (Dec. 1962), 605-14.

Includes a filmography.

SEE ALSO:

#3008(Connor/Jablonski), and #6152(Wilder).

Richard Arnell

2995. Arnell, Richard. "Composing for Animation Film." Composer (London), No. 73 (Summer 1981), 8.

2996. ----------. "'Rain Folly,' A Composed Opera/Film." Hofstra Review, 4, No. 1 (Spring 1969), 1-5.

2997. ----------. "Richard Arnell Discusses His 'Opus 65.'" Music Parade, 2, No. 12 (1952), 6-8.

2998. "'Opus 65': An Essay in Film Music." Musical Opinion, 76 (Nov. 1952), 105.

SEE ALSO:

#82(Manvell/Huntley), and #1368(Kochnitzky).

Malcolm Arnold (1921-)

2999. Keller, Hans. "Film Music and Beyond." <u>Music Review</u>, 19, No. 2 (1958), 150-51.

SEE ALSO:

#1749, 1757(Keller), #1902(Talbert et al.), #1977(Arnold), #2018(Cook), #2167(Steen), and #3086(Collins).

Georges Auric (1899-1983)

3000. Auric, Georges. "Geburt der Filmmusik und Filmmusik heute." <u>Musikerzieh-ung</u>, 6 (1952), 48-49.

   3000a. Also published in <u>Österreichischer Musikzeitschrift</u>, 7 (1952), 294-96.

3001. ----------. "Eine Konfrontierung von Malerei und Musik." <u>Studio</u>, No. 3 (1957).

3002. ----------. "Le Mystère Picasso." <u>Image et son</u>, No. 94 (1956).

3003. ----------. "On Film Music." <u>Mein Film</u>, 22, No. 34 (1952), 1.

3004. Boucourechliev, André. "Auric, Georges." In <u>The New Groves Dictionary of Music and Musicians</u>. Ed. Stanley Sadie. London: Macmillan, 1980, I, pp. 704-05.

     Includes filmography and bibliography.

3005. Cocteau, Jean. <u>Diary of a Film</u>. Trans. Ronald Duncan. London: Dennis Dobson, 1950.

     References to Auric's music for "La Belle et la bête" (1946).

3006. ----------. <u>Entretiens autour du cinématographe: recueillis par André Fraigneau</u>. Paris: Éditions André Bonne, 1951.

     Includes references to music in his films, with special attention to the work of Auric.

   3006. Also published as Cocteau on the Film: A Conversation Recorded by <u>André Fraigneau</u>. Trans. Vera Traill. New York: Roy Publishers, 1954.

       Reprint, New York: Dover, 1972, also includes an introduction by George Amberg.

3007. Comuzio, Ermanno. "Un musicista: Georges Auric." <u>La rivista del cinema italiano</u> (Milan and Rome), No. 1 (Jan.-Mar. 1955).

3008. Connor, Edward, and Edward Jablonski. "The Sound Track." <u>Films in Review</u>, 5, No. 9 (Nov. 1954), 486-87.

     Also includes references to music by Harold Arlen.

3009. Deans, Marjorie. <u>Meeting at the Sphinx</u>. London: MacDonald, 1946.

     Includes references to the music by Auric.

3010. "Georges Auric." <u>Variety</u>, 311 (July 27, 1983), 78.

     Obituary.

3011. Hendricks, Gordon. "Film Music Comes of Age." <u>Films in Review</u>, 3, No. 1 (Jan. 1952), 22-27.

     Music for the film "The Lavender Hill Mob."

     Reprinted in Limbacher, pp. 45-50. See #75.

3012. Irving, Ernest. "Film Music." <u>Tempo</u>, New series, No. 1 (Sept. 1946), 31-32.

     Also includes references to music by Arthur Bliss.

3013. Keller, Hans. "Film Music and Beyond: Georges Auric at Film Music's Best." Music Review, 15, No. 4 (Nov. 1954), 311-13.

3014. Machabey, Armand. "Auric, Georges." In Die Musik in Geschichte und Gegenwart. Ed. Friedrich Blume. Kassel: Bärenreiter, 1955, I, 862-63.

3015. Morton, Lawrence. "On the Hollywood Front." Modern Music, 23, No. 4 (Fall 1946), 313-15.

> Concerning Auric's music for "Caesar and Cleopatra," and "Dead of Night."

3016. Pinchard, Max. "Georges Auric et la musique de film." Musica (Chaix, Fr.), No. 99 (June 1962), 44-48.

3017. Pockriss, Lee J. "Moulin Rouge." Film Music, 12, No. 4 (Mar.-Apr. 1953), 4-7.

3018. Preussner, Eberhard. "Georges Auric als Tonfilmkomponist." Melos, 11, No. 2 (Feb. 1932), 52-53.

3019. Schneider, Marcel. "Le Groupe des Six." Avant-Scène du cinéma (Paris), Nos. 307-308 (May 1, 1983-May 15, 1983), 114-17.

SEE ALSO:

#142(Austin), #1183(Antheil), #1298(Hamilton), #1338(Irving), #1417(Mendez/Hamilton/Brown), #1755(Keller), #1854(Poulenc), #1866(Rattner/Eaton), #1902(Talbert et al.), #4789(Moore), and #4895(Steen).

William Axt

3020. Branscombe, Gena. "The Creative Power of the Sound Film." National Board of Review Magazine, 4 (May 1929), 3-4.

3021. Mendoza, David. "The Theme Song." American Hebrew, 124 (Mar. 15, 1929), 664.

SEE ALSO:

#43(Hagen), #115, and #474(Buchanan).

John Barry (1933-)

3022. Caps, John. "The John Barry Triptych." Film Music Notebook, 2, No. 4 (1976), 6-8.

3023. Knight, Arthur. "A Chat with the Composer." Saturday Review, 55, No. 28 (July 8, 1972), 71.

3024. Snell, Mike. "Romance Amid the 70's." The Max Steiner Journal, No. 2 (1978), 27-28.

> Also includes references to music by Michel Legrand.

SEE ALSO:

#9(Bazelon, pp. 280-86), #1974, #2030(Cook), #2272(Butler), #2303, 2309, 2327, 2331(Cook), #2363(Doherty), #2720(Barbano), #2776(Cook), #2900(Vertlieb), and #3784(Cook).

Yves Baudrier (1906-)

3025. Baudrier, Yves. "A propos de musique de film." La Revue musicale, No. 212 (Apr. 1952), 59-64.

3026. ----------. L'Expression musicale. (Pamphlet.) Paris: I.D.H.E.C., 1944.

3027. ----------. "Image et musique." Polyphonie, Ser. 2, No. 6 (1950), 77-83.

3028. Goldbeck, Frederick. "Current Chronicle: France." Musical Quarterly, 36, No. 3 (July 1950), 457-60.

SEE ALSO:
#8(Baudrier), #1723(Hopkins), #1864, 4449, and 4450(Baudrier).

Arnold Bax (1883-1953)

3029. Cronin, Kathleen. "Bax in the Modern Media." Bax Society Bulletin, No. 4 (Feb. 1969), 57-60.

3030. Foreman, Ronald Lewis Edmund. "Bax and the Score of 'Malta GC.'" Bax Society Bulletin, 2, No. 8 (Apr. 1970), 7-9.
      A description of the holograph score in the National Library of Malta.

3031. Green, Derick M. "'Oliver Twist': Music for the Film." Music in Education (Sept.-Oct. 1948).

3032. Hull, Robin. "Approach to Bax's Symphonies." Music and Letters, 23, No. 2 (Apr. 1942), 101-115.
      A helpful discussion of Bax's style as revealed by an analysis of his symphonies.

3033. Huntley, John. "The Film Music of Sir Arnold Bax." Musical Express (London), (June 25, 1948).

3034. ----------. "Music by Appointment: Sir Arnold Bax and 'Oliver Twist.'" Band Wagon, 7, No. 2 (1948).

3035. ----------. "Oliver Twist." Film Music, 11, No. 1 (Sept.-Oct. 1951), 20-22.
      Reprinted in Limbacher, pp. 99-102. See #75.

3036. Keller, Hans. "Bax's 'Oliver Twist.'" The Music Review, 9 (Aug. 1948).
   3036a. Reprinted in the Bax Society Bulletin, 2, No. 2 (1970), 22-23.

3037. Parlett, Graham. Arnold Bax: A Catalogue of His Music. London: Triad Press, 1972.

3038. Payne, Anthony. "Bax, Arnold." In The New Groves Dictionary of Music and Musicians. Ed. Stanley Sadie. London: Macmillan, 1980, II, pp. 306-10.
      Includes filmography and bibliography.

3039. Scott-Sutherland, Colin. Arnold Bax. London: Dent, 1973.
      Includes bibliography.

SEE ALSO:
#4111(Huntley).

Arthur Benjamin (1893-1960)

3040. Benjamin, Arthur. "Film Music." Musical Times (London), 78 (July 1937), 595-97.

3041. Hendricks, Gordon. "The Sound Track." Films in Review, 5, No. 3 (Mar. 1954), 147-48.
      Film music by Benjamin and others.

3042. Keller, Hans. "The Arthur Benjamin Annual." Musical Opinion (London), 78 (Sept. 1955), 721ff.

SEE ALSO:

#1755, 1756(Keller), and 5533(Hadley).

Richard Rodney Bennett (1936-)

3043. "Additions and Corrections." Film Dope, No. 12 (June 1977), 22a-22d.

3044. Bernstein, Elmer. "A Conversation with Richard Rodney Bennett." Film Music Notebook, 2, No. 1 (1976), 16-25.

3045. Caps, John. "In Conversation with Richard Rodney Bennett." Soundtrack Collectors Newsletter, 2, Nos. 7-8 (1977).

3046. Steen, T. M. F. "The Sound Track." Films in Review, 13, No. 7 (Aug.-Sept. 1962), 435-36.

3047. Tomkins, Les. "Music Gives the Meaning to a Film Says Richard Rodney Bennett." Crescendo International, 20 (June 1982), 16-17.

3048. Walsh, Stephen. "Bennett, Richard Rodney." In The New Groves Dictionary of Music and Musicians. Ed. Stanley Sadie. London: Macmillan, 1980, II, 496-99.

SEE ALSO:

#9(Bazelon, pp. 207-13), #2031(Cook), #2272(Butler), #2315, 2319, and 3823(Cook).

Elmer Bernstein (1922-)

3049. "Additions and Corrections: Elmer Bernstein." Film Dope (London), No. 16 (Feb. 1979), 24b.

3050. Bernstein, Elmer. "The Aesthetics of Film Scoring: A Highly Personal View." Film Music Notebook, 4, No. 1 (1978), 22-27.

3051. ----------. "The Annotated Friedkin." Film Music Notebook, 1, No. 2 (Winter 1974-1975), 10-16.

> Bernstein's response to remarks made by William Friedkin at an AFI Seminar. Concerning Jack Nitzsche, and music for "The Exorcist."

3052. ----------. "A Conversation with George Roy Hill." Film Music Notebook, 1, No. 2 (Winter 1974-1975), 17-25.

3053. ----------. "Film Composers vs. The Studios: A Three Hundred Million Dollar Complaint." Film Music Notebook, 2, No. 1 (1976), 31-39.

3054. ----------. "The Man with the Golden Arm." Film Music, 15, No. 4 (Spring 1956), 3-13.

> Includes references to orchestrations by Fred Steiner.

> Reprinted in Limbacher, pp. 94-95. See #75.

3055. ----------. "The Music of the Movies." AFI Seminar, Mar. 7, 1984 (8:00 p.m.). Tape recording of the seminar is held at the AFI/Louis B. Mayer Library (Los Angeles).

3056. ----------. "On Film Music." University Film Association Journal, 28, No. 4 (Fall 1976), 7-9.

> Transcription of a lecture given at the U.F.A. Conference.

3057. ----------. Seminar on Film Music: AFI/CAFS, Mar. 5, 1975 (3:30 p.m.).
Transcript of the seminar is held at the AFI/Louis B. Mayer Library (Los
Angeles).

3058. ----------. Seminar on Film Music: AFI/CAFS, Nov. 18, 1970 (2:00 p.m.).
Transcript of the seminar is held at the AFI/Louis B. Mayer Library (Los
Angeles).

3059. ----------. "The Ten Commandments." Film and TV Music, 16, No. 2 (Winter
1956), 3-16.
Reprinted in Limbacher, pp. 154-57. See #75.

3060. ----------. "What Ever Happened to Great Movie Music?" High Fidelity and
Musical America, 22, No. 7 (July 1972), 55-58.
3060a. Reprinted in Crossroads to the Cinema. Comp. Douglas Brode.
Boston: Holbrook Press, 1975, pp. 180-86.

3061. Caps, John. "A Conversation with Elmer Bernstein." Soundtrack Collector's
Newsletter, 2 (June 1983), 14-22.

3062. "Composing-for-TV Emerging as New Art Form: Elmer Bernstein's Status."
Variety, 214 (Mar. 4, 1959), 22ff.

3063. Connor, Edward. "The Sound Track." Films in Review, 8, No. 3 (Mar. 1957),
116-17.

3064. ----------, and Gerald Pratley. "The Sound Track." Films in Review, 6,
No. 10 (Dec. 1955), 534-36.
References to music by Bernstein and others.

3065. ----------, and Gerald Pratley. "The Sound Track." Films in Review, 7,
No. 6 (June-July 1956), 296-99.

3066. Cook, Page. "The Sound Track." Films in Review, 26, No. 1 (Jan. 1975), 28-
30, 37.
Also includes references to music by John Cacavas and
John Williams.

3067. ----------. "The Sound Track." Films in Review, 33, No. 5 (May 1982), 311-
13.
Also includes references to music by Mancini and Skinner.

3068. Curley, Joseph. "Elmer Bernstein: How Rock Has Rolled Over Film Scoring."
Millimeter, 8, No. 8 (Aug. 1980), 134-39.
An interview.

3069. Elley, Derek. "The Film Composer: Elmer Bernstein." Films and Filming, 24,
No. 5 (Feb. 1978); and 24, No. 6 (Mar. 1978), 20-24.
Two part interview. Includes filmography.

3070. "Elmer Bernstein Warns of Hazards in Trying to Write Pic Tunes as Pop Hits."
Variety, 237 (Feb. 10, 1965), 55.

3071. Kirk, Cynthia. "Elmer Bernstein." BMI: The Many Worlds of Music (Spring
1975), 46-47.

3072. Lasher, John Steven. "Elmer Bernstein." The Max Steiner Music Society
News Letter, No. 31 (Summer 1972), 2-3.
Includes discography.

3073. Palmer, Christopher. "Bernstein, Elmer." In The New Groves Dictionary of
Music and Musicians. Ed. Stanley Sadie. London: Macmillan, 1980, II,
p. 629.

3074. Pavelek, James ("Pav"). "Film Music Collection: An Appeal for Support."
The Max Steiner Journal, No. 4 (1979), 19-20.
Concerning the activies of Bernstein and the "Film Music
Collection."

3075. "Pressure of Getting Pop Hit Plagues Film Scorer." _Variety_, 245 (Feb. 15, 1967), 43.

3076. Scheff, Michael. "Elmer Bernstein." _Film Music Notebook_, 1, No. 2 (Winter 1974-1975), 5-9.

> Includes filmography.

3077. Vallerand, François. "Musique de films: 'Zulu Dawn,' Elmer Bernstein ... et son club." _Sequences_ (Montreal), No. 102 (Oct. 1980), 49-51.

SEE ALSO:

> #9(Bazelon, pp. 170-80), #43(Hagen), #115, #131, 132(Thomas), #221(Cook), #1602(Beguiristain), #1641(Connor/Jablonski), #1903(Talbert/Schaefer), #2010, 2011, 2018, 2020, 2022, 2035(Cook), #2100(McCutcheon), #2251-2254 (Bernstein), #2294, 2296, 2297, 2305, 2306, 2322(Cook), #2520(Pavelek), #2549(Sharples), #2591(Ulrich/Bernstein), #2771(Cook), #2900(Vertlieb), #2939(Bernstein), #2940(Cook), #2958, 3044, 3270, 3299(Bernstein), #3314 (Godfrey/Bernstein), #3329(Bernstein), #3370(Connor/Pratley), #3479, 3543 (Bernstein), #3636(Cook), #3728(Bernstein), #3732, and #4498(Chase).

Leonard Bernstein (1918-)

3078. Bernstein, Leonard. _The Joy of Music_. New York: Simon and Schuster, 1959.

> Includes references to music in films.

3079. ----------. "The World of Jazz: Script Notes for a TV Program for 'Omnibus.'" _Film and TV Music_, 16, No. 3 (Spring 1957), 20-24.

3080. Hamilton, William. "On the Waterfront." _Film Music_, 14, No. 1 (Sept.-Oct. 1954), 3-14.

> Includes extensive excerpts from the score.
>
> Reprinted in Limbacher, pp. 103-04. See #75.

3081. Hendricks, Gordon. "The Sound Track." _Film Culture_, 1, No. 1 (Jan. 1955), 58-60.

> Concerning Bernstein's score for "On the Waterfront."

3082. Keller, Hans. "On the Waterfront." _Score_ (London), No. 12 (June 1955), 81-84.

SEE ALSO:

> #167(Kingman), #3294(Schwartz/L. Bernstein), #5952(Dienes), and #6002 (Hirsch).

Arthur Bliss (1891-1975)

3083. Bliss, Arthur. "Christopher Columbus." _Film Music Notes_, 9, No. 2 (Nov.-Dec. 1949), 16.

> Reprinted in Limbacher, p. 123. See #75.

3084. Brown, Harold. "The Beggar's Opera." _Film Music_, 13, No. 1 (Sept.-Oct. 1953), 3-5.

3085. Cole, Hugo. "Bliss, Arthur." In _The New Groves Dictionary of Music and Musicians_. Ed. Stanley Sadie. London: Macmillan, 1980, II, pp. 791-94.

3086. Collins, Red. "Sir Arthur Bliss and Malcolm Arnold." _The Max Steiner Music Society News Letter_, No. 33 (Winter 1972), 3-4.

3087. Griffiths, Peter, and David J. Badder. "Sir Arthur Bliss." _Film Dope_ (London), No. 5 (July 1974), 2-5.

3088. Palmer, Christopher. _Bliss_. Novello Short Biographies. Sevenoaks: Novello, 1976.

3089. Wells, H(erbert) G(eorge). _Things to Come_. New York: Macmillan, 1935.
Film script by H. G. Wells, includes as section "The Music,"
pp. x-xi.
Reprint, London: Cresset Press, 1936.

SEE ALSO:
#1258(Dickinson), #1338(Irving), #1356(Keller), and #3012(Irving).

Marc Blitzstein (1905-1964)

3090. Blitzstein, Marc. "Coming -- The Mass Audience!" _Modern Music_, 13, No. 4
(May-June 1936), 23-29.

3091. ----------. "On Writing Music for the Theatre." _Modern Music_, 15, No. 2
(Jan.-Feb. 1938), 81-85.

3092. ----------. "Theatre-Music in Paris." _Modern Music_, 12, No. 3 (Mar.-Apr.
1935), 128-34.

3093. Dietz, Robert J. "Blitzstein, Marc." In _The New Groves Dictionary of Music and Musicians_. Ed. Stanley Sadie. London: Macmillan, 1980, II,
pp. 794-96.

3094. Wörner, Karl H. "Blitzstein, Marc." In _Die Musik in Geschichte und Gegen-
wart_. Ed. Friedrich Blume. Kassel: Bärenreiter, 1955, I, pp. 1934-35.

SEE ALSO:
#603(Hammond), #642(Josephson), #1208(Bowles), #1292(Haggin), #1368(Koch-
nitzky), #1446(Blitzstein), #2978(Antheil), and #6069(Mellers).

Scott Bradley

3095. Bradley, Scott. "Personality on the Sound Track." _Music Educators' Jour-
nal_, 33, No. 3 (Jan. 1947), 28-30.

3096. "An Interview with Scott Bradley." _Pacific Coast Musician_ (May 15, 1937),
12-13.

3097. Mellot, Albert. "'The Two Mouseketeers': With Score Excerpts." _Film Music_,
11, No. 5 (May-June 1952), 9-11.

3098. Winge, John H. "Cartoons and Modern Music." _Sight and Sound_, 17, No. 67
(Autumn 1948), 136-37.

SEE ALSO:
#208(Bradley), #274(Newsom), and #1249(Dahl).

Reiner Bredemeyer (1929-)

3099. Lange, Wolfgang. "Oberstes Prinzip: Dramaturgie." _Film und Fernsehen_ (Berlin, DDR), 7, No. 4 (1979), 15-18.
An interview with Bredemeyer. Includes filmography.

3100. Thiel, Wolfgang. "Reiner Bredemeyers Film- und Fernsehmusiken." _Musik und
Gesellschaft_, 23, No. 11 (Nov. 1973), 648-53.

SEE ALSO:
#4914(Theil).

Joseph Carl Breil

3101. Breil, Joseph Carl. "Making Musical Adaptations." In Opportunities in the Motion Picture Industry. Los Angeles: Photoplay Research Society, 1922, II, pp. 85-87.

   Includes references to the work of Carl Edouarde.

3102. ----------. "Moving Pictures of the Past and Present and the Music Provided for Same." Metronome, 32 (Nov. 1916), 42ff.

3103. "Movie Music and Joseph Carl Breil." Music News (Chicago), 11 (Sept. 26, 1919), 16.

3104. Stern, Seymour. "The Film's Score." Film Culture, 36 (Spring-Summer 1965), 103-32.

   Part of a special issue entitled "Griffith: I. 'The Birth of a Nation.'"

SEE ALSO:
#407(Beynon), #496(B. Cook), #619(Hofmann), and #1085(Breil).

Jacques Brel (1929-)

3105. Barlatier, Pierre. Jacques Brel. Brussels: Labor; and Paris: Solar, 1978.

   Includes filmography and discography.

   -- Rev. in Amis du film et de la télévision (Brussels), No. 269 (Oct. 1978), 38.

3106. Belmans, Jacques. "Jacques Brel ou le Don Quichotte du cinéma de Belgique." Amis du film: Cinéma et télévision, No. 270 (Nov. 1978), 14.

   Includes filmography.

3107. "Jacques Brel." Écran (Paris), No. 75 (Dec. 15, 1978), 67.

   Includes filmography.

3108. "Jacques Brel." Écran (Paris), No. 74 (Nov. 15, 1978), 82.

   Obituary.

3109. "Jacques Brel." Variety, 292 (Oct. 11, 1978), 2ff.

   Obituary.

3110. "Meme au cinéma, Jacques Brel confirma son enorme soif de liberte." Cine Revue (Brussels), 58 (Oct. 12, 1978), 26-27.

3111. Michaud, Christian. "Adieu Jacques Brel!" Cine Revue (Brussels), 58 (Oct. 12, 1978), 2-7.

3112. ----------. "Le mystere Brel." Cine Revue (Brussels), 58 (Aug. 31, 1978), 12-13.

3113. Serenellini, Mario. "Note allo specchio nel cinema del cantoutore." Cinema Nuovo (Turin), 32, No. 281 (Feb. 1983), 36-37.

3114. Temmerman, Jan. "Exterieur, Jacques Brel." Andere Sinema (Antwerp), No. 27 (Nov. 1980), 22-25.

3115. Vandromme, Pol. Jacques Brel: L'Exil du Far West. Brussels: Labor, 1977.

   -- Rev. in Amis du film et de la télévision (Brussels), No. 260 (Jan. 1981), 41.

Benjamin Britten (1913-1976)

3116. Gabbard, James Henry. "Benjamin Britten: His Music, the Man, and his Times." Ed.D. Diss. University of Northern Colorado 1969.

Abstract: DAI 31/01-A, p. 413.

3117. Keller, Hans. "A Film Analysis of the Orchestra." Sight and Sound, 16, No. 61 (Spring 1947), 30-31.

Concerning Britten's "Young People's Guide to the Orchestra" and the film "Instruments of the Orchestra."

3118. Mitchell, Donald, and Hans Keller, eds. Benjamin Britten: A Commentary on His Works from a Group of Specialists. New York: Philosophical Library, 1952.

Includes discography and bibliography.

3119. Schiffer, Brigitte. "Benjamin Brittens neue Fernsehoper." Melos, 38 (July-Aug. 1971), 313-14.

3120. White, Eric Walter. Benjamin Britten: A Sketch of His Life and Works. London: Boosey and Hawkes, 1948.

3120a. Also published as Benjamin Britten: eine Skizze von Leben und Werk. Trans. Bettina Hürlimann and Martin Hürlimann. Zurich: Atlantis, 1948.

3121. Wright, Basil. "Britten and Documentary." The Musical Times, 104 (Nov. 1963), 779-80.

SEE ALSO:

#1408(Mathieson), #1446(Britten), #2662(Evans), #2707(Warrack), #4105 (Britten), #4914(Thiel), and #5542(Hinton).

Mario Castelnuovo-Tedesco (1895-1968)

3122. Abramson, Robert M. "The Brave Bulls." Film Music Notes, 10, No. 4 (Mar.-Apr. 1951), 13.

3123. Keller, Hans. "Film Music: 'Time Out of Mind.'" Contemporary Cinema, 1, No. 8 (Sept. 1947).

Film score by Castelnuovo-Tedesco and Miklos Rozsa.

3124. Scalin, Burton Howard. "Compositions for the Stage by Mario Castelnuovo-Tedesco." Ph.D. Diss. (Music History), Northwestern University.

Work in progress in 1976.

3125. Teichner, Miriam. "The Brave Bulls." Film Music Notes, 10, No. 5 (May-June 1951), 12-13.

SEE ALSO:

#1417(Mendez/Hamilton/Brown), and #1891(Simon).

Charlie Chaplin (1889-1977)

3126. Bloch, Peter. "Charles Chaplin als Filmkomponist." Vier Viertel (Berlin), 7 (1953), 9.

3127. Chaplin, Charles Spencer. My Autobiography. London: The Bodley Head; New York: Simon and Schuster, 1964.

Includes some references to his film music.

3127a. Also published as Die Geschichte meines Lebens. Reutlingen:

S. Fischer, 1964.

3127b. Also published as Histoire de ma vie. Trans. Jean Rosenthal. Paris: R. Laffont, 1964.

3127c. Also published as La mia autobiografia. Trans. Vincenzo Mantovani. Verona: A. Mondadori, 1964.

3127d. Also published as Oma elämä kertani. Helsinki: Söderstrom, 1964.

3127e. Also published as Historia de mi vida. Trans. Julio Gomez de la Serna. Madrid: Taurus, 1965.

3128. Gifford, Denis. Chaplin. Garden City, N.Y.: Doubleday, 1947.

Includes a section "His Musical Career," which provides a listing of his compositions and film scores.

3129. Hickman, C. Sharpless. "Movies and Music." Music Journal, 10, No. 8 (Nov. 1952), 28-29.

3130. Huff, Theodore. "Chaplin as Composer." Films in Review, 1, No. 6 (Sept. 1950), 1-5.

An excerpt from Huff's book, which appeared the following year. See #3130a.

3130a. Also published in Huff's book, Charlie Chaplin. New York: Henry Schuman, 1951.

Chapter 25: "Chaplin as Composer," pp. 235-41.

Reprint, New York: Arno Press, 1972.

3131. Huntley, John. "The Sound Track." Sight and Sound, 22, No. 3 (Jan.-Mar. 1953), 145.

3132. Lyons, Timothy J. Charles Chaplin: A Guide to References and Resources. Boston: G. K. Hall, 1979.

A guidebook to Chaplin materials. Includes a filmography which notes composers, arrangers, and musical directors for the sound films. Also includes an extensive bibliography, and a cue-by-cue listing of musical compositions, pp. 199-202.

3133. Manvell, Roger. Chaplin. Boston: Little, Brown, and Co., 1974.

Includes a few references to Chaplin's musical role.

3134. Metzler, Martina. "Zur Beziehung zwischen Handlung und Musik in Chaplins Film 'City Lights.'" Musik und Bildung, 12 (Dec. 1980), 772-75.

3135. Pavelek, James ("Pav"). "Chaplin Remembered: The Enduring Popularity of Charlie Chaplin's Film Music." The Max Steiner Journal, No. 2 (1978), 7-8.

3136. Raksin, David. "Life with Charlie." Quarterly Journal of the Library of Congress, 40, No. 3 (Summer 1983).

3137. ----------, and Charles M. Berg. "Music Composed by Charles Chaplin: Auteur or Collaborateur?" Journal of the University Film Association, 31, No. 1 (Winter 1979), 47-50.

3138. Sadoul, Georges. Vie de Charlot: Charles Spencer Chaplin, ses films et son temps. Paris: Éditeurs français réunis, 1952.

3138a. Also published as Das ist Chaplin!: sein Leben, seine Filme, seine Zeit. Trans. Peter Loos. Vienna: Globus Verlag, 1954.

3139. Skolsky, Sidney. "Film-Flam: Chaplin's 'Modern Times.'" Hollywood Citizen-News (Nov. 26, 1935).

Also includes references to Chaplin's collaborator, David Raksin.

3140. Thomson, Virgil. "Chaplin Scores." Modern Music, 18, No. 1 (Nov.-Dec. 1940), 15-17.

SEE ALSO:

#142(Austin), #335(Arvey), #487(Chaplin), #794(Petric), #1238(Churchill), #1368(Kochnitzky), #3210(Brecht et al.), and #3751(A. Thomas).

Bill Conti

3141. Curley, Joseph. "A Few Easy Pieces." Millimeter, 7, No. 4 (Apr. 1979), 34-35ff.

Interviews with Bill Conti and Jerry Goldsmith.

3142. McCullaugh, J. "Film Composer's Lot Not Easy: Conti Considers Himself Lucky." Billboard, 89 (Aug. 20, 1977), 18.

3143. Siders, Harvey. "Bill Conti." BMI: The Many Worlds of Music, No. 2 (1977), 34-35.

3144. Wiseman, R. "Bill Conti." Songwriter Magazine (Hollywood, Calif.), 3 (Aug. 1978), 24-31.

SEE ALSO:

#2720(Barbano), and #2868(Quantrill).

Aaron Copland (1900-)

3145. Bazelon, Irwin A. "'The Heiress': A Review of Aaron Copland's Music Score." Film Music Notes, 9, No. 2 (Nov.-Dec. 1949), 17-18.

3146. Berger, Arthur. Aaron Copland. New York: Oxford University Press, 1953.

Includes the chapter "Copland and Hollywood," pp. 85-90.

3147. Copland, Aaron. "The Aims of Music for Films." New York Times (Mar. 10, 1940), Section 11, p. 7.

3148. ----------. "Music on the Soundtracks." Boston Symphony Concert Bulletin, No. 5 (Nov. 18, 1949), 250ff.

3149. ----------. Our New Music. New York: Whittlesey House/McGraw-Hill, 1941.

Part III: "New Musical Media," includes the chapters "Music in the Films," pp. 233-42 (a reworking of Copland's article "Second Thoughts..," see #3151), and "The Composer and Radio," p. 260-75.

Also published in Spanish and German translation.

NOTE: Sections on film music were deleted from the 1968 revision of Copland's book, The New Music. New York: W. W. Norton and Co.

3150. ----------. "Problèmes de la musique de film." La Vie musicale, 1 (Mar. 1951), 5-6.

3151. ----------. "Second Thoughts on Hollywood." Modern Music, 17, No. 3 (Mar.-Apr. 1940), 141-47.

An earlier version of a chapter which appeared in Copland's Our New Music. See #3149.

3152. ----------. "Tip to Moviegoers: Take Off Those Ear-Muffs." New York Times Magazine (Nov. 6, 1949), pp. 28-32.

Also see the response to this article by E. Behrens in Music Clubs Magazine (Indianapolis), 29 (Apr. 1950), 10-11ff.

3153. ----------. What to Listen for in Music. Revised edition. New York: McGraw-Hill, 1957.

Includes Chapter 17: "Film Music," pp. 152-57.

NOTE: This chapter does not appear in the original 1939 edition of Copland's book, nor does it appear in the earlier German, Swedish, Italian, Hebrew, or Spanish editions of his book.

3154. ----------. _Young People's Concert_. New York: Columbia Broadcasting System.

A filmed documentary. Available from CBS-TV, 51 West 52nd St., New York, N.Y., 10019.

3155. Guernsey, Otis L., Jr. "Function of the Movie Musical Score." _New York Herald Tribune_ (Sept. 4, 1949), Section 5, p. 1.

A report on Aaron Copland's remarks on film music.

3156. Hopkins, Antony. "The Music of Copland." _Sight and Sound_, 19, No. 8 (Dec. 1950), 336.

3157. McCarty, Clifford. "Book on Copland Misses Target on His Filmusic." _Down Beat_, 21 (June 16, 1954), 5.

3158. Morton, Lawrence. "'The Red Pony': A Review of Aaron Copland's Score." A special issue of _Film Music Notes_ (Feb. 1949).

3159. Palmer, Christopher. "Aaron Copland as Film Composer." _Crescendo International_, 14 (May 1976), 24-25.

3160. Perlis, Vivian. Interviews with Aaron Copland, 12/23/75 - 12/8/76. Tapes and transcripts are part of the project _Oral History: American Music_. New Haven, Conn.: Yale University, 1976.

3161. Rodakiewicz, Henwar. "Treatment of Sound in 'The City.'" In _The Movies as Medium_. Ed. Lewis Jacobs. New York: Farrar, Straus and Giroux, 1970.

See Jacobs, #4653.

3162. Smith, Julia Frances. "Aaron Copland, His Work and Contribution to American Music: A Study of the Development of His Musical Style and an Analysis of the Various Techniques of Writing He Has Employed in His Works." Ph.D. Diss. (Higher Education), New York University, 1952.

Abstract: DA 13/01, p. 103.

3162a. Published as _Aaron Copland: His Work and Contribution to American Music_. New York: E. P. Dutton, 1955.

Includes Chapter 7, concerning Copland's film music, pp. 184-221, and a list of works, recordings, and writings, pp. 299-322.

3163. Sternfeld, Frederick W. "Copland as a Film Composer." _Musical Quarterly_, 7, No. 2 (Apr. 1951), 161-75.

Concerning Copland's music for William Wyler films; "The Heiress," "Of Mice and Men," and "Our Town."

3164. Thomson, Virgil. "Music in Review: Copland's Score for 'The Red Pony' Hollywood's Best, but Still Hollywood." _New York Herald Tribune_ (Apr. 10, 1949), Drama section, Section 5, p. 5.

SEE ALSO:

#31(Engmann/Copland), #87, #131, 132(Thomas), #142(Austin), #167(Kingman), #642(Josephson), #1208(Bowles), #1224(Carter), #1292(Haggin), #1369(Kochnitzky), #1388, 1390(London), #1446, 1671(Copland), #2050(Dolan), #3395 (Herrmann/Copland), #4464(Bowles), and #4791(Morton).

Carmine Coppola

3165. Karman, Mal. "Carmine Coppola: Scoring with Sound." _Moving Image_, No. 5 (Mar.-Apr. 1982), 30-33.

3166. "'Napoleon' van Gance in Den Bosch." Skoop (Amsterdam), 18 (June 1982), 3.

3167. Soria, Dorle J. "'Napoleon' -- with Music." High Fidelity and Musical America, 31, No. 6 (June 1981), MA6-MA9.

3168. Verstappen, Wim. "Een grote film met: muziek was Napoleon een pacifist?" Skoop (Amsterdam), 18 (June 1982), 26-29.

John Corigliano

3169. Fitzpatrick, John. "Scoring 'Altered States': An Interview with John Corigliano." Pro Musica Sana, 9, No. 2 (Winter 1981-1982), 4-9.

3170. Gagne, Paul R. "The Filming of 'Altered States.'" Cinefantastique, 11 (Fall 1981).

3171. Holland, Bernard. "Highbrow Music to Hum." New York Times Magazine (Jan. 31, 1982), 24-25, 56-57, 65-66, 70.

> Concerning the film "Altered States."

3172. James, David P. "Between the Frames: John Corigliano and 'Altered States.'" Fanfare, 5, No. 4 (Mar.-Apr. 1982), 64-68ff.

3173. ----------. "Modern Music that Works: John Corigliano and 'Altered States.'" Pro Musica Sana, 9, No. 4 (Summer 1982), 2-6.

3174. Silver, R. "Composer John Corigliano Meets Hollywood." Virtuoso, and Keyboard Classics (Paramus, N.J.), 2, No. 2 (1981), 8-9.

Georges Delerue (1925-)

3175. Amy, Dominique. "Delerue, Georges." In The New Groves Dictionary of Music and Musicians. Ed. Stanley Sadie. London: Macmillan, 1980, V, p. 335.

3176. Baker, Bob. "Georges Delerue." Film Dope (London), No. 10 (Sept. 1976), 24-28.

> Includes filmography.

3177. Carcassonne, Philippe, and Bertrand Borie. "Dossier -- La Musique de film: Entretien avec Georges Delerue." Cinematographe (Paris), No. 62 (Nov. 1980), 33-36.

> Includes filmography.

3178. Jomy, Alain. "Musique du film." Cinéma 81, No. 268 (Apr. 1981), 120-21.

3179. ----------, and Dominique Rabourdin. "Rencontre avec Georges Delerue." Cinéma 80, Nos. 259-260 (July-Aug. 1980), 74-84.

> An interview. Includes filmography and discography.

SEE ALSO:

> #2026, 2037, 2045(Cook), #2123(Porcile), #2294, 2295, 2302, 2306, 2333 (Cook), #2465(Lacombe/Delerue), #2868(Quantrill), #4516(Colpi), #4579 (Etzkowitz), and #4894(Steen).

Paul Dessau (1894-1979)

3180. Dessau, Paul. "Moderne Beiprogramm-Musik." Reichsfilmblatt, No. 43 (1928), 21.

3181. Fanck, Arnold. "Der weisse Rausch." Melos, No. 1 (1932), 20.

3182. Hanisch, Michael. "Paul Dessau: Der Filmkomponist und Film-Illustrator." In Dialog 75: Positionen und Tendenzen. Berlin (DDR), 1976.

3183. London, Kurt. "Filmmusik und Kammermusik." Der Film, No. 44 (1929), 3.

SEE ALSO:

#3252, and #4914(Thiel).

Adolph Deutsch (1898-1980)

3184. "Adolph Deutsch." Revue du cinéma/Image et son, No. 348 (Mar. 1980), 8-9.

3185. "Adolph Deutsch." New York Times, 129 (Jan. 3, 1980), Section B, p. 19.
    Obituary.

3186. Castenza, P., et al. "Adolph Deutsch." Classic Film/Video Images, No. 68 (Mar. 1980), 44.

3187. Deutsch, Adolph. "Annie Get Your Gun." Film Music Notes, 9, No. 5 (May-June 1950), 10.
    Irving Berlin's music, with adaptations by Deutsch.

3188. ----------. "Collaboration Between the Screen Writer and the Composer." In Writer's Congress: Proceedings of the Conference Held in October 1943 (by the Hollywood Writer's Mobilization Committee). Berkeley and Los Angeles: University of California Press, 1944, pp. 248-50.
    See #1445.

3189. ----------. "Notes on the Score of 'Whispering Smith.'" Film Music Notes, 8, No. 3 (Jan.-Feb. 1949), 12-14.

3190. ----------. "Three Strangers." Hollywood Quarterly, 1, No. 2 (Jan. 1946), 214-23.
    Comments on the collaboration between the director, screen writer, and composer.

3191. Hamilton, William. "Review of 'Whispering Smith.'" Film Music Notes, 8, No. 3 (Jan.-Feb. 1949), 11.

3192. Morton, Lawrence. "Film Music Profile: Adolph Deutsch." Film Music Notes, 9, No. 2 (Nov.-Dec. 1949), 4-5.

SEE ALSO:

#1276(Forrell/Currie), #1367(Kochnitzky), #1433(Morton), #1902(Talbert et al.), #2007(Connor/Steen), #5957(Edens), and #6048(Lewine).

George W. Duning

3193. Connor, Edward, and Gerald Pratley. "The Sound Track." Films in Review, 7, No. 7 (Aug.-Sept. 1956), 358-60.

3194. Duning, George W. "From Here to Eternity." Film Music, 13, No. 4 (Mar.-Apr. 1954), 3-10.
    Reprinted in Limbacher, pp. 89-90. See #75.

3195. ----------. "'Jolson Sings Again': Composer's Notes." Film Music Notes, 9, No. 1 (Sept.-Oct. 1949), 17-18.

3196. ----------. "The Man from Laramie." Film Music, 14, No. 5 (May-June 1955), 13-18.

3197. ----------. "No Sad Songs for Me." Film Music Notes, 9, No. 4 (Mar.-Apr.

1950), 15-17.
> Reprinted in Limbacher, p. 97. See #75.

3198. ----------. "Picnic." Film Music, 15, No. 3 (Jan.-Feb. 1956), 3-16.
> Includes excerpts from the score.

3199. ----------. "Salome." Film Music, 12, No. 4 (Mar.-Apr. 1953), 8-12.
> Reprinted in Limbacher, pp. 145-46. See #75.
>
> Also includes references to music by Daniele Amfitheatrof.

3200. ----------. "Scoring with the Click Track." ASCAP in Action (New York), (Fall 1979), 46.

3201. ----------. "Two Recent Scores." Film and TV Music, 16, No. 5 (Late Summer 1957), 3-11.
> Includes commentary and excerpts from the scores from "3:10 to Yuma" and "Jeanne Eagels."
>
> Reprinted in Limbacher, p. 93 and p. 111. See #75.

SEE ALSO:
#1817(Morton), and #1902(Talbert et al.).

Brian Easdale (1909-)

3202. Easdale, Brian. "The Movie Scene -- Film Music Series: 'The Red Shoes.'" Film Music Notes, 8, No. 4 (Mar.-Apr. 1949), 7-8.
> Transcribed excerpt from the CBC series.

3203. Gibbon, Monk. The Red Shoes Ballet: A Critical Study. London: Saturn Press, 1948.

3204. Kubik, Gail. "The Red Shoes." Film Music Notes, 8, No. 4 (Mar.-Apr. 1949), 9.

SEE ALSO:
#1326(Huntley), and #1416(Mendez/Hamilton).

Hanns Eisler (1898-1962)

3205. Baker, Bob. "Hanns Eisler." Film Dope (London), No. 14 (Mar. 1978), 25-27.

3206. Betz, Albrecht. Hanns Eisler: Musik einer Zeit, die sich eben bildet. Munich: Edition text und kritik, 1976.

3206a. Also published as Hanns Eisler: Political Musician. Trans. Bill Hopkins. London and New York: Cambridge University Press, 1982.
> Includes the chapters "Practice and Theory: The Project for Film Music," pp. 169-82, and "Hollywood -- A Temporary Refuge," pp. 183-93. Also includes a bibliography, pp. 270-75, and a listing of works (including a filmography) compiled by David Blake, pp. 276-310.

3207. Blake, David. "Eisler, Hanns." In The New Groves Dictionary of Music and Musicians. Ed. Stanley Sadie. London: Macmillan, 1980, VI, pp. 89-94.
> Includes bibliography and filmography.

3208. ----------. "Hanns Eisler." The Listener, 26 (Sept. 15, 1966), 398.

3209. Boehmer, Konrad. "Zu Eislers Text 'Die Erbauer einer neuen Musikkultur.'" Kunst und Gesellschaft (Tübingen), 5, No. 6 (1971), 31ff.

3210. Brecht, Bertolt, et al. "Das ist Chaplin: Zeugnisse von Zeitgenossen." _Film und Fernsehen_ (Berlin, DDR), 6, No. 3 (1978), 32-39.

3211. Brockhaus, Heinz Alfred. "Die Bedeutung der Oktoberrevolution für das Schaffen Hanns Eislers." _Musik und Gesellschaft_, 18, No. 3 (Mar. 1968), 168-70.

3212. ----------. _Hanns Eisler_. Leipzig: Breitkopf und Härtel, 1961.

     Includes bibliography and discography.

3213. Eger, Maria. "Die Zusammenarbeit, Brecht-Eisler, die Stücke betreffend." Ph.D. Diss. (Musicology), Regensburg.

     Work in progress in 1976.

3214. Eisler, Hanns. "Aus meiner Praxis." _Musik und Gesellschaft_, 13 (Sept. 1963), 519-22.

3215. ----------. "The Composer and the Motion Picture." In _The Emergence of Film Art: The Evolution and Development of the Motion Picture as an Art, from 1900 to the Present_. Ed. Lewis Jacobs. Second edition. New York: W. W. Norton, 1979, pp. 198-205.

     An excerpt from _Composing for the Films_ (1947). See #4573a.

3216. ----------. "Conversations with Hanns Eisler." _Sovetskaya muzyka_, 33, Nos. 11-12 (Nov.-Dec. 1969), 92-98.

     An interview (in Russian) with the German literary critic Hans Bunge. Also includes a preface by Bunge, and a foreword by V. Kljuev.

3217. ----------. "Film Music -- Work in Progress." _Modern Music_, 18, No. 4 (May-June 1941), 250-54.

     The "work in progress" here is Eisler's Film Music Project at the New School for Social Research. These efforts ultimately produced _Komposition für den Film_. See #4573.

3218. ----------. _Gesammelte Werke_. Ed. Manfred Grabs. Kassel: Bärenreiter; and Leipzig: VEB Deutscher Verlag für Musik, 1968-.

     Published in several volumes. See also #3220.

3219. ----------. "Music and the Film: Illustration or Creation?" _World Film News_ (May 1936), 23.

     A response to comments by Becce. See #4288.

3220. ----------. _Musik und Politik: Textkritische Ausg. von Günter Mayer_. Munich: Rogner und Bernhard, 1973.

     Includes a discussion of films, film music, and current research.

3220a. Also published as _Musik und Politik. Schriften, 1924-1948. Eisler: Gesammelte Werke_, III, No. 1. Ed. Günter Mayer. Leipzig: VEB Deutscher Verlag für Musik, 1973.

3221. ----------. "Prejudices and New Musical Material." In _Writer's Congress: Proceedings of the Conference Held in October 1943_ (by the Hollywood Writer's Mobilization Committee). Berkeley and Los Angeles: University of California Press, 1944, pp. 260-64.

     See #1445.

3222. ----------. "Probleme der neuen Filmmusik." _Musik und Gesellschaft_, 8 (1958).

3223. ----------. "Reflections on the Future of the Composer." _Modern Music_, 12, No. 4 (May-June 1935), 180-86.

3224. Engelhardt, Jürgen. "Eislers Weg vom Agitprop zum Lehrstück." In _Hanns Eisler: Das Argument_, Sonderband V. Ed. Wolfgang F. Haug. Berlin: Argument, 1975.

     This volume also includes many other important articles on Eisler, and other aspects of his career.

3225. Grabs, Manfred. "Film- und Bühnenmusik im sinfonischen Werk Hanns Eislers." In Sammelbände zur Musikgeschichte der Deutschen Demokratischen Republik, No. 1. Berlin: Verlag Neue Musik, 1969, p. 20.

3226. ----------, ed. Hanns Eisler: A Rebel in Music. New York: International Publishers, 1978.

A collection of articles by Eisler. Includes "Hollywood Seen from the Left," pp. 101-05, "Some Remarks on the Situation of the Modern Composer," pp. 106-13, and others.

-- Rev. in Cineaste (New York), 10, No. 1 (1979-1980), 63-64.

3227. Grützner, Vera. "Das Bild-Ton-Verhältnis in Eislers Musik zu frühen DEFA-Filmen." In Hanns Eisler heute: Berichte-Probleme-Beobachtungen. Ed. Manfred Grabs. Arbeitshefte 19. Berlin: Akademie der Künste der DDR, 1974, pp. 83-85.

References to songs and music from the films "Rat der Götter" (1949), and "Unser täglich Brot" (1950).

3228. Herbort, Heinz Josef. "Hanns Eisler: Porträt eines Nonkonformisten." Die Zeit (Hamburg), (June 14, 1968).

3229. Hübner, Herbert. "Eisler, Hanns." In Die Musik in Geschichte und Gegenwart. Ed. Friedrich Blume. Kassel: Bärenreiter, 1955, III, pp. 1222-23.

3230. Jungheinrich, Hans-Klaus. "Musik und Realismus: einige Aspekte bei Hanns Eisler." In Musik zwischen Engagement und Kunst. Studien zur Wertungsforschung, III. Vienna: Universal-Edition, 1972, p. 69ff.

A paper presented at the Symposium Gesellschaftliches Engagement und Kompositorische Konsequenzen, Oct. 19-25, 1971, in Graz.

3231. Klemm, Eberhardt. "Chronologisches Verzeichnis der Kompositionen von Hanns Eisler." Beiträge zur Musikwissenschaft (Berlin, DDR), 15, No. 1 (1973).

3232. ----------. Hanns Eisler, 1898-1962. Berlin: Kulturbund der DDR, 1973.

Includes bibliography, pp. 59-114, and a catalog of works. The catalog also appears in expanded form in #3231.

3233. Knepler, Georg. "Hanns Eisler und das 'Neue' in der Musik." Musik und Gesellschaft, 8 (1958), 344ff.

3234. Lammel, Inge. "Hanns Eisler und die proletarisch-revolutionäre deutsche Musik der zwanziger Jahre." Musik und Gesellschaft (Berlin), 13 (1963), 25-28.

3235. Laux, Karl. "Filmmusik.". Aufbau: Kulturpolitische Monatschrift mit Literarischen Beiträgen, 6, No. 4 (1950), 377-79.

Remarks concerning the Adorno/Eisler volume Komposition für den Film. See #4573.

3236. Lissa, Zofia. "Hans Eisler." Kuźnica, Nos. 34-35 (1948).

3237. Lück, Hartmut. "Adorno als Geist, Eisler als Praktikus: Filmmusik und die Ursachen." Neues Forum (Vienna), 17 (Jan. 1970), 37-41.

See Adorno/Eisler, #4573.

3238. "Materialistische Kunsttheorie II: Hanns Eisler." A special issue of Alternative (Berlin), 12, No. 69 (1969).

3239. Mayer, Günter. "Hanns Eisler und die Revolution." In Hanns Eisler heute: Berichte-Probleme-Beobachtungen. Ed. Manfred Grabs. Arbeitshefte 19. Berlin: Akademie der Künste der DDR, 1974, pp. 10-12.

A paper presented at the November, 1973, Colloquium on Eisler at the Akademie der Künste.

3240. ----------. "Die Kategorie des musikalischen Materials in den ästhetischen Anschauungen Hanns Eislers. Zur Entwicklung des Theorie und Geschichte des sozialistischen Realismus im Bereich der marxistischen Musikästhetik." Ph.D. Diss. (Musicology), Humboldt University, Berlin 1970.

3241. ----------. "Über die musikalische Integration des Dokumentarischen." In _Bericht über den Internationalen Musikwissenschaftlichen Kongress, Leipzig 1966_. Kassel and Leipzig: Bärenreiter, 1970, pp. 351ff.

3242. McCann, David R. _The Hanns Eisler Hearings: Hollywood, Washington and Beyond_. (Workshop/Pamphlet.) Los Angeles: University of California at Los Angeles, 1971.

3243. Notowicz, Nathan. _Wir reden hier nicht von Napoleon. Wir reden von Ihnen!: Gespräche mit Hanns Eisler und Gerhart Eisler_. Berlin (DDR): Verlag Neue Musik, 1971.

3244. ----------, and Jürgen Elsner. _Hanns Eisler: Quellennachweise_. Hrsg. im Auftrag des Hanns-Eisler-Archives bei der Deutschen Akademie der Künste zu Berlin. Leipzig: Deutscher Verlag für Musik, 1961.

3245. Rösler, Walter. "Angewandte Musik: Notizen zu Bühnenmusiken Hanns Eislers." _Theater der Zeit_, 23, No. 13 (1968), 21-24.

3246. Rubsamen, Walter H. "A Modern Approach to Film Music: Hanns Eisler Rejects the Clichés." _Arts and Architecture_, 61, No. 11 (Nov. 1944), 20, 38.

3247. Rüdiger, Horst. "Vom Kientopp zum Filmpalast: Hanns Eisler schreibt über Probleme der Filmmusik." _Melos_, 17 (1950), 142-45.

> See Adorno/Eisler, #4573.

3248. Rutz, Hans. "Eisler, Hanns." In _Groves Dictionary of Music and Musicians_. Fifth edition. Ed. Eric Blom. London: Macmillan; and New York: St. Martin's Press, 1954, II, pp. 901-02.

3249. Schebera, Jürgen. "Hanns Eisler im USA-Exil: zu den politischen, ästhetischen und kompositorischen Positionen des Komponisten 1938 bis 1948." Ph.D. Diss. Leipzig 1976.

> 3249a. Published version, Berlin: Akademie-Verlag, 1978.
>
> Includes bibliography, pp. 224-29.

3250. Schinsky, Karl. "Der Komponist Hanns Eisler." _Deutsche Filmkunst_, 6, No. 6 (1958).

3251. Siegmund-Schultze, Walther. "Zu einigen Grundfragen der Musikästhetik." _Wissenschaftliche Zeitschrift der Martin-Luther-Universität Halle/Wittenberg_, 11, No. 2 (1962), 167ff.

3252. _Sinn und Form: Beiträge zur Literatur_. Sonderheft Hanns Eisler. Hrsg. von der Deutschen Akademie der Künste. Berlin: Rütten und Loeing, 1964.

> A collection of articles by and about Eisler. Includes contributions by David Blake, Paul Dessau, Jürgen Elsner, Ernst Fischer, Friedrich Goldman, Joris Ivens, Nathan Notowicz, Vladimir Pozner, Grigori Schneerson, Sergei Tretyakov, and others.

3253. Solomon, Maynard. _Marxism and Art: Essays Classic and Contemporary_. Detroit, Mich.: Wayne State University Press, 1973.

> Includes quotations from the 1947 version of Adorno/Eisler (#4573), with critical commentary, pp. 370-82.

3254. Stuckenschmidt, Hans Heinz. "Hanns Eisler." _Musikblätter des Anbruch_ (Vienna), 10 (1928), 163ff.

> 3254a. Reprinted in _Die grossen Komponisten unseres Jahrhunderts_. Munich: R. Piper, 1971, pp. 99ff.

3255. Szerdahelyi, Istvan. "Dramai elem vagy petlek? Adorno-Eisler: Filmzene." _Filmkultura_ (Budapest), 10 (Mar.-Apr. 1974), 82-85.

> See Adorno/Eisler, #4573.

SEE ALSO:

#40, #41(Grützner), #142(Austin), #203(Baxter), #247(Heilbut), #301(Taylor), #701(London), #1347(Jay), #1367(Kochnitzky), #1428, 1436, 1439(Morton), #1446(Eisler), #4416(Allihn), #4418(Amzoll), #4516(Colpi), #4570-

4573(Eisler), #4597(Gallez), #4847(Rosen), #4895(Steen), #4914(Thiel), and #5103(Mayer).

Jerry Fielding (1892-1980)

3256. Fielding, Jerry. "Fielding Tells Everybody Off." _Variety_, 294 (Mar. 21, 1979), 90.

3257. ----------. "Jerry Fielding on the Architecture of the Film Score." _Crescendo International_, 13 (May 1975), 23-24.

3258. "Hot Pursuit of Hit Themes in Films Scored by Composer Jerry Fielding." _Variety_, 263 (June 2, 1971), 42.

3259. "Jerry Fielding." _Revue du cinéma/Image et son_, No. 349 (Apr. 1980), 7.

3260. "Jerry Fielding." _Cinematographe_, No. 56 (1980), 74.

> Obituary.

3261. "Jerry Fielding." _New York Times_, 129 (Feb. 19, 1980), Section B, p. 4.

> Obituary.

3262. Lehman, Peter, and Jonathan Rosenbaum. "Filmmaking: Film Music -- An Interview with Jerry Fielding and Dan Carlin." _Wide Angle_ (Athens, Ohio), 4, No. 3 (1981), 64-68.

3263. Quantrill, Jay Alan. "Jerry Fielding: A Biographical Sketch." _Film Music Notebook_, 3, No. 3 (1977), 9-17.

> Includes filmography.

3264. Seydor, Paul. "Jerry Fielding: The Composer as Collaborator." _Film Music Notebook_, 3, No. 3 (1977), 43-48.

3265. Tomkins, Les. "Film Composer Jerry Fielding Speaking His Mind." _Crescendo International_, 13 (Nov. 1974), 6-7.

> An interview.

3266. ----------. "From the Bands to the Films: Jerry Fielding Tells His Outspoken Story." _Crescendo International_, 13 (Sept. 1974), 22-24.

> An interview.

SEE ALSO:
#131(Thomas), #2309, and 2312(Cook).

Hugo Friedhofer (1902-1981)

3267. Adomian, Lan. "Hugo Friedhofer's Music Score for 'Best Years of Our Lives': An Appreciation." _Film Music Notes_, 6, No. 4 (Feb.-Mar. 1947), 9-10.

3268. Applebaum, Louis. "Hugo Friedhofer's Score to 'The Best Years of Our Lives.'" _Film Music Notes_, 6, No. 5 (1947), 11-15.

> Also includes references to orchestrations by Jerome Moross.
>
> Reprinted in Limbacher, p. 81. See #75.

3268a. Also reprinted in _Film Music_, 13, No. 3 (Jan.-Feb. 1954), 15-18.

3268b. Also published as "The Best Years of Our Lives." Included as an insert accompanying the recording _Hugo Friedhofer: The Best Years of Our Lives_. Entr'acte, EDP 8101, 1979.

3269. Atkins, Irene Kahn. Interview with Hugo Friedhofer. Transcript is part of the AFI/Louis B. Mayer Foundation Oral History Program. Beverly Hills, Calif.: American Film Institute, 1974.

> Includes filmography, pp. 397-494. Also includes references

to film music by Korngold, Newman, and Steiner.

3270. Bernstein, Elmer. "An Interview with Hugo Friedhofer." Film Music Notebook, 1, No. 1 (Autumn 1974), 12-21.

3271. Brown, Royal S. "'The Best Years of Our Lives': The Elements of a Film." Included as an insert accompanying the recording Hugo Friedhofer: The Best Years of Our Lives. Entr'acte, EDP 8101, 1979.

3272. Cook, Page. "Hugo Friedhofer: A Composer for All Seasons." Included as an insert accompanying the recording Hugo Friedhofer: The Best Years of Our Lives. Entr'acte, EDP 8101, 1979.

3273. ----------. "The Sound Track." Films in Review, 26, No. 10 (Dec. 1975), 627-30.

3274. ----------. "The Sound Track." Films in Review, 28, No. 6 (June-July 1977), 369-72.

Concerning Friedhofer's score for "The Companion."

3275. ----------. "The Sound Track." Films in Review, 30, No. 5 (May 1979), 297-99.

3276. ----------. "The Sound Track." Films in Review, 32, No. 7 (Aug.-Sept. 1981), 436-38.

3277. ----------. "The Sound Track." Films in Review, 33, No. 3 (Mar. 1982), 180-85.

Concerning recent soundtrack album releases by Friedhofer, Skinner, and others.

3278. Hamilton, William. "Edge of Doom." Film Music Notes, 10, No. 1 (Sept.-Oct. 1950), 6-15.

Includes excerpts from the score.

Reprinted in Limbacher, p. 88. See #75.

3279. "Hugo Friedhofer." Variety, 303 (May 20, 1981), 130.

Obituary.

3280. Lees, Gene. "Hugo Friedhofer: A 50th Anniversary Tribute." Included as an insert accompanying the recording Hugo Friedhofer: The Best Years of Our Lives. Entr'acte, EDP 8101, 1979.

3281. ----------. "Hugo Friedhofer Scores as Dean of Movie Composers." Los Angeles Times (Mar. 30, 1975), "Calendar" section, p. 24.

3282. ----------. "Hugo Friedhofer -- Still Striving at the Periphery." High Fidelity and Musical America, 25, No. 6 (June 1975), 20ff.

3283. ----------. "Sound Track: The Good Years of Hugo Friedhofer." American Film, 2, No. 8 (June 1977), 77-78.

3284. Morton, Lawrence. "Film Music Profile: Hugo Friedhofer." Film Music Notes, 10, No. 1 (Sept.-Oct. 1950), 4-5.

3285. Palmer, Christopher. "Friedhofer, Hugo." In The New Groves Dictionary of Music and Musicians. Ed. Stanley Sadie. London: Macmillan, 1980, VI, pp. 849-50.

3286. Sternfeld, Frederick W. "Music and the Feature Films." Musical Quarterly, 33, No. 4 (Oct. 1947), 517-32.

Concerning music for "The Best Years of Our Lives," with excerpts from the score.

3286a. Reprinted in Pro Musica Sana, 7, No. 1 (Winter 1978-1979), 7-18.

3287. Thomas, Anthony. "Hugo Friedhofer." Films in Review, 16, No. 8 (Oct. 1965), 496-502.

Includes filmography.

SEE ALSO:

#44(Hagen), #119(Skiles/Friedhofer), #131. 132(Thomas), #1294(Hamilton), #1373(Kubik/Forrell/Hamilton), #1439(Morton), #1795(Lewin/Schaefer), #1817, 1820(Morton), #1903(Talbert/Schaefer), #2050(Dolan), #2099(McCutcheon), #2305, 2317, 2319, 2326(Cook), and #4791(Morton).

Giovanni Fusco (1906-1968)

3288. Badder, David J. "Giovanni Fusco." Film Dope (London), No. 18 (Sept. 1979), 21-23.

Includes filmography.

3289. Comuzio, Ermanno. "Ricordo di Giovanni Fusco." Bianco e nero, 29, No. 5 (May 1968).

3290. Decaux, Emmanuel. "Dossier -- La Musique de film: Une musique -- 'L'Éclipse.'" Cinematographe (Paris), No. 62 (Nov. 1980), 25.

SEE ALSO:

#2115(Pellegrini/Fusco), #4516(Colpi), and #4579(Etzkowitz).

George Gershwin (1898-1937)

3291. Baker, Bob. "George and Ira Gershwin." Film Dope (London), No. 19 (Dec. 1979), 20-24.

Includes an extensive filmography of songs and lyrics.

3292. Jablonski, Edward, and Milton A. Caine. "Gershwin's Movie Music." Films in Review, 2, No. 8 (Oct. 1951), 23-28.

Includes filmography.

3293. Kimball, Robert, and Alfred E. Simon. The Gershwins. New York: Atheneum, 1973.

Includes references to Gershwin's film music and filmed musicals, with a bibliography and discography.

3294. Schwartz, Charles. Gershwin: His Life and Music. With an Appreciation by Leonard Bernstein. Indianapolis, Ind.: Bobbs-Merrill, 1973.

SEE ALSO:

#1492(Rubsamen), #2720(Barbano), #4854(Rubsamen), #5218(Connor/Jablonski), #5220(Crowther), #5244(Green), #5327(Cullaz), #5957(Edens), #5990(Gutowski), #6030(Knox), #6046(Lewine), #6069(Mellers), and #6152(Wilder).

Ernest Gold (1921-)

3295. Gold, Ernest. "The Music of the Movies." AFI Seminar, March 14, 1984 (8:00 p.m.). Tape recording of the seminar is held at the AFI/Louis B. Mayer Library (Los Angeles).

3296. ----------. "Notes from the Cutting Room." Opera News, 26 (Dec. 23, 1961), 8-13.

3297. Lasher, John Steven. "Ernest Gold." The Max Steiner Music Society News Letter, No. 37 (Winter 1973), 4-5.

3298. Reisfeld, Bert. "Filmmusik in America." Musica, 15, No. 11 (Nov. 1961), 621-22.

Concerning Gold's music for "Exodus."

SEE ALSO:

#132(Thomas), #2046(Cook), #2520(Pavelek), #2591(Ulrich/Gold), and #3935 (Cook).

Jerry Goldsmith (1929-)

3299. Bernstein, Elmer. "A Conversation with Jerry Goldsmith." Film Music Notebook, 3, No. 2 (1977), 18-30.

3300. Bohn, Ronald L., et al. "Filmography/Discography: Jerry Goldsmith." Soundtrack Collectors Newsletter, 1 (Sept. 1982), 7-11.

3301. Caps, John. "Serial Music of Jerry Goldsmith." Film Music Notebook, 2, No. 1 (1976), 26-30.

3302. "Cine-disques: Jerry Goldsmith." Amis du film: cinéma et télévision (Brussels), No. 273 (Feb. 1979), 35.

3303. Cook, Page. "The Sound Track." Films in Review, 16, No. 6 (June-July 1965), 378-79.

3304. ----------. "The Sound Track." Films in Review, 23, No. 1 (Jan. 1972), 43-45.

3305. ----------. "The Sound Track." Films in Review, 23, No. 7 (Aug.-Sept. 1972), 423-25.

Also includes references to music by Ron Goodwin.

3306. ----------. "The Sound Track." Films in Review, 26, No. 9 (Nov. 1975), 555-58.

Also includes references to music by John Williams.

3307. ----------. "The Sound Track." Films in Review, 28, No. 5 (May 1977), 307-09.

3308. ----------. "The Sound Track." Films in Review, 29, No. 9 (Nov. 1978), 559-63.

3309. ----------. "The Sound Track." Films in Review, 32, No. 5 (May 1981), 298-300, 304, 309.

Concerning Goldsmith's music for television. Also includes references to music by Lee Holdridge.

3310. ----------. "The Sound Track." Films in Review, 33, No. 10 (Dec. 1982), 631-34.

3311. Elley, Derek. "The Film Composer: Jerry Goldsmith." Films and Filming, 25 (May 1979), 20-24; and 25 (June 1979), 20-27.

An interview.

3312. ----------. "Jerry Goldsmith." Film Dope (London), No. 20 (Apr. 1980), 12-13.

Includes filmography.

3313. Fiedel, Robert D. "Sound Tracks: Digging for Goldsmith." Take One (Montreal), 5, No. 8 (Mar. 1977), 32-33.

Also includes references to music by Bernard Herrmann.

3314. Godfrey, Lionel. "The Music Makers: Elmer Bernstein and Jerry Goldsmith." Films and Filming, 12, No. 12 (Sept. 1966), 36-40.

An interview.

3315. Goldsmith, Jerry. An interview. The Absolute Sound (Sea Cliff, N.Y.), 8, No. 31 (Sept. 1983).

3316. ----------. Seminar on film music: AFI/CAFS Film and Humanities Summer Institute, July 13, 1978. Transcript of the seminar is held at the AFI/

Louis B. Mayer Library (Los Angeles).

3317. ----------. Seminar on film music: AFI/CAFS, April 30, 1975 (3:30 p.m.). Transcript of the seminar is held at the AFI/Louis B. Mayer Library (Los Angeles).

3318. ----------. Seminar on film music: AFI/CAFS, May 5, 1977 (3:30 p.m.). Transcript of the seminar is held at the AFI/Louis B. Mayer Library (Los Angeles).

3319. ----------. "Vital Dialog in Film Making Between Director and Composer." Variety, No. 275 (May 15, 1974), 61.

3320. "The Goldsmith Touch." BMI: The Many Worlds of Music (May 1971), 22-23.

3321. Hutchinson, Ivan. "Soundtracks: Jerry Goldsmith." Cinema Papers (Melbourne, Austr.), No. 11 (Jan. 1977), 277.

Soundtrack album review.

3322. Maffet, James D. "Goldsmith's Oscar Winner: A Milestone." The Thousand Eyes Magazine, 2 (Apr. 1977), 27.

3323. ----------. "'The Omen' -- 'Obsession': Different Approaches to the Supernatural." Film Music Notebook, 3, No. 1 (1977), 32-44.

A comparison of approaches to film scoring by Goldsmith and Bernard Herrmann.

3324. Robbins, A. C. "Composer of the Eighties?" Pro Musica Sana, 9, No. 1 (Summer 1981), 20-21.

3325. Shales, Tom. "Scoring One for the Movies." The Washington Post (May 15, 1977).

Based upon an interview with Goldsmith.

3325a. Excerpts also appear in Music Educator's Journal, 64, No. 1 (Sept. 1977), 31.

3326. Siders, Harvey. "Jerry Goldsmith." BMI: The Many Worlds of Music (Spring 1975), 38-39.

3327. Simels, Steve. "'Star Trek' Soundtrack." Stereo Review, 44, No. 3 (Mar. 1980), 130.

3328. Strachan, Alexander. "Two Forgotten Scores: Jerry Goldsmith in Retrospect." Pro Musica Sana, 8, No. 3 (Summer 1980), 12-14.

Concerning music for the films "The Other," and "The Illustrated Man."

SEE ALSO:

#9(Bazelon, p. 188-92), #44(Hagen), #131, 132(Thomas), #2023, 2034, 2044 (Cook), #2100(McCutcheon), #2312, 2319, 2332, 2337, 2339, 2342(Cook), #2363(Doherty), #2457(Koldys), #2597(Vertlieb), #2720, 2721(Barbano), #2767, 2772, 2776-2778(Cook), #2868(Quantrill), #3141(Curley/Goldsmith), #2900(Vertlieb), #4498(Chase/Goldsmith), and #4528(Cook).

Johnny Green

3329. Bernstein, Elmer. "A Conversation with John Green." Film Music Notebook, 2, No. 4 (1976), 9-21; and 3, No. 1 (1977), 15-31.

Part 1 (Vol. 2, No. 4) includes a filmography.

3330. Eaton, Quaintance. "Rhapsody." Film Music, 13, No. 4 (Mar.-Apr. 1954), 16-17.

Notes on the film with musical direction by Johnny Green, musical adaptation by Bronislau Kaper.

3331. Green, Johnny. "'Raintree County': A Discussion of the Score by Its Composer." Film and TV Music, 17, No. 1 (Fall 1957-Winter 1958), 3-12.

Reprinted in Limbacher, pp. 136-44. See #75.

3332. ----------. Seminar on film music: AFI/CAFS, October 20, 1971 (3:15 p.m.). Transcript of the seminar is held at the AFI/Louis B. Mayer Library (Los Angeles).

3333. Hendricks, Gordon, and Johnny Green. "The Sound Track." Films in Review, 5, No. 5 (May 1954), 246-47.

A reply to an earlier article by Hendricks in which Green comments extensively on the music of Miklos Rozsa.

See Hendricks further reply in FIR, 5, No. 7, #3844.

3334. Hickman, C. Sharpless. "Movies and Music." Music Journal, 12, No. 1 (Jan. 1954), 31, 53-54.

Concerning the music department at M.G.M.

3335. Horwood, Wally, and Jack Carter. "Music as a Visual Art: Johnny Green Concludes His Story." Crescendo International, 10 (Sept. 1971), 12.

3336. "Johnny Green Tells Duties, Functions, and Details of Motion Picture Musical Director." Down Beat, 23 (Aug. 22, 1956), 13ff.

3337. McCarty, Clifford. "Johnny Green." Film and TV Music, 17, No. 1 (Fall 1957-Winter 1958), 19-20.

Includes filmography.

3338. Simon, Alfred E. "The Great Caruso." Film Music Notes, 10, No. 5 (May-June 1951), 4-6.

SEE ALSO:

#119(Skiles/Green), #132(Thomas), #2271(R.S. Brown), #3844(Hendricks), #4498(Chase/Green), #5949(Delamater), #6030(Knox), #6046, 6047(Lewine), #6111(Simon), and #6152(Wilder).

Jean Grémillon (1901-1961)

3339. Bonneau, Jacques. "Jean Grémillon: Habité par la musique, ecrivain scenariste." Cinéma 81, No. 275 (Nov. 1981), 42-47.

3340. Grémillon, Jean. "Jean Grémillon: L'Esthete et le theoricien." Cinéma 81, No. 275 (Nov. 1981), 38-41.

3341. Roland-Manuel. "Grémillon compositeur." Ciné-Club (Paris), No. 4 (1951).

Louis Gruenberg (1884-1964)

3342. Gruenberg, Louis. "Arch of Triumph." Film Music Notes, 7, No. 5 (May-June 1948), 6-7.

Includes excerpts from Gruenberg's score.

3343. ----------. "Music to the Film Audience's Ears." New York Times (Apr. 14, 1940), Section 9, p. 5.

3344. Persichetti, Vincent. "A Concerto Re-Introduces Gruenberg." Modern Music, 22, No. 2 (Jan.-Feb. 1945), 117-19.

Concerning Gruenberg's Concerto for Violin and Orchestra.

SEE ALSO:

#1206, 1210(Bowles), #1222(Carter), #1298(Hamilton), and #1390(London).

Marvin Hamlisch

3345. Curley, Joseph. "Nobody Does It Better: Composers Marvin Hamlisch and Henry Mancini Discuss Their Work." Millimeter, 7, No. 6 (June 1979), 26-30ff.

3346. Grant, Frank. "I Think I Can Talk to You as Friends: An Interview with Marvin Hamlisch." Millimeter, 2 (July-Aug. 1974), 17ff.

3347. "Ragtime and Marvin Hamlisch Put 'The Sting' on Movie Director George Roy Hill." The Ragtimer (Weston, Ontario), (Mar.-Apr. 1974), 13-16.

SEE ALSO:

#2487(Maremaa), and #3655(Vallance).

Leigh Harline (1907-1969)

3348. Care, Ross. "The Film Music of Leigh Harline." Film Music Notebook, 3, No. 2 (1977), 32-48.

Includes filmography.

3349. Morton, Lawrence. "Film Music Profile: Leigh Harline." Film Music Notes, 9, No. 4 (Mar.-Apr. 1950), 13-14.

SEE ALSO:

#212(Care), #1436, and 4791(Morton).

Scott Lee Hart

3350. Cook, Page. "The Sound Track." Films in Review, 26, No. 4 (Apr. 1975), 235-39.

3351. ----------. "The Sound Track." Films in Review, 30, No. 10 (Dec. 1979), 613-15, 624.

Concerning Hart's score for the film "Salderaladon."

SEE ALSO:

#2298, 2312, and 2326(Cook).

Victor Herbert (1859-1924)

3352. Herbert, Victor. "Moving Picture Score by Victor Herbert." Metronome, 32 (June 1916), 16.

An interview with Herbert, concerning his score for "The Fall of a Nation" (1916).

3353. McCarty, Clifford. "Victor Herbert's Filmusic." Films in Review, 8, No. 4 (Apr. 1957), 183-85.

3354. Shirley, Wayne D. "Bugle Call to Arms for National Defense!: Victor Herbert and His Score for 'The Fall of a Nation.'" Quarterly Journal of the Library of Congress, 40, No. 1 (Winter 1983), 26.

SEE ALSO:

#154(Ewen), #496(B. Cook), #726(McCarty), #965(Sinn/Kneeland), #1040(Van Vechten), and #3991(M. Steiner).

Bernard Herrmann (1911-1975)

3355. Baker, Bob. "Bernard Herrmann." Film Dope (London), No. 24 (Mar. 1982), 24-25.

3356. Bartush, Jay. "'Citizen Kane': The Music." Film Reader, No. 1 (1975), 50-54.

3357. "Bernard Herrmann." Cinéma 76 (Paris), No. 206 (Feb. 1976), 190.
     Obituary.

3358. "Bernard Herrmann." Focus on Film, No. 25 (Summer-Autumn 1976), 10.

3359. "Bernard Herrmann." Movie Maker (Gt. Britain), 10 (Mar. 1976), 152.
     Obituary.

3360. "Bernie Herrmann's Posthumous Honor." Variety, 281 (Feb. 4, 1976), 3.

3361. Bertolina, Gian Carlo. "Bernard Herrmann e il 'black and white sound.'" Filmcritica (Rome), 32, No. 315 (June 1981), 289-96.

3362. Broeck, John. "Music of the Fears: Bernard Herrmann." Film Comment, 12, No. 5 (Sept.-Oct. 1976), 56-60.
     Includes discography.

3363. Brown, Royal S. "Bernard Herrmann and the Subliminal Pulse of Violence." High Fidelity and Musical America, 26, No. 3 (Mar. 1976), 75-76.
     Soundtrack album review.

3364. ----------. "Herrmann and Hitch." High Fidelity and Musical America, 28, No. 4 (Apr. 1978), 90-91.

3365. ----------. "Herrmann, Hitchcock, and the Music of the Irrational." Cinema Journal, 21, No. 2 (Spring 1982), 14-49.
     A valuable study of Herrmann's film music. Includes discography.
   3365a. Reprinted in Pro Musica Sana, 10, Nos. 3-4 (Fall 1983), 15-25; and 11, No. 1 (Spring 1984), 6-13.

3366. ----------. "An Interview with Bernard Herrmann." High Fidelity and Musical America, 26, No. 9 (Sept. 1976), 64-67.
     Includes discography.

3367. ----------. "'North by Northwest': By Hitchcock by Herrmann." Fanfare, 3, No. 6 (1980), 12-15.

3368. Carcassone, Philippe. "Dossier -- La Musique de film: Hommage à Bernard Herrmann." Cinematographe (Paris), No. 59 (July-Aug. 1980), 51.

3369. Clarisse, Patrick. "Cine-disques: Bernard Herrmann." Amis du film, cinéma et télévision (Brussels), Nos. 252-253 (May-June 1977), 20.
     Includes discography.

3370. Connor, Edward, and Gerald Pratley. "The Sound Track." Films in Review, 6, No. 5 (May 1955), 245-47.
     Also includes references to music by Elmer Bernstein.

3371. Cook, Page. "Bernard Herrmann." Films in Review, 18, No. 7 (Aug.-Sept. 1967), 398-412.
     Includes filmography.

3372. ----------. "The Sound Track." Films in Review, 15, No. 8 (Oct. 1964), 493-94.
     Also includes references to music by Maurice Jarre.

3373. ----------. "The Sound Track." Films in Review, 21, No. 6 (June-July 1970), 371-73.

3374. ----------. "The Sound Track." Films in Review, 22, No. 9 (Nov. 1971), 562-64.

3375. ----------. "The Sound Track." Films in Review, 25, No. 8 (Oct. 1974), 494-97.

3376. ----------. "The Sound Track." Films in Review, 27, No. 3 (Mar. 1976), 175-78, 180.

3377. ----------. "The Sound Track." Films in Review, 27, No. 4 (Apr. 1976), 234-37.

3378. ----------. "The Sound Track." Films in Review, 27, No. 9 (Nov. 1976), 561-64.

    Concerning Herrmann's score for "Obsession."

3379. ----------. "The Sound Track." Films in Review, 29, No. 5 (May 1978), 307-09.

3380. ----------. "The Sound Track." Films in Review, 31, No. 10 (Dec. 1980), 615-17, 639.

    Concerning new soundtrack albums, with references to music by Herrmann, Rozsa, and John Williams.

3381. De Palma, Brian. "Murder by Moog: Scoring the Chill." Village Voice (Oct. 11, 1973), 85.

  3381a. Reprinted as "Remembering Herrmann" in Take One, 5, No. 2 (May 1976), 40-41ff.

3382. Doherty, Jim. "The Herrmann Zone." Midnight Marquee, No. 31 (Fall 1982), 10-13.

3383. Dorst, Gary D. "Farewell to the Master: Bernard Herrmann." Gore Creatures, No. 25 (Sept. 1976), 19-23.

3384. Duynslaegher, Patrick. "Filmmuziek." Film en televisie (Brussels), No. 234 (Nov. 1976), 26-27.

3385. Gilling, Ted. "Bernard Herrmann: A John Player Lecture (11 June 1972)." Pro Musica Sana, 3, No. 1 (Spring 1974), 10-16; and 3, No. 2 (Summer 1974), 18-27.

3386. ----------. "The Colour of the Music: An Interview with Bernard Herrmann." Sight and Sound, 41, No. 1 (Winter 1971-1972), 36-39.

    Concerning Herrmann's collaborations with Hitchcock and Welles.

3387. Glanville-Hicks, Peggy. "Herrmann, Bernard." In Groves Dictionary of Music and Musicians. Fifth edition. Ed. Eric Blom. London: Macmillan; and New York: St. Martin's Press, 1954, IV, p. 255.

3388. Goldfarb, Phyllis. "Orson Welles's Use of Sound." Take One, 3, No. 6 (July-Aug. 1971), 10-14.

    Concerning the use of sound in "Citizen Kane", "The Magnificent Ambersons", "Lady from Shanghai," and "Touch of Evil." Also includes references to the work of David Raksin and Heinz Roemheld.

3389. Herrmann, Bernard. "The Contemporary Use of Music in Film: 'Citizen Kane,' 'Psycho', 'Fahrenheit 451.'" University Film Study Center Newsletter Supplement (Cambridge, Mass.), 7, No. 3 (Feb. 1977), 5-10. (Incl. bibliog.).

3390. ----------. "From Sound Track to Disc." Saturday Review of Literature, 30, No. 39 (Sept. 27, 1947), 42.

3391. ----------. "Music in Motion Pictures -- A Reply to Mr. Leinsdorf." Music Publisher's Journal, 3, No. 5 (Sept.-Oct. 1945), 17, 69.

    See Leinsdorf's article in the same volume. See #1380.

3392. ----------. "Note on the Composition of the Music for 'Anna and the King of Siam.'" Film Music Notes, 6, No. 1 (Sept.-Oct. 1946), 22.

3393. ----------. "Reminiscence and Reflection: Bernard Herrmann, Composer." In _Sound and the Cinema: The Coming of Sound to American Film_. Ed. Evan William Cameron et al. Pleasantville, N.Y.: Redgrave Publishing, 1980, pp. 117-35.

      See #1139.

3394. ----------. "Score for a Film." _New York Times_ (May 25, 1941), Section 9, p. 6.

      Concerning Herrmann's score for "Citizen Kane."

3394a. Reprinted as "Citizen Kane" in _Film Music Notes_, 1, No. 1 (1941).

3394b. Reprinted as "Score for a Film." In _Focus on Citizen Kane_. Ed. Ronald Gottesman. Englewood Cliffs, N.J.: Prentice-Hall, 1971, p. 69ff.

3394c. Also published as "Eraan elokuvan musiikki." In _Filmihullu_ (Helsinki), No. 5 (1977), 18-19.

3395. ----------, and Aaron Copland. "Is It Bad to be Good?" _Newsweek_, 26 (July 9, 1945), 93.

      In defense of "quality" film music.

3396. Hutchinson, Ivan. "Bernard Herrmann." _Cinema Papers_ (Melbourne, Austr.), 3 (Mar.-Apr. 1976), 375ff.

3397. Johnson, Edward. _Bernard Herrmann: Hollywood's Music-Dramatist_. Traid Bibliographical Series, VI. Rickmansworth, Engl.: Triad Press, 1977.

      Includes bibliography, discography and filmography, and an introduction and Foreword by Miklos Rozsa.

      -- Rev. by Alan Hamer: "A Herrmann Sketchbook." _Pro Musica Sana_, 7, No. 4 (Fall 1979), 18.

3398. Kolodin, Irving. "The Wide Screen World of Bernard Herrmann." _Saturday Review_, 3, No. 11 (Mar. 6, 1976), 35-38.

      Includes discography.

3399. Kresh, Paul. "Top-Drawer Film Scores by Bernard Herrmann." _Stereo Review_ (Boulder, Colo.), 27, No. 4 (Oct. 1971), 81.

3400. Llewellyn, Mark. "Herrmann." _Films in Review_, 27, No. 6 (June-July 1976), 381.

3401. MacDonald, Eric. "A Tribute to the Late Bernard Herrmann." _Films Illustrated_ (London), 6 (Apr. 1977), 318.

      Includes discography.

3402. Malmkjaer, Paul. "Bernard Herrmann." _Kosmorama_ (Copenhagen), 22, No. 129 (1976), 5-6.

3403. McCarty, John. "A Retrospective Look at Bernard Herrmann." _Classic Film/Video Images_, No. 70 (July 1980), 27-28.

      Includes filmography.

3404. Naremore, James. _Filmguide to 'Psycho.'_ Bloomington, Ind.: Indiana University Press, 1973.

      References to Herrmann's music.

3405. Niogret, Hubert. "En hommage à Benny (sur Bernard Herrmann)." _Positif_ (Paris), No. 187 (Nov. 1976), 42-51.

      Includes discography and filmography.

3406. Palmer, Christopher. "American Film Music's Bernard Herrmann." _Crescendo International_, 11 (Apr. 1973), 23-24.

3407. ----------. "Bernard Herrmann, 1911-1975: A Personal Tribute." _Crescendo International_, 14 (Mar. 1976), 8-9.

3408. ----------. "Herrmann, Bernard." In _The New Grove Dictionary of Music and Musicians_. Ed. Stanley Sadie. London: Macmillan, 1980, VIII, pp. 519-20.

Includes filmography and bibliography.

3409. ----------. "I Won't Use Six Musicians If a Film Needs Sixty Says Bernard
Herrmann." Crescendo International, 11 (May 1973), 23.

3410. ----------. "The Music of Bernard Herrmann." Monthly Film Bulletin (BFI,
London), 43, No. 513 (Oct. 1976), 224.

3411. Reisner, Joel. "Cinema Music." Music Journal, 26, No. 9 (Nov. 1968), 6,
12.

Concerning film scores by Herrmann and others.

3412. Sammon, Paul M. "Farewell to the Master: The Fantastic Film Scores of Bernard Herrmann." Photon (New York), No. 27 (1977), 14-17.

Includes filmography and discography.

3413. Sharples, Win, Jr. "Cinescenes: Bernard Herrmann 1911-1975." Filmmakers
Newsletter, 9, No. 12 (Oct. 1976), 12ff.

3414. Steen, T. M. F. "Le Bande-son: De 'Wozzeck' à 'Vertigo.'" Cahiers du cinéma, 26, No. 152 (Feb. 1964), 42-44.

3415. Steiner, Fred. "Bernard Herrmann." Film Music Notebook, 1, No. 4 (Summer
1975), 4-9.

Includes filmography.

3415a. Reprinted as "Bernard Herrmann: An Unauthorized Biographical
Sketch." Film Music Notebook, 3, No. 2 (1977), 6-11.

3416. ----------. "Herrmann's 'Black and White Music' for Hitchcock's 'Psycho.'"
Film Music Notebook, 1, No. 1 (Fall 1974), 28-36; and 1, No. 2 (Winter
1974-1975), 26-46.

3417. Teegarden, John, and Robert A. Wilson, Jr. "Aural Fixations: Soundtracks
in Key." Audience (New York), 9 (Sept. 1976), 11-12.

3418. Teisseire, Guy. "Un coup de cymbales peut quelquefois ... (en guise de requiem pour Bernard Herrmann et quelques autres)." Positif (Paris),
No. 187 (Nov. 1976), 33-39.

Also includes references to music by Korngold, Rozsa,
Steiner, and Waxman.

3419. Vallance, Tom. "On Record." Focus on Film (London), No. 27 (1977), 56ff.

3420. Verstappen, Wim. "Wim Verstappen herinnert zich Bernard Herrmann. Het enige
dat telt is wat de grote doden ervan denken." Skoop (The Hague), 12
(Feb. 1976), 6-9.

3421. Weis, Elisabeth. "The Sound of One Wing Flapping." Film Comment, 14, No. 5
(Sept.-Oct. 1978), 42-48.

Concerning Herrmann's score for Hitchcock's "The Birds."

SEE ALSO:

#9(Bazelon, pp. 232-35), #131, 132(Thomas), #198(Archibald), #1376(La-
touche), #1434(Morton), #2012, 2023, 2041, 2043, 2044(Cook), #2098(Mc
Cutcheon), #2165, 2167(Steen), #2304, 2307, 2317, 2319, 2325-2327(Cook),
#2367(Duynslaegher), #2387(Fiedel), #2407(Garel), #2487(Maremaa), #2777
(Cook), #2852(Norden), #3313(Fiedel), #3323(Maffet), #3873(Pugliese),
#4480(Cameron), #4578(Erens), #4667(Kalinak), #4895(Steen), and #6213(Pru-
ett).

Paul Hindemith (1895-1963)

3422. Hindemith, Paul. "Originalmusik einzig erstrebenswert." Der Film, supplement to No. 47 (1929).

NOTE: Lehrgänge der Rundfunkversuchsstelle bei der Hochschule für Musik Berlin.

3423. ----------. "Zur mechanischen Musik." In Programmheft "Deutsche Kammermusik." Baden-Baden, 1927, pp. 51-55.

3424. "Im Studio 'bei Hindemith.'" Film-Kurier, No. 69 (1930).

SEE ALSO:
#142(Austin).

Frederick Hollander (1896-1976)

3425. Hickman, C. Sharpless. "Movies and Nusic." Music Journal, 11, No. 10 (Oct.
1953), 30.

3426. Hollander, Frederick. (Friedrich Hollaender.) Von Kopf bis Fuss: mein Leben mit Text und Musik. Munich: Kindler, 1965.

3427. Mersmann, Hans. "Tonfilm: 'Der blaue Engel.'" Melos, 9, No. 4 (Apr. 1930),
188.

Arthur Honegger (1892-1955)

3428. Baker, Bob. "Arthur Honegger." Film Dope (London), No. 25 (Nov. 1982), 12-
14.
Includes a detailed filmography.

3429. Chapallaz, G. "Arthur Honegger et la musique de cinéma." Feuilles musicales (Paris), No. 208 (1952).

3430. Delannoy, Marcel F. G. Honegger. Paris: Éditions Pierre Horay, 1953.
Includes a section "Le Film," pp. 155-61, a listing of
works, pp. 241-50 (including a filmography, p. 249), and
a discography, pp. 233-39.

3431. Hoérée, Arthur, and Arthur Honegger. "Particularités du film 'Rapt.'" In
Le Film sonore: L'Écran et la musique en 1935, a special issue of La Revue
musicale, 15, No. 151 (Dec. 1934), 88-91.
Concerning the Hoérée/Honegger collaboration for the film.

3432. Honegger, Arthur. "Du cinéma sonore à la musique réelle." Plans (Paris),
No. 1 (Jan. 1931), 74-79.

3433. ----------. Je suis compositeur. Collection "Mon Métier." Paris: Éditions
du Conquistador, 1951.
Includes a number of references to Honegger's film music.

3433a. Also published as Ich bin Komponist: Gespräche über Beruf,
Handwerk und Kunst in unserer Zeit. Trans. Suzanne Oswald.
Zurich: Atlantis Verlag, 1952.

3433b. Also published as I Am a Composer. Translated from the French
by Wilson O. Clough in collaboration with Allan Arthur Will-
man. London: Faber and Faber; and New York: St. Martin's
Press, 1966.
Also a Japanese (1953), Hebrew (1954), Dutch (1956), and
Hungarian (1960) translation.

3434. ----------. "Les musiciens vus par les cinéastes." Comoedia (Paris),
No. 108 (July 1943).

3435. ----------. "Musique de film." Comoedia (Paris), No. 96 (May 1943).

3436. ----------. "Musique de film." Comoedia (Paris), No. 1 (1944).

3437. ----------. "Musique et cinéma." Masque (Paris), (First Trimester 1946).

3438. Ress, Etta Schneider. "Audio-Visual Forum." <u>Music Educator's Journal</u>, 38, No. 2 (Nov.-Dec. 1951), 40, 42.

> Concerns Honegger's score for "Pacific 231."

3439. Vredenburg, Max. "Over Honeggers Filmervaringen." <u>Mens en melodie</u>, 11 (1956), 5-6.

3440. Vuillermoz, Emile. "Honegger and His Time." <u>Modern Music</u>, 3, No. 1 (Nov.-Dec. 1925), 3-8.

<u>SEE ALSO</u>:

#142(Austin), #480(Calvocoressi), #793(Petit), #1183(Antheil), #1388(London), #2976(Antheil), #4462(Bourgeois), #4464(Bowles), and #5306(Taubman).

Kenyon Hopkins

3441. Bachmann, Gideon. "Composing for Films." <u>Film and TV Music</u>, 16, No. 5 (Late Summer 1957), 15-16.

> An interview with Hopkins.

3442. Feather, Leonard. "From Pen to Screen: Kenyon Hopkins." <u>International Musician</u>, 70 (Sept. 1971), 7ff.

3443. Hopkins, Kenyon. "Notes on Three Scores." <u>Film and TV Music</u>, 16, No. 5 (Late Summer 1957), 12-15.

> Concerning Hopkins' scores for "The Strange One", "Twelve Angry Men," and "Baby Doll."

<u>SEE ALSO</u>:

#1602(Beguiristain).

Jacques Ibert (1890-1962)

3444. Baker, Bob. "Jacques Ibert." <u>Film Dope</u> (London), No. 26 (Jan. 1983), 28-29.

> Includes filmography.

3445. Hamilton, William. "Macbeth." <u>Film Music Notes</u>, 8, No. 2 (Nov.-Dec. 1948).

3446. Ibert, Jacques. "Doléances et suggestions." In <u>Le Film sonore: L'Écran et la musique en 1935</u>, a special issue of <u>La Revue musicale</u>, 15, No. 151 (Dec. 1934), 352-53 (32-33).

> 3446a. Also published as "Lamenti e suggerimenti." <u>Filmcritica</u> (Rome), 31, Nos. 305-306 (May-June 1980), 214-15.

3447. ----------. "'Macbeth': Notes by Composer." <u>Film Music Notes</u>, 8, No. 2 (Nov.-Dec. 1948).

3448. ----------. "Musique et cinéma." In <u>Le Livre d'or du cinéma français</u>. Paris: Agence d'information cinématographique, 1945.

<u>SEE ALSO</u>:

#4460(Boilès).

Maurice Jarre (1924-)

3449. Amy, Dominique. "Jarre, Maurice." In <u>The New Groves Dictionary of Music and Musicians</u>. Ed. Stanley Sadie. London: Macmillan, 1980, IX, p. 559.

3450. Cook, Page. "The Sound Track." Films in Review, 20, No. 6 (June-July 1969), 370-72.

      Also includes references to music by Anthony Bowles.

3451. ----------. "The Sound Track." Films in Review, 23, No. 8 (Oct. 1972), 495-97.

3452. Griffiths, Peter. "Maurice Jarre." Film Dope (London), No. 27 (July 1983), 39-41.

      Includes a detailed filmography.

3453. Jarre, Maurice. "Entretien." Image et son, 6, No. 163 (1963).

3454. McCutcheon, Bill. "The Sound Track." Films in Review, 14, No. 5 (May 1963), 294-95.

      Also includes references to music by Alfred Newman.

    SEE ALSO:

      #2067(Hanson), #2101(McCutcheon), #2123(Porcile/Jarre), #2165(Steen), #2295, 2312, 3372, and 3481(Cook).

Maurice Jaubert (1900-1940)

3455. Amy, Dominique. "Jaubert, Maurice." In The New Groves Dictionary of Music and Musicians. Ed. Stanley Sadie. London: Macmillan, 1980, IX, p. 560.

3456. Baker, Bob. "Maurice Jaubert." Film Dope (London), No. 27 (July 1983), 42-44.

      Includes a detailed filmography.

3457. Bruyr, José. "Jaubert, Maurice." In Die Musik in Geschichte und Gegenwart. Ed. Friedrich Blume. Kassel: Bärenreiter, 1955, VI, pp. 1779-81.

3458. ----------. "Maurice Jaubert." Revue musicale, 22, No. 198 (Feb.-Mar. 1946), 50-51.

3459. Canadian Film Museum. Hommage à Maurice Jaubert. Montreal: La Cinémathèque canadienne, 1967.

      A collection of articles by several contributors.

3460. "Cine-disques: La Musique de 'La chambre verte.'" Amis du film: Cinéma et télévision, Nos. 266-267 (July-Aug. 1978), 35.

3461. Gauthier, Guy. "Cine-parade 1930-1939 de Tino Rossi a Maurice Jaubert." Revue du cinéma/Image et son, No. 330 (July-Aug. 1978), 32.

3462. Gorbman, Claudia Louise. "Film Music: Narrative Functions in French Films." Ph.D. Diss. University of Washington 1978.

      Abstract: DAI 1978, p. 3188A (order #DA 7824455).

      Includes references to the theories of Eisler and Eisenstein, with special focus upon the film music of Maurice Jaubert.

3463. ----------. "Vigo/Jaubert." Ciné-tracts, 1, No. 2 (Summer 1977), 65-80.

      Concerning Jaubert's music for "Zero for Conduct."

3464. Insdorf, Annette. "Maurice Jaubert and François Truffaut: Musical Continuities from 'L'Atalante' to 'L'Histoire d'Adèle H.'" Yale French Studies, No. 60 (1980), 204-18.

3465. Jaubert, Maurice. "Music and Film." World Film News, 1, No. 4 (July 1936), 31.

3466. ----------. "Music on the Screen." In Footnotes to the Film. Ed. Charles Davy. London: Lovat and Dickson; and New York: Oxford University Press, 1937, pp. 101-15.

Reprint, New York: Arno Press, 1970.

3466a. Also published as "La Musique dans le film." In Le Cinéma: Cours et conférences de l'IDHEC (Paris: L'Institute des hautes études cinématographiques), No. 1 (1944).

3466b. Reprinted in Intelligence du cinématographe. Comp. Marcel L'Herbier. Paris: Éditions Corrêa, 1946, pp. 368-71.

See L'Herbier, #4729.

3466c. Also published as "La musica nel film," in Bianco e nero, 28, Nos. 3-4 (Mar.-Apr. 1967), 102-03.

See #2116.

3466d. Reprinted in Filmcritica (Rome), 28, Nos. 279-280 (Dec. 1977), 390-91.

3467. ----------. "Musique de film." L'Écran français (Paris), 3, (June 1946).

3468. ----------. "Petite école du spectateur." Esprit (Paris), 4, No. 1 (Apr. 1936).

3469. "Jaubert Pioneered Artistic Weaving of Music into Films." Variety, 275 (May 15, 1974), 60.

3470. Porcile, François. "François Truffaut en compagnie de Maurice Jaubert." Revue du cinéma/Image et son, No. 327 (Apr. 1978), 37-41.

Includes discography.

3471. ----------. "Jaubert retrouve." Avant-Scene du cinéma, No. 165 (Jan. 1976), 7-9.

3472. ----------. Maurice Jaubert: Musicien populaire ou maudit? Paris: Les Éditeurs français réunis, 1971.

Includes bibliography and discography.

-- Rev. in Schweizerische Musikzeitung, 111, No. 6 (1971), 376-77.

3473. Smith, John. Jean Vigo. London: November Books, 1972.

Includes detailed analysis of Jaubert's scores for Vigo's films.

3474. Via, Baldo. "Maurice Jaubert." Rivista del cinematografo (Rome), 54 (Nov. 1981), 579-82.

SEE ALSO:

#1389(London), #1408(Mathieson), #2367(Duynslaegher), and #4597(Gallez).

Quincy Jones (1933-)

3475. Harrison, Ed. "A Day in the Life of Quincy Jones." Billboard, 90 (July 15, 1978), 75.

3476. Jones, Quincy. "Quincy Jones on the Composer." In Movie People: At Work in the Business of Film. Ed. Fred Baker and Ross Firestone. New York: Douglas Book Corp., 1972, pp. 147-70.

3477. Lees, Gene. "Adventures of a Black Composer in Hollywood." New York Times, 124 (Mar. 16, 1975), Section 2, p. 21.

SEE ALSO:

#44(Hagen), #119(Skiles/Jones), and #4530(Cook).

Bronislau Kaper (1902-1983)

3478. Atkins, Irene Kahn. Interviews with Bronislaw Kaper, July 14-October 14, 1975. Transcript is part of the American Film Institute/Louis B. Mayer Foundation Oral History Program. Beverly Hills, Calif.: AFI, 1975.

Includes filmography, pp. 424-84.

3479. Bernstein, Elmer. "Bronislau Kaper Interview." Film Music Notebook, 4, No. 2 (1978), 12-28.

Includes filmography.

3480. "Bronislau Kaper." Variety, 311 (May 4, 1983), 541.

Obituary.

3481. Cook, Page. "The Sound Track." Films in Review, 16, No. 5 (May 1965), 303-04.

Also includes references to music by Maurice Jarre.

3482. ----------. "The Sound Track." Films in Review, 34, No. 6 (June-July 1983), 375-78.

Includes discography.

3483. ----------. "The Sound Track." Films in Review, 35, No. 3 (Mar. 1984), 184-86.

Concerning Kaper's score for "Lili," and other current soundtrack album releases.

3484. McConnell, Stanlie. "Teaching Possibilities in Current Films: 'Song of Love.'" Film Music Notes, 7, No. 1 (Sept.-Oct. 1947), 5-13.

3485. Palmer, Christopher. "Kaper, Bronislaw." In The New Groves Dictionary of Music and Musicians. Ed. Stanley Sadie. London: Macmillan, 1980, IX, p. 798.

3486. Reisner, Joel. "Cinema Music: Kaper's Film Capers." Music Journal, 26, No. 4 (Apr. 1968), 71, 77.

3487. Ross, Lillian. "Piccolos Under Your Name, Strings Under Mine." In Picture. New York: Avon Discus Books, 1969, pp. 116-74.

Concerning Kaper's music for Huston's "The Red Badge of Courage."

SEE ALSO:

#131(Thomas), #1428(Morton), #1493(Rubsamen), #2029, 2040(Cook), and #3330 (Eaton).

Anton Karas (1906-)

3488. Hamilton, William. "'The Third Man' Music." Film Music Notes, 9, No. 3 (Jan.-Feb. 1950), 5-6.

Reprinted in Limbacher, pp. 109-10. See #75.

3489. Keller, Hans. "Film Music: The Harry Lime Theme." Music Survey, 3 (June 1951), 283-85.

3490. Morton, Lawrence. "Film Music of the Quarter." Hollywood Quarterly, 5, No. 1 (Fall 1950), 49-52.

3491. Onnen, F. "Poging tot analyse van een succes." Mens en melodie (Utrecht), 5 (Apr. 1950), 116-19.

3492. "Thriller with a Zither Theme." Christian Science Monitor Magazine (Feb. 25, 1950), 14.

Concerning music for "The Third Man."

Aram Khachaturian (1903-1978)

3493. Khachaturian, Aram. "Les Griefs du compositeur." Recherches soviétiques,
No. 3 (Apr. 1956), 167-74.

3494. ----------. "Muzyka filma." Iskusstvo kino (Moscow), No. 11 (Nov. 1955),
30-38.

3495. ----------. "Muzyka v kinoiskusstvie i na kinoproisvodstve." Iskusstvo
kino (Moscow), No. 5 (May 1947), 25-27.

3496. ----------. Pesni sovetskogo kino. (Pamphlet.) Moscow, 1950.

3497. Streller, Friedbert. Aram Chatschaturjan. Leipzig: VEB Deutscher Verlag
für Musik, 1968.

> Includes a listing of works (with filmography), a brief
> film music discography, and bibliography, pp. 199-207.

SEE ALSO:
#82(Manvell/Huntley), #4776(McKay), and #4931(Khachaturian).

Erich Wolfgang Korngold (1897-1957)

3498. Behlmer, Rudy. "Erich Wolfgang Korngold." Films in Review, 18, No. 2
(Feb. 1967), 86-100.

3499. Bertolina, Gian Carlo. "La 'golden age' di Erich Wolfgang Korngold." Rivista del cinematografo (Rome), 54 (Nov. 1981), 583-87.

3500. Brown, Royal S. "The Korngold Era." High Fidelity and Musical America, 23,
No. 2 (Feb. 1973), 66, 68.

3501. Carroll, Brendan G. Erich Wolfgang Korngold, 1897-1957: His Life and Works.
Paisley, Scotland: Wilfion Books, 1983.

> A small volume which anticipates a major biography of Korn-
> gold (work in progress in 1983). Includes filmography and
> discography.

3502. ----------. "Korngold, Erich Wolfgang." In The New Groves Dictionary of
Music and Musicians. Ed. Stanley Sadie. London: Macmillan, 1980.

3503. ----------. "The Operas of Erich Wolfgang Korngold." Ph.D. Diss. University of Liverpool 1975.

3504. Colles, H. C. "Korngold, Erich (Wolfgang)." In Groves Dictionary of Music
and Musicians. Ed. Eric Blom. London: Macmillan; and New York: St. Martin's Press, 1954, IV, p. 825.

3505. Cook, Page. "The Sound Track." Films in Review, 23, No. 10 (Dec. 1972),
635-37.

3506. Dale, S. S. "Contemporary Cello Concerti: Korngold and Penderecki." The
Strad, 87, No. 1036 (Aug. 1976), 277-89.

> Includes references to comments by Andre Previn concerning
> the "Devotion" Concerto.

3507. Hammond, Philip J. S. "Erich W. Korngold." The Max Steiner Music Society
News Letter, No. 27 (Summer 1971), 3-6.

3508. Hoffman, R. S. Erich Wolfgang Korngold. Vienna, 1922.

3509. "Korngold Appointed Musical Director of Film 'Magic Fire.'" Musical Courier,
150 (Sept. 1954), 28.

   3509a. Additional information on Korngold's adaptation of Wagner's
music may also be found in "An Important Musical Picture."
Music Clubs Magazine (Indianapolis), 35 (Nov. 1955), 20.

3510. Korngold, Erich Wolfgang. "The Music of Wagner in 'Magic Fire.'" Film Music, 15, No. 3 (Jan.-Feb. 1956), 17.

> Comments concerning the musical supervision for the film.

3511. ----------. "Some Experiences in Film Music." In Music and Dance in California. Comp. William J. Perlman. Hollywood: California Bureau of Musical Research, 1940, pp. 137-39.

> See Perlman, #1467.

3512. Korngold, George. "Recording 'The Adventures of Robin Hood.'" The Cue Sheet (Los Angeles), 1, No. 1 (Jan. 1984), 6-7.

3513. Korngold, Luzi. Erich Wolfgang Korngold: Ein Lebensbild. Österreichische Komponisten des XX. Jahrhunderts, X. Vienna: Verlag Elisabeth Lafiti/ Österreichischer Bundesverlag für Unterricht, Wissenschaft und Kunst, 1967.

> -- Rev. in Composer, No. 29 (Autumn 1968), 3.
> -- Rev. in Music and Letters, 49, No. 2 (1968), 188-89.
> -- Rev. in Neue Zeitschrift für Musik, 129 (July-Aug. 1968), 352.

3514. Korngold, Julius. "About the Fate of Film Music." Musical America, 19 (Feb. 10, 1942), 23ff.

3515. ----------. Child Prodigy. New York: Willard, 1945.

> A biography of Korngold, written by his father.

3516. "Magic Fire." Opera (London), 7 (June 1956), 383-84.

3517. Miller, Frank. "Analysis of the Korngold Cello Concerto." Film Music Notes, 6, No. 4 (Feb.-Mar. 1947), 20-23.

> Includes excerpts from the manuscript.

3518. Moffett, James D. "The Sea Hawk." The Max Steiner Music Society News Letter, No. 33 (Winter 1972), 6-7.

> Review of the soundtrack album.

3519. Pfannkuch, Wilhelm. "Korngold, Julius Leopold, and Erich Wolfgang." In Die Musik in Geschichte und Gegenwart. Ed. Friedrich Blume. Kassel: Bärenreiter, 1955.

3520. Thomas, Anthony. "Erich Wolfgang Korngold." Films in Review, 7, No. 2 (Feb. 1956), 89-90.

3521. ----------. "The Sound Track." Films in Review, 13, No. 3 (Mar. 1962), 177-78.

3522. Vallance, Tom. "The Best of Korngold: Music to Spill Blood By." Film (London), Series 2, No. 4 (July 1973), 8.

> A review of the soundtrack album, and other recent album releases.

SEE ALSO:

> #131, 132(Thomas), #1257(De Vore), #1315(Huntley), #1388(London), #2487 (Maremaa), #3269(Atkins), #3418(Teisseire), #3887(Rozsa), #3983(Snell), #3999(Thomas), and #4667(Kalinak).

Gail Kubik (1914-)

3523. Helm, Everett. "Gail Kubik's Score for 'C-Man': The Sequel." Quarterly of Film, Radio, and Television, 9, No. 3 (Spring 1955), 263-82.

> Concerning Kubik's Pulizer Prize winning "Symphony Concertante," in comparison with the film score for "C-Man."

3524. Kubik, Gail. "The Composer's Place in Radio." Hollywood Quarterly, 1, No. 1 (Oct. 1945), 60-68.

3525. ----------. "Composing for Government Films." Modern Music, 23, No. 3 (Summer 1946), 189-92.

3526. ----------. "Music in Documentary Film." In Writer's Congress: Proceedings of the Conference Held in 1943 (by the Hollywood Writer's Mobilization Committee). Berkeley and Los Angeles: University of California Press, 1944, pp. 256-59.

      See #1445.

    3526a. Reprinted in Musical Opinion (London), 67 (Sept. 1944).

    3526b. Reprinted in Music Publishers' Journal, 3, No. 5 (Sept.-Oct. 1945), 13, 54-56.

3527. Sabin, Robert. "Gerald McBoing Boing Issued in Concert Form." Musical America, 72, No. 8 (Aug. 1952), 32.

3528. Sternfeld, Frederick W. "Current Chronicle: Musical Score of 'C-Man.'" Musical Quarterly, 36 (Apr. 1950), 274-76.

3529. ----------. "Gail Kubik's Score for 'C-Man.'" Hollywood Quarterly, 4, No. 4 (Summer 1950), 360-69.

3530. ----------. "Kubik's McBoing Score: With Excerpts of Score." Film Music Notes, 10, No. 2 (Nov.-Dec. 1950), 8-16.

    SEE ALSO:

       #9(Bazelon, pp. 287-97), #1203, 1204(Bowles), #1369(Kochnitzky), #1373 (Kubik/Forrell/Hamilton), #1435(Morton), #3204(Kubik), #4855 and 4859 (Rubsamen).

Michel Legrand (1932-)

3531. Amy, Dominique. "Legrand, Michel." In The New Groves Dictionary of Music and Musicians. Ed. Stanley Sadie. London: Macmillan, 1980, X, p. 614.

3532. Brown, Royal S. "Music and 'Vivre sa vie.'" Quarterly Review of Film Studies, 5, No. 3 (Summer 1980), 319-33.

3533. Collet, Jean. "An Audacious Experiment: The Soundtrack of 'Vivre sa vie.'" In Focus on Godard. Ed. Royal S. Brown. Englewood Cliffs, N.J.: Prentice-Hall, 1972, pp. 160-62.

3534. Duroy, Alain. "Pour 'Le cadeau,' Clio Goldsmith et Pierre Mondy ont enregistre une chanson en duo, signée Michel Legrand!" Cine Revue (Brussels), 62 (Feb. 25, 1982), 5.

3535. McVay, Douglas. "The Music in 'Les Parapluies.'" Film (London), No. 42 (Winter 1964), 31-32.

3536. Rabourdin, Dominique. "Entretien avec Michel Legrand." Cinéma 81, Nos. 271-272 (July-Aug. 1981), 68-71.

3537. "Vivre sa vie." L'Avant-scene du cinéma, No. 19 (Oct. 15, 1962).

    SEE ALSO:

       #2013, 2043(Cook), #2123(Porcile/Legrand), #2303, 2305, 2327, 2778(Cook), #3024(Snell), and #3620(Steen).

Walter Leigh (1905-1942)

3538. "Walter Leigh." Film Dope (London), No. 21 (Oct. 1980), 32.

Includes filmography.

SEE ALSO:

#687(Leigh), #1205(Bowles), #1379(Leigh), #1389(London), and #1408(Mathieson).

Oscar Levant (1906-1972)

3539. Levant, Oscar. Memoirs of an Amnesiac. New York: G. P. Putnam, 1965.

Levant's autobiography, with many references to his film music, and the world of the Hollywood composer/musician.

3540. ----------. "Movie Music." Town and Country (New York), (Dec. 1939), 90-91, 130-33.

3539a. Reprinted as "A Cog in the Wheel." In A Smattering of Ignorance. New York: Doubleday, 1940, pp. 89-144.

The article appears as Chapter 3 in Levant's autobiography.

Also see comments by Ernest Irving, #1339.

3539b. Reprinted, in part, in Theodore J. Ross' Film and the Liberal Arts, pp. 221-29.

See #4850.

3541. ----------. The Unimportance of Being Oscar. New York: G. P. Putnam's Sons, 1968.

Henry Mancini (1924-)

3542. Berg, Charles. "Henry Mancini: Sounds in the Dark." Down Beat, 45 (Dec. 7, 1978), 14-15ff.

3543. Bernstein, Elmer. "A Conversation with Henry Mancini." Film Music Notebook, 4, No. 1 (1978), 9-16ff.

An interview. Includes filmography.

3544. Binkley, Fred. "Mancini's Movie Manifesto." Down Beat, 37 (Mar. 5, 1970), 16-17.

3545. Brown, Royal S. "'The Pink Panther Strikes Again.': Original Film Soundtrack Recording." High Fidelity and Musical America, 27 (Apr. 1977), 119-20.

3546. Caps, John. "Henry Mancini: On Scoring and Recording." Soundtrack Collector's Newsletter, 2, No. 10 (1977), 3-5.

3547. ----------. "The Lyricism of Mancini." Film Music Notebook, 3, No. 2 (1977), 12-17.

3548. Comuzio, Ermanno. "Blake & Henry." Cineforum (Bergamo), 22, No. 220 (Dec. 1982), 48-54.

Concerning music for Blake Edwards' films.

3549. Cook, Page. "The Sound Track." Films in Review, 26, No. 7 (Aug.-Sept. 1975), 426-28, 432.

3550. Kolodin, Irving. "Have Gunn ..." Saturday Review, 42, No. 15 (Apr. 11, 1959), 55.

Concerning music for the T.V. series "Peter Gunn."

3551. Lees, Gene. "Mancini at Fifty -- Mr. Lucky." High Fidelity and Musical America, 25, No. 7 (July 1975), 11-12.

3552. Mancini, Henry. "An Interview." <u>Dialogue on Film</u> (American Film Institute), 3, No. 3 (1974).

3553. ----------. "The Music of the Movies." AFI Seminar, February 29, 1984 (8:00 p.m.). Tape recording of the seminar is held at the AFI/Louis B. Mayer Library (Los Angeles).

3554. ----------. "Off the Soundtrack." <u>Down Beat</u>, 24 (Aug. 8, 1957), 30.

3555. ----------. "On the Soundtrack." <u>Down Beat</u>, 24 (Oct. 3, 1957), 51-52.

> Concerning Mancini's approach and procedures for scoring a film.

3556. ----------. "On the Soundtrack." <u>Down Beat</u>, 24 (Dec. 26, 1957), 48.

> Concerning techniques for "pre-scoring."

3557. ----------. Seminar on film music: AFI/CAFS Film and Humanities Summer Institute, August 9, 1979. Transcript of the seminar is held at the AFI/Louis B. Mayer Library (Los Angeles).

3558. ----------. Seminar on film music: AFI/CAFS, October 13, 1973 (11:30 a.m.). Transcript of the seminar is held at the AFI/Louis B. Mayer Library (Los Angeles).

3559. ----------. <u>Sounds and Scores: A Practical Guide to Professional Orchestration</u>. New York: Northridge Music, 1962. (Reprint, 1967).

3560. Marrocco, W. Thomas. "Mancini, Henry." In <u>The New Groves Dictionary of Music and Musicians</u>. Ed. Stanley Sadie. London: Macmillan, 1980, XI, p. 603.

3561. Powers, James. "Henry Mancini Seminar." <u>Dialogue on Film</u> (American Film Institute), 3, No. 3 (1974), 2-24.

SEE ALSO:

> #131, 132(Thomas), #154(Ewen), #1922(Watson), #2067(Hanson), #2099(McCutcheon), #2182, #2297, 2310, 2775, 3067(Cook), and #3345(Curley/Hamlisch/Mancini).

Enzo Masetti (1893-1961)

3562. Marshall, James. "Off the Beaten Track: 'Le Fatiche di Ercole.'" <u>Pro Musica Sana</u>, 7, No. 3 (Summer 1979), 21-22.

3563. Masetti, Enzo. <u>Di alcuni aspetti e problemi della musica cinematografica: conferenza</u>. (Pamphlet.) Accademia nazionale di Santa Cecilia, Manifestazioni culturali, 1956.

3564. ----------. "Il realismo musicale nel film." <u>Bianco e nero</u>, 11, No. 3 (Mar. 1950), 32-35.

> A paper which was later read at the 1950 Florence Congress.

3565. ----------. "Introduzione ai problemi della musica nel film." <u>Bianco e nero</u> (Rome), 11, Nos. 5-6 (May-June 1950).

> See #1832.

3565a. Reprinted in <u>La musica nel film</u>. Ed. Luigi Chiarini. Rome: Bianco e nero editore, 1950, pp. 7-29.

> A paper presented at the 1950 Venice conference. See #1627 and #1864.

Norman McLaren

3566. Applebaum, Louis. "Music in the Round." <u>Film Music</u>, 11, No. 2 (Nov.-Dec. 1951), 17-19.

Concerning music for the Telecinema in London, with references to music and experiments in animated sound by McLaren.

3567. "Hen Tracks on Sound Tracks." Popular Mechanics, 91 (Apr. 1949), 168-69.

3568. Jordan, William E. "Norman McLaren: His Career and Techniques." Quarterly
of Film, Radio and Television, 8, No. 1 (Fall 1953), 1-14.

3569. Manvell, Roger, and John Halas. "The Work of Norman McLaren," and "The Pro-
duction Process for Norman McLaren's Films." In The Technique of Film
Animation. London and New York: Focal Press, 1959, pp. 290-303.
See #176.

3570. McLaren, Norman. "Notes on Animated Sound." Quarterly of Film, Radio and
Television, 7, No. 3 (Spring 1953), 223-29.
Concerning McLaren's activities at the National Film Board
of Canada, and his experiments in animated sound.

3571. Pratley, Gerald. "'Blinkity Blank' and Other Canadian News." Film Music,
15, No. 1 (Sept.-Oct. 1955), 20-21.

3572. Vinet, Pierre. "Multi-McLaren." Take One, 1, No. 1 (Sept.-Oct. 1966), 18-
22.

SEE ALSO:
#82(Manvell/Huntley).

Edmund Meisel (1894-1930)

3573. Chowl, Hay. "Interview with Herr Meisel." Close Up (London), 4 (Mar.
1929), 44-48.
References to music for Eisenstein's "Potemkin," and other
films.

3574. Ebert-Obermeier, T. "Kunst im Dienst der Revolution: zur Musik von Edmund
Meisel für den Film 'Panzerkreuzer Potemkin.'" Musik und Gesellschaft,
32, No. 11 (Nov. 1982), 648-53.

3575. Kriegsman, Alan. "A Fusion of Art." The Washington Post (Mar. 24, 1972).
Concerning the music for Eisenstein's "Potemkin."

3576. Meisel, Edmund. Article in Das neue Russland (Apr. 1928).

3576a. Also translated by R. Saxlin, and published as "Yhteistyöni
Eisensteinin kanssa," in Filmihullu (Helsinki), No. 5
(1977), 10-11.

3577. ----------. "Erfahrungen bei der musikalischen Arbeit am Tonfilm." Melos,
9, No. 7 (July 1930), 312-13.

3578. ----------. "Tonfilm in England und Amerika." Melos, 9, No. 4 (Apr. 1930),
182-85.

SEE ALSO:
#464(Bowen), #1839(Neumann), #4303(Borneman), and #4562(Eisenstein).

Ernst Hermann Meyer (1905-)

3579. Müller-Medek, Tilo. "'...solange Leben in mir ist': Einige Gedanken über
die Musik Ernst Hermann Meyers zum Karl-Liebknecht-Film der DEFA." Musik und Gesellschaft, 15 (Dec. 1965), 811-13.

3580. Thiel, Wolfgang. "Ernst Hermann Meyer. Film- und Horspielmusik. Musik zu

speziellen Rundfunksendungen." In Ernst Hermann Meyer: Das kompositor-
ische und theoretische Werk. Ed. Mathias Hansen. Handbücher der Sektion
Musik. Veröffentlichung der Akademie der Kunste de DDR. Leipzig: VEB
Deutscher Verlag für Music; and Mainz: Schott, 1976, pp. 188-202.

> Includes bibliography.

3581. ----------. "Die Filmmusik im Schaffen Ernst Hermann Meyers." Musik und
Gesellschaft, 25, No. 12 (Dec. 1975), 712-16.

3582. Vetter, Walther. "Meyer, Ernst Hermann." In Die Musik in Geschichte und
Gegenwart. Ed. Friedrich Blume. Kassel: Bärenreiter, 1955, IX, pp. 245-
46.

> Includes bibliography.

3583. Young, Percy M. "Meyer, Ernst Hermann." In The New Groves Dictionary of
Music and Musicians. Ed. Stanley Sadie. London: Macmillan, 1980, XII,
pp. 242-44.

> Includes filmography and bibliography.

Michel Michelet

3584. Michelet, Michel. "Atlantis." Film Music Notes, 7, No. 4 (Mar.-Apr. 1948),
7-10.

3585. ----------. "The Man on the Eiffel Tower." Film Music Notes, 9, No. 4
(Mar.-Apr. 1950), 18-19.

3586. ----------. "Notes on the Musical Score Written for 'The Chase.'" Film
Music Notes, 6, No. 3 (Dec. 1946-Jan. 1947), 11-12.

3587. Tozzi, Romano. "The Sound Track." Films in Review, 12, No. 6 (June-July
1961), 364-65.

Darius Milhaud (1892-1974)

3588. Milhaud, Darius. "Deux expériences de film sonore." La Revue du cinéma
(Nov. 15, 1929), 36-40.

> Concerning music for the film "La Petite Lilie."

3588a. Also published in English translation as "Experimenting with
Sound Films," in Modern Music, 7, No. 2 (Feb.-Mar. 1930),
11-14.

3589. ----------. "Film Music." World Film News, 1, No. 1 (Apr. 1936).

3590. ----------. "Music for the Films." Theatre Arts, 31, No. 9 (Sept. 1947),
27-29.

3591. ----------. "Music in French Film." In Writer's Congress: Proceedings of
the Conference Held in October 1943 (by the Hollywood Writer's Mobilization Committee). Berkeley and Los Angeles: University of California
Press, 1944, pp. 272-76.

> See .#1445.

3592. ----------. Notes sans musique. Paris: R. Julliard, 1949.

> Milhaud's autobiography.

3592a. Also published as Notes Without Music. Trans. from the French
by Donald Evans. Ed. Rollo H. Myers. London: Dennis Dobson,
1952.

> > Includes the chapter "Music for the Theatre and the Cine-
> > ma," pp. 204-16.

3593. ----------. "Wagner, Verdi e il film." Cinema (Rome), No. 22 (May 25,
1937), 406-07.

3593a. Reprinted in <u>Atti del secondo congresso internazionale di musica, Firenze-Cremona, 11-26 maggio, 1937</u>. Florence: F. Le Monnier, 1940, pp. 257-59.

Milhaud's commentary was presented at the 1937 Florence Congress, and appears here with synopses in German and French, p. 260. See #1186.

3593b. Also published in English translation by Peter Brooke, in <u>World Film News</u>, 2, No. 4 (July 1937), 27.

3594. Petit, Raymond. "Music Written for French Films." <u>Modern Music</u>, 3, No. 3 (Mar.-Apr. 1926), 32-36.

Also includes references to music by Satie, Honegger, and others. See #793.

3595. "Rotterdam: 'Entr'acte' van Satie-Milhaud." <u>Mens en melodie</u> (Utrecht), 23 (Apr. 1968), 118-20.

3596. Thoresby, C. "Music in Paris." <u>The Strad</u>, 67 (Oct. 1956), 208.

<u>SEE ALSO</u>:

#142(Austin), #603(Hammond), #642(Josephson), #793(Petit), #1184(Applebaum), #1207(Bowles), #1276(Forrell/Currie), #1408(Mathieson), #1671(Milhaud et al.), #1794(Lewin), and #4898(Stern).

Giorgio Moroder

3597. Atkinson, Terry. "Scoring with Synthesizers." <u>American Film</u>, 7, No. 10 (Sept. 1982), 66-71.

Concerning scores by Moroder and Vangelis.

3598. Chin, B. "Riffs: FlashDanceMusic." <u>Village Voice</u>, 28 (Sept. 13, 1983), 55.

3599. Schrader, Paul. "Giorgio Moroder." <u>Interview</u>, 12 (Mar. 1982), 56-58.

3600. Siders, Harvey. "Giorgio Moroder." <u>BMI: The Many Worlds of Music</u>, No. 2 (1979), 22-23.

Ennio Morricone (1928-)

3601. Bertolina, Gian Carlo. "Musica e film: Morricone, precorritore eccelso di generi." <u>Filmcritica</u> (Rome), 33, No. 321 (Jan. 1982), 60-61.

Includes filmography.

3602. Chevassu, François. "Musique et cinéma: Ennio Morricone." <u>Revue du cinéma/Image et son</u>, No. 280 (Jan. 1974), 4-7; and No. 280 (Mar. 1974), 8-9.

Includes filmography and discography.

3603. Clarisse, Patrick. "Ennio Morricone." <u>Amis du film et de la télévision</u>, No. 246 (Nov. 1976), 16-17.

3604. Comuzio, Ermanno. "Il musicista per film come co-autore Ennio Morricone: 'mettiamo le cose a posto.'" <u>Cineforum</u>, No. 217 (Sept. 1982), 37-47.

Includes filmography.

3605. Cumbow, Robert C. "Morricone encomium." <u>Movietone News</u> (Seattle), No. 40 (Apr. 1975), 22-26.

3606. DeMary, Tom. "The Composer -- Ennio Morricone." <u>The Max Steiner Music Society News Letter</u>, No. 47 (Summer 1976), 8-9.

3607. Garel, Alain. "La Musique de films." <u>Écran 78</u>, No. 68 (Apr. 15, 1978), 84-85.

3608. Larson, Randall D. "The Score: Some Thing New from Ennio Morricone." Cine-fantastique, 13, No. 4 (1983), 12.

3609. Niogret, Hubert. "Biofilmodiscographie d'Ennio Morricone." Positif (Paris), No. 266 (Apr. 1983), 8-11.

3610. ----------. "Ennio Morricone sur trois notes." Positif (Paris), No. 266 (Apr. 1983), 2-3.

3611. ----------. "Entretien avec Ennio Morricone." Positif (Paris), No. 266 (Apr. 1983), 4-8.

3612. Reisner, Joel. "Cinema Music." Music Journal, 26, No. 5 (May 1968), 10, 16.

    Concerning a collaboration between composers Morricone and Gillo Pontecorro.

3613. Vallerand, François. "Quelques notes ..." Sequences (Montreal), No. 110 (Oct. 1982), 72-73.

    Also includes references to music by Philippe Sarde.

3614. Wolthius, Julius J. C. "Filmmuziek." Skoop (Amsterdam), 14 (Mar. 1978), 17.

3615. ----------. "Filmmuziek." Skoop (Amsterdam), 14 (Apr. 1978), 40.

3616. ----------. "Morricone: 'Bach schreef toch ook elke dag een muziekstuk?'" Skoop (Amsterdam), 14 (May 1978), 41-43.

    An interview.

SEE ALSO:

    #2331(Cook).

Mario Nascimbene

3617. Cook, Page. "The Sound Track." Films in Review, 18, No. 3 (Mar. 1967), 165-67.

3618. Giusti, Marco. "Con Mario Nascimbene." Filmcritica (Rome), 31, Nos. 305-306 (May-June 1980), 234-35.

    An interview.

3619. Nascimbene, Mario. "L'uso di strumenti insoliti e di effetti realistici nella colonna sonora." Filmcritica (Rome), 31, Nos. 305-306 (May-June 1980), 244-46.

3620. Steen, T. M. F. "The Sound Track." Films in Review, 13, No. 2 (Feb. 1962), 115-16.

    Concerning "satirical" film music by Nascimbene and Michel Legrand.

SEE ALSO:

    #1641, 1642(Connor/Jablonski), #2035(Cook), and #2115(Pellegrini/Nascimbene).

Wilhelm Neef (1916-)

3621. Krause, Ernst. "Die Musik zum Thälmannfilm." Deutsche Filmkunst, 3 (1955), 255-56.

3622. Neef, Wilhelm. "Filmmusik nach wie vor Lückenbüsser." Musik und Gesellschaft, 12, No. 2 (Feb. 1962), 77-79.

3623. ----------. "Filmmusik und Kritik." _Deutsche Filmkunst_, 5 (1957), 114-15.

3624. ----------. "Filmmusik weiter ignoriert: Offener Brief an die Redaktion." _Deutsche Filmkunst_, 4 (1956), 235.

3625. ----------. "Über die Komposition der Musik zu 'Ernst Thälmann -- Sohn seiner Klasse.'" _Deutsche Filmkunst_, 2 (1954), 26-29.

3626. Rebling, Eberhard. "Die Musik zum Thälmannfilm von Wilhelm Neef." _Musik und Gesellschaft_, 4 (1954), 164-66.

3627. Schinsky, Karl. "Der Filmkomponist Wilhelm Neef." _Deutsche Filmkunst_, 7, No. 7 (1959).

3628. ----------. "Wenn der Komponist Eigenes gibt ... Gedanken über die Musik Wilhelm Neefs zu dem DEFA-Film 'Der Hauptmann von Köln.'" _Deutsche Film-kunst_, 5 (1957), 38-40.

Alfred Newman (1901-1970)

3629. "Alfred Newman." _Look_, 10, No. 4 (Feb. 19, 1946), 86-89.

3630. Balinger, Virginia. "Musical Hollywood: Alfred Newman, Fox Music Director, Gives Views on Motion Picture Scores." _Musical Leader_ (Chicago), (Mar. 1943), 5.

3631. Brown, Harold. "A Man Called Peter." _Film Music_, 14, No. 4 (Mar.-Apr. 1955), 3-9.

3632. ----------. "The Robe." _Film Music_, 13, No. 2 (Nov.-Dec. 1953), 3-17.
     Includes extensive excerpts from the score.

3633. Cook, Page. "The Sound Track." _Films in Review_, 16, No. 4 (Apr. 1965), 244-46.

3634. ----------. "The Sound Track." _Films in Review_, 21, No. 4 (Apr. 1970), 234-36.

3635. ----------. "The Sound Track." _Films in Review_, 27, No. 6 (June-July 1976), 369-72, 376.
     Concerning the establishment of the Newman Library.

3636. ----------. "The Sound Track." _Films in Review_, 28, No. 1 (Jan. 1977), 44-46, 55.
     Also includes references to music by Elmer Bernstein.

3637. ----------. "The Sound Track." _Films in Review_, 31, No. 5 (May 1980), 295-97.
     References to music by Newman and others.

3638. Darby, Ken. "Alfred Newman Biography and Filmography." _Film Music Note-book_, 2, No. 2 (1976), 5-13.
     A useful listing, based upon a compilation prepared by Jack Tobin in 1959.

3639. Eaton, Quaintance. "Tonight We Sing." _Film Music_, 12, No. 3 (Jan.-Feb. 1953), 12-13.
     Comments concerning the musical direction by Newman, with musical arrangements by Ken Darby.

3640. Feldman, B. "Stage Fright: Eve's Rhapsody -- The 'Theme' from the Alfred Hitchcock Film." _Musical Opinion_, 73 (Sept. 1950), 701.

3641. Hamer, Alan. "Off the Beaten Track: 'Prince of Foxes.'" _Pro Musica Sana_, 7, No. 2 (Spring 1979), 11-12.

3642. Jacobs, Jack. "Alfred Newman." _Films in Review_, 10, No. 7 (Aug.-Sept. 1959), 403-14.

Includes filmography.

3643. King, William G. "Music and Musicians: A Movie Studio Records Arnold Schoenberg's Quartets -- About Alfred Newman." New York Sun (July 23, 1938), 9.

3644. Morton, Lawrence. "Film Music Profile: Alfred Newman." Film Music Notes, 9, No. 5 (May-June 1950), 15-16.

3645. ----------. "'Prince of Foxes': Some Comments on Alfred Newman's Score." Film Music Notes, 9, No. 3 (Jan.-Feb. 1950), 7-9.

3646. Newman, Alfred. "The Iron Curtain." Film Music Notes, 7, No. 5 (May-June 1948), 19-23.

3647. ----------. "The Razor's Edge." Film Music Notes, 6, No. 3 (Dec. 1946-Jan. 1947), 22-23.

Includes excerpts from the score.

3648. Palmer, Christopher. "Newman, Alfred." In The New Groves Dictionary of Music and Musicians. Ed. Stanley Sadie. London: Macmillan, 1980, XIII, p. 163.

Includes bibliography and filmography.

3649. Pavelek, James ("Pav"). "A Tribute to Alfred Newman." The Max Steiner Journal, No. 2 (1978), 14-16.

3650. Pratt, George. "Music Makers of the Movies: Newman Keeps Screen Brimming with Melody." The Citizen-News (Hollywood, Calif.), (Mar. 21, 1961), 3.

3651. Santelmann, William F. "Stars and Stripes Forever." Film Music, 12, No. 2 (Nov.-Dec. 1952), 19.

Notes on the musical direction by Newman.

3652. Steiner, Frederick. "The Making of an American Film Composer: A Study of Alfred Newman's Music in the First Decade of the Sound Era." Ph.D. Diss. (Musicology), University of Southern California 1981.

Abstract: DAI 42:2359A.

Also see comments by Page Cook, #2775.

NOTE: A brief "Addendum" appears in The Cue Sheet (Los Angeles), 1, No. 1 (Jan. 1984), 9.

3653. Ussher, Bruno David. "Music." Los Angeles Daily News (Jan. 26, 1939), 19.

3654. ----------. "Music in the Films." Los Angeles Daily News (Aug. 5, 1940), 19.

3655. Vallance, Tom. "Soundtrack: The Music of Alfred Newman." Film (London), Series 2, No. 13 (Apr. 1974), 10.

Also includes references to music by Marvin Hamlisch.

3656. Zador, Leslie. "Music and the Movies: Alfred Newman, a Melancholy Man." Los Angeles Free Press (Apr. 2, 1971), 54.

SEE ALSO:

#44(Hagen), #131, 132(Thomas), #198(Archibald), #1206(Bowles), #1277(Forrell/Hamilton), #1294(M. Hamilton), #1296, 1297(Wm. Hamilton), #1373(Kubik/Forrell/Hamilton), #1416(Mendez/Hamilton), #1433(Morton), #1493(Rubsamen), #1866(Rattner/Eaton), #2010, 2016, 2020, 2041(Cook), #2050(Dolan), #2101(McCutcheon), #2301, 2314, 2775(Cook), #3269(Atkins/Friedhofer), #4659(Jones), #4856(Rubsamen), #5935(Cook), and #6038(Kroll).

Alex North (1910-)

3657. Adomian, Lan. "Viva Zapata." Film Music, 11, No. 4 (Mar.-Apr. 1952), 4-14.

3658. Bohn, Ronald L., and Jean-Pierre Pecqueriaux. "Filmography/Discography: Alex North." Soundtrack Collector's Newsletter, 1 (Dec. 1982), 14-16.

3659. Buchanan, Loren G. "The Art of Composing Music Scores for Films: Alex North, an Expert, Comments on His Craft." Motion Picture Herald, 234, No. 8 (Oct. 13, 1965), 12, 36.

Reprinted in Limbacher, pp. 29-31. See #75.

3660. Cook, Page. "The Sound Track." Films in Review, 16, No. 9 (Nov. 1965), 573-75.

Also includes references to music by Jerome Moross.

3661. ----------. "The Sound Track." Films in Review, 31, No. 8 (Oct. 1980), 483-85.

3662. "The Film Career of Alex North." The Max Steiner Music Society News Letter, No. 47 (Summer 1976), 10.

A brief biographical sketch, includes a selective discography.

3663. Hickman, C. Sharpless. "Movies and Music." Music Journal, 11, No. 2 (Feb. 1953), 28-29.

3664. Lewin, Frank. "A Street Car Named Desire." Film Music, 11, No. 3 (Jan.-Feb. 1952), 13-20.

3665. North, Alex. "New Film Directors Accenting Music as Potent Dramatic Angle: Alex North." Variety, 220 (Oct. 12, 1960), 59.

An interview.

3666. ----------. "Notes on 'The Rainmaker.'" Film and TV Music, 16, No. 3 (Spring 1957), 3-15.

Includes excerpts from the score.

3667. ----------. "Notes on the Score of 'The Rose Tattoo.'" Film Music, 15, No. 2 (Winter 1955), 3-15.

Includes excerpts from the score.

3668. ----------. Seminar on film music: AFI/CAFS, October 18, 1971 (3:15 p.m.). Transcript of the seminar is held at the AFI/Louis B. Mayer Library (Los Angeles).

3669. Orowan, Florella. "A Look at Alex North's Use of Historical Source Music." Film Music Notebook, 3, No. 1 (1977), 9-14.

Includes musical examples and a filmography.

3670. Palmer, Christopher. "Film Music Profile: Alex North." Crescendo International, 13 (Apr. 1975), 28-29ff.

An interview.

3670a. Reprinted in Film Music Notebook, 3, No. 1 (1977), 2-8.

Also includes a filmography.

3671. ----------. "North, Alex." In The New Groves Dictionary of Music and Musicians. Ed. Stanley Sadie. London: Macmillan, 1980, XIII, p. 286.

Includes filmography.

3672. Reisner, Joel, and Bruce Kane. "An Interview with Alex North." Cinema (Los Angeles), 5, No. 4 (Dec. 1969), 42-45.

3673. Smith, Scott. "Alex North." Ph.D. Diss. Ball State University.

Work in progress in 1979.

3674. Spolar, Betsey, and Merrilyn Hammond. "How to Work in Hollywood and Still Be Happy!" Theatre Arts, 37 (Aug. 1953), 80.

3675. Sutak, Ken. "A 'Dragonslayer' Inquiry: From Two Heady Notes Toward Some Hard Questions About the Score." Pro Musica Sana, 9, No. 4 (Summer 1982), 7-15.

3676. ----------. "The Return of 'A Streetcar Named Desire.'" Pro Musica Sana,
      3, No. 1 (Spring 1974), 4-10; 3, No. 4 (Winter 1974-1975), 9-15; 4, No. 2
      (1975), 18-24; and 4, No. 3 (1976), 13-18.

          A thorough and valuable analysis of the score.

3677. Wolthuis, Julius J. C. "De port filmmuziek van Stanley Kubrick." Skoop
      (Amsterdam), 16 (Oct. 1980), 38.

          Soundtrack album review.

      SEE ALSO:

      #9(Bazelon, pp.214-23), #119(Skiles/North), #132(Thomas), #221(Cook),
      #1602(Beguiristain), #2010, 2012, 2020, 2040(Cook), #2050(Dolan), #2322,
      2762, 2767(Cook), and #4498(Chase/North).

Clifton Parker (1905-)

3678. Huntley, John. "Clifton Parker." Music Parade, 1, No. 12 (1949), 15-16ff.

3679. ----------. "The Music of 'Treasure Island.'" Film Music Notes, 10, No. 1
      (Sept.-Oct. 1950), 16-17.

          Reprinted in Limbacher, pp. 112-13. See #75.

3680. Parker, Clifton. "The Sword and the Rose." Film Music, 12, No. 5 (May-June
      1953), 14-15.

          Reprinted in Limbacher, p. 105. See #75.

3681. Powell, Mary. "The Story of Robin Hood." Film Music, 12, No. 2 (Nov.-Dec.
      1952), 18.

      SEE ALSO:
      #1326(Huntley).

Andrei P. Petrov (1930-)

3682. Belyavski, Oleg. "Two-Way Process: Reflections on a Profession: Composer
      Andrei Petrov." Soviet Film (Moscow), No. 206 (No. 7), (July 1974), 35-
      36.

          An interview.

3683. Petrov, Andrei. "Talking About My Profession: The Secrets of Music in
      Films." Soviet Film (Moscow), No. 233 (No. 10), (Oct. 1976), 24-25.

3684. ----------, and Dora Romadinova. "Kinokompozitor -- èto professiya?: Krit-
      ičeskie dialogi." Sovetskaya muzyka, 36, No. 6 (June 1972), 16-22.

3685. ----------, et al. "Nuzhna khoroshaia melodiia." Iskusstvo kino, No. 10
      (Oct. 1980), 84-96.

André Previn (1929-)

3686. Bookspan, Martin, and Ross Yockey. André Previn: A Biography. Garden City
      N.Y.: Doubleday, 1981.

          Includes many references to Previn's film music in the
          sections "The Hollywood Life, " pp. 3-96, and "The Jazz
          Life," pp. 99-222.

3687. Cook, Page. "The Sound Track." Films in Review, 15, No. 10 (Dec. 1964),
      628-29.

3687. ----------. "The Sound Track." Films in Review, 17, No. 4 (Apr. 1966), 241-42.

3688. Kraus, Milton M. "Kim." Film Music Notes, 10, No. 3 (Jan.-Feb. 1951), 6.

3689. Manson, Eddy. "It's Always Fair Weather." Film Music, 15, No. 1 (Sept.-Oct. 1955), 18-19.

3690. Morton, Lawrence. "Film Music Profile: Andre Previn." Film Music Notes, 10, No. 3 (Jan.-Feb. 1951), 4-5.

3691. Previn, André. "'Invitation to the Dance': Ring Around the Rosy Sequence." Film Music, 15, No. 5 (Summer 1956), 8-16.

> Includes excerpts from the score.

3692. ----------, and Antony Hopkins. Music Face to Face. London: Hamish Hamilton; and New York: Scribner's, 1971.

3693. Ruttencutter, Helen Drees. "Profiles: A Way of Making Things Happen." New Yorker, 58 (Jan. 10, 1983), 36-79.

> Part 1, includes references to Previn's film music.

3694. Steen, T. M. F. "The Sound Track." Films in Review, 13, No. 1 (Jan. 1962), 47-49.

> Also includes references to music by Russ Garcia.

SEE ALSO:

#2009, 2010(Cook), #2098, 2100(McCutcheon), #3506(Dale), #3821(Cook), #3943(Burton), and #5244(H. Green).

Serge Prokofiev (1891-1953)

3695. Bowes, Malcolm Eugene. "Eurhythmics and the Analysis of Visual-Musical Synthesis in Film: An Examination of Sergei Eisenstein's 'Alexander Nevsky.'" Ph.D. Diss. Ohio University 1978.

> Abstract: DAI 1978: 2593A (order #DA 7821173).

3696. Eisenstein, Sergei M. "Alexander Nevsky." In Soviet Films, 1938-39: The Soviet Historical Film. Moscow: State Publishing House for Cinema and Literature, 1939.

> NOTE: Reprinted in Izbranniye stat'i (see #4565a). Reprinted in translation in Notes of a Film Director (see #4565).

3697. ----------. "Iz perepizki S. Prokof'yeva i S. Eyzhenshteyna." Sovetskaya muzyka, 25, No. 4 (Apr. 1961), 105-13.

> NOTE: Also published in German and English translation. See #3700 and #3706.

> Excerpts from the correspondence, 1939-1946.

3698. ----------. "P-R-K-F-V." An introduction to Sergei Prokofiev: His Musical Life by Israel Nestyev. Trans. Jay Leyda. New York: Alfred A. Knopf, 1946.

> See Nestyev, #3710. Eisenstein's introduction, however, is dated November 1942.

> NOTE: An expanded Russian version appears in Izbranniye stat'i (see #4565a), and is translated in Notes of a Film Director, pp. 149-67 (see #4565).
> Also reprinted in Prokofiev's autobiography (see #3712a), and in Limbacher, pp. 159-63 (see #75).
> Appears also in German, translated from the Russian by Lothar Fahlbusch in Ausgewählte Aufsätze (see #4565b).

3698a. Also published as "P R K F V," in Soviet Film (Moscow), No. 167 (No. 4), (Apr. 1971), 35-37.

3698b. Also translated by M. Koski in Filmihullu (Helsinki), No. 1

3699. ----------. "Prokofjew als Filmkomponist." Musik und Gesellschaft, 21 (Apr. 1971), 245-48.

> Reprinted from an earlier issue of MuG. See #3700.

3700. ----------. "Prokofjew als Filmkomponist," and "Aus dem Briefwechsel zwischen Prokofjew und Eisenstein." Musik und Gesellschaft, 12, No. 2 (Feb. 1962), 85-87.

> NOTE: Portions of the Prokofiev/Eisenstein correspondence are translated from the version which appeared in Sovetskaya muzyka. See #3697.

> Also see #3699.

3701. ----------. "Vertikalny montash." Iskusstvo kino (Moscow), No. 1 (1941), 29-38.

> Concerning the film "Alexander Nevsky."

> Translated as "Form and Content: Practice," in The Film Sense, pp. 157-216. See #4562c.

3702. "Fil'm o Prokof'eve." Sovetskaya muzyka, 25, No. 4 (Apr. 1961), 206.

> Concerning the film "Kompozitor Sergey Prokof'ev."

3703. Gallez, Douglas W. "The Prokofiev-Eisenstein Collaboration: 'Nevsky' and 'Ivan' Revisited." Cinema Journal, 17, No. 2 (Spring 1978), 13-35.

3704. Helman, Alicja. "Filmy Eisensteina i Prokofiewa jako nowa forma sztuki syntetycznej." Kwartalnik Filmowy, 10, No. 2 (1960).

3705. Jurenev, Rostislav, comp. and ed. Ėjzenštejn v vospominanijah sovremennikov. Moscow: Iskusstvo, 1974.

> Eisenstein is recalled by his "contemporaries," Prokofiev, Boris Vol'skij, Samuil Samosud, and Galina Ulanova.

3706. Levaco, Ronald. "The Eisenstein-Prokofiev Correspondence." Cinema Journal, 13, No. 1 (Fall 1973), 1-16.

> Also includes translations of some of the letters. See #3697.

3707. Lissa, Zofia. "Sergiusz Prokofiew (w 60-lecie urodzin)." Muzyka, No. 7 (1951), 13-18.

3708. Martin, Andre. "Serge Prokofieff: la musique rencontre le cinéma." Cahiers du cinéma, 4, No. 23 (May 1953), 24-32.

3709. Medvedev, A. "Filmova povidka u Prokofjevovi." Hudební Rozhledy (Prague), 14, No. 20 (1961), 863.

> Concerning the film "Skladate Sergej Prokofjev."

3710. Nestyev, Israel Vladimirovich. Sergei Prokofiev: His Musical Life. Trans. Rose Prokofieva. New York: Alfred A. Knopf, 1946.

> Many references to Prokofiev's film music throughout, with bibliographic references, and an introduction by Sergei Eisenstein (see #3698).

3711. Palmer, Christopher. "Film Composing and Prokofiev." Crescendo International, 15 (Mar. 1977), 10-11.

3712. Prokofiev, Sergei. "Muzyka k kartine 'Alexandr Nevski.'" In Soviet Films, 1938-39: The Soviet Historical Film. Moscow: State Publishing House for Cinema and Literature (Iskusstvo), 1939.

> 3712a. Also published as "Music for 'Alexander Nevsky,'" in S. Prokofiev: Autobiography, Articles, Reminiscences. Comp. S. Shlifstein. Trans. Rose Prokofieva. Moscow: Foreign Language Publishing House, n.d., pp. 112-14.

>> NOTE: This volume also includes a listing of works, including film scores, and a reprint of Eisenstein's essay "P-R-K-F-V," pp. 252-63 (see #3698).

3713. ----------. ("My Work on the Film 'Ivan the Terrible.'") VOKS Musical

Chronicle (Vsesoiuznoe Obshchestvo Kul'turnoi Sviazi), (Oct. 1944).

3714. Roberts, Philip D. "Prokofiev's Score and Cantata for Eisenstein's 'Alexander Nevsky.'" Semiotica (The Hague), 21, Nos. 1-2 (1977), 151-66.

3715. Rubsamen, Walter H. "Music in the Cinema." Arts and Architecture, 62, No. 8 (Aug. 1945), 24, 50, 52.

3716. Schwarz, Boris. Music and Musical Life in Soviet Russia, 1917-1970. New York: W. W. Norton, 1972.

    Also includes references to film music by Shostakovich.

3717. Seelmann-Eggebert, Ulrich. "Prokofjew und die Filmmusik." Neue Zeitschrift für Musik, 125, No. 12 (Dec. 1964), 522-27.

3718. Seroff, Victor. Sergei Prokofiev -- A Soviet Tragedy: The Case of Sergei Prokofiev, His Life and Work, His Critics, and His Executioners. New York: Funk and Wagnalls, 1968.

    Includes bibliography, pp. 331-32.

   3718a. Also published as Sergei Prokofiev: A Soviet Tragedy. London: Leslie Frewin, 1969.

    Includes bibliography, pp. 377-78.

3719. Sharova, E. ("Sergei Prokof'ev's Film Music.) In Iz istorii russkoi i sovetskoi muzyki, III. Comp. Mikhail Pitkus and Irina Givental'. Moscow: Muzyka, 1978.

    In Russian.

3720. Sheren, Paul. "Eisenstein (Eyzenshteyn), Sergey (Mikhaylovich)." In The New Groves Dictionary of Music and Musicians. Ed. Stanley Sadie. London: Macmillan, 1980.

    Includes bibliography for Eisenstein.

3721. Shklovskiĭ, Viktor Borisovich. Eyzenshteyn. Moscow: Iskusstvo, 1973.

    Includes many references to his collaboration with Prokofiev.

3722. Stegemann, Michael. "Sergej Eisenstein und Sergej Prokofieff: Protokoll einer Zusammenarbeit." Melos: Neue Zeitschrift für Musik, New series, 4, No. 6 (Nov.-Dec. 1978), 495-500.

3723. Stevens, Bernard. "Alexander Nevsky: Prokoviev's 'Nevsky' Cantata." Music Survey, 2, No. 3 (Winter 1950), 187-88.

3724. Torganov, I. Muzyka S. S. Prokof'eva k kinofilmam. Moscow, 1963.

3725. Troitskaya, Galina. "Prokof'ev -- kompozitor kino." Sovetskaya muzyka, 42, No. 9 (Sept. 1978), 95-101.

    A special focus upon music for Eisenstein's "Ivan Groznyj."

3726. Vasina-Grossman, Vera. "Muzyka k filmu 'Ivan Grosny.'" Sovetskaya muzyka, 22, No. 3 (Mar. 1958).

    SEE ALSO:

    #31(Engmann/Prokofiev), #142(Austin), #1183(Antheil), #1388(London), #1494(Rubsamen), #1854(Poulenc), #4562, 4566, 4567(Eisenstein), #4812 (Peatman), #1898(D. Stern), #5231(Elias), #5277(Michaut), #5580(Roger), and #5673(Pensdorfova).

David Raksin (1912-)

3727. Atkins, Irene Kahn. Interviews with David Raksin, 12/6/76 - 2/15/77. Tapes and transcripts are part of the project Oral History: American Music. New Haven, Conn.: Yale University, 1977.

3728. Bernstein, Elmer. "A Conversation with David Raksin." Film Music Notebook,

2, No. 2 (1976), 14-21; and 2, No. 3 (1976), 9-18.

Part II (Vol. 2, No. 3) includes a filmography.

3729. Collura, Joe. "Dialogue in L.A. with David Raksin." Classic Film/Video Images, No. 68 (Mar. 1980), 24.

3730. Cook, Page. "The Sound Track." Films in Review, 22, No. 8 (Oct. 1971), 501-05.

Concerning the film "What's the Matter with Helen?"

Reprinted in Limbacher, pp. 114-19. See #75.

3731. ----------. "The Sound Track." Films in Review, 32, No. 6 (June-July 1981), 365-67, 372.

Includes comments by Raksin concerning his score for "Separate Tables."

3732. "David Raksin Biography and Filmography." Film Music Notebook, 2, No. 3 (1976), 3-8.

Also includes comments by Elmer Bernstein.

3733. Hamilton, William. "The Bad and the Beautiful." Film Music, 12, No. 3 (Jan.-Feb. 1953), 4-11.

Includes excerpts from the score.

Reprinted in Limbacher, pp. 77-80. See #75.

3734. Hickman, C. Sharpless. "Movies and Music." Music Journal, 13, No. 2 (Feb. 1955), 36, 38.

3735. Morton, Lawrence. "Film Music Profile: David Raksin." Film Music Notes, 9, No. 1 (Sept.-Oct. 1949), 14-15.

3736. ----------. "'Force of Evil': A Review of David Raksin's Score." Film Music Notes, 8, No. 3 (Jan.-Feb. 1949), 7-10.

3737. Newsom, Jon. "David Raksin: A Composer in Hollywood." Quarterly Journal of the Library of Congress, 35, No. 3 (July 1978), 142-72.

Concerning the films "Force of Evil", "Carrie", "Separate Tables," and"The Redeemer." Includes 2 7-inch 45 rpm discs of musical examples. Available from the Superintendent of Documents, GPO, Washington, D.C., 20402.

3738. Raksin, David. "Carrie." Film Music, 12, No. 1 (Sept.-Oct. 1952), 13-17.

Includes excerpts from the score.

Reprinted in Limbacher, pp. 82-84. See #75.

3739. ----------. "Come ho musicato 'Carrie.'" Cinema (Rome), New series, No. 102 (1953).

3740. ----------. "Film Music: Beauty and the Beast? Raksin Raps State of Art." Variety, 275, No. 1 (May 15, 1974), 59ff.

3741. ----------. "'Forever Amber' -- Notes on the Musical Score." Film Music Notes, 7, No. 2 (Nov.-Dec. 1947), 5-9.

3742. ----------. "The Music of the Movies." AFI Seminar, February 22, 1984 (8:00 p.m.). Tape recording of the seminar is held at the AFI/Louis B. Mayer Library (Los Angeles).

3743. ----------. "The Next Voice You Hear." Film Music Notes, 9, No. 5 (May-June 1950), 5-7.

3744. ----------. "A Note on the Music of 'Force of Evil.'" Film Music Notes, 8, No. 3 (Jan.-Feb. 1949), 6.

3745. ----------. "A Note on the Score of 'Suddenly.'" Film Music, 14, No. 2 (Nov.-Dec. 1954), 3-11.

Includes extensive excerpts from the musical score.

3746. ----------. "Notes on the Musical Score: 'Forever Amber.'" Film Music

Notes, 7, No. 3 (Jan.-Feb. 1948), 6-11.

3747. ----------. "Raksin on Film Music." Journal of the University Film Association, 26, No. 4 (1974), 68-70, 79.

3748. ----------. "Talking Back: A Hollywood Composer States Case for His Craft." New York Times (Feb. 20, 1949), Section 2, p. 7.

   3748a. Reprinted in Film Music Notes, 10, No. 4 (Mar.-Apr. 1951), 14-15.

3749. ----------. "Whatever Became of Movie Music?" Film Music Notebook, 1, No. 1 (Fall 1974), 22-26.

      Originally published in Daily Variety.

3750. Steen, T. M. F. "The Sound Track." Films in Review, 11, No. 5 (May 1960), 307-09.

3751. Thomas, Anthony. "David Raksin." Films in Review, 14, No. 1 (Jan. 1963), 38-41.

      Includes filmography, and comments on Raksin's "collaboration" with Charlie Chaplin.

    SEE ALSO:

    #9(Bazelon, pp. 236-47), #87(Raksin et al.), #131, 132(Thomas), #274(Newsom), #1817(Morton), #1988(Bock), #2034, 2041(Cook), #2050(Dolan), #2307 (Cook), #2520(Pavelek), #2591(Ulrich/Raksin), #2868(Quantrill), #3136, 3137(Raksin), #3139(Skolsky), #3388(Goldfarb), #4666, 4667(Kalinak), and #4854(Rubsamen).

Alan Rawsthorne (1906-1971)

3752. Dickinson, A. E. F. "The Progress of Alan Rawsthorne." Music Review, 12, No. 1 (1951), 87-104.

3753. Hendricks, Gordon. "'Ivory Hunter's' Music." Films in Review, 3, (Aug.-Sept. 1952), 342-45.

      A critical analysis.

3754. Huntley, John. "Alan Rawsthorne." Music Parade, 2, No. 2 (1950), 12-14.

3755. Keller, Hans. "Film Music and Beyond." Music Review, 17, No. 1 (Feb. 1956), 95-96.

      Concerning the film "The Drawings of Leonardo da Vinci."

3756. ----------. "Film Music: Rawsthorne's 'Leonardo.'" Musical Times, 97 (Jan. 1956), 29.

3757. Rawsthorne, Alan. "The Celluloid Plays a Tune." In Diversion: Twenty-Two Authors on the Lively Arts. Ed. John Sutro. London: Max Parrish, 1950, pp. 25-34.

    SEE ALSO:

    #56(Irving), and #1755(Keller).

Hugo Riesenfeld (1883-1939)

3758. Desilets, Elliott Michael. "F. W. Murnau's 'Sunrise': A Critical Study." Ed.D. Diss. Columbia University Teacher's College 1979.

      Abstract: DAI 1979, p. 1725A (order # DA 7923581).

3759. "The Picture Drama, a New Field for Composers." Musician (Boston), 29

(July 1924), 11.

3760. Riesenfeld, Hugo. "The Advancement in Motion Picture Music." American Hebrew, 116 (Apr. 3, 1925), 632.

3761. ----------. "Film Music." Modern Music, 3, No. 2 (Jan.-Feb. 1926), 30-31.

> Concerns the film "The Cabinet of Dr. Caligari" (1919).

3762. ----------. "Music and Motion Pictures." In The Motion Picture in Its Economic and Social Aspects (American Academy of Political and Social Science, Annals, Vol. 128, November 1926). Ed. Clyde L. King and Frank A. Tichenor. Philadelphia: The Academy, 1926.

3763. Russell, Alexander. "A Scholarly Musician Examines Sound Films." Theatre, 50 (Aug. 1929), 21, 60-62.

3764. Vila, Josephine. "Hugo Riesenfeld Tells How He Scores a Film." Musical Courier (Feb. 17, 1927), 48.

SEE ALSO:

#274(Newsom), #407, 421, 450(Beynon), #821(Rogers), #978(Sinn/Stuckey), #1123(Riesenfeld et al.), and #1283(Geduld/Gottesman).

Ann Ronell

3765. Denison, Alva Coil, and Ann Ronell. "The River." Film Music, 11, No. 3 (Jan.-Feb. 1952), 4-10.

> Concerning music for the Indian film "The River" by Ann Ronell.

3766. Geller, Harry. "An Article on 'Love Happy': Part I. Comments on Ann Ronell's Score." Film Music Notes, 9, No. 4 (Mar.-Apr. 1950), 5-10.

3767. Ronell, Ann. "'The Great Adventure': Notes." Film Music, 15, No. 1 (Sept.-Oct. 1955), 3-13.

> Includes the cue sheet and extensive excerpts from the score.

3768. ----------. "'Love Happy': Composer's Notes." Film Music Notes, 9, No. 4 (Mar.-Apr. 1950), 4-5.

3769. ----------. "So You Want to Be a Music Director?: Notes on 'Main St. to Broadway.'" Film Music, 12, No. 5 (May-June 1953), 3-9.

3770. Smith, Paul. "An Article on 'Love Happy': Part II. On Precision Timing." Film Music Notes, 9, No. 4 (Mar.-Apr. 1950), 10-12.

SEE ALSO:
#1877(Ronell).

Leonard Rosenman (1924-)

3771. "Composer Juggles Film Work, Serious Music in Celluloid Jungle." Variety, 311 (May 25, 1983), 71.

3772. Fitzpatrick, John. "Rosenman's Ring." Pro Musica Sana, 7, No. 2 (Spring 1979), 10-11.

> Concerning the film "Lord of the Rings."

3773. Palmer, Christopher. "Leonard Rosenman and the James Dean Sound." Crescendo International, 14 (Sept. 1975), 26-27.

3774. ----------. "Rosenman, Leonard." In The New Groves Dictionary of Music and Musicians. Ed. Stanley Sadie. London: Macmillan, 1980, XVI, p. 201.

Includes filmography.

3775. Rosenman, Leonard. "Notes from a Sub-Culture." Perspectives of New Music, 7, No. 1 (1968), 122-35.

3776. ----------. "Notes on the Score to 'East of Eden.'" Film Music, 14, No. 5 (May-June 1955), 3-12.

Reprinted in Limbacher, pp. 86-87. See #75.

3777. ----------. Seminar on film music: AFI/CAFS, February 14, 1979 (3:45 p.m.). Transcript of the seminar is held at the AFI/Louis B. Mayer Library (Los Angeles).

3778. Siders, Harvey. "Leonard Rosenman." BMI: The Many Worlds of Music (Spring 1976), 42-43.

SEE ALSO:

#9(Bazelon, pp. 181-87), #131, 132(Thomas), #1602(Beguiristain), #2296, 2298, 2337(Cook), #2721(Barbano), #2768(Cook), and #4096(Connor/Pratley).

Nino Rota (1911-1979)

3779. Carcassonne, Philippe. "Musique et film: Nino Rota, careme-prenant." Cine-matographe (Paris), No. 47 (May 1979), 59-60.

3780. Care, Ross B. "Scoring: Nino Rota." Take One, 7, No. 6 (1979), 46-47.

Includes discography.

3781. Champenier, Serge. "L'Heritage de Nino Rota (1911-1979): une originalite limitée." Revue du cinéma/Image et son, No. 342 (Sept. 1979), 28-32.

Includes filmography and discography.

3782. Comuzio, Ermanno. "Fellini/Rota: un matrimonio concertato." Bianco e nero, 40 (July-Aug. 1979), 62-94.

3783. Connor, Edward, and Gerald Pratley. "The Sound Track." Films in Review, 7, No. 8 (Oct. 1956), 422-25.

Also includes references to current filmed musicals.

3784. Cook, Page. "The Sound Track." Films in Review, 19, No. 9 (Nov. 1968), 571-73.

Also includes references to music by John Barry and Roman Vlad.

3785. ----------. "The Sound Track." Films in Review, 22, No. 6 (June-July 1971), 361-63.

3786. D'Amico, Fedele. "Rota, Nino." In The New Groves Dictionary of Music and Musicians. Ed. Stanley Sadie. London: Macmillan, 1980, XVI, p. 256.

3787. D'Andrea, Renzo. "Le musiche di Rota da Visconti a Fellini." Cinema Nuovo (Turin), 30, No. 274 (Dec. 1981), 57-59.

3788. Fellini, Federico. "Maaginen ystava." Filmihullu (Helsinki), No. 2 (1980), 18-19.

3789. ----------. "Nino Rota." Iskusstvo kino, No. 11 (Nov. 1979), 167.

3790. ----------. "Eine ungewöhnliche Bekanntschaft." Film und Fernsehen (Ber-lin, DDR), 11, No. 4 (1983), 43-44.

3791. Gorbman, Claudia. "Music as Salvation: Notes on Fellini and Rota." Film Quarterly, 28, No. 2 (Winter 1974-1975), 17-25.

Concerns the film "Nights of Cabiria."

3792. Mazurelle, Julien. "Cine disques: une dernier repetition d'orchestre pour Nino Rota." Amis du film: Cinéma et télévision (Brussels), Nos. 278-279 (July-Aug. 1979), 39.

> Soundtrack album review.

3793. Miceli, Sergio. "Musica e film: proposta per un'analisi audiovisiva attraverso il rapporto Rota-Fellini." Ph.D. Diss. (Musicology), Firenze 1976.

> In Italian, with summaries in English, French, and German.

3794. Moret, Henry. "Nino Rota." Écran 79, No. 80 (May 15, 1979), 85.

> Obituary.

3795. "Nino Rota." Cinéma 79, Nos. 247-248 (July-Aug. 1979), 190.

> Obituary. Includes a filmography.

3796. "Nino Rota." Cine Review (Brussels), 59 (Apr. 19, 1979), 61.

> Obituary. Includes a filmography.

3797. Philbert, Bertrand. "Un hommage à Nino Rota." Cinematographe, No. 80 (July-Aug. 1982), 80.

3798. Rizzo, Eugene. "Fellini's Musical Alter Ego, Nino Rota: How They Work." Variety, 279 (May 21, 1975), 28.

3799. Rota, Nino. "The Background Music of the Film 'War and Peace.'" The Max Steiner Music Society News Letter, No. 32 (Autumn 1972), 7.

3800. ----------. "The Background Music of 'War and Peace.'" Film and TV Music, 16, No. 1 (Fall 1956), 8-10.

3801. Volta, Ornella. "Huit entretiens autour du 'Casanova de Fellini.'" Positif (Paris), No. 191 (Mar. 1977), 6-15.

3802. Wolthius, Julius J. C. "Filmmuziek: Nino Rota dood." Skoop (Amsterdam), 15 (June 1979), 19.

> Includes filmography.

SEE ALSO:
> #2026(Cook), #2115(Pellegrini/Rota), #2322, 2323, 2777(Cook), #2837(Lardeau), and #3815(Cook).

Miklós Rózsa (1907-)

3803. Applebaum, Ralph. "Storytelling: Nicholas Meyer in an Interview with Ralph Applebaum." Films and Filming, 26, No. 4 (Jan. 1980), 8-18.

> Includes references to Rozsa's music for Meyer's "Time After Time."

3804. Bassoff, Lawrence. "Rozsa, Miklos: 150 Fanfares from an Uncommon Man." Los Angeles Times (Dec. 28, 1979), Part 4, p. 27.

3805. Bertolina, Gian Carlo. "Miklos Rozsa e Billy Wilder: storia di una collaborazione." Filmcritica, 33, Nos. 329-330 (Nov.-Dec. 1982), 594-602.

3806. Borie, Bertrand. "Entretien: Alain Resnais." Journal of L'Association Miklos Rozsa France (1977).

> Concerning the film "Providence."

3806a. Also published as "Alain Resnais -- Interviewed by Bertrand Borie." Trans. John Fitzpatrick. Pro Musica Sana, 6, No. 3 (Summer 1978), 5-9.

3807. ----------. "A propos de la bande sonore de 'Providence.'" Positif (Paris), Nos. 244-245 (July-Aug. 1981), 45-49.

> An interview.

3808. ----------. "Discographie de Miklos Rozsa." Cinéma 80, Nos. 259-260 (July-
Aug. 1980), 82-83.

3809. ----------. "Miklos Rozsa: grandeur et passion." Écran 78 (Paris), No. 74
(Nov. 15, 1978), 37-48.

     An interview. Includes filmography.

3810. ----------. "La Musique de Miklos Rozsa." Positif (Paris), Nos. 244-245
(July-Aug. 1981), 50-51.

3811. Brown, Royal S. "'Providence': Original Film Soundtrack Recording." High
Fidelity and Musical America, 27, No. 11 (Nov. 1977), 134.

     Soundtrack album review.

3812. ----------. "'The Thief of Bagdad': Original Film Score by Miklos Rozsa."
High Fidelity and Musical America, 27, No. 9 (Sept. 1977), 116.

     Soundtrack album review.

3813. Caps, John. "A Correspondence with Miklos Rozsa." Film Music Notebook, 2,
No. 1 (1976), 2-5.

     Includes filmography.

3814. Connor, Edward, and Edward Jablonski. "The Sound Track." Films in Review,
9, No. 3 (Mar. 1958), 150-51, 154.

3815. Cook, Page. "The Sound Track." Films in Review, 14, No. 9 (Nov. 1963),
556-57.

     Concerns scores by Rozsa and Nino Rota. Significant also,
as it is Cook's first article in the continuing series for
Films in Review.

3816. ----------. "The Sound Track." Films in Review, 20, No. 7 (Aug.-Sept.
1969), 435-38, 441.

3817. ----------. "The Sound Track." Films in Review, 25, No. 6 (June-July
1974), 362-66.

3818. ----------. "The Sound Track." Films in Review, 27, No. 7 (Aug.-Sept.
1976), 434-37.

3819. ----------. "The Sound Track." Films in Review, 28, No. 3 (Mar. 1977),
175-77, 185.

     Concerns Rozsa's score for "Providence."

3820. ----------. "The Sound Track." Films in Review, 29, No. 10 (Dec. 1978),
627-30.

3821. ----------. "The Sound Track." Films in Review, 30, No. 6 (June-July
1979), 358-61, 366.

     Also includes references to the work of Andre Previn.

3822. ----------. "The Sound Track." Films in Review, 30, No. 7 (Aug.-Sept.
1979), 416-19.

3823. ----------. "The Sound Track." Films in Review, 30, No. 9 (Nov. 1979),
551-53.

     Also includes references to the music of Richard Rodney
Bennett.

3824. ----------. "The Sound Track." Films in Review, 31, No. 6 (June-July
1980), 361ff.

3825. ----------. "The Sound Track." Films in Review, 32, No. 8 (Oct. 1981),
499-500, 502.

     Concerns Rozsa's score for "The Eye of the Needle."

3826. ----------. "The Sound Track." Films in Review, 33, No. 1 (Jan. 1982),
52-54, 57.

     Comments on Rozsa's recently published autobiography. See

#3877.

3827. ----------. "The Sound Track." Films in Review, 33, No. 7 (Aug.-Sept. 1982).

3828. Dale, S. S. "Contemporary Cello Concerti: Miklos Rozsa, Hendrik Herman Badings." The Strad, 87, No. 1041 (Jan. 1977), 735-45.
>Includes comments on both the film and concert music.

3829. DeWald, Frank. "The Concert Music on Records: A Checklist and Commentary." Pro Musica Sana, 7, No. 4 (Fall 1979), 4-17.
>A useful discography.

3830. ----------. "'Time After Time': An Analysis." Pro Musica Sana, 8, No. 4 (Fall 1980), 3-19.

3831. ----------. "Two from Tony Thomas." Pro Musica Sana, 10, Nos. 3-4 (Fall 1983), 11-15.
>Concerns two new Rozsa soundtrack albums. The article also includes a listing of choral music in Rozsa's films, with publication data, etc.

3832. Doeckel, Ken. "The Four Concertos of Miklós Rózsa." Miklós Rózsa Society Newsletter (Pro Musica Sana), 1, No. 4 (1972), 9.

3833. ----------. "Miklos Rozsa." Films in Review, 16, No. 9 (Nov. 1965), 536-48.
>A biographical sketch. Includes filmography.

3834. Duynslaegher, Patrick. "Filmmuziek." Film en Televisie (Brussels), No. 232 (Sept. 1976), 24-25.

3835. Elley, Derek. "The Film Composer: Miklos Rozsa." Films and Filming, 23, No. 8 (May 1977), 20-24; and 23, No. 9 (June 1977), 30-34.
>An interview.

>3835. Reprinted in Pro Musica Sana, 7, No. 3 (Summer 1979), 4-19.

3836. Eyquem, Olivier, and Jacques Saada. "Rencontre avec Miklos Rozsa." Positif (Paris), No. 189 (Jan. 1977), 49-56.
>Includes filmography.

3837. Fitzpatrick, John. "First Notes on 'Young Bess.'" Pro Musica Sana, 1, No. 1 (Spring 1972), 5-8.

3838. ----------. "More Notes on 'Young Bess.'" Pro Musica Sana, 5, No. 1 (Aug. 1976), 12-15.

3839. ----------. "Rozsa on Disc. Part 2: The Film Music." Pro Musica Sana, 2, No. 2 (Summer 1973), 11-21.

3840. ----------, and Mark Koldys. "The Films of Miklos Rozsa: Checklist, Tapeography and Commentary." Pro Musica Sana, 5, No. 3 (1977), 11-25.

3841. Hamer, Alan. "'Eye of the Needle': The London Sessions." Pro Musica Sana, 9, No. 1 (Summer 1981), 18-19.

3842. Harrison, Lou. "Composers, Singers, Chamber Music." Modern Music, 21, No. 2 (1944), 99ff.

3843. Hendricks, Gordon. "The Sound Track." Films in Review, 5, No. 4 (Apr. 1954), 198-99.

3844. ----------. "The Sound Track." Films in Review, 5, No. 7 (Aug.-Sept. 1954), 370-71.
>Hendrick's response to comments made by Johnny Green in an earlier issue of FIR. See #3333.

3845. Hickman, C. Sharpless. "Heard While Seeing." Music Journal, 10, No. 3 (Mar. 1952), 70.
>Concerns Rozsa's music for "Quo Vadis."

3846. ----------. "Movies and Music." Music Journal, 10, No. 9 (Dec. 1952), 32.

3847. Huntley, John. "The Sound Track." Sight and Sound, 21, No. 4 (Apr.-June 1952), 183.

    Concerning music for the film "Quo Vadis."

3848. ----------. "The Sound Track." Sight and Sound, 23, No. 4 (Apr.-June 1954), 219.

    Includes brief comments on the music for "Julius Caesar."

3849. Jones, Preston Neal. "'Dead Men's' Diary." Pro Musica Sana, 9, No. 3 (Spring 1982), 4-21.

    Concerns the recording sessions for "Dead Men Don't Wear Plaid."

3850. Jouvet, Pierre. "Festival: à Thonon-les-Bains." Cinematographe (Paris), No. 63 (Dec. 1980), 59-60.

3851. Koldys, Mark. "Miklos Rozsa and 'Ben-Hur.'" Pro Musica Sana, 3, No. 3 (Fall 1974), 3-20.

3852. ----------. "The Power of 'The Power.'" Pro Musica Sana, 2, No. 4 (Winter 1973-1974), 11-18.

3853. Kraft, David, and Richard Kraft. "A Conversation with Miklos Rozsa and Carl Reiner." Soundtrack Collector's Newsletter, 1 (Sept. 1982), 13-22; and 1 (Dec. 1982), 17-23.

3854. McConnell, Stanlie. "Teaching Possibilities in Current Films: 'Song of Scheherazade.'" Film Music Notes, 6, No. 5 (Apr.-May 1947), 16.

3855. Meyer, Nicholas. "Miklos Rozsa: The Maestro Scores Again." New West Magazine, 4, No. 20 (Sept. 24, 1979), SC-5.

    Concerns Rozsa's music for "Time After Time."

3856. "Miklos Rozsa." Bollettino Bibliografico Musicale (Milan), 7 (1932).

3857. Morton, Lawrence. "Film Music Profile: Miklos Rozsa." Film Music Notes, 10, No. 4 (Mar.-Apr. 1951), 4-6.

3858. ----------. "Rozsa's Music for 'Quo Vadis.'" Film Music, 11, No. 2 (Nov.-Dec. 1951), 11-13.

3859. Niogret, Hubert. "La musique de Miklos Rozsa." Positif (Paris), No. 189 (Jan. 1977), 42-48.

    A discography.

3860. "An Oscar for Who?" Down Beat, 26 (Feb. 19, 1959), 11.

3861. Pal, George. "Master of Cinema Music." Music Journal, 26, No. 1 (Jan. 1968), 48.

3862. Palmer, Christopher. "Hollywood in London." Crescendo International, 14 (July 1976), 10-11.

    Concerns the Polydor anthologies of Rozsa's film works.

3863. ----------. "Miklos Rozsa Biography." Film Music Notebook, 2, No. 1 (1976), 6-15.

    Reprinted from Palmer's monograph. See #3865.

3864. ----------. "Miklos Rozsa." Performing Right (London), No. 55 (May 1971), 11-13.

3865. ----------. Miklós Rózsa: A Sketch of His Life and Work. London and Wiesbaden: Breitkopf und Härtel, 1975.

    Includes a listing of works, with publication data, and filmography.

    Portions are reprinted in Film Music Notebook. See #3863.

3866. ----------. "Miklos Rozsa on 'The Thief of Bagdad.'" Film Music Notebook, 2, No. 4 (1976), 25-28.

    An interview.

  3866a. Reprinted in Crescendo International, 15 (Jan. 1977), 10-11ff.

3867. ----------. "The Music of Miklos Rozsa." Monthly Film Bulletin (BFI, London), 45, No. 530 (Mar. 1978), 60.

3868. ----------. "The Rozsa Touch." Crescendo International, 13 (Jan. 1975), 26-27.

3869. ----------. "Satisfaction and Scores: Miklos Rozsa." Crescendo International, 13 (Feb. 1975), 26-27.

    An interview.

3870. ----------. "A True Composer for the Screen: Miklos Rozsa." Crescendo International, 11 (Jan. 1973), 12-13.

3871. ----------, and John S. Weissmann. "Rózsa, Miklós." In The New Groves Dictionary of Music and Musicians. Ed. Stanley Sadie. London: Macmillan, 1980, XVI, p. 288-89.

    Includes bibliography and filmography.

3872. Peatman, Mary. "'Providence I' -- The Film." Pro Musica Sana, 5, No. 3 (1977), 9-18.

    Concerns Rozsa's music for the Resnais film, with comments on the soundtrack album.

3873. Pugliese, Roberto. "Due maestri hollywoodiani: Rozsa e Herrmann." Filmcritica, 28, Nos. 279-280 (Dec. 1977), 379-85.

    Also includes a filmography, pp. 385-86.

3874. Rabourdin, Dominique. "Entretien avec Miklos Rozsa." Cinéma 80, No. 258 (June 1980), 55-67.

    Includes filmography.

3875. Reid, Charles. "Notes from Abroad." High Fidelity, 10, No. 1 (Jan. 1960), 18, 20, 22.

    Concerns the film "Ben Hur."

3876. "Rozsa Conducts Rozsa." High Fidelity and Musical America, 27 (Nov. 1977), 134-35.

    A review of the anthology album.

3877. Rózsa, Miklós. Double Life: The Autobiography of Miklós Rózsa. Foreword by Antal Doráti. Tunbridge Wells, Kent, U.K.: Midas Books; and New York: Hippocrene Books, 1982.

    Includes filmography and discography.

    See comments by Page Cook in Films in Review. See #3826.

    -- Rev. by John Fitzpatrick: "Some Reflections on 'Double Life.'" Pro Musica Sana, 10, No. 2 (Spring 1983), 6-9.

3878. ----------. "The Growing Art." In Music and Dance in California and the West. Ed. Richard Drake Saunders. Hollywood: Bureau of Musical Research, 1948, pp. 79, 133.

    See #1496.

3879. ----------. "An Interview with Miklos Rozsa." Starlog, 4, No. 31 (Feb. 1980), 47-49.

3880. ----------. "Jules Cesar." Positif (Paris), No. 189 (Jan. 1977), 57-59.

3881. ----------. "Julius Caesar." Film Music, 13, No. 1 (Sept.-Oct. 1953), 7-13.

    Reprinted in Limbacher, pp. 132-35. See #75.

3882. ----------. "Lust for Life." Film and TV Music, 16, No. 1 (Fall 1956), 3-7.

3883. ----------. "More Music for Historical Films." Film Music, 12, No. 2 (Nov.-Dec. 1952), 13-17.

    Concerns music for the films "Ivanhoe" and "Plymouth Adventure."

    Reprinted in Limbacher, pp. 125-27. See #75.

3884. ----------. "The Music in 'Quo Vadis.'" Film Music, 11, No. 2 (Nov.-Dec. 1951), 4-10.

    Reprinted in Limbacher, pp. 147-53. See #75.

3885. ----------. "The Music of the Movies." AFI Seminar, February 15, 1984 (8:00 p.m.). Tape recording of the seminar is held at the AFI/Louis B. Mayer Library (Los Angeles).

3886. ----------. "Teaching Composition for the Cinema." Film Music Notes, 7, No. 3 (Jan.-Feb. 1948), 4-5.

3887. ----------. "The Transplanted Composer." Los Angeles Times (May 1950).

    A series of three articles which focus upon the work and career of Erich Korngold.

3888. ----------. "University Training for Motion Picture Musicians." Etude, 64 (June 1946), 307, 360.

3889. Rubsamen, Walter H. "Music in the Cinema." Arts and Architecture, 62, No. 3 (Mar. 1945), 22, 24-25.

    Concerns the filmed biography of Chopin, "A Song to Remember."

3890. ----------. "Music in the Cinema." Arts and Architecture, 63, No. 2 (Feb. 1946), 22-23, 59.

3891. Sebestyén, János, and Miklós Rózsa. Életem történeteiböl. Budapest: Zenemükiadó, 1980.

    A series of interviews presented over a period of about 10 years on Hungarian Radio.

3892. "Soundtracks." Fanfare, 4, No. 3 (1981), 235-36.

    Concerning Rozsa's recorded soundtrack for "Knights of the Round Table."

3893. Sternfeld, Frederick W. "The Strange Music of 'Martha Ivers.'" Hollywood Quarterly, 2, No. 3 (Apr. 1947), 242-51.

3894. Vallerand, Francois. "An Interview with Miklos Rozsa." 24 Images (Quebec), No. 12 (Apr. 1982).

3895. Warner, Alan. "Miklos Rozsa: Lecture in London (October 1972)." Pro Musica Sana, 3, No. 4 (Winter 1974-1975), 15-25; and 4, No. 1 (Spring 1975), 21-30.

3896. Weissmann, John S. "Rózsa, Miklós." In Groves Dictionary of Music and Musicians. 5th edition. Ed. Eric Blom. New York: St. Martin's Press; and London: Macmillan, 1954, VII, pp. 286-87.

3897. ----------. "Rózsa, Miklós." In Die Musik in Geschichte und Gegenwart. Ed. Friedrich Blume. Kassel: Bärenreiter, 1955, XI, pp. 1029-30.

3898. Wescott, Steven D. Interview with Miklós Rózsa, 1/10/84. Tapes and transcript are part of the project Oral History: American Music. New Haven, Conn.: Yale University, 1984.

3899. ----------. "Miklós Rózsa: A Portrait of the Composer as Seen Through an Analysis of His Early Works for Feature Films and the Concert Stage." Ph.D. Diss. (Musicology), University of Minnesota.

    Work in progress in 1983.

3900. Wheelwright, D. Sterling. "An Interview with Miklos Rozsa." Music News (Chicago), 44 (Oct. 1952), 15.

SEE ALSO:

#32(Evans), #82(Manvell/Huntley), #131, 132(Thomas), #198(Archibald),
#221(Cook), #278(Palmer), #281(Porfirio), #1203, 1210(Bowles), #1276(For-
rell/Carrie), #1296(Hamilton), #1368(Kochnitzky), #1427, 1438(Morton),
#1455(Nelson), #1490(Rubsamen), #1522(A. Thomas), #1720(Hickman), #1980
(Assayas), #2010, 2034, 2037, 2041(Cook), #2099(McCutcheon), #2299, 2301,
2322, 2324, 2325, 2328, 2334, 2336, 2342(Cook), #2363(Doherty), #2387(Fiedel), #2457(Koldys), #2487(Maremaa), #2549(Sharples), #2596, 2597(Vertlieb), #2767, 2768, 2772(Cook), #2900(Vertlieb), #3123(Keller), #3333(Hen-
dricks/Green), #3380(Cook), #3397(Johnson/Rózsa), #3418(Teisseire), #3983
(Snell), #4191(Cook), #4460(Boilès), and #4485(Carcassone).

Hans J. Salter (1896-)

3901. Jones, Preston Neal. "The Ghost of Hans J. Salter: The Man Who Brought Harmony to the House of Frankenstein." Cinefantastique, 7, No. 2 (1978), 10-
25.

> An interview. Includes filmography.

3902. Pavelek, James ("Pav"). "Hans J. Salter: More Than 'Master of Terror and
Suspense.'" The Max Steiner Journal, No. 5 (1980), 27.

> Includes a partial filmography.

SEE ALSO:

#131(Thomas).

Philippe Sarde

3903. Clarisse, Patrick. "Cine-disques: Philippe Sarde." Amis du film, cinéma
et télévision (Brussels), No. 250 (Mar. 1977), 14-15.

3904. Lacombe, Alain. "Music Lovers: La musique de films." Écran, No. 30 (Nov.
1974), 86-87.

3905. Pede, Ronnie. "Filmmuziek." Film en Televisie (Brussels), No. 298 (Mar.
1982), 27-29.

3906. Sineux, Michel. "Entretien avec Philippe Sarde sur Claude Sautet et quelques autres." Positif (Paris), No. 214 (Jan. 1979), 13-15.

3907. Tessier, Max. "Sur 'Tess': propos de Philippe Sarde." Écran, No. 86
(Dec. 15, 1979), 56-57.

SEE ALSO:

#2762, 2767, 2772(Cook), and #3613(Vallerand).

Erik Satie (1866-1925)

3908. Gallez, Douglas W. "Satie's 'Entr'acte': A Model of Film Music." Cinema
Journal, 16, No. 1 (Fall 1976), 36-50.

> Concerns Satie's music for René Clair's "Relâche" (1924),
> and includes cue sheets and musical examples.

3909. Mellers, Wilfred. "Erik Satie et la musique 'fonctionelle.'" La Revue musicale, No. 214 (June 1952), 33-37.

SEE ALSO:

#793(Petit), #3595, and #4898(Stern).

Lalo Schifrin (1932–)

3910. Mangodt, Daniel. "Filmography/Discography: Lalo Schifrin." Soundtrack Collector's Newsletter, 2 (June 1983), 24-25.

3911. Schifrin, Lalo. "Lalo Schifrin and the Music from 'Che!'" Jazz and Pop, 8 (Aug. 1969), 30.

3912. ----------. "Them and Us." BMI: The Many Worlds of Music, No. 2 (1982), 22.

3913. Siders, Harvey. "Keeping Score on Schifrin." Down Beat, 36 (Mar. 6, 1969), 16-17ff.

3914. Tomkins, Les. "It's Exciting to Be a Musical Alchemist Says Lalo Schifrin." Crescendo International, 15 (Oct. 1976), 15-16.

3915. ----------. "My Approaches to the Film Score by Lalo Schifrin." Crescendo International, 15 (Sept. 1976), 8-10.

SEE ALSO:

#9(Bazelon, pp. 224-31), #44(Hagen), #132(Thomas), #2033, and 2331(Cook).

Dimitri Shostakovich (1906–1975)

3916. Arnshtam, Lev. "Muzyka geroicheskogo." Iskusstvo kino, No. 3 (1976), 96-104.

3917. Fedorov, Georgi Alekseevich. "Vnimanie: tretiy zhanr!" Sovetskaya muzyka, 42, No. 4 (Apr. 1978), 66-73.
     Concerns the film "Vospominanie o Shostakoviche."

3918. Kozintsev, Grigorii. "La Fin des années vingt." Trans. by Barbara Meyer. Cahiers du cinéma, No. 230 (July 1971), 5-14.
     Concerns the film "La Nouvelle Babylone."

3919. ----------. "Iz rabochikh tetradei." Iskusstvo kino, No. 1 (Jan. 1979), 102-11.

3920. ----------. "Iz rabochikh tetradei Pis'ma." Iskusstvo kino, No. 4 (Apr. 1980), 96-112.

3921. ----------. "Šostakovič: musica per 'Babilonia.'" Trans. and with an introduction by Laura Persichini. Filmcritica, 31, Nos. 305-306 (May-June 1980), 189-99.

3922. Lehel, György D. "Sosztakovics zenéje a 'Feledhetetlen 1919' c. filmhez." Uj zenei szemle (Budapest), 4, No. 3 (1953), 13-17.

3923. Markowski, Liesel. "Schostakowitsch filmporträtiert." Musik und Gesellschaft, 18 (Mar. 1968), 191-93.

3924. Nikel'berg, S. ("'Hamlet': The Film Music by Dmitrij Šostakovič.") In Iz istorii russkoj i sovetskoj muzyki, III. Comp. Mikhail Pitkus and Irina Givental'. Moscow: Muzyka, 1978.
     In Russian.

3925. Shostakovich, Dmitri. "Dmitri Shostakovich: We Get Along Well Together." Soviet Film (Moscow), No. 232 (1976), 11.
     Includes filmography.

3926. ----------. "Jeschtscho ras o kinomuzyke." Iskusstvo kino, No. 1 (Jan. 1954), 85-89.

3927. ----------. Kino kak schkola dlja kompositorov. Moscow, 1950.

3928. ----------. ("On the Music for 'New Babylon.'") Sovietskii ekran (Moscow),

(Mar. 12, 1929), 5.

In Russian.

3929. ----------. "Sur la musique de cinéma." _Recherches soviétiques_ (Paris), (Apr. 3, 1956), 175-82.

3930. ----------. _Testimony: The Memoirs of Dmitri Shostakovich, as Related to and Edited by Solomon Volkov._ Trans. from the Russian by Antonina W. Bouis. New York: Harper and Row; and London: H. Hamilton, 1979.

-- Rev. in _Music and Musicians_, 28 (Mar. 1980), 23.

-- Rev. in _High Fidelity and Musical America_, 30 (Mar. 1980), MA12-13.

3930a. Also published as _Testimonianza: Memorie raccolte e curate da Solomon Volkov._ Milan: Edizioni Mondadori, 1979.

3930b. Also published as _Zeugenaussage: die Memoiren des Dmitrij Schostakowitsch._ Comp. and ed. Solomon Volkov. Hamburg: A Knaus, 1979.

-- Rev. in _Neue Musikzeitung_, No. 1 (Feb.-Mar. 1980), 1ff.

3931. Troitskaya, Galina. "Muzyka Shostakovich v kino." _Iskusstvo kino_, No. 12 (Dec. 1981), 54-67.

3932. Walker, Robert Matthew. "Dmitri Shostakovich: The Film Music." _Music and Musicians_, 28 (Apr. 1980), 34ff.

3933. Yurchenko, V. D. "Shostakovich's New Movie Score." _High Fidelity and Musical America_, 21 (June 1971), 12ff.

3934. Zinkevič, E. "Prochtenie shekspira." _Sovetskaya muzyka_, 35 (Sept. 1971), 41-47.

Concerns the filmed version of "King Lear."

3934a. Also published as "Sostakovicuv Shakespeare," in _Hudební Rozhledy_, 25, No. 3 (1972), 133-36.

SEE ALSO:

#142(Austin), #1261(Eremin), #1446(Shostakovich et al.), #2018(Cook), #2978(Antheil), #3716(Schwarz), #4898(Stern), #4931(Shostakovich), and #5331(Frid).

Frank Skinner (1898-1968)

3935. Cook, Page. "The Sound Track." _Films in Review_, 16, No. 8 (Oct. 1965), 506-07.

Also includes references to music by Ernest Gold.

SEE ALSO:

#120(Skinner), #1204(Bowles), #1296(Hamilton), #2019, 2022, 3067, and 3277(Cook).

Max Steiner (1888-1971)

3936. Bender, Albert K., ed. _Just for Max._ Bakersfield, Calif.: Max Steiner Music Society, 1981.

The final publication of the MSMS, this pamphlet is a memorial tribute to the composer, with short contributions by several composers and leaders of the film industry.

3937. ----------. "Max Steiner." _Film Music Notebook_, 1, No. 1 (Fall 1974), 5-11.

Includes filmography.

3938. ----------. "Max Steiner -- The Humorist." The Max Steiner Annual, No. 8 (1974), 20-21.

3939. ----------, and Edward A. Schmidt. "The Max Steiner Chronology." The Max Steiner Annual, No. 1 (1967), 3-8.

   3939a. Reprinted in The Max Steiner Journal, No. 1 (1977), 27-33.

      Also includes a filmography: "The Films of the Steiner Years," pp. 31-33, and "Max Steiner's Songs from the Movies," p. 33.

3940. Bertolina, Gian Carlo. "Max Steiner, il decano." Rivista del cinematografo (Rome), 54 (Dec. 1981), 649-59.

3941. Bradbury, Ray. "The Film, The Music, and the Man." The Max Steiner Music Society News Letter, No. 41 (Winter 1974), 6-7.

3942. Brown, Harold. "The Miracle of Our Lady of Fatima." Film Music, 12, No. 1 (Sept.-Oct. 1952), 4-10.

      Includes excerpts from the score.

3943. Burton, Geoff. "In Defence of Max Steiner." The Max Steiner Journal, No. 5 (1980), 7-9.

      A defense against comments made by Andre Previn.

3944. Bush, Richard H. "A Musical Review of the Film 'King Kong.'" The Max Steiner Music Society News Letter, No. 19 (Summer 1969), 3.

3945. Carcassonne, Philippe. "Musique et film: en ecoutant 'Le Grand sommeil.'" Cinematographe (Paris), No. 42 (Dec. 1978), 71-73.

3946. Comuzio, Ermanno. "La lezione di Max Steiner." Cineforum (Bergamo), (Oct. 1971).

3947. Cook, Page. "John Paul Jones." The Max Steiner Annual, No. 4 (1970), 11-14.

3948. ----------. "The Music from 'Gone with the Wind.'" The Max Steiner Annual, No. 1 (1967), 11.

3949. ----------. "Steiner Film Score Reviews: 'The Adventures of Don Juan.'" The Max Steiner Annual, No. 1 (1967), 13-14.

3950. ----------. "The Sound Track." Films in Review, 16, No. 1 (Jan. 1965), 42-43.

      Concerning current scores by Steiner and others.

3951. ----------. "The Sound Track." Films in Review, 18, No. 9 (Nov. 1967), 569-71.

3952. Deke, R. F. "Glass Menagerie." Film Music Notes, 10, No. 1 (Sept.-Oct. 1950), 17-18.

3953. Farrant, Bernard. "A Film Score Review: 'Distant Drums.'" The Max Steiner Journal, No. 5 (1980), 33-34.

3954. Fichter, Gerald. "The Hanging Tree." The Max Steiner Journal, No. 4 (1979), 11.

3955. Fiedel, Robert D. "Music by Max Steiner." In The Girl in the Hairy Paw: King Kong as Myth, Movie and Monster. Ed. Ronald Gottesman and Harry M. Geduld. New York: Avon Books, 1976, pp. 191-97.

3956. ----------. "Sound Track: And the Beast Goes On." American Film, 2, No. 5 (Mar. 1977), 71-72.

      Concerning the reconstruction of Steiner's score for 'King Kong' for a new recording.

3957. Goldner, Orville, and George E. Turner. The Making of King Kong: The Story Behind a Film Classic. New York: A.S. Barnes, 1975.

Includes many references to Steiner's music for the film.

3958. Gorbman, Claudia. "The Drama's Melos: Max Steiner and 'Mildred Pierce.'" Velvet Light Trap, No. 19 (1982), 35-39.

3959. Green, Stu. "Reflections on the "King Kong' Score." The Max Steiner Journal, No. 5 (1980), 23-25.

3960. Hammond, Philip J. S. "Max Steiner's Music for 'Little Women' (1933)." The Max Steiner Annual, No. 8 (1974), 10-14.

3961. ----------. "Max Steiner's Music for the Bette Davis Films." The Max Steiner Annual, No. 6 (1972), 2-14.

Includes a Bette Davis filmography.

3962. ----------. "Max Steiner's Music for the Errol Flynn Films." The Max Steiner Annual, No. 5 (1971), 2-6.

3963. ----------. "Max Steiner's Music for 'Virginia City' (1940)." The Max Steiner Annual, No. 9 (1975), 2-8.

3964. ----------. "Riding the Sagebrush Trail with Max Steiner." The Max Steiner Annual, No. 4 (1970), 2-3.

Originally appeared, in part, in Films and Filming (Dec. 1969).

3965. ----------. "Transatlantic Title Changes." The Max Steiner Annual, No. 7 (1973), 12-13.

A listing of the American and British titles for Steiner's films.

3966. ----------. "The World of Max Steiner." The Max Steiner Annual, No. 8 (1974), 2-9.

Hammond introduces a collection of "Tribute" to Steiner, including contributions by Reginald J. Otter, John Mann, James "Pav" Pavelek, Samuel Steinberg, Hans-Paul Zimmer, Albert K. Bender, and George A. Lazarou.

3967. Haun, Harry, and George Raborn. "Max Steiner." Films in Review, 12, No. 6 (June-July 1961), 338-51.

Includes filmography.

3968. Lasher, John Steven. "'Now, Voyager': The Classic Film Scores of Max Steiner." The Max Steiner Music Society News Letter, No. 36 (Autumn 1973), 6-7; and No. 37 (Winter 1973), 6.

A review of the soundtrack album.

3969. Lazarou, George A. Max Steiner and Film Music: An Essay. Athens, Greece: The Max Steiner Music Society, 1971.

A pamphlet, incorporates portions of Steiner's unpublished autobiography. See #3992.

Includes a bibliography, pp. 38-40.

3970. Lichtenberger, Robert S. "Behind the Scenes with Max Steiner." The Max Steiner Music Society News Letter, No. 45 (Winter 1975), 4.

3971. Littman, Bill. "The 'King Kong' Score: Primitive Rhythms on Skull Island." Gore Creatures, No. 23 (Jan. 1975), 10-13.

3972. Mitchell, Richard. "Max Steiner: Composer of Action." The Max Steiner Music Society News Letter, No. 43 (Summer 1975), 3-4.

3973. ----------. "'Without Honor': Back from Obscurity." The Max Steiner Journal, No. 5 (1980), 45-46.

3974. Morgan, John W. "Max Steiner Discography." The Max Steiner Annual, No. 9 (1975), 14-17.

3975. Palmer, Christopher. "Steiner, Max(imilian Raoul Walter)." In The New Groves Dictionary of Music and Musicians. Ed. Stanley Sadie. London:

Macmillan, 1980, XVIII, pp. 109-10.

Includes filmography and bibliography.

3976. Pugliese, Roberto. "Filmografia completa di Max(imilian) Raoul Walter Steiner." Filmcritica, 30, Nos. 296-297 (Aug. 1979), 255-62.

Includes filmography and bibliography.

3977. ----------. "Steiner: 'Via col vento' e/è la sua musica." Filmcritica (Rome), 30, Nos. 296-297 (Aug. 1979), 247-54.

An analysis of the score for "Gone with the Wind."

3978. Rosenberg, Bernard, and Harry Silverstein. The Real Tinsel. New York: Macmillan, 1970.

Includes an interview with Max Steiner, pp. 387-98, and with sound engineer Douglas Shearer, pp. 373-84.

3979. Rubsamen, Walter H. "Music in the Cinema." Arts and Architecture, 62, No. 5 (May 1945), 18, 42, 44.

Concerning the use of Welsh folk music in Steiner's films.

3980. Snell, Mike. "Compliments to Kate." The Max Steiner Journal, No. 1 (1977), 3-9.

Concerning Steiner's scores for films starring Katharine Hepburn.

3981. ----------. "From York to Roark: Max Steiner's Scores for Gary Cooper." The Max Steiner Journal, No. 5 (1980), 17-20.

3982. ----------. "'Home Before Dark' and Other 'Unknown' Steiner Credits." The Max Steiner Journal, No. 4 (1979), 10, 26, 41.

3983. ----------. "'Max Steiner Revisited' and 'Beyond the Forest': Special MSMS Albums Continue on Citadel." The Max Steiner Journal, No. 4 (1979), 42-46.

Also includes commentary on new recordings of music by Rozsa and Korngold.

3984. ----------. "Music in Technicolor: Max Steiner's Score for 'The Garden of Allah.'" The Max Steiner Journal, No. 5 (1980), 2-5.

3985. ----------. "'Now, Voyager' Revisited." The Max Steiner Journal, No. 2 (1978), 9-11.

3986. ----------. "Out of the Blue: Max Steiner's Score for 'Bird of Paradise.'" The Max Steiner Journal, No. 2 (1978), 2-5.

3987. ----------. "Play the Part that I Like." The Max Steiner Journal, No. 1 (1977), 10-13.

3988. ----------. "Symphony of Six Million." The Max Steiner Journal, No. 4 (1979), 2-9.

3989. Steiner, Max. "Isn't That the Music You Used in Another Film?", "Scoring for the TV Film," and "My Father and the Masters." The Max Steiner Annual, No. 8 (1974), 22-26.

Anecdotes related by the composer.

3990. ----------. "Max Steiner and the Birth of a Star," and "Jolson or Not Jolson." The Max Steiner Annual, No. 7 (1973), 3-5.

Anecdotes from Steiner's days as a musical comedy conductor. (The "star" mentioned here is Rudolph Valentino.)

3991. ----------. "My Association with the Great Victor Herbert." The Max Steiner Annual, No. 6 (1972), 15-16.

3992. ----------. Notes to You. Unpublished autobiography in typescript, ca. 1963.

Portions have been published in The Max Steiner Music Society Newsletter (see Lazarou, #3969), and in Thomas's

Film Score (see #131).

3993. ----------. "Music in the Cinema." New York Times (September 29, 1935),
    Section 10, p. 4.

3994. ----------. "Scoring the Film." In We Make the Movies. Ed. Nancy Naum-
    berg. New York: W. W. Norton, 1937, pp. 216-38.

  3994a. Reprinted in issues of The Max Steiner Music Society News
      Letter, No. 36 (Autumn 1973), 2-3; No. 37 (Winter 1973),
      2-3; No. 38 (Spring 1974), 2-3; No. 39 (Summer 1974), 2-
      3; No. 40 (Autumn 1974), 2-3; and No. 41 (Winter 1974),
      3-5.

3995. ----------. "Scoring the Film 'Bird of Paradise.'" The Max Steiner Jour-
    nal, No. 2 (1978), 6.

3996. ----------. "Sh-h-h, Quiet Please!", "Max Steiner on the Music from Sum-
    mer Place," and "The Crystal Cup." The Max Steiner Annual, No. 5 (1971),
    6-7.

      Anecdotes related by the composer.

3997. ----------. "This Is Cinerama." The Max Steiner Annual, No. 7 (1973),
    13-15.

3998. Thomas, Anthony. "The Sound Track." Films in Review, 14, No. 7 (Aug.-
    Sept. 1963), 429-30.

      Concerns Steiner's "collaboration" with David O. Selznick.

3999. Thomas, Tony. "Flynn and Film Music." The Max Steiner Annual, No. 5
    (1971), 12-13.

      A brief survey of scores for films starring Errol Flynn
      including scores by Steiner and Erich Korngold.

4000. ----------. "Music and Film -- The Odd Coupling, Part 2." The Max Steiner
    Music Society News Letter, No. 32 (Autumn 1972), 3-4.

4001. Vallance, Tom. "Current Releases." Film (London), Series 2, No. 10 (Jan.
    1974), 21.

      Soundtrack album review.

4002. Vertlieb, Steve. "The Horror and Fantasy Films of Max Steiner." The Max
    Steiner Annual, No. 4 (1970), 4-6.

SEE ALSO:

    #28(Corper), #43(Hagen), #115, #131, 132(Thomas), #221(Cook), #357(Beat-
    on), #1178, 1180(Antheil), #1213(Brown), #1223(Carter), #1276(Forrell/
    Currie), #1297, 1298(Hamilton), #1373(Kubik/Forrell/Hamilton), #1439(Mor-
    ton), #1522(Thomas), #1645(Connor/Pratley), #2013, 2314(Cook), #3269(At-
    kins/Friedhofer), #3418(Teisseire), #4215(Connor/Pratley), #4217(Mitchell),
    #4666 and 4667(Kalinak).

Leith Stevens (1909-1970)

4003. "First Entirely Jazz Background on Pic Set on Coast by Stevens." Variety,
    195 (Aug. 11, 1954), 45.

4004. Hamilton, James Clifford. "Leith Stevens: A Critical Analysis of His
    Works." D.M.A. Diss. University of Missouri - Kansas City 1976.

      Abstract: DAI 37:2481A (order #DA 7625145).

4005. Kelley, F. "Leith Stevens: Unsung Hero." Metronome, 71 (Sept. 1955), 20ff.

4006. Lucraft, Howard. "First Jazz Score." Music U.S.A., 76 (June 1959), 7.

4007. McCarty, Clifford. "Leith Stevens." Film and TV Music, 16, No. 2 (Winter
    1956), 21.

Includes filmography and selected discography.

4008. Steiner, Fred. "An Examination of Leith Stevens' Use of Jazz in 'The Wild One.'" Filmmusic Notebook, 2, No. 2 (1976), 26-35; and 2, No. 3 (1976), 26-34.

4009. Stevens, Leith. "The Promotion of Film Music in the Concert Hall." Opera, Concert, and Symphony (Aug. 1947).

4010. ----------. "Radio vs. Movie Underscoring." Opera, Concert, and Symphony (Jan. 1948).

4011. ----------. "Storm Over Hollywood." Down Beat, 26 (Oct. 15, 1959), 16-17ff.

4012. ----------. "The Wild One." Film Music, 13, No. 3 (Jan.-Feb. 1954), 3-7.
Reprinted in Limbacher, pp. 120-22. See #75.

SEE ALSO:
#1355(Keller).

Herbert Stothart (1885-1949)

4013. Hammond, Philip J. S. "The Career of Herbert Stothart (1885-1949)." The Max Steiner Annual, No. 7 (1973), 10-12.
Also see the addenda in The Max Steiner Annual, No. 8 (1974), 15; and No. 9 (1975), 17. These include a filmography.

4013a. Reprinted (including the addenda) in The Max Steiner Journal, No. 4 (1979), 30-41.

4014. ----------. "Herbert Stothart: An Encore." The Max Steiner Journal, No. 5 (1980), 13-16, 31-32.

4015. Harmetz, Aljean. The Making of "The Wizard of Oz." New York: Alfred A. Knopf, 1977.
Concerns Stothart's adaptation of the musical score.

4016. McCarty, Clifford. "Herbert Stothart Filmography." The Cue Sheet (Los Angeles), 1, No. 1 (Jan. 1984), 2.

4017. Palmer, Christopher. "Stothart, Herbert." In The New Groves Dictionary of Music and Musicians. Ed. Stanley Sadie. London: Macmillan, 1980, XVIII, p. 185.

4018. Rosar, William H. "Herbert Stothart: A Biographical Sketch." The Cue Sheet (Los Angeles), 1, No. 1 (Jan. 1984), 3-5.

4019. Stothart, Herbert. "Film Music." In Behind the Screen: How Films Are Made. Ed. Stephen Watts. New York: Dodge Publishing Co., 1938; and London: Arthur Barker, Ltd., 1939, pp. 139-44.

4020. ----------. "Il problema della musica nel film storico." Cinema (Rome), No. 17 (1937), 178.

4021. Stothart, Herbert, Jr. "Herbert Stothart." Films in Review, 21, No. 10 (Dec. 1970), 622-30.
Includes filmography.

4022. "'The Yearling': Frederick Delius and Herbert Stothart." Film Music Notes, 6, No. 4 (Feb.-Mar. 1947), 11.

SEE ALSO:
#501(Cousins), #1203(Bowles), #1428 and 1433(Morton).

Mikis Theodorakis (1925-)

4023. Giannaris, George. _Mikis Theodorakis: Music and Social Change_. New York: Praeger, 1973.

4024. Minuzzo, Nerio. "Intervista con Theodorakis." _L'Europeo_ (Milan), (June 1969).

4025. ----------. "Theodorakis racconta perché ha lasciato il Partito comunista: Perché non sono piú comunista." _L'Europeo_ (Milan), 28, No. 17 (Apr. 1972), 72-75.

4026. Theodorakis, Mikis. _Les fiances de Penelope: Conversations avec Denis Bourgeois_. With a foreword by François Mitterrand. Paris: Grasset, 1975.
-- Rev. in _Amis du film et de la télévision_, No. 238 (Mar. 1976), 38.

SEE ALSO:
#2296(Cook).

Virgil Thomson (1896-)

4027. Achter, Barbara Zuck. "Americanism and American Art Music, 1930-1945." Ph.D. Diss. (Musicology), University of Michigan.

Work in progress in 1976.

4028. Brown, Harold. "Music Chronicle: Two Film Scores." _Partisan Review_, 16, No. 2 (Feb. 1949), 193-95.

A comparison of Thomson's "Louisiana Story" and the film "Kalpana," a study of Uday Shankar, with musical score by Shirali.

4029. Huntley, John. "The Sound Track." _Sight and Sound_, 21, No. 1 (Aug.-Sept. 1951), 47.

4030. Keller, Hans. "Louisiana Story." _Music Survey_, 2, No. 2 (Autumn 1949), 101-02; and 2, No. 3 (Winter 1950), 188-89.

4031. Peatman, Mary. "A New 'Louisiana Story.'" _Pro Musica Sana_, 2, No. 3 (Fall 1973), 7-11.

Analysis of a new soundtrack album.

4032. Perlis, Vivian. Interviews with Virgil Thomson, 9/28/77 and 1/10/78. Tapes and transcripts are part of the project _Oral History: American Music_. New Haven, Conn.: Yale University, 1978.

4033. Snyder, Robert L. _Pare Lorentz and the Documentary Film_. Norman, Oka.: University of Oklahoma Press, 1968.

Includes Chap. 2: "The Plow that Broke the Plains," pp. 21-49; Chap. 3: "The River," pp. 50-78; and Chap. 8: "An Evaluation of the Films of Merit," pp. 177-201.

4034. Sternfeld, Frederick W. "Current Chronicle." _Musical Quarterly_, 35 (Jan. 1949), 115-121.

4035. ----------. "Louisiana Story: A Review of Virgil Thomson's Score." _Film Music Notes_, 8, No. 1 (Sept.-Oct. 1948), 5-14.

4035a. Reprinted in _Music Journal_, 7 (Mar.-Apr. 1949), 21ff.

4036. Thomson, Virgil. "Films Seen in New York." _Modern Music_, 14, No. 4 (May-June 1937), 239-40.

4037. ----------. "A Little About Movie Music." _Modern Music_, 10, No. 4 (May-June 1933), 188-91.

4038. ----------. The State of Music. New York: William Morrow, 1939.

        Includes the chapter "Music and Photography," pp. 173-90.

        Second revised edition, New York: Random House, 1962. Includes the same chapter, pp. 157-71.

4039. ----------. "On the Screen -- Music: 'Fantasia.'" New York Herald Tribune (Nov. 14, 1940), p. 20.

4040. ----------. "Processed Music." Music Publishers Journal, 3, No. 5 (Sept.-Oct. 1945), 33, 60.

SEE ALSO:

        #82(Manvell/Huntley), #132(Thomas), #167(Kingman), #1178(Antheil), #1389 (London), #1446, 2961(Thomson), #2978(Antheil), #3140, and 3164(Thomson).

Dimitri Tiomkin (1899-1979)

4041. Bazelon, Irwin A. "'Cyrano de Bergerac': A Review of Dimitri Tiomkin's Score." In a Special Bulletin of Film Music Notes (Jan. 1951), 2-8.

4042. Carcassonne, Philippe. "Dimitri Tiomkin." Cinematographe, No. 53 (1979), 77.

        Obituary.

4043. Corneau, Ernest N. "Genius of Movie Music: Dimitri Tiomkin." Classic Film Collector, No. 57 (Winter 1977), 20ff.

4044. del Valle, John. "Composer Problems." Film Music Notes, 8, No. 3 (Jan.-Feb. 1949), 18.

4045. "Dimitri Tiomkin." Cine Revue (Brussels), 59 (Nov. 22, 1979), 61.

        Obituary. Includes filmography.

4046. Epstein, Dave A. "Back Stage with the Film Music Composer." Etude, 71, No. 2 (Feb. 1953), 19, 60-61.

        An interview with Tiomkin.

4047. Hamilton, William. "Current Films." Film Music Notes, 8, No. 5 (May-June 1949), 17.

        Reprinted as "'Champion' and 'Home of the Brave,'" in Limbacher, p. 85. See #75.

4048. ----------. "High Noon." Film Music, 12, No. 1 (Sept.-Oct. 1952), 19-20.

        Reprinted in Limbacher, pp. 91-92. See #75.

4049. Hickman, C. Sharpless. "Movies and Music." Music Journal, 13, No. 4 (Apr. 1955), 46-47.

4050. Jomy, Alain, and Dominique Rabourdin. "Adieu Monsieur Tiomkin." Cinéma 80, No. 253 (Jan. 1980), 66-70.

        Includes discography and filmography.

4051. Jordan, Robert. "Dimitri Tiomkin." The Max Steiner Journal, No. 1 (1977), 17-18.

4052. Lewin, Frank. "Land of the Pharoahs." Film Music, 14, No. 5 (May-June 1955), 19.

4053. "The Melody Lingers On." Newsweek, 44, No. 10 (Sept. 6, 1954), 50-51.

        Concerns Tiomkin's use of "theme songs."

4054. Moret, Henry. "Dimitri Tiomkin." Écran, No. 86 (Dec. 15, 1979), 76-77.

        Obituary.

4055. Palmer, Christopher. "Dimitri Tiomkin: A Biographical Sketch." Film Music Notebook, 4, No. 2 (1978), 29-33.

> Includes filmography.

4056. ----------. "Dimitri Tiomkin in London." Crescendo International, 14 (Jan. 1976), 24-25.

4057. ----------. "Dimitri Tiomkin: The Composer in the Cinema, Part 1." Film (London), No. 64 (Winter 1971), 19-21; and "Dimitri Tiomkin: The Composer in the Cinema, Part 2." Film (London), No. 65 (Spring 1972), 18-20.

> Part 2 includes filmography.

4058. ----------. "Dimitri Tiomkin: Master of the Symphonic Film Score." Crescendo International, 10 (July 1972), 18-19.

4059. ----------. "The Function of Film Music." Crescendo International, 11 (Aug. 1972), 26-27.

> An interview with Tiomkin.

4060. ----------. "Profile: Dimitri Tiomkin." Performing Right (London), No. 53 (May 1970), 24-26, 32.

4061. ----------. "St. Petersburg to Hollywood." Music and Musicians, 21 (Apr. 1973), 18-20.

> Concerns the film "Tchaikovsky" (U.S.S.R.).

4062. ----------. "Tiomkin as Russian Composer." Film Music Notebook, 4, No. 2 (1978), 34-39.

4063. ----------. "Tiomkin, Dimitri." In The New Groves Dictionary of Music and Musicians. Ed. Stanley Sadie. London: Macmillan, 1980, XIX, p. 1.

> Includes filmography and bibliography.

4064. ----------. "Tiomkin's 'Tchaikovsky.'" Musical Opinion, 95, No. 1131 (Dec. 1971), 122-24.

4065. Rosar, William H. "'Lost Horizon': An Account of the Composition of the Score." Film Music Notebook, 4, No. 2 (1978), 40-52.

4066. Sokol'sky, Matias. "'Chaykovskiy' i ... Chaykovskiy." Sovetskaya muzyka, 35 (Mar. 1971), 63-67.

> See #4067.

4067. ----------. "Der Film 'Tschaikowski' und der wahre Tschaikowski." Kunst und Literatur (Berlin), 20 (Mar. 1972), 319-26.

> See #4066.

4068. Sutak, Ken. "'The Alamo' Remembered." Soundtrack Collectors Newletter, 2, Nos. 7 and 8 (1977).

> A thorough explication of Tiomkin's score.

4069. Tiomkin, Dimitri. "Composing for Films." Films in Review, 2, No. 9 (Nov. 1951), 17-22.

> Reprinted in Limbacher, pp. 55-60. See #75.

> Reprinted in Theodore J. Ross Film and the Liberal Arts pp. 230-37. See #4850.

4070. ----------. "Don't Underestimate Filmusic." Variety, 229 (Dec. 5, 1962), 42.

4071. ----------. "The Maturity of Music for Motion Pictures." Variety, 213 (Jan. 7, 1959), 212.

4072. ----------. "Music for the Films." Music Journal Annual (1967), 29ff.

4073. ----------. "The Music of Hollywood." Music Journal, 20, No. 8 (Nov.-Dec. 1962), 7, 87.

4074. ----------. "On Motion Picture Music." Variety, 221 (Jan. 4, 1961), 207.

4075. ----------. "Theme Song." Time, 62 (Sept. 14, 1953), 108.

4076. ----------. "Writing Symphonically for the Screen." Music Journal, 17, No. 1 (Jan. 1959), 26, 106.

4077. ----------, and Prosper Buranelli. Please Don't Hate Me. Garden City, N.Y.: Doubleday, 1959. (Reprint, 1961.)

     Autobiography of Tiomkin.

4078. "Tiomkin's Plea: Give Film Music More 'Liberty.'" Variety, 205 (Jan. 30, 1957), 4ff.

4079. Vallerand, François. "Dimitri Tiomkin." Sequences (Montreal), No. 99 (Jan. 1980), 47-48.

     Obituary.

SEE ALSO:

    #131, 132(Thomas), #221(Cook), #1276(Forrell/Currie), #1339(Irving), #1621(Cerulli), #2009, 2030(Cook), #2067(Hanson), #2098(McCutcheon), #2272(Butler), #2406(Gardiner), and #4482(Capra).

Vaclav Trojan (1907-)

4080. Bor, Vladimir, and Stepanem Luckym (Stepan Lucky). "La Musique de film de Vaclav Trojan." Hudební Rozhledy (Prague), 9, Nos. 2 and 3 (1955).

4081. ----------, and Stepanem Luckym. Trojan, filmová hudba. Prague: Státní nakl. krásné literatury, hudby a umění, 1958.

4082. Deke, R. F. "The Emperor's Nightingale." Film Music Notes, 10, No. 5 (May-June 1951), 8-9.

4083. Hepner, Arthur. "The Emperor's Nightingale." Film Music Notes, 10, No. 5 (May-June 1951), 7-8.

Georges van Parys (1902-1971)

4084. Fleuret, Maurice. "Un musicien heureux: Georges van Parys." Musica (Chaix, France), No. 104 (Nov. 1962), 21-27.

4085. Hendricks, Gordon. "The Sound Track." Films in Review, 5, No. 6 (June-July 1954), 311-12.

4086. van Parys, Georges. "Le Compositeur de musique." In Le Livre d'or du cinéma français. Paris: Agence d'information cinématographique, 1945.

4087. ----------. "La Musique de film." France Illustration, No. 51 (Sept. 1946).

4088. ----------. "Musique et cinéma." Les Annales, 62, No. 57 (1955), 25-38.

4089. ----------. "'Le Silence c'est d'or' vu par le musicien." Ciné-Club (Paris), (1947).

SEE ALSO:

    #137(van Parys), and #2167(Steen).

Ralph Vaughan Williams (1872-1958)

4090. Bergsagel, John Dagfinn. "The National Aspects of the Music of Ralph Vaughan Williams." Ph.D. Diss. Cornell University 1957.

An important stylistic analysis, with references to
music for films.

Abstract: DA 17/09:2026.

4091. Pratley, Gerald. "Ralph Vaughan Williams' 'Sinfonia Antartica': A Radio
Program in Two Parts." Film Music, 14, No. 2 (Nov.-Dec. 1954), 12-16.

A transcription of programs recorded for the weekly
series "Music from the Films" (Canadian Broadcasting
Corporation).

4092. Schwartz, Elliott Shelling. "The Symphonies of Ralph Vaughan Williams: An
Analysis of their Stylistic Elements." Ed.E. Diss. Columbia University
1962.

Abstract: DA 23/08:2938.

4093. Vaughan-Williams, Ralph. Some Thoughts on Beethoven's Choral Symphony,
with Writings on Other Musical Subjects. London: Oxford University
Press, 1953.

Includes the essay "Composing for the Films," pp. 107-15.

4094. ----------. "Film Music." Royal College of Music Magazine (London), 40,
No. 1 (1944).

4094a. Reprinted in Piping Times, 4, No. 1 (1944).

4094b. Reprinted in Film Music Notes, 6, No. 3 (Dec. 1946-Jan.
1947), 7-10.

4094c. Reprinted in Film Music Notebook, 2, No. 2 (1976), 22-25.

4095. ----------. National Music and Other Essays. London: Oxford University
Press, 1963.

Includes the essay "Composing for the Films," pp. 160-65.

SEE ALSO:
#56(Irving), and #1408(Mathieson).

Roman Vlad (1919-)

4096. Connor, Edward, and Gerald Pratley. "The Sound Track." Films in Review,
6, No. 4 (Apr. 1955), 193-95.

Also includes references to music by Leonard Rosenman.

4097. Vlad, Roman. "Como ho scritto la musica per 'Giulietta e Romeo.'" Cinema
(Rome), No. 143 (1957).

4098. ----------. "Il compositore e la musica per film." In Musica e film.
Ed. S. G. Biamonte. Rome: Edizioni dell'Ateneo, 1959, pp. 197-202.

A paper presented at the 1950 Florence Congress. See
Biamonte (#1606) and the Proceedings (#1864).

4099. ----------. "La musica nel cinema." Bianco e nero, 10, No. 4 (Apr. 1949).

4100. ----------. "Musica per film." L'Illustrazione Italiana (Christmas 1954).

4101. ----------. "Notes on the Music for 'Romeo and Juliet.'" Film Music, 14,
No. 3 (Jan.-Feb. 1955), 3-5.

4102. ----------. "Tecnica della musica per film." Bianco e nero, 10, No. 8
(Aug. 1949).

4103. ----------. "Tecnica della musica per film." In Modernità e tradizione
nella musica contemporanea. Turin: Edizione Einaudi, 1955.

4104. "Voci per un dizionario di compositori viventi: Roman Vlad." Rassegna
musicale (Rome), 20, No. 1 (Jan. 1950).

SEE ALSO:

#139(Vlad), #1698(Hendricks), #1752(Keller), #1794(Lewin), #1915, 1916 (Vlad), #2115(Pellegrini/Vlad), and #3784(Cook).

William Walton (1902-)

4105. Britten, Benjamin. "As You Like It." World Film News, 1, No. 7 (Oct. 1936), 46.

4106. Clifford, Hubert. "Walton's 'Henry V' Music." Tempo (London), (Dec. 1944).

4107. Connor, Edward, and Gerald Pratley. "The Sound Track." Films in Review, 7, No. 5 (May 1956), 228-31.

4108. Diether, Jack. "'Richard III': The Preservation of a Film." Quarterly of Film, Radio, and Television, 11, No. 3 (Spring 1957), 280-93.

4109. Geduld, Harry M. Filmguide to "Henry V." Bloomington, Ind.: Indiana University Press, 1973.

> Includes references to Walton's music throughout, but especially in the chapter "Music," pp. 63-65. Also includes bibliography and discography.

4110. Greenfield, Edward. "The Battle of Britain." Bedside Guardian, 18 (1969), 163-65.

4111. Huntley, John. "The Music of 'Hamlet' and 'Oliver Twist.'" Penguin Film Review, No. 8 (Jan. 1949), 110-116.

> Also see #1315a.

4112. ----------. "Tchaikowsky, Walton, Addinsell." Sound Illustrated (London), (May 1945).

4113. Hutton, C. Clayton. Henry V. London: Punch Bowl Press, 1945.

> Includes a section on Walton's score for the film.

4114. Keller, Hans. "Music for the Film 'Hamlet.'" Monthly Film Review, 6, No. 7 (1948).

4115. Lewin, Frank. "Richard III." Film and TV Music, 16, No. 1 (Fall 1956), 11-12.

4116. Leyda, Jay. "The Evil That Men Do ..." Film Culture, 2, No. 1 (1956), 21-23.

> Concerns Walton's "Richard III," and Mussorgsky's "Boris Gudonov."

4117. Lichtenberger, Robert S. "The Film Music of Sir William Walton: A Brief Survey." The Max Steiner Annual, No. 7 (1973), 6-9.

4118. Mathieson, Muir. "Note on 'Hamlet.'" Film Music, 13, No. 3 (Jan.-Feb. 1954), 19.

> Reprinted from an earlier issue of Film Music Notes.
>
> Reprinted in Limbacher, p. 131. See #75.

4119. ----------. "Recording the Music." In The Film "Hamlet": A Record of Its Production. Ed. Brenda Cross. London: Saturn Press, 1948, pp. 63-64.

4120. McCarty, Clifford. "William Walton." Film and TV Music, 16, No. 1 (Fall 1956), 12-13.

> Includes filmography, bibliography, and selected discography.

4121. Palmer, Christopher. "Walton's Film Music." Musical Times, 113, No. 1549 (Mar. 1972), 249-52.

4122. Rawlinson, Harold. "Music and the Film: 'Oliver Twist.'" British Journal of Photography (Aug. 6, 1948).

4123. "Sir William Walton." Variety, 310 (Mar. 16, 1983), 196.

Obituary.

4124. "Sir William Walton's Shakespeare Film Scores." American Record Guide (Washington, D.C.), (May 1964), 881-83.

Includes discography and filmography.

4125. Walton, William. "Excerpts from the Score for 'Hamlet.'" Film Music Notes, 9, No. 2 (Nov.-Dec. 1949), 7-15.

A facsimile reproduction of the "Prelude" to the film, entitled "To Be or Not To Be."

4126. ----------. "Music for Shakespearean Films." Film Music, 15, No. 4 (Spring 1956), 20.

Reprinted in Limbacher, pp. 128-30. See #75.

4127. ----------. "The Music of 'Hamlet.'" In The Film "Hamlet": A Record of Its Production. Ed. Brenda Cross. London: Saturn Press, 1948, pp. 60-62.

4127a. Partially reprinted in Film Music, 8, No. 4 (Mar.-Apr. 1949), 4.

SEE ALSO:

#56(Irving), #82(Manvell), #87(Walton et al.), #1258(Dickinson), #1315, 1326(Huntley), #1441(Morton), #1650(Connor/Pratley), #1755(Keller), and #2976(Antheil).

Franz Waxman (1906-1967)

4128. Abramson, Robert M. "A Place in the Sun." Film Music, 11, No. 2 (Nov.-Dec. 1951), 20.

4129. Applebaum, Louis. "Waxman and 'Humoresque.'" Film Music Notes, 6, No. 3 (Dec. 1946-Jan. 1947), 5-6.

4130. Brown, Harold. "The Silver Chalice." Film Music, 14, No. 3 (Jan.-Feb. 1955), 20-21.

4131. Cook, Page. "A Capsule Biography: Franz Waxman, 1906-1967." The Max Steiner Annual, No. 5 (1971), 17.

4132. ----------. "Franz Waxman." Films in Review, 19, No. 7 (Aug.-Sept. 1968), 415-30.

4133. Frankenstein, Alfred V. "Franz Waxman's Music for 'The Silver Chalice.'" Film Music Notebook, 1, No. 3 (Spring 1975), 27-35.

Includes a Waxman filmography.

4134. "Franz Waxman." Film Music Notebook, 1, No. 3 (Spring 1975), 6-9.

Filmography.

4135. Hendricks, Gordon, and James Chapin. "The Sound Track." Films in Review, 5, No. 8 (Oct. 1954), 437-38.

References to music by Waxman and others.

4136. Hickman, C. Sharpless. "Heard While Seeing." Music Journal, 10, No. 1 (Jan. 1952), 36-37.

4137. Littman, Bill. "Music for the Bride: Franz Waxman's Score for 'The Bride of Frankenstein.'" Gore Creatures, No. 25 (Sept. 1976), 63-66.

4138. Morton, Lawrence. "Film Music Profile: Franz Waxman." Film Music Notes, 9, No. 3 (Jan.-Feb. 1950), 10-11.

4139. ----------. "'Music from the Films': A CBC Broadcast." Hollywood Quarterly, 5, No. 2 (Winter 1950), 132-37.

Transcription of an interview with Waxman recorded for
the Canadian Broadcasting Corporation.

4139a. Reprinted in Pro Musica Sana, 8, No. 1 (Winter 1979-1980),
4-9.

4140. ----------. "The Music of 'Objective: Burma.'" Hollywood Quarterly, 1,
No. 4 (July 1946), 378-95.

An important, thorough analysis of the score.

4141. Palmer, Christopher. "Waxman (Wachsmann), Franz." In The New Groves Dictionary of Music and Musicians. Ed. Stanley Sadie. London: Macmillan,
1980, XX, p. 236.

4142. Waxman, Franz. "Progress in Development of Film Music Scores." Music Publishers' Journal, 3, No. 5 (Sept.-Oct. 1945), 9, 66-67.

SEE ALSO:

#131, 132(Thomas), #1207(Bowles), #1296(Hamilton), #1428, 1438, 1820(Mor-
ton), #1902(Talbert et al.), #1903(Talbert/Schaefer), #2019(Cook), #2100
(McCutcheon), #2165(Steen), #3418(Teisseire), and #4462(Bourgeois).

Roy Webb (1888-197-)

4143. "The Film Music Career of Roy Webb." The Max Steiner Music Society News
Letter, No. 22 (Spring 1970), 4-5.

Includes a selective filmography.

4144. Morton, Lawrence. "Composing for a Film Score: 'The Last of the Badmen.'"
Film Music Notes, 8, No. 2 (Nov.-Dec. 1948).

Includes excerpts from the score.

4145. Palmer, Christopher. "Roy Webb -- Film Score Veteran." Crescendo International, 11 (Mar. 1973), 12ff.

4146. ----------. "Write It Black: Roy Webb, Lewton and 'film noir.'" Monthly
Film Bulletin (London), 48 (Aug. 1981), 168.

4147. Webb, Roy. "The Development of Descriptive and Dramatic Musical Scores
in Motion Pictures." The Max Steiner Music Society News Letter, No. 22
(Spring 1970), 2-3.

4148. ----------. "Mechanical Aids in Films." In Music and Dance in California.
Comp. William J. Perlman. Hollywood: Bureau of Musical Research, 1940,
pp. 126-27.

See Perlman, #1467.

4149. ----------. "Scissors Save the Score." In Music and Dance in California
and the West. Ed. Richard Drake Saunders. Hollywood: Bureau of Musical
Research, 1948, pp. 85, 144.

SEE ALSO:

#1223(Carter), and #1417(Mendez/Hamilton/Brown).

John Whitney

4150. Brick, Richard. "John Whitney Interview, Conducted by Richard Brick,
12/30/69." Film Culture, Nos. 53-54-55 (Spring 1972), 39-73.

This issue also contains a Whitney bibliography and
filmography, pp. 80-83.

4151. Clarke, Sheila. "Computer Turns Director ... an Interview with John Whitney." Kilobaud, No. 7 (July 1977), 34-40.

4152. Claus, Jürgen. Expansion der Kunst: Beiträge zu Theorie und Praxis öffentlicher Kunst. Reinbeck-Hamburg: Rowohlt-Taschenbuch-Verlag, 1970.

    Includes the chapter "Die Computerfilme von John Whitney."

4153. Franke, Herbert W. Computer Graphics. Computer Art. New York: Phaidon, 1971.

    References to the work of John Whitney. See pp. 93-97.

4154. Hein, Birgit. Film im Underground. Frankfurt: Ullstein, 1971.

    References to works by John Whitney.

4155. Lamont, Austin. "An Interview with John Whitney." Film Comment, 6, No. 3 (Fall 1970), 28-33.

4156. Moritz, William. "Beyond 'Abstract' Criticism." Film Quarterly, 31, No. 3 (Spring 1978), 29-39.

4157. Rondolino, Gianni. Storia del cinema d'animazione. Turin: Edizione Einaudi, 1974.

    References to the work of John Whitney. See pp. 339-47.

4158. Rubsamen, Walter H. "Music in the Cinema." Arts and Architecture, 62, No. 11 (Nov. 1945), 22, 25.

4159. Whitney, James A., and John H. Whitney. "Film Notes on 'Five Film Exercises.'" In Art in Cinema. Ed. Frank Stauffacher. San Francisco: Museum of Art, 1947, pp. 60-61. (Reprint, New York: Arno Press, 1968.)

  4159a. The article is reprinted as "Audio-Visual Music and Program Notes, 1946," in Whitney's Digital Harmony, pp. 144-50. See #4168.

4160. Whitney, John H. "An Abstract Film-maker's View of the Belgium Experimental Film Competition (1963) and All." Film Culture, No. 37 (Summer 1965), 24-26.

4161. ----------. "A.S.I.D. Talk -- Design Conference, Catalina, 1962." Film Culture, No. 37 (Summer 1965), 21-24.

  4161a. Reprinted as "The Raw and the Cooked Sit and Dance or Dance and Sit." Interface, 1, No. 4 (Mar. 1976), 29-31.

  4161b. Reprinted as "ASID Talk and Belgian Competition, 1963," in Whitney's Digital Harmony, pp. 156-66. See #4168.

4162. ----------. "Cranbrook Essay, 1973." In Digital Harmony: On the Complementarity of Music and Visual Art. Peterborough, N.H.: Byte Books, 1980, pp. 198-206.

    Transcription of an address to the Computer Arts Society of America, presented at the Cranbrook Art Academy, Michigan, May, 1973. See #4168.

4163. ----------. "Back to Baroque." Interface, 1, No. 5 (Apr. 1976), 43-44.

4164. ----------. "Computational Periodics." In Artist and Computer. Ed. Ruth Leavitt. New York: Harmony, 1976, p. 80.

    Reprinted as "Computational Periodics, 1975," in Whitney's Digital Harmony, pp. 210-12. See #4168.

4165. ----------. "A Computer Art for the Video Picture Wall." Art International, 15, No. 7 (Sept. 20, 1971), 35-38.

    Reprinted in Whitney's Digital Harmony, pp. 190-97. See #4168.

4166. ----------. "Culture for Computers." Interface, 1, No. 2 (Jan. 1976), 51.

4167. ----------. "Democratizing the Audio-Visual Arts." Program notes from the U.S.A. International Animation Festival, New York, January, 1974.

> Reprinted in Whitney's Digital Harmony, pp. 207-09. See #4168.

4168. ----------. Digital Harmony: On the Complementarity of Music and Visual Art. Peterborough, New Hampshire: Byte Books, 1980.

> Includes an "Interview with John Whitney, 1970," pp. 174-82, "Film Music, 1977," p. 216, and reprints of many articles by Whitney: see #4159, 4161, 4162, 4164, 4165, 4167, 4169, 4175, 4178, and 6180-6182.

> Also includes a bibliography, pp. 220-24, and a filmography, pp. 225-26.

> -- Rev. by John Halas in Film (London), No. 104 (Mar. 1982), 10.

4169. ----------. "Digital Pyrotechnics: The Computer in Visual Arts." First Computer Faire Proceedings (San Francisco), 1977, pp. 14-16.

> Based upon two earlier articles in Interface (see #4172), and Beyond Baroque (see #4173).

> Reprinted as "Digital Pyrotechnics, 1977," in Whitney's Digital Harmony, pp. 213-15. See #4168.

4170. ----------. "Discussion with John Whitney Recorded at the 1969 Flaherty Film Seminar, Standish Lawder, Moderator." Film Comment, 6, No. 3 (Fall 1970), 34-38.

4171. ----------. "Excerpts from a Talk Given at California Institute of Technology -- 3/21/68." Film Culture, Nos. 53-54-55 (Spring 1972), 73-78.

4172. ----------. "Fireworks: Ancient and Modern." Interface, 1, No. 6 (May 1976), 30-33ff.

> An early version of Whitney's "Digital Pyrotechnics." See #4169.

4173. ----------. "Fireworks: Ancient and Modern." Beyond Baroque, New series, 8, No. 3 (May 1977), 12-13.

> An early version of Whitney's "Digital Pyrotechnics." See #4169.

4174. ----------. "Further Reflections of a Culture Savage." Interface, 1, No. 3 (Feb. 1976), 22-23.

4175. ----------. "John Whitney at Cal Tech." In Experiments in Art and Technology, an issue of Survey (Los Angeles), 5 (Summer 1970), 8-9.

> Reprinted as "John Whitney at Cal Tech, 1968," in Whitney's Digital Harmony, pp. 170-73. See #4168.

4176. ----------. "Music Space -- Computer Time." Los Angeles Institute of Contemporary Arts Journal, 15 (July-Aug. 1977), 34-36.

4177. ----------. "Notes on 'Permutations' and 'Matrix.'" Film Culture, Nos. 53-54-55 (Spring 1972), 78-80.

4178. ----------. "On Order and Disorder." In Proceedings of the 17th International Design Conference at Aspen, Colorado, 1967.

> Reprinted as "Aspen Design Conference, 1967," in Whitney's Digital Harmony, pp. 167-69. See #4168.

4179. ----------. "Permutations." In Cybernetic Serendipity, a special issue of Studio International. Ed. Jasia Reichardt. New York: Praeger, 1968, p. 65.

4180. ----------. "Reflections on Art." Page: Bulletin of the Computer Arts Society (London), 21 (Mar. 1972), 4.

4181. ----------. "There Isn't Even a Name for It." Page: Bulletin of the Computer Arts Society (London), 24 (July 1972), 1.

SEE ALSO:
  #165(Jacobs), #1809(Manvell), #2092, #2134(Renan), #2557(Sitney), #4972 (Youngblood), #6159, #6161(Becker), #6163(Citron/Whitney), #6164(Curtis/ Francis), #6166(Davis), #6169(Hein/Herzogenrath), #6170(Langsner), #6171 (LeGrice), #6172(Leyda), #6175(Potter), #6176(Russett/Starr), and #6180- 6183(Whitney).

Jean Wiener (1896-1982)

4182. Amy, Dominique. "Wiener, Jean." In The New Groves Dictionary of Music and Musicians. Ed. Stanley Sadie. London: Macmillan, 1980, XX, p. 380.
  Includes filmography.

4183. Carcassonne, Philippe, and Renaud Bezombes. "Dossier -- La Musique de film: Entretien avec Jean Wiener." Cinematographe (Paris), No. 62 (Nov. 1980), 28-32.

4184. Wiener, Jean. Allegro Appassionato. Paris: P. Belfond, 1978.
  Includes discography, pp. 213-22.
  -- Rev. by Jacques Courcier in Cinéma 80, No. 255 (Mar. 1980), 67.

4185. ----------. "Muzyka tylko dlja filmu." Film na Świecie, No. 4 (1956).

4186. ----------. "Le rôle de la musique dans le film." In Cinéma: Cours et conférences d'l'IDHEC (Paris: L'Institute des hautes études cinématographiques), (Apr. 1945).

John Williams (1932-)

4187. Bertolina, Gian Carlo. "John Williams: La musica la trascendenza." Filmcritica (Rome), 34, No. 333 (Apr. 1983), 161-63.

4188. Caps, John. "John Williams: Scoring the Film Whole." Film Music Notebook, 2, No. 3 (1976), 19-25.

4189. ----------. "Keeping in Touch with John Williams." Soundtrack Collectors Newsletter, 1 (Mar. 1982), 3-7.
  An interview.

4190. Clarisse, Patrick. "Cine-disques: John Williams." Amis du Film, Cinéma et Télévision (Brussels), No. 251 (Apr. 1977), 20-21.

4191. Cook, Page. "The Sound Track." Films in Review, 28, No. 7 (Aug.-Sept. 1977), 422-24, 426.
  Concerns William's score for "Star Wars," with additional references to music by Miklos Rozsa.

4192. ----------. "The Sound Track." Films in Review, 30, No. 8 (Oct. 1979), 484-86.

4193. ----------. "The Sound Track." Films in Review, 31, No. 7 (Aug.-Sept. 1980), 423-25.
  Concerns William's scores for the "Star Wars" sequels.

4194. Elley, Derek. "The Film Composer: John Williams." Films and Filming, 24 (July 1978), 20-24; and 24 (Aug. 1978), 30-33.
  An interview. Includes filmography.

4195. Fiedel, Robert D. "It's 'Superman!'" High Fidelity and Musical America, 29, No. 6 (June 1979), 75-76.

4196. Garel, Alain. "Music Lovers: La Musique de films." Écran 79, No. 81 (June 15, 1979), 83-84.

4197. Hume, Paul. "Close Encounters with the Music of the Spheres." The Washington Post, Arts/Entertainment Section, pp. Ll, L14.

4198. Koldys, Mark. "'Star Wars.'" Pro Musica Sana, 5, No. 3 (1977), 4-6.

4199. Littman, Bill. "'Jaws': Music to Digest By." Gore Creatures, No. 24 (Oct. 1975), 33-36.

4200. Milano, D. "'Star Wars' Sounds." Contemporary Keyboard (San Diego, Calif.), 4 (Feb. 1978), 10-12ff.

4201. Oatis, Greg. "The Score: John Williams Strikes Back, Unfortunately." Cinefantastique, 10, No. 2 (1980), 8.

4202. Palmer, Christopher. "Williams, John T(owner)." In The New Groves Dictionary of Music and Musicians. Ed. Stanley Sadie. London: Macmillan, 1980, XX, p. 435.

4203. Pugliese, Roberto. "John Towner Williams, l'extraterrestre." Filmcritica (Rome), 34, No. 333 (Apr. 1983), 164-73.
    Includes filmography and discography.

4204. ----------. "'Shining': suoni 'altri.'" Filmcritica (Rome), 32, No. 315 (June 1981), 301-06.

4205. Simels, Steve. "'Star Wars': The Soundtrack." Stereo Review, 39 (Sept. 1977), 95.

4206. Snell, Mike. "But What Does He Do for an Encore?" The Max Steiner Journal, No. 2 (1978), 23-26.

4207. Stevens, John. "The Music from the Film 'Superman.'" The Max Steiner Journal, No. 4 (1979), 22-23.

4208. Terry, Kenneth. "Williams Brings New Repertoire to Pops: Continues Scoring Films, Now Working on Spielberg 'Ark.'" Variety, 302 (Feb. 18, 1981), 79ff.

4209. Thompson, Kenneth. "Why 'Jaws' Scores." Films Illustrated, 5 (Apr. 1976), 318.

4210. Tynan, John. "John Williams." BMI: The Many Worlds of Music (Spring 1975), 42-43.

4211. Vallerand, François. "Musique de films: John Williams et 'The Empire Strikes Back.'" Sequences (Montreal), No. 101 (July 1980), 49-50.

4212. Weiss, Paulette. "Musical Trips." Stereo Review, 40, No. 2 (Feb. 1978), 58, 60.
    Soundtrack album review, concerns the music for "Close Encounters of the Third Kind."

4213. Whitman, Mark. "Records." Films Illustrated, 7 (Jan. 1978), 194.
    An interview.

SEE ALSO:

#9(Bazelon, pp. 193-206), #2031, 2304, 2307, 2312, 2334, 2336, 2337, 2339, 2342(Cook), #2407(Garel), #2457(Koldys), #2596(Vertlieb), #2720, 2721(Barbano), #2771, 2772, 2776, 2777, 3066, 3306, 3380(Cook), and #4275(Williams).

Victor Young (1900-1956)

4214. Bertolina, Gian Carlo. "L'eta di Victor Young." Rivista del cinematografo (Rome), 54 (Jan. 1981), 16-21.
    Includes filmography.

4215. Connor, Edward, and Gerald Pratley. "The Sound Track." Films in Review, 7, No. 10 (Dec. 1956), 531-33.

>   Also includes references to music by Max Steiner.

4216. McCarty, Clifford. "Victor Young." Film and TV Music, 16, No. 5 (Late Summer 1957), 21-22.

>   Includes filmography and discography.

4217. Mitchell, Richard. "'China Gate': A Rarity in Filmusic History." The Max Steiner Journal, No. 5 (1980), 21-22.

>   Concerns music for the score begun by Victor Young, but completed by Max Steiner.

4218. Palmer, Christopher. "Young, Victor." In The New Groves Dictionary of Music and Musicians. Ed. Stanley Sadie. London: Macmillan, 1980, XX, p. 581.

4219. Wilkinson, Scott. "The Quiet Man." Film Music, 12, No. 1 (Sept.-Oct. 1952), 11.

4220. Young, Victor. "Confessions of a Film Composer." Music Journal, 14, No. 7 (Sept. 1956), 16, 38.

>   An interview.

   4220a. Reprinted in Film and TV Music, 16, No. 2 (Winter 1956), 23-24.

   SEE ALSO:

>   #132(Thomas), #1213(Brown), #1294(Hamilton), #1795(Lewin/Schaefer), #1822(Morton), and #4485(Carcassonne).

Additional Composer Profiles

4221. "Adolph Green." Film Dope (London), No. 21 (Oct. 1980), 2-3.

>   Includes filmography.

4222. Afanas'eva, Lidija. "Vmestimost' duši." Molodoj Kommunist, 9 (Sept. 1973), 100-06.

>   Concerns the songs and film music of the Belo-russian composer Igor Lučenok (b. 1937).

4223. Atkins, Irene Kahn. Interview with Joseph Gershenson, March 4 - March 15, 1976. Transcript is part of the American Film Institute/Louis B. Mayer Foundation Oral History Program. Beverly Hills, Calif.: AFI, 1976.

>   Includes filmography, pp. 127-250.

4224. ----------. Interviews with Ray Heindorf, 10/10/77, 11/16/77, and 12/6/77. Tapes and transcripts are part of the project Oral History: American Music. New Haven, Conn.: Yale University, 1977.

4225. Arnaudova, B. "The Composer Georgi Genkov." Bǎlgarska muzyka, 20, No. 2 (Feb. 1969).

>   Concerns Genkov's music for the films "Bednata ulica," "Margaritka", "Mama i az", " V kraja na ljatoto," and "Pǎtešestvie meždu dva brjaga."

4226. Baker, Bob. "Gerald Fried." Film Dope (London), No. 18 (Sept. 1979), 14-15.

4227. ----------. "Hans Werner Henze." Film Dope (London), No. 24 (Mar. 1982), 21.

4228. ----------. "John Dankworth." Film Dope (London), No. 9 (Apr. 1976), 30-31.

4229. Barrier, Mike. "An Interview with Carl Stalling." Funnyworld (Spring

1971).

4230. Blackmore, Bob. "The Film Career of Stanley Black." The Max Steiner Journal, No. 4 (1979), 24-26.

Includes filmography and discography.

4231. Boganova, Tat'ĩana Vasil'evna. Kinomuzyka T. N. Chrennikova. Moscow: Sovetskij kompozitor, 1961.

4232. Carcassonne, Philippe. "Musique et film: entretien avec Antoine Duhamel." Cinematographe (Paris), No. 48 (June 1979), 64-66.

Includes filmography.

4233. Chandavarkar, Bhaskar. "Satyajit Ray, from 'Kanchenjunga' to 'Land of the Diamond King.'" Cinema Vision India, 1, No. 4 (Oct. 1980), 20-21.

See #61.

4234. Chłopecki, Andrzej. "Penderecki i film." Kino (Warsaw), 9, No. 12 (Dec. 1974), 25-30.

4235. Cocumarolo, Enzo. "Carlo Rustichelli." Soundtrack Collectors Newsletter, 3, No. 11 (1977), 3-10, 13-16.

4236. Comuzio, Ermanno. "Ildebrando Pizzetti e il cinema." Cineforum (April 1968).

4237. Cook, Page. "Ken Darby." Films in Review, 20, No. 6 (June-July 1969), 335-56.

Includes filmography and additional composer credits.

4238. Crowther, Bosley. "Songs of India." New York Times, 112 (May 5, 1963), Section 2, p. 1.

Concerns music for films by composer/film-maker Satyajit Ray.

4239. Delcheva, Vicleta. "Tam, kudeto svurshva slovoto: Razgovor s kompozitora Boris Karadimchev." Kinoiskusstvo (Sofia), 34 (July 1979), 29-33.

4240. Gant, Liz. Interview with William Grant Still, 11/22/72. Tapes and transcript from the Hatch/Billops Collection are part of the project Oral History; American Music. New Haven, Conn.: Yale University, 1972.

4241. Giusti, Marco. "L'arte di colorar caramelle (alla W. B.)." Filmcritica (Rome), 30, Nos. 296-297 (Aug. 1979), 263-69.

Concerns music for Warner Brothers' films by Carl W. Stalling.

4242. ----------. "Con Angelo Lavagnino." Filmcritica (Rome), 31, Nos. 305-306 (May-June 1980), 230-33.

4243. ----------. "Dialogo sulla musica con Carlo Rustichelli e Alessandro Cicognini." Filmcritica (Rome), 31, Nos. 305-306 (May-June 1980), 239-42.

An interview.

4244. Griffiths, Peter. "Duke Ellington." Film Dope (London), No. 14 (Mar. 1978), 29-32.

Includes filmography.

4245. Grützner, Vera. "Ein Drehbuch hat keine Noten: Werkstattgespräch mit Karl-Ernst Sasse." Film und Fernsehen (Berlin, DDR), 4, No. 9 (1976), 18-20ff.

4246. Hammond, Philip J. S. "The Career of W. Franke Harling (1887-1958)." The Max Steiner Journal, No. 1 (1977), 25-26.

4247. Heinz, Wolfgang. "Vom klaren Pathos des Revolutionärs: Ernst Busch zum 80. Geburtstag." Film und Fernsehen (Berlin, DDR), 8, No. 2 (1980), 2.

4248. Jameux, Dominique. "Fano, Michel." In The New Groves Dictionary of Music and Musicians. Ed. Stanley Sadie. London: Macmillan, 1980, VI, p. 380.

4249. Lamb, Andrew. "Stolz, Robert." In The New Groves Dictionary of Music and Musicians. Ed. Stanley Sadie. London: Macmillan, 1980, XVIII, p. 172-73.

4250. Lanjean, Marc. Jean Françaix: musicien français. Paris: Contact, 1961.

4251. Laura, Ernesto G. "Glauco Pellegrini: Un'esperienza di lavoro." Bianco e nero, 28, Nos. 3-4 (Mar.-Apr. 1967), 54-78.

   Biography of Pellegrini, includes filmography.

4252. Liškou, Zdeňkem. "O filmové hudbé se Zdeňkem Liškou." Hudební Rozhledy (Prague), 25, No. 10 (Oct. 1972), 457-58.

   An interview.

4253. Marshall, James, et al. "Filmography/Discography: Roy Budd." Soundtrack Collectors Newsletter, 1 (Mar. 1982), 21-23.

4254. Moritz, Al. "Louis Levy: Film Music Composer-Conductor (1893-1957)." The Max Steiner Journal, No. 5 (1980), 44.

4255. Nick, Edmund. "Edmund Nick." In Die Musik in Geschichte und Gegenwart. Ed. Friedrich Blume. Kassel: Bärenreiter, 1955, IX, p. 1444-45.

   Includes filmography.

4256. Orledge, Robert. "Charles Koechlin and the Early Sound Film, 1933-38." Proceedings of the Royal Music Association, 98 (1971-1972), 1-16.

4257. ----------. "A Study of the Composer Charles Koechlin (1867-1950)." Ph.D. Diss. (Musicology), Cambridge University 1973.

   Includes bibliography.

4258. Palmer, Christopher. "Popular Appeal Plus Musical Purpose: The Film Music of Jerome Moross." Crescendo International, 11 (June 1973), 25-27.

4259. ----------, and Peggy Glanville-Hicks. "Moross, Jerome." In The New Groves Dictionary of Music and Musicians. Ed. Stanley Sadie. London: Macmillan, 1980, XII, p. 590-91.

   Includes filmography.

4260. Pecqueriaux, Jean-Pierre. "Filmography/Discography: Vladimir Cosma." Soundtrack Collectors Newsletter, 1 (Mar. 1982), 9-11.

4261. Pilka, Jiří. Filmová hudba Jiřího Srnky. Prague: Verband tsch. Komponisten, 1957.

   A survey of the film music of Jiří Srnka.

4262. ----------. Otázky filmové hudby. Filmová hudba Jiřího Srnky. Prague: Diplomarbeit, 1956.

4263. Pinchard, Max. "Maurice Thiriet à la recherche du spectacle total." Musica (Chaix, France), No. 112 (July 1963), 48-52.

4264. Prox, Lothar. "Anmerkungen zum Werk von Wolfgang Zeller." Film-Korrespondenz, No. 9 (1978), 15-17.

4265. ----------. "Komponist zwischen 'Jud Süss' und 'Ehe im Schatten.'" Film-Korrespondenz (Cologne), 24, No. 9 (Sept. 1978), 15-17.

   Concerns film music scores by Wolfgang Zeller.

4266. Roshal, Grigory. "Dmitri Kabalevski." Soviet Film (Moscow), No. 211 (No. 12), (Dec. 1974), 38-39.

4267. Schinsky, Karl. "Der Filmkomponist Joachim Werzlau." Deutsche Filmkunst, 7, No. 2 (1959).

4268. Schnebel, Dieter. Mauricio Kagel: Musik, Theater, Film. Cologne: DuMont-Schauberg, 1970.

   -- Rev. in Nutida Musik (Stockholm), 14, No. 3 (1970-

1971), 46-47.

-- Rev. in _Musica_ (Kassel), 25, No. 2 (1971), 170-71.

-- Rev. in _Musik und Bild_, 3 (Nov. 1971), 567.

4269. Scofield, Tom. "Les Baxter." _The Max Steiner Music Society News Letter_, No. 42 (Spring 1975), 3-5.

Includes a selective filmography.

4270. Shaw, Arnold. "Nelson Riddle." _BMI: The Many Worlds of Music_ (Spring 1975), 40-41.

4271. Solar, Jean. _Maurice Thiriet_. Musiciens d'aujourd'hui. Paris: Éditions Ventadour, 1957.

Includes a listing of "radio works" and other compositions, along with a filmography and discography.

4272. Stanley, Raymond. "John Dankworth." _Cinema Papers_, No. 12 (Apr. 1977), 332-35.

Includes filmography.

4273. Thomas, Tony. "David Shire." _The Max Steiner Journal_, No. 5 (1980), 29-30.

4274. Vil'ner, Natal'ja. "Zrelost'." _Sovetskaya muzyka_, No. 12 (Dec. 1978), 28-33.

Concerns the mature works, including the film music, of composer Vadim Bibergan.

4275. Williams, John, and Daniel Mangodt. "Filmography/Discography: Carl Davis." _Soundtrack Collectors Newsletter_, 1 (Dec. 1982), 9-11.

4276. Willson, Meredith. _And There I Stood with My Piccolo_. Garden City, N.Y.: Doubleday, 1948.

An autobiography.

SEE ALSO:

#259(Kułakowska - Markowski), #1964(Land - Hollingsworth), #2057(Galling - Freed), #2196(Whittenberg - Ussachevsky), #2231(Alexander - Asher), #2239 (Atkins - Stoloff), #2257(Borchert - Sasse), #2292(G.R. Cook - Small), #2330, 2341(P. Cook - Dawson), #2355(DeMary - Shire), #2381(Feather - Ellis), #2382(Feather - Karlin), #2383(Feather - Werner), #2384(Feather - McIntosh), #2401(Fraccaro - Hambro), #2402(Fraccaro - Lockhart), #2412 (Goldovskaia - Paatshvili), #2419(Guiod - de Roubaix), #2420(Gusev), #2423(Harmetz - Warren), #2431(Hutchinson - May), #2445(Kemp - Lutyens), #2454(Kirk - Goldenberg), #2467(Lange - Matthus), #2491(Mayr - Richards), #2492(Mazurelle - Moraz), #2511(Norquist - Tartaglia), 2514(Palmer - Cordell), #2525(Predal - de Roubaix), #2550(Sherman), #2564(Stamelman - Shire), #2588(Thiel - Asriel), #2595(Vercelli - Grusin), #2608(Wiseman - Fox), #2618(Wolthius - Otterloo), #2622(Zimmerer - Ciani), #2623(Zlotnik - Babajanian), #2663(Feather - Hagen), #2664(Feather - Johnson), #2666 (Feather - P. Williams), #2667(Feather - Manne), #2668(Feather - Wilson), #2672(Gough - Blyton), #2709(Acher - Furey), #2736(Caps - Gowers), #2761 (Cook - Zeliff), #2779(Cook - Morris), #2797(Fried - Slevin), #2798(Frolova - Pauls), #2823(Jomy/Rabourdin - Dzierlatka), #2846(Matveyev - Ptichkin), #2878(Sartor - Lai), #2897(Vallerand - Dompierre), #2925(Honickel - Raben), and #4352(Koechlin).

III. AESTHETICS

Silent and Early Sound Era

4277. Arnheim, Rudolf. "Contrappunto sonoro." La Stampa (Turin), (June 20, 1932).

4278. ----------. Film als Kunst. Berlin: Ernst Rowohlt-Verlag, 1932.

> Includes the chapters "Film und Musik", "Der Tonfilm," and many references to film music throughout.

> Reprinted, Munich: Carl Henser Verlag, 1974.

4278a. Published again as Film als Kunst. With a Foreword to the new edition by Rudolf Arnheim, and Afterword by Helmut H. Diederichs. Fischer Cinema Series. Frankfurt am Main: Fischer-Taschenbuch-Verlag, 1979.

4278b. Also published as Film. Translated from the German by L. M. Sieveking and Ian F. D. Morrow, with a Preface by Paul Rotha. London: Faber and Faber, 1933.

> See especially Part V: "Film and Music," pp. 270-75, and "The Sound Film," pp. 201-08.

4278c. Also published as Film as Art. Berkeley: University of California Press, 1957. (Reprint, 1967.)

> The greater part of this volume is an adaptation of the 1933 translation (see #4278b), but the section on "The Sound Film" is omitted.

> Also includes the essay "A New Laocoön: Artistic Composites and the Talking Film," pp. 199-230. See #4425.

4278d. Also published as Kino kak iskusstvo. Moscow, 1960.

4279. ----------. "Sound Commands." Intercine (Rome), 7 (Mar. 1935), 167.

4280. Arnold, H. "Die Filmmusik auf künstlerischen Wegen." Zeitschrift für Musik, 96 (1929), 83-84.

4281. Assagioli, Roberto. "La musica come mezzo di cura con riferimento agli effetti del cinema sonoro." La rivista internazionale del cinema educatore (Rome), (Sept. 1933).

4282. Bagier, Guido. "Der akustiche Film: sein Wesen und seine Bedeutung." Melos, 7, No. 4 (Apr. 1928), 163-66.

4283. ----------. "Musikalische Probleme des Films." Die Musik, 17, No. 5 (Feb. 1925), 349-53.

4284. Balázs, Béla. Der Geist des Films. Halle (Saale): W. Knapp, 1930.

> Concerns the problems of the "sound revolution," with a plea for the use of asynchronous sound. Includes the chapter "Tonfilm," pp. 142-85.

> Reprint, Frankfurt: Makol, 1972.

4285. ----------. "Proportionen des Filmbildes und der Filmmusik." Film-Kurier, No. 220 (1924).

4286. ----------. Der sichtbare Mensch: oder, die Kultur des Films. Leipzig and Vienna: Deutsch-Österreichischer Verlag; and Halle: Verlag Wilhelm Knapp, 1924.

> Includes the chapter "Musik ins Kino," pp. 143-44.

> Reprint, Hamburg: Medienladen, 1977.

4287. Baroncelli, Jacques de. <u>Pantomime, musique, cinéma</u>. (Pamphlet.) Paris, 1915.

    4287a. Reprinted as "Définition du cinéma: Pantomime -- Musique -- Cinéma." In <u>Anthologie du cinéma: rétrospective par les textes de l'art muet qui devint parlant</u>. Ed. Marcel La-pierre. Paris: La Nouvelle édition, 1946, pp. 123-29.

4288. Becce, Giuseppe. "Der Film und die Musik: Illustration oder Komposition?" <u>Melos</u>, 7, No. 4 (Apr. 1928), 170-72.

    See comments by Hanns Eisler in <u>World Film News</u>, #3219.

4289. Beynon, George W. "Music for the Picture." <u>The Moving Picture World</u>, 35 (Feb. 23, 1918), 1093-94.

    Includes the articles "Proper Presentation of Pictures Musically" and "Fitting the Scenic."

4290. ----------. "Music for the Picture." <u>The Moving Picture World</u>, 35 (Mar. 2, 1918), 1241-42.

    Includes the article "The Art in Musical Settings."

    This article, and those which follow (#4290-4294), also include information for the silent film accompan-ist, including suggestions for music to accompany sel-ected current film releases.

4291. ----------. "Music for the Picture." <u>The Moving Picture World</u>, 36 (Apr. 6, 1918), 89-90.

    Includes the article "Atmosphere in Music and Perfor-mance."

4292. ----------. "Music for the Picture." <u>The Moving Picture World</u>, 36 (Apr. 20, 1918), 393-94.

    Includes the article "Color in Picture Playing."

4293. ----------. "Music for the Picture." <u>The Moving Picture World</u>, 36 (May 11, 1918), 853-54.

    A plea for "original" filmscores, entitled "Music of the Future."

4294. ----------. "Music for the Picture." <u>The Moving Picture World</u>, 37 (July 13, 1918), 212-13.

    Includes the article "Proper Presentation of Pictures Musically: Playing the Pictorial."

4295. ----------. "Music for the Picture." <u>The Moving Picture World</u>, 38 (Oct. 12, 1918), 225-34.

    Includes the article "The Dramatic Effect of Silence."

    This article, and those which follow (#4295-4300), in-clude cue sheets for current film releases, prepared by George W. Beynon, James C. Bradford, Louis F. Gott-schalk, S. M. Berg, and Harley Hamilton.

4296. ----------. "Music for the Picture." <u>The Moving Picture World</u>, 38 (Oct. 19, 1918), 379-88.

    Includes the article "The Abuse of Silence," along with a discussion of the use of "animated song sheets" for community singing in theaters.

4297. ----------. "Music for the Picture." <u>The Moving Picture World</u>, 38 (Oct. 26, 1918), 511-19.

    Includes the article "The Choice of Incidental Music."

4298. ----------. "Music for the Picture." <u>The Moving Picture World</u>, 38 (Nov. 2, 1918), 589-93.

    Includes the article "The Choice of Incidental Music, Part 2."

4299. ----------. "Music for the Picture." <u>The Moving Picture World</u>, 39

(Jan. 25, 1919), 497-502.

Concerns questions of musical "atmosphere."

4300. ----------. "Music for the Picture." The Moving Picture World, 39 (Feb. 15, 1919), 909-14.

Includes the article "Through Evolution in Picture Music the Scenic Comes into Its Own."

4301. Biermann, Franz Benedict. "Tonfilm und Musik." Die Musik, 24 (1931), 250-54.

4302. Blum, Karl Robert. "Film, Musik und Rhythmus in ihrer künstlerisch technischen Wechselbeziehung." Der Stein der Weisen (1927), 561.

4303. Borneman, Ernest J. "Sound Rhythm and the Film: Recent Research on the Compound Cinema." Sight and Sound, 3, No. 10 (Summer 1934), 65-67.

Concerns the problems of "sound montage," with references to the work of Meisel, Eisenstein, and the German Film Research Institute in Berlin (D.F.I.).

4304. Breton, André. Manifest du surréalisme: Poisson soluble. Paris: Éditions du Sagittaire, 1924.

Many reprints.

4305. Bush, W. Stephen. "Giving Musical Expression to the Drama." The Moving Picture World, 9 (Aug. 12, 1911), 354-55.

4306. Busoni, Ferruccio. Entwurf einer neuen Ästhetik der Tonkunst. Leipzig and Berlin: Insel-bücherei, 1907. (Second enlarged edition, 1916.)

With implications for film music.

4306a. Reprinted, with a Foreword by Arnold Schoenberg, and an Afterword by Hans Heinz Stuckenschmidt, Frankfurt am Main: Suhrkamp Verlag, 1974.

4307. Clair, René. "Rythme." Les Cahiers du mois (Paris), Nos. 16-17 (1925).

4307a. Reprinted in Intellegence du cinématographe. Comp. Marcel L'Herbier. Paris: Éditions Corrêa, 1946, pp. 291-93.

See #4729.

4308. Coeuroy, André. "Problèmes intérieurs et extérieurs de Radio." In Atti del primo congresso internazionale di musica, Firenze, 30 april - 4 maggio 1933. Florence: F. Le Monnier, 1935, pp. 52-60.

A paper presented at the 1933 Florence Congress. Includes a synopsis in Italian: "Problemi interni ed esterni della Radio." See #339.

4309. Diebold, B. "Das Kino als Kunst?" Ostdeutsche Monatshefte des Buhnenvolksbundes (1924).

4310. Dulac, Germaine. "L'Essence du cinéma: L'Ideé visuelle." Les Cahiers du mois (Paris), Nos. 16-17 (1925).

4311. ----------. "Les esthétiques, les entraves, la cinégraphie intégrale." In L'Art cinématographique, II. Paris: Librarie Félix Alcan, 1927, pp. 29-50.

4312. Eïkhenbaum, Boris Mikhaïlovich, ed. Poetika kino. Moscow, 1927.

4313. Eisenstein, Sergei Mikhaïlovich. "Outside the Frame." An Afterword to Yaponskoye kino by Nikolai Kaufman. Moscow, 1929, pp. 72-92.

4313a. Reprinted in Transition (Paris), No. 6 (June 1930).

4313b. Reprinted as "The Cinematographic Principle and the Ideogram," in Film Form, pp. 28-44.

See #4562a.

4314. ----------, Vsevolod I. Pudovkin, and G. Alexandrov. "Sayavka: Buduschtscheye svukovogo filma." Sovyetski Ekran (Moscow), No. 32 (1928).

4314a. Also published in Zhizn iskusstva (Leningrad), 32 (Aug. 5, 1928), 4-5.

4314b. Also published as "The Future of Sound Films, a Statement," in the New York Herald Tribune (Sept. 21, 1928).

    Reprinted in Film Form, pp. 257-60. See #4562a.

4314c. Also published as "Manifesto sull'asincronismo," in Cinema (Rome), No. 108 (1941).

4314d. Also published as "Contrepoint orchestral." In Anthologie du cinéma: rétrospective par les textes de l'art muet qui devint parlant. Ed. Marcel Lapierre. Paris: La Nouvelle édition, 1946, pp. 243-46.

4314e. Also published as "Il manifesto dell'asincronismo," in Bianco e nero, 28, Nos. 3-4 (Mar.-Apr 1967), 89-90.

    See #2116.

4315. Elman, --. "Musikkritischer Querschnitt." Lichtbildbühne, No. 268 (1930).

4316. Epstein, Jean. La cinématographie vu de'l'Etna. Paris: Les Écrivains réunis, 1926.

4317. Erdmann, Hans. "Abschied von der Filmmusik." Filmtechnik, No. 14 (1930), 13.

4318. ----------. "Auf der Suche nach einer Filmschrift." Filmtechnik (1928), 478.

4319. ----------. "Filmmusikalische Formen." Reichsfilmblatt, No. 17 (1926), 16.

4320. ----------. "Die Grundidee der Filmmusik." Der Film, No. 34 (1922), 36.

4321. ----------. "Illustration oder Komposition?" Reichsfilmblatt, No. 8 (1927), 32.

4322. ----------. "Der künstlerische Spielfilm und seine Musik: Versuch einer kritischen Umschau." In Das deutsche Lichtspieltheater. Ed. Rudolf Pabst. Berlin: Prisma Verlag, 1926, pp. 100-16.

    Includes bibliography.

4323. ----------. "Licht -- Raum -- Ton." Filmtechnik (1927), 391.

4324. ----------. "Reform." Reichsfilmblatt, No. 17 (1928), 23.

4325. ----------. "Die Schwierigkeit der deskriptiven Musik." Reichsfilmblatt, No. 38 (1927), 29.

4326. ----------. "Zur Grundlage der Beziehungen zwischen Film und Musik, I." Reichsfilmblatt, No. 25 (1926), 26.

4327. ----------. "Zur Grundlage der Beziehungen zwischen Film und Musik, II." Reichsfilmblatt, No. 26 (1926), 16.

4328. Ettinger, Max. "Gedanken über Film und Musik." Erwachen (1928), 317-23.

4329. Frankenstein, Alfred V. "Music and Radio." Golden Book (Chicago), 10 (July 1929), 55, 113.

    Includes references to comments by Potamkin. See #800.

4330. Fürst, Leonhard. "Mechanische Musik: Filmgestaltung aus der Musik." Melos, 12, No. 1 (Jan. 1933), 18-22.

    Basis for an essay later presented at the 1933 Congress in Florence. See #4331.

4331. ----------. "Prinzipien musikalischer Gestaltung im Tonfilm." In Atti del primo congresso internazionale di musica, Firenze, 30 aprile - 4 maggio 1933. Florence: F. Le Monnier, 1935, pp. 216-21.

    A paper presented at the 1933 Florence Congress, with a synopsis in Italian: "Principi d'una forma musicale nel film sonoro," pp. 221-22. See #339.

4332. Giovannetti, Eugenio. "Musica per il centauro." La rivista internazionale del cinema educatore (Rome), 5 (May 1933), 324-27.

> Also includes an English translation "Must We First Educate the Film Director? Music for the Centaurs."

4333. Goodwin, James Edward. "Sergei Eisenstein's Ideological Aesthetics: The Silent Films." Ph.D. Diss. Rutgers University 1973.

> Abstract: DA 34/05:2624 (order #DA 7327930).

4334. Grempe, F. M. "Die Bedeutung der Musikwerke für den Kinobetrieb." Der Kinematograph (Berlin), No. 655 (1919).

4335. Grierson, John. "Pudovkin on Sound." Cinema Quarterly, 2, No. 2 (Winter 1933-1934), 106-10.

> See Pudovkin's writings, #4382.

4336. Gronostay, Walter. "Die Möglichkeiten der Musikanwendung im Tonfilm." Melos, 8, No. 7 (July 1929), 317-18.

4337. ----------. "Die Technik der Geräuschanwendung im Tonfilm." Die Musik, 22, No. 1 (Oct. 1929), 42-44.

4338. Gutman, Hanns. "Der tönende Film." Melos, 7, No. 1 (Jan. 1928), 6-9.

4339. Hackenschmied (Hammid), Alexander. "Film and Music." Translated from the Czech by Karel Santar. Cinema Quarterly (Edinburgh), 1, No. 3 (Spring 1933), 152-55.

> Includes filmography.

4339a. Reprinted in Film Culture, Nos. 67-68-69 (1979), 238-41.

4340. Häfker, Hermann. Kino und Kunst. Lichtbühnen - Bibliothek, II. Berlin: M. Gladbach: Lichtbilderei Volksvereins-Verlag G.m.b.H., 1913.

4341. Harms, Rudolf. Philosophie des Films: Seine ästhetischen und metaphysischen Grundlagen. Leipzig: Verlag von Felix Meiner, 1926.

> Includes the chapters "Der Film als Kollektivkunst," pp. 35ff., "Film und Musik," pp. 64-76, and many references to film music throughout. Bibliography, p. 188.
>
> Reprint, Zurich: Verlag Hans Rohr, 1970.

4342. ----------. Untersuchungen zur Ästhetik des Spielfilms. Leipzig: typescript, 1925.

> Harm's doctoral dissertation from the University of Leipzig.

4343. Hoérée, Arthur. "Essai d'esthétique du sonore." In Le Film sonore: l'écran et la musique en 1935, a special issue of La Revue musicale, 15, No. 151 (Dec. 1934), 365-382 (45-62).

4344. ----------. "Le Travail du film sonore." In Le Film sonore: l'écran et la musique en 1935, a special issue of La Revue musicale, 15, No. 151 (Dec. 1934), 63-79.

4345. Hohenemser, Richard. "Über Komik und Humor in der Musik." In Jahrbuch der Musikbibliothek Peters 1917, XXIV. Ed. Rudolf Schwartz. Leipzig: C. F. Peters, 1918, pp. 65-83.

> With implications for music in film. Also see later articles on this subject by Antony Hopkins (#4642) and Zofia Lissa (#4737).

4346. Ingarden, Roman. Das literarische Kunstwerk: eine Untersuchung aus dem grenzgebiet der Ontologie, Logik und Literaturwissenschaft. Halle: M. Niemeyer, 1931.

> Ingarden's aesthetic and ontological writings provide a foundation for several important studies of film music aesthetics.

4347. Irzykowski, Karol. Dziesiąta Muza. Zagadnienia estetyczne kina. Krakow: Krakowska spółka wydawnicza, 1924.

Reprint, Warsaw: Wydawnictwo Artystyczne i Filmowe, 1960.

4348. Jaques-Dalcroze, Émile. "Le Cinéma et sa musique." Bibliothèque univer-
sitaire et Revue de Genève, 2 (1925), 1448-65.

4348a. Also published as "The Cinema and Its Music." In Eurhythmics, Art and Education. Trans. Frederick Roth-
well, ed. Cynthia Cox. London: Chatto and Windus;
and New York: Barnes and Co., 1930, pp. 192-210.

Reprint, New York: Benjamin Blom, 1972.

Reprint, New York: Arno Press, 1976 and 1980.

4349. Kahlenberg, Friedrich P. "Der wirtschaftliche Faktor 'Musik' im Theater-
betrieb der UFA in den Jahren 1927 bis 1930." In Stummfilmmusik Gestern
und Heute. Ed. Walther Seidler. Berlin: Verlag Volker Spiess, 1979,
pp. 51-71.

Includes bibliographic references.

See Seidler, #875.

4350. "Die Kinos als Stätten guter Musik." Reichsfilmblatt, No. 14 (1929), 13.

4351. Klein (Cornwell-Clyne), Adrian Bernard. Colour-Music: The Art of Light.
London: Lockwood, 1926.

Includes bibliography.

4352. Koechlin, Charles. "Réflexions d'un musicien." In Le Film sonore:
l'écran et la musique en 1935, a special issue of La Revue musicale,
15, No. 151 (Dec. 1934), 4-18.

4353. Kurtz, Rudolf. Expressionismus und Film. Berlin: Verlag der Lichtbildbühne, 1926.

4354. Landsberger, H. "Verfilmte Musik oder musikalischer Film?" Nationalzeit-
ung (Sept. 14, 1920).

4355. Laszlo, A. "Musik zum Film und ihre künstlerische Bedeutung." Leipziger
Neueste Nachrichten (Jan. 27, 1927).

4356. Leigh, Henry. "The Filming of Music." Musical News and Herald (Mar. 11,
1922), 314.

4357. Lion, A. "Erreichtes und Erreichbares: Zur Frage der natürlichen Klang-
wiedergabe im Tonfilm." Die Musik, 22, No. 6 (Mar. 1930), 473-74.

4358. Lissa, Zofia. "O zagadnieniach krytyki muzycznej." Przegląd Filmowy i
Teatralny, Nos. 31-32 (1929).

4359. London, Kurt. "Filmstil und Filmmusik." Melos, 11, No. 12 (Dec. 1932),
404-06.

4360. ----------. "Gedanken zum Problem der Filmmusik." Allgemeine Musikzeitung, 51 (1924), 60-62.

4361. ----------. "Kinoorchester und Tonfilm: Organisationsfragen der Filmmusik." Melos, 9, Nos. 5-6 (May-June 1930), 247-50.

4362. ----------. "Problem der Filmmusik." Frankfurter Zeitung (Aug. 6, 1926).

4363. Luedtke, Hans. "Filmmusik und Kunst." Melos, 7, No. 4 (Apr. 1928), 167-
70.

4364. Lunacharskiĭ, Anatoliĭ Vasil'evich. Kino na zapade i u nas. Moscow:
Teakdnodechat, 1928.

4365. Luz, Ernst. "The Musician and the Picture." Moving Picture News (Oct. 9,
1912), 20-21.

4366. ----------. "Picture Music." Moving Picture News (Aug. 16, 1913), 31.

4367. Marinetti, Filippo Tommaso. Le futurisme. Paris: E. Sansot, 1911.
Aesthetic fundamentals, with implications for film music.

4368. ----------. Manifesto sul cinéma futurista. Milan: Direzione del Movimento futurista, 1916.

4369. Martens, Frederick H. "Funning the Films." Musical Observer, 14, No. 1 (1916), 58-59.

4370. Meckbach, W. "Grundgedanken zur Filmmusik." Melos, 8, No. 1 (Jan. 1929), 24-29.

4371. Medina, P. "Die Utopie der Filmmusik." Der Kinematograph (Berlin), No. 847 (1923).

4372. Mersmann, Hans. Angewandte Musikästhetik. Berlin: M. Hesse, 1926.

4373. Messter, Oskar. Mein Weg mit dem Film. Berlin: Max Hesses Verlag, 1936.

> Includes the chapter "Musik beim Film," pp. 61ff., and a bibliography, pp. 148-50.

4374. Mila, Massimo. "Musica e ritmo nel cinematografo." In Atti del primo congresso internazionale di musica, Firenze, 30 aprile - 4 maggio 1933. Florence: F. Le Monnier, 1935, pp. 209-15.

> A paper read at the 1933 Florence Congress. See #339.

> Also see Mila's report on the Congress, #738.

4375. Moussinac, Léon. "Du rythme cinégraphique." In Le Cinéma, a special issue of Le Crapouillot (Paris), (Mar. 16, 1923), 9-12.

> 4375a. Reprinted in Intelligence du cinématographe. Comp. Marcel L'Herbier. Paris: Éditions Corrêa, 1946, pp. 250-56.

>> See #4729.

4376. Müller, Maximilian (Max Mühlenau). "Zur Reform der Kinomusik." Reichsfilmblatt, No. 5 (1924), 13.

4377. Ostrezov, A. "Muzyka i svukovoye kino." Sovetskaya muzyka, 1, No. 1 (Jan. 1933).

4378. ----------. "Problemy muzykalnoi dramaturgii v tonfilmach." Sovetskaya muzyka, 2, No. 11 (Nov. 1934), 5-11.

4379. Pierre-Quint, Léon. "Signification du cinéma." In L'Art cinématographique, II. Paris: Librarie Félix Alcan, 1927.

4380. Pudovkin, Vsevolod Illarïonovich. Akter v fil'me. Leningrad: Gos. akademie iskusstvoznanie, Sektsne kinovedenie, 1934.

> Concerning the use of sound and music in film.

> 4380a. Also published as Film Acting: A Course of Lectures Delivered at the State Institute of Cinematography, Moscow. Trans. from the Russian by Ivor Montagu. London: George Newnes, 1935.

>> Includes the chapter "Dual Rhythm of Sound and Image," pp. 90-98, which also appears in #4381, pp. 308-16.

> 4380b. Also published as L'attore nel film, a cura del Centro sperimentale di cinematografia. With a Preface by Luigi Freddi. Rome: Edizioni di Bianco e nero, 1939.

4381. ----------. Film Techniques and Film Acting. Trans. and ed. Ivor Montagu. London: Lear, 1949.

> This volume includes the English texts of both major works: Kinorezhisser i kinomaterial (see #4382), and Akter v fil'me (see #4380).

> Reprint, London: Vision Press, 1954.

> Revised and enlarged edition, London: Vision Press, 1958. (Reprint, New York: Grove Press, 1976.)

4382. ----------. Kinorezhisser i kinomaterial. Moscow: Kinodechat, 1926.

> 4382a. Also published as Filmregie und Filmmanuskript. Trans. Georg and Nadia Friedland. Berlin: Verlag der Licht-

bildbühne, 1928.

4382b. Also published as <u>On Film Technique: Three Essays and an Address</u>. Translated and annotated by Ivor Montagu. London: Victor Gollancz, 1929.

4382c. Also published as <u>Film Technique: Five Essays and Two Addresses</u>. Enlarged edition. Trans. Ivor Montagu. London: George Newnes, 1933.

> Includes the sections "Asynchronism as a Principle of Sound Film," and "Rhythmic Problems in My First Sound Film," which also appear in #4381, pp. 183-93, and pp. 194-202, respectively.

> Also see comments by John Grierson, #4335.

4382d. Also published as <u>Film e fonofilm</u>. Rome: Edizioni d'Italia, 1935.

4382e. Also published as <u>Wybór pism</u>. Warsaw, 1956.

4383. Raskin, Adolf. "Grundsätzliches zum Klangfilmproblem." <u>Melos</u>, 8, Nos. 5-6 (May-June 1929), 249-51.

4384. Read, Herbert. "Experiments in Counterpoint." <u>Cinema Quarterly</u> (Edinburgh), 3, No. 1 (Autumn 1934), 17-21.

> Concerns the use of sound and music in British documentaries.

4385. Richter, Herbert. <u>Der Spielfilm: Aufsätze zu einer Dramaturgie des Films</u>. Berlin: H. Reckendorf, 1920.

4386. Roland, Marc. "Das Problem der Film-Musik." <u>Der Kinematograph</u> (Berlin), No. 851 (1923).

4387. Schirmann, Alexander. "Wie entsteht eine künstlerische und sinngemässe Filmmusik?" <u>Der Kinematograph</u> (Berlin), No. 536 (1917).

4388. Schlechtriem, --. "Das Problem der Film-Musik." <u>Der Kinematograph</u> (Berlin), No. 851 (1923).

4389. Schmidl, Poldi. "Filmmusikfolgen als künstlerische Arbeit." <u>Der Kinematograph</u> (Berlin), No. 806-807 (1922).

4390. ----------. "Filmmusikprobleme und filmmusikalischer Fortschritt." <u>Der Kinematograph</u> (Berlin), No. 739 (1921).

4391. ----------. "Kinomusikalische Streifzüge." <u>Der Kinematograph</u> (Berlin), Nos. 642-643 (1919).

4392. ----------. "Kinomusikalische Streifzüge: Neue Filmmusik aus alter Zeit." <u>Der Kinematograph</u> (Berlin), No. 826 (1922).

4393. ----------. "Technische und künstlerische Gesetze der Filmmusik." <u>Der Kinematograph</u> (Berlin), No. 661 (1919).

4394. Sinn, Clarence E. "Music for the Picture." <u>Moving Picture World</u>, 7 (Dec. 31, 1910), 1531.

4395. ----------. "Music for the Picture." <u>Moving Picture World</u>, 8 (Jan. 7, 1911), 27.

4396. ----------. "Music for the Picture." <u>Moving Picture World</u>, 8 (Jan. 21, 1911), 135.

> Concerns the use of "Wagnerian" leitmotifs in film scoring.

4397. ----------. "Music for the Picture." <u>Moving Picture World</u>, 8 (Apr. 1, 1911), 707.

> Concerns the "appropriate role" for the silent film drummer.

4398. ----------. "Music for the Picture." <u>Moving Picture World</u>, 18 (Dec. 20, 1913), 1396-97.

4399. ----------. "Music for the Picture." <u>Moving Picture World</u>, 22 (Dec. 19,

1914), 1690-91.

Includes the article "Music Drama of the Future."

4400. ----------, and Norman Stuckey. "Music for the Picture." _Moving Picture World_, 31 (Jan. 6, 1917), 77.

4401. ----------, and Norman Stuckey. "Music for the Picture." _Moving Picture World_, 31 (Feb. 17, 1917), 1004.

Includes the article "The Expression of Human Emotion in the Works of Richard Wagner."

4402. ----------, and Norman Stuckey. "Music for the Picture." _Moving Picture World_, 32 (Apr. 28, 1917), 618.

Concerns the topic of "individuality" in motion picture accompaniments.

4403. ----------, and Norman Stuckey. "Music for the Picture." _Moving Picture World_, 32 (May 12, 1917), 970.

4404. Stein, Richard H. "Probleme der Rundfunkmusik." _Die Musik_, 18, No. 4 (Jan. 1926), 263-69.

4405. Stuckey, Norman. "Music for the Picture." _Moving Picture World_, 32 (Apr. 7, 1917), 98.

Includes the article "The Importance of Tone Coloring in Relation to Musical Interpretation."

4406. Terakawa Makoto. _Eiga oyobi eigageki_. Ōsaka: Ōsaka Mainichi, 1925.

4407. Trystan, L. "Kino jako muzyka wzrokowa: Estetyka kinematografu." _Film polski_ (Warsaw), Nos. 4-5 (1923).

4408. Valéry, Paul. "La Conquête de l'ubiquité." In _De la musique avant toute chose_. Ed. Roger Wild. Paris: Éditions du Tambourinaire, 1929.

4408a. Also published in English translation by Ralph Mannheim in Valéry's _Aesthetics_. New York: Pantheon, 1964, p. 225.

4409. Vuillermoz, Émile. "La Musique des images." In _L'Art cinématographique_, III. Paris: Librarie Félix Alcan, 1927.

4410. Weyl-Nissen, Ali. "Stilprinzipien des Tonfilms -- Versuch einer Grundlegung." _Die Musik_, 21 (Sept. 1929), 905-07.

4411. "Zur Reform der Kinomusik." _Reichsfilmblatt_, No. 10 (1924), 10.

Includes a reply by Maximilian Müller.

4412. "Zuviel Musik." _Reichsfilmblatt_, No. 51 (1927), 21.

SEE ALSO:

#326(Amzoll), #345(Bagier), #356(Baughan), #394(S.M. Berg), #408, 409, 426, 428(Beynon), #478(Bush), #480(Calvocoressi), #499(Corradini), #556 (L. Fischer), #585(Gregor), #587(Grierson), #643(Kahan), #646(Kautzenbach), #678, 679(Lambert), #695(Lindsay), #698(London), #773(Ogden), #800 (Potamkin), #860(Schmidl), #914, 917(Sinn), #992(I. Smith), #1037, #1039 (Urgiss), #1041(Van Vechten), #1118(Rapée), #1165(Pitkin), #3446(Ibert), #4669, #4754(Luciani), #4789(Moore), #4898(Stern), #4974(Zahorska), #4975 (Zakošanskaya/Straženkova), #4976(Zawadzki), #4987(Brillouin), and #5018 (Lissa).

Sound Era

Form and Function : Aural / Visual Relationships in Film Art

4413. Adorno, Theodor W. "Fragment über Musik und Sprache." In Quasi una fantasia: musikalische Schriften II. Frankfurt am Main: Suhrkamp Verlag, 1963, pp. 9-16.

4414. ----------. "Über Jazz." In Moments musicaux: neu gedruckte Aufsätze 1928-1962. Frankfurt am Main: Suhrkamp Verlag, 1964, pp. 84-124.

    Includes references to the use of jazz in film.

4415. Agel, Henri. Esthétique du cinéma. Paris: Presses universitaires de France, 1957.

4416. Allihn, Ingeborg. "Eislers Bühnenmusik zu Friedrich Schillers 'Wilhelm Tell': Bemerkungen einem musikästhetischen Problem." In Hanns Eisler heute: Berichte - Probleme - Beobachtungen. Arbeitshefte 19. Ed. Manfred Grabs. Berlin: Akademie der Künste der DDR, 1974, pp. 94-99.

    Concerns the music for "William Tell" and corresponding scenes from the films "Rat der Götter" (1950), and "Unser Präsident -- Wilhelm Pieck" (1952).

4417. Altman, Rick. "Cinema/Sound: An Introduction." Yale French Studies, No. 60 (1980), 3-15.

    4417a. Reprinted, with an Introduction by John Fitzpatrick, in Pro Musica Sana, 9, No. 1 (Summer 1981), 3-17.

4418. Amzoll, Stefan. "Dramaturgischer Kontrapunkt in der Filmmusik: Zur Konzeption von Hanns Eisler und Theodor Adorno." Musik und Gesellschaft, 26, No. 11 (Nov. 1976), 659-63.

    See Adorno/Eisler, #4573.

4419. ----------. "Vom Einbruch des Terrors in Stille und Reinheit." Musik und Gesellschaft, 27, No. 10 (Oct. 1977), 583.

4420. Anderson, William. "The Invisible Music." Stereo Review, 33, No. 3 (Sept. 1974), 4.

4421. Andrew, Dudley. "Sound in France: The Origins of a Native School." Yale French Studies, No. 60 (1980), 94-114.

4422. Apon, Annette, and Ton de Graaff. "Esthetiek en techniek: Louis Andriessen." Skrien (Amsterdam), No. 95 (Mar. 1980), 8-15.

    An interview.

4423. Ariscarco, G. Storia delle teoriche del film. Turin, 1960.

4424. Arnheim, Rudolf. "Art Today and the Film." In Aesthetics and the Arts. Ed. Lee A. Jacobus. New York: McGraw-Hill, 1968, p. 291.

4425. ----------. "Nuovo Lacoonte." Bianco e nero, 2, No. 8 (Aug. 31, 1938), 3-33.

    4425a. Also published as "A New Laocoön: Artistic Composites and the Talking Film." In Film. Berkeley and Los Angeles: University of California Press, 1957; and London: Faber and Faber, 1958, pp. 199-230. (Reprint, 1971.)

        See #4278c.

    4425b. Also published as "Neuer Laokoon: Die Verkoppelung der künstlerischen Mittel, untersucht anlässlich des Sprechfilms." In Kritiken und Aufsätze zum Film. Ed. Helmut H. Diederichs. Munich: Carl Hanser Verlag, 1977, pp. 81-112.

        The first publication of the original German text.

4426. Arsenov, P. "V čem istinnaya specifika žanra?" Sovetskaya muzyka, 32, No. 11 (Nov. 1968), 84-88.

4427. "An Art from Within a Craft." BMI: The Many Worlds of Music (Oct. 1966), 2.

4428. Asaf'ev, Boris Vladimirovich. Muzykalnaya forma kak prozes, II. Moscow: Goc. myz. izd-vo, 1947.

4429. Auer-Sedak, Eva. "Funkcionalnost moderne muzike." Zvuk, No. 55 (1962), 519-24.

4430. Bacalov, Luis. "Il 'collage musicale.'" Filmcritica (Rome), 31, Nos. 305-306 (May-June 1980), 243-44.

4431. Bächlin, P. "Der Film als Ware." Ph.D. Diss. Universität Basel 1947.

    4431a. Published, with the same title, Frankfurt am Main: Athenäum Fischer Taschenbuch Verlag, 1975.

4432. Bachmann, Claus-Henning. "Hat der Musikfilm eine Zukunft?" Neue Literarische Welt, 4, No. 10 (1953).

4433. Backer, Thomas E., and Eddy Lawrence Manson. "In the Key of Feeling." Human Behavior Magazine (1978).

    4433a. Reprinted in International Musician, 77 (Nov. 1978), 14ff.

4434. Baird, T. "Odpowiedź na ankietę 'Rola muzyki w dziele filmowym.'" Kwartalnik Filmowy, 11, No. 2 (1961).

    Also see the article by Komeda-Tryciński, #4690.

4435. Balázs, Béla. "The Acoustic World." In The Movies as Medium. Ed. Lewis Jacobs. New York: Farrar, Straus and Giroux, 1970.

    See Jacobs, #4653.

4436. ----------. Filmkultúra: a film művészetfilozófiája. Budapest: Szikra, 1948.

    4436a. Also published as Iskusstvo kino. Moscow, 1945.

        Appears also in a Yugoslavian edition (1947).

    4436b. Also published as Der Film: Werden und Wesen einer neuen Kunst. Vienna: Globus-Verlag, 1949.

    4436c. Also published as Il film: evoluzione ed essenza di un'arte nuova. Trans. Grazia e Fernaldo Di Grammatteo. Turin: G. Einaudi, 1952.

        Translated from the German.

    4436d. Also published as Theory of the Film: Character and Growth of a New Art. Trans. from the Hungarian by Edith Bone. London: Dennis Dobson, 1952; and New York: Roy Publ., 1953.

        Reprint, New York: Dover, 1970.

        Includes Chap. 16: "Sound," pp. 194-220, Chap. 17: "Dialogue," pp. 221-31, Chap. 18: "Problem of the Sound Comedy," pp. 232-41, and Chap. 23: "Musical Forms," pp. 275-82.

    4436e. Also published as Wybór pism. Warsaw, 1957.

4437. ----------. "Zhanroviye problemy muzykalnogo filma." Iskusstvo kino (Moscow), No. 9 (Sept. 1940), 44-51.

4438. Bal'ozov, Rumen. "Muzikalniyat obraz v kinoto i novite bulgarski igralni filmi." Bulgarska Muzika (Sofia), 28 (Oct. 1977), 60-62.

4439. ----------. "Za musikalnoto oformlenie na kinokhronika." Bulgarska Muzika (Sofia), 32 (May 1981), 83-85.

4440. Band, Lothar. "Der Musikfilm." Die Musik-Woche, 15 (1955), 7-9.

4441. Barbaro, Umberto. Il problema estetico del film. Rome: Edizioni di Bianco e nero, 1939, III.

4442. Baronijan, Vartkes. "Vizuelizacija muzike i zvuk kao dimenzija slike i pokreta." _Zvuk_ (Sarajevo), Nos. 124-125 (1972), 112-17.

4443. Baronnet, Jean. "Le Bande-Son: Eloge de la phonie." _Cahiers du cinéma_, 26, No. 152 (Feb. 1964), 37-41.

4444. Barthes, Roland. _Image -- Music -- Text_. Trans. Stephen Heath. New York: Hill and Wang, 1977.

> Includes the chapter "Musica Practica," pp. 149-54.

4445. Bassan, Raphaël. "Emergence d'un autre langage cinématographique." _Revue du cinéma/ Image et son_, No. 363 (July-Aug. 1981), 82-88.

4446. Battenberg, Hermann. "Dramaturgische und ideologische Funktionen der Musik in der Fernsehserie 'Bonanza.'" In _Schulfach Musik_. Veröffentlichungen des Institut für Neue Musik und Musikerziehung, XVI. Ed. Rudolf Stephan. Mainz: Schott, 1976.

> Transcription of a lecture presented at the Institut fur Neue Musik und Musikerziehung conference in Darmstadt, March 20-25, 1975.

4447. ----------. "Musik als Einwegkommunikation: zur Krimi-Musik im Fernsehen." _Musica_, 32, No. 3 (1978), 241-45.

4448. Bauche, Dieter. "Über die musikalische Gestaltung in der Aktuellen Kamera." _Diskussionsmaterialien zur Theorie und Praxis des Fernsehens_, No. 1 No. 1 (1960).

4449. Baudrier, Yves. _Les Signes du visible et de l'audible, première partie: Le Monde sonore_. Esthétique et critique, XII. Paris: Cours et publications de l'IDHEC, 1964.

> NOTE: Part 2, "La Musique et l'art cinématographique," was apparently never published.

4450. ----------. "Technique et esthétique de la musique de film." _Cinéma: Cours et conférences de l'IDHEC_ (Paris: L'Institute des hautes études cinématographiques), (Oct.-Nov. 1944).

4451. Bazin, André. "L'Eau danse." _Cahiers du cinéma_, 2, No. 7 (Dec. 1951), 58-59.

> Concerns Jean Mitry's film, "Images pour Debussy."

4452. ----------. "Le langage de notre temps." In _Regards neufs sur le cinéma_. Peuple et culture. Paris: Éditions du Seuil, 1953.

4453. ----------. "Néo-réalisme, opéra et propagande." _Cahiers du cinéma_, 1, No. 4 (July-Aug. 1951), 46-51.

> Concerns Curzio Malaparte's film, "Il Cristo Proibito."

4454. ----------. _Qu'est-ce que le cinéma?_, I-IV. 7ème Art. Paris: Éditions du Cerf, 1958-1962. (Reprint, 1975.)

> Includes many brief references to music throughout.

> Four volumes: I. Ontologie et langage, II. Le Cinéma et les autres arts, III. Cinéma et sociologie, and IV. Une esthétique de la réalité: le néoréalisme.

4454a. Also published as _¿Qué es el cine?_ Trans. José Luis López Muñoz. Madrid: Ediciones Rialp, 1966.

4454b. Also published as _What is Cinema?_ Trans. Hugh Gray. Los Angeles and Berkeley, Calif.: University of California Press, 1967-1971.

4455. Beese, Henriette. "Notizen zum Tönenden am Tonfilm." _Filmkritik_ (Munich), 21 (Dec. 1977), 612-21.

4456. Bellour, Raymond. "The Unattainable Text." _Screen_ (London), 16, No. 3 (Autumn 1975), 19-27.

4457. Biamonte, S. G. "Il 'rilancio' della musica da film." _Bianco e nero_, 28, Nos. 3-4 (Mar.-Apr. 1967), 109-11.

> See #2116.

4457a. Also published in Cinema ridotto (Apr. 1967).

4458. Bluestone, George. Novels into Film. Berkeley and Los Angeles: University of California Press, 1966.

4459. Blum, Robert. "Die Musik im Film: Wesen, Aufgabe und Entstehung." Schweizerische Musikzeitung, 100, No. 2 (1960), 66-70.

4460. Boilès, Charles Lafayette. "La Signification dans la musique de film." Trans. François LaTraverse. Musique en jeu, 19 (June 1975), 71-85.

 Concerns the use of "leitmotifs" in Ibert/Welles' "Macbeth" (1948), and the variation processes employed in Rozsa/Minnelli's "Lust for Life" (1956).

4461. Bordwell, David. "The Musical Analogy." Yale French Studies, No. 60 (1980), 141-82.

4462. Bourgeois, Jacques. "Musique dramatique et cinéma." La Revue du cinéma (Paris), New series, 2, No. 10 (Feb. 1948), 25-33.

 Includes references to music by Honegger and Waxman.

4463. ----------. "Wagner und die Filmmusik." Dionysos (1948).

4464. Bowles, Paul. "On the Film Front." Modern Music, 17, No. 1 (Oct.-Nov. 1939), 60-62.

 Includes references to music by Honegger and Copland.

4465. Bragaglia, Anton Giulio. "Dal visivo alla musica." Bianco e nero, 28, Nos. 3-4 (Mar.-Apr. 1967), 96-100.

 See #2116.

4466. Brakhage, Stanley. "The Silent Sound Sense." Film Culture, No. 21 (Summer 1960), 65-67.

4467. ----------. "Stan Brakhage on Music, Sound, Color, and Film." Film Culture, Nos. 67-68-69 (1979), 129-35.

 Concerns the film "Scenes from Under Childhood."

4468. Brelet, Gisèle. "L'Interprétation." Contrepoint II (Paris), (1957).

4469. ----------. Le Temps musical: Essai d'une esthétique nouvelle de la musique. Paris: Presses Universitaires de France, 1949.

 Includes Part I: "La forme sonore," Part II: "La forme rythmique," and Part III: "La forme musicale," concerning the principles of musical aesthetics, with a number of references to music in films.

4470. Brichetto, Attilio. "Una semantica della musica nel melodramma filmato." Cinema Nuovo (Turin), 26, No. 250 (Nov.-Dec. 1977), 417-19.

4471. Bronchain, Christian M. "Du sens de l'étude des significations de la musique dans le film." APEC - Revue Belge du cinéma, 19 (Dec. 1980 - Jan.-Feb. 1981), 9-17.

 Includes bibliography.

4472. Browning, Mortimer. "Establishing Standards for Evaluation of Film Music." Music Publishers' Journal, 3, No. 5 (Sept.-Oct. 1945), 23, 63-64.

4473. Buchanan, George. "Rhythm and Experience: The Expanding Art of Rhythm in Novel and Film." Ph.D. Diss. University of Chicago 1973.

4474. Bukofzer, Max. Die musikalische Gemütsbewegung: erlebnisse, erkenntnisse, bekenntnisse. Leipzig: Breitkopf und Härtel, 1935.

4475. Burch, Noël. Praxis du cinéma. Paris: Édition Gallimard, 1969.

 Includes the chapter "De l'usage structural du son."

4475a. Also published as Theory of Film Practice. Trans. Helen R. Lane. New York: Praeger, 1973.

 Chap. 6: "On the Structural Use of Sound," pp. 90-101.

4476. ----------. _To the Distant Observer: Form and Meaning in the Japanese Cinema_. London: Scholar Press; and Berkeley: University of California Press, 1979.

> Includes references to the role of music in film.

4477. Burt, Warren. "On the Relation of Sound and Image in 'Moods.'" _Cantrill's Filmnotes_, Nos. 35-36 (Apr. 1981), 56-64.

4478. Cacia, Nino. "Funzione e problemi della musica nel film." _Ferrania_ (Milan), No. 10 (1958).

4479. Cage, John. "A Few Ideas About Music and Films." _Film Music Notes_, 10, No. 3 (Jan.-Feb. 1951), 12-15.

> Concerns Cage's music for the Calder film.

4479a. Reprinted in _Film Culture_, No. 29 (Summer 1963), 35-37.

4480. Cameron, Evan William. "'Citizen Kane': The Influence of Radio Drama on Cinematic Design." In _Sound and the Cinema: The Coming of Sound to American Film_. Ed. Evan William Cameron et al. Pleasantville, N.Y.: Redgrave Publishing, 1980, pp. 202-16.

> See #1139.

4481. Canby, Edward Tatnall. "Music for Background." _Saturday Review of Literature_, 32 (Jan. 8, 1944), 29.

4482. Capra, Frank. _The Name Above the Title_. New York: Bantam Books, 1971.

> References to the use of music in film, with special attention to the music of Dimitri Tiomkin.

4483. Caps, John. "The Third Language: The Art of Film Music." _Film Music Notebook_, 1, No. 3 (Spring 1975), 10-13.

4484. ----------. "A Word About Film Music Criticism." _Pro Musica Sana_, 9, No. 2 (Winter 1981-1982), 9-12.

4485. Carcassonne, Philippe. "Dossier -- La Musique de film: La loi du plus fort." _Cinématographe_ (Paris), No. 62 (Nov. 1980), 38-41.

> Concerns the use of quotations from "serious composers" in film scoring by Victor Young, Miklos Rozsa, and others.

4486. ----------. "Musique sans paroles." _Cinématographe_ (Paris), No. 64 (Jan. 1981), 20-21.

4487. Cardinale, Robert Lee. "Identification and Explanation of the Aesthetic Variables of the Motion Picture." Ed.D. Diss. Arizona State University 1977.

> Abstract: DAI 38/11:6363 (order #DDK 7805384).

4488. Carsalade du Pont, Henri de. "Musique et cinéma." _Études_ (Paris), 91, No. 298 (July-Sept. 1958), 82-94.

4489. Casini, Claudio. "L'impiego nella colonna sonora della musica elettronica e della musica concreta." In _Musica e film_. Ed. S. G. Biamonte. Rome: Edizioni dell'Ateneo, 1959, pp. 179-93.

> See Biamonte, #1606.

4490. Cavalcanti, Alberto. "Music: Music Can Provide Only Interior Rhythm." _World Film News_, 2, No. 4 (July 1937), 26-27.

> A paper presented at the 1937 Florence Congress.

4490a. Also published in _Atti del secondo congresso internazionale di musica, Firenze-Cremona, 11-26 maggio, 1937_. Florence: F. Le Monnier, 1940, pp. 265-70.

> > Includes synopses in Italian, French, and German, pp. 270-71.
> > See #1186.

4491. Cavazzuti, Enrico. "Problemi della registrazione sonora e del missaggio." _Bianco e nero_, 11, Nos. 5-6 (May-June 1950), 105-14.

See #1832.

4491a. Also published in La musica nel film. Ed. Luigi Chiarini. Rome: Bianco e nero editore, 1950, pp. 97-106.

See Chiarini, #1627.

4492. Caveing, Maurice. "Dialectique du concept du cinéma." Revue internationale de filmologie (Paris), 1, No. 1 (July-Aug. 1947), 71-78; and 1, Nos. 3-4 (Oct. 1948), 343-50.

4493. Cavell, Stanley. "The Thought of Movies." Yale Review (New Haven, Conn.), 72, No. 2 (1983), 181-200.

4494. Chailly, Luciano. "Musica da film." Bianco e nero, 28, Nos. 3-4 (Mar.-Apr. 1967), 101.

See #2116.

4495. Chanan, Michael. "Death in Venice." Art International, 15, No. 7 (Sept. 1971), 31-32, 57.

Concerns the use of Mahler's music in the Visconti film.

4496. Chandavarkar, Bhaskar. "The Great Film Song Controversy." Cinema Vision India, 1, No. 4 (Oct. 1980), 66-75.

See #61.

4497. Charent, Brian. "A Kind of Awareness." Motion (Toronto), 4, No. 2 (1975), 16-18.

4498. Chase, Donald, ed. Filmmaking: The Collaborative Art. Boston: Little, Brown and Co., 1975.

Includes Chapter 9, "The Composer," pp. 271-91, based upon interviews with Bernstein, Goldsmith, Green, and North, conducted as part of the AFI Oral History Project.

4499. Chateau, Dominique. "Projet pour une sémiologie des relations audio-visuelles dans le film." Musique en jeu, No. 23 (Apr. 1976), 82-98.

A semiological theory of film sound and music.

4500. Cheremukhin, M. "O realistitscheskom stile v muzyke kino." Iskusstvo kino (Moscow), No. 5 (May 1936), 52-54.

4501. Cherkasova, Natal'ya. "Zametki o muzyke indiyskogo kino." Sovetskaya Muzyka, 42, No. 8 (Aug. 1978), 101-04.

Observations on music in Indian films.

4502. Chevassu, François. Article in Le son au cinéma, a special issue of Image et son, No. 215 (Mar. 1968).

4503. Chiarini, Luigi. "Cenni sull'estetica del suono." In La registrazione del suono. Ed. Libero Innamorati and Paolo Uccello. Rome: Edizioni di Bianco e nero, 1939.

4504. ----------. "La musica." In Il film nei problemi dell'arte. Rome: Edizioni dell'Ateneo, 1949.

4505. Chirkov, B. "S pesney po zhizni shagaya ..." Sovetskaya muzyka, 27, No. 1 (Jan. 1963), 9-14.

4506. Cicognini, Alessandro. "La musica d'atmosfera nel film storico e nel film neorealista." In Musica e film. Ed. S. G. Biamonte. Rome: Edizioni dell'Ateneo, 1959, pp. 163-69.

See Biamonte, #1606.

4507. Clair, René. Cinéma d'hier, cinéma d'aujourd'hui. Paris: Éditions Gallimard, 1970.

Includes many references to film music, and a filmography.

4507a. Also published as Cinema Yesterday and Today. Trans. Stanley Applebaum. Ed. and with an introduction and annotations by R. C. Dale. New York: Dover, 1972.

4508. Clair, René. Réflexion faite: notes pour servir à l'histoire de l'art cinématographique de 1920 à 1950. Paris: Gallimard, 1951.

> Includes the chapter "L'Art du son."

4508a. Also published as Vom Stummfilm zum Tonfilm: kritische Notizen zur Entwicklungsgeschichte des Films, 1920-1950. Trans. Eva Fehsenbecker. Munich: C. H. Beck, 1952.

4508b. Also published as Reflections on the Cinema. Trans. Vera Traill. London: William Kimber, 1953.

> The chapter "The Art of Sound" is reprinted in Film: A Montage of Theories. Ed. Richard Dyer MacCann. New York: E. P. Dutton, 1966, pp. 38-44. See #2093.

4508c. Also published as Razmyshleniya o kinoiskusstve. Moscow, 1958.

4509. Clancier, Georges Emmanuel. "La Poésie et les nouveaux moyens d'expression." In Un siècle de radio et de télévision. Ed. Pierre Descaves and A. V. J. Martin. Paris: O.R.T.F., 1965, pp. 304-16.

> See Descaves, #149.

4510. Cocteau, Jean. "La Machine se moque de nous." In Un siècle de radio et de télévision. Ed. Pierre Descaves and A. V. J. Martin. Paris: O.R.T.F., 1965, pp. 263-66.

> See Descaves, #149.

4511. ----------. "Vom Wunderbaren zur Lichtspielkunst." Melos, 31, No. 2 (Feb. 1964), 42-46.

4512. Cogni, Giulio. "La musica, la parola, l'immagine." Bianco e nero (Rome), 5 (1941), 7-8.

4513. Cohen-Séat, Gilbert. Essai sur les principes d'une philosophie du cinéma. Paris: Presses universitaires de France, 1946.

> Part I: "Introduction générale: Notions fondamentales et vocabulaire de filmologie."

4514. Colacicchi, Luigi. "Problemi del cinema sonoro: Il 'parlato' come recitativo." La rassegna musicale, 10 (1937), 60-63.

4515. Colpi, Henri. Défense et illustration de la musique dans le film. Panoramique, I. Lyon: Société d'édition de recherches et de documentation cinématographiques, 1963.

> Includes filmography.

> Also see #4516.

> -- Rev. in Jazz Magazine, 9 (June 1963), 34-35.

> -- Rev. in Variety, 230 (May 1, 1963), 65.

4516. ----------. "Musique d''Hiroshima.'" Cahiers du cinéma, 18, No. 103 (Jan. 1960), 1-14.

> Concerns the music for Resnais' "Hiroshima, mon amour," with references to Hanns Eisler, Georges Delerue, and Giovanni Fusco. Includes musical examples and cue sheets.

> Reprinted in Défense et illustration ..., see #4515.

4516a. Also published as "La musica de 'Hiroshima, mi amor," in Boletín de programas, 19, No. 193 (1960), 18-24; and 19, No. 194 (1960), 21-24.

4517. ----------. "Réflexions sur la fonctionnalité de la musique au cinéma." Revue musicale de Suisse Romande (Lausanne), (Many-June 1964).

4518. Comolli, Jean-Louis. "Technique et idéologie: Effacement de la profondeur/avènement de la parole." Cahiers du cinéma, Nos. 234-235 (Dec. 1971 - Jan.-Feb. 1972), 94-100.

4519. Comuzio, Ermanno. "Colonna sonora: partitura per film - parte II." Revista del cinematografo, 54 (Feb.-Mar. 1981), 121.

4520. ----------. "Colonna sonora: Wagner, Ravel, Fauré complici o alleati?"

Revista del cinematografo, 54 (Nov. 1981), 612.

4521. ----------. "Schiavitu e trasgressioni negli stereotipi della musica per film." Cineforum (Bergamo), No. 202 (Feb.-Mar. 1981), 12-15.

4522. ----------. "Visconti e Wagner." Cineforum (Bergamo), (Mar. 1970).

4523. Confalonieri, Giulio. "La visualizzazione della musica." In Musica e film. Ed. S. G. Biamonte. Rome: Edizioni dell'Ateneo, 1959, pp. 21-33.

See Biamonte, #1606.

4524. Connor, Edward, and Edward Jablonski. "The Sound Track." Films in Review, 9, No. 9 (Nov. 1958), 521-22, 526.

Concerns the "dissonance" in recent scores.

4525. Connor, Edward, and Robert B. Kreis. "The Sound Track." Films in Review, 10, No. 1 (Jan. 1959), 45-48.

Concerns the use of "classical" music in films.

4526. Contamine, Claude. "Essence de la télévision." In Un siècle de radio et de télévision. Ed. Pierre Descaves and A. V. J. Martin. Paris: O.R.T.F., 1965, pp. 282-84.

See Descaves, #149.

4527. Cook, Page. "The Sound Track." Films in Review, 24, No. 4 (Apr. 1973), 229-32.

4528. ----------. "The Sound Track." Films in Review, 27, No. 8 (Oct. 1976), 495-99.

Includes references to music by Jerry Goldsmith.

4529. ----------. "The Sound Track." Films in Review, 32, No. 1 (Jan. 1981), 38-39, 45.

4530. ----------. "The Sound Track: Film Music as Noise." Films in Review, 19, No. 3 (Mar. 1968), 162-63, 166.

References to the work of Neil Hefti, Quincy Jones, and others.

Reprinted in Theodore J. Ross' Film and the Liberal Arts, pp. 244-47. See #4850.

4531. Cornelis, Eefie, and Frank Zaagsma. "Göde Filmmuziek möt je niet kuunnen horen: Interview met Ruud Bos, componist." Skoop (The Hague, Neth.), 11 (Apr. 1975), 14-16.

4532. Costarelli, Nicola. "Aspetti della musica nel film." In La musica nel film. Ed. Luigi Chiarini. Rome: Bianco e nero editore, 1950, pp. 30-34.

A paper presented at the 1950 Venice conference. See #1627.

4533. Curran, Trisha. "A New Note on the Film: A Theory of Film Criticism Derived from Suzanne K. Langer's Philosophy of Art." Ph.D. Diss. Ohio State University 1978.

Abstract: DAI 1978:4556A (order #DA 7902105).

4534. Czeczot-Gawrak, Zbigniew. Jean Epstein: Studium natury w sztuce filmowej. Warsaw: Wydawnictwo Artystyczne i Filmowe, 1962.

Includes bibliography, pp. 246-58.

4535. Daehn, Hans-Georg. "Verhalten des Musikhörers: Aufgabe für den Musikproduzenten." In Tonmeistertagung (10.) 19.-22. November 1975, Köln: Bericht. Cologne: Welzel und Hardt, 1976.

See #2654.

4536. d'Amico, Fedele. "Musica e cinematografo: Un connubio difficile." Rassegna musicale, 16, No. 2 (Feb. 1943), 43-49.

4537. Dane, Jeffrey. "The Significance of Film Music." American Cinematographer, 42, No. 5 (May 1961), 302ff.

4538. Debenedetti, Giacomo. "In sala o sullo schermo?" In Atti del secondo congresso internazionale di musica, Firenze-Cremona, 11-26 maggio, 1937. Florence: F. Le Monnier, 1940, pp. 245-50.

A paper presented at the 1937 Florence Congress, with synopses in French and German, pp. 250-51. See #1186.

4539. ----------. "La musica e il cinematografo." Cinema (Rome), No. 15 (1937).

4540. DeBlasio, A. "Funzione della musica nel film." Biblio-cinema (Rome), Nos. 6-9 (1958).

4541. Decker, J. de. "Entretien avec André Delvaux." Degrés, 4 (1973), e-e15.

4542. De Coster, M. "L'Exemple de la musique classique enrégistrée." International Review of the Aesthetics and Sociology of Music (Zagreb), 6 (1975), 255ff.

4543. Desson, Guy. "La Télévision n'est pas du cinéma." In Un siècle de radio et de télévision. Ed. Pierre Descaves and A. V. J. Martin. Paris: O.R.T.F., 1965, pp. 285-91.

See Descaves, #149.

4544. De Vore, Nicolas. "Movie Mirrors Music-Mindedness." Musician, 43 (Apr. 1938), 75.

4545. Döhring, Sieghart. "Franz Schreker und die grosse musiktheatralische Szene." Die Musikforschung, 27, No. 2 (1974), 175-86.

A discussion of Schreker's stageworks as an important link between 19th century opera and the mixed- and multimedia genres.

4546. Dorigo, Francesco. Civilta è cinema. Venice: Stabilimento Zincografico S. Marco, 1959.

4547. Douin, Jean-Louis. "La Musique de film est-elle du papier peint?" Télérama (Feb. 28, 1971).

4548. Dreyer, R. "Słowo w filmie." In Zagadnienia estetyki filmowej. Warsaw, 1955.

See #4973.

4549. Drĭscoll, John. "Music Is for Beauty." Journal of the University Film Association, 13, No. 1 (Fall 1960), 2-4.

4550. Duvillars, Pierre. "Musique et cinéma: Enquête." L'Age nouveau, 51 (June 1950), 34-60.

4551. Dvorničenko, Oksana Ivanovna. "Chtoby udach bylo bol'she!" Sovetskaya muzyka, 44, No. 7 (July 1980), 64-70.

4552. ----------. "Muzyka kak element ekrannogo sinteza." Ph.D. Diss. (Music and Dramatic Arts), Vsesojuzhyi inst. kinematografii, Moscow 1975.

Concerns the role of music as an element in the synthesis of film and musical structure. Also deals with the problem of musical performance on film.

4553. Dziębowska, Elżbieta, Zofia Helman, Danuta Idaszak, and Adam Neuer, eds. Studia Musicologica: Aesthetica, Theoretica, Historica. Krakow: Polskie Wydawnictwo Muzyczne, 1979.

Festschrift in honor of Professor Zofia Lissa on the 70th Anniversary of her birthday. Includes a bibliography of her works, pp. 11-47, many of which deal with the aesthetics of film music.

4554. Eckert, Gerhard. "Gestaltung eines literarischen Stoffes in Tonfilm und Hörspiel." Ph.D. Diss., Berlin 1936.

4554a. Published with the same title, Berlin: Junker und Dünnhaupt, 1937.

4555. Eckert, Gerhard. Die Kunst des Fernsehens. Emsdetten: Lechte, 1953.

"Quellen und Hinweise," pp. 103-05.

4556. Eggebrecht, Hans Heinrich. "Funktionale Musik." Archiv für Musikwissen-schaft (Wiesbaden), 30, No. 1 (1973), 1-25.

Includes bibliographic references.

4557. Eisenstein, Sergei Mikhailovich. "Aanielokuvaa ennakoimassa." Trans. A. Tiusanen. Filmihullu (Helsinki), No. 5 (1977), 9-10.

4558. ----------. "Again on Structure." Iskusstvo kino, No. 6 (1940), 27-32.

In Russian.

4558a. Reprinted and translated as "More Thoughts on Structure," in Film Essays, pp. 92-108.

See #4561.

4559. ----------. "Colour and Music: The Colour Genealogy of 'Moscow 800.'" In Mosfilm: Articles. Moscow: Iskusstvo, 1961, pp. 239-45.

Drawn from a manuscript dated Nov. 29, 1946.

4560. ----------. "Film -- eine Kunst der Synthese." In Synthese der Künste und Kunst der Synthese in der Theorie und Praxis Sergej Eisensteins. Berlin: Deutschen Akademie der Künst, 1970.

4561. ----------. Film Essays with a Lecture. Edited and translated by Jay Ley-da, with a Foreword by Grigorii Kozintsev. London: Dobson Books, 1968.

See #4558 and #4567.

4562. ----------. "Film Form: Essays in Film Theory," and "The Film Sense." Edited and translated from the Russian by Jay Leyda. New York: Meridian Books, 1957 (Reprint, 1959); and Cleveland: World Publishing Co., 1965.

Contains the full text of two collections of essays by Eisenstein, #4562a and #4562c:

4562a. ----------. Film Form: Essays in Film Theory. Edited and translated by Jay Leyda. New York: Harcourt, Brace, and World, 1949.

Includes many references to film music, with special attention to Prokofiev's score for "Alexander Nevsky."

Includes the essays "The Structure of the Film," pp. 150-78, and "A Statement on the Sound-Film by Eisenstein, Pudovkin, and Alexandrov," pp. 257-60 (see #4314).

4562b. Also published as Forma e tecnica del film e lizioni di regia. Trans. Paolo Gobetti. Turin: G. Einaudi, 1964.

4562c. ----------. The Film Sense. Edited and translated by Jay Leyda. New York and London: Harcourt, Brace, and World, 1942. (Reprint, 1947.)

Reprint, New York: Meridian, 1967.

Includes the essays "Synchronization of the Senses," pp. 69-109 (see #4568), "Color and Meaning," pp. 113-53 (see #4569), and "Form and Content: Practice," pp. 157-216 (see #3701).

Also see comments by Roger Manvell, #81.

4562d. Also published as Tecnica del cinema. Turin: G. Einaudi, 1950.

4562e. Also published as Wybór písm. Trans. R. Dreyer. Warsaw, 1959.

4563. ----------. "Il montaggio del film sonoro: origini." Bianco e nero, 28, No. 5 (May 1967).

4564. ----------. "In Place of Speech." Kino (Warsaw), (Mar. 11, 1936).

Concerns questions of "formalism" and "naturalism" in the arts.

4565. ----------. Notes of a Film Director. Comp. and ed. Rostislav N. Jurenev.

Trans. X. Danko. Moscow: Foreign Languages Publishing House, 1946. (Reprint, London: Lawrence, 1958.)

4565a. Also published as Izbranniye stat'i. Redaktor-sostavitel', avtor vstup. stat'i i primechanii R. N. IUrenev. Moscow: Iskusstvo, 1956.

    Includes reprints of several important essays, see #3696, #3698, and #4567.

4565b. Also published as Ausgewählte Aufsätze. Trans. Lothar Fahlbusch. Berlin: Henschelverlag, 1960.

4566. ----------. "O stroyenii veshchei." Iskusstvo kino (Moscow), No. 6 (June 1939).

    In Russian.

4566a. Reprinted and translated as "The Structure of the Film," in Film Form, pp. 150-78.

    See #4562a.

4567. ----------. "Problems of Composition." Stenographic record of a lecture given on Dec. 25, 1946.

    Reprinted in Izbranniye stat'i. See #4565a.

    Translated in Film Essays, pp. 155-83. See #4561.

4568. ----------. "Vertikalny montash." Iskusstvo kino (Moscow), No. 9 (1940), 16-25.

    Translated as "Synchronization of the Senses," in The Film Sense, pp. 69-109. See #4562c.

4569. ----------. "Vertikalny montash." Iskusstvo kino (Moscow), No. 12 (1940), 27-35.

    Translated as "Color and Meaning," in The Film Sense, pp. 113-53. See #4562c.

4570. Eisler, Hanns. "Aikamme musiikki ja elokuva." Trans. M. Koski. Filmihullu (Helsinki), No. 5 (1977), 12-13.

4571. ----------. "Hudební skladba pro film." Hudební rozhledy, 26, No. 4 (1973), 182-87.

4572. ----------. Materialien zu einer Dialektik der Musik. Musik und Musiktheater. Ed. Manfred Grabs. Leipzig: Verlag Philipp Reclam, 1973.

    Includes a "Statement über die Untersuchungen von Musik und Film," pp. 176-80.

4573. ----------, and Theodor W. Adorno. Komposition für den Film. Unpublished, 1944.

    A significant analysis of the use and function of music in film, together with an account of Eisler's own research, enabled by support from the Rockefeller Foundation. This original draft was not published until 1969 (see #4573e), but appeared first in several differing versions. See #4573a-4573d.

    See Eisler's own comments on the work, #3217.

    Also see comments by Stefan Amzoll (#4418), and Horst Rüdiger (#3247).

4573a. Eisler, Hanns. Composing for the Films. Translated from the German by Hanns Eisler, in collaboration with George McManus and Norbert Guterman. New York: Oxford University Press; and London: Dennis Dobson, 1947. (Reprint, 1951.)

    NOTE: For primarily political reasons, Adorno was not credited as co-author of the work until the 1969 edition. (See #4573e.)

    Portions of this edition are quoted in Lewis Jacob's Emergence of Film Art (see #3215) and, with commentary, in Maynard Solomon's Marxism and Art (see #3253).

-- Rev. by Lawrence Morton: "Hanns Eisler, Composer and Critic." In Hollywood Quarterly, 3, No. 2 (Winter 1947-1948), 208-11.

-- Rev. by René Leibowitz: "Un nouveau genre musical? La Musique de film." In Critique (Paris), 5, No. 37 (June 1949), 501-10.

-- Rev. in Musical Times, 93 (Sept. 1952), 405-07.

4573b. Reprinted as Composing for the Films: With a Translation of the Postscript from the German Language Edition. Freeport, N.Y.: Books for Libraries Press, 1971.

> A reprint of the 1947 version, includes a translation of Adorno's 1969 postscript for the work. See #4573e.

4573c. Eisler, Hanns. Komposition für den Film. Berlin: Henschelverlag, 1949.

> The first German edition, greatly revised by Eisler, reflecting a marked anti-American, pro-Soviet tone.

> Also see comments by Karl Laux, #3235.

4573d. Also published as Hudební skladba pro film: Učební texty vysokých škol. Prague: Státní pedagogické nakladatelství, 1965.

4573e. Eisler, Hanns, and Theodor W. Adorno. Komposition für den Film. Munich: Verlag Rogner und Bernhard, 1969.

> Adorno's German edition, actually the first printing of the 1944 manuscript. Also includes a Postscript by Adorno: "Zum Erstdruck der Originalfassung," pp. 212-13.

> See comments by Hartmut Lück, #3237.

> Also see an important analysis of this volume by Philip Rosen, #4847.

-- Rev. in Neue Musikzeitung, 18, No. 5 (1969), 12.

-- Rev. by Alphons Silberman in Kölner Zeitschrift für Soziologie und Sozialpsychologie, 22 (1970), 809-13.

-- Rev. in Das Orchester (Hamburg), 18 (Oct. 1970), 482-83.

-- Rev. by Rudolf Stephan in Die Musikforschung, 25, No. 4 (1972), 567-68.

4573f. Also published as Musique de cinéma: Essai. Trad. de l'allemand. Trans. Jean-Pierre Hammer. Paris: Édition l'Arche, 1972.

-- Rev. by Olivier-René Veillon in Cinématographe (Paris), No. 62 (Nov. 1980), 37.

4573g. Also published as Filmszene. Trans. László Báti. Budapest: Zenemükiadö, 1973.

> Also see comments by Istvan Szerdahelyi, #3255.

-- Rev. by Péter Balassa in Magyar zene, 15, No. 3 (Sept. 1974), 321-23.

4573h. Also published as La musica per film. Trans. P. Bertini. Rome: Newton Compton, 1975.

-- Rev. by Luca Lombardi in Nuova rivista musicale italiana, 11, No. 1 (Jan.-Mar. 1977), 116-19.

4573i. Eisler, Hanns, and Theodor W. Adorno. Komposition für den Film. Gesammelte Werke: Hanns Eisler, III, No. 4. Leipzig: VEB Deutscher Verlag für Musik, 1977.

> Includes commentary on the dual authorship of the work.

-- Rev. in Musik und Gesellschaft, 28 (July 1978), 418-20.

-- Rev. in Opus Musicum (Brno, Czech.), 11, No. 2 (1979), 60-61.

4574. Embler, Jeffrey. "The Structure of Film Music." _Films in Review_, 4, No. 7 (Aug.-Sept. 1953), 332-35.

>Concerns the use of "theme music" and "leitmotifs."

>Reprinted in Limbacher, pp. 61-65. See #75.

4575. Emmer, Huib. "The Principle of Montage." _Key Notes Donemus_ (Amsterdam), No. 12 (1980), pp. 42-46.

4576. Epstein, Jean. _Esprit de cinéma_. Geneva and Paris: Éditions Jeheber, 1955.

>A collection of essays, includes "Le Cinéma pur et le film sonore," pp. 137-41, "Le Contrepoint du son," pp. 146-49, and "Le gros plan du son," pp. 150-60. Also includes filmography, noting composers and sound editors, pp. 181-215.

4577. Erdely, M. "Mozgó jelentés: Zenei szervezés lehetösége a filmben." _Valo-sag_, 11 (1973), 78-86.

4578. Erens, Patricia. "Patterns of Sound." _Film Reader_, No. 1 (1975), 40-49.

>Concerns the film "Citizen Kane," with music by Herrmann.

4579. Etzkowitz, Janice. "Toward a Concept of Cinematic Literature: An Analysis of 'Hiroshima, Mon Amour.'" Ph.D. Diss. Columbia University 1978.

>Includes references to the music of Giovanni Fusco and Georges Delerue. Abstract: DAI 1978:1886A (order #DA 7819334).

4580. Fano, Michel. "L'Attitude musicale dans 'Glissements progressif du plaisir.'" _Ça_, 1, No. 3 (1974), 20-22.

4581. ----------. "Le Bande-son: Vers une dialectique du film sonore." _Cahiers du cinéma_, 26, No. 152 (Feb. 1964), 30-36.

4582. ----------. _La Musique en projet_. Paris: Gallimard, 1975.

>4582a. A portion of this work is also published as "Musica e film." Trans. Enrico Ghezzi. _Filmcritica_ (Rome), 30, Nos. 296-297 (Aug. 1979), 288-91.

4583. Fey, Wilhelmine. "Die Verwertung musikschöpferischer Werke: insbesondere bei Funk, Film und Schallplatte." Ph.D. Diss., Munich 1941.

>Published version, Würzberg: Triltsch, 1941.

4584. "Filmmusik gewinnt an Wert und Bedeutung." _Musikhandel_, 6 (1955), 358-59.

4585. Fischer, Jan F. "I hudba je součástí filmového umění." _Hudební rozhledy_, 14, No. 15 (1961), 631-35.

4586. Fothergill, Richard. "Putting Music in Its Place." _Films and Filming_, 5, No. 6 (Mar. 1959), 10-11, 33.

4587. Frances, R. "Musique et image." _Cahiers d'Études de Radio-Télévision_, 18 (1958), 3-29.

4588. Franz, Erich A. "Die Aufgabe der Musik im Film." _Musikhandel_, 12, No. 5 (1961), 260.

4589. ----------. '"Die Filmmusik -- ihr Wesen und ihre Aufgabe." _Der Volksmu-siklehrer_, 19 (1970), 215-16.

4590. Freisburger, Walther. _Theater im Film: Eine Untersuchung über die Grundzüge und Wandlungen in den Beziehungen zwischen Theater und Film_. Emsdetten: H. & B. Lechte, 1936.

>Includes many references to film music throughout, and a "Verzeichnis der benutzten Literatur." pp. 88-90.

4591. Frith, Simon. "Music for Pleasure." _Screen Education_, No. 34 (Spring 1980), 51-61.

4592. Frolov, Ivan Dmitrievich. "O muzykalnoi dramaturgii kino." _Sovetskaya muzyka_, 24, No. 9 (Sept. 1960), 114-19.

4593. Frye, Northrupe. "Music in the Movies." Canadian Forum, 22, No. 263 (Dec. 1942), 275-76.

> Also see reader response to this article in Vol. 22, No. 264 (Jan. 1943), 303; and 22, No. 265 (Feb. 1943), 330-31.

4594. Fuhrmann, Peter. "Musik: die keiner kennen will." Neue Musikzeitung (Regensburg), 26, No. 6 (1977), 4.

4595. Fürst, Leonhard. "Der eigengesetzliche Tonfilm." Süddeutsche Monatshefte, 33 (1936), 216-19.

4596. Gallez, Douglas W. "Facing the Music in Scripts." Cinema Journal, 11, No. 1 (Fall 1971), 57-62.

4597. ----------. "Theories of Film Music." Cinema Journal, 9, No. 2 (Spring 1970), 40-47.

> Includes references to composers and theorists Eisler, Jaubert, Kracauer, and Pudovkin.

4598. Gauthier, Guy. Article in Le Son au cinéma, a special issue of Image et son, No. 215 (Mar. 1968).

4599. Gavazzeni, Gianandrea. "Impiego della musica nel film." Cinema (Rome), (1938).

4600. ----------. "Un connubio impossibile." La Ruota (Rome), (Jan. 1943).

4601. Gawrak (Czeczot-Gawrak), Zbigniew. "Jean Epstein jako teoretyk i filozof filmu." Kwartalnik Filmowy, 8, No. 4 (1958).

4602. ----------. "Narodziny filmologii." Kwartalnik Filmowy, 8, No. 2 (1958).

4603. Geduld, Harry M. "Film: A Discussion of Film Music -- Stravinsky and Film Music." Humanist, 39 (July-Aug. 1979), 55.

4604. Gelmetti, Vittorio. "Connotazioni plebee della musica per film." Cinema Nuovo (Turin), 24, No. 234 (Mar.-Apr. 1975), 90-97.

4605. Genkov, Georgi, et al. "Kino, kompozitor, rezhis'or." Bulgarska Muzika (Sofia), 32 (Mar. 1981), 39-46.

4606. Germain, Jean. "La Musique et le film." In L'Univers filmique. Bibliothèque d'esthétique. Ed. Etienne Souriau. Paris: Flammarion, 1953, pp. 137-55.

4607. Gessner, Robert. The Moving Image. New York: E. P. Dutton, 1968.

> Chapter 2: "The Auditory Image."

4608. Ghatak, Ritwik. "Sound in Film: Ghatak on Ghatak." Cinema Vision India, 1, No. 4 (Oct. 1980), 25-26.

> See #61.

4609. Gheorghiu, M. "Film -- Filmologie." Revue Roumaine d'Histoire de l'Art (Bucarest), 10, No. 1 (1973), 95-97.

4610. Ghezzi, Enrico. "De la musique avant toute chose." Filmcritica (Rome), 28, Nos. 279-280 (Dec. 1977), 359-62.

4611. ----------. "Senza parole." Filmcritica (Rome), 30, Nos. 296-297 (Aug. 1979), 242-44.

4612. ----------, and Marco Giusti. "La paura la musica il cinema." Filmcritica (Rome), 32, No. 312 (Feb. 1981), 89-95.

4613. Giannetti, Louis D. Understanding Movies. Englewood Cliffs, N.J.: Prentice-Hall, 1972.

> Includes the chapter "Sound," pp. 103-30.

4614. Gill, R. "The Soundtrack of 'Mme. Bovary': Flaubert's Orchestration of Aural Imagery." Literature/Film Quarterly, 1, No. 3 (1973), 206-17.

4615. Giovanni, A. B. Il cinema e il problema estetico. Messina, 1954.

4616. Girnus, Wilhelm. Von der unbefleckten Empfängnis des Ästhetischen. Berlin, 1972.

> Includes the chapter "Kunst und Geschichte," p. 83ff.

4617. Gmelin, Otto. Philosophie des Filmsehens. Pfullingen: Altes Zollhaus Selbstverlag, 1967.

> Concerns the special musical problems of television broadcasting.

4618. Goléa, Antoine. Esthétique de la musique contemporaine. Paris: Presses universitaires de France, 1954.

4619. Gómez Mesa, Luis. Autenticidad del cinema: Teorías sin trampa. Madrid: Galo Sáez, 1936.

4620. Gorbman, Claudia. "Clair's Sound Hierarchy and the Creation of Auditory Space." Film Studies Annual (West Lafayette, Ind.: Purdue Research Foundation, 1976), 113-23.

> Concerns the film "Sous les toits de Paris."

4621. ----------. "'Cleo from Five to Seven': Music as Mirror." Wide Angle, 4, No. 4 (1981), 38-49.

4622. ----------. "Narrative Film Music." Yale French Studies, No. 60 (1980), 183-203.

4623. ----------. "Teaching the Soundtrack." Quarterly Review of Film Studies, 1, No. 4 (Nov. 1976), 446-52.

4624. Gorodinskii, V. Muzyka dukhovnoĭ nishchety. Moscow: Gos. muzykal'noe izd-vo, 1950.

> 4624a. Also published as Geistige Armut in der Musik. Halle, 1953.

4625. Gressieker, H. "Das sinfonische Prinzip." Deutsches Filmschaffen (1943).

4626. Gruillas, G. "Estetica generale della cinematografia sonora." Cinema (Rome), (1936).

4627. Grützner, Vera. "Bemerkungen zur Musikdramaturgie in neueren Spielfilmen der DEFA." Musik und Gesellschaft, 24, No. 10 (Oct. 1974), 613-21.

4628. ----------. "Die dramaturgische Funktion der Musik im Spielfilm." In Urheberrecht und Musik: Aufsätze -- Referate -- Beiträge zur Diskussion. Berlin: Akademie der Künste der DDR, 1975, pp. 91-94.

4629. Guernsey, Otis L., Jr. "Hört der Kinobesucher die Filmmusik?" Österreichischer Autorenzeitung, 3, Nos. 8-9 (1951), 11.

4630. Guillot de Rode, François. "La dimension sonore." In L'Univers filmique. Bibliothèque d'esthétique. Ed. Etienne Souriau. Paris: Flammarion, 1953, 119-35.

> See #4890.

4631. Hagemann, Walter. Der Film: Wesen und Gestalt. Heidelberg: K. Vowinckel, 1952.

> Includes bibliography, pp. 219-23.

4632. Hamilton, William. "Music in Art Films." Film Music, 12, No. 4 (Mar.-Apr. 1953), 19-23.

4633. ----------. "Music in Art Films, Part 2." Film Music, 12, No. 5 (May-June 1953), 20-23.

> Includes a listing of films, with composers, and a selective discography.

4634. Hartmann, Nicolai. Ästhetik. Berlin: Walter de Gruyter, 1953.

> A fundamental statement of aesthetic theory, with important implications for the study of film and music.

See especially the chapter "Schichten des Musikwerkes," pp. 197-211.

4635. Hazumi Tsuneo. *Eiga to minzoku*. Tokyo: Eiga Nihonsha, 1943.

Includes many references to the use of music in Japanese films.

4636. Helman, Alicja. "Probleme der Musik in Film." *Film* (Frankfurt), 5 (1964), 687-707.

Includes a discussion of film music literature.

4637. ----------. "Rola filmu w upowszechnianiu muzyki." *Kino* (Warsaw), 15 (Mar. 1980), 32-34.

4638. ----------. "Rola muzyki w filmie." Ph.D. Diss., Warsaw 1964.

4638a. Published as *Rola muzyki w filmie*. Instytut Sztuki Polskiej Akademii Nauk. Z prac Zakladu Historii i Teorii Filmu. Warsaw: Wydawnictwa Artystyczne i Filmowe, 1964.

-- Rev. by Zofia Kułakowska in *Kwartalnik Filmowy*, 15, No. 3 (1965), 15-22.

-- Rev. by Zofia Lissa in *Studia Estetyczne*, 2 (1965), 355-58.

4639. ----------. *Z tajemnic X muzy*. Warsaw: Wydawnictwo Zwiazkowe CRZZ, 1968.

Includes the chapter "Muzyka," pp. 81-89.

4640. Hengst, Heinz. "Von den Medien umstellt: Sprechen, Sehen, Hören in der Fernseh-Kino-Stereo-Welt." *Medium* (Frankfurt am Main), 9 (July 1979), 3-8.

4641. Hoérée, Arthur. "Morceaux de musique et musique en morceaux." *L'Écran français* (Paris), 4 (May 1947).

4642. Hopkins, Antony. "Irony and Humour in Film-Music." *Chesterian*, 25 (July 1950), 7-11.

An article later presented at the 1950 Florence Congress. See the *Proceedings ...*, #1864.

4642a. Also published as "Ironia e umorismo nella musica da film." In *Musica e film*. Ed. S. G. Biamonte. Rome: Edizioni dell'Ateneo, 1959, pp. 207-11.

See #1606.

4643. Húbaček, Alois. "Nástin teorie audiovizuálnich technických prostředků." *Prolegomena scénografické encyklopedie*, 7 (1971), 80-85.

4644. Huntley, John. "Film Music." *Penguin Film Review*, No. 4 (Oct. 1947), 17-20.

See #1315a.

4645. ----------. "Music in Films." *The Musical Times*, 98, No. 1378 (Dec. 1957), 662-63.

4646. Hussey, Dyneley. "Music in the Cinema." *Spectator*, 154 (Feb. 15, 1935), 247.

4647. Ikonomov, Bojan. "Muzikata v dramaturgiceskata tukan na filma." *Muzika*, Nos. 9-10 (1951), 23-26.

4648. Imamura Taihei. *Nihon geijutsu to eiga*. Tokyo: Suga Shoten, 1941.

4649. Internationales Musikzentrum, Vienna. *IMZ Report: Hearing and Seeing -- Music in the Technical Media*. Salzburg: IMZ, 1971.

In English, German, and French.

4650. Irving, Ernest. "Music in Films." *Music and Letters*, 24, No. 4 (Oct. 1943), 223-35.

A defense of film music. Includes an "Appendix: Short Description of the Method for Recording Sound upon Film."

4651. Jacchia, Paolo. "Appunti per una poetica cinematografica del motivo musicale." _Bianco e nero_, 9, No. 7 (July 1948).

4652. Jackiewicz, Aleksander. "Scenografia i muzyka: narodziny dziela filmowego (IV)." _Kino_ (Warsaw), 14 (June 1979), 25-27.

4653. Jacobs, Lewis, ed. _The Movies as Medium_. New York: Farrar, Straus and Giroux, 1970.

Includes the section "Sound," pp. 243-96, a collection of essays by Jacobs, Rodakiewicz (see #3161), Balázs (see #4435), and Weill (see #4954). Also contains a bibliography, pp. 323-28.

4654. Jelinek, Hanns. "Musik in Film und Fernsehen: Einige Betrachtungen zu einem aktuellen Thema." _Österreichische Musikzeitschrift_, 23, No. 3 (Mar. 1968), 122-35.

Concerns the view of music itself as a "visual image."

4655. Jinks, William. _The Celluloid Literature: Film in the Humanities_. New York: Delacorte Press, 1965.

Includes a chapter on the use of sound.

4656. Joffe, Judah A. "Sintetitscheskaya istoriya iskusstv." In _V Vedeniye v istoriyu chudoshestvennogo myschleniya_. Leningrad, 1933, pp. 546-68.

4657. Johnson, William. "Face the Music." _Film Quarterly_, 22, No. 4 (Summer 1969), 3-19.

4658. Jolivet, Jean. "Note sur le temps au cinéma." _Revue internationale de filmologie_ (Paris), 1, Nos. 3-4 (Oct. 1948), 331-34.

4659. Jones, Isabel Morse. "Emotional Power of Music Revealed." _Los Angeles Times_ (June 20, 1937), Section 3, p. 9.

4660. Jujka, Andrzej. "O ontologicznej strukturze filmu dźwiekowego." _Studia Estetyczne_, 12 (1975), 171-80.

A refutation of Roman Ingarden's concept of the multi-layered structure of film which was later applied by Zofia Lissa.

Includes summaries in Russian and English.

4661. Julien, Jean Remy. "Elements methodologiques pour une typologie de la musique de film." _Revue de musicologie_, 66, No. 2 (1980), 179ff.

4662. ----------. "Musique en images." _Harmonie_ (Paris), No. 156 (Mar. 1980), 46-50.

4663. Jungk, Klaus. _Musik im technischen Zeitalter: von der Edison-Walze zur Bildplatte_. Buchreihe des Sender Freies Berlin, XI. Berlin: Haude und Spenersche Verlagsbuchhandlung, 1971.

An extremely valuable work, touching upon nearly every aspect of film music and music-and-media.

4664. Kabalevskij, Dmitrij. "Dve vstreči s Aleksandrom Petrovičem Dovženko." _Sovetskaya muzyka_, 38, No. 12 (Dec. 1974).

Kabalevsky's interviews with Dovženko, concerning the films "Aèrograd" and "Ščors."

4665. Kadieva, P. "Za njakoi problemi na muzikata v animacionnija film." _Bŭlgarska Muzika_, 24, No. 2 (Feb. 1973), 53-55.

4666. Kalinak, Kathryn M. "The Fallen Woman and the Virtuous Wife: Musical Stereotypes in 'The Informer', 'Gone with the Wind,' and 'Laura.'" _Film Reader_, No. 5 (1982), 76-82.

An interesting view of the music by Raksin and Steiner.

4667. ----------. "Music as Narrative Structure in Hollywood Film." Ph.D. Diss. University of Illinois at Urbana-Champaign 1982.

Abstract: DAI 42/11:4626A (order #DA 8209593).

4668. Kaltofen, Günter. Das Bild, das deine Sprache spricht: Fernsehspiele. Berlin: Henschelverlag, 1962.

"Dramatische Kunst auf dem Bildschirm," p. 17ff.

4669. "Kansas Exhibitor Wants Special Music." The Moving Picture World, 31 (Jan. 13, 1917), 264.

A demand for original scores designed to fit each new film.

4670. Kaziów, Michał. "Znaczenie fonicznego tworzywa słuchowiska radiowego." Studia estetyczne, 11 (1974), 245-61.

Concerns the significance of the "phonic medium" in radio drama. Includes summaries in Russian and English.

4671. Keller, Hans. "Film-Musical Atmosphere." Contemporary Cinema, 1, No. 9 (Oct. 1947).

4672. ----------. "Film Music: Problems of Integration." Musical Times, 96, No. 1349 (July 1955), 381-82.

4673. ----------. "Film Music: Theme Song and Leading Motif." Film Monthly Review (Jan. 1948).

4674. ----------. "'Lease on Life': A New Formal Principle of Dramatic Music." Musical Opinion, 78 (Dec. 1954), 151ff.

4675. ----------. The Need for Competent Film Music Criticism: A Pamphlet for Those Who Care for Film as Art, with a Final Section for Those Who Do Not. (Pamphlet.) London: British Film Institute, 1947.

4676. Kenedi, János, ed. Film + zene = filmzene?: Írások a filmzenéről. Budapest: Zeneműkiadó, 1978.

A collection of essays by Sergei Eisenstein, Zofia Lissa, Jacques Bourgeois, Arnold Schoenberg, Frank Martin, Kurt Weill, and John Cage. Also includes bibliographic references.

4677. Kershaw, D. "Tape Music with Abstract Animated Film." Ph.D. Diss. (Music), York.

Work in progress in 1976.

4678. Khristova, Yuliya. "Khorova pesen, filmova i estradna muzika." Bŭlgarska Muzika (Sofia), 28 (Feb. 1977), 20-21.

4679. Kilenyi, Edward. "Film Music of Recent Pictures." Film Music Notes, 10, No. 2 (Nov.-Dec. 1950), 20.

4680. Kinder, Marshe, and Beverle Houston. Closeup. New York: Harcourt, Brace, Jovanovich, 1972.

Includes many references to film music throughout, with a section on the use of sound, pp. 51-65.

4681. Kirschner, Klaus. "Die Anwesenheit von Musik bei Filmen." Neue Musikzeitung (Regensburg), 28, No. 4 (1979), 23.

4682. Kishi Matsuo. Nihon eiga ron. Tokyo: Komatendō, 1935.

4683. ----------. Nihon eiga yōshiki kō. Tokyo: Kawade Shobō, 1937.

4684. Klangstruktur der Musik: neue Erkenntnisse musik-elektronischer Forschung. Berlin: Verlag für Radio - Foto - Kinotechnik, 1955.

A collection of articles by H. Eimert, P. Boulez, L. Kestenberg, W. Meyer-Eppler, and others. Includes contributions by Boris Blacher and F. Enkel.

4685. Kneif, Tibor. "Das triviale Bewusstsein in der Musik." In Studien zur Trivialmusik des 19. Jahrhunderts. Ed. Carl Dahlhaus. Regensburg: Bosse, 1967, pp. 29-52.

4686. Koch, Gerhard R. "Vom Sehen und Hören. Einiges über Filmmusik." HiFi-

Stereophonie, 13, No. 4 (Apr. 1974), 368-78.

4687. Kofin, Ewa. "Muzyka telewizyjna: cechy i funkcje." *Ruch Muzyczny* (Warsaw), 23, No. 20 (1979), 16.

4688. ----------. "Muzyka telewizyjna: deformacja czyli adaptacia." *Ruch Muzyczny* (Warsaw), 23, No. 16 (1979), 6-7.

4689. ----------. "Muzyka telewizyjna: wspolzaleznosci." *Ruch Muzyczny* (Warsaw), 23, No. 17 (1979), 17ff.

4690. Komeda-Trzciński, K. "Odpowiedź na ankietę 'Rola muzyki w dziele filmowym.'" *Kwartalnik Filmowy*, 11, No. 2 (1961).
    Also see #4434.

4691. Kominek, Mieczysław. "Podstawy nowej integracji audiowizvalnej w filmie współczesnym." *Muzyka*, 20, No. 4 (1975), 49-57.

4692. Kotoński, W. "Odpowiedź na ankietę 'Rola muzyki w dziele filmowym.'" *Kwartalnik Filmowy*, 11, No. 2 (1961).
    Also see #4434.

4693. Kozlov, Leonyid. "A kulcs: a Tx szimfonia: a klasszikus szovjet film esztetikajahoz." *Filmkultura* (Budapest), 13 (Sept.-Oct. 1977), 69-75.

4694. Kracauer, Siegfried. (Zigfrid Krakauer.) "Film i muzika." *Zvuk*, No. 94 (1969), 150-67.

4695. ----------. *From Caligari to Hitler: A Psychological History of the German Film*. Princeton: Princeton University Press, 1947. (Reprint, 1971.)
    Includes several references to music in film.
  4695a. Also published as *Von Caligari bis Hitler: ein Beitrag zur Geschichte des deutschen Films*. Hamburg: Rowohlt, 1958.

4696. ----------. "L'Immagine ha bisogno della musica." *Cinema nuovo*, No. 104 (1957).

4697. ----------. "La musica nell'immagine." *Cinema nuovo*, No. 108 (1957).

4698. ----------. *Theory of Film: The Redemption of Physical Reality*. New York and London: Oxford University Press, 1960. (Reprint, 1965.)
    Includes Chapter 7: "Dialogue and Sound," pp. 102-32, and Chapter 8: "Music," (with the subsections "Physiological Functions," and "Aesthetic Functions"), pp. 133-56.
  4698a. Also published with the title *Nature of Film: The Redemption of Physical Reality*. London: Dennis Dobson, 1961.
  4698b. Also published as *Theorie des Films: die Errettung der äusseren Wirklichkeit*. Trans. Friedrich Walter and Ruth Zellschan. Frankfurt am Main: Suhrkamp, 1964.

4699. Kühn, Hellmut. "Analyse von Rundfunkprogrammen nebst einem Anhang über Ausdruckscharaktere in der Filmmusik sowie Hinweisen auf die Struktur eines Medieninstituts." *Schulfach Musik* (1976), 62-69.

4700. ----------. "Hinweise auf eine Analyse von Filmmusik." In *Musik in den Massenmedien, Rundfunk und Fernsehen: Perspectiven und Materialien*. Ed. Hans-Christian Schmidt. Mainz: B. Schotts Söhne, 1976, pp. 120-25.

4701. Kuna, Milan. "Ke kritice filmové hudby." *Hudební Rozhledy* (Prague), 15, No. 20 (1962), 862.

4702. ----------. "K problémům estetiky filmové hudby." *Hudební Rozhledy* (Prague), 14, No. 22 (1961), 946-48.

4703. ----------. "Otazky formy ve filmové hudbe." *Hudební Rozhledy* (Prague), 15, No. 18 (1962), 778.

4704. Kupsch, Horst. "Musik wird störend oft empfunden." *Film und Ton*, 24 (Nov. 1978), 30.

4705. Kurčenko, Alexandr. "Dokazyvat' i ne soglašat'sja, iskat' i myslit'..." *Sovetskaya muzyka*, 38, No. 5 (May 1974), 51-59.

Concerns the films "Andrey Rublev," and "Solyaris."

4706. Labroca, Mario. "Corsi e ricorsi negli incontri fra il cinematografo e la musica." In *Musica e film*. Ed. S. G. Biamonte. Rome: Edizioni dell' Ateneo, 1959, pp. 11-20.

See #1606.

4707. Lacombe, Alain, and Claude Rocle. "Les paramètres d'un silence indésirable." *Musique en jeu*, No. 33 (Nov. 1978), 41-58.

4708. Lajtha, László. "Music and Films." *The Chesterian*, 23, No. 155 (July 1948), 1-7.

4709. Lambert, Gavin. "Sight and Sound." *Sequence* (Summer 1950).

4709a. Reprinted in *Film: A Montage of Theories*. Ed. Richard Dyer MacCann. New York: E. P. Dutton, 1966, pp. 45-52.

See #2093.

4710. La Motte-Haber, Helga de. "Filmmuziek." *Adem* (Louvain, Belgium), 14, No. 3 (May-June 1978), 133-37.

4711. ----------. "Filmmusik." *Musik und Bildung*, 9, No. 1 (Jan. 1977), 19-22.

Originally published in a collection edited by Roland Posner and Hans-Peter Reinecke. *Zeichenprozesses -- Semiotische Forschung in den Einzelwissenschaften*.

4712. ----------. "Fünf Thesen zur Filmmusik." *Melos: Neue Zeitschrift für Musik*, 4, No. 2 (New series, Mar.-Apr. 1978), 111-13.

4713. ----------. "Funktionelle Musik." In *Die Wertproblematik in der Musikdidaktik*. Ed. W. Krützfeld. Ratingen, 1973, pp. 65ff.

4714. ----------. "Komplementarität von Sprache, Bild und Musik. Am Beispiel des Spielfilms." *Sprache im technischen Zeitalter*, 16, No. 1 (1976), 57-64.

4715. Landry, Lionel. "Le Commentaire musical." In *Le Film sonore: l'écran et la musique en 1935*, a special issue of *La Revue musicale*, 15, No. 151 (Dec. 1934), 340-47.

4716. Lange, Arthur. "The Epigrammatic Nature of Motion Picture Music." *Score*, 4 (Mar. 1950), 8-9.

4717. Langer, Suzanne K. "A Note on the Film." In *Feeling and Form*. New York: Charles Scribner's Sons, 1953, pp. 411-15.

4717a. Reprinted in *Film: A Montage of Theories*. Ed. Richard Dyer MacCann. New York: E. P. Dutton, 1966, pp. 199-204.

See #2093.

4718. ----------. "On Significance in Music." In *Aesthetics and the Arts*. Ed. Lee A. Jacobus. New York: McGraw-Hill, 1968, pp. 182-212.

A presentation of aesthetic foundations which bear upon the study of film music.

4719. Langham Smith, Richard. "Debussy and the Art of the Cinema." *Music and Letters*, 54, No. 1 (Jan. 1973), 61-70.

Drawn from newspaper articles by Debussy, displays his interest in film, and poses cinema as a possible renewal for 20th century music.

4720. Lawson, John Howard. *Film: The Creative Process: The Search for an Audio-Visual Language and Structure*. New York: Hill and Wang, 1964.

Includes many references to film music. Also includes a Preface by Jay Leyda, and a bibliography, pp. 361-68.

4721. Lefèvre, R. Article in *Le Son au cinéma*, a special issue of *Image et son*,

No. 215 (Mar. 1968).

4722. Lemaître, Henri. "L'Animation des tableaux et les problèmes du film sur l'art." In L'Univers filmique. Bibliothèque d'esthétique. Ed. Etienne Souriau. Paris: Flammarion, 1953, pp. 157-78.

    See #4890.

4723. Lenartowicz, Stanislaw. "Organizacja czasu i przestrzeni w utworze filmowym." In Zagadnienia estetyki filmowej. Warsaw. 1955.

    See #4973.

4724. Lewicki, B. "Gramatyka języka filmowego." Kwartalnik Filmowy, 9, No. 1 (1959).

4725. ----------. "Percepcyjne uwarunkowanie estetyki filmowej." Kwartalnik Filmowy, 8, No. 2 (1958).

4726. ----------. "Podstawowe zagadnienia budowy dziela filmowego." In Zagadnienia estetyki filmowej. Warsaw, 1955.

    See #4973.

4727. ----------. "Problematyka rodzajów i gatunków w sztuce filmowej." In Zagadnienia rodzajów literackich, II. Łódz, 1960.

4728. Lexman, Juraj. "Estetická väzba obrazu a hudby vo filme." Slovenské divadlo, 23, No. 4 (1975), 470-95.

    Includes summaries in English and Russian.

4729. L'Herbier, Marcel, comp. Intelligence du cinématographe. Paris: Éditions Corrêa, 1946.

    A collection of essays, includes contributions by Maurice Jaubert (see #3466), René Clair (see #4307), Léon Moussinac (see #4375), and Paul Valéry (see #4935).

4730. ----------. "Que demande le cinéma à la musique?" Journal musical français (Paris), (Sept. 25, 1952).

4731. Liess, Andreas. Die Musik im Weltbild der Gegenwart: Erkenntnis und Bekenntnis. Vienna and Lindau im Bodensee: Frisch und Perneder, 1949.

4732. Lippold, Eberhard. Zur Frage der ästhetischen Inhalt - Form - Relationen in der Musik. Beiträge zur musikwissenschaftlichen Forschung in der DDR, III. Leipzig: Deutscher Verlag für Musik, 1971.

4733. Lissa, Zofia. Estetyka muzyki filmowej. Krakow: Polskie Wydawnictwo Muzyczne, 1964.

    An important analysis of the form and function of music in film. Includes a filmography, and an extensive bibliography.

    -- Rev. by Ludwik Erhardt in Nowe Książki, No. 2 (1965), 78.

    -- Rev. in Hudebni Rozhledy, No. 16 (1964), 723.

    -- Rev. by Bohdan Pociej in Ruch Muzyczny, 16 (1964), 17-18.

    -- Rev. by Zofia Kułakowska in Kwartalnik Filmowy, 15, No. 3 (1965), 15-22; and in Muzyka, 9, Nos. 3-4 (1964), 147-51.

    -- Rev. by Alicja Helman in Studia Estetyczne, 2 (1965), 345-49.

    -- Rev. by A. Farbštejn in Sovetskaya Muzyka, 29, No. 12 (1965), 140-42.

4733a. Also published as Ästhetik der Filmmusik. Berlin: Henschelverlag, 1965.

    Includes a section "Literatur über den Tonfilm," pp. 9-16, filmography, pp. 425-44, and bibliography, pp. 409-24.

-- Rev. by Reimar Hollmann in Opernwelt, 7, No. 2
(1966), 8.

-- Rev. by Herbert M. Schueller in The Journal of
Aesthetics and Art Criticism, 24, No. 4 (Summer
1966), 605-06.

-- Rev. by Fritz Bose in Musica, 20 (1966), 142.

-- Rev. by Ulrich Seelmann-Eggebert in Neue Zeitschrift für Musik, 128, No. 5 (May 1967), 216-
18.

-- Rev. by Péter Várnai in Studia Musicologica, 9,
Nos. 1-2 (1967), 236-40.

-- Rev. by Heinz Alfred Brockhaus in Musik und Gesellschaft, 17, No. 2 (1967), 132-35.

-- Rev. by Claudio Giorgini in Rivista de Estetica,
13 (1968), 300-01.

-- Rev. by Friedbert Streller in Beiträge zur Musikwissenschaft, 11, No. 2 (1969), 141-44.

4733b. Also published as Éstetika kinomuzyki. Moscow: Muzyka,
1970.

4734. ----------. "Formprobleme der Filmmusik." In Festschrift Karl Gustav
Fellerer zum sechzigsten Geburtstag am 7. Juli 1962. Ed. Heinrich
Hüschen. Cologne and Regensburg: Gustav Bosse Verlag, 1962, pp. 321-35.

4735. ----------. "Funkcje muzyki w filmie a w innych gatunkach syntetycznych."
Muzyka, 7, No. 2 (1962), 3-14.

4736. ----------. "Funkcje muzyki w utworze filmowym." In Księga pamiątkowa
III Polskiego Zjazdu Filozofów w Krakowie, a special issue of Przegląd
Filozoficzny, No. 4 (1936), 457-59.

4737. ----------. "Die Kategorie des Komischen in der Musik." In Bericht über
den 7. Musikwissenschaftlichen Kongress Köln 1958. Kassel: Bärenreiter,
1959, pp. 181-83.

4738. ----------. "Leninowska teoria odbicia a estetyka muzyczna." Materialy
do Studiów i Dyskusji (Warsaw), Special issue (1950), 95-159.

Reprinted in Podstawy estetyki muzyzynej. See #4743.

4739. ----------. "Musikalisches Geschichtsbewusstsein -- Segen oder Fluch?"
In Neue Aufsätze zur Musikästhetik. Berlin: Wilhelmshaven: Heinrichs-
hofens Verlag, 1975, p. 153.

4740. ----------. Muzyka i film: Studium z pogranicza ontologii, estetyki i
psychologii muzyki filmowej. Lwow: Lwów Księgarnia Lwowska, 1937.

-- Rev. by Stefania Zahorska: "Książka o muzyce i filmie."
Wiadomości Literackie, 32 (1938), 771.

-- Rev. by K. Regamey in Muzyka Polska, No. 5 (1938),
226-30.

-- Rev. by S. Frank in Sygnaly, No. 37 (1938), 11.

4741. ----------. Niektóre zagadnienia estetyki muzycznej w świetle artykułów
Józefa Stalina o marksizmie w językoznawstwie. Krakow: Polskie Wydawnictwo Muzyczne, 1952.

4741a. Reprinted in Studia Muzykologiczne, 1 (1953), 11-154.

-- Rev. by P. Beylin: "Z zagadnień estetyki muzycznej."
Myśl Filozoficzna, No. 3 (1953), 259-66.

4741b. Also published as Fragen der Musikästhetik: Einige Probleme der Musikästhetik im Lichte der Arbeit J. W.
Stalins "Der Marxismus und die Fragen der Sprachwis-
senschaft." Berlin: Henschelverlag, 1954.

4741c. Also published in Japanese translation, Tokyo: Tokyo Sa-
niti Senobe, 1956.

4741d. Also published in Chinese translation, Peking, 1962.

4742. ----------. "O zainteresowanie muzyka filmowa." Ruch Muzyczny, 5, No. 5

(1961), 15-16.

4743. ----------. Podstawy estetyki muzyzynej, I-II. Warsaw: Polskie Wydawnictwo Naukowe, 1953.

    A collection of essays by Lissa, including a reprint
of "Leninowskiej teorii..." (see #4738), and others.

    -- Rev. by Stefania Łobaczewska in Studia Muzykologiczne,
3 (1954), 536-48.

4744. ----------. "Problem 'czasu przedstawionego' w muzyce filmowej." Kwartalnik Filmowy, 9, No. 1 (1959), 23-33.

4744a. Also published as "Das Problem der 'dargestellten Zeit' in
der Filmmusik." Musik und Gesellschaft, 12, No. 2 (Feb.
1962), 66-76.

4745. ----------. "Problem odzwierciedlenia rzeczywistości w muzyce." Materialy
do Studiów i Dyskusji (Warsaw), No. 5 (1951), 164-83.

4745a. Also published in a collection of Lissa's essays: Muzyko-
logia polska na przełomie. Krakow: Polskie Wydawnictwo
Muzyczne, 1952, pp. 157-93.

4746. ----------. Szkice z estetyki muzycznej, I. Krakow: Polskie Wydawnictwo
Muzyczne, 1965.

    Includes a number of references to music in film.

    -- Rev. by Malgorzata Komorowska in Ruch Muzyczny,
No. 8 (1966), 5-6.

4746a. Also published as Aufsätze zur Musikästhetik. Berlin:
Henschelverlag, 1969.

4746b. Also published as Zene és csend. Zeneesztétikai tanulmán-
yok. Budapest: Gondolat, 1973.

4747. ----------. "Über das Wesen des Musikwerks." Die Musikforschung, No. 2
(1968), 157-82.

4748. ----------. "Wychowawcza rola filmu w zakresie muzyki." Kultura i Spo-
łeczeństwo, 3, No. 2 (1963), 67-80.

4748a. Reprinted as "Wychowawcza rola muzyki filmowej." In
Wychowanie przez sztukę. Warsaw, 1965, pp. 288-305.

4748b. Also published as "Die musikerzieherische Rolle des Films."
Musik und Gesellschaft, 15, No. 3 (Mar. 1965), 162-73.

4749. Litle, Michael. "Sound Track: 'The Rules of the Game.'" Cinema Journal,
13, No. 1 (Fall 1973), 35-44.

    An analysis of the use of sound and music in Jean Renoir's
film.

4750. Łobaczewska, Stefania. Style muzyczne, I-II. Krakow: Polskie Wydawnictwo
Muzyczne, 1960-1961.

    Includes references to the function of music in film.

4751. Lohmann, Hans. "Filmdramatisches Erzählen, Konflikt - Fabel - Genre."
Aus Theorie und Praxis des Films, No. 4 (1972), 29.

4752. Longo, Achille. "La critica cinematografica e la musica nel film." In
La musica nel film. Ed. Luigi Chiarini. Rome: Bianco e nero editore,
1950, pp. 86-90.

    A paper presented at the 1950 Venice conference. See
Chiarini, #1627.

4753. Lucchesi, Joachim. "Zur Funktion und Geschichte der zeitgenössischen
Schauspielmusik und zu einigen Aspekten der schauspielmusikalischen
Praxis." Ph.D. Diss., Berlin 1977.

    Includes references to music in film, and many implications
for the study of film music.

4754. Luciani, Sebastiano A. L'antiteatro: il cinema come arte. Rome: Edizioni
La Voce, 1928.

4755. ----------. "L'estetica del film." Bianco e nero, 28, Nos. 3-4 (Mar.-
        Apr. 1967), 91-93.
            See #2116.

4756. ----------. Il cinema e le arti. Siena: Ticci Editore, 1942.

4757. ----------. "La musica del film." Bianco e nero, 2, No. 12 (Dec. 1938).

4758. ----------. "La musica e il film." Bianco e nero, 1, No. 6 (June 1937),
        3-17.
            The first article on film music to appear in this im-
            portant Italian periodical.

4759. ----------. "La musica e il film." Bianco e nero, 2, No. 6 (June 1938).

4760. Ludwig, Ernst. "Film und Kunst." Deutsches Musikjahrbuch (1937), 136-38.

4761. Luft, Friedrich. "Film-Musik -- Musikfilm." Musik und Dichtung (1953),
        110.

4762. Lundgren, Henrik. "Det sublimerede lystspil." Kosmorama (Copenhagen), 22,
        No. 129 (1976), 50-58.

4763. Malipiero, Gian-Francesco. "La musica nel cinematografo di domani." In-
        ternational Review of Educational Cinematography (Rome), 7, Nos. 8-9
        (Aug.-Sept. 1935), 138-40.
            Includes a synopsis in English: "Cinema Music of Tomor-
            row," pp. 141-42.

4764. Maniewicz, J., and L. Rogozyna. "O teorii i praktike svukovogo filma."
        Iskusstvo kino (Moscow), No. 5 (May 1948).

4765. Marcel, Gabriel. "Possibilités et limites de l'art cinématographique."
        Revue internationale de filmologie (Paris), 5, Nos. 18-19 (July-Dec.
        1954), 163-76.

4766. Marie, Michel. Lectures du film. Paris: Éditions Albatros, 1977.
            A collection of articles by various authors, includes
            three sections by Marie: "Comédie musicale," pp. 51-60,
            "Muet," pp. 164-73, and "Son," pp. 198-211. Each sec-
            tion is accompanied by a brief selective bibliography.
        4766a. Also published as Attraverso il cinema. Trans. Antonio
            Costa. Milan: Longanesi, 1978.

4767. ----------. "'Muriel,' un film sonore, un film musical, un film parlant."
        In "Muriel": Histoire d'une recherche, by Claude Bailblé, Michel Marie,
        and Marie-Claire Ropars-Wuilleumier. Paris: Éditions Galilée, 1975,
        pp. 61-122.

4768. Marinuzzi, Gino. "Aspetti della musica nel film." In La musica nel film.
        Ed. Luigi Chiarini. Rome: Bianco e nero editore, 1950, pp. 35-38.
            A paper presented at the 1950 Venice conference. See
            Chiarini, #1627.

4769. Martin, Marcel. Le Langage cinématographique. 7ème art. Paris: Éditions
        du Cerf, 1955.
            Includes the chapter "Les Phénomènes sonores," and many
            references to the use of music and sound in film. Also
            includes a bibliography, pp. 243-44.
            Reprint, Paris: Les Editeurs Français Réunis, 1977.
            Translated into 10 different languages, including a
            Russian edition: Yazyk kino. Moscow, 1959.

4770. Mast, Gerald. Film/Cinema/Movie: A Theory of Experience. New York: Har-
        per and Row, 1977.
            Includes Chapter 8: "(Recorded) Sound," pp. 206-37, and
            many other references to film music.

4771. Matter, Jean. "Présence de la musique à l'écran." Schweizerische Musikzeitung, 110 (1970), 367-70.

4772. ----------. "Réflexions sur la fonctionnalité de la musique au cinéma."
Schweizerische Musikzeitung, 104, No. 3 (1964), 180-86.

4773. May, Renato. L'avventura del film: Immagini, suono, colore. Rome: Bianco
e nero editore, 1952.

4774. ----------. Il linguaggio del film. Biblioteca cinematografica Series,
No. 1; Saggi critici, Vol 3. Milan: Poligono, 1947.

Includes bibliography, pp. 203-04.

4775. Mayer, Günter. "Gesellschaftlicher und musikalischer Fortschritt." Beiträge zur Musikwissenschaft, Nos. 1-2 (1973), 7.

4776. McKay, Frances Thompson. "Movement in Time and Space: The Synthesis of
Music and Visual Imagery in Luchino Visconti's 'Death in Venice' and
Stanley Kubrick's '2001: A Space Odyssey.'" D.M.A. Diss. Peabody Con-
servatory of Music (Johns Hopkins University) 1982.

Abstract: DAI 43/04:955A (order #DA 8220057).

4777. Medvedev, A. "Obraz kompozitorov na ekrane." Sovetskaya muzyka, 17,
No. 3 (Mar. 1953), 83-90.

4778. Mele, Rino. "La musica, un'attrice astratta." Filmcritica (Rome), 30,
Nos. 296-297 (Aug. 1979), 278-87.

An interview with Memè Perlini.

4779. Mellers, Wilfred H. "Problemas formales de la musica cinematografica."
Nuestra Musica, 6, No. 24 (1951), 254-63.

A paper presented at the 1950 Florence Congress. See
#1864.

4780. Metz, Christian. "Aural Objects." Yale French Studies, No. 60 (1980), 24-
32.

4781. ----------. Essais sur la signification au cinéma. Paris: Klincksieck,
1968.

Includes references to the function of music in film,
and an important paradymn for the study of film music.

4781a. Also published as Semiologie des Films. Trans. Renate
Koch. Munich: Wilhelm Fink, 1972.

4781b. Also published as Film Language: A Semiotics of the Cinema. Trans. Michael Taylor. New York: Oxford University
Press, 1974.

4782. Meyer, Leonard B. Emotion and Meaning in Music. Chicago: University of
Chicago Press, 1956.

With implications for the study of film music. See especially the chapter "Notes on Image Processes, Conno-
tations and Moods," pp. 256-72.

4783. Meyer-Eppler, W. "Wie lassen sich Klänge und Geräusche in Film und Rundfunk 'elektronisch' gestalten?" Die Umschau in Wissenschaft und Technik
(Frankfurt am Main), 54 (1954), 81-83.

4784. Milano, Paolo. "Music in the Film: Notes for a Morphology." Journal of
Aesthetics and Art Criticism, 1, No. 1 (Spring 1941), 89-94.

4785. Mitry, Jean. Esthétique et Psychologie du cinéma, I-II. Paris: Éditions
universitaires, 1963-1965.

Volume II includes Chapter 12: "La Parole et le son."

4786. ----------. "Musique et cinéma." In Cinéma: theorie, lectures. Comp.
Dominique Noguez. A special issue of Revue d'esthétique, 26, Nos. 2-4
(1973), 311-28.

Concerns the relationship between music and the visual
image.

4786a. Also published as "Music and Cinema." Trans. W. Frawley.

In Film Reader, 3 (Feb. 1978), 136-49.

4787. Moholy-Nagy, László. Vision in Motion. Chicago: Paul Theobald, 1947.

Concerns the work of the Chicago Institute of Design, with just a few comments on sound and music in films in the section "Motion Pictures," pp. 270-91.

4788. Moll, A. Teorii informatsii i esteticheskoe vospriyatie. Moscow, 1966.

4789. Moore, Douglas. "Music and the Movies." Harper's Magazine, 171 (July 1935), 181-88.

References to the music of Georges Auric.

4790. Morton, Lawrence. "Film Music in the Mainstream." Hollywood Quarterly, 3, No. 1 (Fall 1947), 101-04.

In part, a review of Claire Reis's 1947 edition of Composers in America. See #1479.

4790a. Portions are reprinted in Film Music Notes, 7, No. 5 (May-June 1948), 5.

4791. ----------. "Film Music of the Quarter." Hollywood Quarterly, 3, No. 4 (1948-1949), 395-402.

An argument for well-formed film music criticism, with references to music by Friedhofer, Harline, and Copland.

4792. ----------. "Film Music of the Quarter." Hollywood Quarterly, 4, No. 3 (Spring 1950), 289-92.

4793. ----------. Foreword to Clifford McCarty's Film Composers in America: A Checklist of Their Work. Glendale, Calif.: John Valentine, 1953, pp. xi-xvi.

See #6270.

4794. ----------. "On the Hollywood Front." Modern Music, 22, No. 4 (May-June 1945), 274-75.

4795. Müller, Gottfried. Dramaturgie des Theaters und des Films. Mit einem Beitrag von Professor Wolfgang Liebeneiner. Würzburg: K. Triltsch Verlag, 1941.

References to the role of music in film.

Many reprints. The sixth edition, entitled Dramaturgie des Theaters, des Hörspiels und des Films (1954), also includes a bibliography, pp. 233-34.

4796. Müller-Medek, Tilo. "Musik und Geräusch im Hörspiel." In Probleme der Realismustheorie. Berlin: Hauptkommission Musikwissenschaft des Verbandes Deutscher Komponisten und Musikwissenschaftler, 1970, pp. 111-12.

4797. Nelson, Gene. "Values of Film Music." Music Journal, 26, No. 6 (June 1968), 24, 50-51.

4798. Nelson, Robert U. "Film Music: Color or Line?" Hollywood Quarterly, 2, No. 1 (Oct. 1946), 57-65.

Concerns the factor of "emotion" and "intellect" in the perception of film music.

4799. Nesthus, Marie. "The Influence of Olivier Messiaen on the Visual Art of Stan Brakhage in 'Scenes From Under Childhood, Part One.'" Film Culture, Nos. 63-64 (1977), 39-51, 179-80.

4800. Newlin, Dika. "Music for the Flickering Image: American Film Scores." Music Educator's Journal, 64, No. 1 (Sept. 1977), 24-35.

Excerpts from an interview with Earle Hagen, and an article by Tom Shales in The Washington Post.

Also includes bibliography and discography.

4801. Nick, Edmund. "Die Widersacher der Filmmusik." Deutsches Filmschaffen (1943).

4802. Nicoll, Allardyce. _Film and Theatre_. New York: Thomas Y. Crowell, 1936. Reprint, London: Harrup, 1939.

Includes the chapter "The Sound Film," pp. 120-63, and a film bibliography, pp. 195-249.

4803. Obraztsov, Sergeĭ Vladimirovich. "Estafeta iskusstv." _Iskusstvo kino_ (Moscow), No. 6 (June 1975), 78-101.

4804. ----------. "Film und Theater." In _Von der Filmidee zum Drehbuch_. Berlin, 1949.

4805. Odin, Roger. "A Propos d'un couple de concepts 'son in' vs 'son off.'" In _Linguistique et sémiologie, VI_. Lyon: Presses universitaires de Lyon, 1979.

4806. "O roli muzyki w filmie -- mowi Waldemar Kazanecki." _Ruch Muzyczny_ (Warsaw), 17, No. 14 (1973), 18.

4807. Otto, Irmgard. "Tonfilmmusik -- ein Problem?" _Die Musik_ (Berlin), 28 (1935), 111-17.

4808. Palmer, Christopher. "The Problems of Film Music Criticism." _Crescendo International_, 13 (June 1975), 25-26.

4809. Pasolini, Pier Paolo, and Vratislav Dejmek. "Sub specie musicae: poznamky k hudebni dramaturgii -- filmoveho debutu." _Hudební Rozhledy_ (Prague), 23, No. 2 (1970), 84-87.

4810. Paul, William. "Art, Music, Nature, and Walt Disney." _Movie_, 24 (Spring 1977), 44-52.

4811. Pauli, Hansjörg. "Filmmusik." _Schweizerische Musikzeitung_ (_Revue musicale Suisse_), 114, Nos. 5-6 (Sept.-Nov. 1974), 265-70.

4812. Peatman, Mary Madeline. "Sergei Eisenstein's 'Ivan the Terrible' as a Cinematic Realization of the Concept of the Gesamtkunstwerk." Ph.D. Diss. Indiana University 1975.

Abstract: DAI: 36/11:7013A (order #DAH 7611438).

4813. Percheron, Daniel. "Le Son au cinéma dans ses rapports à l'image et à la diégèse." _Ça/Cinéma_, 1, No. 2 (Oct. 1973), 81-86.

4813a. Also published as "Sound in Cinema and Its Relationship to Image and Diegesis." _Yale French Studies_, No. 60 (1980), 16-23.

4814. Petri, Horst. "Probleme der Amalgamierung von Sprache und Musik im Hörspiel." _Akzente_, 16 (1969), 87-95.

4815. Petric, Vlada. "Sight and Sound: Counterpoint or Entity?" _Filmmakers Newsletter_, 6, No. 7 (May 1973), 27-31.

4816. Philippot, Michel J. "Musik und Technik." In _50 Jahre Musik im Hörfunk: Beiträge und Berichte_. Ed. Kurt Blaukopf et al. Vienna: Jugend und Volk, 1973, pp. 28-39.

Translated by Renate Barth-Wehrenalp. See Blaukopf, #207.

4817. Pietrangeli, A. "Asincronismo." _La critica cinematografica_ (Parma), No. 2 (Mar. 6, 1947).

4818. Pitts, Lilla Belle. "Film Music." _Film Music Notes_, 10, No. 5 (May-June 1951), 19.

4819. Piva, Franco. _Musica e cinema: problemi di un rapporto_. Padua: Edizioni Rebellato, 1966.

4820. Pizzetti, Ildebrando. "Musica necessaria." _Bianco e nero_, 10, No. 8 (Aug. 1949).

4821. Popova, Manya. "Filmi, kompozitori, vuzgledi, idei." _Bulgarska Muzika_ (Sofia), 29 (May 1978), 55-57.

4822. Pratley, Gerald. "A Consideration of Film Music Away from the Screen." In The Technique of Film Music by John Huntley and Roger Manvell. Revised and enlarged by Richard Arnell and Peter Day. London: Focal Press, 1975, pp. 287-88.

    See #82.

4823. Previn, Dory. Seminar on film music: AFI/CAFS, January 29, 1975 (3:30 p.m.). Transcript of the seminar is held at the AFI/Louis B. Mayer Library (Los Angeles).

4824. Prieberg, Fred K. Musica ex Machina: über das Verhältnis von Musik und Technik. Berlin: Verlag Ullstein, 1960.

    Includes the chapter "Filmmusik," pp. 234-43, and other related sections, including a discussion of experiments with "animated sound." Also includes a discography, pp. 263-81, and bibliography, pp. 295-98.

  4824a. Also published in Italian translation, Turin: Edizioni G. Einaudi, 1963.

4825. ----------. "Die musikalische Kulisse." In Die drei grossen "F": Film, Funk, Fernsehen. Musik der Zeit, Neue Folge, II. Ed. Heinrich Lindlar and Reinhold Schubert. Bonn: Boosey & Hawkes, 1958.

    See Lindlar, #78.

4826. Prohorov, E. ("Creative Forms of Mass Media.") In Muzy XX veka. Ed. Natal'ya Zorkaya and Jurij Bogomolov. Moscow: Iskusstvo, 1978.

    In Russian. See Zorkaya, #2624.

4827. Prox, Lothar. "Im Stadium der Kindheit: Skizzen zur Filmmusik." Musica, 32, No. 3 (1978), 229-35.

    Includes references to the role of music in both silent and sound films.

4828. Pudovkin, Vsevolod I. "Montage und Ton." Die Quelle, 1, No. 3 (1947), 43-57.

4829. Pulwer, A. "Muzyka -- element dramaturgii." Iskusstvo kino (Moscow), No. 5 (May 1936).

4830. Quantrill, Jay Alan. "How Not to Be a Film Music Critic." Film Music Notebook, 3, No. 3 (1977), 33-42.

    Concerns the work of Page Cook.

4831. ----------. "Why Have Filmmusic at All?" The Thousand Eyes Magazine, 2 (Mar. 1977), 29-30.

4832. Quinto, Lenard. "Some Questions for Music Educators on Film Music." Music Publishers Journal, 3, No. 5 (Sept.-Oct. 1945), 27, 60-63.

4833. Rabenalt, Arthur Maria. Mimus ohne Maske. (Pamphlet.) Berlin: O. Hellwig, 1947.

  4833a. Also appears in a collection of writings by Rabenalt: Vom Sein im Schein: Essays, 1944-1948. Berlin: O. Hellwig, 1950.

4834. Ragghianti, Carlo L. Cinema, arte figurativa. Turin: Edizioni G. Einaudi, 1952.

    Includes the section "Documentari sulle arti figurative," pp. 225-38.

4835. Rehlinger, Bruno. Der Begriff filmisch. Emsdetten: H. und J. Lechte, 1938.

4836. Ringger, Rolf Urs. "Filmmusik sucht sich selbst." Melos, 33, No. 10 (Oct. 1966), 313-19.

4837. Riniéri, Jean-Jacques. "La Réversion du temps filmique." In L'Univers filmique. Bibliothèque d'esthétique. Ed. Etienne Souriau. Paris: Flammarion, 1953, pp. 75-84.

See #4890.

4838. Robbe, Friedrich G. "Die Einheitlichkeit von Bild und Klang im Tonfilm: Untersuchung über das Zusammenwirken der verschiedene Sinnorgane und seine Bedeutung für die tonfilmische Gestaltung." Ph.D. Diss., Hamburg 1940.

    4838a. Published edition, Hamburg: Niemann und Moschinski, 1940.

4839. Roggensack, Delinda. "Teaching Appreciation for Motion Pictures." Film Music, 12, No. 3 (Jan.-Feb. 1953), 23.

4840. Roland-Manuel. "La musique à l'écran ou la complainte des Fualdés." L'Écran français (Paris), 3, No. 36 (Mar. 1946).

4841. ----------. "La Musique prise dans le sujet, élément materiel du film et la musique composée pour le film, élément formel de l'oeuvre d'art." In Atti del secondo congresso internazionale di musica, Firenze-Cremona, 11-26 maggio, 1937. Florence: F. Le Monnier, 1940, pp. 253-55.

    A paper presented at the 1937 Florence Congress. Includes synopses in Italian and German, p. 256. See #1186.

4842. ----------. "Rhythme cinématographique et musical." In Cinéma: Cours et conférences d'l'IDHEC (Paris: L'Institut des hautes études cinématographiques), No. 2 (1945), 3-5.

4843. Ropars-Wuilleumier, Marie-Claire. "The Disembodied Voice ('India Song')." Yale French Studies, No. 60 (1980), 241-68.

4844. Rosati, Giuseppe. "Aspetti della musica nel film." In La musica nel film. Ed. Luigi Chiarini. Rome: Bianco e nero editore, 1950, pp. 39-42.

    A paper presented at the 1950 Venice conference. See Chiarini, #1627.

4845. Rosbaud, Hans. "Problem der Programmgestaltung und der Künstlerischtechnischen Wiedergabe im deutschen Rundfunk." In Atti del primo congresso internazionale di musica, Firenze, 30 aprile - 4 maggio 1933. Florence: F. Le Monnier, 1935, pp. 118-24.

    A paper presented at the 1933 Florence Congress. Includes a synopsis in Italian: "Programmi musicali delle radiotrasmissioni in Germania." See #339.

4846. Rosen, Claude-Emile. "Le Bruit." Revue d'esthétique, 8, No. 2 (1955).

4847. Rosen, Philip. "Adorno and Film Music: Theoretical Notes on 'Composing for the Films.'" Yale French Studies, No. 60 (1980), 157-82.

    See Adorno/Eisler, #4573.

4848. Rösing, Helmut. "Die Bedeutung der Klangfarbe in traditioneller und elektronischer Musik." In Schriften zur Musik, XII. Munich, 1972.

4849. ----------. "Funktion und Bedeutung von Musik in der Werbung." Archiv für Musikwissenschaft, 32, No. 2 (1975), 139-55.

4850. Ross, Theodore J. Film and the Liberal Arts. New York: Holt, Rinehart and Winston, 1970.

    Includes the section "Film and Music," pp. 217-47, an anthology of articles , including essays by Antheil (see #2973), Levant (see #3540), Tiomkin (see #4069), and Page Cook (see #4530).

4851. Rotha, Paul, Sinclair Road, and Richard Griffith. Documentary Film: The Use of the Film Medium to Interpret Creatively and in Social Terms the Life of the People as It Exists in Reality. London: Faber and Faber, 1935. (Many reprints.)

    Third edition, revised and enlarged, London: Faber and Faber, 1952, includes the chapter "Sound: Raw Materials, Creative Uses," pp. 163-74, along with many additional references to the role of music in documentary films.

4852. Rubsamen, Walter H. "Contemporary Music in Films." Arts and Architecture, 62, No. 7 (July 1945), 34, 46.

>The conclusion of a discussion begun in Vol. 62, No. 6 (see #4860).

4852a. Reprinted in Film Music Notes, 5 (May 1946).

4853. ----------. "The Devices of Descriptive Music." Arts and Architecture, 63, No. 1 (Jan. 1946), 10, 19, 22, 51-54.

4854. ----------. "Music as Dramatic Device." Arts and Architecture, 62, No. 10 (Oct. 1945), 46, 52.

>Concerns the Gershwin, Weill, Raksin collaboration for "Where Do We Go From Here?"

4855. ----------. "Music in the Cinema." Arts and Architecture, 61, No. 6 (June 1944), 9, 12.

>Concerns the "appropriate" use of film music, with references to music for documentaries by Gail Kubik.

>The first in a series of monthly articles which continued in A&A for two years.

4856. ----------. "Music in the Cinema." Arts and Architecture, 61, No. 9 (Sept. 1944), 13, 38.

>References to music by Alfred Newman.

4857. ----------. "Music in the Cinema." Arts and Architecture, 61, No. 10 (Oct. 1944), 13, 37.

>Also includes references to recent filmed musicals.

4858. ----------. "Music in the Cinema." Arts and Architecture, 61, No. 12 (Dec. 1944), 15, 40.

>Concerns the subject of humor in music, with more commentary on filmed musicals.

4859. ----------. "Music in the Cinema." Arts and Architecture, 62, No. 4 (Apr. 1945), 17-18.

>Music for documentary films, with references to scores by Gail Kubik and David Buttolph.

4860. ----------. "Music in the Cinema: Contemporary Music in Films." Arts and Architecture, 62, No. 6 (June 1945), 15-16.

>Concerns the use of 20th-century musical techniques, popular idioms, and jazz in film scoring. Part 1. See conclusion in Vol. 62, No. 7 (#4852).

4861. Schaeffer, Pierre. À la recherche d'une musique concrète. Paris: Éditions du Seuil, 1952.

>Includes references to music for film, and film as a vehicle for musical performance.

4862. ----------. "Le Contrepoint du son et de l'image." Cahiers du cinéma, 18, No. 108 (June 1960), 7-22.

4862a. Reprinted in Cahiers d'études de Radio - Télévision, 27-28 (1960), 107-21.

4863. ----------. "L'Élément non-visuel au cinéma. I: Analyse de la bande 'son.'" Revue du cinéma (Paris), New series, 1, No. 1 (Oct. 1946), 45-48.

4864. ----------. "L'Élément non-visuel au cinéma. II: Conception de la musique." Revue du cinéma (Paris), New series, 1, No. 2 (Nov. 1946), 62-65.

4864a. Also published as "Element pozawizualny w filmie." Kwartalnik Filmowy, 11, No. 2 (1961).

4865. ----------. "Les Nouvelles techniques sonores et le cinéma." Cahiers du cinéma, 7, No. 37 (July 1954), 54-56.

Concerns the use of electronic music in films, with
references to experiments in animated sound.

4866. Schall, Edgar. "Filmmusik auf neuen Wegen." Neue Zeitschrift für Musik,
116 (Oct. 1955), 37-38.

4867. ----------. "Probleme der Filmmusik: Das 10. Filmfestival von Cannes."
Schweizerische Musikzeitung, 97 (July 15, 1957), 301-02.

4868. Schepelern, Peter. "Ingmar Bergman og musikken." Kosmorama (Copenhagen),
24, No. 137 (1978), 44-46.

4869. Schering, A. "Symbol in der Musik." Zeitschrift für Ästhetik, 21 (1941).

4870. Schinsky, Karl. "Filmmusik: kritisch betrachtet." Musik und Gesellschaft,
9 (Mar. 1959), 30-38.

4871. Schmalenbach, Werner. "Dialogues et bruitages dans le film." In Cinéma
d'aujourd'hui. Bâle: Les Trois Collines, 1946.

4872. Schmalstieg, Peter. "Filmmusik -- unter semiotischem Aspekt." Ph.D.
Diss. (Musicology), Freiburg.

Work in progress in 1976.

4873. Schmidt, Hans-Christian. "Autonomie und Funktionalität von Musik: Gedanken zu einer ästhetischen Polarisierung und ihrer didaktischen Bedeutung." Revue musicale Suisse / Schweizerische Musikzeitung, 117,
No. 5 (Sept.-Oct. 1977), 267-72.

4874. ----------. "Didaktik der Filmmusik." Musik und Bildung, 12 (Mar. 1980),
158-61.

Includes bibliography.

4875. ----------. "Wesensmerkmale und dramaturgische Funktion der Musik in Roman Polanskis Film 'Rosemaries Baby' (1968)." In Musik in der Massenmedien, Rundfunk und Fernsehen: Perspektiven und Materialien. Ed. Hans-
Christian Schmidt. Mainz: B. Schotts Söhne, 1976, pp. 250-75.

Concerns the work of Krzysytof Komeda.

See Schmidt, #5117.

-- Rev. in Medien und Erziehung (Munich), 22, No. 1
(1978), 63-65.

4876. Schmitt, Rainer. "Musik in der Werbung: Ein Beitrag zu ihrer Didaktik."
Musik und Bildung, 8, No. 6 (1976), 327-31.

4877. Schnebel, Dieter. "Sichtbare Musik." In Musik auf der Flucht vor sich
selbst. Reihe Hanser, XXVIII. Munich: Hanser Verlag, 1969.

4878. Schneider, H. J. "Die Rezeption von Musik im Vergleich von Musik im
filmischen Kontext." Staatsexamensarbeit Siegen (FB 4 Kunst- und Musikpädagogik), 1976.

4879. Schoen, Max. The Understanding of Music. New York and London: Harper and
Bros., 1945.

Aesthetic considerations applied to music in combination
with the other arts, with implications for film music.

4880. Schoenberg, Arnold. "Art and the Moving Picture." California Arts and
Architecture (Apr. 1940), 12ff.

4880a. Reprinted as "Art and the Moving Pictures." In Style and
Idea. Ed. Leonard Stein. New York: St. Martin's Press,
1975, pp. 153-57.

4881. Schröder, Rolf Xago. "Komische Stoffe - komische Wendungen." Filmwissenschaftliche Mitteilungen (1972), 165.

4882. Segond, Joseph. "Rythme inhérent au film." Revue internationale de filmologie (Paris), 1, No. 2 (Sept.-Oct. 1947), 159-60.

4883. Shaindlin, Jack. "Of the Film and Music." Film Music, 13, No. 5 (May-

June 1954), 9-10.

4884. Sharples, Win, Jr. "The Aesthetics of Film Sound: The Importance of Being Audible." Filmmakers Newsletter, 8, No. 5 (Mar. 1975), 27-32.

4885. Shilova, Irina Mikailovna. "Muzyka otkryvaet, vyyasnyaet, razgadyvaet ..." Sovetskaya muzyka, 33, No. 4 (Apr. 1969), 55-58.

4886. Silber, Frederic. "The State of the Art: The Film Soundtrack as Contemporary Music -- Contemporary Music as Film Score." Fanfare, 4, No. 1 (1980), 309-17.

4887. Sokol'sky, Matias. "Im Einklang mit der Musik." Sowjetwissenschaft: Kunst und Literatur (Berlin), 7 (1959), 424-28.

4888. Souriau, Etienne. La correspondance des arts: Éléments de esthétique comparée. Bibliothèque de philosophie scientifique. Paris: Flammarion, 1947.

   Concerns the aesthetics of interacting art forms. Inludes the chapter "Musique et arts plastiques," pp. 187-240, with bibliographic references.

4889. ----------. "Filmologie et esthétique comparée." Revue internationale de filmologie (Paris), 3, No. 10 (Apr.-June 1952), 113-41.

4890. ----------, ed. L'Univers filmique. Bibliothèque d'esthétique. Paris: Flammarion, 1953.

   Includes Souriau's article "Rythme et unanimité: compte rendu d'une expérience," pp. 203-07, together with articles by J. J. Riniéri (see #4837), J. Germain (see #4606), F. Guillot de Rode (see #4630), H. Lemaître (see #4722), and H. Agel (see #4980).

4891. Steen, T. M. F. "The Sound Track." Films in Review, 11, No. 1 (Jan. 1960), 33-34.

   Concerns the role of silence in film scoring.

4892. ----------. "The Sound Track." Films in Review, 11, No. 3 (Mar. 1960), 175-76.

   A discussion of music as "sound" in film.

4893. ----------. "The Sound Track." Films in Review, 11, No. 7 (Aug.-Sept. 1960), 434-36, 440.

4894. ----------. "The Sound Track." Films in Review, 12, No. 4 (Apr. 1961), 243-44.

   Concerns the use of "classical" music in films. Also includes references to a score by Georges Delerue.

4895. ----------. "The Sound Track." Films in Review, 13, No. 5 (May 1962), 303-06.

   Concerns musical "form" as a structural element in film. Includes references to music by Eisler, Auric, and Herrmann.

4896. ----------, and Don Miller. "The Sound Track." Films in Review, 11, No. 10 (Dec. 1960), 623-27.

4897. Stephenson, Ralph, and J. R. Debroix. The Cinema as Art. Harmondsworth, Engl.: Penguin Books, 1965.

   Includes the chapter "The Fifth Dimension: Sound," pp. 174-200.

4898. Stern, Dietrich. "Komponisten gehen zum Film: zum Problem angewandter Musik in den 20er Jahren." In Angewandte Musik der 20er Jahre: exemplarische Versuche gesellschaftsbezogener musikalischer Arbeit fur Theater, Film, Radio, Massenveranstaltung. Argument-Sonderbände, XXVI. Ed. Dietrich Stern. Berlin: Argument-Verlag, 1977, pp. 10-58.

   Includes references to the music of Shostakovich, Satie, Prokofiev, and Milhaud.

-- Rev. in Neue Musikzeitung (Regensburg), 28, No. 6
(1979), 58.

4899. Stolowitsch, L. N. "Die Schönheit als Wert und der Wert der Schönheit."
Deutsche Zeitschrift für Philosophie, No. 12 (1966).

4900. Strobel, Heinrich. "Meinungen deutscher Komponisten zum Thema: Musik und
Film." Melos, 17, No. 6 (June 1950), 163-67.

Includes references to the work of Werner Egk, Wolfgang
Fortner, and Hans Werner Henze.

4901. Stuckenschmidt, Hans Heinz. "Lenkt das Fernsehen von Kunstmusik ab und
zu Unterhaltungsmusik hin?" In Vierzehn Mutmassungen über das Fernseh-
en. Ed. A. R. Katz. Munich, 1963, pp. 83-88.

4902. Sun, R. F. "The Esthetics of Film Music." College Music Symposium (SUNY),
19, No. 1 (1979), 216-20.

4903. Supičič, Ivo. La Musique espressive. Bibliothèque internationale de musicologie. Paris: Presses Universitaires de France, 1957.

4904. Taddei, Nazareno. "Funzione estetica della musica nel film." Bianco e
nero, 10, No. 1 (Jan. 1949), 5-11.

4905. Tagg, Philip. "'Kojak' - 50 Seconds of Television Music: Toward the Analysis of Affect in Popular Music." Ph.D. Diss. (Musicology), Göteborg
1979.

4905a. Published as part of the series Skrifter från Musikveten-
skapliga inst. Goteborg, II. Göteborg, Sweden: Univ.
Musikventenskapliga Institutionen, 1979.

Includes a bibliography, pp. 270-82.

-- Rev. in Svensk Tidskrift foer Musikforskning, 61,
No. 1 (1979), 101-06.

-- Rev. in Studia Musicologica, 24, Nos. 1-2 (1982),
255ff.

4906. Takenaka Tsutomu. Nihon eiga judan, I-III. Tokyo: Shirakawa Shoin, 1974-
1976.

Includes many references to the use of music in Japanese
film.

4907. Tannenberg, G. "Beziehungen zwischen Filmmusik und Musik im Hörspiel."
Die Musik (Berlin), 29 (1937), 275-78.

4908. Tardos, Béla. "Gondolatok egy filmzenei vita után." Uj zenei szemle, 6,
No. 4 (1955), 28-31.

4909. Tariverdiev, Mikael. "Kompozitor rabotaet v kino." Sovetskaya muzyka, 27,
No. 1 (Jan. 1963), 14-16.

4910. ----------. "Muzika kao komponenta filma." Zvuk, No. 71 (1967), 37-38.

4911. Tasalov, Vladimir Il'ich. Estetika teknitsizma: kriticheskii ocherk. Moscow: Iskusstvo, 1960.

4912. Tempo, Claudio. "Appunti di un discorso sulla musica per film." Teatro
e cinema (Genoa), No. 1 (Jan.-Mar. 1967).

4913. Thiel, Wolfgang. "Ästhetische und historiographische Beiträge zur Geschichte und Theorie der Film- und dramatischen Fernsehmusik." Ph.D.
Diss. (Musicology), Berlin (DDR) 1975.

4914. ----------. "Bausteine zu einer Ästhetik der Dokumentarfilmmusik." In
Dokument und Kunst: Vietnam bei H. & S. -- eine Werkstatt. Arbeitshefte
Akademie der Künste der DDR, XXVII. Berlin: Akademie der Künste der DDR,
1977, pp. 52-57.

Concerning Vietnam documentaries, 1966-1976, from the
Heynowski and Scheumann Studios. Includes references to
the theories of Siegfried Kracauer, and composers Hanns
Eisler, Reiner Bredemeyer, Paul Dessau, S. Ortega, and
Benjamin Britten.

4915. ----------. "Beiträge zu einer Ästhetik und Geschichte der Fernsehfilm-musik." In Sammelbände zur Musikgeschichte der DDR, IV. Berlin: Neue Musik, 1975, pp. 134-69.

Includes bibliographic references.

4916. ----------. "Die dramaturgische Funktion der Musik in DDR-Fernsehfilmen." Musik und Gesellschaft, 22, No. 4 (Apr. 1972), 205-13.

4917. ----------. "Gedanken und Gespräch über filmmusikalische Gestaltung." Musik und Gesellschaft, 30, No. 10 (Oct. 1980), 584-89.

4918. ----------. "Probleme der Fernsehfilmmusik." Beiträge zur Musikwissen-schaft, 15, No. 3 (1973), 173-78.

4919. ----------. "Wie hört man Musik im Film?" Musik und Gesellschaft, 24, No. 4 (Apr. 1974), 193-98.

4920. ----------. "Zur dramaturgischen Funktion der Musik in Fernsehfilmen der DDR." Musik und Gesellschaft, 22, No. 4 (Apr. 1972), 205-13.

4921. Thomas, Tony. "Music and the Film -- The Odd Coupling, Part 1." The Max Steiner Music Society News Letter, No. 31 (Summer 1972), 4.

4922. Thompson, Kristin. "Early Sound Counterpoint." Yale French Studies, No. 60 (1980), 115-40.

4923. Tommasini, Vincenzo. "Aspetti della musica nel film." In La musica nel film. Ed. Luigi Chiarini. Rome: Bianco e nero editore, 1950, p. 43.

A paper presented at the 1950 Venice conference. See Chiarini, #1627.

4924. Tondorf, Franz-Josef. "Über die begleitende Verwendung von Musik in tech-nischen Medien." Zeitschrift für Musikpädagogik, 3, No. 6 (1978), 13-26.

Includes a summary in English.

4925. Trantow, Herbert. "Film-Musik: Über die Möglichkeiten des Musikeinsatzes im Film." Der Musik-Student, 4 (1952), 67-69.

4926. Troitskaya, Galina. "Muzykal'no-szeničeskij obraz na ekrane." Sovetskaya muzyka, 18, No. 11 (Nov. 1954), 83-89.

4927. ----------. "Musik als Gestaltungsmittel im Fernsehen." Trans. Rahel Strassberg. Musik und Gesellschaft, 12, No. 2 (Feb. 1962), 88-89.

Originally appeared in Sovetskaya muzyka.

4928. ----------. "Zarubezhnoe kino i klassicheskaya muzyka." Sovetskaya mu-zyka, 24, No. 2 (Feb. 1960), 121-24.

4929. Turim, Maureen. "Symmetry/Asymmetry and Visual Fascination." Wide Angle (Athens, Ohio), 4, No. 3 (1981), 38-47.

4930. Turkin, V. A. Dramaturgiya kino: Otscherki po teorii i praktike kino-szenariya. Moscow, 1938. (Reprint, 1945.)

4931. Über die Musik im Film: Vier Aufsätze Sowjetischer Autoren. Beiträge zu Fragen der Filmkunst, II. 2nd revised edition. Ed. Tamara Krause. Ber-lin: Henschelverlag, 1954.

Includes essays by Isaak Dunayevsky, Aram Khatchaturian, and Dimitri Shostakovich.

4932. Ulner, Martin. Zukunftsfragen der Filmtontechnik. Berlin: Detmold, 1951.

4933. Ushihara Kyohiko. Kyohiko eigafu gojunen. Tokyo: Kyoho Shobō, 1968.

Includes references to music in Kyohiko's films.

4934. Ussher, Bruno David. "Some Functions and Problems of Film Music." In Proceedings for 1942. Series 37. Pittsburgh: Music Teacher's National Association, 1943, pp. 162-81.

Part of the "Report of the Committee on Functional Music"

by Warren D. Allen, prepared for the M.T.N.A.

4935. Valéry, Paul. "Cinématographe." In Intelligence du cinématographe. Comp. Marcel L"Herbier. Paris: Éditions Corrêa, 1946, pp. 35-36.

See #4729.

4936. Vanslov, Viktor Vladimirovich. Ob otrazheni deĭstvitel'nosti v muzyke: ocherki. Moscow: Gos. muz. izd-vo, 1953.

4937. Varese, Edgard. "Organized Sound Film." Commonweal, 33 (Dec. 13, 1940), 204-05.

4938. Vartanov, Anri Surenovich. ("Methodology in the Art-Historical Study of Mass Media.") In Muzy XX veka. Ed. Natal'ya Zorkaya and Jurij Bogomolov. Moscow: Iskusstvo, 1978.

In Russian. See Zorkaya #2624.

4939. Vecchiali, Paul. "Musica: oggetto o soggetto?" Filmcritica (Rome), 30, Nos. 296-297 (Aug. 1979), 245-46.

In Italian and French.

4940. Venžer, N. ("The Communicative Possibilities of Animated Cartoons.") In Muzy XX veka. Ed. Natal'ya Zorkaya and Jurij Bogomolov. Moscow: Iskusstvo, 1978.

In Russian. See Zorkaya #2624.

4941. Verdone, Mario. "Forme pure del fonofilm." La critica cinematografica (Parma), No. 7 (1947).

4942. ----------. "Lubitsch ou l'idéal de l'homme moyen." Revue du cinéma (Paris), New series, 2, No. 17 (1948).

4943. ----------. "Per la storia dei rapporti tra musica e cinema e per la storia dell' 'avanguardia' nel film." Bianco e nero, 28, Nos. 3-4 (Mar.-Apr. 1967), p. 89.

See #2116.

4944. ----------. "Problemi estetici della musica per film." Bianco e nero, 28, Nos. 3-4 (Mar.-Apr. 1967), 104-08.

See #2116.

4945. Veretti, Antonio. "Aspetti della musica nel film." In La musica nel film. Ed. Luigi Chiarini. Rome: Bianco e nero editore, 1950, pp. 44-48.

A paper presented at the 1950 Venice conference. See Chiarini, #1627.

4946. ----------. "Varie forme di musica nel film." In Atti del secondo congresso internazionale di musica, Firenze-Cremona, 11-26 maggio, 1937. Florence: F. Le Monnier, 1940, pp. 228-31.

A paper presented at the 1937 Florence Congress, with synopses in French and German, pp. 231-32. See #1186.

4947. Vidor, King. King Vidor on Film Making. New York: David McKay, 1972.

Includes Chapter 9: "Film Music," pp. 139-45.

4948. Vietta, Egon. "'Was lebenswahr ist, bestimmt die jeweilige Epoche?' Der Verismus einst auf der Bühne - heute im Film." Das Musikleben, 8 (Feb. 1955), 47-49.

4949. Vladimirov, L. "Muzyka i dramaturgiya chudoshestvennogo filma." Iskusstvo kino (Moscow), No. 3 (Mar. 1952), 81-86.

4950. Vlasov, Vladimir A. "Khoroshim fil'mam: khoroshuyu muzyku." Sovetskaya muzyka, 27, No. 1 (Jan. 1963), 7-9.

4951. Wanderscheck, Hermann. "Eigengesetzlichkeit der Filmmusik." Das Musikleben, 3 (1950), 244-51.

4952. Wangermée, Robert. "Über Wesen und Formen des Musikhörens." In 50 Jahre

Musik im Hörfunk: Beiträge und Berichte. Ed. Kurt Blaukopf et al. Vienna: Jugend und Volk, 1973, pp. 19-27.

> See Blaukopf, #207.

4953. Watts, Stephen. "Alfred Hitchcock on Music in Film." Cinema Quarterly (Edinburgh), 2, No. 2 (Winter 1933-1934), 80-83.

> An interview.

4954. Weill, Kurt. "Music in the Movies." Harper's Bazaar (Sept. 1946), 257, 398-400.

4954a. Reprint in The Movies as Medium. Ed. Louis Jacobs. New York: Farrar, Straus, and Giroux, 1970.

> See #4653.

4955. Well, Bernhard. "Funktion und Metafunktion von Musik im Fernseh-Serien-film, dargestellt au 'Der Fall von nebenan' ARD. Eine Modell-Analyse." In Musik in den Massenmedien, Rundfunk und Fernsehen: Perspektiven und Materialien. Ed. Hans-Christian Schmidt. Mainz: B. Schotts Söhne, 1976, pp. 276-95.

> See Schmidt, #5117.

4956. Werzlau, Joachim. "Probleme der Filmmusik." Musik und Gesellschaft, 3 (1953), 213-15.

4957. Whitaker, Rod. The Language of Film. Englewood Cliffs, N.J.: Prentice-Hall, 1970.

> Includes the chapter "The Audio Content," pp. 99-112.

4958. ----------. "The Role of Movie Music." Music Journal Annual (1966), 68ff.

4960. Wiese, Epi (Ellen P.) "The Shape of Music in 'The Rules of the Game.'" Quarterly Review of Film Studies, 7, No. 3 (Summer 1982), 199-209.

> Concerns the "musical structure" of the film.

4960. Williams, Martin T. "The Audible Image." Films in Review, 5, No. 7 (Aug.-Sept. 1954), 371-73.

> Concerns the use of "sound similes" which mimic the "action" of films.

4961. Winckel, Fritz Wilhelm. Klangstruktur der Musik. Berlin-Borsigwalde: Verlag fur Radio-Foto-Kinotechnik, 1955.

> Includes references to the use of music in film and experiments in the concept of "animated sound."

4962. Winter, Klas. "Film ist Musik: über die Bedeutung der Filmmusik." Film und Ton, 26 (Nov. 1980), 24-31.

> Includes discography.

4963. ----------. "Filmmusik -- Musik zum Weghören?" Film und Ton, 25 (Mar. 1979), 11-16.

4964. ----------. "Der Soundtrack macht den Film Komplett." Film und Ton, 25 (Aug. 1979), 30-35.

4965. Wissum, K. "Film og musik: Nogle tanker om filmmusikkens psykologi og oestetik·(Part 5)." Dansk Musiktidsskrift (Copenhagen), 24, No. 5 (1949), 110-13.

4966. Wolkow-Lanit, L. "Kinomuzyka i jejo teoretiki." Iskusstvo kino (Moscow), No. 8 (Aug. 1939).

4967. Wonde, Jürgen. "Die Platte als Drehbuch (12. Schallplattenfilm -- Wett-bewerb)." Film und Ton, 25 (June 1979), 32-33.

4968. "The World and the Theater: Research in Sound Reproduction." Theater Arts (March 1930), 185-89.

> Concerns the theories of V. I. Pudovkin on silent and sound film, with quotes from his writings.

4969. Worringer, Wilhelm. _Abstraction and Empathy: A Contribution to the Psychology of Style_. New York: International Universities Press, 1967.

>Includes references to experiments with "animated sound."

4970. Wüsthoff, Klaus. _Die Rolle der Musik in der Film- und Fernsehwerbung_. Berlin (BRD): Merseburger Verlag, 1978.

>-- Rev. in _Gottesdienst und Kirchenmusik_, No. 5 (Sept.-Oct. 1978), 190.

4971. Yakubov, Manashir Ya, Galina Troitskaya, Tomas I. Korganov, M. Ziv, and I. Jakušenko. "Muzykal'nyi fil'm i ego problemy." _Sovetskaya muzyka_, 32, No. 9 (Sept. 1968), 54-61.

>A discussion of music in films and filmed musicals.

4972. Youngblood, Gene. _Expanded Cinema_. With an Introduction by R. Buckminster Fuller. New York: E. P. Dutton, 1970.

>Includes the sections "The Audience and the Myth of Entertainment," pp. 45-74, and "Computer Films," pp. 207-39, a discussion of the work of James and John Whitney. Also includes a bibliography, pp. 421-25.

4973. _Zagadnienia estetyki filmowej_. Warsaw, 1955.

>A collection of articles by B. Lewicki (see #4726), S. Lenartowicz (see #4723), R. Dreyer (see #4548), and others.

4974. Zahorska, Stefania. "Zagadnienia formalne filmu." _Przegląd Filozoficzny_ (Warsaw), (1928).

4975. Zakošanskaya, L., and I. Straženkova. "Kogda vidno litso avtora ..." _Sovetskaya muzyka_, 32, No. 4 (Apr. 1968), 26-30.

>Concerns music by Boris A. Tchaikovsky for the film "Aibolit - 66."

4976. Zawadzki, B. "Przegląd krytyczny wazniejszych teorii komizmu." _Przegląd Filozoficzny_ (Warsaw), 1 and 2 (1929).

4977. Zecchi, Adone. "Note sul sonoro nel film." _Bianco e nero_, 12, No. 5 (May 1951), 23-27.

4978. ----------. "Particolare rilievo della musica in alcuni film." In _La musica nel film_. Ed. Luigi Chiarini. Rome: Bianco e nero editore, 1950, pp. 49-55.

>A paper presented at the 1950 Venice conference. See Chiarini, #1627.

4979. Zuckerkandl, Victor. _Sound and Symbol: Music and the External World_. Princeton, N.J.: Princeton University Press, 1969.

SEE ALSO:

#4(Arnshtam), #9(Bazelon), #19(Cockshott), #20(Comuzio), #35(Frid), #39 (Grigoriu), #40(Grützner), #46, 47(Helman), #49(Hoérée), #52(Huntley), #59(Irving/Keller/Mellers), #60(Joffe), #65(Korganov/Frolov), #69(Kuna), #71(la Motte-Haber/Emons), #77(Lindgren), #79(London), #93(Palmer/Gillett), #96, 98(Pauli), #101(Pilka), #104(Prendergast), #110(Sabaneev), #111(H.-C. Schmidt), #126(Thiel), #166(Joffe), #189, #210(Bujacz), #222 (Cook), #235(Fano), #259(Kułakowska), #281(Porfirio), #283(Ranade), #292 (Sineux), #302(Thiel), #304(Troitskaya), #1219(Carbonara), #1228(Cavalcanti), #1248(Culshaw), #1384, 1385, 1386(Lissa), #1399(Manvell), #1516 (Stravinsky), #1517(Stravinsky/Dahl), #1559(K. Cameron), #1581(Bowman), #1611(Blasetti/Serandrei/Luciani), #1676(Fulchignoni), #1754(Keller), #1895(Spottiswoode), #1925(Weinert), #2054(Fischer), #2069(Helman), #2085 (Kraft), #2087(Kuna), #2093(MacCann), #2180(J. Thiel), #2223(Rhotert), #2358(DePrez), #2489(Maurelli), #2536(Roberts/Sharples), #2587(Thiel), #2673(Gräter), #2687, 2688(H.-C. Schmidt), #2703(Thiel), #2762, 2768 (Cook), #2945(Alwyn), #2971(Antheil), #3001(Auric), #3011(Hendricks), #3020(Branscombe), #3026, 3027(Baudrier), #3050(E. Bernstein), #3150

(Copland), #3215, 3216, 3219, 3220, 3222(Eisler), #3227(Grützner), #3237 (Lück), #3240, 3241(Mayer), #3251(Siegmund-Schultze), #3286(Sternfeld), #3365(R. S. Brown), #3414(Steen), #3416(F. Steiner), #3446(Ibert), #3462 (Gorbman), #3466(Jaubert), #3563, 3564, 3565(Masetti), #3593(Milhaud), #3619(Nascimbene), #3622(Neef), #3695(Bowes), #3701(Eisenstein), #3775 (Rosenman), #3791(Gorbman), #3793(Miceli), #3813(Caps), #3908(Gallez), #3929(Shostakovich), #3958(Gorbman), #4008(F. Steiner), #4020(Stothart), #4059(Palmer), #4073(Tiomkin), #4102, 4103(Vlad), #4168, 4172, 4173, 4175, 4176, 4180(Whitney), #4186(Wiener), #5031(H.-C. Schmidt), #5046(Berten), #5323(Bornoff), #5343(Lissa), #5384(Cobb), #5437, 5438(Palmer), #5519 (Cantrick), #5549, 5551(Koster), #5563, #5816(H.-C. Schmidt), #5891(Altman), #5926(Charness), #6050(Lissa), #6101(Scheurer), and #6154(Witte).

Psychology and Perception : The Aural/Visual Experience

4980. Agel, Henri. "Activité ou passivité du spectateur." In L'Univers filmique. Bibliothèque d'esthétique. Ed. Etienne Souriau. Paris: Flammarion, 1953, pp. 47-58.

See #4890.

4981. Arnheim, Rudolf. Art and Visual Perception: A Psychology of the Creative Eye. Berkeley and Los Angeles: University of California Press; and London: Cambridge University Press, 1954.

4982. ----------. Radio: An Art of Sound. Trans. Margaret Ludwig and Herbert Read. New York: Da Capo Press, 1972.

Reprint of the original 1936 edition, with a new preface by Arnheim.

4983. Bekesy, G. von. "Über die Entstehung der Enfernungsempfindung beim Hören." Akustische Zeitschrift, 3 (1938), 21ff.

4984. Besseler, Heinrich. Das musikalische Hören der Neuzeit. Berlin: Akademie der Wissenschaften zu Leipzig-Verlag, 1959.

4985. Blaustein, L. "Przyczynki do psychologii widza kinowego." Kwartalnik Psychologiczny, 4 (1933).

4986. Brillouin, Jacques. "Éléments psycho-physiologiques du problème de la musique à l'écran." In Atti del secondo congresso internazionale di musica, Firenze-Cremona, 11-26 maggio, 1937. Florence: F. Le Monnier, 1940, pp. 219-26.

A paper presented at the 1937 Florence Congress, with synopses in Italian and German, pp. 226-27. See #1186.

4987. ----------. "Quelques remarques." In Le Film sonore: l'écran et la musique en 1935, a special issue of La Revue musicale, 15, No. 151 (Dec. 1934), pp. 355-60.

4988. Cantril, Hadley, and Gordon W. Allport. The Psychology of Radio. New York: Harper, 1935.

Includes a discussion of music in radio and radio-music, pp. 217-20.

4989. Cohen-Séat, Gilbert. Problèmes du cinéma et de l'information visuelle. Paris: Presses Universitaires de France, 1961.

Observations on the perception of film, by the Director of the Institut de Filmologie de l'Universite de Paris. Includes implications for the study of film music.

4990. Dauriac, Lionel. "Des Images suggérées par l'audition musicale." Revue philosophique de la France et de l'etranger (Paris), 54, No. 2 (July-Dec. 1902), 488-503.

4991. Eberhard, Fritz. "Warum Hörerforschung? und wie?" In Publizistik: Festschrift für Emil Dovifat. Ed. Günter Kieslich and Walter J. Schütz. Bremen: B. C. Heye, 1960, pp. 32-40.

4992. Edmonds, Robert. The Sights and Sounds of Cinema and Television: How the Aesthetic Experience Influences Our Feelings. With a Foreword by Alberto Cavalcanti. New York: Teachers College Press, 1982.

Includes Chapter 15: "The Characteristics of Music," pp. 125-29, and Chapter 17: "The Mutual Modification of Elements," pp. 135-44.

4993. English, Horace B. "'Fantasia' and the Psychology of Music." Journal of Aesthetics and Art Criticism, 2, No. 7 (Winter 1942-1943), 27-31.

4994. Fulchignoni, Enrico. "Filmologie et psychologie enfantine." Revue du cinéma (Paris), New series, 4 (1949).

4995. Gallez, Douglas W. "The Effect Upon Cognitive Learning of Background Music in Instructional Films." Ph.D. Diss. University of California, Berkeley 1975.

Abstract: DAI 37/01:101A (order # DA 7615187).

4996. Garroni, Emilio. "Linguaggio verbale e componenti non-verbali nel messaggio filmico-televisivo." Filmcritica, 28, Nos. 279-280 (Dec. 1977), 143-58.

4997. Gerrero, Richard Henry. "Music as a Film Variable." Ph.D. Diss. Michigan State University 1969.

Abstract: DAI 30/06:2555A (order # DA 6920859).

-- Rev. by Thomas S. Brown in Council for Research in Music Education Bulletin, No. 25 (Summer 1971), 49-52.

4998. Griffin, Thomas Solomon. "An Experimental Study of the Effectiveness of Functional Music in Instructional Television." Ph.D. Diss. New York University 1968.

Abstract: DAI 29:3169A (order # DA 693174).

4999. Hanslick, Eduard. "The Effects of Music." In Aesthetics and the Arts. Ed. Lee A. Jacobus. New York: McGraw-Hill, 1968, p. 170.

An important view of the question of musical perception, with implications for the study of film music.

5000. Heinlein, C. P. "The Affective Character of Music." Proceedings of the Music Teachers National Association, 33 (1939), 218-26.

With implications for the study of film music.

5001. Hevner, Kate. "The Affective Character of the Major and Minor Modes in Music." American Journal of Psychology, 47, No. 1 (Jan. 1935), 103-18.

With implications for the study of film music.

5002. ----------. "The Affective Value of Pitch and Tempo in Music." American Journal of Psychology, 49, No. 4 (Oct. 1937), 621-30.

With implications for the study of film music.

5003. ----------. "Experimental Studies in the Elements of Expression in Music." American Journal of Psychology, 48, No. 2 (Apr. 1936), 246-68.

With implications for the study of film music.

5004. ----------. "Expression in Music: A Discussion of Experimental Studies and Theories." Psychological Review, 42, No. 2 (Mar. 1935), 186-204.

With implications for the study of film music.

5005. Huber, Kurt. Der Ausdruck musikalischer Elementarmotive: eine experimentalpsychologische Untersuchung. Leipzig: J. A. Barth, 1923.

5006. Husson, Raoul. "Le Conditionnement psychophysiologique de l'esthétique musicale." La Revue musicale, Numero special, No. 236 (1957), 94-102.

5007. Karwoski, Theodore F., and Henry S. Odbert. "Color Music." Psychological Monographs, 50, No. 2 (Whole Number 222), (1938), 60pp.

   With implications for the study of film music.

5008. ----------, Henry S. Odbert, and C. E. Osgood. "Studies in Synesthetic Thinking: II. The Role of Form in Visual Responses to Music." Journal of General Psychology, 26 (Apr. 1942), 199-222.

5009. Kofin, Ewa. "Muzyka telewizyjna: percepcja." Ruch Muzyczny (Warsaw), 23, No. 19 (1979), 15-16.

5010. Kötter, E. Der Einfluss übertragungstechnischer Faktoren auf das Musikhören. Veröffentlichung des Staatlichen Instituts für Musikforschung, III. Cologne: Staatlichen Instituts für Musikforschung, 1968.

5011. Kurth, Ernst. Musikpsychologie. Berlin: M. Hesse Verlag, 1931.

   With implications for the study of film music.

5012. La Motte-Haber Helga de. "'Erkennen Sie die Melodie?': Gedanken zur gewaltsamen Zerstörung von Kunstwerken." Musik und Bildung, 5, No. 4 (Apr. 1973), 178-81.

5013. ----------. "Wirkungen der Filmmusik auf den Zuschauer." Musica, 34, No. 1 (1980), 12-17.

5014. Licart, A. Théâtre et cinéma: Psychologie du spectateur. Brussels, 1937.

5015. Lissa, Zofia. "O ewolucji percepcji muzycznej." Ruch Muzyczny (Warsaw), New series, 3, No. 12 (June 1959), 7-12; and 3, No. 13 (July 1959), 8-12.

   5015a. Reprinted as "O historycznej zmienności percepcji muzycznej," in Przegląd Humanistyczny, No. 4 (1959), 43-56.

   5015b. Also published in Japanese translation in Ongaku Gaku (Tokyo), No. 12 (1961), 28-42.

   5015c. Also published as "Zur historischen Veränderlichkeit der musikalischen Apperzeption." In Festschrift für Heinrich Besseler. Leipzig, 1961, pp. 475-88.

   5015d. Also published as "On the Evolution of Musical Perception," in Journal of Aesthetics and Art Criticism, No. 2 (1965), 273-86.

5016. ----------. "O roli ciszy i pauzy w muzyce." Muzyka, No. 4 (1960), 12-42.

   Includes references to the role of music in film.

   5016a. Reprinted as "Estetycznych funkcjach ciszy i pauzy w muzyce," in Estetyka (Warsaw), 2 (1961), 77-102.

   5016b. Also published as "Die ästhetische Funktionen der Stille und Pause in der Musik." In Studien zur Musikwissenschaft, XXV: Festschrift für Erich Schenk. Graz, 1962, pp. 315-46.

   5016c. Also published as "Aesthetic Functions of Silence and Rests in Music," in Journal of Aesthetics and Art Criticism, No. 4 (1964), 443-54.

5017. ----------. "O słuchaniu i rozumieniu utworów muzycznych: Z zagadnień psychologii muzyki." Wiedza i Życie (Warsaw), No. 6 (1937), 383-95.

   5017a. Reprinted in Ruch Muzyczny (Warsaw), Nos. 19-20 (1947), 2-6; and No. 21 (1947), 6-10.

   5017b. Reprinted in the collection Jak słuchać muzyki by S. Szuman and Zofia Lissa. Warsaw, 1948, pp. 71-134.

        -- Rev. by Józef M. Chomiñsky in Kwartalnik Muzyczny, No. 24 (1948), 176-80.

5018. ----------. "Psychologiczne podstawy muzyki filmowej." Lwowskie Wiadomości Muzyczne i Literackie, No. 78 (1933).

5019. ----------. "Znaczenie kojarzeú w percepcji dzieł muzycznych." Studia i Materiały do dyskusji (Warsaw), No. 17 (1954).

5020. Malraux, André. Esquisse d'une psychologie du cinéma. Paris: Éditions Gallimard, 1946.

5021. Meyerhoff, Horst. Tonfilm und Wirklichkeit: Grundlagen zur Psychologie des Films. Berlin: B. Henschel, 1949.

Includes a bibliography, p. 96.

5022. Michel, Paul. Probleme der Realismustheorie. Berlin: Hauptkommission Musikwissenschaft des Verbandes Deutscher Komponisten und Musikwissenschaftler, 1970.

Includes the chapter "Komponist und Hörer," p. 127ff.

5023. Odbert, Henry S., Theodore F. Karwoski, and A. B. Eckerson. "Studies in Synesthetic Thinking: I. Musical and Verbal Associations of Color and Mood." Journal of General Psychology, 26 (Jan. 1942), 153-73.

Also see #5008.

5024. Pech, K. "Hören im 'optischen Zeitalter.'" Musik und Gesellschaft, 19, No. 5 (May 1969).

5025. Ribot, Théodule Armand. Problèmes de psychologie affective. Paris: Félix Alcan, 1910.

With implications for the study of film music.

5025a. Also published as Podstawowe zagadnienia psychologii uezué. Lwow, 1912.

5026. Rigg, Melvin G. "The Effect of Register and Tonality Upon Musical Mood." Journal of Musicology, 2, No. 2 (Sept. 1940), 49-61.

With implications for the study of film music.

5027. ----------. "Speed as a Determiner of Musical Mood." Journal of Experimental Psychology, 27, No. 5 (Nov. 1940), 566-71.

With implications for the study of film music.

5028. Rink, Otho P. "An Investigation into the Effects of Background Music in a Dramatic Television Presentation on University Students' Perception and Retention of Cognitive Content." Ed.D. Diss. East Texas State University 1974.

Abstract: DAI 35:4139A (order #DA 75-1601).

5029. Roemer, Michael. "The Surfaces of Reality." In Aesthetics and the Arts. Ed. Lee A. Jacobus. New York: McGraw-Hill, 1968, p. 297.

With implications for the study of film music.

5030. Schaeffer, Pierre. "L'Élément non-visuel au cinéma, III: Psychologie du rapport vision-audition." Revue du cinéma (Paris), New series, 1, No. 3 (Dec. 1946), 51-54.

5031. Schmidt, Hans-Christian. "Musik als Einflussgrösse bei der filmischen Wahrnehmung." In Musik in den Massenmedien, Rundfunk und Fernsehen: Perspektiven und Materialien. Ed. Hans-Christian Schmidt. Mainz: B. Schotts Söhne, 1976, pp. 126-69.

Concerns the impact of music in documentary films.

See Schmidt, #5117.

-- Rev. in Medien und Erziehung (Munich), 22, No. 1 (1978), 63-65.

5032. Schoen, Max. The Psychology of Music: A Survey for Teacher and Musician. New York: The Ronald Press Co., 1940.

With implications for the study of film music. Includes a selective bibliography, pp. 241-51.

5033. Schwartz, Stanley. "Film Music and Attitude Change: A Study to Determine the Effect of Manipulating a Musical Soundtrack upon Changes in Attitude toward Militarism-Pacifism Held by Tenth Grade Social Studies Students." Ph.D. Diss. Syracuse University 1970.

Abstract: DAI 31/11:5677A (order #DA 7110977).

5034. Simkins, John D., and Jack A. Smith. "Effects of Music on Source Evalua-
tions." Journal of Broadcasting, 18, No. 3 (Summer 1974), 361-67.

Concerns the influence of music in advertising.

5035. Tannenbaum, P. H. "Music Background in the Judgement of Stage and Television Drama." Audio-Visual Communication Review (Washington, D.C.),
4 (1956), 92ff.

5036. Tieplow, B. Psychologia zdolności muzycznych. Warsaw: Nasza Księgarnia,
1952.

Translated from the Russian.

5037. Valentini, Ernesto. "Perspectives psychologiques en filmologie." Revue
internationale de filmologie, 7, No. 25 (Jan.-Mar. 1956), 3-18.

5038. Wallon, Henri. "L'Acte perceptif et le cinéma." Revue internationale de
filmologie (Paris), 4, No. 13 (Apr.-June 1953), 97-110.

5039. Washburn, Margaret F., and G. L. Dickinson. "The Sources and the Nature
of the Affective Reaction to Instrumental Music." In The Effects of
Music. Ed. Max Schoen. New York: Harcourt Brace, 1927.

With implications for the study of music in silent and
sound films.

5040. Wellek, Albert. "Der Raum in der Musik." Archiv für die gesamte Psychologie (Leipzig), 91, Nos. 3-4 (Aug. 1934), 395-443.

With implications for the study of film music.

5041. Willems, Edgar. Le Rythme musical: étude psychologique. Paris: Presses
Universitaires de France, 1954.

With implications for the study of film music. Includes
bibliographic references.

5042. Williams, Michael. "Demoralizing Use of Musical Backgrounds with News-
reels of the War." Commonweal, 35 (Mar. 6, 1942), 485-86.

5043. Wintle, Regie Rae. "Emotional Impact of Music on Television Commercials."
Ph.D. Diss. University of Nebraska 1978.

Abstract: DAI 39/08:5115A (order #DA 7901953).

-- Rev. by E. Ostleitner in Council for Research in
Music Education Bulletin, No. 74 (Spring 1983),
88-90.

SEE ALSO:

#44(Hagen), #454(Bingham), #1141(Cass), #2217(Jungheinrich), #2679
(Meissner), #2687(H.-C. Schmidt), #4424(Arnheim), #4499(Chateau), #4670
(Kaziów), #4714(La Motte-Haber), #4725(Lewicki), #4740(Lissa), #4785
(Mitry), #4838(Robbe), #4919(Thiel), #4965(Wissum), #4969(Worringer),
#4970(Wüsthoff), and #5045(Benjamin).

Sociology and Culture : The Impact of Industry and Art

5044. Bahadur, Satish. The Context of Indian Film Culture. Study Material Series, II. Poona: National Film Archive of India, 1978.

5045. Benjamin, Walter. "L'Oeuvre d'art à l'époque de sa reproduction mécani-
sée." Zeitschrift für Sozialforschung, 5, No. 1 (1936), 40ff.

Concerns the perception of film and film music, and the
political ramifications of the new art.

5045a. Also published as "Das Kunstwerk im Zeitalter seiner Technischen Reproduzierbarkeit." In Schriften, I. Ed. T. W.

Adorno. Frankfurt am Main: Suhrkamp Verlag, 1955, pp. 366-405.

5045b. Also published in Illuminationen: ausgewählte Schriften. Ed Siegfried Unseld. Frankfurt am Main: Suhrkamp, 1961, pp. 148-84. (Reprint, 1963.)

5045c. Also published in Lesezeichen. Leipzig: Reclams Universal-Bibliothek, 1970.

5045d. Also published as "The Work of Art in the Age of Mechanical Reproduction." In Illuminations. Edited, and with an Introduction by Hannah Arendt. Trans. Harry Zohn. New York: Harcourt, Brace, World, 1968.

5046. Berten, Walter Michael. Musik und Mikrophon: zur Soziologie und Dramaturgie der Musikweitergabe durch Rundfunk, Tonfilm, Schallplatte und Fernsehen. Dusseldorf: Schwann, 1951.

Includes the chapters "Neuer Musikgebrauch," pp. 17-44, and "Musik im Gesamtkunstwerk Tonfilm," pp. 137-97.

-- Rev. in Musica, 6 (Apr. 1952), 174-75.

-- Rev. in Zeitschrift für Musikwissenschaft, 113 (Feb. 1952), 102.

5047. Bischoff, F. "Fernsehen als kulturelle Aufgabe." Melos, 22 (July-Aug. 1955), 195-96.

5048. Blacher, Boris. "Musik im technischen Zeitalter." Beiträge zur Musikwissenschaft 1968/69 (1969), 67-71.

5049. Boatwright, Howard. Indian Classical Music and the Western Listener. Bombay: Bharatiya Vidya Bhavan, 1960.

Includes references to the role of film music in Indian culture.

5050. Boisdeffre, Pierre de. "Rôle de la Radio comme promoteur d'une culture vivante." In Un siècle de radio et de télévision. Ed. Pierre Descaves and and A. V. J. Martin. Paris: O.R.T.F., 1965, pp. 279-81.

See Descaves, #149.

5051. Bornoff, Jack, in collaboration with Lionel Salter. Music and the Twentieth Century Media. International Music Council Publications in Music and Communication, III. Florence: Leo S. Olschki, 1972.

Many references to film music, including the sections "Music in Television Programmes," pp. 111-30, "From Opera to Music Theatre on Stage, Film and Television," pp. 131-62, and a bibliography, pp. 213-16.

Also published in a French language edition: La Musique et les moyens techniques, du vingtième siècle. Florence: Leo S. Olschki, 1972.

-- Rev. in Variety, 269 (Nov. 15, 1972), 64.

-- Rev. in the Australian Journal of Music Education, No. 13 (Oct. 1973), 55.

-- Rev. in Revue Musicale de Suisse Romande, 26, No. 1 (1973), 3.

-- Rev. in Neue Zeitschrift für Musik, 134, No. 11 (Nov. 1973), 752.

-- Rev. in The World of Music (UNESCO), 15, No. 1 (1973), 72-81.

5052. Breckoff, Werner. "Soziologisch-historische Anmerkungen zur Pop-Musik." Medien und Erziehung, 24, No. 5 (1980), 258-67.

5053. Brock, Hella, Bernhardt Günther, Horst Langer, and Heinz Quitzsch. "Zu einigen Fragen der Wechselbeziehung der Künste." Wissenschaftliche Zeitung der Ernst - Moritz - Arndt - U. Griefswald, 21, No. 2 (1972), 103-13.

Concerns the role of "multimedia" in the "developing socialist society."

5054. Brudny, Wolfgang. "Musik im Jugendfilm." Musik im Unterricht, 49 (1958), 288-90.

5055. Carrera, Alessandro. "Musica e pubblico giovanile: La creativitá ambigua." Cineforum, No. 164 (Apr. 1977), 259-66.

5056. ----------. "Musica e pubblico giovanile: L'evoluzione del Gusto (dai Beatles a Braxton)." Cineforum, No. 165-166 (May-June 1977), 342-47.

5057. ----------. "Musica e pubblico giovanile." Cineforum, No. 166 (July-Aug. 1977), 409-19.

5058. ----------. "Musica e pubblico giovanile (dai Beatles a Braxton), 5: il jazz italiano." Cineforum, No. 177 (Sept. 1978), 495-507.

5059. ----------. "Musica e pubblico giovanile: L'evoluzione del Gusto -- L'accostamento al Jazz." Cineforum, No. 170 (Dec. 1977), 747-59.

5060. ----------. "Musica e pubblico giovanile: L'evoluzione del Gusto, 4: ascesa e caduta dei grandi raduni (dai Beatles a Braxton)." Cineforum, No. 172 (Mar. 1978), 97-107.

5061. ----------. "La politica della sinistra in campo musicale." Cineforum, No. 162 (Feb. 1977), 86-105.

5062. Collaer, Paul. "La culture musicale par la radiophonie." In Atti del secondo congresso internazionale di musica, Firenze-Cremona, 11-26 maggio, 1937. Florence: F. Le Monnier, 1940, pp. 145-54.

    A paper presented at the 1937 Florence Conference, with synopses in Italian and German, pp. 154-55. See #1186.

5063. Coppola, Carlo. "Politics, Social Criticism and Indian Film Songs: The Case of Sahir Ludhianvi." Journal of Popular Culture, 10, No. 4 (1977), 897-902.

5064. Coppola, Piero. "La funzione educatrice del disco." In Atti del secondo congresso internazionale di musica, Firenze-Cremona, 11-26 maggio, 1937. Florence: F. Le Monnier, 1940, pp. 166-70.

    A paper presented at the 1937 Florence Congress, with synopses in French and German, p. 171. See #1186.

5065. de Saxe, Rudy. "Studio and Symphony Players." Music Publishers Journal, 3, No. 5 (Sept.-Oct. 1945), 40, 69.

5066. Dunajewski, Isaak. "Musik der Massen." In Über die Musik im Film: Beiträge zu Fragen der Filmkunst, II. Berlin.

5067. Erdmann, Hans. "Politik, Kunst, Bühne, Film, Musik." Filmtechnik (1927), 358.

5068. Ermash, Filipp T., et al. "O povyshenii roli kino v kommunisticheskom vospitanli trudiashchikhsia v svete Postanovleniia Ts K KPSS 'O dal'neishem uluchshenii ideologicheskoi politiko-vospitatel' noi raboty.'" Iskusstvo kino, No. 8 (Aug. 1980), 4-50.

    Includes references to the music of E. N. Ptichkin.

5069. Fabian, Imre. "Der Film, ein Mittel zur Demokratisierung der Oper." Opernwelt, 19, No. 8 (1978), 16.

5070. Farnsworth, Paul R. The Social Psychology of Music. New York: Holt, Rinehart and Winston, 1958.

    Second edition, Ames, Iowa: The Iowa State University Press, 1969.

    With implications for the study of film music.

5071. Fassett, J. H. "What Radio is Doing for Serious American Music." In Proceedings for 1939. Series 34. Pittsburgh, 1940.

5072. Faulkner, Robert Roy. "Dilemmas in Commercial Work: Hollywood Film Composers and Their Clients." Urban Life, 5 (Apr. 1976), 3-32.

5073. ----------. Music on Demand: Composers and Careers in the Hollywood Film

Industry. New Observations Series. New Brunswick, N.J.: Transaction Books, 1983.

> An important sociological study. Includes a foreword by Fred Steiner, pp. 1-8.

5074. ----------. "Studio Musicians: Their Work and Career Contingencies in the Hollywood Film Industry." Ph.D. Diss. (Sociology), U.C.L.A. 1968.

> Abstract: DAI 1968:2809A (order #DA 69-1108).

5074a. Published as Hollywood Studio Musicians: Their Work and Careers in the Recording Industry. Chicago: Aldine - Atherton, 1971.

> -- Rev. in Ethno, 14 (1970), 173.

> -- Rev. in American Record Guide (Washington, D.C.), 37 (May 1971), 647-48.

> -- Rev. in Music Journal, 29, No. 10 (Oct. 1971), 8.

5075. Feather, Leonard. "Black Blues in Studios." Down Beat, 34 (Feb. 9, 1967), 13.

> Concerns racial discrimination in the recording studio. Also see responses to this article by F. Kofsky (#2081) and B. Shank (#5121).

5076. Feldmann, Erich. Theorie der Massenmedien: Presse, Film, Funk, Fernsehen. Munich and Basel: E. Reinhardt, 1962.

> Includes the chapter "Film- und Fernsehforschung im System der Wissenschaften," p. 126ff.

5077. Franchère, Lucille C. "The Rebirth of Music." Catholic World, 174 (Oct. 1951), 36-39.

> Concerns the impact of the introduction of Vitaphone.

5078. Gillett, John, and Roger Manvell. Music and Social Change. New York: Praeger, 1973.

5079. Goldsmith, Alfred N., and Austin C. Lescarboura. This Thing Called Broadcasting. New York: Holt, 1930.

> Includes the chapter "Creating a Musical Consciousness," pp. 185-93.

5080. Goslich, Siegfried. "Rundfunk und Musikerziehung." Rundfunk und Fernsehen, 8 (1960), 241-46.

5081. Helm, Everett Burton. Composer, Performer, Public: A Study in Communication. International Music Council Publications in Music and Communication, I. Florence: Leo S. Olschki, 1970.

> Concerns the role of the composer in contemporary media. Includes bibliography, pp. 207-09.

> Also published in a French language edition: Le Compositeur, l'interprète, le public: Une étude d'intercommunication. Florence: Leo S. Olschki, 1970.

5082. Helman, Alicja. "Związki kultury muzycznej i filmowej." Kwartalnik Filmowy, 14, Nos. 1-2 (1964), 72-84.

5083. Internationales Musikzentrum, Vienna. IMZ Report: 6. Internationaler Kongress des IMZ (Zagreb, May 10-13, 1967) -- Die Schallplatte in der Musikkultur der Gegenwart. Vienna: IMZ, 1967.

> A collection of articles concerning the dissemination of music through the phonographic medium, with implications for the study of film music.

> See an article by V. Seljan, #5119.

> In German, English, and French.

5084. International Music Council. The Composer of Today and the Public. Rotterdam: IMC, 1966.

> A collection of papers presented at the IMC Congress in

Rotterdam, June, 1966.

5085. ----------. The Music Critic and the Mass Media. Florence: IMC, 1969.

5086. ----------. The Promotion of Classical and Contemporary Music in the Modern World. Cannes: IMC, 1970.

In English, German, and French.

5087. ----------, and the Internationales Musikzentrum, Vienna. IMZ Report: Coexistence or Integration -- A Musical Alternative. Stuttgart: IMC/IMZ, 1966.

A collection of papers presented at the IMC Congress in Stuttgart, October, 1966. In English, French, and German.

5088. ----------, and the Internationales Musikzentrum, Vienna. IMZ Report: The Technical Media and the Presentation of Music to the General Public. Rome: IMC/IMZ, 1962.

In English, French, and German.

5089. ----------, the International Library Association, and the U.S. National Commission for UNESCO. Music and Communication. New York: IMC, 1968.

Proceedings of the Congress held in New York and Washington, D.C., September 6-15, 1968. Includes an introduction by Oliver Daniel, and a summation by Everett Helm.

5090. Jenke, Manfred. "Hörfunk heute und sein Auftrag kunstlerische Substanz zu erhalten." In Tonmeistertagung (10.) 19.-22. November 1975, Köln: Bericht. Cologne: Welzel und Hardt, 1976.

See #2654.

5091. Joshi, G. N. "The Phonograph Comes to India." Cinema Vision India, 1, No. 4 (Oct. 1980), 40-50.

See #61.

5092. Kabalevskij, Dmitrij. "Technical Media for Mass Dissemination of Music and the Musical Culture of Our Time." International Music Educator (Oldenburg, Ger.), No. 18 (Oct. 1968), 609-18.

5093. Karaev, Kara. ("Musical Culture and Television.") In Muzyka i televidenie, I. Ed. Galina Troitskaya. Moscow: Sovetskij Kompozitor, 1978.

In Russian. See Troitskaya, #5834.

5094. Kaufmann, Nicholas. Filmtechnik und Kultur. Wege der Technik. Stuttgart: J. G. Cotta'sche Buchhandlung Nachfolger, 1931.

Concerns the role of film in education.

5095. Kind, S. Mikrophon, Orchester, Hörer. Zurich, 1946-1947.

5096. Klausmeier, Friedrich. Jugend und Musik im technischen Zeitalter: eine repräsentative Befragung in einer westdeutschen Grossstadt. Bonn: H. Bouvier, 1968.

A treatise on the sociological effects, with implications for music and education, and music in the media. Includes a bibliography, pp. 300-08.

5097. Koch, Ludwig. "Schallplattenmusik." In Atti del primo congresso internazionale di musica, Firenze, 30 aprile - 4 maggio 1933. Florence: F. Le Monnier, 1935, pp. 109-17.

A paper presented at the 1933 Florence Congress, with a synopsis in Italian: "Musica per dischi." See #339.

5098. Lissa, Zofia. "Radio we współczesnej kulturze muzycznej: Psychologiczne, artystyczne, społeczne i pedagogiczne problematy radia." Kwartalnik Muzyczny, No. 16 (1932), 643-59.

5098a. Also published as "Radio a nauczanie muzyki," in Muzyka w szkole, No. 2 (1932), 29-33.

5099. ----------. "Społeczna rola radia w kulturze muzycznej." Przegląd Społeczny, No. 6 (1934), 130-35.

5100. Mager, Jörg. Eine neue Epoche der Musik durch Radio. Berlin: Selbstverlag des verfassers, 1924.

5101. Maletzke, Gerhard. Psychologie der Massenkommunikation: Theorie und Systematik. Hans Bredow-Institut für Rundfunk und Fernsehen an der Universität Hamburg. Hamburg: Verlag Hans Bredow-Institut, 1963.

Includes bibliography, pp. 255-94.

5102. Manvell, Roger. The Effects of the Cinema on Adult and Juvenile. London: Film Pican Books, 1946.

5103. Mayer, Günter. "Massenkommunikation und sozialistische Kunstprogrammatik: zur Medienkonzeption Hanns Eislers." Musik und Gesellschaft, 25, No. 11 (Nov. 1975), 662-68.

5104. McLaughlin, Robert Guy. "Broadway and Hollywood: A History of Economic Interaction." Ph.D. Diss. University of Wisconsin 1970.

5105. Melichar, Alois. Die unteilbare Musik: Betrachtungen zur Problematik des modernen Musiklebens. Vienna: J. Weinberger, 1952.

Includes the chapter "Musik und Film."

5106. Mittenzwei, Werner. Wechselwirkung technischer und kultureller Revolution. Berlin, 1966.

Includes the chapter "Die Entwicklung neuer Kunstmittel in der technischen Revolution," p. 323ff.

5107. Mooser, R.-Aloys. "La Radio et son influence sur le goût musical." In Atti del secondo congresso internazionale di musica, Firenze-Cremona, 11-26 maggio, 1937. Florence: F. Le Monnier, 1940, pp. 129-33.

A paper presented at the 1937 Florence Congress, with synopses in Italian and German, pp. 133-34. See #1186.

5108. Music and Media: Report of the Canadian Music Council. Toronto: CMC, 1967.

5109. Ottenbacher, Albert. "Massenkultur ist nicht geschichtlos: Bemerkungen zur Historie von Pop-Musik." Medien und Erziehung, 25, No. 1 (1981), 29-38.

5110. Reich, Willi. "Il gusto musicale nella luce della statistica." In Atti del secondo congresso internazionale di musica, Firenze-Cremona, 11-26 maggio, 1937. Florence: F. Le Monnier, 1940, pp. 113-16.

A paper presented at the 1937 Congress, with synopses in French and German, p. 117. See #1186.

5111. Reinecke, Hans Peter. "Massenmedien und Musikkultur." Musik und Bildung, 4, No. 6 (June 1972).

5112. Reinold, H. "Musik im Rundfunk." Kölner Zeitschrift für Soziologie und Sozialpsychologie, 7 (1955).

5113. Rosbaud, Hans. "Der Rundfunk als Erziehungsmittel für das Publikum." In Atti del secondo congresso internazionale di musica, Firenze-Cremona, 11-26 maggio, 1937. Florence: F. Le Monnier, 1940, pp. 135-43.

A paper presented at the 1937 Florence Congress, with synopses in Italian and French, pp. 143-44. See #1186.

5114. Sarris, Andrew. "The Cultural Guilt of Music Movies." Film Comment, 13, No. 5 (Sept.-Oct. 1977), 39-41.

Concerns Al Jolson, "The Jazz Singer," and similar feature films.

5115. Schaffner, André. "Le disque: sa portée, ses defaillances, ses conséquences." In Atti del secondo congresso internazionale di musica, Firenze-Cremona, 11-26 maggio, 1937. Florence: F. Le Monnier, 1940, pp. 156-64.

A paper presented at the 1937 Florence Congress, with

synopses in Italian and German, pp. 164-65. See #1186.

5116. Schmidt, Hans-Christian. "Erziehung zum Musikhören: Fernsehen." Musik und Bildung, 8, No. 1 (Jan. 1976), 24-32.

5117. ----------, ed. Musik in den Massenmedien, Rundfunk und Fernsehen: Perspektiven und Materialien. Mainz: B. Schotts Söhne, 1976.

> A collection of articles, includes contributions by J. Augustin and R. Sailer (see #5719), L. Gerhartz (see #2635), H. Kühn (see #4700), H. Pauli (see #97), P. Rocholl (see #5808), H.-C. Schmidt (see #2687, #4875, #5031), and B. Well (see #4955). Also includes bibliography, pp. 319-36.
>
> -- Rev. by Rainer Wagner in Musica, 32, No. 1 (Jan. 1978), 65-66.
>
> -- Rev. in Das Musikhandel (Bonn), 29, No. 6 (1978), 314.

5118. Schopen, Edmund. Das Kulturproblem des Films. Munich, 1929.

5119. Seljan, Vladimir. "Record, Radio and Television." In IMZ Report: Die Schallplatte in der Musikkultur der Gegenwart. Vienna: Internationales Musikzentrum, 1967, pp. 99-100.

> In English, French, and German. See #5083.

5120. Semaines Musicales de Paris. Les nouvelles structures musicales constituent-elles un phénomène social? Paris, 1962.

> A collection of papers presented at the Colloque International pour une sociologie de la musique in Paris, November, 1962.

5121. Shank, Bud. "A Reply to Leonard Feather." Down Beat, 34 (Mar. 23, 1967), 6ff.

> A response to Feather's article, see #5075.

5122. Silbermann, Alphons. La Musique, la radio et l'auditeur. Paris, 1954.

5122a. Also published as Musik, Rundfunk und Hörer. Cologne and Opladen, 1958.

5123. ----------. "Unter soziologischem Aspekt." Musik der Zeit, No. 2 (1958).

5124. Sittner, Hans. "The Importance of Technical Media for the Dissemination of the Music of the World." International Music Educator (Oldenburg, Ger.), No. 17 (Mar. 1968), 582-89.

> In English, French, and German.

5125. Smith, Warren Storey. "Music for the Moving Pictures: A New Art and a New Profession." Musician (Boston), 25 (Mar. 1920), 12.

> Concerns the effect of film music on the public's "musical taste."

5126. Der sowjetische Film: eine Vortragsreihe. Trans. Erich Salewski. Berlin: Dietz Verlag, 1953. (Reprint, 1974.)

> A collection of lectures on the theory and function of film in Russian society, presented at the State Institute for Cinematography in Moscow, 1950. Includes references to the work of V. I. Pudovkin and others.

5127. Spaeth, Sigmund. "Film Music and the Public." Music Publisher's Journal, 3, No. 5 (Sept.-Oct. 1945), 10, 58-59.

5128. ----------. "Music and the Movies: Its Growth and a Prophecy." Arts and Decoration, 13 (May 25, 1920), 36, 64.

> Concerns the role of the cinema in developing the musical tastes of America.

5129. ----------. "Winning Friends for Opera." Opera News, 30 (Dec. 11, 1965), 8-11.

5130. Sternberg, Samuel P. "The Circadian and Monthly Biological Rhythms as Models for the State of Health and Sickness." Ph.D. Diss. Baintridge Forest School (Haywards Heath, Sussex), 1977.

With a "suggestion for their application and maintenance through filmmusic."

5131. Supičič, Ivo. Musique et société: perspectives pour une Sociologie de la musique. Zagreb, 1971.

5132. Thiel, Wolfgang. "Bemerkungen zum Einsatz und zur dramaturgischen Funktion von Arbeiter- und Massenliedern im Spielfilm." In Arbeiterklasse und Musik: Internationale Tagung der Akademie der Künste der DDR, Wissenschaftliche Abteilung. Musik, Arbeiterliedarchiv, 4.-6. Dezember 1974, Teil 2. Arbeitshefte/Akademie der Kunste der DDR, XXII. Ed. Charlotte Albrecht, Inge Lammel, Ilse Schütt, and Marlene Weller. Berlin: Henschelverlag, 1977, pp. 136-39.

5133. Der Tonfilm: eine Gefahr für den Musikerberuf und für die Musikkultur. Umschlagtext: Aufklarungs- und Werbeschriften des Deutsches Musikverbandes. (Pamphlet.) Berlin: Deutscher Musikverband, 1930.

5134. Troitskaya, Galina. "A People's War, a Sacred War, Is Going On." Soviet Film (Moscow), No. 216(No. 5), (May 1975), 43.

5135. United Nations Educational, Scientific, and Cultural Organization. The Composer in the Technological Era. Stockholm: UNESCO, 1970.

5136. Vogel, Amos. Film as a Subversive Art. New York: Random House, 1974.

Includes references to music in films.

5137. Votterle, K. "Soziale Umschichtung und die Funktion der Musik." Hausmusik, 15 (Nov.-Dec. 1951), 153-56.

5138. Vuillermoz, Émile. "La Musique mécanique et la culture musicale." In Atti del primo congresso internazionale di musica, Firenze, 30 aprile - 4 maggio 1933. Florence: F. Le Monnier, 1935, pp. 93-104.

A paper presented at the 1933 Florence Congress, with a synopsis in Italian: "La musica meccanica e la cultura musicale." See #339.

5139. Wangermée, Robert. "La vulgarisation de la musique par la radio." Cahier d'études de Radiodiffusion - Télévision (Paris), Nos. 3-4 (n.d.), 538.

5140. Weaver, S. L. "Enlightenment Through Exposure is NBC Technique." Musical America, 76 (Feb. 15, 1956), 25.

5141. Westphal, K. "Wird klassische Musik durch ihre Aufführung in Café und Kino entweiht?" Allgemeine Musikzeitung, 53 (1926), 885-86.

5142. Weyer, Reinhold. "Musikunterich und Film: Kritische Anmerkungen zu einem vernachlässigten Thema." Musik und Bildung, 9 (Dec. 1977), 681-85.

5143. Zorkaya, Natal'ya. ("The Origin of the 'So-Called' Technical Arts.") In Muzy XX veka. Ed. Natal'ya Zorkaya and Jurij Bogomolov. Moscow: Iskusstvo, 1978.

In Russian. See #2624.

SEE ALSO:

#1(Acosta), #27(Comuzio), #81(Manvell), #91(Paiva), #112(Scholes), #133 (Tinhorão), #149(Descaves/Martin), #150, #159(Gregor), #160(Griffith/Mayer), #173(Leyda), #178(Mussulman), #203(Baxter), #207(Blaukopf), #244 (Goslich), #247(Heilbut), #264(Mapp), #273(Narducy), #287(Salter), #298 (Stelzer), #299(Still), #301(Taylor), #313(Westphal), #327, #348(Baldwin), #388(Berg), #427, 432, 440, 444(Beynon), #454(Bingham), #459(Blum), #461(Boblitz), #491, #518(Dykema), #558(Fleischer), #611(Hatschek), #616 (Hildebrandt), #674(Kühn), #688(Lenvoc), #715(Maine), #735(Mermey), #746 (Mooser), #783(Panovsky), #821(Rogers), #918(Sinn), #1030, #1150, 1152 (Gomery), #1191(Baxter), #1200(Bondeville), #1251(Daugherty), #1273(Finston), #1299(Hartwell), #1334(Inglis), #1347(Jay), #1445, #1498(Schoenberg), #1547(Wall), #1802(Lissa), #1949, #2085(Kraft), #2220(Müller-Me-

dek), #2222(Novick), #2223(Rhotert), #2264(Broughton), #2438, #2602
(Weissman), #2619(Young/Young), #2624(Zorkaya/Bogomolov), #2679(Meissner),
#2703(Thiel), #2875(Rogge), #2972(Antheil), #3090(Blitzstein), #3206
(Betz), #3209(Boehmer), #3216, 3220, 3221, 3223(Eisler), #3224(Engel-
hardt), #3227(Grützner), #3234(Lammel), #3240(Mayer), #3249(Schebera),
#3762(Riesenfeld), #3887(Rozsa), #3927(Shostakovich), #4009(Stevens),
#4023(Giannaris), #4026(Theodorakis), #4166(Whitney), #4296(Beynon),
#4350, #4414(Adorno), #4431(Bächlin), #4452, 4454(Bazin), #4573(Eisler/
Adorno), #4617(Gmelin), #4640(Hengst), #4643(Húbaček), #4649(IMZ), #4738,
4741, 4748(Lissa), #4824(Prieberg), #4898(Stern), #4901(Stuckenschmidt),
#4913(Thiel), #4938(Vartanov), #4972(Youngblood), #5042(M. Williams),
#5181(Best/Russell), #5205(Biondo), #5321(Boll), #5322, 5323(Bornoff),
#5343(Lissa), #5363, 5364(UNESCO), #5452(Veillon), #5512, #5526, 5527
(Fickler), #5569(Mokry), #5597, 5598(Taubman), #5607(Adler), #5612,
#5616, 5617(Bornoff), #5630, 5631(Fickler), #5662(Kuusisto), #5670(Pauli),
#5684(Salter), #5688(Schaefer), #5702(UNESCO), #5712(Adler), #5715(Ander-
son), #5739(Coolidge), #5751, #5760(Gräter), #5769(Kirchberg), #5778
(Kozhukharov), #5796(Muggler), #5807(Rich), #5827(J. Thiel), #5834(Troitskaya), #5837(Veri/Jamanis), #5850(Ely), #5875(Reinecke), #5876(Rockwell),
#5877(Röhrig), #5910(Bowles), #5964-5967(Feuer), #5990(Gutowski), #6014,
#6032(Kothes), #6051(Lughi), #6056, #6128-6130(Telotte), #6154(Witte),
#6304, and #6326.

IV. SPECIAL TOPICS

Musical Performance on Film

Silent and Early Sound Era

5144. Andreevsky, Alexander von. "Was soll der Opernfilm?" Weser Zeitung (Bre-
    men), (May 15, 1930).

5145. Bierstadt, E. H. "Opera in Moving Pictures." Opera Magazine (Oct. 1915).

5146. "'Elektra' on the Screen." The Moving Picture World (Apr. 23, 1910), 634.

5147. "Filmoper und Musik." Umschau (Frankfurt am Main), (1921), 173.

5148. Franke, C. W. "Verfilmte Musik." Reichsfilmblatt, No. 19 (1923), 11.

5149. Gueule, P. "Zur Frage des Opernfilms und der Filmoper." Bühnentechnische
    Rundschau, No. 3 (1930), 17.

5150. Heinsheimer, Hans W. "Film Opera -- Screen vs. Stage." Modern Music, 8,
    No. 3 (Mar.-Apr. 1931), 10-14.

5151. Hofmannsthal, Hugo von, and Richard Strauss. "Der Rosenkavalier": Fassung-
    en -- Filmszenarium -- Briefe. Edited, and with an Introduction by Willi
    Schuh. Frankfurt am Main: S. Fischer, 1971.

        Includes sketches, the scenario, program book, and pic-
        tures of the silent film version which premiered in 1926.

        -- Rev. in Das Orchester (Hamburg), 20 (Mar. 1972), 157-
           58.

        -- Rev. in Your Musical Cue (Bloomington, Ind.), 1, No. 1
           (1973), 51-52.

-- Rev. by Barbara Peterson in Notes, 29, No. 3 (Mar. 1973), 461-63.

5152. Holl, K. "Opernfilm oder Filmoper." Deutsche Allgemeine Zeitung (Dec. 7, 1930).

5153. ----------. "Opernfilm und Filmoper." Neue Züricher Zeitung (Dec. 11, 1930).

5154. Hörth, Fr. L. "Oper und Film." Deutsche Tonkünstlerzeitung, 27 (1929), 513.

5155. ----------. "Oper und Film." Hallesche Nachrichten (May 29, 1929).

5156. Kulakowski, L. "Opera i svukovoye kino." Sovetskaya muzyka, 1, No. 4 (Apr. 1933).

5157. "Lohengrin im Film." Der Kunstwart, 29 (Feb. 1916), 155.

5158. Mascagni, Pietro. "Tonfilm und Oper." Chemnitzer Tageblatt und Anzeiger (Sept. 15, 1929).

5159. ----------. "Tonfilm und Oper." Schwäbischer Merkur (Strassburg), (Sept. 14, 1929).

5160. Rachmann, S. "Auf dem Wege zur Filmoper." Berliner Tageblatt (Oct. 3, 1925).

5161. Roth, --. "Filmmusik und Konzertmusik." Die Musik, 21 (1929), 750.

5162. Rotha, Paul. Celluloid: The Film To-Day. London and New York: Longmans, Green, 1933.

     Includes an extensive analysis of the film production of Weill's "Die Dreigroschenoper," pp. 105-19.

5163. Scheufele, Theodor. "From a Comedy for Music to a Novel in Pictures: Hofmannsthal's Media Consciousness in the Film Adaptation of 'Der Rosenkavalier.'" 1978 Film Studies Annual. West Lafayette, Ind.: Purdue University, 1979, pp. 21-29.

     Also includes references to Weill's "Three Penny Opera."

5164. Schmitz, P. A. "Filmoper und sprechender Film." Der Gral, 21 (1927), 521-23.

5165. Servaes, F. "Der Tonfilm und die Opernbühnen im Reich." Mecklenburgische Zeitung (Schwerin), (May 10, 1930).

5166. Sinn, Clarence E. "Music and the Picture." The Moving Picture World, 7 (Dec. 31, 1910), 1518-19.

     Concerns Pathé's music for Verdi's "Il Trovatore."

5167. ----------. "Music for the Picture." The Moving Picture World, 9 (July 22, 1911), 116.

     Concerns music for "Il Trovatore" (1910), "Faust" (1910), and "Dante's Inferno" (1911).

5168. "Tonfilm als Opernersatz." Thüringische Allgemeine Zeitung (Erfurt), (May 10, 1930).

5169. "Tonfilm, Opernfilm, Filmoper." Frankfurter Zeitung (May 23, 1930).

5170. "'Trovatore' Begins Lyric Reform." The Moving Picture World, 8 (Mar. 4, 1911), 474.

5171. Urgiss, Julius. "Die deutsche Lichtspieloper." Der Kinematograph (Berlin), No. 474 (1916).

5172. Vertun, H. "Der Tonfilm und die Opernbühnen." Hallesche Nachrichten (May 12, 1929).

5173. Wallerstein, L. "Zum Problem der Opernverfilmung." Neue freie Presse (Vienna), (May 17, 1930).

5174. "Was soll der Opernfilm?" Magdeburger General-Anzeiger (May 15, 1930).

5175. Weill, Kurt. Article in Die Musik, 21 (Mar. 1929), 420ff.

5176. Withrington, L. "Correspondence: 'Der Rosenkavalier.'" Gramophone (Gt. Brit.), 47 (Oct. 1969), 689.
       Concerns Strauss' participation in the 1926 film production.

5177. Witt, Bertha. "Die Kinooper." Neue Zeitschrift für Musik, 85, Nos. 46-47 (Nov. 21, 1918), 296-97.

5178. Wolff, H. "Probleme des Operntonfilms." Hamburger Fremdenblatt (July 3, 1930).

SEE ALSO:

#204(Beckley), #234(Ehrenstein/Reed), #251(Jenkinson/Warner), #255(Kennington), #373(Berg), #442(Beynon), #474(Buchanan), #496(B. Cook), #518 (Dykema), #703(London), #774(Orme), #946(Sinn), #1005(Stokowski), #1040 (Van Vechten), #4399(Sinn), #4545(Döhring), #5894(Bardèche/Brasillach), #6085(Parker), #6117(Sonnenschein), and #6122(Steinke).

1935-1949

5179. Adorno, Theodor W. "The Radio Symphony: An Experiment in Theory." In Radio Research, 1941. Ed. Paul F. Lazarsfeld and Frank N. Stanton. New York: Duell, Sloan, and Pearce, 1941, pp. 110-39.

5180. Berchtold, William E. "Grand Opera Goes Hollywood." North American Review, 239, No. 2 (Feb. 1935), 138-46.

5181. Best, Katherine, and Frederick Russell. "Opera: Pro bono publico." Stage, 12 (May 1935), 11-12.

5182. Brecht, Bertolt. "Dreigroschenprozess." In Schriften zur Literatur und Kunst, I. Ed. Werner Hecht. Frankfurt am Main: Suhrkamp Verlag, 1967. pp. 185ff.

5183. Danilova, Alexandra. "Classical Ballet and the Cinema." Sight and Sound, 4, No. 15 (Autumn 1935), 107-08.
       Concerns the filming of the Russian Ballet.

5184. "'Die Dreigroschenoper' von Kurt Weill als Farbfilm." Melos, 30, No. 4 (Apr. 1963), 128-29.
       A photographic study.

5185. Erskine, John. "On Turning an Opera into a Film." The New York Times (Feb. 4, 1940), Section 9, p. 7.

5186. Fisher, T. "Opera into Film." Musical Times, 90 (June 1949), 204-06.

5187. Hamilton, Marie L. "16 mm. Films." Film Music Notes, 8, No. 3 (Jan.-Feb. 1949), 22-23.

5188. Jurenev, Rostislav. "Tri filma o P. Tschaikovskom." Iskusstvo kino (Moscow), No. 6 (June 1940).

5189. Keller, Hans. "Revolution or Retrogression?" Sight and Sound, 16 (Summer 1947), 63-64.

5190. Kiepura, Jan. "L'opera lirica sullo schermo." Cinema (Rome), No. 33 (1937).

5191. Lehar, Franz. "L'operetta cinematografica." Cinema (Rome), No. 23 (1937).

5192. London, Kurt. "'L'Arlésienne': ein Tonfilm mit Musik von Bizet." Melos, 11, No. 2 (Feb. 1932), 53-54.

5193. Luciani, Sebastiano A. "L'opera in film." Bianco e nero, 2, No. 4 (Apr. 1938).

5194. Pandolfi, Vito. "Wedekind, Berg e Pabst: Tre 'Lulu.'" Cinema (Milan), New series, No. 26 (1949).

5195. Rubsamen, Walter H. "Music in the Cinema." Arts and Architecture, 61, No. 7 (July 1944), 16.

> Includes references to the music of Ernst Toch.

5196. ----------. "Music in the Cinema: Ballet, Folk Dance, and Pantomime." Arts and Architecture, 62, No. 1 (Jan. 1945), 24, 48.

5197. Schott, M. "Film und Oper." Musica Aeterna (Zurich), (1948).

5198. Spaeth, Sigmund. "Grand Opera on the Screen." Film Music Notes, 8, No. 1 (Sept.-Oct. 1948), 17.

5199. Vesselo, Arthur. "L'opera filmata." Cinema (Rome), No. 21 (1937).

SEE ALSO:

#687(Leigh), #1194(Berman), #1199(Black), #1259(Doniol-Walcroze/Bourgeois), #1336(Iros), #1389(London), #1452(Myers), #1491(Rubsamen), #1514, 1515(Stokowski), #4039(Thomson), #4436(Balázs), #4538(Debenedetti), #4993 (English), #5894(Bardèche/Brasillach), #5926(Charness), #5986(Green), #6016(Janowski), #6029(Knight), #6074(Mueller), #6117(Sonnenschein), #6122(Steinke), and #6308(Comuzio).

1950's

5200. Alpert, H. "Strictly for the Art Houses." Saturday Review, 34 (Apr. 28, 1951), 27-28.

> Concerns the filmed version of "The Tales of Hoffmann."

5201. Apostolov, P. "Fil'm-opera 'Evgeniy Onegin.'" Sovetskaya muzyka, 23, No. 6 (June 1959), 124-27.

> Concerns the filmed version of Tchaikovsky's opera.

5202. Arundell, D. "The Salzburg Conference in Radio, Television and Films." Opera (London), 7 (Nov. 1956), 670-75.

5203. Berner, Alfred, and Gertrud Pliquett. "Zwei Betrachtungen anlässlich eines Konzertfilms." Musikblätter, 2 (1950), 31-36.

> Concerns the film "Concert Magic."

5204. Berthelot, R. "Reflexions sur les films musicaux." La Vie musicale, 1 (June 1951), 9.

5205. Biondo, Charles Anthony. "Stream-Lined Music Education." Film Music, 12, No. 2 (Nov.-Dec. 1952), 22-23.

5206. Boll, André. "Oper in Funk, Fernsehen und Film." Antares (Baden-Baden), 4, No. 8 (1956), 34-36.

5207. Bollert, W. "Bemerkungen zu einem Musikfilm." Musica, 8 (May 1954), 211-12.

> Concerns the film "Horch auf die Musik."

5208. "Boris Godunoff im Film." Neue Zeitschrift für Musik, 119 (Sept. 1958), 534.

5209. Bornoff, Jack. "The Salzburg Congress on Opera and Ballet in Television and Film." _Opera_ (London), 10 (Oct. 1959), 661ff.

   5209a. Reprinted in _The World of Music_ (UNESCO), No. 4 (Dec. 1959), 61-63.

5210. Brunello, R. "Il film - baletto." In _Musica e film_. Ed. S. G. Biamonte. Rome: Edizioni dell'Ateneo, 1959.

       See Biamonte, #1606.

5211. Chochlovkina, A. "Opera 'Don Žuan' na ekrane." _Sovetskaya muzyka_ (Moscow), 20, No. 6 (June 1956), 94-95.

5212. Christmann, Arthur. "Faust and the Devil." _Film Music Notes_, 9, No. 5 (May-June 1950), 8-9.

       Concerns a filmed version of Gounod's opera.

5213. Colton, H. "'Of Men and Music' Marks Latest Attempt to Sell Classic Melodies Via Films." _New York Times_, 100 (Feb. 11, 1951), Section 2, p. 5.

5214. "Concerts on Film." _Instrumentalist_ (Evanston, Ill.), 11 (Dec. 1956), 74.

5215. "Concerts on Film: A Series of 16 mm. Films Presenting Performances of Music by Some of the World's Greatest Concert Artists (Beverly Hills, Calif., World Artists)." _Journal of Research_, 3 (Fall 1955), 160-62.

5216. Connor, Edward. "The Sound Track." _Films in Review_, 8, No. 2 (Feb. 1957), 86-87.

5217. ----------. "The Sound Track." _Films in Review_, 8, No. 4 (Apr. 1957), 182-83.

5218. ----------, and Edward Jablonski. "The Sound Track." _Films in Review_, 9, No. 2 (Feb. 1958), 96-98.

       Concerns music for Disney films, and a filmed production of Gershwin.

5219. Crowther, Bosley. "A Ballet on Film." _New York Times_, 105 (Apr. 8, 1956), Section 2, p. 1.

       Concerns the filmed version of "Romeo and Juliet."

5220. ----------. "Fitness of Folk Opera." _New York Times_, 108 (June 28, 1959), Section 2, p. 1.

       Concerns the filmed version of Gershwin's "Porgy and Bess."

5221. ----------. "Opera on the Screen." _New York Times_, 104 (Nov. 14, 1954), Section 2, p. 1.

       Concerns the contrasting difficulties posed by filmed and televised opera.

5222. Cuenca, Carlos F. _El cine y la danza_. Madrid: Filmoteca Nacional de España, 1959.

5223. Deke, R. F. "The Medium." _Film Music_, 11, No. 1 (Sept.-Oct. 1951), 13-15.

       An opera by Gian Carlo Menotti.

5224. ----------. "Tales of Hoffmann." _Film Music Notes_, 10, No. 4 (Mar.-Apr. 1951), 7-9.

       Music by Jacques Offenbach.

5225. Downes, O. "Menotti: Pioneer." _New York Times_, 100 (Sept. 16, 1951), Section 2, p. 9.

       Concerns the opera "The Medium."

5226. Druskin, Mikhail Semenovich. _Opernaya dramaturgiya_. Moscow, 1956.

5227. Eaton, Quaintance. "Grand Opera Feature Films." _Film Music_, 12, No. 5 (May-June 1953), 15-18.

5228. ----------. "Of Men and Music." _Film Music Notes_, 10, No. 3 (Jan.-Feb.

1951), 7-10.

5229. ----------. "Opera in the Camera's Eye." Opera News, 17 (Feb. 16, 1953), 13-15.

5230. Eisner, Lotte H. "De la pièce et du film au ... ballet d'opéra." Cahiers du cinéma, 6, No. 36 (June 1954), 33-37.

Concerns G. W. Pabst's production "L'Opéra de Quat'Sous." Also includes references to music by Menotti and Weill.

5231. Elias, Albert J. "The Ballet of 'Romeo and Juliet.'" Film and TV Music, 16, No. 1 (Fall 1956), 10.

Music of Serge Prokofiev.

5232. Eyquem, Olivier. "'Carmen Jones': un film d'Otto Preminger." Avant-Scene du cinéma (Paris), Nos. 211-212 (July-Sept. 1978), 67-79.

Includes a shot-analysis of the 1954 production, with music by Georges Bizet, and musical direction by Herschel Burke Gilbert.

5233. Fiechtner, H. A. "Chinesische Oper als Tonfilm." Musica, 8 (Dec. 1954), 555-56.

5234. "Film Opera: A Field Waiting for Exploration." Musical America, 71 (Nov. 1, 1951), 14.

5235. Forrell, Gene. "A Time for Bach." Film Music Notes, 9, No. 3 (Jan.-Feb. 1950), 16-17.

Reprinted in Limbacher, pp. 164-65. See #75.

5236. Franks, Arthur Henry. Ballet for Film and Television. London: Pitman, 1950.

Includes a bibliography, pp. 73-77, and a catalog of dance and ballet films, pp. 78-82.

5237. "Geigenbau im Film." Musica, 11 (Mar. 1957), 178.
    5237a. Also published in Neue Zeitschrift für Musik, 118 (Apr. 1957), 244.

5238. Georges, Horst. "Oper als Film: Improvisation über ein grundsätzliches Problem." Zeitschrift für Musik, 111 (1950), 135-37.

5239. Gibbon, Monk. "The Tales of Hoffman": A Study of a Film. London: Saturn Press, 1951.

Includes extensive references to the music of Offenbach.

5240. Gilliat, Sidney. "Gilbert and Sullivan." Film Music, 13, No. 2 (Nov.-Dec. 1953), 18-19.

5241. Gordon, Paul. "Gefilmte Konzerte: Revolution im Konzertsaal." Das Musikleben, 3 (1950), 78-80.

5242. ----------. "Gefilmte Musik." Das Musikleben, 3 (1950), 251-53.

5243. Green, Harris. "Celluloid Mozart." Opera News, 23 (Feb. 9, 1959), 31.

5244. ----------. "Porgy and Bess." Opera News, 24 (Dec. 12, 1959), 26.
        Concerns the musical direction by André Previn.

5245. ----------. "'Tosca' in CinemaScope." Opera News, 23 (Dec. 15, 1958), 14.
        Concerns the Cinecitta production of Puccini's opera.

5246. Grodman, Jeanette, and Maria De Monte. "Opera of the Future: Hollywood's Opera Films." Opera News, 19, No. 24 (Apr. 18, 1955), 8-9.

5247. Hamilton, William. "St. Matthew Passion." Film Music, 11, No. 3 (Jan.-Feb. 1952), 10-11.

5248. Haney, G. R., and George Vedegis. "Concerts on Film." Film Music, 13,

No. 5 (May-June 1954), 14-15.

5249. Harth, Walther. "Oper zwischen Montage und Breitwand." Melos, 24, No. 1 (Jan. 1957), 7-8.

5250. Haskell, Arnold L. "Paul Czinner's Film of the Bolshoi Ballet." London Musical Events, 12 (June 1957), 24-26.

5251. Helm, Everett. "International Conference on Opera in Radio, T.V. and Film." Musical Times (London), 98 (Feb. 1957), 87-89.

5252. Helpmann, Robert. "The Orchestration of Movement." In Diversion: Twenty-Two Authors on the Lively Arts. Ed. John Sutro. London: Max Parrish, 1950, pp. 198-206.

5253. Hickman, C. Sharpless. "Movies and Music." Music Journal, 11, No. 1 (Jan. 1953), 63.

   Concerns the "inadequacies" of the film media as a vehicle for opera.

5254. Ĭārustovskiĭ, Boris M. Opernaya dramaturgiya P. I. Tschaikovskogo. Moscow: Gos. muzykal'noe izd-vo, 1957.

5255. International Music Council. Opera and Ballet in T.V. and Film. Salzburg: IMC, 1959.

5256. ----------, and the Internationales Musikzentrum, Vienna. IMZ Report: Opera in Radio, T.V., and Film -- Report on the International Music Council Congress. Salzburg: IMC/IMZ, 1956.

   In English, French, and German.

5257. Keller, Hans. "Film Music and Beyond: Carmen à la Hollywood." Music Review, 16, No. 2 (1955), 153-55.

5258. ----------. "Film Music and Beyond: The Civilization of Musical Refuse through 'The Medium' of Menotti." Music Review, 14, No. 2 (1953), 141-43.

5259. ----------. "Film Music and Beyond: Tales from the Vienna Hollywoods." Music Review, 15, No. 2 (1954), 140-41.

5260. ----------. "Film Music: The Operatic Problem." Musical Times, 96, No. 1352 (Oct. 1955), 549.

5261. Knight, Arthur. "Opera Week at the Movies." Saturday Review, 39 (Mar. 24, 1956), 31-32.

5262. Kracauer, Siegfried. "Opera on the Screen." Film Culture, 1, No. 2 (Mar.-Apr. 1955), 19-21.

5263. Kroll, Nathan. "Carmen Jones." Film Music, 14, No. 2 (Nov.-Dec. 1954), 20.

   Concerns the musical direction of Herschel Burke Gilbert for the Otto Preminger film.

5264. Laine, Juliette, Mary Jane Matz, Frank Merkling, and M. E. Peltz. "Four Dimensions for the Opera Screen." Opera News, 20, No. 21 (Mar. 26, 1956), 10-13.

5265. Lavrovski, L. "Balet v kino." Iskusstvo kino (Moscow), No. 4 (Apr. 1954).

5266. Livingston, D. D. "The Dance in Films." Film Music Notes, 9, No. 4 (Mar.-Apr. 1950), 20-21.

5267. Loft, Abram. "Two New Films on Music." Film Music, 15, No. 3 (Jan.-Feb. 1956), 21.

5268. London, George. "Grand Opera on the Screen." Music Journal, 15, No. 9 (Nov.-Dec. 1957), 7, 46.

5269. Luft, Friedrich. "Musikalische Film-Experimente: Maskerade mit Musique concrete und der gefesselte Debussy." Das Musikleben, 7 (Mar. 1954),

104-05.

5270. ----------. "Verfilmtes 'Tiefland.'" *Das Musikleben*, 7 (Oct. 1954), 360-61.

5271. Lunghi, Fernando Ludovico. "Il film-opera." In *Musica e film*. Ed. S. G. Biamonte. Rome: Edizioni dell'Ateneo, 1959, pp. 35-48.
    See Biamonte, #1606.

5272. Martin, John. "Soviet Ballet on the Screen." *New York Times*, 107 (Dec. 1, 1957), Section 2, p. 7.

5273. Marx, H. "Music Films." *Music News*, 43 (Mar. 1951), 4.

5274. ----------. "Music Films: Past, Present and Future." *Music News*, 43 (Nov. 1951), 3-4ff.

5275. Maxwell, M. "Noteworthy." *Music Journal*, 9 (Oct. 1951), 3.
    Concerns the filmed versions of Offenbach's "Tales of Hoffmann," and Menotti's "The Medium."

5276. Michaut, Pierre. *Della danza di attrazione alla cinecoreografia*. Rome, 1952.

5277. ----------. "Un film ballet: 'Roméo et Juliette.'" *Cahiers du cinéma*, 9, No. 49 (July 1955), 29-31.
    Concerns the filmed version of Prokofiev's ballet.

5278. Mitchell, Donald. "The St. Matthew Passion on Film." *Musical Opinion*, 79 (Feb. 1956), 289.

5279. Morton, Lawrence. "Film Music of the Quarter." *Hollywood Quarterly*, 4, No. 4 (Summer 1950), 370-74.
    Concerns the problems of filming an opera production, with references to Verdi's "Il trovatore."

5280. "Music and Movies." *Music News*, 43 (Oct. 1951), 11-12.

5281. "New Italian Opera Films." *Opera News*, 18 (Dec. 28, 1953), 32.

5282. "Of Men and Music." *Music Clubs Magazine* (Indianapolis), 30 (Feb. 1951), 6-7.

5283. dall'Ongaro, Giuseppe. "Due film da John Gay." In *Musica e film*. Ed. S. G. Biamonte. Rome: Edizioni dell'Ateneo, 1959, pp. 155-62.
    See Biamonte, #1606.

5284. Onnen, F. "Een balletfilm op muziek van Ravel." *Mens en Melodie* (Utrecht, Neth.), 5 (May-June 1950), 181-83.

5285. "Opera in Mass Media." *Musical America*, 74 (Dec. 1, 1954), 4.

5286. Pilka, Jiří. "Problém zfilmované opery." *Hudební Rozhledy* (Prague), 9, No. 19 (1956), 800-03.
    Concerns the filmed version of Smetana's "Dalibor."

5287. Polyakova, Lyudmila. "'Evgeniy Onegin' na ekrane." *Sovetskaya muzyka*, 23, No. 6 (June 1959), 119-23.
    Concerns the filmed version of Tchaikovsky's opera.

5288. "Problems of Filming Opera Unresolved." *Musical America*, 76 (Mar. 1956), 4.

5289. "Proposed Film Concerts by Noted Artists Offer an Intriguing Program Suggestion." *Music Clubs Magazine* (Indianapolis), 33 (Nov. 1953), 19.

5290. Rattner, David S. "Don Juan." *Film Music*, 15, No. 3 (Jan.-Feb. 1956), 17-18.
    Concerns a filmed version of the Mozart opera.

5291. ----------. "Opera and Films." *Film Music*, 15, No. 4 (Spring 1956), 21-22.

5292. Rondi, Brunillo. "Il film-balletto." In Musica e film. Ed. S. G. Biamonte. Rome: Edizioni dell'Ateneo, 1959, pp. 49-64.

   See Biamonte, #1606.

5293. Rutz, Hans. "Die Oper der Zukunft: Ein Kongress von Kunst, Film, Funk und Fernsehen." Musica, 10, No. 11 (Nov. 1956), 744-47.

5294. ----------. "Zum 'Matthäus-Passion' -- Film." Musica, 4 (Jan. 1950), 31-32.

5295. Sabin, Robert. "Film Version of 'The Medium' Directed by Menotti in Rome." Musical America, 71 (Apr. 15, 1951), 21.

5296. Schab, G. "Problematischer Opern-Farbfilm." Musikleben, 4 (Nov. 1951), 323-24.

5297. Shebalin, Vissarion. "O kinoopere." Iskusstvo kino (Moscow), No. 3 (Mar. 1953), 90-94.

5298. Skelton, G. D. "The 'Matthew Passion' Filmed." Musical Opinion, 75 (Mar. 1952), 341ff.

5299. Sokol'sky, Matias. "Film 'Mussorgski' i nekotoriye voprosy muzykosnaniya." Sovetskaya muzyka, 15, No. 2 (Feb. 1951), 25-33.

5300. ----------. "Opera Mussorgskogo na ekrane." Sovetskaya muzyka, 20, No. 4 (Apr. 1956), 133-40.

5301. Spaeth, Sigmund. "From the Reviewing Stand." Music Clubs Magazine (Indianapolis), 34 (Nov. 1954), 13.

   Concerns the filmed version of "Aida."

5302. ----------. "From the Reviewing Stand." Music Clubs Magazine (Indianapolis), 35 (Mar. 1956), 12.

5303. ----------. "Motion Picture Music." Music Clubs Magazine (Indianapolis), 33 (Mar. 1954), 19.

5304. Steglich, R. "Bachs Matthäuspassion und das Filmtheater." Musik und Kirche (Kassel), 22 (May-June 1952), 117-19.

5305. Taubman, Howard. "The 'Don' in Films: Two Movies Lack Art of Mozart Masterpiece." New York Times, 105 (Mar. 11, 1956), Section 2, p. 9.

5306. ----------. "Give It a Hearing: Public Should Be Allowed to See Film Version of Claudel-Honegger Work." New York Times, 104 (May 22, 1955), Section 2, p. 7.

   Concerns the film "Jean d'Arc au Bucher."

5307. Terry, W. "The Dance." Etude, 74 (May-June 1956), 17ff.

   Concerns the filmed version of Prokofiev's "Romeo and Juliet."

5308. Tuggle, R. A. "Eugene Onegin." Opera News, 24 (Dec. 12, 1959), 26.

5309. Ujfalussy, József. "Operák filmen." Uj zenei szemle, 3, No. 2 (1952), 4-5.

5310. Vyborny, Z. "'Dalibor' im Film." Musica, 11, No. 1 (Jan. 1957), 53-54.

   Concerns the filmed version of Bedrich Smetana's opera.

5311. ----------. "Prague." Opera (London), 8 (Apr. 1957), 232.

   Concerns the filmed version of Smetana's "Dalibor."

5312. Wedekind, Joachim. "Operettenfilm? -- Filmoperette!" Vier Viertel, 7, No. 7 (1957), 5.

5313. Weiler, A. H. "'Beggar's Opera': A British Musical Film Version of Gay's Work." New York Times, 102 (Aug. 30, 1953), Section 2, p. 1.

5314. Werker, Gerard. "'Fanfare': een muzikale speelfilm." Mens en Melodie (Utrecht, Neth.), 13 (Nov. 1958), 341-43.

5315. Wexler, J. "Opera Taken Out of Mothballs, Given Exciting Vitality by NBC." _Billboard_, 63 (Oct. 13, 1951), 3.

5316. ----------. "Whither Music in Television?" _Billboard_, 62 (Nov. 25, 1950), 1ff.

5317. Wörner, Karl Heinrich. "Unsere Stimme dem musikalischen Kulturfilm." _Neue Zeitschrift für Musik_, 118 (July-Aug. 1957), 457-58.

SEE ALSO:

#1600(Becker/Rutz/Bornoff), #1614(Bowers), #1718, 1719(Hickman), #1744 (Jennings), #1803(Livingston), #1810(Marcorelles), #1854(Poulenc), #1879, #1907(Tilton), #2983(Reisfeld), #3193, 3370(Connor/Pratley), #3414(Steen), #3509, #3510(Korngold), #4116(Leyda), #4453(Bazin), #4861(Schaeffer), #4948(Vietta), #5046(Berten), #5105(Melichar), #5522(Chochlov), #5538, 5539(Helm), #5702(UNESCO), #5906(Borgelt), #5926(Charness), #5986(Green), #6007(Hollingsworth), #6117(Sonnenschein), #6259, and #6308(Comuzio).

1960's

5318. Aranovsky, M. "Kinoopera VI: Uspenskogo." _Sovetskaya muzyka_, 31, No. 1 (Jan. 1967), 27-29.

5319. Bleier-Brody, Agnes. "The Dancing Screen." In _Catalogue: Ten Years of Films on Ballet and Classical Dance, 1956-1965_. Paris: UNESCO, 1968.

5320. Blyth, Alan. "Karajan's Filmed 'Carmen.'" _Opera_ (England), 20 (Jan. 1969), 84.

5321. Boll, André. "Le Cinéma au secours de l'opera." _Musica_ (Chaix, Fr.), No. 112 (July 1963), 12-17.

5322. Bornoff, Jack. "Music and Mechanics." (Typescript.)

A paper presented at the Zagreb Biennale of Contemporary Music, 1963.

5323. ----------. _Music Theater in a Changing Society: The Influence of the Technical Media_. Paris: UNESCO, 1968.

A collection of papers from a "round table" of the International Music Council, Internationales Musikzentrum, and UNESCO, in Salzburg, August, 1965.

Includes the articles "Sound Radio and Music Theater -- Mutual Accommodation," pp. 64-70, "Characteristics of Film and Television," pp. 71-75, "Opera in Film and Filmed Opera," pp. 76-80, "Opera in Television and Television Opera," pp. 81-106, and "Ballet and Dance in Film and Television," pp. 126-34. Also includes a bibliography, p. 144.

5324. ----------. _Rapporteur-General's Report on the Fourth International Congress of the IMC on "Dance, Ballet and Pantomime in Film and Television" and UNESCO Colloquium on "Technical Media and Contemporary Music Theater."_ Salzburg: International Music Centre, 1965.

Also see the IMZ Report, #5335.

5325. Braun, Susan. "Dance Films Association, Inc., and How It Grew." _Performing Arts Review_ (New York), 1, No. 1 (1969), 119-26.

5326. Connor, Edward. "The Sound Track." _Films in Review_, 13, No. 4 (Apr. 1962), 242-43.

5327. Cullaz, M. "Porgy and Bess." _Jazz Hot_ (Paris), No. 226 (Dec. 1966), 7.

5328. Czinner, Paul. "Documenting the Stage." _Opera News_, 27 (Dec. 22, 1962), 28-29.

5329. Dienes, Gideon. "A Hattyuk tava--filmen." _Muzsika_ (Budapest), 12 (Dec. 1969), 17-18.

Concerns the filmed version of Tchaikovsky's "Swan Lake."

5330. Diether, Jack. "'Queen of Spades' Filmed." _Musical America_, 81 (Nov. 1961), 40.

Concerns the filmed version of Tchaikovsky's opera.

5331. Frid, Emiliĩa Lazarevna. "Na zkrane 'Katerina Izmailova.'" _Sovetskaya muzyka_, 31, No. 12 (Dec. 1967), 70-75.

Concerns the filmed version of Shostakovich's opera.

5332. Green, Harris. "Celluloid Imports." _Opera News_, 28 (Mar. 14, 1964), 35.

Includes references to music by Mozart, Johann Strauss, and Alban Berg.

5333. ----------. "Florestan Unrecognized." _Opera News_, 26 (Feb. 3, 1962), 34.

Concerns the filmed version of Beethoven's "Fidelio."

5334. Hennenberg, F. "'Die Schöne Lurette' auf der Leinwand." _Musik und Gesell-schaft_, 11 (June 1961), 369-70.

5335. Internationales Musikzentrum, Vienna. _IMZ Report: Dance, Ballet and Panto-mime in Film and T.V._ Salzburg: IMZ, 1965.

In English, French, and German.

Also see the report on the congress by Jack Bornoff, #5324.

5336. Jacobs, Arthur D. "'Khovanshchina' -- Opera and Film." _Opera_, 13 (Aug. 1962), 520ff.

Concerns the filmed version of the Mussorgsky opera.

5337. ----------. "Two Opera Films." _Opera_ (England), 20 (Sept. 1969), 818, 820.

Concerns Beethoven's "Fidelio" and Kodály's "Hary Janos."

5338. Kerr, Russell. "'Der Rosenkavalier' on Film." _Music Magazine_ (Toronto), 164 (Oct. 1962), 59.

5339. Klado, N. "Balet na ekrane ili kinobalet?" _Iskusstvo kino_ (Moscow), No. 11 (Nov. 1960).

5340. "Kongresse in Salzburg: Der 4. Internationale Kongress für Tanz, Ballett und Pantomime in Film und Fernsehen." _Osterreichische Musikzeitschrift_, 20 (Oct. 1965), 551-52.

Also see #5324 and #5335.

5341. Kotek, Josef. "Jasnou obrazovku, jasnejsi vyhledy!" _Hudební Rozhledy_, 13, No. 6 (1960), 223-24.

5342. Kuna, Milan. "Dramaturgie filmove 'Rusalky.'" _Hudební Rozhledy_ (Prague), 16, Nos. 10-11 (1963), 447-48.

5343. Lissa, Zofia. "Film a opera: Z zagadnień krzyżowania konwencji gatunkowych w sztuce." _Estetyka_, 4 (1963), 199-217.

Includes a summary in English.

5344. ----------. "Opera w filmie czy opera filmowa?" _Muzyka_, 6 (1961).

5345. Lüdemann, Lutz. "4. Internationaler Kongress 'Tanz, Ballett und Pantomime in Film und Fernsehen' und das UNESCO-Colloquium 'Technische Medien und zeitgenössisches Musiktheater.'" _The World of Music_ (UNESCO), 7, No. 6 (1965), 121-22.

Also see #5324 and #5335.

5346. MacFarland, D. "Ballet on Film." _Music Journal_, 24, No. 9 (Nov. 1966), 70.

5347. Marcus, Michael. "'Rosenkavalier': Paul Czinner's Filmed Version." _Music _and Musicians_, 10 (July 1962), 16-17ff.

5348. McVay, Douglas. "The Art of the Actor." _Films and Filming_, 12, No. 12 (Sept. 1966), 43-50.

5349. Neuhaus, R. "Zwei Balletfilme -- zwei Positionen." _Melos_, 28, No. 3 (Mar. 1961), 81-83.

    Concerns the ballet-films "Romeo and Juliet" and "Undine."

5350. Payne, Anthony. "Wide-Screen Rimsky." _Music and Musicians_, 15 (Mar. 1967), 32-33.

    Concerns the filmed version of "The Tsar's Bride."

5351. Rivette, Jacques, and François Wezergans. "Le Bande-Son: Entretien avec Pierre Boulez." _Cahiers du cinéma_, 26, No. 152 (Feb. 1964), 19-29.

5352. Runeborg, Björn, and Björn W. Hallberg. "Kring tvaa nya svenska operor." _Nutida Musik_ (Stockholm), 13, No. 2 (1969-1970), 19-24.

5353. Ryzkin, I. "Opera a film." _Hudební Rozhledy_ (Prague), 14, No. 5 (1961), 195-96.

5354. Sabin, Robert. "Russians Film Complete 'Swan Lake.'" _Musical America_, 80 (Feb. 1960), 251.

5355. Schaefer, Hansjürgen. "Experiment von internationalen Rang: Wagner's 'Fliegender Holländer' als DEFA-Film." _Musik und Gesellschaft_, 15 (Mar. 1965), 181-84.

5356. Schelp, Arend. "'Ludwig van': de Beethovenfilm van Mauricio Kagel." _Mens en Melodie_ (Utrecht, Neth.), 26 (Feb. 1971), 52-53.

5357. Schonberg, Harold C. "Casals on Film." _New York Times_, 110 (May 14, 1961), Section 2, p. 9.

5358. Sutcliffe, Tom. "Opera on the Screen." _Music and Musicians_, 16 (July 1968), 24-25.

5359. ten Zijthoff, Reg. "De Bach-Film van Jean Marie Straub." _Mens en Melodie_ (Utrecht, Neth.), 23 (Apr. 1968), 98-102.

5360. Thomas, Ernst, ed. _Contemporary Music Theatre: Report on Congress of the International Music Centre, Hamburg, 1964_. Hamburg: Deutscher Musikrat, 1966.

5361. Tinterov, S. Stefanov. "'Traviata' na ekrana." _Bulgarska Muzika_ (Sofia), 19, No. 8 (1968), 81-82.

5362. Tumanina, N. V. "'Khovanshchina' v kino." _Sovetskaya muzyka_, 24, No. 1 (Jan. 1960), 96-101.

    Concerns the filmed version of Mussorgsky's opera.

5363. United Nations Educational, Scientific and Cultural Organization. _Ballett und Tanz in Film und Fernsehen (Salzburg 1965): einem Katalog_. Paris: UNESCO, 1968.

    -- Rev. in _Musikalische Jugend_ (Regensburg), 17, No. 5 (1968), 6.

5364. ----------. _Film and Television in the Service of Opera and Ballet_. Reports and Papers on Mass Communication, XXXII. Edited, and with contributions by G. Freund, P. Angerer, and Paul Becker. Paris: UNESCO, 1960.

5365. Vajda, Igor. "Film." _Slovenska Hudba_ (Bratislava, Czech.), 10, No. 6 (1966), 279.

    Concerns the filmed version of Wagner's "Der Fliegende Holländer."

5366. Verdone, Mario. _Répertoire Films sur la danse_. Rome: CIDALC, 1961.

5367. Ward, Harry. "Opera/Concert Talk." _Music Journal_, 23, No. 8 (Nov. 1965), 18-22.

    Concerns the filmed La Scala production of Puccini's

"La Bohême."

5368. Weiss, Norbert. "Film and 'Lulu.'" Opera, 17 (Sept. 1966), 707-09.

5369. ----------. "Film in der Oper." Schweizerische Musikzeitung, 106, No. 4 (1966), 208-10.

5370. ----------. "Film in Opera." Opera Canada (Toronto), 9, No. 4 (1968), 16-17.
> Concerns the filmed version of Alban Berg's "Lulu."

5371. Wright, Kenneth A. "From Flop to Pop: Some Thoughts on Bizet's 'Carmen.'" Music (Schools Music Association, Oxford), 3, No. 1 (1969), 6-8.
> Concerns Herbert von Karajan's version of the opera.

SEE ALSO:
> #2073(IMZ), #2132(Reisner), #2179(J. Thiel), #2996(Arnell), #3414(Steen), #3702, #3923(Markowski), #4654(Jelinek), #4819(Piva), #5086(IMC), #5087 (IMC/IMZ), #5092(Kabalevskij), #5129(Spaeth), #5135, 5702(UNESCO), #5926 (Charness), #5946(Cutts), #6002(Hirsch), #6117(Sonnenschein), #6259, #6264, 6265(IMZ), #6273(UNESCO), and #6308(Comuzio).

1970's

5372. Ayanova, Ekaterina. "Muzika kum bulgarski filmi." Bulgarska Muzika (Sofia), 26, No. 3 (Mar. 1975), 69-70.

5373. Bazarov, K. "Grand Cinema." Music and Musicians, 20 (Oct. 1971), 20-22.

5374. Beck, Joseph George. "Education Film for the Fine and Performing Arts." Ed.D. Diss. St. Louis University 1979.
> Abstract: DAI 40/04:1822 (order #DEL 79-23639).

5375. Bernsdorff-Engelbrecht, C. "Recklinghausen: Revolution der Oper im Film." Neue Zeitschrift für Musik, 132, No. 6 (June 1971), 317-19.

5376. Bertz-Dostal, Helga. Oper und Ballett im Film / Opera and Ballet on Film / Opéra et ballet au film. Trans. (English) Christopher Norton-Welsh, and (French) Rosy Weiss. Vienna: Ges. für Musiktheater, 1973. (Reprint, 1975.)

5377. Bestehorn, Wilfried. "Musikprogramme im Funk -- richtig, proportioniert?" Musik und Gesellschaft, 28, No. 12 (Dec. 1978), 714-19.

5378. Blyth, Alan. "Karajan's 'Otello.'" Opera (England), 25 (Dec. 1974), 1124.

5379. Bor, Vladimir. "Nad Smetanovskym filmen." Hudební Rozhledy, 25, No. 2 (1972), 62.

5380. Borev, V. ("Audio-Visual Resources in Mass Media.") In Muzy XX veka. Ed. Natal'ya Zorkaya and Jurij Bogomolov. Moscow: Iskusstvo, 1978.
> In Russian. See Zorkaya, #2624.

5381. Boyum, Joy Gould. "Bergman Takes Us to an Opera." Wall Street Journal, 56 (Nov. 17, 1975), p. 15.
> Concerns the filming of Mozart's "Magic Flute."

5382. Carcassone, Philippe. "Dossier -- La Musique de film: cinéma et opéra -- tombeaux de Mozart." Cinématographe, No. 52 (Nov. 1979), 11-15.

5383. Cardon, Charlotte. "Hong Kong Letter." Take One (Montreal), 3, No. 7 (Sept.-Oct. 1971), 38-40.
> Concerns opera films produced in China.

5384. Cobb (Norwood), Hazel Louanne. "A Delineation of Three Sources of Artistic Output in the Production of Dance Art Films." Ph.D. Diss. Texas Women's University 1977.

5385. Comuzio, Ermanno. "Ingmar Bergmans 'Il flauto magico.'" Cineforum (Bergamo), No. 160 (Dec. 1976), 790-96.

5386. Csobadi, Peter. "Die Massenmedien der musikalischen Information: Herbert von Karajan antwortet Peter Csobadi." Neue Zeitschrift für Musik, 131 (May 1970), 223-24.

5387. Cuel, François. "Dossier: Cinéma italien et culture populaire. Figaro ci, Garibaldi la." Cinématographe, No. 30 (Sept. 1977), 7-11.
     Includes a bibliography.

5388. Davis, Peter G. "Opera on Film: Pitfalls Aplenty." High Fidelity and Musical America, 20 (Oct. 1970), MA12-13.

5389. Decaux, Emmanuel. "Dossier: Cinéma et opera -- fascination de l'irreel." Cinématographe, No. 52 (Nov. 1979), 2-7.

5390. ----------, and Bruno Villien. "Dossier: Cinéma et opera -- entretien avec Patrice Chereau." Cinématographe, No. 52 (Nov. 1979), 19-24.

5391. Demers, Pierre. "Filmographie succincte de la musique traditionelle au Quebec." Cinéma Quebec, 4, Nos. 9-10 (1976), 29.

5392. ----------. "La vitalite d'un courant musical de chez nous." Cinéma Quebec, 4, Nos. 9-10 (1976), 27-28.

5393. Demin, V. ("Indirect Ancestry.") In Muzy XX veka. Ed. Natal'ya Zorkaya and Jurij Bogomolov. Moscow: Iskusstvo, 1978.
     In Russian. See Zorkaya, #2624.

5394. Dvorničenko, Oksana Ivanovna. "Dmitriy Kabalevskiy: Muzyka, Razmyshleniya, Vospominaniya." Sovetskaya muzyka, 38, No. 12 (Dec. 1974), 37-39.

5395. Epertiere, Renard. "Mozart selon Bergman et Losey." Harmonie (Paris), No. 152 (Nov. 1979), 34-39.

5396. Evans, Colin. "Film of the Music." Times Educational Supplement (London), No. 3244 (Aug. 5, 1977), 26.

5397. Fieschi, Jacques. "Dossier: Cinéma et opera -- l'air de la folie." Cinématographe, No. 52 (Nov. 1979), 8-10.

5398. "Filming the Blues: The Films of Les Blank." Jazz Forum (Stockholm), No. 20 (Dec. 1972), 40-41.

5399. Flothuis, Marius. "Een gemiste kans." Mens en Melodie (Utrecht, Neth.), 31, No. 5 (May 1976), 135-36.
     Concerns the filming of Mozart's "Die Zauberflöte."

5400. Fuhrmann, Peter. "Henzes freimütige Bekenntnisse." Neue Musikzeitung (Regensburg), 26, No. 1 (1977), 2.
     Concerns the filmed version of "Die verbotene Schönheit," by Hans Werner Henze.

5401. Furceva, S. ("Film and TV: The Effect of the Audience.") In Muzy XX veka. Ed. Natal'ya Zorkaya and Jurij Bogomolov. Moscow: Iskusstvo, 1978.
     In Russian. See Zorkaya, #2624.

5402. Gevaudan, Frantz. "La Musique aux 'Yeux fertiles.'" Cinéma 77, Nos. 224-225 (Aug.-Sept. 1977), 116-17.

5403. Ghezzi, Enrico. "Vedere la musica: 'Il margine' (e 'Il flauto magico')." Filmcritica (Rome), 28, No. 273 (Mar. 1977), 108-11.

5404. Gielen, Michael. "Bericht über die Wiener Tonaufnahmen im April/May 1974: Schoenbergs 'Moses und Aron.'" Filmkritik (Munich), 19 (May-June 1975), 276-78.

5405. Grier, Harry. "Multi-media: 'Les Troyens.'" Filmmaker's Newsletter, 7 (Jan. 1974), 19-21.

5406. Hayford, Aba. "Traditional Music and Dance in the Visual Media (TV and Film)." The World of Music (UNESCO), 18, No. 4 (1976), 43-48.

5407. Higgins, Jon B. "Film Review: Four Color Films on Hindustani Music." Asian Music, 3, No. 2 (1972), 58-60.
    An ethnomusicological study, with implications for the study of problems of filming musical performances.

5408. Hoack, Paul A. "Focus on Opera: A Series of Five Motion Pictures -- 'The Barber of Seville', 'Rigoletto', 'La traviata', 'Tales of Hoffmann,' and 'Gagliacci.'" Music Journal, 35, No. 4 (Apr. 1977), 36.

5409. Horning, Joseph. "Shooting a Live Symphony Orchestra." American Cinematographer, 59, No. 3 (Mar. 1978), 264-65.

5410. Istiushina, Marina. "Bicentennial: The Bolshoi on Film." Soviet Film (Moscow), No. 226 (No. 3), (Mar. 1976), 21-25.

5411. Keating, L. "Jazz on the Screen." Jazz Journal International (London), 31 (Jan.-Feb. 1978), 34.
    Includes references to the music of Scott Joplin.

5412. ----------. "Jazz on the Screen." Jazz Journal International (London), 32 (Mar. 1979), 18-19.

5413. Kirchberg, Klaus. "Der Musik gehorsame Töchter: zu Ingmar Bergmans 'Zauberflöten'-Film." Musica, 30, No. 6 (1976), 503-05.

5414. Kluge, Alexander, et al. "Theorie und Praxis: die Opernhäuser als Produktionswerkstätten der Massenmedien." Opernwelt, 12, No. 7 (July 1971), 40-43.

5415. Koch, Gerhard R. "Immer noch Konfliktstoff? 'Moses und Aron': Jean Marie Straubs Film und Michael Gielens Schallplatten." Musica, 29, No. 3 (1975), 247-49.

5416. ----------. "Kritische Utopie: Max Ophuls Film 'Die Verkaufte Braut.'" Opernwelt, No. 1 (Jan. 1973), 44-45.

5417. Kolodin, Irving. "The Film as Opera (and Vice Versa)." Saturday Review, 2 (Aug. 23, 1975), 54-55.
    Concerns the employment of "cinematic" techniques in staging opera productions.

5418. ----------. "Magical 'Flute,' Marriageable 'Figaro.'" Saturday Review, 3, No. 7 (Jan. 10, 1976), 65-66.

5419. Krause, Ernst, and Clemens Kohl. Felsenstein auf der Probe. Berlin: Henschelverlag, 1971.
    A photographic study, includes 168 pp. of illustrations from the opera productions and operatic films.

5420. Landry, Robert J. "Baryshnikov's 'Nijinsky' Moves Ballet Boom to Big Screen." Variety, 292 (Oct. 4, 1978), 3ff.

5421. Le Pavec, Jean-Pierre. "La Part du cinéma." Cinéma 79, No. 244 (Apr. 1979), 48-50.

5422. Lever, Yves. "'Jean Carignan, Violoneux' de Bernard Gosselin et la musique traditionnelle au Quebec." Cinéma Quebec, 4, Nos. 9-10 (1976), 25-27.

5423. Lienert, K. R. "Zur Bergman-Verfilmung von W. A. Mozarts 'Zauberflöte.'" Schweizerische Musikzeitung, 116, No. 2 (1976), 102.

5424. Lossmann, H. "Teheran: Opernverfilmungen -- aber wie?" Die Bühne (Vienna), No. 239 (Aug. 1978), 16-17.
    Concerns the Internationales Festival der Musikfilme in Teheran.

5425. Lučaj, G. ("From Scenic Views to Stereo Tele-Journeys.") In Muzy XX veka. Ed. Natal'ya Zorkaya and Jurij Bogomolov. Moscow: Iskusstvo, 1978.

In Russian. See Zorkaya, #2624.

5426. Mielke, Georg. "Zur Positionsbestimmung der Opernadaption." Film und Fernsehen (Berlin, DDR), 3, No. 1 (1975), 14-18ff.

5427. ----------. "Zwischen Reportage und Studiogastspiel: zur positionsbestimmung der Opernadaption." Film und Fernsehen (Berlin, DDR), 3, No. 2 (1975), 43-45.

5428. Milnes, Rodney. "'Cavalleria Rusticana' and 'I Pagliacci': Queen Elizabeth Hall." Opera (England), 22 (Oct. 1971), 924-26.

Concerns the filming of operas by Pietro Mascagni and Ruggiero Leoncavallo.

5429. ----------. "Film Opera." Opera (England), 23 (Sept. 1972), 864ff.

5430. Mordden, Ethan C. "Film." Opera News, 40, No. 8 (Dec. 20-27, 1975), 36.

Concerns the film production of Bergman's "Magic Flute."

5431. Mueller, John. "Films: Choreographing for Camera." Dance Magazine, 52, No. 4 (Apr. 1978).

5432. ----------. Films on Ballet and Modern Dance: Notes and a Directory. New York: American Dance Guild, 1977.

-- Rev. in Saturday Review, 5 (Oct. 15, 1977), 44.

5433. Müller-Blattau, Wendelin. "Chormusik in Film und Fernsehen." Musik und Bildung, 7, No. 4 (Apr. 1975), 176-78.

5434. Nordon, Vincent. "Dossier: Cinéma et opera -- le realisme social de Wagner." Cinématographe, No. 52 (Nov. 1979), 28-30.

5435. Oms, Marcel. "Une esthétique d'opera." Cahiers de la cinématheque, Nos. 26-27 (1979), 132-37.

5436. Osborne, Conrad L. "The 'Flute' on Film: It Works, Bergman's Camera Captures Mozart." High Fidelity and Musical America, 26 (Feb. 1976), MA16-18.

5437. Palmer, Christopher. "The Cinema and the Concert Hall." Crescendo International, 14 (Dec. 1975), 24-25.

Includes a discussion of the music for "2001 - A Space Odyssey."

5438. ----------. "When the Concert Hall Meets the Cinema Screen." Crescendo International, 14 (Nov. 1975), 26-27.

5439. Pauly, Reinhard G. Music and the Theater: An Introduction to Opera. Englewood Cliffs, N.J.: Prentice-Hall, 1970.

Includes a bibliography.

5440. Phraner, Leighton. "Spotlight." Music Journal, 32, No. 5 (May 1974), 48.

Notes on the "renovation" of "Der Rosenkavalier."

5441. Pleasants, Henry. "The Screen and the Voice." Opera News, 34 (Jan. 17, 1970), 8-13.

5442. Rickey, Carrie. "Seeing Ideas: Straub and Huillet's 'Moses und Aron.'" Artforum (New York), 16 (Nov. 1977), 66-69.

5443. Rogers, Joel. "Le Son au cinéma." Cahiers du cinéma, Nos. 260-261 (Oct. 1975), 5-84.

An interview with Jean-Marie Straub and Danièle Huillet. Concerns the filming of Schoenberg's "Moses und Aron."

Reprinted in Jump Cut (see #5454).

5444. Schadhauser, Sebastian, Elias Chaluja, Gianna Mingrone, and Jacques Fillion.

"Entretien avec Jean-Marie Straub et Danièle Huillet." Cahiers du ciné-ma, No. 223 (Aug.-Sept. 1970), 48-57; and No. 224 (Oct. 1970), 40-42.

Concerns the film "Othon."

5445. Schonberg, Harold C. "Films -- A New Dimension for Opera." New York Times, 124 (April 20, 1975), Section 2, p. 19.

5446. Schutte, Wolfram. "Sur la musique: questions a Michael Gielen." Trans. Jacques Aumont. Cahiers du cinéma, Nos. 260-261 (Oct.-Nov. 1975), 54-56.

Translation of an article which originally appeared in Kirche und Film (May 1975). Includes references to Schoenberg's "Moses und Aron."

5447. "Simfonicheskomu orkestru kinematografii." Iskusstvo kino, No. 12 (Dec. 1974), 85.

5448. Soria, Dorle J. "Artist Life." High Fidelity and Musical America, 29, No. 5 (May 1979), MA5-7ff.

Concerns the filming of Mozart's "Don Giovanni."

5449. Strässner, M. "Musikalisches Elementarerlebnis Bach's 'h-moll Messe' als Film mit der Gächinger Kantorei unter Helmuth Rilling." Musica, 33, No. 6 (June 1979), 577-78.

5450. Thiel, Wolfgang. "'Tage aus einem Leben,' erster Beethoven-Film der DEFA." Musik und Gesellschaft, 27, No. 1 (Jan. 1977), 17-19.

5451. Ungari, Enzo. "Sur le son: Entretien avec Jean-Marie Straub et Danièle Huillet." Cahiers du cinéma, Nos. 260-261 (Oct.-Nov. 1975), 48-53.

Concerns the filming of Schoenberg's "Moses und Aron."

5452. Veillon, Olivier-Rene. "Dossier: Cinéma et opera -- transformation d'un heritage." Cinématographe, No. 52 (Nov. 1979), 31-33.

5453. Villien, Bruno. "Dossier: Cinéma et opera -- de l'influence des cameras sur le comportement des tenors." Cinématographe, No. 52 (Nov. 1979), 34-35.

5454. Walsh, Martin. "'Moses and Aaron': Straub and Huillet's Schoenberg." Jump Cut, Nos. 12-13 (Dec. 30, 1976), 57-64.

Includes an interview with Jean-Marie Straub and Danièle Huillet, conducted by Joel Rogers, reprinted from Cahiers du cinéma (see #5443).

5455. Walter, Edith. "Tête d'affiche: Rolf Liebermann." Harmonie (Paris), No. 152 (Nov. 1979), 28-33.

An interview. Concerns the filming of "Don Giovanni."

5456. Weiler, A. H. "Film Forum: Charles Ives and Harry Partch, Two Originals." New York Times, 126 (April 22, 1977), Section C, p. 11.

5457. Woods, Gregory. "Ein Arbeitsjournal." Filmkritik (Munich), 19 (May-June 1975), 254-75.

5458. Zachary, Ralph. "Films: 'Prince Igor.'" Opera News, 37, No. 17 (Mar. 3, 1973), 27.

Concerns the Russian film version of Borodin's opera.

SEE ALSO:

#306(Troitskaya), #2233(Amzoll), #2247(Bayne), #2374(Fabian), #2398(Forrest), #2440(M. Jones), #2567(Sterritt), #2607(Wimbush), #3917(Fedorov), #4442(Baronijan), #4552(Dvorničenko), #4649(IMZ), #4663(Jungk), #4868 (Schepelern), #5051(Bornoff/Salter), #5069(Fabian), #5086(IMC), #5142 (Weyer), #5926(Charness), #5989(Grover), #6082(Olschausen), #6117(Sonnenschein), #6265(IMZ), #6266(Intl. Folk Music Council), and #6308(Comuzio).

1980's

5459. Bachmann, Claus Henning. "Eine Filmoper, die Kundry heisst: Hans Jürgen Syberbergs 'Parsifal' Version." Schweizerische Musikzeitung (Zurich), 122, No. 5 (1982), 338ff.

5460. ----------. "Hundert Jahre danach: eine Filmoper, die Kundry heisst." Musikhandel (Bonn), 33, No. 6 (1982), 251-53.

    Concerns H. J. Syberberg's production of "Parsifal" at Bayreuth.

5461. Chevassu, Francois. "Vous avez dit: Mozart?" Revue du cinéma/Image et son, No. 346 (Jan. 1980), 65-72.

5462. Comuzio, Ermanno. "Colonna sonora: l'opera filmata come 'operazione nostalgia.'" Revista del cinematografo, 54 (Sept.-Oct. 1981), 536-37.

5463. ----------. "Mozart musicista cinematografico." Cineforum, No. 213 (Apr. 1982), 25-36.

5464. ----------. "La musica: la sostanza tragica di Mozart." Cineforum (Bergamo), No. 193 (Apr. 1980), 190-94.

5465. ----------. "Werner Herzog: 'Woyzeck.'" Cineforum (Bergamo), No. 196 (July-Aug. 1980), 496-501.

5466. Corrigan, Timothy. "Werner Schroeter's Operatic Cinema." Discourse (Berkeley, Calif.), No. 3 (Spring 1981), 46-59.

    Includes a filmography.

5467. Corwin, Betty L. "Theatre on Film and Tape Preserving Stage Performances." Variety, 297 (Jan. 9, 1980), 26-29.

5468. Deisinger, H. "Viel Freud und Schmerz um Schumanns 'Frühlingssinfonie'; zum Peter-Schamoni-Film der Warner Columbia." Neue Zeitschrift für Musik, 144, No. 7-8 (July-Aug. 1983), 4-7.

5469. Drubachevskaya, G. "Priroda, muzyka, stikhi." Sovetskaya muzyka, 44, No. 8 (Aug. 1980), 90-91.

5470. Ely, Norbert. "Film als Fortsetzung des Lebens mit anderen Mitteln." Neue Zeitschrift für Musik, 143, No. 8 (Aug. 1982), 4-7.

    Concerns Hans Jürgen Syberberg's film of "Parsifal."

5471. Fabian, Imre. "Amerikanisches Opern-Tagebuch." Opernwelt, 21, No. 1 (1980), 47-48.

5472. ----------. "Mozarts 'Titus' verfilmt: zur Inszenierung von Jean-Pierre Ponnelle." Opernwelt, 22, No. 5 (1981), 13.

    Concerns the filmed version of "Clemenza di Tito."

5473. ----------. "Die Schallplattenaufnahme zum Jubilaeum: Wagners 'Parsifal' unter Armin Jordan -- die Musikaufnahme zu H. J. Syberbergs 'Parsifal' Film." Opernwelt Jahrbuch, 23 (1982), 62-63.

5474. Fenoglio, P. "'Don Giovanni' e l'Eros malinconico." Rassegna Musicale Curci (Milan), 33, No. 3 (1980), 41-42.

5475. Fierz, G. "'Don Giovanni' in Renaissance-Architektur: Bemerkungen zu Joseph Loseys Film anlässlich seiner deutschen Premiere." Opernwelt, 21, No. 4 (1980), 6-7.

5476. Germani, Sergio Grmek. "Il doppio e il nero." Filmcritica, 31, Nos. 305-306 (May-June 1980), 212-13.

    Concerns the filmed version of "Don Giovanni."

5477. Grodanov, V. "Liudi, professiia, zhizn'." Iskusstvo kino, No. 1 (1983), 85-97.

5478. Heinsheimer, Hans W. "'Don Giovanni' als Film." Neue Zeitschrift für Musik, 142, No. 1 (Jan.-Feb. 1980), 43-45.

5479. Holthof, Marc. "De abnormale opera: pathos en trivialiteit." Andere Sinema (Antwerp), No. 17 (Mar. 1980), 30-32.

5480. Ishaghpour, Youssef. "La realite de l'art et l'art de la realite: opera, roman." Positif (Paris), No. 259 (Sept. 1982), 2-10.

5481. Jungheinrich, Hans Klaus. "Stadtoper in der Landschaft: Joseph Loseys Filmversion von Mozarts 'Don Giovanni.'" Neue Zeitschrift für Musik, 142, No. 2 (Apr.-May 1980), 2.

5482. Knotik, C. "Opernfilm-Festival im Wiener Künstlerhaus." Österreichische Musikzeitschrift, 38 (Apr.-May 1983), 271.

5483. Leirens, Jean. "Mozart, Losey, Bergman." Amis du film: Cinéma et télévision, No. 284 (Jan. 1980), 16-17.

5484. Leukel, Jürgen. "Puccinis kinematographische Tecknik." Neue Zeitschrift für Musik, Nos. 6-7 (June-July 1982), 24-26.

5485. Lindberg, Ib. "Don Giovanni." Kosmorama (Copenhagen), 28, Nos. 159-160 (Aug. 1982), 100-03.

5486. Lindemann, Klaus. "Die Sehnsucht nach dem höchsten Ausdruck: zu meiner filmischen Umsetzung von Henzes 'Tristan' Romantik, ein imaginärer Dialog." Neue Zeitschrift für Musik, 142, No. 3 (May-June 1980), 218-20.
     Concerns the filming of Hans Werner Henze's "Tristans Klage."

5487. Loney, Glenn. "Film." Opera News, 47 (Mar. 12, 1983), 42-43.
     Concerns the filmed version of "Parsifal."

5488. Losey, Joseph. "Notre 'Don Giovanni.'" La Revue musicale (Paris), Nos. 338-339 (1981), 133-35.

5489. Loundine, Tamara. "La danza e il cinema." Filmcritica, 31, Nos. 305-306 (May-June 1980), 215-17.

5490. Mahlke, S. "Traumbild 'Elektra': der Opernfilm von Karl Böhm und Goetz Friedrich und eine Dokumentation seiner Entstehung." Opernwelt, 23, No. 11 (1982), 31-32.

5491. Mai, C. "Ein neuer Opernfilm: Franco Zeffirelli arbeitet an der Verfilmung von Verdis 'Traviata.'" Opernwelt, 23, Nos. 8-9 (1982), 8-9.

5492. Michot, P., and P. Albera. "'Don Giovanni,' film de Joseph Losey." Schweizerische Musikzeitung (Zurich), 120, No. 1 (1980), 40-43.

5493. Osborne, Conrad L. "Zeffirelli's Film, 'La Traviata.'" High Fidelity and Musical America, 33 (Aug. 1983), MA15-18.

5494. Persche, G. "In Schönheit zu sterben: Franco Zeffirellis Verfilmung von Verdis 'La Traviata.'" Opernwelt, 24, No. 5 (1983), 56-58.

5495. ----------. "Kommt der Opern-Film-Sänger?" Opernwelt, 24, No. 5 (1983), 56.

5496. Pisarenko, O. "'Parsifal' Syberga czyli naruszenie tabu." Ruch Muzyczny (Warsaw), 27, No. 15 (1983), 20-21.
     Concerns the work of Hans Jürgen Syberberg.

5497. Raitmayr, B. "Film: Abenteuer im Kopf." Die Bühne (Vienna), No. 290 (Nov. 1982), 9-10.

5498. ----------. "Opernfilm: Vor allem kulinarisch." Die Bühne (Vienna), No. 293 (Feb. 1983), 7.

5499. Rasponi, L. "Dream 'Traviata.'" Opera News, 47 (Mar. 12, 1983), 8-12ff.
     Concerns the film version by Franco Zeffirelli.

5500. Rockwell, John. "Why Does Opera Lure Filmmakers?" New York Times, 132
      (May 8, 1983), Section 2, p. 1ff.

5501. Sainderichin, Guy-Patrick. "Voyage a Munich." Cahiers du cinéma, No. 331
      (Jan. 1982), 22-29.

5502. Schlesinger, Arthur. "Coppola's Self-Appointed Epic." Saturday Review, 7
      (Jan. 5, 1980), 44.
           Concerns Francis Ford Coppola's "Don Giovanni."

5503. Schött, Hans Joachim. "'Don Giovanni' 1980: oder, Die Liebe zur klass-
      ischen Architektur." Opernwelt Jahrbuch (1980), 107-10.

5504. Schreiber, Ulrich. "Das Gold im Zahn oder, Die andere Zugehörigkeit: zu
      den Mozart-Filmen von Ingmar Bergman und Joseph Losey." Hifi-Stereophon-
      ie, 20 (Mar. 1981), 240-42.

5505. Syberberg, Hans Jürgen. "Parsifal": ein Filmessay. Munich: W. Heyne, 1982.
           -- Rev. in Musikhandel, 34, No. 3 (1983), 174.

5506. Thiel, Wolfgang. "Klischees aus dem Künstlerleben." Film und Fernsehen
      (Berlin, DDR), 11, No. 2 (1983), 12-15.

      SEE ALSO:

      #260(La Balbo), #2783(Daney/Fargier), #2877(Rothstein), and #6098(Sasa-
      now).

Musical Performance on Television

1935-1949

5507. Gardner, B. B. "Television for Music Lovers." Music Parade (London), 1,
      No. 13 (1949), 11-12.

5508. Graf, Herbert. "Opera in Television." In Music in Radio Broadcasting. Ed.
      Gilbert Chase. New York: McGraw-Hill, 1946, pp. 138-45.

5509. ----------. "Television: Its Potentialities for Grand Opera." Musical A-
      merica, 69 (Feb. 1949), 10-11.

5510. Morgan, A. L. "Some Notes on Radio and Television." Etude, 67 (July 1949),
      406ff.

5511. "Televising the Opera." Opera Notes, 13 (Jan. 24, 1949), 30.

5512. "What Will Television Do for Music?" Etude, 67 (June 1949), 339ff.

      SEE ALSO:

      #238(Ford), #267(Matejka), #280(Philippot), #287(Salter), #313(Westphal),
      #1300(Haver), #1449, #1514(Stokowski), #1582(Bowman), #1584(Chotzinoff),
      #1585(Cooke), #1587(Menotti), #4915(Thiel), and #5621(Burke).

1950's

5513. Abegg, F. F. "Musikalische Möglichkeiten des Fernseh-Funkes." Das Musik-leben, 5 (Sept. 1952), 253.

5514. Adler, Peter Herman. "Opera on Television." Music Journal, 17, No. 4 (Apr.-May 1959), 18ff.

5515. ----------. "Opera on Television: The Beginning of an Era." Musical America, 72 (Feb. 1952), 29.

5516. ----------. "T.V. in the Opera Picture." Film Music, 15, No. 3 (Jan.-Feb. 1956), 23.

5517. Ameringen, S. van. "Elektronische Fernsehoper." Musica, 13, No. 10 (Oct. 1959), 661-62.

5518. Breuer, Robert. "Wird die Fernsehoper die Oper 'retten?'" Österreichisch-er Musikzeitschrift, 12 (Sept. 1957), 360-61.

5519. Cantrick, Robert. "Music, Television, and Aesthetics." Quarterly of Film, Radio, and Television, 9, No. 1 (Fall 1954), 60-78.
        Concerns the telecasting of musical performances.

5520. Carner, M. "The Right Opera for the Microphone." BBC Quarterly (London), (1951-1952), 288.
        Concerns the problems of broadcasting opera on radio.

5521. Cartier, Rudolph. "Producing Television Opera." Opera (London), 8 (Nov. 1957), 679-84.

5522. Chochlov, J. "Klassičeskuyu operu -- na ekran." Sovetskaya muzyka, 16, No. 4 (Apr. 1952), 69-74.

5523. Eaton, Quaintance. "NBC Television Series Offers 'Carmen' as Initial At-traction." Musical America, 71 (Jan. 1, 1951), 25.

5524. Evans, E. G. "Music Appreciation by Television." Music Educators' Jour-nal, 41 (Nov.-Dec. 1954), 28-29ff.

5525. Faltinova, E. "Hudobne vysielanie v bratislavskej televizii." Slovenska Hudba (Bratislava), 3 (Nov.-Dec. 1959), 488-90.

5526. Fickler, August. "Oper und Operette im Rundfunk und deutschen Fernsehen: eine statistische Übersicht." Neue Zeitschrift für Musik, 118, Nos. 7-8 (July-Aug. 1957), 418-24.

5527. ----------. "Oper und Operette in Rundfunk und Fernsehen 1957: eine sta-tistische Übersicht." Neue Zeitschrift für Musik, 119, No. 5 (May 1958), 282-88.

5528. Fierz-Bantli, Gerold. "Helvetisches Wellenmosaik." Musica, 13 (July-Aug. 1959), 486-87.

5529. Foa, George R. "A Few Technical Problems." Opera (London), 8 (Nov. 1957), 685-86.
        Concerns the problems of opera on television.

5530. Fuchs, Viktor. "Thoughts About Television Opera." Music of the West Maga-zine (Pasadena, Calif.), 13 (July 1958), 5ff.

5531. Gill, G. "Serious Music and Television in Britain." The Chesterian, 31 (Summer 1956), 24-27.

5532. Goléa, Antoine. "'Don Giovanni' ein 'Musical?' Der Salzburger Kongress." Neue Zeitschrift für Musik, 120, No. 10 (Oct. 1959), 524-26.

5533. Hadley, M. "Arthur Benjamin's 'Prima Donna' on TV." London Musical Events, 7 (Oct. 1952), 26-28.

5534. Harth, Walther. "Das Bild auf dem Schirm." _Melos_, 22 (July-Aug. 1955), 209-12.

5535. Haskell, Arnold L. "The Dance on Television." _London Musical Events_, 12 (Apr. 1957), 22-23.

5536. Heidt, W. "The Challenge of Operatic Performance on Television." _Etude_, 71 (Nov. 1953), 14ff.

5537. Heimann, Mogens. "Seriøs musik i TV." _Dansk Musiktidsskrift_ (Copenhagen), 34, No. 8 (1959), 253-58.

5538. Helm, Everett B. "Opera for TV and Film." _Saturday Review_, 42 (Sept. 26, 1959), 67-68.
    Concerns the Salzburg Congress.

5539. ----------. "Salzburg Congress Debates Value of TV and Film Opera." _Musical America_, 79 (Oct. 1959), 7.

5540. Herrmann, Joachim. "Das Gesetz der Linse." _Musica_, 13, No. 4 (Apr. 1959), 237-38.

5541. Heylbut, Rose. "What TV Opera Needs, by Peter H. Adler." _Etude_, 69 (Sept. 1951), 14-15ff.

5542. Hinton, J. "'Billy Budd' on Television in U.S.A." _Musical Times_, 93 (Dec. 1952), 564-65.
    Concerns the television broadcast of Britten's opera.

5543. Holde, Artur. "Die Fernseh-Oper." _Musikleben_, 4 (June 1951), 167-70.

5544. ----------. "Radio und Television in USA." _Das Musikleben_, 6 (Oct. 1953), 337-44.

5545. Joachim, Heinz. "Fernsehen darf auf Opern nicht verzichten." _Neue Zeitschrift für Musik_, 120, No. 3 (Mar. 1959), 150-51.

5546. Junkers, Herbert. "Repertoire und Methode der Fernsehoper." _Musica_, 13, No. 4 (Apr. 1959), 235-37.

5547. Kirstein, Lincoln. "Television Opera in U.S.A." _Opera_ (London), 3 (Apr. 1952), 198-202ff.

5548. Kostelanetz, Andre. "Music's Potentialities in Television." _Variety_, 185 (Jan. 2, 1952), 224.

5549. Koster, Ernst. "Auf dem Wege zur Fernsehopern-Ästhetik." _Neue Zeitschrift für Musik_, 116, No. 11 (Nov. 1955), 94-95.

5550. ----------. "Beobachtungen am Bildschirm." _Musica_, 13, No. 11 (Nov. 1959), 720-21.

5551. ----------. "Fernseh-Dämmerung." _Musica_, 10, No. 3 (Mar. 1956), 193-97.

5552. ----------. "Fernsehopern: international betrachtet." _Musica_, 13, No. 11 (Nov. 1959), 727-29.
    Reactions to the Congress in Salzburg.

5553. ----------. "Musiktheater -- Ferngesehen." _Musica_, 10, Nos. 7-8 (July-Aug. 1956), 525-27.

5554. ----------. "Musiktheater im Fernsehen." _Das Musikleben_, 6 (Oct. 1953), 351-53.

5555. ----------. "Television Opera in Germany." _Opera_ (London), 8 (Dec. 1957), 755-59.

5556. ----------. "Um den Fernseh-Stil." _Musica_, 8 (Sept. 1954), 412-13.

5557. ----------. "Zur Synästhesie von Bild und Musik." _Musica_, 13, No. 4 (Apr. 1959), 240-42.

5558. ----------. "Von der Probe bis zur Sendung: wie entsteht ein Fernseh-
        spiel?" Das Musikleben, 8 (Feb. 1955), 52-54.

5559. Krebs, H. "Opera i radioen." Dansk Musiktidsskrift, 29 (1954), 65.

5560. Kukharsky, V. "Muzyka i televidenie." Sovetskaya muzyka, 23 (Aug. 1959),
        3-10.

5561. Labroca, Mario. "Das Opernglas für alle." Melos, 22 (July-Aug. 1955),
        198-200.

5562. Lawrence, Harold. "Music on TV." Audio, 41 (Mar. 1957), 56-57.

5563. "Leo Blechs 'Versiegelt': zur Ästhetik der Fernsehoper." Das Musikleben,
        7 (Sept. 1954), 319-20.

5564. Marie, Jean-Etienne. "Pour ou contre la musique pure à la télévision."
        Cahiers d'études de Radio-Télévision, 24 (1959), 355-76.

    5564a. Also published in German translation in Rundfunk und Fern-
            sehen, 8 (1960), 247-66.

5565. Martin, John. "The Dance: TV Ballet." New York Times, 103 (Jan. 10, 1954),
        Section 2, p. 7.

5566. Marx, H. "TV and Music." Music News, 43 (June 1951), 9.

5567. Matz, Mary Jane. "Opera of the Future: 'Tosca' for Tomorrow." Opera News,
        19, No. 24 (Apr. 18, 1955), 10-12.

5568. Mindermann, Earl. "Television and the Symphony." Music Journal, 12,
        No. 9 (Sept. 1954), 25, 65-66.

5569. Mokry, Ladislav. "Hudobna kultura a prostriedky masovej komunikacie."
        Slovenska Hudba (Bratislava), 9, No. 9 (1955), 401-02.

5570. Mul, Jan. "De toekomst der televisieopera." Mens en Melodie (Utrecht,
        Neth.), 14 (Oct. 1959), 313-15.

5571. Paulu, Burton. "Televising the Minneapolis Symphony Orchestra." Quarterly
        of Film, Radio and Television, 8, No. 2 (Winter 1953-1954), 157-71.

5572. Podest, Ludvik. "Hudba v televizi." Hudební Rozhledy (Prague), 12,
        No. 23 (1959), 968-71.

5573. ----------. "Kongres o opere a baletu v televizi." Hudební Rozhledy
        (Prague), 12, No. 19 (1959), 810-11.

5574. Reisfeld, Bert. "Ferngesehene Musik." Musica, 7 (Sept. 1953), 408-10.

5575. ----------. "Fernseh-Oper in Gefahr." Musica, 8, No. 3 (Mar. 1954), 114-
        15.

5576. ----------. "Menottis 'Maria Golovin.'" Musica, 13, No. 5 (May 1959),
        320-21.

5577. ----------. "Oper im Fernsehen." Musica, 7 (June 1953), 271-73.

5578. Rinaldi, Mario. "Milano: la prima opera televistiva -- 'Le Campane' di
        Rossellini." Musica d'Oggi (Milan), 2 (June 1959), 255.

5579. Robin, Harry. "The State of Music in Television." Film and TV Music, 16,
        No. 1 (Fall 1956), 22-23.

5580. Roger, Kurt George. "Prokofieffs 'Krieg und Frieden' als Fernsehoper."
        Österreichische Musikzeitschrift, 12 (Mar. 1957), 119-20.

5581. Rotondo, Peter. "Decorating Music for Television." Music Journal, 16,
        No. 6 (Sept. 1958), 20ff.

5582. Ruppel, Karl H. "Orffs 'Bernauerin' als Fernsehspiel." Melos, 26 (Mar.
        1959), 94-95.

5583. Sahl, H. "Glanz und Elend der Television." Das Musikleben, 5 (Apr. 1952),

97-100.

5584. Salter, Lionel. "Music in Television." Musical Times (London), 98 (Jan. 1957), 12-15.

5585. ----------. "Opera on Television." Opera (London), 8 (Nov. 1957), 673-79.
Includes a listing of operas produced by the B.B.C.

5586. Schlüter, Karl Heinz. "Blick in die Produktion." Musica, 13, No. 4 (Apr. 1959), 239-40.

5587. Schubert, Reinhold. "Strawinskys 'Geschichte vom Soldaten' im Fernsehen." Melos, 21 (May 1954), 147-48.

5588. Shavin, Norman. "Music: Television's Stepchild." Music Journal, 15, No. 6 (July-Aug. 1957), 12, 24.

5589. Shayon, R. L. "It's Opera, But Is It Grand?" Saturday Review, 36 (Mar. 13, 1954), 39.

5590. Sieburg, F. "Klangkulisse zum Bildschirm." Melos, 22 (July-Aug. 1955), 196-98.

5591. Smith, N. "'The Magic Flute' on TV." The Canon (Australia), 9 (Apr. 1956), 258-59.

5592. Sosnik, Harry. "TV Has Set Music Back 20 Years Because 'Picture' Is Main Thing." Variety, 184 (Sept. 26, 1951), 29.

5593. Spaeth, Sigmund. "As a Medium for Good Music." Music Clubs Magazine (Indianapolis), 30 (Oct. 1950), 22.

5594. Stahl, B. "'Carmen' on TV Comes Off Successfully, Showing Staging, Transmitting Needs." Variety, 189 (Dec. 17, 1952), 4ff.

5595. Strobel, Heinrich. "Die neue chance." Melos, 22 (July-Aug. 1955), 193-95.

5596. Taubman, Howard. "Problems of Music on TV." New York Times, 102 (Jan. 25, 1953), Section 2, p. 7.

5597. ----------. "Reaching a Public: Many Questions Posed by New Mass Media." New York Times, 106 (Jan. 13, 1957), p. 9.

5598. ----------. "Why More and More Like Opera." New York Times Magazine, 102 (Mar. 8, 1953), 18ff.

5599. "Two Opera Films Shown on Television." Musical America, 77 (Nov. 1, 1957), 30.
Concerns the television broadcasts of Verdi's "La traviata" and Mascagni's "Cavalleria rusticana."

5600. Van Volkenburg, J. L. "Provide Serious Musical Programs Through Integration." Musical America, 76 (Feb. 15, 1956), 27.

5601. Várady, László. "A Rádió operafelvételei." Uj zenei szemle, No. 3 (1952).

5602. Werker, Gerard. "Twee Nederlandse televisieopera's." Mens en Melodie (Utrecht, Neth.), 14 (July 1959), 217-22.

5603. Willey, George A. "Opera on Television." Music Review, 20, No. 2 (May 1959), 152-58.

5604. Wright, Kenneth A. "Television and Opera." Tempo (London), No. 45 (Autumn 1957), 8-14.

5605. Zillig, Winfried. "Hat Musik im Fernsehen eine Chance?" Melos, 24, Nos. 7-8 (July-Aug. 1957), 207-11.

SEE ALSO:

#238(Ford), #267(Matejka), #280(Philippot), #287(Salter), #1595(Barrett), #1600(Becker/Rutz/Bornoff), #1879, #1944, 1945(Bowman), #1950(Dahlgren),

#1955(Harman), #1956(Hijman), #1958(Holde), #1960(Koster), #1963(Lalou), #1965(Rigault), #1967(Seymour), #3079(L. Bernstein), #3154(Copland), #4915(Thiel), #5047(Bischoff), #5140(Weaver), #5202(Arundell), #5206 (Boll), #5209(Bornoff), #5221(Crowther), #5236(Franks), #5249(Harth), #5251(Helm), #5255(IMC), #5256(IMC/IMZ), #5315, 5316(Wexler), and #5621 (Burke).

1960's

5606. Adler, Peter Herman. "A Cruel Medium." Opera News, 33 (June 14, 1969), 8-11.

5607. ----------. "Music: The Silent Stepchild." Saturday Review, 52 (Apr. 26, 1969), 22-25ff.

5608. Adorno, Theodor W. "Musik im Fernsehen ist Brimborium." Der Spiegel, 9 (1968).

5609. Araoz Badi, J. "Visto y oido." Buenos Aires Musical, 18, No. 297 (1963), 5.

5610. Bamboschek, Giuseppe. "Televised Opera?" Musical Courier, 162 (Oct. 1960), 9.

5611. Baronijan, Vartkes. "Muzika i televizija: problemi vizuelizacije zvuka." Zvuk (Sarajevo), Nos. 92-93 (1969), 115-16.

5612. "The BBC as a Patron of Music." Bulletin of the European Broadcasting Union (1968).

A paper presented at the Royal Society of Arts, London.

5613. Black, Peter. "Opera on the Television Screen." Opera (London), 19 (Mar. 1968), 197-201.

5614. Blankenburg, Walter. "Nochmals: Zur Fernsehübertragung der Johannes-Passion." Musik und Kirche (Basel), 33, No. 4 (1963), 174-76.

5615. Blaukopf, Kurt, ed. IMZ Report: Music in T.V. -- Stage Management, Scenery and Costume in the T.V. Music Programme. Vienna: Internationales Musikzentrum, 1964.

In English, French, and German.

5616. Bornoff, Jack. "Music: A Challenge to Television." The World of Music (UNESCO), 11, No. 1 (1969), 17-31.

5617. ----------. "Die technischen Medien: Musik in Funk und Fernsehen." Neue Zeitschrift für Musik, 124, No. 12 (Dec. 1963), 473-76.

5618. Brasch, Alfred. "Berg's 'Wozzeck' ist eine Fernseh-Oper -- Inszenierung des WDR." Neue Zeitschrift für Musik, 126, No. 11 (Nov. 1965), 442.

5619. ----------. "Das Schönste aus 'Aida': Anmerkungen zur Oper im Fernseh-Programm." Neue Zeitschrift für Musik, 123, No. 4 (Apr. 1962), 172-74.

5620. ----------. "Wege und Irrwege der Fernsehoper." Neue Zeitschrift für Musik, 122 (Apr. 1961), 167-69.

5621. Burke, Richard Cullen. "A History of Televised Opera in the United States." Ph. D. Diss. University of Michigan 1963.

Abstract: DAI 25:6878A (order #DA 64-6658).

5622. Chailly, Luciano. "La Musique classique a la télévision italienne." The World of Music (UNESCO), 5, Nos. 1-2 (1963), 38.

5623. Colfescu, Alexandru. "Muzica la televiziune." Muzica (Bucarest), 14 (May-

June 1964), 92-94.

5624. Culshaw, John. "The Sight of Music." _Music and Musicians_, 17 (Nov. 1968), 24-25.

    An interview.

5625. Dirckinck-Holmfeld, Gregers. "Samtale omkring en TV-ballet." _Dansk Musiktidssktift_ (Copenhagen), 40, No. 2 (1965), 39-41.

5626. Dwyer, Edward Joseph. "American Video Opera: An Introduction and Guidebook to Its Production." Ph.D. Diss. Columbia University 1963.

    Abstract: DAI 24:5450A (order #DA 64-5680).

5627. Ebert, K. "Rundfunk und Fernsehen." _Musica_, 16, No. 1 (Jan. 1962), 31.

5628. Erhardt, Ludwik. "Oprawcy do wiezienia." _Ruch Muzyczny_ (Warsaw), 4 (Feb. 1, 1960), 11.

5629. ----------. "Telewizja od tylu." _Ruch Myzyczny_ (Warsaw), 4 (Feb. 15, 1960), 9-11.

5630. Fickler, August. "Oper und Operette in Rundfunk und Fernsehen 1961: eine statistische Übersicht." _Das Orchester_ (Hamburg), 10 (June 1962), 193-97.

5631. ----------. "Oper und Operette in Rundfunk und Fernsehen 1962: eine statistische Übersicht." _Das Orchester_ (Hamburg), 11 (July-Aug. 1963), 235.

5632. "Fjernsynet og musikken." _Norsk Musikerblad_ (Oslo), 49 (Sept. 1960), 1-2.

5633. "Fra talemaskin til fargefjernsyn." _Norsk Musikerblad_ (Oslo), 49 (Mar. 1960), 2-3.

5634. Fröhlich, W. "Musiktheater - Fernsehgerecht?" _Musica_, 19, No. 6 (June 1965), 313-14.

5635. Gattermeyer, H. "'Musik im Fernsehen': zum Fernsehkongress 1962 in Salzburg." _Musikerziehung_, 16, No. 3 (1963), 154-55.

5636. Goodwin, Noël. "'The Rise and Fall of the City of Mahagonny': BBC-2." _Opera_ (London), 16 (Apr. 1965), 307-08.

    Concerns the television broadcast of Kurt Weill's opera.

5637. Goslich, Siegfried. "Musik im Fernsehen." _Medium_, 2 (1965), 85ff.

5638. Gotlib, A. "Kogda telezritel' stanovitsya teleslushatelem." _Sovetskaya muzyka_, 26, No. 5 (May 1962), 122-24.

5639. Gräter, Manfred. "Musik in der 'television totale.'" _Neue Zeitschrift für Musik_, 129, No. 12 (Dec. 1968), 548-50.

    Also see a response to this article by Peter Rocholl, #5681.

5640. Hanus, Jan. "Televizni opera zatim netelevizne." _Hudebni Rozhledy_, 13, No. 5 (1960), 204.

5641. Hausswald, Günter. "Oper in Funk und Fernsehen." _Musica_, 18, No. 3 (Mar. 1964), 115-19.

5642. Havlicek, Dusan. "Stara opereta s novymi problemy." _Hudebni Rozhledy_, 16, No. 4 (1963), 172.

5643. ----------. "Svetla a stiny televizni zabavy." _Hudebni Rozhledy_, 17, No. 12 (1964), 520-22.

5644. ----------. "Umeni hudebni interpretace v televizi." _Hudebni Rozhledy_, 14, No. 3 (1961), 114-15.

5645. Helm, Everett. "Ima li televiziska opera buducnost? Povodom medunarodnih razgovora u Salzburgu." _Zvuk_ (Sarajevo), Nos. 35-36 (1960), 263-64.

5646. Holzamer, Karl. "Fernsehen in Konkurrenz mit dem Theater und dem Konzertsaal." Neue Zeitschrift für Musik, 130, No. 1 (Jan. 1969), 30-32.

5647. Honolka, Kurt. "Wo bleibt die Funk- und Fernsehoper?" Musica, 18, No. 1 (Jan. 1964), 32-33.

5648. Hrckova, Nada. "Hudba a televizia." Slovenska Hudba (Bratislava), 7, No. 2 (1963), 41-45.

5649. ----------. "Opera v televizli." Slovenska Hudba (Bratislava), 9, No. 9 (1965), 412-15.

5650. ----------. "Vzajomna podmienenost' televiznej opery a spolocnosti." Slovenska Hudba (Bratislava), 5 (July-Aug. 1961), 311-15.

5651. Hruba, J. "K opernym inscenaciam Bratislavskej televizie." Hudební Rozhledy (Prague), 13, No. 10 (1960), 437.

5652. "Hudba pro dva miliony: rozhovor s televiznimi pracovniky." Hudební Rozhledy (Prague), 16, No. 3 (1963), 97-101.

5653. Internationales Muzikzentrum, Vienna. IMZ Report: Music -- A Challenge to T.V. Salzburg: IMZ, 1968.

5654. ----------. IMZ Report: Music in T.V. Salzburg: IMZ, 1962.

In English, French, and German.

5655. Juhasz, J. E. "Dallapiccola: 'Ejszakai Repüles' -- bemutato a televizioban." Muzsika (Budapest), 7 (Jan. 1964), 8-9.

Concerns the television production of Luigi Dallapiccola's "Volo di notte."

5656. Jurik, Marian. "Hudba ako piate koleso v televizii." Slovenska Hudba (Bratislava), 11, No. 3 (1967), 136-38.

5657. Karman, Gyoergy. "A televizio opera: es balettmusorairol." Muzsika (Budapest), 12 (June 1969), 20-22.

5658. Koch, Karl O. "Die Technik der Opernproduktion im Fernsehen." Neue Zeitschrift für Musik, 123 (Apr. 1962), 168-72.

5659. Konzelmann, G. "Das Fernsehen und die Oper." Neue Zeitschrift für Musik, 127 (July-Aug. 1966), 263-64.

5659a. Also published in Das Orchester (Hamburg), 14 (Sept. 1966), 329-31.

5660. Korykhalova, N. "Dorogu novomu zhanru!" Sovetskaya Muzyka, 32, No. 12 (Dec. 1968), 61-65.

5661. Kotek, Josef. "Operni obrazovka nebo televizni jeviste?" Hudební Rozhledy (Prague), 13, No. 21 (1960), 876-80.

5662. Kuusisto, Ilkka. "Radions och TV: s roll i dagens finska musikliv." Musikrevy (Stockholm), 21, No. 6 (1966), 241-43.

5663. Lewinski, Wolf Eberhard von. "Fernsehoper nach Büchner." Musica, 18, No. 2 (Feb. 1964), 74-75.

5664. Majerska, Nada. "Niekol'ko problemov televiznej opery." Slovenska Hudba (Bratislava), 4 (June 1960), 276-78.

5665. Mehler, Walter. "Mit der Fernsehkamera im Konzertsaal." Musik und Gesellschaft, 10, No. 9 (Sept. 1960), 522-25.

5666. Merkulov, V. "Opera prikhodit v dom." Sovetskaya muzyka, 28, No. 12 (Dec. 1964), 27-28.

5667. Mul, Jan. "Televisie en muziek." Mens en Melodie (Utrecht, Neth.), 17 (Dec. 1962), 377-79.

5668. Müller, Hans Peter. "Musiksendungen im Deutschen Fernsehfunk." Musik und Gesellschaft, 18 (Jan. 1968), 45-46.

5669. ----------. "Zwischen Probe und Premiere: 'Bitte, nicht stören!' und 'Der Günstling.'" Musik und Gesellschaft, 18 (Apr. 1968), 265-68.

5670. Pauli, Hansjörg. "Das Hörbare und das Schaubare -- Fernsehen und jüngste Musik." In Musik auf der Flucht vor sich selbst. Reihe Hanser, XXVIII. Munich: Hanserverlag, 1969.

5671. ----------. "Musik im Fernsehen." Melos, 35 (July-Aug. 1968), 290-99.

5672. Pechotsch, Josef. "Musik zum Anschauen." Österreichische Musikzeitschrift, 23, No. 3 (Mar. 1968), 135-40.

5673. Pensdorfova, Eva. "Prokofjev v televizi." Hudební Rozhledy (Prague), 16, No. 14 (1963), 571-72.

5674. Pilka, Jiří. "Hudební filmy nasi televize." Hudební Rozhledy (Prague), 20, No. 18 (1967), 558-61.

5675. ----------. "Hudební vysilani televize: zezadu." Hudební Rozhledy (Prague), 18, No. 12 (1965), 487-90.

5676. ----------. "Nove formy pocuvania hudby predovsetkym v televizii." Slovenska Hudba (Bratislava), 12, Nos. 9-10 (1968), 412-17.

5677. Pociej, Bohdan. "Telewizja od przodu." Ruch Muzyczny (Warsaw), 4 (Feb. 15, 1960), 8-11.

5678. Pospisil, Vilem. "Televize, hudba, technika, vzdelani." Hudební Rozhledy, 13, No. 14 (1960), 582-83.

5679. ----------. "Televizni opera o Fucikovi." Hudební Rozhledy (Prague), 14, No. 14 (1961), 610.

5680. Rekai, A. "Szeljegyzet egy TV operafilmhez." Muzsika (Budapest), 7 (Mar. 1964), 28-29.

5681. Rocholl, Peter. "Zu Manfred Gräters Diskussionsbeitrag über 'Musik in der television totale.'" Neue Zeitschrift für Musik, 130, No. 4 (Apr. 1969), 185.

        See Gräter's article, #5639.

5682. Romadinova, Dora. "Opera? Muzykal'naya novella." Sovetskaya muzyka, 28, No. 1 (Jan. 1964), 100-03.

5683. Russell, Thomas L. "Televising a Symphony Orchestra." Music Journal, 25, No. 10 (Oct. 1967), 48ff.

5684. Salter, Lionel. "Opera at Home." Bulletin of the European Broadcasting Union (1966).

5685. ----------. "Television Operas at Salzburg." Opera (London), 13 (Dec. 1962), 817-18.

5686. Salzman, Eric. "'The Flood' von Igor Stravinsky in New York." Melos, 29 (Oct. 1962), 331-34.

5687. Schack, Erik. "Hvorfor opera i TV?" Dansk Musiktidsskrift, 44, Nos. 5-6 (1969), 113-14.

5688. Schaefer, Hansjürgen. "Verheissungsvoller Auftakt: Bemerkungen zu den Musiksendungen des Deutschen Fernsehfunks um die Jahreswende." Musik und Gesellschaft, 12, No. 2 (Feb. 1962), 90-92.

5689. ----------. "Versuch einer Fernsehfilm-Oper." Musik und Gesellschaft, 13, No. 2 (Feb. 1963), 78-80.

5690. Scheib, Wilfried. "Musik im Fernsehen." Österreichische Musikzeitschrift, 20 (Jan. 1965), 62-65.

5691. Schwinger, E. "Fernseh-Feuilleton: Musiksendungen im Deutschen Fernsehfunk." Musik und Gesellschaft, 16, No. 3 (Mar. 1966), 164-71.

5692. Shetler, Donald J. "First International Congress on Music in Television."

Music Educators' Journal, 49, No. 3 (1963), 54ff.

5693. ----------. "The Salzburg Opera Prize and the Congress on 'Music in Television.'" *The World of Music* (UNESCO), 4, No. 5 (1962), 101-02.

5694. Sibirsky, V. "Pesnya igoluboy ekran." *Sovetskaya muzyka*, 28, No. 6 (June 1964), 112-14.

5695. Siebler, Helmut. "Musik im Fernsehen." *Neue Zeitschrift für Musik*, 125, No. 6 (June 1964), 261-64.

   5695a. Also published in *Das Orchester* (Hamburg), 12 (July-Aug. 1964), 244-47.

5696. Sittner, Hans. "Internationaler Kongress 'Musik im Fernsehen' in Salzburg." *Österreichische Musikzeitschrift*, 17 (Oct. 1962), 491.

5697. Spingel, Hans Otto. "Erkennen, was jenseits von Form und Farbe verborgen ist." *Opernwelt*, 9, No. 5 (May 1968), 19-20.

   An interview with Herbert von Karajan.

5698. Stokowska, M. "O audycjach umuzykalniajacych w telewizii." *Ruch Muzyczny* (Warsaw), 8, No. 20 (1964), 12-13.

5699. Stuckenschmidt, Hans Heinz. "Gefahren und Möglichkeiten." *Opernwelt*, 8, No. 5 (May 1967), 27-29.

   An interview with Herbert von Karajan.

5700. Todorov, Manol. "Bulgarskata narodna muzika po Radio Sofiya i televiziyata." *Bulgarska Muzika* (Sofia), 17 (Aug. 1966), 49-54.

5701. Troitskaya, Galina. "Televidenie i muzyka." *Sovetskaya muzyka*, 24, No. 9 (Sept. 1960), 145-48.

5702. United Nations Educational, Scientific, and Cultural Organization. *Film and Television in the Service of Opera and Ballet*. Reports and Papers on Mass Communications, XXXII. Paris: UNESCO, 1960.

   See #5364.

5703. Vaislov, V., M. Mordvinov, A. Cholminov, E. Uyern'a et al. "Tribuna: Tele-opera i ee problemy." *Sovetskaya muzyka*, 33, No. 7 (July 1969), 28-43.

   Contributions presented at a conference of the Union of Composers in Moscow.

   5703a. Also published as "Die Fernsehoper und ihre Probleme," in *Sowjetwissenschaft: Kunst und Literatur* (Berlin), 18, No. 6 (June 1970), 653-64.

5704. Volek, Tomislav. "Dovetek televizniho kritika." *Hudební Rozhledy*, 18, No. 17 (1965), 731-32.

5705. ----------. "O hudebnim vysilani nasi televize." *Hudební Rozhledy*, 13, No. 19 (1960), 798-99.

5706. Werker, Gerard. "Opera en televisie: Mozarts 'Ontvoering uit het Serail.'" *Mens en Melodie*, 18 (Oct. 1963), 297-99.

5707. Whelen, Christopher. "Thoughts on Television Opera." *Composer* (London), No. 24 (Summer 1967), 15-17.

5708. Wicke, Andreas. "Musik und Geräusch in Fernsehreportagen." *Theorie und Praxis* (Berlin-Adlershof), No. 29 (n.d.), 24-25.

5709. Willnauer, Franz. "'Ausgerechnet und Verspielt': eine Fernsehoper von Ernst Krenek." *Neue Zeitschrift für Musik*, 123, No. 9 (Sept. 1962), 417-18.

5710. Winters, Ken. "'Elektra' on CBC Television." *Canadian Music Journal*, 5, No. 3 (1961), 30-33.

5711. Zillig, Winfried. "Des Fernsehens Opernsorgen." In *Vierzehn Mutmassungen über das Fernsehen*. Ed. A. R. Katz. Munich, 1963, pp. 89-99.

SEE ALSO:

#238(Ford), #267(Matejka), #280(Philippot), #287(Salter), #2073(IMZ), #2122(Pleasants), #2212(Breuer), #2216(Eastwood), #2222(Novick), #2224 (Rinaldi), #2229, #4654(Jelinek), #4901(Stuckenschmidt), #4915(Thiel), #5086(IMC), #5087(IMC/IMZ), #5092(Kabalevskij), #5135(UNESCO), #5323, 5324(Bornoff), #5335(IMZ), #5340, #5345(Lüdemann), #5363, 5364(UNESCO), and #6264(IMZ).

1970's

5712. Adler, Peter Herman. "Can TV Save Opera?" New York Times, 119 (Sept. 13, 1970).

    5712a. Reprinted in the National Music Council Bulletin (New York), 31, No. 1 (1970), 6-8.

5713. Afonina, N. ("Portrait of a Television Musician: A Conversation with Dan- iil Shafran.") In Muzyka i televidenie. Ed. Galina Troitskaya. Moscow: Sovetskij Kompositor, 1978.

    In Russian. See Troitskaya, #5834.

5714. ----------, and Galina Troitskaya, comps. Muzyka i televidenie, I. Moscow: Sovetskij Kompositor, 1978.

    -- Rev. in Sovetskaya muzyka, 45, No. 1 (Jan. 1981), 102-04.

5715. Anderson, William. "Opera as a Spectator Sport." Stereo Review, 36, No. 6 (June 1976), 4.

5716. Andreeva, D. "Chutiy posrednik." Sovetskaya muzyka, 36, No. 7 (July 1972), 101-05.

5717. Angelov, Petur. "Televiziyata otrazyava muzikalniya zhivot." Bulgarska Mu- zika (Sofia), 29 (May 1978), 44-46.

5718. Applebaum, Louis. "The Paradox and Puzzle of Music on Canadian Television." The Canadian Composer/Le Compositeur Canadien (Toronto), No. 137 (Jan. 1979), 18-23ff.

5719. Augustin, Joachim, and Rudolf Sailer. "Probleme der musikalischen Vermitt- lung von 'ernster' Musik im Fernsehen." In Musik in den Massenmedien, Rundfunk und Fernsehen: Perspektiven und Materialien. Ed. Hans-Christian Schmidt. Mainz: B. Schotts Söhne, 1976, pp. 67-73.

    See Schmidt, #5117.

5720. Averbach, E. ("Musical Concerts in Television.") In Muzy XX veka. Ed. Natal'ya Zorkaya and Jurij Bogomolov. Moscow: Iskusstvo, 1978.

    In Russian. See Zorkaya, #2624.

5721. Bark, Jan. "Paa spark genom Sahara: om musik i television." Ballade, 3, No. 1 (1979), 6-10.

5722. Barkauskas, Vytautas. ("The Creative Process and TV.") In Muzyka i tele- videnie. Ed. Galina Troitskaya. Moscow: Sovetskij Kompositor, 1978.

    In Russian. See Troitskaya, #5834.

5723. Barnes, John W. "Musical Dramatic Works on the Television Screen." The Canadian Music Book (Ottawa), 9 (Autumn-Winter 1974), 161-64.

5724. Bastide, François Regis. "Sortir de l'élite." Harmonie (Paris), No. 135 (Mar. 1978), 33-36.

5725. Benvenga, Nancy. "Bergman's TV 'Flute.'" Opera (England), 26 (July 1975), 693-95.

5726. Bertz-Dostal, Helga. "Oper im Fernsehen: Grundlagenforschung im Rahmen des Forschungsprogramms des Instituts für Theaterwissenschaft an der Universität Wien." Ph.D. Diss. (Theater and Musicology), University of Vienna 1970-1971.

> A history and index of televised operas produced from 1936-1970, including operas commissioned for T.V. Also includes a bibliography.

> Published in two volumes, Vienna: Gesellschaft für Musiktheater, 1970. Vol. 1: "Text und Bildteil," and Vol. 2: "Registerteil."

> -- Rev. in Opera Journal, 6, No. 2 (1973), 20-21.

> -- Rev. in Neue Zeitschrift für Musik, 135, No. 11 (Nov. 1974), 718-19.

5727. Bogomolov, Jurij. ("Representation: The Function of Television.") In Muzy XX veka. Ed. Natal'ya Zorkaya and Jurij Bogomolov. Moscow: Iskusstvo, 1978.

> In Russian. See Zorkaya, #2624.

5728. Bornoff, Jack. "Lisbon." The World of Music (UNESCO), 14, No. 3 (1972), 57-60.

> Concerns the Symposium on Music and the 20th Century Media. In English, French, and German.

5729. Brasch, Alfred. "Der aktuelle Musikbericht." Melos/Neue Zeitschrift für Musik, 4, No. 3 (1978), 243-44.

5730. ----------. "'Figaro': 20 Jahre Manipulation." Melos/Neue Zeitschrift für Musik, 3, No. 2 (1977), 150-51.

5731. ----------. "Musik für Zuschauer." Melos/Neue Zeitschrift für Musik, 4, No. 2 (1978), 141-42.

> Concerns the broadcasting of "classical" music on T.V.

5732. ----------. "Musik für Zuschauer: Oper im Fernsehen -- Internationales Symposion in Wien." Melos/Neue Zeitschrift für Musik, 4, No. 4 (1978), 334-36.

5733. ----------. "Musik für Zuschauer: zwanzig Jahre Fernseh-Oper -- ein Rückblick in Stichworten." Neue Zeitschrift für Musik, 133 (May 1972), 280-81.

5734. ----------. "Musik für Zuschauer von morgen: Fernsehopernpreis und IMZ-Kongress in Salzburg." Neue Zeitschrift für Musik, 135, No. 10 (Oct. 1974), 640-43.

5735. ----------. "Salzburg: Wege ser Oper im Fernsehen." Melos/Neue Zeitschrift für Musik, 3, No. 6 (1977), 531-33.

5736. Cemino, R. "Musica por TV." Buenos Aires Musical, 31, No. 491 (1976), 1ff.

5737. Chanan, Michael. "Opera for a Small Screen." Music and Musicians, 20 (Jan. 1972), 24-26.

5738. Chernova, Natal'ya. ("In Search of Contacts: Remarks on the Special Features of the Medium.") In Muzyka i televidenie, I. Ed. Galina Troitskaya. Moscow: Sovetskij Kompozitor, 1978.

> In Russian. See Troitskaya, #5834.

5739. Coolidge, Richard A. "Soap Culture: or, Art Music in the Heat of the Day." Southwestern Musician and Texas Music Educator, 42, No. 10 (May 1974), 16-17.

> Includes a bibliography.

5740. Coppage, Noel. "The Oddest Couple of All -- Music and TV." Stereo Review, 36, No. 6 (June 1976), 64-68.

5741. Cowie, Peter. "TV Opera: Ingmar Bergman Shows How It Should Be Done." High Fidelity and Musical America, 25 (June 1975), 66-70.

5742. Culshaw, John. "Music and the Media." Australian Journal of Music Education, No. 22 (Apr. 1978), 9-15.

An address delivered at the University of Western Australia.

5743. Davlekamova, S. "O balete." Sovetskaya muzyka, 42, No. 11 (Nov. 1978), 96-100.

5744. Dimov, B. "Praktische Fernseharbeit in Köln." Melos, 37 (July-Aug. 1970), 290-95.

5745. Docheva, Ekaterina. "Televiziya, muzyka, estetichesko vuzpitanie." Bulgarska Muzika (Sofia), 28 (Dec. 1977), 23-25.

5746. Dusek, Peter. "Zittern um das hohe C: Reflexionen über den Siegeszug der Fernseh - Live - Oper." HiFi Stereophonie, 18 (Nov. 1979), 1542-43.

5747. Dvorničenko, Oksana. ("A Televised Interpretation of Music.") In Muzyka i televidenie. Ed. Galina Troitskaya. Moscow: Sovetskij Kompositor, 1978.

In Russian. See Troitskaya, #5834.

5748. Efimov, A. "Muzyka, teleekran, slushatel'." Sovetskaya muzyka, 41, No. 8 (Aug. 1977), 63-66.

5749. Epertiere, Renard. "Quatre aus de retransmissions lyriques a la télévision." Harmonie - Antenne (Feb. 1979), 14-19.

5750. "Eshche raz o muzyke v efire." Sovetskaya muzyka, 35, No. 3 (Mar. 1971), 47-51.

5751. "Fernsehen in Deutschland: ein preiswertes Vernügen -- Gebührenhöhe und Programmangebot im internationalen Vergleich." Media - Perspektiven (Frankfurt am Main), (Dec. 1973).

5751a. Reprinted in Das Orchester (Hamburg), 22 (Apr. 1974), 232-36.

5752. Fomin, V. "Smotrite i slushayte simfoniyu." Sovetskaya muzyka, 38, No. 12 (Dec. 1974), 84-88.

5753. Frederiksen, Steen. "Janacek: en omtale af den herhjemme relativt ukendte komponist i anledning af TV-operaens opfoerelse af 'Katja Kabanova.'" Dansk Musiktidsskrift, 47, No. 1 (1971), 1-5.

5754. Friedrich, Heinz. "Symfonie na obrazovce." Hudební Rozhledy (Prague), 26, No. 3 (1973), 123-24.

5755. Fuga, Sandro. "Alcune considerazioni sui programmi musicali radio-televisivi." Rassegna Musicale Curci (Milan), 31, No. 2 (1978), 35-36.

5756. Gibson, Gordon R. "A Chance to Compare." The Opera Journal (University of Mississippi), 5, No. 2 (1972), 19-23.

5757. ----------, and Thomas H. Philips. A Manual of Television Opera Production. Albuquerque: New Mexico University Press, 1973.

-- Rev. in Music Educators' Journal, 61 (Oct. 1974), 90ff.

5758. Gotlib, A. "O kamernoy muzyke na teleekrane." Sovetskaya muzyka, 37 (July 1973), 53-56.

5759. Grassi, P. "La musica nei programmi radiotelevisivi." Rassegna Musicale Curci (Milan), 30-31, Nos. 3-1 (1977-1978), 43-47.

5760. Gräter, Manfred. "The Future of Music Lies in TV." The World of Music (UNESCO), 13, No. 4 (1971), 20-31.

In English, French, and German.

5761. Grünewald, Helge. "Musik im Fernsehen: Stiefkind der Optik?" Neue Musikzeitung (Regensburg), 21, No. 2 (1972), 3.

5762. Grzybowski, Jan. "Music in Television." Polish Music/Polnische Musik (Warsaw), 10, No. 4 (1975), 11-16.

In English and German.

5763. Helm, Everett B. "Lissabon: Die Musik und die Medien -- ein Kolloquium." Neue Zeitschrift für Musik, 133, No. 9 (Sept. 1972), 525-26.

5764. Hess, Joachim. "Oper im Fernsehen." Musica, 32, No. 3 (Mar. 1978), 237-40.

5765. Jenke, Manfred. "Die neuen audiovisuellen Medien und das Fernsehen." Börsenblatt für den Deutschen Buchhandel, No. 69 (1971).

   5765a. Reprinted in Musikhandel (Bonn), 22, No. 7 (1971), 323-25.

5766. Johnson, Bengt Emil. "Pendereckis djaevlar: engagerad musikdramatik eller vaaldspornografi?" Nutida Musik (Stockholm), 15, No. 4 (1971-1972), 50-52.

5767. "Der Kameramann kannte die Instrumente nicht." Instrumentenbau Musik International, 30, No. 4 (1976), 351.

5768. Kerner, L. "Music: Opera and TV -- Scenes from a Stormy Marriage." Village Voice, 23 (Aug. 21, 1978), 102-03.

5769. Kirchberg, Klaus. "Fast ein Musik-Frühling." Neue Zeitschrift für Musik, No. 5 (Sept.-Oct. 1979), 509-10.

5770. Kisun'ko, V. ("The Richness of Sound.") In Muzy XX veka. Ed. Natal'ya Zorkaya and Jurij Bogomolov. Moscow: Iskusstvo, 1978.

        In Russian. See Zorkaya, #2624.

5771. Klein, Rudolf. "Ein überdimensionales Unternehmen: Bizets 'Carmen' an der Wiener Staatsoper." Opernwelt, 20, No. 2 (1979), 20-22.

5772. Klotyns, Arnold. ("The Aesthetics of the Televised Musical Setting.") In Muzyka i televidenie, I. Ed. Galina Troitskaya. Moscow: Sovetskij Kompositor, 1978.

        In Russian. See Troitskaya, #5834.

5773. Kofin, Ewa. "Muzyka telewizyjna -- koncert." Ruch Muzyczny (Warsaw), 23, No. 18 (1979), 17-18.

5774. Kopecka, M. "Opery na obrazovce." Hudební Rozhledy (Prague), 30, No. 4 (1977), 150-51.

5775. Korčegina, E. ("The Television Performance: Technology of Preparation and Artistic Evolution.") In Muzy XX veka. Ed. Natal'ya Zorkaya and Jurij Bogomolov. Moscow: Iskusstvo, 1978.

        In Russian. See Zorkaya, #2624.

5776. Koreshkova, L., and A. Barannikov. "S litse kum slushatelya." Bulgarska Muzika (Sofia), 29 (Feb. 1978), 83-85.

5777. Korykhalova, N. ("Instrumental Music on TV.") In Muzyka i televidenie, I. Ed. Galina Troitskaya. Moscow: Sovetskij Kompositor, 1978.

        In Russian. See Troitskaya, #5834.

5778. Kozhukharov, Slav. "Nasha muzikalna kultura i bulgarskata televiziya." Bulgarska Muzika (Sofia), 29 (May 1978), 46-51.

5779. Kul'berg, V. ("The Influence of Television's Specific Features on Staging Ballet.") In Muzyka i televidenie. Ed. Galina Troitskaya. Moscow: Sovetskij Kompositor, 1978.

        In Russian. See Troitskaya, #5834.

5780. Lager, G. "Soekelys paa NORDSAT." Ballade, 2, No. 3 (1978), 8-9.

5781. Lange, Wolfgang. "Von Brecht bis Marlitt: Marginalien zum 'Kulturmagazin.'" Film und Fernsehen (Berlin, DDR), 6, No. 7 (1978), 11-13.

5782. Lewinski, Wolf Eberhard von. "Grosse Oper -- nah gesehen: zu aktuellen Bestrebungen des Fernsehens, Opern zu senden." Opernwelt, 20, No. 9 (1979), 10-11.

5783. Lindemann, Klaus. "Ohren zu, Augen auf: Musik im Fernsehen." Neue Zeitschrift für Musik, 26, No. 1 (Jan. 1977), 3.

5784. Lorber, Richard. "Toward an Aesthetics of Videodance." Arts in Society (University of Wisconsin, Madison), 13, No. 2 (1976), 242-53.

5785. Malyshev, Jucij. ("Television and Musicians.") In Muzyka i televidenie, I. Ed. Galina Troitskaya. Moscow: Sovetskij Kompozitor, 1978.

      In Russian. See Troitskaya, #5834.

5786. Mark, Elisabeth. "Musik im Fernsehen: ein Gespräch mit Klaus Lindemann." Neue Zeitschrift für Musik, 134, No. 10 (Oct. 1973), 637-39.

5787. Markowski, Liesel. "Internationale Fernseh-Kooperation: Verdis 'Rigoletto.'" Musik und Gesellschaft, 22 (July 1972), 444-45.

5788. Mayer, Martin. "About Television: Music and the Medium." American Film, 3 (Feb. 1978), 55ff.

5789. Menaker, Daniel. "Television: How to Take Pictures of Music." Film Comment, 15 (Mar.-Apr. 1979), 76-77.

5790. Mercer, Ruby. "Plan of Action: TV Opera." Opera Canada (Toronto), 18, No. 4 (1977), 12-14.

      An interview with Armand Landry and Peter Symcox.

5791. Mielke, Georg F. "Musik im Fernsehen: 'Pehello' -- Dokumentation oder Musikfilm?" Musik und Gesellschaft, 20, No. 3 (Mar. 1970), 188-90.

5792. ----------. "'Xerxes': Vergleich zweier Fernsehproduktionen." Musikbühne (Berlin, DDR), 77 (1977), 75-87.

      Concerns the problems of television opera, through a valuable analysis of Handel's "Xerxes."

5793. Miller, Allan. "Symphony Orchestras on Television: Do We Have a Model for the Future?" Symphony News (Virginia), 24, No. 3 (1973), 8ff.

5794. Moscati, Italo. "Dopo il teatro e il cinema la TV secondo Carmelo." Cineforum (Bergamo), No. 178 (Oct. 1978), 593-99.

5795. Mosusova, Nadezda. "Savremena muzika na televiziji." Zvuk (Sarajevo), No. 2 (Summer 1973), 213-14.

5796. Muggler, Fritz. "Rundfunk und Fernsehen als Kulturträger." Schweizerische Musikzeitung, 110, No. 1 (1970), 8-13.

5797. Nunes, E. "Musica, opera e ballet na TV." Celuloide (Portugal), 24, No. 278 (June 1979), 171-72.

5798. "Orchestral Broadcasting, Television and Recording in Britain." In A Report on Orchestral Resources in Great Britain. London: Arts Council of Great Britain, 1970, pp. 48-54.

   5798a. Reprinted in Performing Arts Review (New York), 3, No. 2 (1972), 351-64.

5799. Panek, Waclaw. "Muzyczne postawy telewidzow." Ruch Muzyczny (Warsaw), 18, No. 3 (1974), 4-5.

5800. ----------, and Andrzej Witkowski. "Wychowanie muzyczne w radiu i telewizji: Miedzynarodowe Seminarium w Warszawie 18-22 maja." Ruch Muzyczny (Warsaw), 16, No. 15 (1972), 3-5.

5801. Pash, Donald A. "What Can an American University Contribute to Music in Television?" The Canada Music Book (Ottawa), 11-12 (Autumn/Winter-Spring/Summer 1975-1976), 97-103.

      An address delivered to the 16th IMC General Assembly.

5802. Pauli, Hansjörg. "Hudba poslechem i pohledem." Hudební Rozhledy (Prague), 25, No. 3 (1972), 118-20.

5803. ----------. "Music: Heard and Seen." The World of Music (UNESCO), 13, No. 4 (1971), 32-47.

      In English, French, and German.

5803a. Reprinted as "Musik: gehört und gesehen," in Musikhandel
        (Bonn), 24, No. 7 (1973), 297-98; and 24, No. 8 (1973),
        350.

5804. Philips, Thomas H., and Gordon R. Gibson. "Television: The Challenge of a
        New Medium." The Opera Journal (University of Mississippi), 5, No. 1
        (1972), 5-8.

5805. Popova, Manya. "Purvi televizionen tsikul za bulgarska muzika." Bulgarska
        Muzika, 29 (Apr. 1978), 83.

5806. Potter, Keith. "Radio and Television." Music and Musicians, 24, No. 8
        (Apr. 1976), 26-28.
        Concerns Ingmar Bergman's "Die Zauberflöte." Also in-
        cludes references to other current operatic and con-
        cert works on radio and television.

5807. Rich, Alan. "Music: Television Culture -- A Jaundiced Look." New York
        Magazine (Boulder, Colo.), 11 (Mar. 13, 1978), 61-62.

5808. Rocholl, Peter. "Fragen der unterschiedlichen Vermittlung von Musikwerken
        in den Medien: Gründe, Tendenzen, Auswirkungen." In Musik in den Massen-
        medien, Rundfunk und Fernsehen: Perspektiven und Materialien. Ed. Hans-
        Christian Schmidt. Mainz: B. Schötts Sohne, 1976, pp. 74-90.

        See Schmidt, #5117.

5809. Romadinova, Dora. "O muzykal'nykh telefil'makh." Sovetskaya muzyka, 35,
        No. 5 (May 1971), 21-27.

5810. Rubinstein, Leslie. "Live from the Met." Opera News, 44 (Sept. 1979), 10-
        14ff.
        Concerns the process of adaptation from stage to screen.

5811. Salter, Lionel. "The Birth of TV Opera." Opera (England), 28 (Mar. 1977),
        234-39.

5812. ----------. "The Infancy of TV Opera." Opera (England), 28 (Apr. 1977),
        340-44.

5813. Savinov, N. "Opera na golubom ekrane." Sovetskaya muzyka, 36 (July 1972),
        97-101.

5814. Scheib, Wilfried. "Musik im Fernsehen: Gedanken zum neuen Schema." Öster-
        reichische Musikzeitschrift, 34 (Dec. 1979), 619-21.

5815. ----------. "Oper im Fernsehen: ein internationales Symposium." Öster-
        reichische Musikzeitschrift, 33 (July-Aug. 1978), 393-94.

5816. Schmidt, Hans-Christian. "Zum Dilemma der Visualisierung von Musik im
        Fernsehen." Das Orchester (Hamburg), 25 (Dec. 1977), 835-60.

5817. Schneider, Frank. "Musiksendungen im Deutschen Fernsehfunk." Musik und
        Gesellschaft, 22, No. 5 (May 1972), 295-300.

5818. Schroth, Gerhard. "Blachers einschichtige Fernseh-Musik." Neue Zeitschrift
        für Musik, 24, No. 6 (June 1975), 28.

5819. Shantyr, Grigory Mikhailovich. "Byt' li teleopere?" Sovetskaya muzyka, 43,
        No. 7 (July 1979), 48-50.

5820. Shilova, Irina M. ("Classical Opera and Television.") In Muzyka i televi-
        denie, I. Ed. Galina Troitskaya. Moscow: Sovetskij Kompozitor, 1978.
        In Russian. See Troitskaya, #5834.

5821. Slivin'sky, Zdzislaw, et al. "Na opernoy stsene, v kontsertnom zale i v
        efire." Sovetskaya muzyka, 35, No. 6 (June 1971), 127-29.

5822. Statelova, Roz Mari. "Da se zabavlyavame s televiziya." Bulgarska Muzika
        (Sofia), 25, No. 2 (1974), 41-44.

5823. Sutermeister, Henri. "Henri Sutermeister nous parle -- une nouvelle forme
        d'art: l'opera pour la television." Revue Musicale de Suisse Romande

(Yverdon, Switz.), 24, No. 4 (1971), 13-14.

5824. Swallow, Norman. "Images with Melodious Intent." <u>Music and Musicians</u>, 19 (Feb. 1971), 22-24.

5825. "Television española y la musica." <u>Monsalvat</u> (Barcelona), No. 52 (July-Aug. 1978), 440.

5826. "Television: A Medium for Music." <u>Musicanada</u> (Ottawa), No. 37 (Nov. 1978), 13-14.

> Concerns the Canadian Music Council Conference on "Music and Television." In English and French.

5827. Thiel, Jörn. "Die musikalische Szene des Fernsehens im internationalen Vergleich." <u>Musik und Bildung</u>, 7, No. 4 (Apr. 1975), 170-73.

5828. Thiel, Wolfgang. "Konzerte auf dem Bildschirm." <u>Musik und Gesellschaft</u>, 26, No. 5 (May 1976), 298-99.

5829. ----------. "Musikästhetische Medienspezifik: dreimal getanztes Fernsehkonzert." <u>Musik und Gesellschaft</u>, 27, No. 8 (Aug. 1977), 506-08.

5830. ----------. "Vermischte Sendungen im Fernsehen." <u>Musik und Gesellschaft</u>, 27, No. 11 (Nov. 1977), 684-86.

5831. Tournier, Michel. "Ecouter mieux la musique." <u>Harmonie</u> (Paris), No. 135 (Mar. 1978), 40-43.

5832. Trenczak, Heinz. "Mehr andere Musik in Fernsehen." <u>HiFi Stereophonie</u>, 17 (June 1978), 688-90.

5833. Troitskaya, Galina. ("A Little Trip through History and Music and Urgent Questions of Television.") In <u>Muzyka i televidenie, I</u>. Ed. Galina Troitskaya. Moscow: Sovetskij Kompositor, 1978.

> In Russian. See Troitskaya, #5834.

5834. ----------, ed. <u>Muzyka i televidenie, I</u>. Moscow: Sovetskij Kompositor, 1978.

> A collection of articles, with contributions by N. Afonina (#5713), V. Barkauskas (#5722), N. Chernova (#5738), O. Dvorničenko (#5747), K. Karaev (#5093), A. Klotyns (#5772), N. Korykhalova (#5777), V. Kul'berg (#5779), J. Malyshev (#5785), I. Shilova (#5820), and G. Troitskaya (#5833).

5835. Tsuker, A. "Sovetskaya muzyka v televizionnoy interpretatsii." <u>Sovetskaya muzyka</u>, 43, No. 6 (June 1979), 57-62.

5836. Tumilowicz, Bronislaw. "Muzyka w telewizji." <u>Ruch Muzyczny</u> (Warsaw), 22, No. 13 (1978), 3-6.

5837. Veri, Frances, and Michael Jamanis. "Creating a New Audience." <u>Music Journal</u>, 33 (Oct. 1975), 24-25.

5838. Walter, Edith. "Arnaud Teneze à la télévision: Le Probleme de la musique, c'est l'image." <u>Harmonie-Antenne</u> (Nov. 1979), 8-12.

> An interview.

SEE ALSO:

#63(Kofin), #238(Ford), #267(Matejka), #287(Salter), #2233(Amzoll), #2240 (Bachmann), #2374(Fabian), #2434(IMZ), #2585(Theodor), #2594(Vartanov), #2624(Zorkaya/Bogomolov), #2662(P. Evans), #2674(Irvine), #2675(King), #2686(Rocholl), #2707(Warrack), #4649(IMZ), #4663(Jungk), #4915(Thiel), #5051(Bornoff/Salter), #5086(IMC), #5093(Karaev), #5116(H.-C. Schmidt), #5380(Borev), #5386(Csobadi), #5401(Furceva), #5406(Hayford), #5414(Kluge et al.), #5425(Lučaj), #5433(Müller-Blattau), #5951(Dexter), #6125(Stoyanova), and #6265(IMC).

1980's

5839. Aakerberg, Yngve. "Video paa gott och ont." Musikern (Stockholm), No. 2 (Feb. 1982), 27-31.

5840. Abadzhiev, Aleksandur. "Muzikalni aktsenti v televiziyata." Bulgarska Muzika, 33, No. 9 (1982), 93-96.

5841. Andersen, Mogens. "Fra opera i TV til TV-opera." Dansk Musiktidsskrift (Copenhagen), 56, No. 6 (1982), 253-55.

5842. Ardoin, John. "A 'Ring' Diary." Opera Quarterly, 1, No. 2 (1983), 4-10.

   Concerns the 1980 T.V. production of Wagner's "Ring" by Patrice Chereau and Pierre Boulez.

5843. Auerbakh, L. "Ya smotryu simfonicheskiy kontsert." Sovetskaya muzyka, 46, No. 3 (Mar. 1982), 61-63.

5844. Bartels, Karsten. "Fernsehen: Janaceks 'Katja Kabanova.'" Musik und Gesellschaft, 32, No. 11 (Nov. 1982), 692-94.

5845. Boltz, Klaus. "Beleuchtungstechnische Adaptationen für die Aufzeichnung des vollständigen 'Ring des Nibelungen' aus dem Festspielhaus Bayreuth." Fernseh- und Kino-Technik (Berlin, BDR), 34 (Dec. 1980), 459-61.

5846. Bonnesen, Michael. "'Stalten Mette': noter til en fjernsynsopera." Dansk Musiktidsskrift (Copenhagen), 56, No. 6 (1982), 248-53.

5847. Carcassonne, Philippe. "Dossier -- La Musique de film: Grand musique, petites images." Cinématographe (Paris), No. 62 (Nov. 1980), 26.

5848. Chizhek, L. "Muzikalnite predavaniya v chekhoslovashkata televiziya." Bulgarska Muzika (Sofia), 32 (Apr. 1981), 100-03.

5849. Dvorničenko, Oksana I. "Muzykanty v svete yupiterov." Sovetskaya muzyka, 46, No. 3 (Mar. 1982), 54-61.

5850. Ely, Norbert. "Oper im Fernsehen -- eine neue Massenkunst?" Neue Zeitschrift für Musik, 144, No. 4 (Apr. 1983), 10-12.

5851. Engstrom, John. "Television: Wagner on the Tube -- 'Ring' Around the Color." Film Comment, 19 (Jan.-Feb. 1983), 78-79.

5852. Fabian, Imre. "Das Interview: Karlheinz Hundorf." Opernwelt, 23, No. 6 (1982), 26-28.

5853. Foti, L. H. "Sight and Sound: Music Video -- Growth of a New Art Form." Rolling Stone, No. 404 (Sept. 15, 1983), 90.

5854. Kenyon, Nicholas. "Musical Events: Small Screen." New Yorker, 58 (July 5, 1982), 93-96.

   Concerns T.V. performances of operas by Monteverdi.

5855. Kneif, Tibor. "Filmmern, Glamour, Ignoranz: warum ich keine Rocksendungen anschaue." Neue Zeitschrift für Musik, No. 1 (Jan.-Feb. 1981), 14-16.

5856. Kochetkov, A. "Televidenie -- interpretator muzykal'noy zhizni." Sovetskaya muzyka, 45, No. 7 (July 1981), 84-88.

5857. Kokoreva, L. "Eshche raz o problemakh zhanra." Sovetskaya muzyka, 46, No. 6 (June 1982), 49-51.

5858. Konicek, Frantisek. "Vazna hudba v nasi televizi." Hudební Rozhledy, 33, No. 11 (1980), 523-25.

5859. Kopecka, M. "Televize." Hudební Rozhledy, 34, No. 9 (1981), 409-11.

5860. ----------. "Vysilala televize." Hudební Rozhledy, 35, No. 5 (1982), 209-11.

5861. Kuneva, Rada. "Na opera po domashni pantofi." _Bulgarska Muzika_ (Sofia), 32 (Jan. 1981), 72-74.

5862. Lendvay, Kamillo. "A zene es a vizualitas ujszeru kapcsolata: operakompon-alas televiziora." _Filmkultura_ (Budapest), 16 (Mar.-Apr. 1980), 70-72.

5863. Lipton, Gary. "If He Were Alive Today, Wagner Would Use TV." _New York Times_, 132 (Jan. 23, 1983), Section 2, p. 25.

5864. Livingston, William. "Audio - Video Wagner." _Stereo Review_, 48 (Mar. 1983), 6.

5865. Loskill, J. "King Kong am Rhein: Karajans TV-Version von 'Rheingold.'" _Opernwelt_, 22, No. 7 (1981), 8.

5866. Mayer, Martin. "TV Opera Hits a High Note." _American Film_, 6 (Jan.-Feb. 1981), 53-55.

5867. Moses, Kurt. "Opera on Television: The Problems and Strengths." _American Record Guide_ (Washington, D.C.), 44 (July-Aug. 1981), 2-5.

5868. Musaeva, F. "Teleopera: problemy zhanra." _Sovetskaya muzyka_, 44, No. 1 (Jan. 1980), 78-82.

5869. Öpen, Heinz. "Klassische Musik im Fernsehen." _Musica_, 34, No. 1 (1980), 18-20.

5870. ----------. "Oper im Fernsehen: Bemerkungen zur Situation in der BRD." _Österreichische Musikzeitschrift_, 36 (Oct.-Nov. 1981), 563-66.

5871. Penney, Phyllis Annette. "Ballet and Modern Dance on Television in the Decade of the 70's." Ed.D. Diss. University of North Carolina (Greensboro) 1981.

   Abstract: DAI 42:4962A (order #DA 8210367).

5872. Pitts, Eugene, and Walter I. Seigal. "Fifty Years of T.V." _Audio_ (Boulder, Colo.), 65 (July 1981), 28-32.

5873. Popova, Manya. "Zlatnata antena na muzikalna vulna." _Bulgarska Muzika_ (Sofia), 33 (Feb. 1982), 42-45.

5874. Preuschoff, Gisela. "Musik im Fernsehen: Herausforderung an den Musikunterricht." _Musik und Bildung_, 12 (Mar. 1980), 151-58.

5875. Reinecke, Hans Peter. "Das Fernsehen und der vermeintliche Niedergang der Musikkultur." _Neue Zeitschrift für Musik_, 142, No. 1 (Jan.-Feb. 1981), 6-9.

   5875a. Reprinted in _Der Kirchenmusiker_, 32, No. 5 (1981), 157-60.

5876. Rockwell, John. "Music View: The Impact of TV on Opera." _New York Times_, 130 (Jan. 25, 1981), Section 2, p. 1ff.

5877. Röhrig, Wolfram. "Musikalische Koexistenz oder Integration? Probleme der E- und U-Musik in den technischen Medien." _Musica_, 37, No. 4 (1983), 322-25.

5878. Sailer, Rudolf. "Zeitgenössische Musik im ZDF." _Neue Zeitschrift für Musik_, 143, No. 1 (Jan. 1982), 16-18.

5879. Scheib, Wilfried. "Steigende Beliebtheit der Oper beim Fernsehen." _Österreichische Musikzeischrift_, 35 (Oct. 1980), 548-49.

   Concerns the 13th Internationalen Musikzentrums Congress in Salzburg.

5880. Schendel, Peter. "Die heitere Muse im DDR-Fernsehen." _Musik und Gesellschaft_, 30, No. 3 (Mar. 1980), 136-41.

5881. Schmidt, Hans-Christian. "Wer nicht hören will, muss sehen." _Musik und Bildung_, 12 (May 1980), 330-32.

5882. Schwartz, Lloyd. "Music: Opera on Television." _Atlantic Monthly_, 251 (Jan. 1983), 84-86ff.

5883. Symcox, Peter. "Four Faces of Opera." Opera Canada (Toronto), 22, No. 4 (1981), 14-17ff.

5884. Thiel, Jörn. "Musik im Fernsehen: Glossen zu einem unerschöpflichen Thema." Musica, 34, No. 1 (Jan. 1980), 9-11.

5885. Tsanovski, Krasimir. "Muzikalno-stsenichniyat zhanr l televiziyata." Bulgarska Muzika (Sofia), 32 (Oct. 1981), 60-63.

5886. Vartanov, Anri Surenovich. "Mnogoobrazie poiska." Sovetskaya muzyka, 45, No. 6 (June 1981), 50-56.

5887. Wagner, Manfred. "Musik in Fernsehen und Hörfunk vor neuen Ansätzen? Ein Diskussionsbeitrag." Österreichische Musikzeitschrift, 35, No. 1 (Jan. 1980), 39-41.

5888. Werba, E. "Mozarts 'Entführung' als ideale Fernseh-Oper." Österreichische Musikzeitschrift, 35, No. 6 (June 1980), 318-19.

5889. Zuber, Barbara. "'Sonntags immer ...' -- Über Musiksendungen im Fernsehen." Neue Zeitschrift für Musik, No. 1 (Jan.-Feb. 1981), 9-13.

          SEE ALSO:

          #63(Kofin), #238(Ford), #267(Matejka), #2936(Williamson/Hachem), and #4915(Thiel).

Film Musicals

5890. Adler, Thomas P. "The Musical Dramas of Stephen Sondheim: Some Critical Approaches." Journal of Popular Culture, 12, No. 3 (Winter 1978-1979), 513-25.

5891. Altman, Charles F. "The American Film Musical: Paradigmatic Structure and Mediatory Function." Wide Angle (Athens, Ohio), 2, No. 2 (1978), 10-17.

5892. Altman, Rick, ed. Genre: The Musical. BFI Readers in Film Studies. London and Boston: British Film Institute and Routledge-Kegan Paul, 1982.

          -- Rev. by Douglas McVay in Film (London), No. 104 (Mar. 1982), 10.

          -- Rev. in Village Voice, Supplement to Vol. 27 (Mar. 9, 1982), 5.

          -- Rev. by Eric Gobbers in Andere Sinema (Antwerp), No. 40 (June 1982), 35.

          -- Rev. by Jonathan Rosenbaum: "Four Books on the Hollywood Musical." Film Quarterly, 35, No. 4 (1982), 34-36.

          -- Rev. by Steve Neale: "Authors and Genres." Screen (London), 23, No. 2 (1982), 84-89.

          -- Rev. by Philip M. Taylor and Susan Heward in Historical Journal of Film, Radio and Television (Oxford), 2, No. 2 (1982), 207-08.

5893. Bakshy, Alexander. "Screen Musical Comedy." Nation, 130 (Feb. 1930), 158, 160.

5894. Bardèche, Maurice, and Robert Brasillach. Histoire du cinéma. Paris: Denoël et Steele, 1935.

          Includes the section "Opérettes et films viennois," along with other references to film musicals throughout.

          Reprinted in two volumes, Paris: André Martel, 1954.

    5894a. Also published as The History of Motion Pictures. Edited and translated by Iris Barry. New York: W. W. Norton and the Museum of Modern Art, 1938.

Includes the section "Operetta and Viennese Films," pp. 346-47.

5895. Becvar, William. "The Stage and Film Career of Rouben Mamoulian." Ph.D. Diss. University of Kansas 1973.

5896. Belach, Helga, ed. Wir tanzen um die Welt: Deutsche Revuefilme 1933-1945. Munich: Carl Hanser Verlag, 1979.

A collection of articles published on the occasion of the Retrospective dedicated to dance musical films at the Conference in Berlin, 1979. Includes bibliographic references and a filmography.

-- Rev. in Cinema 79, No. 252 (Dec. 1979), 102.

5897. Belton, John. "The Backstage Musical." Movie (London), No. 24 (Spring 1977), 36-43.

5898. Benayoun, Robert. "Re-examen de Mamoulian." Positif (Paris), Nos. 64-65 (1964).

5899. Bidaud, Anne-Marie. "Le Discours ideologique dans la comedie musicale americaine." Cinéma 78, Nos. 236-237 (Aug.-Sept. 1978), 38-60.

5900. Birrell, Francis. "Musical Comedies." New Statesman and Nation (London), 3, No. 59 (Apr. 9, 1932), 452.

5901. Bitsch, Charles, and Jacques Rivette. "Rencontre avec Gene Kelly." Cahiers du cinéma, 20, No. 85 (July 1958).

5902. ----------, and Jean Domarchi. "Entretien avec Vincente Minnelli." Cahiers du cinéma, 19, No. 74 (Aug.-Sept. 1957).

5903. Bizet, Jacques-Andre. "Le Musical americain." Cinéma 74, No. 184 (Feb. 1974), 34-55.

Includes bibliography and filmography.

5904. Borde, Raymond. "Eloge du style américain." Positif (Paris), Nos. 50-51-52 (Mar. 1963).

5905. ----------. "Importance de Lloyd Bacon." Positif (Paris), No. 27 (Feb. 1958).

5906. Borgelt, Hans. "Der ideale Musikfilm und seine bisherigen Erscheinungsformen." Theater der Zeit, 6, No. 7 (July 1951), 36-40.

5907. Bortolussi, Stefano. "Effetto video." Filmcritica (Rome), 32, Nos. 319-320 (Nov.-Dec. 1981), 542-43.

5908. ----------. "Non c'e sortilegio che possa resuscitare il musical." Cineforum, No. 207 (Sept. 1981), 50-54.

5909. Bosseur, Jean-Yves. "Vers un theatre musical." Musique de tous les temps, No. 9 (Sept. 1972), 14-17.

5910. Bowles, Stephen E. "'Cabaret' and 'Nashville': The Musical as Social Comment." Journal of Popular Culture, 12, No. 3 (Winter 1978-1979), 550ff.

5911. Boyum, Joy Gould. "Reliving the Sunny Days of the Aquarian Age." Wall Street Journal, 59 (Mar. 30, 1979), 15.

Concerns the filmed version of "Hair."

5912. Brauner, Ludwig. "Filmmusikalein." Der Kinematograph (Berlin), No. 662 (1919).

5913. Bricusse, Leslie. "Bricusse Looks at Musicals." BMI: The Many Worlds of Music (Dec. 1970), 14.

5914. "British Swing to Production of Filmusicals." Variety, 212 (Oct. 22, 1958), 13.

5915. Burton, Jack. The Blue Book of Hollywood Musicals: Songs from the Sound

Tracks and the Stars Who Sang Them since the Birth of the Talkies a Quarter-Century Ago. Watkins Glen, N.Y.: Century House, 1953.

-- Rev. in Score, 5, Nos. 2-3 (1953), 13.

5916. Byrne, Connie, and William O. Lopez. "Nashville." Film Quarterly, 29, No. 2 (1976), 13-25.

Concerns the work of composer Richard Baskin.

5917. Cameron, Julia. "Milos Forman and 'Hair.'" Rolling Stone, No. 289 (Apr. 19, 1979), 82-85.

5918. Carcassonne, Philippe. "Dossier -- La Musique de film: 'All That Jazz.'" Cinématographe (Paris), No. 62 (Nov. 1980), 27.

5919. Casper, Joseph A. Vincente Minnelli and the Film Musical. South Brunswick, N.J.: A. S. Barnes; and London: Tantivy, 1977.

-- Rev. in Films Illustrated (London), 7 (Apr. 1978), 318.

5920. ----------. "A Critical Study of the Film Musicals of Vincente Minnelli." Ph.D. Diss. University of Southern California 1973.

Abstract: DAI 34:6787A.

5921. Castell, David. "A Change of Tune: Report on the Musical Boom of the '80's." Films Illustrated (London), 9 (Aug. 1980), 427-30.

5922. Castello, Giulio Cesare. "Canzoni, reviste, operette nella storia del cinema." In Musica e film. Ed. S. G. Biamonte. Rome: Edizioni dell'Ateneo, 1959, pp. 65-103.

See Biamonte, #1606.

5923. ----------. "Rouben Mamoulian." Bianco e nero, 35, No. 3 (Mar. 1964).

Reprinted in French translation in Cinéma 65 (Paris), Nos. 92-93 (Jan.-Feb. 1965).

5924. Castle, Hugh. "The 'Talkie' Melody." Close Up (London), 5, No. 3 (Sept. 1929), 185-93.

5925. Caussou, Jean-Louis. "Entrez dans la danse." Cinéma 56, No. 11 (May 1956).

5926. Charness, Casey. "Hollywood Cine-Dance: An Explanation of the Interrelationship of Camerawork and Choreography in Films by Stanley Donen and Gene Kelly." Ph.D. Diss. New York University 1977.

5927. Choubachy, Ali. "Le Drame du cinéma egyptien." Positif (Paris), No. 151 June 1973), 1-8.

5928. Cicognini, Alessandro. "Il film musicale." In La musica nel film. Ed. Luigi Chiarini. Rome: Bianco e nero editore, 1950, pp. 61-62.

A paper presented at the 1950 Venice conference. See Chiarini, #1627.

5929. Comuzio, Ermanno. "Il film musicale." Bollettino per Biblioteche (dell' Amministrazione Provinciale di Pavia), (June 1978).

5930. ----------. "Il 'musical' americano degli Anni Trenta in bilico fra Depressione e 'New Deal.'" Cineforum, Nos. 141-142 (Feb.-Mar. 1975), 134-54.

5931. ----------. "Il 'rock-movie' e un genere cinematografico?" Rivista del cinematografo (Rome), 54 (July 1981), 336-38.

5932. Connor, Edward. "The Sound Track." Films in Review, 6, No. 1 (Jan. 1955), 39-40.

5933. ----------. "The Sound Track." Films in Review, 10, No. 5 (May 1959), 305-06.

5934. ----------, and Don Miller. "The Sound Track." Films in Review, 10, No. 8 (Oct. 1959), 497-500.

5935. Cook, Page. "The Sound Track." <u>Films in Review</u>, 18, No. 10 (Dec. 1967), 639-40.

Concerns the filmed version of "Camelot," with musical direction by Alfred Newman.

5936. ----------. "The Sound Track." <u>Films in Review</u>, 24, No. 1 (Jan. 1973), 43-45.

5937. ----------. "The Sound Track." <u>Films in Review</u>, 24, No. 3 (Mar. 1973), 175-78.

5938. ----------. "The Sound Track." <u>Films in Review</u>, 25, No. 5 (May 1974), 294-97.

Includes references to the work of Jerry Herman.

5939. ----------. "The Sound Track." <u>Films in Review</u>, 26, No. 5 (May 1975), 300-03.

Includes referneces to the work of Jerry Herman.

5940. ----------. "The Sound Track." <u>Films in Review</u>, 29, No. 7 (Aug.-Sept. 1978), 426-29ff.

5941. ----------. "The Sound Track." <u>Films in Review</u>, 34, No. 10 (Dec. 1983), 614-16.

Concerns Jerry Herman's music for "La Cage aux Folles."

5942. Coursodon, Jean-Pierre. "Stanley Donen." <u>Cinéma 59</u>, No. 39 (Aug.-Sept. 1959.

5943. Croce, Arlene. "Film Musicals -- A Crisis of Form." <u>Film Culture</u>, 2, No. 2 (1956), 25-26.

Includes references to Hammerstein's "Carousel."

5944. Cros, Jean-Louis. "Festival du film musical." <u>Revue du cinéma/Image et son</u>, No. 373 (June 1982), 6.

5945. Cushman, Robert. "Rodgers and Hart." <u>Sight and Sound</u>, 51, No. 3 (Summer 1982), 202-03.

5946. Cutts, John. "Bye Bye Musicals." <u>Films and Filming</u>, 10, No. 2 (Nov. 1963), 42-45.

Concerns the problem of musicals adapted from the stage, but not designed for the screen.

5947. Dale, Charles. "Mr. Ziegfeld Talks About Show Business." <u>Theatre</u>, 52 (Oct. 1930), 15-16.

Ziegfeld's comments on the filming of his New York stage productions.

5948. Deer, Harriet, and Irving Deer. "Musical Comedy: from Performer to Performance." <u>Journal of Popular Culture</u>, 12, No. 3 (Winter 1978-1979), 406-20.

5949. Delamater, Jerome Herbert. "A Critical and Historical Analysis of Dance as a Code of the Hollywood Musical." Ph.D. Diss. Northwestern University 1978.

Abstract: 1978:4556A (order #DA 7903244).

Includes references to the work of Johnny Green.

5950. de la Roche, Catherine. "Song and Dance." <u>Films and Filming</u>, 1, No. 1 (Oct. 1954), 12-13.

Concerns the changing styles of Hollywood musicals in the 1930's and 1940's.

5951. Dexter, Dave. "Bergman's First to Compose for an Original TV Musical Drama." <u>Billboard</u>, 86 (Nov. 23, 1974), 6.

Concerns the work of Marilyn Bergman.

5952. Dienes, Gideon. "A West Side Story - filmen." <u>Muzsika</u> (Budapest), 16 (May

1973), 46-47.

5953. Dietz, Howard. _Dancing in the Dark: Words by Howard Dietz_. With an Intro-
    duction by Alan Jay Lerner. New York: Quadrangle, 1974.

> Includes reminiscences, song lyrics, and pictures; a
> personal portrait of the business.

> -- Rev. in _Velvet Light Trap_, No. 18 (Spring 1978),
>   53-56.

5954. Domarchi, Jean, and Jean Douchet. "Rencontre avec Vincente Minnelli." _Ca-
    hiers du cinéma_, 24, No. 128 (Feb. 1962).

5955. Douchet, Jean, and Bertrand Tavernier. "Interview with Rouben Mamoulian."
    Positif (Paris), Nos. 64-65 (1964).

5956. Druxman, Michael B. _The Musical: From Broadway to Hollywood_. South Bruns-
    wick, N.J.: A. S. Barnes, 1980.

> -- Rev. by Douglas McVay in _Film_ (London), No. 88 (Aug.
>   1980), 10.

5957. Edens, Roger. "Labor Pains." _Film and TV Music_, 16, No. 3 (Spring 1957),
    18-20.

> Concerns the film "Funny Face," with music by George
> Gershwin and Adolph Deutsch.

5958. Eels, George. _The Life that Late He Led_. New York: Berkley Publishing,
    1967.

> A biography of Cole Porter.

5959. Emge, C. "More, Gaudier Filmusicals Hollywood's Reply to TV." _Down Beat_,
    18 (Sept. 21, 1951), 9.

5960. Everson, William K. "The History of the Musical." _Film Review, 1957-1958_,
    ed. F. Maurice Speed (1958), 17-21.

5961. Fel'senštejn, Val'ter. "Problemy muzykal'nogo fil'ma." _Sovetskaya muzyka_,
    33, No. 4 (Apr. 1969), 53-54.

5962. Ferrini, Franco, ed. "Musical." _Bianco e nero_ (Rome), 35, Nos. 3-4 (Mar.-
    Apr. 1974), 99-109.

> Includes bibliography.

5963. Feuer, Jane. _The Hollywood Musical_. Bloomington, Ind.: Indiana University
    Press, 1982.

> -- Rev. in _Film_ (London), No. 112 (Jan. 1983), 11.

> -- Rev. by Jonathan Rosenbaum in _Film Quarterly_, 36,
>   No. 4 (Summer 1983), 54-55.

> -- Rev. by Jerome Delamater in _University Film Associa-
>   tion Journal_ (Houston, Texas), 35, No. 1 (1983), 65-
>   66.

5964. ----------. "The Hollywood Musical: The Aesthetics of Spectator Involve-
    ment in an Entertainment Form." Ph.D. Diss. University of Iowa 1978.

> Abstract: DAI 1978: 4557A (order #DA 7902900).

5965. ----------. "Hollywood Musicals: Mass Art as Folk Art." _Jump Cut_, No. 23
    (Oct. 1980), 23-25.

5966. ----------. "The Self-Reflective Musical and the Myth of Entertainment."
    Quarterly Review of Film Studies, 2, No. 3 (1977), 313-26.

5967. ----------. "The Theme of Popular vs. Elite Art in the Hollywood Musical."
    Journal of Popular Culture, 12, No. 3 (Winter 1978-1979), 491-99.

5968. Fieschi, Jacques. "Dossier: Le Rêve a l'écran -- Memoire musicale." _Ciné-
    matographe_ (Paris), No. 34 (Jan. 1978), 14-18.

5969. "The Film Musical: Golden 13." _Action_, 9, No. 3 (May-June 1974), 4-9.

5970. Fischer, Lucy. "'Applause': The Visual and Acoustic Landscape." In Sound and the Cinema: The Coming of Sound to American Film. Ed. Evan William Cameron et al. Pleasantville, N.Y.: Redgrave Publishing, 1980, pp. 182-201.

Concerns Rouben Mamoulian's innovative use of sound and music.

5971. Fleuret, Maurice. "Musique et cinéma." Musica (Chaix, France), No. 121 (Apr. 1964), 48-49.

5972. ----------. "Musique et cinéma." Musica (Chaix, France), No. 122 (May 1964), 46-47.

5973. Fontenla, César Santos. El musical americano. Madrid: Akal Editor, 1973.

A survey of American musicals, with references to film musicals, and a "who's-who" of performers and creators.

5974. Fordin, Hugh. "Film Musicals: Rock Calls the Tune." New York Times, 127 (Mar. 12, 1978), Section 2, p. 1ff.

5975. ----------. The World of Entertainment!: Hollywood's Greatest Musicals. Garden City, N.Y.: Doubleday, 1975.

Concerns the films of Arthur Freed. Includes filmography.

-- Rev. in Producer's Guild of America Journal, 17, No. 3 (1975), 27.

-- Rev. in Academy of Motion Picture Arts and Sciences Bulletin, No. 9 (Spring 1975), 6.

-- Rev. in Audience, 8 (Sept. 1975), 11-13.

-- Rev. in Positif (Paris), 80, No. 1 (Apr. 1976), 76-77.

-- Rev. in Cinema Journal, 16, No. 1 (1976), 79-80.

-- Rev. in Velvet Light Trap, No. 18 (Spring 1978), 53-56.

5976. ----------, and Robin Chase. "Hollywood Puts On Its Dancing Shoes Again." New York Times (June 25, 1978), Section 2, p. 8.

5977. Freed, Arthur. "Making Musicals." Films and Filming, 2, No. 4 (Jan. 1956), 9-12, 30.

5977a. Also published as "O pracy nad filmen muzycznym." Film na świecie, No. 3 (1956).

5978. Fumento, Rocco. "Those Busby Berkeley and Astaire-Rogers Depression Musicals: Two Different Worlds." American Classic Screen, 5, No. 4 (1981), 15-18.

5979. Gardner, Paul. "Bob Fosse." Action, 9, No. 3 (May-June 1974), 22-27.

5980. Gerstein, Evelyn. "Films: Musical Talkies." Nation (New York), 133, No. 3458 (Oct. 14, 1931), 407-08.

5981. Giachetti, Romano. "L'evasione impura del nuovo musical americano." Cinema Nuovo (Turin), 27, No. 253 (May-June 1978), 183-93.

5982. Gill, Brendan. Cole: A Biographical Essay. Ed. Robert Kimball. London: Michael Joseph, 1972.

A biography of Cole Porter.

5983. Gillette, Don Carle. "Whatever Happened to Filmusicals?" Producers Guild of America Journal, 18, No. 3 (1976), 19-20ff.

5984. Godfrey, Lionel. "A Heretic's Look at Musicals." Films and Filming, 13, No. 6 (Mar. 1967), 5-10.

5985. Goodman, Alfred A. Musik im Blut: Amerikanische Rhythmen erobern die Welt. Die Südwest-Bibliothek, VI. Munich: Südwest Verlag, 1968.

A survey of American music from the Puritans to the present. Includes references to music and musical films, with bibliographic references.

5986. Green, Stanley. "Hammerstein's Film Career." Films in Review, 8, No. 2 (Feb. 1957), 68-77.

5987. ----------. "Richard Rodger's Filmusic." Films in Review, 7, No. 8 (Oct. 1956), 398-405, 420.

5988. ----------. The World of Musical Comedy. New York: A. S. Barnes; and London: Thomas Yoseloff, 1968.

5989. Grover, Stephen. "Making Broadway Hit into a Movie Involves Much Work, Big Risks: 'A Little Night Music.'" Wall Street Journal, 57 (Dec. 23, 1976), 1ff.

5990. Gutowski, Lynda Diane. "George Gershwin's Relationship to the Search for an American Culture During the Nineteen-Twenties." M.A. Thesis, University of Maryland 1967.

5991. Haeggqvist, Björn. "Om discofilm." Musikrevy (Stockholm), 35, No. 8 (1980), 387-88.

5992. Hanisch, Michael. Vom Singen im Regen: Filmmusical gestern und heute. Berlin: Henschelverlag Kunst und Gesellschaft, 1980.

> Includes bibliographic references.
>
> -- Rev. by Ralf Schenk in Film und Fernsehen (Berlin, DDR), 9, No. 9 (1981), 42-43.
>
> -- Rev. in Musik und Gesellschaft, 31 (June 1981), 372-73.

5993. Harcourt-Smith, Simon. "Vincente Minnelli." Sight and Sound, 21, No. 3 (Jan.-Mar. 1952).

5994. Hasbany, Richard. "'Saturday Night Fever' and 'Nashville': Exploring the Comic Mythos." Journal of Popular Culture, 12, No. 3 (Winter 1978-1979), 557ff.

5995. Hauduroy, Jean-François. "Writing for Musicals: Comden and Green Interview." Cahiers du cinéma in English, No. 2 (1966), 43-50.

> An interview with scenarists Betty Comden and Adolph Green. Includes a filmography compiled by Patrick Brion.

5996. Henderson, Brian. "A Musical Comedy of Empire." Film Quarterly, 35, No. 2 (Winter 1981-1982), 2-14.

> Includes references to early film musicals.

5997. Hendricks, Gordon. "The Sound Track." Films in Review, 5, No. 1 (Jan. 1954), 38-39.

5998. Henriksson, S. A. "'American Hot Wax': pophistorisk film on Alan Freed." Musikrevy (Stockholm), 33, No. 4 (1978), 145.

5999. Herring, Robert. "The Implications of Revue." Close Up (London), 5, No. 3 (Sept. 1929), 199-209.

6000. Hertel, Franz Paul. "Das Phänomen Robert Stolz: Zur Entwicklung der Operette im 20. Jahrhundert, gezeigt am Beispiel des Komponisten Robert Stolz." Ph.D. Diss. (Theater Arts), Universität Wien 1978.

> Includes references to the nearly 100 filmscores by Stolz, with a bibliography and a thematic catalog.

6001. Higham, Charles. "George Sidney." Action, 9, No. 3 (May-June 1974), 17-23.

> Concerns the films and film musicals of director George Sidney.

6002. Hirsch, Nicole. "Un chef-d'oeuvre du film musical: 'West Side Story.'" Musica (Chaix, France), No. 100 (July 1962), 51-54.

6003. Hirschhorn, Clive. The Hollywood Musical. New York: Crown, 1981.

> -- Rev. by Torsten Manns in Filmrutan (Liding, Sweden), 24, No. 4 (1981), 40.

-- Rev. by Seymour Peck: "Suddenly the Talkies Could Sing," in The New York Times, 131 (Nov. 15, 1981), Section 7, p. 13ff.

-- Rev. by Peter S. Prescott: "Books: Volumes of Comfort and Joy," in Newsweek, 98, No. 25 (Dec. 21, 1981), pp. 78-79.

-- Rev. by Arlene Croce: "Books: Going Hollywood," in The New Yorker, 57 (Jan. 18, 1982), 128-29.

-- Rev. by Jonathan Rosenbaum: "Four Books on the Hollywood Musical," in Film Quarterly, 35, No. 4 (1982), 34-36.

-- Rev. by Alain Masson in Positif (Paris), No. 264 (Feb. 1983), 90-92.

6004. Hoberman, J. "Scanners: All Singing, Some Dancing." Village Voice, 27 (Mar. 9, 1982), 57.

Concerns new musical releases on video cassette.

6005. Hodenfield, Chris. "'New York, New York': Martin Scorsese's Back-Lot Sonata." Rolling Stone, No. 241 (June 16, 1977), 36-44.

6006. Hodgkinson, Anthony W. "'Forty-Second Street' New Deal: Some Thoughts About Early Film Musicals." Journal of Popular Film, 4, No. 1 (1975), 33-46.

6007. Hollingsworth, Wills. "Gilbert and Sullivan." Film Music, 13, No. 2 (Nov.-Dec. 1953), 20-21.

6008. Hopkins, Antony. "Music: Letter from an Unknown Critic." Sight and Sound, 19, No. 10 (Feb. 1951), 416.

6009. Horgan, Paul. "Ruben Mamoulian: The Start of a Career." Films in Review, 24, No. 7 (Aug.-Sept. 1973), 402-13.

6010. Hrusa, Bernard. "On the Musical." Film (London), No. 14 (Nov.-Dec. 1957); and No. 15 (Jan.-Feb. 1958).

6011. Huntley, John. "The Sound Track." Sight and Sound, 22, No. 1 (July-Sept. 1952), 45.

Concerns Lennie Hayton's score for "Singin' in the Rain."

6012. Ieperen, Ab van. "Discofilms! Rockfilms! Musicals!" Film en Televisie (Brussels), No. 262 (Mar. 1979), 12-14.

6013. Internationaler Musikfilm, 1930-1945. Internationale Filmfestspiele, X. Berlin, 1960.

6014. International Institute for Music, Dance and Theatre in the Audio-Visual Media. Research Project: The Public for Music Theatre, 1965.

6015. Jablonski, Edward. "Film Musicals." Films in Review, 6, No. 2 (Feb. 1955), 56-69.

6016. Janovski, M. "Komedia revyu operetta." Iskusstvo kino (Moscow), Nos. 1-2 (Jan.-Feb. 1940).

6017. Jélot-Blanc, Jean-Jacques. Le Cinéma musical -- Du Rock au Disco, I: 1953-1967. Collection Têtes d'affiche. Paris: Éditions PAC, 1978.

Includes filmography, pp. 153-231.

-- Rev. by Ermanno Comuzio in Cineforum, No. 201 (Jan. 1981), 77-78.

6018. ----------. Le Cinéma musical -- Du Rock au Disco, II: 1968-1979. Collection Têtes d'affiche. Paris: Éditions PAC, 1978.

6019. Jenkinson, Philip. "The Great Busby." Film, 45 (Spring 1966).

6020. Jennings, C. Robert. "Cahn and Van Heusen: Hollywood's Tin Pan Aladdins." Show, 3 (July 1963), 76-77ff.

6021. Johnson, Albert. "Conversation with Roger Edens." _Sight and Sound_, 27, No. 4 (Spring 1958), 179-82.

6022. ----------. "The Films of Vincente Minnelli." _Film Quarterly_, 13, No. 2 (Winter 1958); and 13, No. 3 (Spring 1959).

6023. ----------. "The 10th Muse in San Francisco." _Sight and Sound_, 26, No. 1 (Summer 1956).

> A report on a lecture delivered by Gene Kelly at the San Francisco Museum of Art. Also includes an interview with Stanley Donen.

6024. Jones, Allan. "A New Age of Film Musicals." _Music Journal_, 21, No. 1 (Jan. 1963), 65, 67.

6025. Kasha, Al, and Joel Hirschhorn. "The Making of a Movie Musical." _Songwriter Magazine_ (Hollywood, Calif.), 3 (Nov. 1977), 19-23.

> Concerns the filming of Disney's "Pete's Dragon."

6026. Kehr, Dave. "Can't Stop the Musicals." _American Film_, 9, No. 7 (May 1984), 32-37.

6027. Kichin, Valerij. "Chrezyvchainoe proisshestvie." _Istkusstvo kino_, No. 4 (Apr. 1975), 50-59.

6028. Knight, Arthur. "Busby Berkeley." _Action_, 9, No. 3 (May-June 1974), 11-16.

6029. ----------. "Dancing in Films." _Dance Index_, 6, No. 8 (1947), 193ff.

6029a. Also published as "Danse et cinéma," in _La Revue du cinéma_, New series, 3, No. 14 (June 1948), 25-37.

6030. Knox, Donald. _The Magic Factory_. New York: Praeger, 1973.

> Includes many references to the film "An American in Paris," with music by George Gershwin and Johnny Green. Based upon material drawn from the AFI Oral History Project.

6031. Kobal, John. _Gotta Sing, Gotta Dance: A Pictorial History of Film Musicals_. New York and London: Hamlyn, 1970.

> A broad survey, with many pictures and a good deal of information. Includes a bibliography, pp. 319-20.

6032. Kothes, Franz-Peter. _Die theatralische Revue in Berlin und Wien, 1900-1938: Typen, Inhalte, Funktionen_. Taschenbücher zur Musikwissenschaft, XXIX. Wilhelmshaven: Heinrichshofen, 1977.

> Includes references to film musicals.
>
> -- Rev. in _Film und Fernsehen_ (Berlin), 6 (May 1978), 44.

6033. Kraus, Milton M. "Lullaby of Broadway." _Film Music Notes_, 10, No. 4 (Mar.-Apr. 1951), 12.

> References to the music direction of Ray Heindorf.

6034. Kreuger, Miles. "The Birth of the American Film Musical." _High Fidelity and Musical America_, 22, No. 7 (July 1972), 42-48.

6035. ----------. "Dubbers to the Stars." _High Fidelity and Musical America_, 22, No. 7 (July 1972), 49-54.

6036. ----------. "Extravagant! Spectacular! Colossal!: Movie Musicals in the Thirties." _High Fidelity and Musical America_, 24, No. 4 (Apr. 1974), 66-73.

6037. ----------. _The Movie Musical from Vitaphone to "42nd Street": as Reported in a Great Fan Magazine_. New York: Dover, 1975.

> A collection of reproductions from _Photoplay_ magazine, includes nearly every reference to musical films which appeared from July 1926 to early 1933. Also includes many record reviews, and a discography.
>
> -- Rev. in _Films in Review_, 27 (Oct. 1976), 491.

6038. Kroll, Nathan.   "Call Me Madam." Film Music, 12, No. 4 (Mar.-Apr. 1953), 13-14.

    Includes references to music by Irving Berlin and Alfred Newman.

6039. Lacombe, Alain, and Claude Rocle.   De Broadway à Hollywood, L'Amérique et sa comédie musicale: Anthropologie et dictionaire biofilmographie de la comédie musicale. In collaboration with the Foundation pour l'action culturelle internationale en montagne. Paris: Cinéma, 1980.

    Includes a discography, pp. 332-45.

    -- Rev. by Louis Skorecki: "Qu'est-ce que vous avez sur Mamoulian?" Cahiers du cinéma, No. 321 (Mar. 1981), xiv-xv.

    -- Rev. by Christian Bosseno: "De Broadway à Hollywood." Revue du cinéma/Image et son, No. 362 (June 1981), 131.

6040. La Polla, Franco. "Chi e morto a 'Brigadoon.'" Filmcritica (Rome), 30, Nos. 296-297 (Aug. 1979), 275-77.

6041. Lees, Gene. "In Memory of Mercer." American Film, 2, No. 3 (Dec.-Jan. 1978), 64-65.

    Concerns the work of lyricist Johnny Mercer.

6042. Leonard, William T., and James Robert Parish. Hollywood Players: The Thirties. New York: Arlington House, 1976.

6043. Lerner, Alan Jay. The Street Where I Live. New York: W. W. Norton, 1978.

6044. "Let's Bring Back the Movie Musical." Show (New York), 3 (Oct. 1963), 50.

6045. Levy, Louis. "Britain Can Make Good Musicals." Films and Filming, 2, No. 4 (Jan. 1956), 13, 30.

    A brief survey history of the musical in Britain.

6046. Lewine, Richard. "An American in Paris." Film Music, 11, No. 2 (Nov.-Dec. 1951), 14-16.

    Concerns the music by Gershwin, and musical direction by Johnny Green.

6047. ----------. "Because You're Mine." Film Music, 12, No. 3 (Jan.-Feb. 1953), 14.

    Concerns the musical director, Johnny Green.

6048. ----------. "Showboat." Film Music Notes, 10, No. 5 (May-June 1951), 10-11.

    Concerns the musical director, Adolph Deutsch.

6049. ----------. "Singin' in the Rain." Film Music, 11, No. 4 (Mar.-Apr. 1952), 15-16.

    Concerns the musical director, Lennie Hayton.

6050. Lissa, Zofia. "O muzyce w filmie muzycznym." Film, No. 13 (1951).

6051. Lughi, Paolo. "La mitologia anti-urbana nel musical Hollywoodiano." Cineforum, No. 200 (Dec. 1980), 838-42.

6052. Macpherson, Sandy. Sandy Presents. London: Home and Van Thal, 1950.

6053. Mander, Raymond, and Joe Mitchenson. Musical Comedy. London: Peter Davies, 1969.

6054. ----------, and Joe Mitchenson. Revue. London: Peter Davies, 1969.

6055. Manson, Eddy. "Anything Goes." Film Music, 15, No. 3 (Jan.-Feb. 1956), 19.

6056. Manuale dello spettacolo: Il cinematografo e il teatro nella legislazione fascista. Rome: C. Colombo, 1936.

6057. Marinucci, V.   ("Italian Musical Films.")   Il film italiano, 9, No. 24
      (1958), 41.

6058. Marshall, Michael.   Top Hat and Tails: The Story of Jack Buchanan.   London:
      Elm Tree Books, 1978.

      A biography of the performer, relates a good deal of the
      history of the genre. Includes a discography and a biblio-
      graphy, pp. 259-61.

6059. Martin, David.   The Films of Busby Berkeley.   San Francisco: David Martin,
      1965.

6060. Masson, Alain.   La Comédie musicale.   Paris: Éditions Stock, 1981.

      -- Rev. by Michel Chion: "La Comédie musicale: un amour
         pudique." Cahiers du cinéma, No. 331 (Jan. 1982), xv.

      -- Rev. by Jean-Loup Bourget in Positif (Paris), No. 250
         (Jan. 1982), 89-91.

      -- Rev. by Claude Arnaud in Cinématographe (Paris), No. 76
         (Mar. 1982), 76-77.

      -- Rev. by Dominique Rabourdin in Cinéma 82, No. 288 (Dec.
         1982), 13.

6061. ----------.   "L'Eclat de l'artifice (sur George Sidney)." Positif (Paris),
      No. 180 (Apr. 1976), 48-54.

6062. ----------.   "Le Style de Busby Berkeley." Positif (Paris), No. 173 (Sept.
      1975), 41-48.

6063. Mathieson, Muir.   "The British Musical Film." Melody Maker (London), (Jan.
      1947).

6064. Mazilu, Teodor.   "Musicalul si istoria." Cinema (Romania), 13, No. 11 (Nov.
      1975), 9.

6065. McVay, Douglas.   "Mainly About Musicals." Focus on Film, No. 36 (Oct. 1980),
      21-26.

6066. ----------.   The Musical Film.   International Film Guide Series.   London:
      A. Zwemmer, Ltd.; and New York: A. S. Barnes, 1967.

      A selective chronological survey of the musical, 1927-
      1964. Includes bibliography, pp. 165-69.

6067. Meirer, David.   "Films: From the Big Bands to the Beatles." Classic Film
      Collector, No. 52 (Fall 1976), 49.

6068. Mellancamp, Patricia.   "Spectacle and Spectator: Looking Through the Ameri-
      can Musical Comedy." Ciné-Tracts (Montreal), 1, No. 2 (1977), 27-35.

6069. Mellers, Wilfred.   "Music, Theatre and Commerce: A Note on Gershwin, Menotti
      and Marc Blitzstein." Score (London), No. 12 (June 1955), 69-76.

6070. Michener, Charles.   "Words and Music -- by Sondheim." Newsweek, 81, No. 17
      (Apr. 23, 1973), 54-56, 61, 64.

6071. Milne, Tom.   Rouben Mamoulian.   Bloomington, Ind.: University of Indiana
      Press, 1969.

6072. Minnelli, Vincente, with Hector Arce.   I Remember It Well.   Garden City,
      N.Y.: Doubleday, 1974.

6073. Mordden, Ethan.   The Hollywood Musical.   New York: St. Martin's Press, 1981.

      -- Rev. by Arlene Croce: "Books: Going Hollywood." The
         New Yorker, 57 (Jan. 18, 1982), 128-29.

      -- Rev. by Lawrence O'Toole: "Books: Musicals Are Mord-
         den Merry." Film Comment, 18 (May-June 1982), 76-77.

      -- Rev. by Terry Teachout: "Books in Brief: The Holly-
         wood Musical." National Review, 34 (Sept. 3, 1982), 1101.

      -- Rev. by Jonathan Rosenbaum: "Four Books on the Holly-
         wood Musical." Film Quarterly, 35, No. 4 (1982), 34-36.

6074. Mueller, John. "The Filmed Dances of Fred Astaire." Quarterly Review of Film Studies, 6, No. 2 (Spring 1981), 135-54.

6075. Murray, William. "The Return of Busby Berkeley." New York Times Magazine (Mar. 2, 1969), p. 7ff.

6076. "Musical Films Shrink." Variety, 117 (Jan. 1, 1935), 33.

6077. Myrsine, Jean. "Gene Kelly: auteur de films et homme-orchestre." Cahiers du cinéma, 2, No. 14 (July-Aug. 1952).

6078. National Board of Review of Motion Pictures' Better Films National Council. Selected Pictures, 1934/35. Annual Catalog, No. 20. New York: National Board of Review, 1935.

> Includes a listing of films from 1934-1935, with significant data in the section "Musical Comedies and Operettas."

6079. "Ein neuer Weg zum Musikfilm." Der Kinematograph (Berlin), No. 971 (1925).

6080. Newton, Douglas. "Poetry in Fast and Musical Motion." Sight and Sound, 22, No. 1 (July-Sept. 1952), 35-37.

> Concerns the musical "Singin' in the Rain" and a few others, with reference to the work of Lennie Hayton.

6081. ----------. "Un mito moderno nei film musicali." Cinema (Rome), New series, No. 115 (1953).

6082. Olshausen, Uli. "Ein Meilenstein in der Verfilmung von Popmusik: Ken Russells Film 'Tommy.'" Musik und Bild, 7 (Sept. 1975), 464.

> Originally printed in the Frankfurter Allgemeine Zeitung (Apr. 21, 1975).

6083. Ortman, Marguerite Gonda. Fiction and the Screen. With an Introduction by Lewis Worthington Smith. Boston: Marshall Jones, 1935.

> Includes brief references to musical films in the section "Musical Plays," pp. 69-72.

6084. Palas, Daniel, and Bertrand Tavernier. "Entretien avec Stanley Donen." Cahiers du cinéma, 25, No. 143 (May 1963).

6085. Parker, David L. "The Singing Screen: Remembering Those Movies That Not Only Talked But Sang ..." American Classic Screen, 7 (Mar.-Apr. 1983), 22-26.

6086. Pede, Ronnie. "Cannes 1980: New Musicals." Film en Televisie, Nos. 278-279 (July-Aug. 1980), 13.

6087. Perez, Michel. "The Golden Age of the Hollywood Musical." Positif (Paris), No. 149 (Apr. 1973), 86.

6088. Piper, Rudolf. Filmusical brasileiro e chanchada: posters e ilustrações. Second edition. São Paulo: Global, 1977.

6089. Pitts, Michael R. "Popular Singers and the Early Movie Musicals." Classic Film/Video Images, No. 72 (Nov. 1980), 10-11.

6090. Powell, Stephen. "The Mighty Musical Makes Its Comeback." Millimeter, 7, No. 1 (Jan. 1979), 24-40.

> A view of contemporary trends in film musicals, with a brief historical survey of the genre.

6091. Pyr'ev, Ivan Aleksandrovich. Izbrannye proizvederiia v 2-kh tomakh: kinematograficheskoe nasledie. Ed. B. F. Andreev et al. Moscow: Iskusstvo kino, 1978.

> -- Rev. in Iskusstvo kino, No. 8 (Aug. 1979), 154-61.

6092. Reisner, Joel. "Cinema Music." Music Journal, 26, No. 6 (June 1968), 54.

6093. ----------. "Cinema Music." Music Journal, 26, No. 8 (Oct. 1968), 10, 12.

6094. ----------. "Cinema Music." Music Journal, 27, No. 4 (Apr. 1969), 4.

6095. Rockwell, John. "Nights and Days of Cole Porter on Screen." New York Times, 129 (July 4, 1980), Section C, p. 18.

6096. Roth, Mark. "Some Warner's Musicals and the Spirit of the New Deal." Velvet Light Trap, No. 1 (Spring 1971).

      Reprinted in Velvet Light Trap, No. 17 (Winter 1977), 1-7.

6097. Rothel, David. The Singing Cowboys. South Brunswick, N.J.: A. S. Barnes; and London: Tantivy Press, 1978.

      Includes filmography and bibliography, pp. 264-65.

      -- Rev. in Films Illustrated (London), 8 (Mar. 1979), 274.

      -- Rev. in Focus on Film, No. 32 (Apr. 1979), 55.

6098. Sasanow, Richard. "Scoring with Mozart." American Film, 8, No. 10 (Sept. 1983), 13.

      Concerns the screen version of Peter Shaffer's "Amadeus."

6099. Scher, Saul N. "The American Film Musical: Golden Age, Neglected Art." Audience, 7, No. 4 (Apr. 1975), 2-4; and 7, No. 5 (May 1975), 11-13.

6100. ----------. "Irving Berlin's Filmusic." Films in Review, 9, No. 5 (May 1958), 225-34.

      Includes a filmography.

6101. Scheurer, Timothy E. "The Aesthetics of Form and Convention in the Movie Musical." Journal of Popular Film, 3, No. 4 (1974), 306-24.

6102. ----------. "I'll Sing You a Thousand Love Songs: A Selected Filmography of the Musical Film." Journal of Popular Film, 8, No. 1 (Spring 1980), 61-67.

6103. Schmidl, Poldi. "Neue musikal: Werte für den Film." Filmtechnik (1926), 100.

6104. Schultz, Jacque. "Categories of Song." Journal of Popular Film and Television, 8, No. 1 (1980), 15-25.

6105. Schumach, Murray. "Hollywood Musicals." New York Times, 108 (Apr. 26, 1959), Section 2, p. 7.

6106. Sennett, Ted. Hollywood Musicals. New York: Harry N. Abrams, 1982.

      A huge volume with many pictures, provides a broad survey of the genre and a good deal of useful information. Includes a selected bibliography and filmography.

      -- Rev. in The New Yorker, 57 (Jan. 18, 1982), 128.

      -- Rev. by Doug McClelland in Films in Review, 32 (Dec. 1981), 637.

      -- Rev. by Jonathan Rosenbaum: "Four Books on the Hollywood Musical." Film Quarterly, 35, No. 4 (1982), 34-36.

      -- Rev. in Central Opera Service Bulletin (New York), 24, No. 1 (1982), 38.

6107. Shout, John D. "The Film Musical and the Legacy of Show Business." Journal of Popular Film, 10, No. 1 (1982), 23-26.

6108. Sidney, George. "The Three Ages of the Musical." Films and Filming, 14, No. 9 (June 1968), 4-7.

      The three "ages" noted are: "Busby Berkeley", "The 1940's Musicals," and the "Big Stage Adaptations."

6109. Siegel, J. E. "'Love Is the Exception to Every Rule, Is It Not?': The Films of Vincente Minnelli and Alan Jay Lerner." Bright Lights (Los Angeles), 3, No. 1 (No. 9), (1980), 7-11ff.

6110. Silke, James R., ed. Rouben Mamoulian: "Style Is the Man." Washington,

D.C.: American Film Institute, 1971.

6111. Simon, Alfred E. "Brigadoon." _Film Music_, 14, No. 1 (Sept.-Oct. 1954), 19.

    Includes references to the musical direction by Johnny Green.

6112. ----------. "Guys and Dolls." _Film Music_, 15, No. 2 (Winter 1955), 15-16.

    Concerns the film version with music adapted by Cyril J. Mockridge, and musical supervision by Jay Blackton.

6113. ----------. "The King and I." _Film Music_, 15, No. 5 (Summer 1956), 17.

    References to the music of Richard Rodgers.

6114. ----------. "The Merry Widow." _Film Music_, 12, No. 1 (Sept.-Oct. 1952), 18.

    Concerns the filmed version of Lehar's music.

6115. "Der singende Film." _Frankfurter Nachrichten_ (June 19, 1922).

6116. Skala, Pavel. "Film: 'My Fair Lady.'" _Hudební Rozhledy_, 21, No. 20 (1968), 621-22.

6117. Sonnenshein, Richard. "Dance: Its Past and Its Promise on Film." _Journal of Popular Culture_, 12, No. 3 (Winter 1978-1979), 500-06.

6118. Sosnik, Harry. "Screen Musicals Killed Conductors, and Replaced Them with Engineers." _Variety_, 285 (Jan. 5, 1977), 9.

6119. Springer, John. _All Talking! All Singing! All Dancing!: A Pictorial History of the Movie Musical_. New York: Citadel Press, 1966.

    -- Rev. in _New York Folklore Quarterly_, 23, No. 1 (1967), 72.

    6119a. Also published as _La Comédie musicale_. Paris: Éditions Henri Veyrier, 1975.

        Includes filmography.

        -- Rev. in _Revue du cinéma/Image et son_, No. 342 (Sept. 1979), 37.

6120. Squarini, Peter. "Is the Movie Musical Coming Back?" _Classic Film/Video Images_, No. 71 (Sept. 1980), 3.

6121. Steinhauer, Walter. "Musik in Film und Fernsehen." _Film und Ton_, 20 (Mar. 1974), 39-40.

6122. Steinke, Gary Lee. "An Analysis of the Dance Sequence in Busby Berkeley's Films: 'Forty-Second Street', 'Footlight Parade,' and 'Gold Diggers of 1935.'" Ph.D. Diss. University of Michigan 1979.

    Abstract: DAI 40/02: 506A (order #DEL 79-16819).

6123. Stern, Lee Edward. _The Movie Musical_. New York: Pyramid Communications, 1974.

    6123a. Also published as _Il musical_. Milan: Milano Libri, 1977.

        -- Rev. in _Cineforum_, No. 165 (May-June 1977), 398-99.

6124. Sterritt, David. "Screen Musical's Last Gasp?" _Christian Science Monitor_, 70 (Mar. 27, 1978), 22.

    Concerns the film version of Sondheim's "A Little Night Music."

6125. Stoyanova, Svetla. "Televizionen myuzikul: realnost i perspektivi." _Bulgarska Muzika_ (Sofia), 28 (Oct. 1977), 57-59.

6126. Suchianu, D. I. "A fost odata un Hollywood." _Cinema_ (Romania), 13, No. 7 (Aug. 1975), 12.

6127. Taylor, John Russell, and Arthur Jackson. _The Hollywood Musical_. New York: McGraw-Hill; and London: Secker and Warburg, 1971.

Perhaps the best survey to date. Concerns the role of
music and dance in film musicals. Includes indices of
film titles and songs, along with a good deal of biographical material and a filmography.

-- Rev. in Performing Arts Review, 3, No. 4 (1972),
689-93.

-- Rev. in The Triangle of Mu Phi Epsilon, 66, No. 4
(1972), 34.

6128. Telotte, J. P. "A 'Gold Digger' Aesthetic: The Depression Musical and Its
Audience." Post Script, 1, No. 1 (1981), 18-24.

6129. ----------. "Self and Society: Vincente Minnelli and Musical Formula."
Journal of Popular Film, 9, No. 4 (1982), 181-93.

6130. ----------. "A Sober Celebration: Song and Dance in the 'New' Musical."
Journal of Popular Film, 8, No. 1 (1980), 2-14.

6131. Thomas, Lawrence B. The MGM Years. New York: Columbia House, 1972.

Includes an introduction by Sidney Skolsky, and a commentary on sound-track recording by Jesse Kaye. Also includes a discography and bibliography, p. 136.

-- Rev. in Journal of Popular Culture, 6, No. 3 (1973),
627.

-- Rev. in Velvet Light Trap, No. 18 (Spring 1978), 53-
56.

6132. Thomas, Tony. Harry Warren and the Hollywood Musical. With a Foreword by
Bing Crosby. Secaucus, N.J.: Citadel Press, 1975.

A survey history and criticism of the genre, with musical
excerpts and piano scores. Also includes a "catalog" of
films, pp. 331-41.

-- Rev. in Variety, 281 (Dec. 10, 1975), 70.

6133. ----------, and Jim Terry, with Busby Berkeley. The Busby Berkeley Book.
Greenwich, Conn.: New York Graphic Society; and London: Thames and Hudson,
1973.

Includes a Foreword by Ruby Keeler.

-- Rev. in Films in Review, 24, No. 8 (Oct. 1973), 495-96.

-- Rev. by Louise G. Boundas in Stereo Review, 32, No. 3
(Mar. 1974), 12.

-- Rev. in Audience, 8 (Oct. 1975), 10-11.

6134. Torok, J.-P., and J. Quincey. "Vincente Minnelli." Positif (Paris),
Nos. 50-51-52 (Mar. 1963).

6135. Tozzi, Romano. "Jerome Kern's Film Music." Films in Review, 6, No. 9 (Nov.
1955), 452-59.

Includes filmography.

6136. Traubner, Richard. "Between the Wars: A Musical Theater Survey -- Central
Europe." American Record Guide (Washington, D.C.), 44 (May 1981), 2-6.

6137. ----------. "Escapist Movies from Wartime Germany." New York Times, 128
(Mar. 11, 1979), Section 2, p. 19ff.

6138. ----------. "The Sound and the Führer." Film Comment, 14, No. 4 (July-
Aug. 1978), 17-23.

Concerns the role of musicals and entertainment films in
Nazi Germany.

6139. Truchaud, François. Vincente Minnelli. Classiques du cinéma, XXIII. Paris: Éditions Universitaires, 1966.

6140. Turroni, Giuseppe. "Hollywood e la morte: dove va il musical?" Filmcritica (Rome), 28, No. 277 (Oct. 1977), 263-66.

6141. Ulrichsen, Erik, and Jørgen Stegelmann. Showfilmens forvändling: Musicals i Hollywood och pa andra plaster. Stockholm, 1958.

6142. Vallance, Tom. The American Musical. New York: A. S. Barnes; and London: Zwemmer, 1970.

A brief alphabetical listing of films and film personalities.

6143. ----------. "Melody Always Wins: Jule Styne." Focus on Film (London), No. 21 (Summer 1975), 14-26.

6144. ----------, and Douglas McVay. "Gotta Sing! Gotta Dance!" Film (London), 40 (Summer 1964).

6145. Vaughan, David. "After the Ball." Sight and Sound, 26, No. 2 (Autumn 1956), 89-91.

Includes references to the musicals of Gene Kelly.

6146. Vernhes, Monique. "Festivals et rencontres, Paris. 1930: L'Allemagne chante et danse." Cinéma 74, No. 189 (July-Aug. 1974), 28-30.

6147. Walldov, Lars. "Musikalen under 60-talet." Filmrutan (Sweden), 18, No. 1 (1975), 3-26.

Includes a filmography, discography, and bibliography.

6148. Warner, Alan. Article in Films and Filming, 18, No. 1 (Oct. 1971), 18-33.

6149. Weinberg, Harman G. The Lubitsch Touch. New York: E. P. Dutton, 1968.

6150. Wiener, Thomas. "The Rise and Fall of the Rock Film." American Film, 1, No. 2 (Nov. 1975), 25-29.

6151. ----------. "The Rise and Fall of the Rock Film: From 'Woodstock' to 'Stardust,' the Parade's Gone By." American Film, 1, No. 3 (Dec. 1975), 58-63.

6152. Wilder, Alec. American Popular Song: The Great Innovators, 1900-1950. Edited, and with an Introduction by James T. Maher. New York: Oxford University Press, 1972.

Includes sections on the music of Jerome Kern, Irving Berlin, George Gershwin, Richard Rogers, Cole Porter, Harold Arlen, Johnny Green, and others.

6153. Wilk, Max. They're Playing Our Song. New York: Atheneum, 1973.

A survey of American songwriters; Broadway and Hollywood.

6154. Witte, Korsten. "Visual Pleasure Inhibited: Aspects of the German Revue Film." New German Critique, Nos. 24-25 (Fall-Winter 1981-1982), 238-63.

6155. Wolf, William. "On Film: Encores for the Movie Musical." New York Magazine, 15, No. 2 (Jan. 11, 1982), 73-74.

6156. "Yank Musicals Flop on German Cinema Screens." Variety, 200 (Sept. 7, 1955), 12.

6157. Zadan, Craig. Sondheim & Co. New York: Avon Books, 1976.

6158. Zimmermann, C. "Oberhausen: Melodie des Broadway -- 100 Jahre Musical." Oper und Konzert (Munich), 21, No. 2 (1983), 21-22.

SEE ALSO:

#74(Levy), #79(London), #81(Manvell), #103(Porcile), #125(Taylor), #151 (Eames), #152-154(Ewen), #167(Kingman), #201(Atkins), #229(Craig), #232 (Domarchi), #243, #256(Knopf), #273(Narducy), #282(Ramin), #300(Struck), #305(Troitskaya), #336(Arvey), #357(Beaton), #493(Connor/Miller), #665 (Knight), #706, 707(Low), #716(Mamontowicz-Łojek), #743(Modern), #1046 (Viviani), #1262(Ericsson), #1414(Melichar), #1480(Rideout), #1486(Rotha/ Griffith), #1487(Rotha/Manvell), #1544(Wilson), #1547(Woll), #1593(Asklund/Grayson), #1595(Barrett), #1678(Gallone), #1777(Kögler), #1810(Marcorelles), #1902(Talbert/Simon/Smith), #1903(Talbert/Schaefer), #1918(Volodin), #1929(Zurbach), #2013(Cook), #2052(Eswar), #2057(Galling), #2295,

2315(Cook), #2390, #2397(Fong-Torres), #2398(Forrest), #2443(Kasha/Kostal/Hirschhorn), #2464(Lacombe), #2512(Oliva), #2713(Ales), #2782(Dagneau), #2993(Jablonski), #2994(Jablonski/Sweigert), #3105(Barlatier), #3113(Serenellini), #3115(Vandromme), #3187(Deutsch), #3292(Jablonski/Caine), #3293(Kimball/Simon), #3535(McVay), #3686(Cook), #3783(Connor/Pratley), #4015(Harmetz), #4276(Willson), #4515(Colpi), #4766(Marie), #4854, 4857, 4858(Rubsamen), #4947(Vidor), #4971(Yakubov), #5046(Berten), #5051(Bornoff/Salter), #5104(McLaughlin), #5114(Sarris), #5191(Lehar), #5220(Crowther), #5240(Gilliat), #5244(H. Green), #5273, 5274(Marx), #5323(Bornoff), #5327(Cullaz), #5348(McVay), #5360(E. Thomas), #5553, 5554(Koster), #6249(Salem), #6261, 6262(Farren), #6271(Parker/Siegel), #6274(Aros), #6309(D'Amico/Savio), #6312(Gifford), #6314(S. Green), #6316, #6323(Kinkle), #6324(Lewine/Simon), #6336(Reinert/Brack/Portmann), #6338(Shapiro), and #6340(Woll).

Animated Sound and Musical Graphics

6159. "The Art of Motion Graphics." Computing Report, 5, No. 2 (Mar. 1969), 10-13.

    Includes references to the work of John Whitney.

6160. Association of Computing Machinery. Experiments in Motion Graphics. IBM Monograph (Fall 1969).

6161. Becker, Leon. "Synthetic Sound and Abstract Image." Hollywood Quarterly, 1, No. 1 (Oct. 1945), 95-96.

    Includes references to the work of John Whitney.

6162. C., A.-j. "Musique cinégraphique." Néo - Ciné - Art, No. 4 (1948).

6163. Citron, Jack, and John Whitney. "CAMP - Computer Assisted Movie Production." Proceedings of the Fall Joint Computer Conference, San Francisco, 1968, pp. 1299-1305.

6164. Curtis, David, and Richard Francis, eds. Film as Film: Formal Experiment in Film, 1910-1975. London: Hayward Gallery, 1979.

    Includes references to experiments in animated sound, with special attention to the work of John Whitney.

6165. Damas, --. "La Musique, fil d'Ariane du dessin animé." Stars et films (Paris), No. 22 (1948).

6166. Davis, Douglas. Art and the Future: A History/Prophecy of the Collaboration between Science, Technology and Art. New York: Praeger, 1973.

    Includes references to experiments in animated sound.

    Also see comments by John Whitney in #4168, pp. 98-99.

6167. Eimert, H. "Was ist electronische Musik?" Melos, 20 (1953).

    Also see comments by Christopher Palmer, #6173.

6168. "The Handwritten Sound Track." Music Educator's Journal, 55, No. 3 (Nov. 1968), 114ff.

6169. Hein, Birgit, and Wulf Herzogenrath, eds. Film als Film: 1910 bis Heute. Cologne: Kölnischer Kunstverein, 1978.

    Includes references to experiments in animated sound, with special attention to the work of John Whitney.

6170. Langsner, Jules. "Kinetics in L.A." Art in America, 60, No. 3 (May-June 1967), 107-09.

    Includes references to the work of John Whitney.

6171. LeGrice, Malcolm. Abstract Film and Beyond. Cambridge, Mass.: MIT Press,

1977.

    Includes references to animated and computer sound, with special attention to the work of John Whitney.

6172. Leyda, Jay. "Exploration of New Film Techniques." Arts and Architecture, 62, No. 12 (Dec. 1945), 38-39, 56.

    Includes references to the work of John Whitney.

6173. Palmer, Christopher. "Electronic Origins." The Musical Times, 113 (June 1972), 557.

    Includes references to an article by H. Eimert, see #6167.

6174. Popper, Paul. "Synthetic Sound: How Sound Is Produced on the Drawing Board." Sight and Sound, 2, No. 7 (Autumn 1933), 82-84.

6175. Potter, Ralph K. "Audivisual Music." Hollywood Quarterly, 3, No. 1 (Fall 1947), 66-78.

    Includes references to works by Walt Disney, James and John Whitney, and others.

6176. Russett, Robert, and Cecile Starr, eds. Experimental Animation: An Illustrated Anthology. New York: Van Nostrand, 1976.

    Includes references to the work of John Whitney.

6177. Schnebel, Dieter. "Werk-Stücke/Stück-Werk (Debris d'oeuvre/Oeuvre en debris)." Melos, 36, No. 3 (Mar. 1969), 111-15.

    6177a. Reprinted in Musique en jeu, No. 1 (Nov. 1970), 4-7.

6178. Solev, V. "Absolute Music." Sight and Sound, 5, No. 18 (Summer 1936), 48-50.

    Concerns the early concept of "designed sound" on the soundtrack, with references to the work of Avraamov, Pfenniger, Sholpo, and Voinoff.

6179. Spinello, Barry. "Notes on Soundtrack." Source: Music of the Avant Garde, Issue No. 7 (Vol. 4, No. 1), (Nov. 1970), 50-51.

    A composition by Spinello.

6180. Whitney, James A., and John H. Whitney. "Audio Visual Music." In Art in Cinema. Ed. Frank Stauffacher. San Francisco: Museum of Art, 1947, pp. 31-34.

    Reprint, New York: Arno Press, 1968.

    6180a. Article is reprinted with different illustrations in Circle, No. 10 (Summer 1948), 4-10.

    6180b. Reprinted in The Avant-Garde Film: A Reader of Theory and Criticism. Ed. P. Adams Sitney. New York: New York University Press, 1978, pp. 83-86.

    6180c. Reprinted as "Audio-Visual Music and Program Notes, 1946," in Whitney's Digital Harmony, pp. 144-50. See #4168.

6181. ----------, and John H. Whitney. "Color Music - Abstract Film - Audio-Visual Music." Arts and Architecture, 61, No. 12 (Dec. 1944), 25, 42.

    Reprinted in Whitney's Digital Harmony (1980), pp. 138-43. See #4168.

6182. Whitney, John H. "Animation Mechanisms." American Cinematographer, 52, No. 1 (Jan. 1971), 26-31.

    Reprinted as "Animation Mechanisms, 1971," in Whitney's Digital Harmony (1980), pp. 183-89. See #4168.

6183. ----------. "Moving Pictures and Electronic Music, 1959." In Digital Harmony: On the Complementarity of Music and Visual Art. Peterborough, N.H.: Byte Books, 1980, pp. 151-55.

    The first printing of the original English text. See #4168.

    6183a. Also published as "Bewegungsbilder und elektronische Musik." In Die Reihe, VII: Information über serielle Musik -- Form -

Raum. Vienna: Universal, 1960, pp. 62-72.

6183b. Also published as "Moving Pictures and Electronic Music."
In Die Reihe, VII: Form - Space, Information about Serial Music. Bryn Mawr: Presser, 1965, pp. 61-71.

6184. Winckel, Fritz Wilhelm. Musik in optischer Gestaltung." Melos, 10, No. 11
(Nov. 1931), 365-68.

SEE ALSO:

#82(Manvell/Huntley), #165(Jacobs), #188(Scheugl/Schmidt), #312(Weiland),
#832(Sabaneev), #1809(Manvell), #2557(Sitney), #3566(Applebaum), #3567,
#3568(Jordan), #3569(Manvell/Halas), #3570(McLaren), #3571(Pratley), #3572
(Vinet), #4152(Claus), #4153(Franke), #4157(Rondolino), #4158(Rubsamen),
#4164, 4168, 4169, 4175(Whitney), #4663(Jungk), #4677(Kershaw), #4824
(Preiberg), #4865(Schaeffer), #4961(Winckel), #4969(Worringer), and #5672
(Pechotsch).

V. RESEARCH

Surveys of Film Music Research

6185. Diederichs, Helmut H. "Die schweigende Muse: alte und neue Bücher zum
Stummfilm." Medium (Frankfurt am Main), 10 (May 1980), 39-41

A brief survey of the literature of silent films.

6186. ----------. "Stummfilm und Musik: neue Diskussion über ein altes Thema."
Medium (Frankfurt am Main), 10 (Aug. 1980), 40-42.

6187. ----------. "Zur Geschichte des Stummfilms: und dem Anteil der Frauen das
Westberliner Symposium und etliche Bücher." Medium (Frankfurt am Main),
11 (Sept. 1981), 38-43.

Concerns the research conducted by Herbert Birett and
others.

6188. Fiedel, Robert D. "Saving the Score -- Wanted: A National Film Music Archive." American Film, 3, No. 1 (Oct. 1977), 32, 71.

6189. Fitzpatrick, John, and Martin Marks. "A Note on Film Music Scholarship:
A Special Supplementary Guide to Research in the Field." Pro Musica Sana,
6, No. 4 (Fall 1978), 17-19.

6190. Geduld, Harry M. "Film Music: A Survey." Quarterly Review of Film Studies,
1, No. 2 (May 1976), 183-204.

A very general introduction to the study of film music.
Includes a brief selected bibliography and discography.

6191. Gorbman, Claudia. "Film Music." Quarterly Review of Film Studies, 3, No. 1
(Winter 1978), 105-13.

Concerns the current state of film music literature.

6192. Helman, Alicja. "Literatura muzyki filmowej." Kwartalnik Filmowy, 11,
No. 2 (1961), 58-72.

6193. Hickman, C. Sharpless. "Movies and Music." Music Journal, 12, No. 10 (Oct.
1954), 78, 80.

Concerns the current state of film music research.

6194. Huntley, John. "Film Music." Penguin Film Review, No. 2 (Jan. 1947), 21-25.

> Concerns methodology for the study of film music.
>
> Reprinted in Manvell (#1315a).

6195. Marks, Martin. "Film Music: The Material, Literature, and Present State of Research." Music Library Association Notes, 36 (Dec. 1979), 314-25.

> An outstanding survey of the history of film music scholarship. Includes a highly accurate, annotated bibliography.

6195a. Also published, with a few corrections and additions, in University Film Association Journal, 34, No. 1 (1982), 3-40.

6196. Symposium on the Methodology of Film History, a special issue of Cinema Journal, 14, No. 2 (Winter 1974-1975).

> A special issue devoted to the current state of film research, with directives for the future, and implications for the study of film music.

SEE ALSO:

> #699(London), #883(Shepard), #1512(Sternfeld), #2498, #2549(Sharples), #3635(Cook), #4636(Helman), and #6208(Lebeau).

Guides to Primary Sources

6197. Allen, Nancy. Film Study Collections. New York: Frederic Ungar, 1979.

> A survey of libraries that house film collections, includes brief synopses of the holdings of major archives.

6198. American Film Institute. Catalog of Holdings of the American Film Institute Collection and the United Artists Collection at the Library of Congress. Washington, D.C.: The American Film Institute, 1978.

6199. Armour, Robert A. Film: A Reference Guide. Westport, Conn.: Greenwood Press, 1980.

> A general introduction to reference materials for film research. Includes a section "Film and Music," p. 83.

6200. Birett, Herbert. Stummfilm-Musik: Materialsammlung. Berlin: Deutsche Kinemathek, 1970.

> Includes listings of published musical numbers composed for films, film music reviews, and listings of silent films with information concerning production companies, composers, conductors, etc. Also provides a useful bibliography, pp. 90-105 (reprinted, with a few additions, in Seidler, #875).
>
> Also includes facsimile reprints of articles by Franz Wallner, taken from columns in the Leipziger Illustrierte Zeitung, Berliner Tageblatt, and others, pp. 161-87, and the article "Die Untermalung zu 'Menschen am Sonntag,'" by Otto Stenzel, pp. 189-90.

6201. Cohn, Arthur. "Film Music in the Fleischer Collection of the Free Library of Philadelphia." Film Music Notes, 7, No. 4 (Mar.-Apr. 1948), 11-13.

6202. Cowie, Peter, ed. International Film Guide, 1979. London: Tantivy Press, 1978, pp. 400-04.

> A listing of major international film archives.

6203. Davies, John Howard. "Organismes de la radiodiffusion: bibliothèques et archives sonores. I:Radio and Television Music Libraries." In Neuvième congrès international des bibliothèques musicales, St-Gall, 22-28 août 1971, a special issue of Fontis Artis Musicae, 19, No. 3 (Sept.-Dec. 1972), 1113-48.

6204. "Early Film Music Collections in the Library of Congress." Main Title (Entr'acte Recording Society Newsletter), 2, No. 2 (1976), 8ff.

6205. International Federation of Library Associations, International Section for Performing Arts Libraries and Museums. Performing Arts Libraries and Museums of the World. Ed. André Veinstein, with revisions by Cécile Giteau, 1967.

6206. Kula, Sam. Bibliography of Film Librarianship. Library Association Bibliographies, VIII. London: Library Association, 1967.

A guide to current activities of the film libraries and archives, with a bibliography of articles on current problems and procedures, cataloguing, copyright, etc.

6207. ----------. "Literature of Film Librarianship." Aslib Proceedings (Association of Special Libraries and Information Bureaux), 14 (Apr. 1962), 91-93.

6208. Lebeau, Elisabeth. "Le Problème des publications originales de musique non imprimées, à propos de la recherche de la musique de film." Fontes artis musicae, 12 (1965), 150-52.

6209. Mehr, Linda Harris, ed. Motion Pictures, Television, and Radio: A Union Catalogue of Manuscript and Special Collections in the Western United States. Boston: G. K. Hall, 1977.

A significant research tool, lists the holdings, including film music collections, for most of the major museums and libraries in the Western U.S.

-- Rev. in American Film, 3 (May 1978), 77.

6210. Motion Pictures: A Catalogue of Books, Periodicals, Screenplays, and Production Stills. Boston: G. K. Hall, 1972.

Facsimile reproduction of the card catalogue from the Reference Library and the Cinema/Theater Arts Library at U.C.L.A.

6210a. Second edition, revised and expanded, published as Motion Pictures: A Catalogue of Books, Periodicals, Screenplays, Television Scripts, and Production Stills. Boston: G. K. Hall, 1976.

6211. Nelson, R. A. "Germany and the German Film, 1930-1945: An Annotated Research Bibliography. Part III: Research Libraries, Archives and Other Sources." University Film Association Journal, 30, No. 1 (1978), 53-72.

6212. "Our Resources for Scholarship." Film Quarterly, 16, No. 2 (Winter 1962-1963), 34-50.

A guide to some of the major archives and libraries in the U.S., with contributions by Eileen Bowser, James Card, Arthur Knight, George Freedley, Richard Dyer Mac-Cann, and Raymond Fielding.

6213. Pruett, James W. "Notes for Notes: Recent Acquisitions." Notes (Music Library Association), 33, No. 3 (Mar. 1977), 575-80.

Concerns acquisitions at California State and the Library of Congress, with references to works by Bernard Herrmann.

6214. Rose, Ernest D. World Film and Television Study Resources: A Reference Guide to Major Training Centers and Archives. Bonn - Bad Godesburg: Friedrich-Ebert-Stiftung, 1974.

Includes a bibliography, pp. 383-411.

6215. Sargent, Ralph N. Preserving the Moving Image. Ed. Glen Fleck. Washington, D.C.: Corporation for Public Broadcasting, and the National Endowment for the Arts, 1974.

A source of technical information for film archivists.

6216. Tsukada Yoshinobu. _Eiga shi shiryō hakkutsu, I-VII_. Tokyo: Tsukada Yoshinobu, 1969.

> Concerns the materials and techniques for the historical study of Japanese film.

6217. Weber, Olga S., and Deirdre Boyle. _North American Film and Video Directory_. New York: R. R. Bowker, 1976.

> A general guidebook to the major film archives.

6218. Wheaton, Christopher D., and Richard B. Jewell. _Primary Cinema Resources: An Index to Screenplays, Interviews and Special Collections at the University of Southern California_. Boston: G. K. Hall, 1975.

SEE ALSO:

#1647(Connor/Pratley), #1727(Huntley), and #4596(Gallez).

Bibliographies

6219. Alvarez, Max Joseph. _Index to Motion Pictures Reviewed by 'Variety,' 1907-1980_. Metuchen, N.J.: Scarecrow Press, 1982.

> A listing of film reviews, arranged alphabetically by film title.

6220. Batty, Linda, ed. _Retrospective Index to Film Periodicals, 1930-1971_. New York: R. R. Bowker; and London: Crown, 1975.

> A selective listing, with brief annotations. See entries under "Music, Film," pp. 311-12, "Musicals," pp. 312-13, "Dance and the Cinema", "Opera on the Screen," p. 319, and individual composer names.

6221. Besterman, Theodore. _Music and Drama: A Bibliography of Bibliographies_. Totawa, N.J.: Rowman and Littlefield, 1971.

> A listing of bibliographic materials relating to opera, theater, and dramatic music.

> -- Rev. by Guy A. Marco in _American Reference Books Annual_ (1973), 390.

6222. Beuick, Marshall, comp. _Bibliography of Radio Broadcasting_. New York: the author (mimeo.), 1947.

6223. _Bibliographie des Musikschrifttums, 1950-_. Staatlichen Institut für Musikforschung. Mainz: B. Schotts Söhne, 1951-.

> See entries under "Filmmusik." Volumes continue from 1951 into the 1980's. A useful source for European titles.

6224. Bowles, Stephen Eugene. "Critical Film Reviews in British and American Film Periodicals: A Study and an Index." Ph.D. Diss. Northwestern University 1979.

> Abstract: DAI 40/06: 2948A (order #DA 7927301).

6224. Published as _Index to Critical Film Reviews in British and American Film Periodicals_, together with _Index to Critical Reviews of Books about Film, 1930-1972_. 3 vols. New York: Burt Franklin Publishing, 1974.

> An immense project, cataloging 20,000 film reviews from selected periodicals, arranged alphabetically by film title. Also includes some 6,000 reviews of books on the subject of film.

6225. British Film Institute. _Catalogue of the Book Library of the British Film_

Institute, III: Subject Catalogue. Boston: G. K. Hall, 1975.

See entries under "Film Music", "Sound", "Animation," and related topics.

6225a. Revised and updated in Book Library Bibliography, No. 5: Film Music. London: British Film Institute, 1977.

6226. "Composers on Film Music: A Bibliography." Films: A Quarterly of Discussion and Analysis, 1, No. 4 (Winter 1940), 21-24.

Reprinted in Kirstein (#1362).

6227. Ellis, Jack C., Charles Derry, and Sharon Kern. The Film Book Bibliography: 1940-1975. Metuchen, N.J.: Scarecrow Press, 1979.

A listing of English language books on film. See entries under "Music," pp. 85-87, "Sound," pp. 92-93, and "Collective Biography," pp. 349-69. Also includes information on research collections, film societies, etc.

-- Rev. by Harry M. Geduld in Quarterly Review of Film Studies, 5, No. 3 (Summer 1980), 403-06.

6228. Elsas, Diana, ed. Factfile: Film Music. Washington, D.C.: American Film Institute, 1977-.

An intermittent mimeographed update from the AFI which appears from 1977 into the 1980's.

6229. Eschbach, Achim, and Wendelin Rader. Film Semiotik: Eine Bibliographie. Munich: Verlag Dokumentation Saur KG, 1978.

A listing of works which analyze film (and film music) according to a semiotic paradigm.

6230. Fielding, Raymond, comp. A Bibliography of Theses and Dissertations on the Subject of Film, 1916-1979. U. F. A. Monograph, No. 3. Houston: University Film Association at the School of Communication, University of Houston, 1979. (Pamphlet.)

A cumulative listing of graduate studies on the subject of film, previously published in the Journal of the University Film Association, 20, No. 2 (1968); 21, No. 4 (1969); 24, No. 3 (1972); and 26, No. 3 (1974).

Available from the Publications Office of the University Film and Video Association, Southern Illinois University, Dept. of Cinema and Photography, Carbondale, Illinois, 62901.

Also see #6231.

6231. ----------. "Sixth Bibliographic Survey of Theses and Dissertations on the Subject of Film Filed at U.S. Universities 1916-1981." Journal of the University Film and Video Association, 34, No. 1 (Winter 1982), 41-54.

An update of the original listing. See #6230.

6232. Film Literature Index, 1974-. Ed. Vincent J. Aceto, Jane Graves, and Fred Silva. Albany and New York: Film and Television Documentation Center (Filmdex), SUNY (Albany), 1975-.

A quarterly listing with annual accumulations, continues from 1974 into the 1980's. The most recent editor is Linda Provinzano.

See entries under "Music", "Composers", "Opera", "Television Music", "Bibliography," and individual composer names.

6233. Gerlach, John, and Lana Gerlach. The Critical Index: A Bibliography of Articles on Film in English, 1946-1973. New York: Teacher's College Press, 1974.

See entries under "Sound", "Music," and "Music for Silents," pp. 516-20.

6234. Gorbman, Claudia. "Bibliography on Sound in Film." Yale French Studies, No. 60 (1980), 269-86.

An extremely accurate listing of carefully selected
sources which deal with sound and music in film. Entries appear under the headings, I: General Theory and
Aesthetics, II: Technology (A. General, and B. History -
The Coming of Sound), and III. Music.

6235. Imamura Miyo'o. _Nihon eiga bunken shi_. Tokyo: Kyōho Shobō, 1967.

A chronological bibliography of the Japanese film.

6236. Jones, Karen, ed. _International Index to Film Periodicals, 1972-_. New
York: R. R. Bowker, 1973 and 1974; and New York: St. Martin's Press,
1975-.

An annotated listing which continues from 1972 into the
1980's. See entries under "Music" and "Sound."

6237. Langer, Y. "Bibliographie sommaire de la musique mecanisée." _Polyphonie_,
2nd series, No. 6 (1950), 144-49.

6238. Leonard, Harold, ed. _The Film Index: A Bibliography. I: The Film as Art_.
New York: Work Projects Administration, Writer's Program, New York, The
Museum of Modern Art Film Library, and the H. W. Wilson Co., 1941.

A highly selective, but heavily annotated listing of
American and British sources. See entries under "Sound,"
pp. 231-49, "Music: Silent Era, Sound Era," pp. 202-211,
and "Musical Films," pp. 468-72.

Reprint, New York: Arno Press, 1966.

Essentially updated and expanded by the MacCann and
Perry volume (see #6241).

6239. Leyda, Jay. "Film Literature, 1945." In _Annual Communications Biblio-
graphy_, a supplement to _Hollywood Quarterly_, 1 (1946), 4.

See entries on the subject of film sound under "Part 1:
Film Techniques."

6240. Lichtenwager, William, Carolyn Lichtenwager, and Wayne D. Shirley, comp.
Modern Music: An Analytic Index. New York: Ames Press, 1976.

An annotated guide to the periodical _Modern Music_,
which contains many articles dealing with all aspects
of film music.

6241. MacCann, Richard Dyer, and Edward S. Perry, eds. _The New Film Index: A
Bibliography of Magazine Articles in English, 1930-1970_. New York: E.P.
Dutton, 1975.

A supplement to Harold Leonard's _Film Index_, see #6238.

See entries under "Music for Films", "Theory and Function
of Music", "History of Music", "Technical Aspects of Music", " Technical Aspects of Sound", "Case Studies and
Criticism," and "Dubbing."

6242. _The Music Index: A Subject-Author Guide to Current Music Periodical Litera-
ture_. Ed. Florence Kretzschmar et al. Detroit: Information Coordinators,
1949-.

See entries under "Moving Picture Music", "Film Music,"
"Films", "Television Music," and "Televising."

A monthly listing with annual accumulations, continues
from 1949 into the 1980's.

6243. _The New York Times Film Reviews, 1913-1968_. New York: The New York Times,
1970.

In six volumes. Vols. 1-5 are reviews. Vol. 6 is an appendix and index.

6243a. Also published as _The New York Times Film Reviews: A One-
Volume Selection, 1913-1970, Chosen from the 7-Volume
Set, with an Introduction and Six Original Essays by
George Amberg_. New York: Arno Press, 1971.

6244. Rehrauer, George. _Cinema Booklist_. Metuchen, N.J.: Scarecrow Press, 1972.

A listing of 4,000 books on film (52 relate to the subject of film music). Additional supplements published in 1974 and 1977.

6245. RILM Abstracts of Music Literature (International Inventory of Music Literature), 1967-. Ed. Barry S. Brook. New York: City University of New York (International RILM Center); and Kassel: Bärenreiter-Verlag, 1967-.

A quarterly listing with annual accumulations. See entries under "Dramatic Arts," and related areas: "Radio," "Television", "Sound Recording and Reproduction," and "Mass Media."

6246. Rose, Oscar. Radio and Television: A Bibliography. New York: Wilson, 1947.

A bibliography of sound technology.

6247. Rubsamen, Walter H. "Literature on Music in Film and Radio: Addenda, 1943-1948." Hollywood Quarterly, 3, No. 4 (Summer 1949), 403-04.

A supplement to the Rubsamen and Nelson listing, see #6248.

6248. ----------, and Robert U. Nelson. "Literature on Music in Film and Radio." In Annual Communications Bibliography, a supplement to Hollywood Quarterly, 1 (1946), 40-45.

See Rubsamen's "Addenda," #6247.

6248a. Reprinted, combined with the 1949 addenda, in Hinrichsen's Musical Yearbook, 6 (1950), 318-31.

6249. Salem, James M. A Guide to Critical Reviews, II: The Musical, 1909-1974. 2nd edition. Metuchen, N.J.: Scarecrow Press, 1976.

A valuable guide to reviews of Broadway (and filmed Broadway) musicals. Includes composers, lyricists, staging and set designers, and an extremely useful composer index.

-- Rev. in Quarterly Review of Film Studies, 4, No. 1 (1979), 79-85.

6250. ----------. A Guide to Critical Reviews, IV: The Screenplay from "The Jazz Singer" to "Dr. Strangelove." Metuchen, N.J.: Scarecrow Press, 1971. 2 volumes.

A valuable guide to reviews of Hollywood films.

6251. Seidman, S. A. "On the Contributions of Music to Media Productions." Educational Communication and Technology Journal, 29 (Spring 1981), 60-61.

6252. Sharples, Win, Jr. "Motion Picture Music: A Select Bibliography." Film Music Notebook, 4, No. 1 (1978), 28-32.

6253. ----------. "Motion Picture Music: A Select Bibliography." In Film Score: The View from the Podium by Tony Thomas. South Brunswick and New York: A. S. Barnes and Co., 1979, pp. 260-66.

See #131.

6254. ----------. "A Selected and Annotated Bibliography of Books and Articles on Music in the Cinema." Cinema Journal, 17, No. 2 (Spring 1978), 36-67.

The most extensive film music listing to this date. Also includes a listing of film music clubs, sources for obtaining soundtrack recordings, films on film music, and a selected list of film music periodicals.

6255. Verdone, Mario, comp. "Nota bibliografica." In La musica nel film. Ed. Luigi Chiarini. Rome: Bianco e nero editore, 1950, pp. 139-45.

See Chiarini, #1627.

NOTE: Most English titles are taken from the listing by John Huntley in British Film Music, see #51. The entire bibliography also appears in Revue Musicale erroneously attributed to Enrico Fulchignoni. See #1676.

6256. Vincent, R. C. "A Bibliography of Film Reference Resources." University Film Association Journal, 29, No. 3 (1977), 43-56.

6257. Zuckerman, John V. "A Selected Bibliography on Music for Motion Pictures." *Hollywood Quarterly*, 5, No. 2 (Winter 1950), 195-99.

> A revised version of the listing which first appeared in *Technical Report: Rapid Mass Learning, SDC 269-7-2: Music in Motion Pictures: Review of Literature with Implications for Instructional Films*. Prepared by the Instructional Film Research Program at Pennsylvania State College. Port Washington, N.Y.: Special Devices Center of the Office of Naval Research, May 15, 1949.

> SEE ALSO:

> #20(Comuzio), #34, #42(Hacquard), #43a(Hagen), #51(Huntley), #73(Lavagnino), #80(Mahesvari), #82(Manvell/Huntley), #84(Miceli), #86(Moser), #89(Nick), #93(Palmer/Gillet), #100(Petrova), #103(Porcile), #104(Prendergast), #117(Shilova), #122(Sternfeld), #127(Thiel), #131(Thomas), #133 (Tinhorão), #140(Weber), #201(Atkins), #254(Kellog), #255(Kennington), #364(Berg), #618(Hofmann), #626(Hunsberger), #716(Mamontowicz-Łojek), #778(Ottenheym), #789(Pauli), #791(Peeples), #1113(Mills), #1457(Noble), #1676(Fulchignoni), #1759, 1760(Keller), #2377(Farren), #2505(Nau), #2527 (Prox), #2643(Leipp), #2650(Rosenbaum), #2916(Lockhart), #3389(Herrmann), #4168(Whitney), #4322(Erdmann), #4471(Bronchain), #4733(Lissa), #4766 (Marie), #4800((Newlin), #4824(Prieberg), #4874(H.-C. Schmidt), #4905 (Tagg), #5051(Bornoff/Salter), #5081(Helm), #5117(H.-C. Schmidt), #5236 (Franks), #5323(Bornoff), #5387(Cuel), #5726(Bertz-Dostal), #5739(Coolidge), #5903(J.-A. Bizet), #5962(Ferrini), #5992(Hanisch), #6031(Kobal), #6058(Marshall), #6066(McVay), #6097(Rothel), #6106(Sennett), #6131(L.B. Thomas), #6147(Walldov), #6189(Fitzpatrick/Marks), #6190(Geduld), #6192 (Helman), #6195(Marks), #6200(Birett and Siedler (see #875)), #6211(R.A. Nelson), #6263(Hippenmeyer), #6269(Limbacher), #6308(Comuzio), #6323(Jäggi), and #6336(Reinert/Brack/Portmann). NOTE: For bibliographies of individual composers and topics, see entries cited in the INDEX.

Filmographies

6258. Armatys, Leszek. "Polska muzyka filmowa, 1943-1960." *Kwartalnik Filmowy*, 11, No. 2 (1961), 73-79.

6259. *Catalogue: Ten Years of Films on Ballet and Classical Dance, 1956-1965.* Paris: UNESCO; and New York: UNIPUB, 1968.

> Includes a Preface by Gerhard Brunner, and the article "The Dancing Screen" by Agnes Bleier-Brody (see #5319).

6260. Cincotti, Guido. "Filmografia." In *Musica e film*. Ed. S. G. Biamonte. Rome: Edizioni dell' Ateneo, 1959, p. 235.

> See Biamonte, #1606.

> Includes American films, apparently dubbed into Italian.

6261. Farren, Jonathan. "Cinéma et rock and roll: filmographie (suite et fin)." *Cinéma 75*, Nos. 201-202 (Sept.-Oct. 1975), 56-59.

6262. ----------. "Filmographie (cinéma and rock n'roll)." *Cinéma 75*, No. 200 (July-Aug. 1975), 44-54.

6263. Hippenmeyer, Jean-Roland. *Jazz sur films -- ou 55 années de rapports jazz-cinéma vus à travers plus de 800 films tournés entre 1917 et 1972: Filmographie critique.* Yverdon, Switz.: Éditions de la Thièle, 1973.

> Includes a bibliography.

> -- Rev. by Carl Gregor zu Mecklenburg in *Jazzforschung*, 5 (1974), 200.

> -- Rev. in *Positif* (Paris), No. 162 (Oct. 1974), 76-77.

6264. Internationales Musikzentrum, Vienna. *Films for Music Education and Opera Films: An International Selective Catalogue.* Paris: UNESCO, 1962.

Includes a general introduction by Egon Kraus, and an introduction to opera films by Jack Bornoff. See #6273.

6265. ----------. Music in Film and Television: An International Selective Catalogue, 1964-1974. Paris: UNESCO; and Vienna and Munich: Jugend und Volk, 1975.

> A listing of operas, concerts, and music education programs broadcast via television, with pertinent information concerning their production, and a catalogue of films devoted to the performing arts.
>
> -- Rev. by Alfred Brasch in Melos/Neue Zeitschrift für Musik, 2, No. 3 (1976), 239.
>
> -- Rev. by Stephen M. Fry in Notes (Music Library Association), 33, No. 1 (Sept. 1976), 83.

6266. International Folk Music Council. Films on Traditional Music and Dance. Ed. Peter Kennedy. New York: UNESCO Publications Center, 1970.

> A listing of films, arranged by country.
>
> -- Rev. in Music Educator's Journal, 57 (Sept. 1970), 83.

6267. Lacombe, Alain, and Nicole Lacombe. Des compositeurs pour l'image. Paris: Musique et promotion éditeur, 1982.

> A survey of music in French films, with an extensive and useful filmography of French film music composers.

6268. Leebron, Elizabeth, and Lynn Gartley. Walt Disney: A Guide to References and Resources. Boston: G. K. Hall, 1979.

> Includes a filmography, pp. 15-112, detailing film credits, composers, arrangers, conductors, and sound editors.

6269. Limbacher, James L. Keeping Score: Film Music, 1972-1979. Metuchen, N.J.: Scarecrow Press, 1981.

> A valuable, though selective reference work. Prepared as a supplement to Violins to Video (see #75), includes bibliography and discography.

6270. McCarty, Clifford, comp. and ed. Film Composers in America: A Checklist of Their Work. Glendale, California: J. Valentine, 1953. (Reprint, New York: Da Capo, 1972.)

> Perhaps the most valuable research tool available to the film music scholar, the eagerly awaited 2nd edition and update of this work has been in preparation for nearly 35 years! Includes a Foreword by Lawrence Morton.
>
> -- Rev. in Music Journal, 11 (Sept. 1953), 48.
>
> -- Rev. in Notes (Music Library Association), 11 (Dec. 1953), 105.
>
> -- Rev. in Score, 5, Nos. 2-3 (1953), 13.
>
> -- Rev. by Kenneth Thompson in The Musical Times, 114, No. 1565 (July 1973), 705.

6271. Parker, David L., and Esther Siegel. Guide to Dance in Film: A Catalogue of U.S. Productions Including Dance Sequences, with Names of Dancers, Choreographers, and Directors. New York: Gale Research, 1978.

6272. Rangoonwalla, Firoze, and Vishwanath Das. Indian Filmography: Silent and Hindi Films (1897-1969). Bombay: J. Udeshi, 1970.

> A chronological listing of films, with pertinent information about their production, including music directors.

6273. United Nations Educational, Scientific, and Cultural Organization. Films for Music Education and Opera Films: An International Selective Catalogue. Paris: UNESCO, 1962.

> Includes introductions by Egon Kraus and Jack Bornoff. See #6264.

SEE ALSO:

#13(Canadian Film Museum), #20(Comuzio), #30(Elley), #65(Korganov/Frolov), #70(Lacombe/Rocle), #82b(Manvell/Huntley), #103(Porcile), #117(Shilova), #130(H.A. Thomas), #132(T. Thomas), #133(Tinhorão), #136(van de Ven), #251(Jenkinson/Warner), #338(Atkins), #674(Kühn), #1271, #1318(Huntley), #1419(Miller/Huntley/Mathieson), #1479(Ries), #1606(Biamonte), #1696(Hamraaz), #2057(Galling), #2123(Porcile), #2162(Staehling), #2366(Dostie), #2467(Lange), #2564(Stamelman), #2588(Thiel), #2591(Ulrich), #2725(Bertolina), #2780(Costabile), #2806(Giusti), #2835(Lafaye), #4168(Whitney), #4515(Colpi), #4576(Epstein), #4733(Lissa), #5236(Franks), #5391(Demers), #5432(Mueller), #5466(Corrigan), #5896(Belach), #5903(J.-A. Bizet), #6017, 6018(Jélot-Blanc), #6091(Pyr'ev), #6097(Rothel), #6102(Scheurer), #6106 (Sennett), #6119(Springer), #6127(Taylor/Jackson), #6142(Vallance), #6147 (Walldov), #6305(Blaedel), #6306(Burton), #6308(Comuzio), #6311(Garel/Lacombe/Tessier), #6323(Jäggi), #6327, 6328(Meeker), and #6336(Reinert/ Brack/Portmann). NOTE: For filmographies of individual composers and topics, see entries cited in the INDEX.

Discographies

6274. Aros, Andrew A. Broadway and Hollywood Too. Diamond Bar, Calif.: Applause Publications, 1980.

6275. Cook, Page, comp. "Film Music Discography: Since 1970." In Film Score: A View from the Podium, by Tony Thomas. South Brunswick and New York: A. S. Barnes and Co., 1979, pp. 245-59.

> See #131.

6276. Harris, Steve, ed. Recorded Music for Motion Pictures, TV and the Stage. Los Angeles: A-1 Record Finders, 1976.

> A listing of recordings produced from 1940-1975.

6277. Harrison, Louis H., and Michael R. Pitts. Hollywood on Record: The Film Stars' Discography. Metuchen, N.J.: Scarecrow Press, 1978.

> A listing of recordings, arranged by performer.

> -- Rev. in Notes (Music Library Association), 35, No. 4 (1979), 877-78.

> -- Rev. by Harry M. Geduld: "A Scarecrow for Each Field." Quarterly Review of Film Studies, 5, No. 3 (Summer 1980), 403-06.

6278. Limbacher, James L., comp. "Film and TV Scores on Long-Playing Records, Part 1." Film and TV Music, 16, No. 4 (Summer 1957), 22-23.

6279. ----------. "Film and TV Scores on Long-Playing Records, Part 2." Film and TV Music, 16, No. 5 (Late Summer 1957), 23-24.

6280. ----------. "Film and TV Scores on Long-Playing Records, Part 3." Film and TV Music, 17, No. 1 (Fall-Winter 1957-1958), 22-23.

6281. ----------. A Selected List of Recorded Musical Scores from Radio, Television, and Motion Pictures. (Pamphlet.) Dearborn, Mich.: Dearborn Public Library, Audio-Visual Division, 1960-.

> Annotated listings of film music recordings. Several editions appeared between 1960 and 1967.

6282. Morrison, Alen. "Film Music on Record." Film Music, 14, No. 4 (Mar.-Apr. 1955), 19-22.

6283. ----------. "Film Music on Records." Film Music, 13, No. 1 (Sept.-Oct. 1953), 14-16.

6284. Pratley, Gerald. "Film Music on Records (as of July 1951)." Quarterly of

Film, Radio and Television, 6, No. 1 (Fall 1951), 73-98.

6285. ----------. "Film Music on Records: Part 2." Quarterly of Film, Radio and
Television, 7, No. 1 (Fall 1952), 100-07.

6286. ----------. "Film Music on Records." Quarterly of Film, Radio and Television, 8, No. 2 (Winter 1953), 194-205.
Part 3.

6287. ----------. "Film Music on Records." Quarterly of Film, Radio and Television, 9, No. 2 (Winter 1954), 195-208.
Part 4.

6288. ----------. "Film Music on Records." Quarterly of Film, Radio and Television, 10, No. 2 (1955), 186-207.
Part 5.

6289. Preston, Mike. Tele-tunes. London: Record Information Centre, 1979.
-- Rev. in Film (London), No. 75 (July 1979), 4.

6290. Raymond, Peter Craig. "Film Music on Record." Sight and Sound, 18, No. 69
(Spring 1949), 53.

6291. Reid, Robert H., ed. The Gramophone Shop Encyclopedia of Recorded Music.
3rd. revised and enlarged edition. New York: Crown Publishers, 1948.
A useful source for early film music recordings.

6292. Rose, Edward. Soundtrack Record Collectors' Guide. Minneapolis, Minn.:
Dored Co., 1978.
-- Rev. by Ronald L. Bohn in Pro Musica Sana, 8, No. 1
(Winter 1979-1980), 11.

6293. Rust, Brian, and Allen G. Debus. The Complete Entertainment Discography:
From the Mid-1890's to 1942. New Rochelle, N.Y.: Arlington House, 1973.
A useful source for information about early soundtrack
recordings.

6294. "The Score: On the Record." BMI: The Many Worlds of Music, No. 1 (1974),
34-43.
Accompanies the documentary film "The Score." See #114.

6295. Smolian, Steven, comp. A Handbook of Film, Theater, and Television Music
on Record, 1948-69. 2 volumes. New York: Record Undertaker, 1970.
-- Rev. in Association for Recorded Sound Collections
Journal, 3, No. 1 (1970-1971), 38-40.
-- Rev. by Philip L. Miller in Notes (Music Library
Association), 28, No. 3 (Mar. 1972), 450.
-- Rev. in Recorded Sound (London), No. 61 (Jan. 1976),
510.

6296. Thomas, Anthony. "Film Music Available on Disc." Film Music Notes, 10,
No. 3 (Jan.-Feb. 1951), 16-19.

6297. Viviani, C. "Discographie: série 'Classic Film Scores' (R.C.A. Red Seal)."
Positif (Paris), No. 187 (Nov. 1976), 39-41.

SEE ALSO:

#43a(Hagen), #51(Huntley), #70(Lacombe/Rocle), #72(Larson), #82(Manvell/
Huntley), #103(Porcile), #131, 132(Thomas), #136(van de Ven), #237(Fiedel), #1318(Huntley), #1333, #1658(Debnam), #1696(Hamraaz), #1701(Hentoff), #1852, #2072, #2482(Magliozzi), #2823(Alain/Rabourdin), #4633(Hamilton), #4800(Newlin), #4824(Prieberg), #4962(Winter), #6037(Kreuger),
#6039(Lacombe/Rocle), #6058(Marshall), #6131(L.B. Thomas), #6147(Wall-
dov), #6190(Geduld), #6269(Limbacher), #6301(ASCAP), #6306(Burton), and
#6325(Markewich). NOTE: For discographies of individual composers and
topics, see entries cited in the INDEX.

Reference Materials: Biography/Film Credits

6298. American Society of Composers, Authors and Publishers. ASCAP Biographical Dictionary of Composers, Authors and Publishers. Ed. Daniel I. McNamara. New York: Thomas Y. Crowell, 1948.

> An alphabetical listing of names, with brief biographical information and filmography.

> Second edition, 1952.

6299. ----------. ASCAP Biographical Dictionary of Composers, Authors and Publishers. Third edition. Compiled and edited by the Lynn Farnol Group. New York: ASCAP, 1966.

6300. ----------. ASCAP Biographical Dictionary. Fourth edition. Compiled by Jacques Cattell Press. New York: R. R. Bowker, 1980.

6301. ----------. ASCAP: 30 Years of Motion Picture Music -- The Big Hollywood Hits from 1928-1958. New York: ASCAP, 1958. (Reprint, 1967.)

> A chronological listing of songs, with information concerning the performers, recordings, and publishers.

6302. ----------. List of Members of the American Society of Composers, Authors and Publishers and Similar Foreign Societies as of January 1st, 1936. New York: ASCAP, 1936.

> An alphabetical directory, includes a listing of performing rights societies.

6303. Asian Film Directory and Who's Who, 1956. Ed. V. Doraiswamy. New Dehli, 1952.

> The first of several volumes with this title published in New Dehli and Bombay.

6304. Basic Facts and Figures: International Statistics Relating to Education, Culture and Mass Communication. Paris: UNESCO, 1952.

> The first of a series of UNESCO publications, culminating in the current UNESCO Statistical Yearbooks. Each provides information concerning film production, T.V. and radio statistics, and measurements of the social impact of the mass media.

6305. Blaedel, Michael, et al. "Finland; Norge; Sverige: leksikon." Kosmorama (Copenhagen), 23, No. 134 (1977), 113-24.

> Includes composer biographies and filmographies.

6306. Burton, Jack. Blue Book of Tin Pan Alley: A Human Interest Anthology of American Popular Music. Watkins Glen, N.Y.: Century House, 1950.

> A useful listing of songs and recordings, arranged by period (from Minstrelsy to the present) and composer, with indices of composers and lyricists. See especially the section "Sound Track, Loud Speaker and Juke Box," pp. 405-94.

6307. Clason, W. E., comp. Dictionary of Cinema, Sound and Music. Amsterdam: Elsevier Publishing Co., 1956.

> A dictionary of terms in English, French, Spanish, Italian, Dutch, and German.

6307a. Also published as Dizionario del cinema, acustica e musica. Florence: Edizioni Sansoni, 1956.

6308. Comuzio, Ermanno. Film Music Lexicon. Pavia: Varesina Grafica e Amministrazione Provinciale di Pavia, 1980.

> An alphabetical listing of composers, with biographical information and filmographies. Also includes listings of selected filmscores, musicals, jazz, filmed opera, pop and rock, arranged chronologically and by region,

pp. 213-87, together with a bibliography, pp. 289-98.

6309. D'Amico, Silvio, and Francesco Savio, eds. Enciclopedia dello spettacolo.
Nine volumes, 1954-1962.

Additional volumes edited by Francesco Savio include:
Appendice di aggiornamento: Cinema, 1963; and Aggiornamento 1955-1965, 1966.

6310. Eisner, Lotte H., and Heinz Friedrich, eds. Film, Rundfunk, Fernsehen.
Das Fischer Lexicon, IX. Frankfurt am Main: Fischer Bücherei, 1958.

Includes bibliographies.

6311. Garel, Alain, Alain Lacombe, and Max Tessier. "Dictionaire: quelques di-
zaines de musiciens." In Cinéma et musique, 1960-1975, a special issue
of Écran 75, No. 39 (Sept. 15, 1975), 45-59.

A biographical dictionary with useful filmographies,
especially for recent releases and for European films.

See #2463.

6312. Gifford, Denis. The British Film Catalogue, 1895-1970: A Reference Guide.
New York: McGraw-Hill; and London: David and Charles, 1973.

Essentially a listing of every British film ever produced. Provides some useful material for the study of
film musicals in Gt. Britain.

6313. Gough-Yates, Kevin, and M. Tarratt. The Film Music Book: A Guide to Film
Composers. New Rochelle, N.Y., 1978.

6314. Green, Stanley. Encyclopaedia of the Musical Film. New York: Oxford University Press, 1981.

Information concerning people, productions, and songs
from Hollywood musical features and cartoons, together
with a listing of British musical films and selected
original television musicals.

-- Rev. in Billboard, 93 (Sept. 5, 1981), 50.

-- Rev. by Martin Sutton in Films and Filming, No. 329
(Feb. 1982), 38.

-- Rev. in Notes (Music Library Association), 38, No. 4
(1982), 846-47.

-- Rev. in Central Opera Service Bulletin (New York), 24,
No. 1 (1982), 38.

6315. Handbook of the Indian Film Industry. Bombay: Motion Picture Society of
India, 1949.

6316. The Hollywood Musical: A Catalogue. London: The Cinema Bookshop, 1971.

6317. Indian Films, 1966. Poona and Bombay: B. V. Dharap Publ., and Allied Publishers Private Limited Distributors, 1966.

The first of a series of annual compilations of film
facts. Include information on music and dance directors, song writers, etc.

6318. Indian Motion Picture Almanac and Who's Who, 1953. Bombay: Film Federation of India, 1953.

6319. International Who Is Who in Music. Fifth (Mid-Century) edition. Ed.
J. T. H. Mize. Chicago: Who Is Who in Music, Ltd., 1951.

6320. International Who's Who in Music and Musicians' Directory. Eighth edition.
Ed. Adrian Gaster. Cambridge, Engl.: Melrose Press, 1977.

6321. Iwasaki Akira, et al., eds. Eiga hyakka jiten. Tokyo: Hakuyōsha, 1954.

An encyclopedia of film.

6322. Jäggi, Bruno. "Petit dictionnaire des cineastes bulgares." Cinema (Zurich), 22, No. 4 (1976), 80-90.

Includes biographical information, filmographies, and a bibliography of Bulgarian film.

6323. Kinkle, Roger D. The Complete Encyclopedia of Popular Music and Jazz 1900-1950. Four volumes. New Rochelle, N.Y.: Arlington House, 1974.

Vol. 1: a year-by-year chronology of new music, Vol. 2-3: biographies, Vol. 4: alphabetical indices of titles, musicals, and personalities. Vol. 4 also includes a listing of "Academy Award Winners and Nominees for Music: 1934-1972," pp. 2029-39.

-- Rev. in Coda (Toronto), 12, No. 6 (1975), 27-28.

-- Rev. in Popular Music and Society, 4, No. 2 (1975), 111-12.

-- Rev. by Stanley Dance in Music Journal, 33, No. 2 (Feb. 1975), 29.

-- Rev. by Felicity Howlett in Notes (Music Library Association), 32, No. 1 (Sept. 1975), 44-46.

6324. Lewine, Richard, and Alfred Simon. Songs of the American Theater. With an Introduction by Stephen Sondheim. New York: Dodd and Mead, 1973.

A comprehensive listing of more than 12,000 theatrical songs from 1900-1925 and 1925-1971, including selected titles from film and television.

6325. Markewich, Reese. The Definitive Bibliography of Harmonically Sophisticated Tonal Music. New York: the author, 1970.

A listing of songs, with information concerning publishers, recording companies, etc.

6326. Mass Media in India, 1978. New Dehli: Ministry of Information and Broadcasting, 1978.

6327. Meeker, David. Jazz in the Movies: A Guide to Jazz Musicians, 1917-1977. London: Talisman, 1977.

An encyclopedic listing of musicians and films. Supercedes the Tentative Index (#6328).

Also see comments by Tom Milne, #269.

-- Rev. in Skrien (Amsterdam), No. 70 (Dec. 1977), 40-41.

-- Rev. in Audience, 10 (Summer 1978), 31-32.

6328. ----------. Jazz in the Movies: A Tentative Index to the Work of Jazz Musicians in the Cinema. London: British Film Institute, 1972.

See #6327.

-- Rev. in Jazz and Blues, 2 (July 1972), 26.

-- Rev. in Orkester Journalen (Stockholm), 40 (Sept. 1972), 22.

-- Rev. in Jazz Forum, No. 20 (Dec. 1972), 100-101.

6329. Morley, Glenn. "The Guild" and "Professional Directory of Canadian Film Composers." Cinema Canada (Montreal), No. 60-61 (Dec. 1979-Jan. 1980), 51-53.

6330. Munden, Kenneth W., ed. American Film Institute Catalogue 1921-1930. New York and London: R. R. Bowker, 1971.

A useful resource for silent and early sound films.

6331. New York Times Directory of the Film. New York: Random House and Arno Press, 1973.

6332. Nihon eiga sakuhin taikan, I-VII. Tokyo: Kinema Jumpō, 1960-61.

A comprehensive directory of Japanese film, 1896-1945.

6333. Noble, Peter, ed. British Film Yearbook. London: Skelton Robinson British Yearbooks, 1946-1947.

Includes film music information, and the article "Music

and the Film Script" by Ernest Irving. See #1341.

The first in an irregular series of annuals which include information on composers, musical directors, etc.

6334. Ragan, David, ed. Who's Who in Hollywood 1900-1976. New York: Arlington House, 1976.

6335. Rangoonwalla, Firoze. Indian Films Index (1912-1967). Compiled by Vishwanath Das. Bombay: J. Udeshi, 1968.

6336. Reinert, Charles, ed., in association with Johann Paul Brack and Paul F. Portmann. Kleines Filmlexikon: Kunst, Technik, Geschichte, Biographie, Schrifttum. Einsiedeln-Zurich: Verlagsanstalt Benziger & Co., 1946.

See entries under "Filmmusik", "Musikerfilm," and "Musiktrickfilm." Also includes a listing "Schweitzerische Spielfilme 1933-1945, " with information concerning composers, music directors, etc., pp. 417-23, and an extensive bibliography, pp. 383-411.

6336a. Also published in an Italian edition, compiled by Francesco Pasinetti. Milan: Filmeuropa, 1948.

6337. La Revue du cinéma/Image et son: Hors série. Revue éditée par l'U.F.O.L.E. I.S. (Ligue Française de l'Enseignement et de l'Education Permanente).

An annual publication , provides synopses of current films with production information, including composers, sound editors, performers, etc.

6338. Shapiro, Nat, ed. Popular Music: An Annotated Index of American Popular Songs. 5 volumes. New York: Adrian Press, 1964-1969.

A listing of songs, including music from films and film musicals, 1920-1964.

6339. Slonimsky, Nicolas, ed. Baker's Biographical Dictionary of Musicians. 6th revised edition. New York: Schirmer Books, 1978.

6340. Woll, Allen L. Songs from Hollywood Musical Comedies, 1927 to the Present: A Dictionary. Garland Reference Library in the Humanities, 44. New York: Garland Publishing, 1976.

Includes a listing of films with song titles, credits, etc., with some bibliographic references.

-- Rev. in Journal of Popular Film, 6, No. 1 (1977), 90-91.

-- Rev. in Cinéma 78, No. 234 (June 1978), 106.

SEE ALSO:

#30(Elley), #70(Lacombe/Rocle), #243, #245(Hannemann), #728(McDonald), #1044, #1479(Reis), #1496(Saunders), #1696(Hamraaz), #2434(IMZ), #2694-2702, 2226-2228(BMI), #2891(Spurgeon), #2934-2935(BMI), #3132(Lyons), #5236(Franks), #5585(Salter), #5621(Burke), #5726(Bertz-Dostal), #5915 (Burton), #5973(Fontenla), #6013, #6078(Natl. Board of Review), #6127(Taylor/Jackson), #6200(Birett), #6249(Salem), #6256(Vincent), #6268(Leebron/ Gartley), #6269(Limbacher), #6271(Parker/Siegel), and #6272(Rangoonwalla/ Das).

VI. INDEX

NOTE: "Author" entries first note books or articles written by the person cited. These are followed by a listing of additional sources which provide information concerning his/her work (underlined).

Film music composers are designated by an asterisk (*).

ADDENDUM: